CHRONICLES
OF WASTED TIME

THE MALCOLM MUGGERIDGE SOCIETY

The Malcolm Muggeridge Society was founded on the 100th anniversary of the birth of Malcolm Muggeridge and some thirteen years after his death. This coincided with a successful two-day seminar entitled 'Muggeridge Rediscovered' held at Wheaton College, Illinois in May 2003, bringing together people from many parts of the world with an interest in the work of Malcolm Muggeridge – his life and his times.

The aims of the Society can be summarised as follows:

- Providing information for those researching the life and work of Malcolm Muggeridge
- Keeping writings in print and to encourage the publication of new critiques and scholarship
- Providing fellowship and virtual forum for admirers to discuss Muggeridge's work
- Publishing a regular newsletter
- Facilitating republication of his books and publication of unpublished material
- Providing linkage with other societies where mutual interest exists
- Increasing awareness of papers, writings and other memorabilia held in Special Collections at Wheaton College, Illinois
- Developing a web presence
- Organising social, dramatic and literary events
- Encouraging new writing about Muggeridge

In preserving and utilising the literary and broadcast legacy, the Society provides a focus for those wishing to learn more about this famous author, journalist, soldier-spy, broadcaster, and Christian apologist. The Society publishes a quarterly literary journal called *The Gargoyle,* distributed to members.

www.malcolmmuggeridge.org

CHRONICLES OF WASTED TIME

MALCOLM MUGGERIDGE

FOREWORD BY IAN HUNTER

REGENT COLLEGE PUBLISHING
• VANCOUVER, BRITISH COLUMBIA •

For my ever-dear children:
Leonard, John and Valentine,
And the other three that have
come to us through them:
Sylvia, Anne and Gerrit-Jan

Chronicles of Wasted Time was originally published in two volumes:
Chronicle I: The Green Stick
Chronicle II: The Infernal Grove

This edition, including Chronicle III, published 2006 by
Regent College Publishing
5800 University Blvd., Vancouver, BC V6T 2E4 Canada

Views expressed in works published by Regent College Publishing are those
of the author and do not necessarily represent the official position of Regent
College <www.regent-college.edu>.

Cover portrait by Michael Noakes

Library and Archives Canada Cataloguing in Publication

Muggeridge, Malcolm, 1903-1990.
Chronicles of wasted time / Malcolm Muggeridge.

Includes index.
Some material previously published under the titles *The Green Stick,* and
The Infernal Grove.
Includes the previously unpublished *The Right Eye.*

ISBN 1-57383-376-2

1. Muggeridge, Malcolm, 1903-1990. 2. Authors, English—20th
century—Biography. 3. Journalists—Great Britain Biography. I. Muggeridge,
Malcolm, 1903-1990. Green stick. II. Muggeridge, Malcolm, 1903-1990.
Infernal grove. III. Muggeridge, Malcolm, 1903-1990. Right eye. IV. Title.

PR6025.U5Z463 2006 070.92 C2006-903785-X

Contents

Foreword

THE RE-ISSUANCE of Malcolm Muggeridge's autobiography, *Chronicles of Wasted Time,* including, for the first time, the fragment with which he intended to begin his oft-contemplated third volume, will be welcomed by readers familiar with the compulsively-readable Muggeridge and, one hopes, will serve to introduce a new generation to a journalist and author whose life spanned the 20th century and who chronicled its turbulent ups and downs in matchless prose.

Volume I, *The Green Stick* – the title drawn from a saying of Leo Tolstoy's that somewhere there was buried a green stick inscribed with words that would destroy evil in the hearts of men and bring them happiness - was first published by William Collins in 1972. *The Sunday Times* hailed it as '. . . one of the greatest autobiographies of our time.' Volume II, *The Infernal Grove,* a chastened title taken from William Blake's 'Songs of Experience', appeared a year later (1973).

These two volumes carry Muggeridge's life story only to the end of the second World War. For the next two decades, autobiographical silence. So much of Muggeridge's career, including his dominance of the early years of BBC television, lay ahead; so why no third volume?

In part, it may have been due to mental exhaustion; Muggeridge was nearly 70 when he completed *The Infernal Grove.* In part, it was because many of the people who would populate his third volume were still alive, sensitive to criticism, and not beyond a threat of libel. Malcolm told me once that he could never write about his once close friendship with novelist Anthony Powell as long as Powell was alive; as it happened Powell was to outlive Muggeridge by a decade. Then, too, it is clear that Malcolm wanted to switch the tone and substance of his memoirs; from events to their significance, from the ways of the world to his vision of God. Indeed, his highly autobiographical 1969 bestseller, *Jesus Rediscovered,* had already begun the process.

In the last years of his life, writing was simply beyond him. Muggeridge's eyesight failed and his memory, once so acute, began to fail. The spirit may have been willing but the flesh was weak. So the fragmentary, rather tentative opening of *The Right Eye* – a title intended to remind us that while the left eye sees only time and man, the right eye sees eternity – is all we shall have. What is most remarkable is that Malcolm's prophetic instincts never left him. In my last visit to him, a couple of years before his death in 1990, he was still following world events and very shrewd about their direction and eventual outcome.If Muggeridge was sometimes mocked and seldom heeded – well, that is the fate of prophets, as Jeremiah discovered when, for his insights, he got himself chucked down a well. Prophets unsettle our preconceptions and disturb our complacency. Muggeridge never claimed to be a prophet. When others, like Cardinal Manning of Los Angeles, applied that label to him, he demurred: 'I am no prophet, no, nor prophet's son', he said, then adapting Amos; 'I was a journalist and the Lord took me as I sat at my typewriter.' Yet no perceptive reader of the ensuing pages will fail to be struck by Muggeridge's prophetic genius.

His instincts were on display in the winter months of 1932-33 when he served as stand-in correspondent for the *Manchester Guardian* in Moscow. He did a daring thing: he had his Russian interpreter buy him a railway ticket to the Ukraine and North Caucasus. What Muggeridge saw on that extended rail trip he never forgot; years later he wrote that it 'remained in my mind as a nightmare memory.' And he did his best to make sure the world did not forget.

He saw the richest wheat lands of Europe turned into a wilderness. He saw famine – 'planned and deliberate; not due to any natural catastrophe like failure of rain or cyclone or flooding. An administrative famine brought about by the forced collectivization of agriculture . . . abandoned villages, the absence of livestock, neglected fields: everywhere, famished, frightened people.'

In a German settlement, a little oasis of prosperity in the collectivized wilderness, he saw peasants kneeling down in the snow, weeping, and asking for bread. In his diary he wrote: "Whatever else I may do or think in the future, I must never pretend that I haven't seen this. Ideas will come and go; but this is more than an idea. It is peasants kneeling down in the snow and asking for bread. Something that I have seen and understood.'

In a series of articles, Muggeridge wrote of what he had seen; on February 26, 1933: '. . . to say there is a famine in some of the most fertile parts of Russia is to say much less than the truth; there is not only famine . . . but a state of war, a military occupation . . . the grain collection has been carried out with such thoroughness and brutality that the peasants are now quite without bread.' The next month he wrote a three part series tracing how the 'Dictatorship of the Proletariat' had become the Dictatorship of Joseph Stalin; then how the Dictatorship of Stalin became the 'Dictatorship of the General Idea'.

His reporting produced a chorus of denunciation. The policy of the British government, and the inclination of the chattering classes, was wholehearted support for what was then called 'the Soviet experiment'. Muggeridge was denounced as 'an hysterical liar' by such eminent personages as the Very Rev. Hewlett Johnson, Dean of Canterbury, who, from his pulpit had praised Stalin's '. . . steady purpose and kindly generosity'; by Harold Laski, who assured all who would listen that the show trials of the Old Bolsheviks were models of judicial fairness. George Bernard Shaw, who had just returned from a visit to Russia, contradicted Muggeridge's accounts of famine by describing granaries full to overflowing, attended by apple-cheeked granary maids. Even Malcolm's aunt by marriage, Beatrice Webb, joined the chorus, repudiating Muggeridge's assertion that forced labour existed in the Soviet Union; though when pressed in private conversation, she did acknowledge, almost wistfully Malcolm noted, 'In Russia, people disappear.'

Within Russia, Muggeridge's reporting was contradicted preeminently by Walter Duranty, Moscow correspondent for the *New York Times,* a man whom Muggeridge later called 'the greatest liar I have ever met' – a reporter who nonetheless was awarded a Pulitzer Prize for journalism.

If vindication was a long time coming, it came when Susan Taylor, in her 1990 biography of Duranty, *Stalin's Apologist* (Oxford University Press), wrote this: 'But for Muggeridge's eyewitness accounts of the famine in the spring of 1933 and his stubborn chronicle of the event, the effects of the crime upon those who suffered it might well have remained as hidden from scrutiny as its perpetrators intended. Little thanks he has received for it over the years, although there is a growing number who realize what a singular act of honesty and

courage his reportage constituted.' Alas, by the time Susan Taylor wrote that, Muggeridge was dead.

Vindication came again from Alexander Solzhenitsyn; when Joseph Pearce interviewed Solzhenitsyn for his biography (*Solzhenitsyn: a Soul in Exile*, Baker Books, 2001) Solzhenitsyn commended Muggeridge as '. . . a man able to travel that difficult path of freeing himself from socialist lies and attaining spiritual heights.'

It was Malcolm's Russian experience that first prompted a re-evaluation of Christianity. As Muggeridge put it four decades later: 'My disillusionment with the notion of a predestined progress towards a kingdom of heaven on earth led me inexorably back to the kingdom not of this world proclaimed in the Christian revelation.'

Malcolm made a prophetic remark to me in 1978 when I happened to be staying with him at the time a conclave in Rome chose Karol Wojtyla to become Pope John Paul II. 'It is the end of the Soviet Union,' Muggeridge said, 'they will not be able to withstand the moral authority of a Pope from the Communist bloc.' Another prophecy that he did not live to see fully vindicated.

Nothing in Muggeridge's controversial journalistic career ever rivaled his 'Royal Soap Opera' article that appeared in the *Saturday Evening Post* on October 19, 1957. His theme was that materialist societies like ours are especially prone to hero-worship; having by and large ceased to believe in God, they pay increasing obeisance to a Queen or Royal family, making of a symbol ('no bad thing in itself') a kind of substitute or ersatz religion.

The Queen happened to be touring America when the article appeared (it had been written nearly two years before) and the British press smelled blood. Muggeridge's article was described as '. . . treasonous . . . ruthless . . . shocking . . . patronizing . . . gruesome' to quote only a few epithets. Muggeridge received death threats and his home was vandalized. As he walked along the seafront in Brighton, a passer-by spat in his face. He was banned from the BBC, and his newspaper column dropped.

We who have lived to watch the authority of the Monarchy reduced to a ribald joke – soap opera indeed – can but marvel at Muggeridge's prescience and courage. If even he could not have imagined a character quite so ludicrous as Princess Di, he could nevertheless say, paraphrasing Kipling, 'I saw the sunset ere most men saw the dawn.'

In the 1960s and 70s Muggeridge operated as a sort-of freelance

world correspondent; as he put it, he had taken up the hazards of street-walking in preference to the security of being an inmate of a licensed house. He wrote for papers and magazines in the U.K., the U.S., Canada, Australia, and elsewhere. His television programs were broadcast through the English-speaking world. Even to summarize his utterances in this hectic period is to shortchange his prophetic gifts. Nevertheless, here, without comment, are a few delicious Muggeridgisms:

> In our time the genius of man has gone into science, where it has achieved the most astounding results – far, far greater in my lifetime than in the whole of the rest of recorded time. In literature and the arts, in mysticism and religion, nothing has been done that will be of any major interest to posterity, and a good deal that will invite derision and even contempt. (1967)

> The twentieth century's version of Descartes' famous dictum is, 'I screw, therefore I am.' (1969)

> Man is a fugitive from reality who must somehow be persuaded to confront his own imperfection and despair (1976)

> The State, in fact, is the greatest of all tyrants, the ultimate tyrant. Kings can be executed, oligarchies can be broken up, millionaires can be despoiled of their money, Popes can be defied and heresies persisted in, but the State is, in principle, ourselves, and how can we put down ourselves? We who are the Leviathan cannot slay it. (1954)

> The most highly educated society in Western Europe elected Hitler and the highest density of Universities per acre and per person is to be found in California. Need I say more? (1978)

> A key to our present discontents is simply that the burden of being free has come to seem to heavy to be borne, and that, consciously or unconsciously, willfully or under duress, the prevailing disposition is to lay it down. In a famous scene in Dostoevsky's novel *The Brothers Karamazov*, the Chief Inquisitor turns away the returned Christ because he brings with him the dreaded gift of freedom. Governments, as it seems to me, whatever their ideology, are going to show themselves of a like mind with the Grand Inquisitor. (1978)

When Pope John Paul ll issued his encyclical *Humanae Vitae* in 1978, Muggeridge wrote a supportive letter to *The Times:* 'I do not doubt that in the history books, when our squalid moral decline is recounted, with the final breakdown in law and order that must follow (for without a moral order, there can be no order) the Pope's courageous and just, though I fear in the event largely ineffectual, stand will be accorded the respect and admiration it deserves.'

Four years after he wrote this, Muggeridge was received into the Roman Catholic church.

Death was a topic about which Malcolm frequently thought and wrote. At the age of 76, he wrote: 'Like a prisoner awaiting his release, like a schoolboy when the end of term is near, like a migrant bird ready to fly south . . . I long to be gone. Extricating myself from the flesh I have too long inhabited, hearing the key turn in the lock of time so that the great doors of eternity swing open, disengaging my tired mind from its interminable conundrums, and my tired ego from its wearisome insistencies. Such is the prospect of death.'

Alas, Malcolm's death was not to be the easeful passage from time to eternity that he had hoped for; at the end his mind disintegrated, he grew suspicious and quarrelsome, at the last he was confined to a nursing home.

He died on November 14, 1990 at the age of 87. He was buried in the village cemetery at Whatlington in Sussex and on his gravestone was incised the epitaph VALIANT FOR TRUTH. It is an apt inscription; Malcolm Muggeridge had earned the right to echo the words of Bunyan's Mr. Valiant-For-Truth:

> Though with great difficulty I am got hither, yet now I do not repent me of all the trouble I have been at to arrive at where I am. My sword I give to him that shall succeed me in my pilgrimage, and my courage and skill to him that can get it. My marks and scars I carry with me, to be a witness for me, that I have fought his battles who will now be my rewarder. And so he passed over, and all the trumpets sounded for him on the other side.

Dr. Ian Hunter is Professor Emeritus in the Faculty of Law at the University of Western Ontario; he is the author of the first biography of Malcolm Muggeridge [*Malcolm Muggeridge, A Life*], and editor of two Muggeridge anthologies: *Things Past* (1978) and *The Very Best of Malcolm Muggeridge* (1998).

LONG AGO I copied out from a Life of the French sculptor, Rodin, a letter he addressed to his wife, Rose, dated 24 August, 1913. It occurs to me now that in it he says to her exactly what I should wish to say to my wife, Kitty, and that there could be no better place for saying it than here. So, transposing the names·

My dear Kitty,
This letter is just to tell you that my mind is full of the greatness of God's gift to me when He put you at my side. Keep this thought of mine in your generous heart.
Your,
M.

Chronicle I:

THE
GREEN
STICK

I used to believe that there was a green stick, buried on the edge of a ravine in the old Zakaz forest at Yasnaya Polyana, on which words were carved that would destroy all the evil in the hearts of men and bring them everything good.

—Leo Tolstoy

1 *A Part in Search of a Play*

Nous ne vivons jamais, mais nous espérons de vivre; et, nous disposant toujours à être heureux, il est inévitable que nous le soyons jamais.

– Pascal

WE COMMUNICATORS – vendors of words, to use St Augustine's expression – tend to accumulate a lot of waste matter as we go along. I mean press-cuttings, maybe pasted up in books, or just stuffed into envelopes; old letters, whether of personal significance, recording some moment of ostensible drama in one's life, or from unknown correspondents, flattering or abusive (television appearances bring in sackfuls of these), in both cases ministering to one's self-esteem. Books once considered to be of special interest, or just review copies for some reason unsold to the knackers; for that matter, one's own books, still standing in tattered dust-jackets on one's shelves. Photographs, souvenirs, presentations, certificates; even – a mania of my own – all the different passes, *laissez-passers*, visas and other such documents needed to make one's way about this increasingly obstructed world. The rags and tatters of a professionally exhibitionist ego. After half a century in the business, I have a mountain of such junk.

The fact that I have allowed these, what the French police call *pièces justificatives*, to accumulate at all, indicates, I suppose, that I attach a certain value to them, and have an intention some day to sort them out and arrange them chronologically with a view to their preservation, maybe at some American university, grateful for any pabulum to fill its air-conditioned, dust-and-damp-proof vaults. I doubt, though, whether I shall ever bring myself to undertake the task. The odds are I shall die with it still undone, and I see no reason why anyone else should bother with it. Unless my beloved Kitty, if she outlives me (as I pray she may, rather than leaving me, desolate, behind), were for love of me to cherish them, staple or sew them together, and stow them away in

boxes in her neat, methodical way. Then perhaps one of my children or grandchildren might subsequently have a look at them. Or flog them for what they would fetch – which would not, I fear, be much; apart from an occasional signature or letter from someone distinguished enough to be considered worthy of 'collecting' in the saleroom sense. My years of journalism have, in any case, inculcated in me a strong and, as I consider, on the whole salutory resistance to re-reading or re-considering anything done earlier than yesterday. With a few special exceptions, I have had no wish to renew acquaintance with my past writings, whether published or unpublished. Even when they have been re-issued, I have not cared to revise them, or, if the truth be told, read them. That mysterious saying *Let the dead bury their dead* applies, as far as I am concerned, with particular force to words, which exist like insects in the tropics, buzzing briefly round a hurricane lamp and then piling up in dead heaps on the ground.

Nonetheless, from the very beginning of my life I never doubted that words were my *métier*. There was nothing else I ever wanted to do except use them; no other accomplishment or achievement I ever had the slightest regard for, or desire to emulate. I have always loved words, and still love them, for their own sake. For the power and beauty of them; for the wonderful things that can be done with them. I had a memorable example of this once when I was in Darwin, Australia. A message came to me that a man in hospital there had expressed a wish to see me. It seemed he had heard something I said on the radio that had taken his fancy. So I went along. He turned out to be a wizened old fellow who had spent much of his life in the bush, and now was obviously soon going to die. Also, he was quite blind. At first, I just couldn't think of anything to say and felt the silent reproach of his dead eyes. Then, suddenly, there came into my mind what Gloucester says in *King Lear* when Edgar commiserates with him on his blindness – 'I stumbled when I saw.' Just five simple, ordinary words, but the effect was immediate and terrific. My man loved them, and kept saying them over and over. As I went out of the ward I could hear him still repeating them in a loud, joyous voice: 'I stumbled when I saw.'

So, as a child, a writer was in my eyes a kind of god; any writer, no matter how obscure, or even bogus, he might be. To compare a writer with some famous soldier or administrator or scientist or politician or actor was, in my estimation, quite ludicrous. There was no basis for comparison; any more than between, say, Francis of Assisi and Dr Spock. Perhaps more aware of this passion than I realised, when I was

still a schoolboy my father took me to a dinner at a Soho restaurant at which G. K. Chesterton was being entertained. I remember that the proprietor of the restaurant presented me with a box of crystallised fruits which turned out to be bad. As far as I was concerned, it was an occasion of inconceivable glory. I observed with fascination the enormous bulk of the guest of honour, his great stomach and plump hands; how his pince-nez on a black ribbon were almost lost in the vast expanse of his face, and how when he delivered himself of what he considered to be a good remark he had a way of blowing into his moustache with a sound like an expiring balloon. His speech, if he made one, was lost on me, but I vividly recall how I persuaded my father to wait outside the restaurant while we watched the great man make his way down the street in a billowing black cloak and old-style bohemian hat with a large brim. I only saw him once again. That was years later, shortly before he died, when on a windy afternoon he was sitting outside the Ship Hotel at Brighton, and clutching to himself a thriller in a yellow jacket. It, too, like the pince-nez, seemed minute by comparison with his immensity. By that time, the glory of the earlier occasion had departed.

Long before I could read them, or even properly identify the letters, I used to turn over the pages of my father's books. Also, I regularly scrutinised our newspaper, the *Daily News*, more particularly because my father told me it had once been edited by Dickens, though its contents, too, were largely as mysterious to me as Egyptian hieroglyphics. I even remember the arrival of the first issue of the *New Statesman*, my father being an original subscriber. Its rather soggy paper – almost like blotting-paper – could, I discovered, be used to make ersatz cigarettes. I puffed at it before I began to read it, still less to write in it, deriving, I dare say, more solid satisfaction from it then than ever I did subsequently. On one of my early birthdays I was given a toy printing-set with whose large rubber letters I was able to print off my first composition. It was a story of a train going along very fast and, to the satisfaction of the passengers, racing through the small stations along the track without stopping. Their satisfaction, however, turned to dismay, and then to panic fury, as it dawned on them that it was not going to stop at *their* stations either when it came to them. They raged and shouted and shook their fists, but all to no avail. The train went roaring on. At the time I had no notion what, if anything, the story signified. It just came into my mind, and the rubber letters dropped into place of themselves. Yet, as I came to see, and see now more clearly than ever, it is the story I have been writing ever since; the story

of our time. The imagination, at however rudimentary a level, reaches into the future. So its works have a prophetic quality. A Dostoevsky foresees just what a revolution will mean in Russia – in a sense, foresees the Soviet regime and Stalin; whereas a historian like Miliukov and his liberal-intellectual friends envisage the coming to pass of an amiable parliamentary democracy. Similarly, a Blake or a Herman Melville sees clearly through the imagination the dread consequences industrialism and technology must have for mankind, whereas, as envisaged in the mind of a Herbert Spencer or an H. G. Wells, they can bring only expanding wealth and lasting well-being. It was not until much later that I came to identify the passengers in my train as Lord Beveridge, Sidney and Beatrice Webb, Kingsley Martin, Eleanor Roosevelt, and any number of progressive prelates, mahatmas, millionaires, regius professors and other such eminent persons.

Words being my single pursuit, I have to accept my output of them as being, as it were, my gross personal product. And what an output! – millions and millions, on all manner of subjects and in all manner of contexts. Declamatory leading articles and little ridiculous gossip paragraphs; sonorous obituaries, news stories of all shapes and sizes; miscellaneous book reviews, feature articles, captions, commentaries and scripts. If, after aeons of time in hell or heaven or purgatory, I were to be asked what earthly life was like, I should still, I am sure, say it was a sheet of paper fixed in a typewriter and needing to be covered with words; not to-morrow, or next week, or next year, but *now*. I should say it was a clapper-board snapped to, followed by a peremptory voice pronouncing the word: 'Action!' A floor-manager's hand raised, then dramatically falling; a camera advancing with bloodshot eye. Voice, hand and camera equally demanding instant words.

Surveying now this monstrous Niagara of words so urgently called for and delivered, I confess they signify to me a lost life. Possibilities vaguely envisaged but never realised. A light glimpsed, only to disappear. Something vaguely caught, as it might be distant music or an elusive fragrance; something full of enchantment and the promise of ecstasy. Far, far away, and yet near; at the very farthermost rim of time and space, and in the palm of my hand. In any case, whether strained after in the remote distance, or reached for near at hand – unattained. No light seen more enduring than a match flickering out in a dark cave. No lasting ecstasy experienced, only a door closed, and footsteps echoing ever more faintly down stone stairs.

I am not for one moment suggesting, let me hasten to add, that this

sense of a lost life is due to there being no *Times Literary Supplement-*certified or Leavis-sanctified *Oeuvre* among my remains. My grave is quiet; I have no regrets for masterpieces unwritten, for genius unfulfilled. It has long seemed abundantly clear to me that I was born into a dying, if not already dead, civilisation, whose literature was part of the general decomposition; a heap of rubble scavenged by scrawny Eng.Lit. vultures, and echoing with the hyena cries of Freudians looking for their Marx and Marxists looking for their Freud. This, despite adam's apples quivering over winged collars to extol it, and money, money, money, printed off and stuffed into briefcases to finance it. At the beginning of a civilisation, the role of the artist is priestly; at the end, harlequinade. From St Augustine to St Ezra Pound, from Plainsong to the Rolling Stones, from El Greco to Picasso, from Chartres to the Empire State Building, from Benvenuto Cellini to Henry Miller, from Pascal's *Penseés* to Robinson's *Honest to God*. A Gadarene descent down which we all must slide, finishing up in the same slough.

By the same token, a strange certainty has possessed me, almost since I can remember, that the Lord Mayor riding in his coach, the Lord Chancellor seated on his Woolsack, Honourable and Right Honourable Members facing one another across the floor of the House of Commons, were somehow the end of a line. That soon there would be no more Lord Mayors, Lord Chancellors, Honourable and Right Honourable Members, the Mother of Parliaments having reached her time of life or menopause, and become incapable of any further procreation. That figure in a velvet-trimmed gown with a floppy black hat on his head leading a procession of familiar celebrities similarly attired – he can't really be a Vice-Chancellor, can he? Any more than that red-tabbed one is a general. Or that braided one an admiral. Surely the old gentleman in the purple cassock so weirdly grimacing – surely he's an extra, hurriedly fitted out by the wardrobe mistress at the last moment and pushed on to the stage. Even the cash – yes, even the cash – so eagerly or earnestly accumulated and stowed away in the great bank-refrigerators, won't last; there's been a power-cut, the electric current has gone off, and it's melting away.

As for literature and the arts, as cherished by Jennie Lee, and nestling under Lord Goodman's downy wing, listen to the *Missa Solemnis* after the Beatles, and be thankful to Cage for his soundless concertos and symphonies. Likewise, render hearty thanks to Beckett for his wordless, actionless, mindless play after taking a look at *Oh Calcutta!* Corbusier's high-rises are sweet, but those unbuilt are sweeter. After Bacon's

canvases, blessings on those empty ones trendy curators delight to buy for vast sums of money and hang in their galleries! Where are the Parnassians of yesteryear; the dear, drunken Americans gathering in Paris at the Shakespeare Bookshop with Sylvia Beach to care for them, Gertrude Stein or Alice B. Toklas to bore them? Or drying out their hangovers in the Riviera sun? Alas, poor Scott, and poorer Zelda, and Ernest with a self-made hole in his head; the only shot he ever fired that found its target! Whether back into the dark unconscious with Lawrence, or to the end of the night with Céline; whether forward with Marcuse, or sideways with McLuhan, or all over the place with Sartre – no matter. Existentialists of the world uniting, and old Shaw lighting the way to the Good Fabian, Stalin. Oh, Brecht, where is thy sting?

Doubtless other glories lie ahead. Bigger and better capsules carried to the moon; down in the test-tube something stirs; 'I think, therefore, you're not,' says the computer. We all know, though, in our hearts, that our old homestead is falling down; with death-watch beetles in the rafters, and dry rot in the cellar, and unruly tenants whose only concern is to pull the place to pieces. Thus placed, my own inclination has been to join in the buffoonery, but the more scholastically inclined may emulate T. S. Eliot and construct a Wasteland out of bits and pieces culled from Donne, Milton and many a metaphysical compilation. As the Romans, when they were no longer capable of constructing triumphal arches, would still erect one to celebrate some fraudulent hero's home-coming, using for their material bits and pieces taken from old fallen triumphal arches put up in the days of Rome's greatness.

Nor is my sense of a lost life due to repining over opportunities missed, hopes unrealised, happiness vainly pursued. There are no human causes I wish I had served better, no wonders I wish I had seen, no women I wish I had seduced – or, for that matter, wish I had not seduced; no books I wish I had read, languages I wish I had learnt; no events whose outcome I wish I could know. I have never greatly cared for the world, or felt particularly at home in it. Just walking along the road we lived in when I was a child I would find myself wondering, with a poignancy I find it difficult now to convey, who I was and how I came to be in that place. As though it were a foreign land and I a stranger, knowing no one and unable to speak the language. On occasions later, when I was in some sort of position of authority – say, in an editorial chair – I found myself likewise wondering how it could possibly have happened that decisions should be referred to, of all people, me. As it might be looking at dummies or roughs of drawings,

finding things to say – I like it, I don't much care for it, it might be better thus and thus. Ultimately deciding to go with that and that rather than that and the other; but lacking any true conviction or involvement. Not truly participating, even though ostensibly deciding.

Again, in the ultimate fantasy of war, wondering: What's that on my shoulder? Pips? A crown? Hands raised to their caps to salute me, mine raised to salute others. Why? Or yet again, in the even more ultimate fantasy of sex – Whose is this body lying beside mine? To what end? How did it get here? How, for that matter, did I? Watching my own body making bizarre movements, emitting strange groans, in relation to this other body, as though I were in no way concerned. Like seeing oneself on television – a figure on a screen, a stranger, a speaking shadow whose words seem to come out of some immense cave; dry and remote and dead. In this sense, it is possible to look back on a life as so much footage. Or, better – a scene that has often come into my mind, both sleeping and waking – I am standing in the wings of a theatre waiting for my cue to go on stage. As I stand there I can hear the play proceeding, and suddenly it dawns on me that the lines I have learnt are not in this play at all, but belong to a quite different one. Panic seizes me; I wonder frenziedly what I should do. Then I get my cue. Stumbling, falling over the unfamiliar scenery, I make my way on to the stage, and there look for guidance to the prompter, whose head I can just see rising out of the floor-boards. Alas, he only signals helplessly to me, and I realise that of course his script is different from mine. I begin to speak my lines, but they are incomprehensible to the other actors and abhorrent to the audience, who begin to hiss and shout: 'Get off the stage!' 'Let the play go on!' 'You're interrupting!' I am paralysed and can think of nothing to do but to go on standing there and speaking my lines that don't fit. The only lines I know.

There are so many plays to have a part in. As it might be a great love scene; flesh to flesh, and eternity in your eyes. Nonsense! That comes from *Antony and Cleopatra*. Or a great drama of action; firing off-stage, alarums and excursions, a dashing salute. 'Sir, I caught the spy!' Nonsense, again! Leave that to Fleming. Or a political satire, Trollopian, Disraelian, with the part of an *eminence grise* for me. Or rather, *déclivité*. No, that will never do either; render unto Snow the things that are Snow's. Or a majestic voice on the telly – a voice, though, that is for ever Dimbleby. Or a typewriter mightier than the sword; meaning Don Quixote's, of course. So many and so varied plays, but never a one with my lines in it. Yet I remain ever more convinced that

at last I shall find the play my lines belong to, and speak them. Like choristers waiting to sing; hearing unfamiliar music rumbling from the organ; poised ready, and then – the notes they are waiting for, the tune they know. Uplifted, their faces shining and glorious, they pour out their song, filling the air with confident, full-throated notes.

How can I ever explain to those who insist that we must believe in the world to love it that it is *because* I disbelieve in the world that I love every breath I take, look forward with ever-greater delight to the coming of each spring, rejoice ever more in the companionship of my fellow-humans, to no single one of whom – searching my heart – do I wish ill, and from no single one of whom do I wish to separate myself, in word or thought or deed, or in the prospect of some other existence beyond the ticking of the clocks, the vista of the hills, the bounds and dimensions of our earthly hopes and desires? To accept this world as a destination rather than a staging-post, and the experience of living in it as expressing life's full significance, would seem to me to reduce life to something too banal and trivial to be taken seriously or held in esteem. The only thing that could make me falter in taking a position of extreme, if not de-mented, optimism about our human condition and prospects would be if one of the prospectuses for an earthly paradise – whether Scandi-navian-Styled, British-Beveridge, old Stalin-Ware, Dollar-Reinforced, Mao-Special, Tito- or Castro-ised – looked like providing a satisfying or fulfilled way of life. On this score I see no cause for present anxiety. To attempt to expose and ridicule the fraudulence of such prospectuses is no more life-denying than exposing the fraudulence of one for building a housing estate on the slopes of Etna would be shelter-denying.

In other words, the Christian proposition that he that loves his life in this world shall lose it, and he that hates his life in this world shall see it projected and glorified into eternity, is for living, not for dying. After all, it was a St Francis who truly loved the world he so gaily abjured, as his enchanting prayers and canticles convey; not a Père Goriot who so cherished its commodities. It is misers and Don Juans who moan; spendthrifts and saints are always laughing. As the writer of Ecclesiastes so delightfully puts it: 'For to him that is joined to all the living there is hope; for a living dog is better than a dead lion.' All I can claim to have learnt from the years I have spent in this world is that the only happiness is love, which is attained by giving, not receiving; and that the world itself only becomes the dear and habitable dwelling place it is when we who inhabit it know we are migrants, due when the time comes to fly away to other more commodious skies.

I have never, I should add, learnt anything from any exhortation or homily; any political, ethical, theological or philosophical exposition; any presentation in any form of plans, programmes or blue-prints for happy living. Nor from any supernatural visitation or sudden Damascus Road prostration. Only from the experience of living itself, or – what is the same thing – the distillation of that experience in the visions of mystics and the productions of great writers and artists. Learning from experience means, in practice, learning from suffering; the only schoolmaster. Everyone knows that this is so, even though they try to persuade themselves and their fellows otherwise. Only so is it possible to understand how it came about that, through all the Christian centuries, people have been prepared to accept the Cross, ostensibly a symbol of suffering, as the true image and guarantee of their creator's love and concern for them. To climb the highest, stoniest mountain to set it on its peak; to carry it to the remotest, darkest, most forbidding corners of the earth; to build great cathedrals to glorify it; to find in it the inspiration for the most sublime achievements and noblest lives over the last two thousand years.

'I desire to set before my fellows the likeness of a man in all truth of nature, and that man myself,' Rousseau begins his *Confessions*, and then proceeds to construct a vast, serpentine edifice of lies and fantasies. The hazards in the way of telling the truth are, indeed, very great. Seeking it, one can so easily become enmeshed in lies; 'A truth that's told with bad intent/Beats all the lies you can invent,' Blake wrote. Every man the centre of his own universe; insensibly, we sub-edit as we go along, to produce headlines, cross-heads, a story line most favourable to our egos. How indestructible, alas, is that ego! Thinking to have struck it down once and for all, I find its hissing cobra-head lifted again, deathless.

Yet even so, truth is very beautiful; more so, as I consider, than justice – to-day's pursuit – which easily puts on a false face. In the nearly seven decades I have lived through, the world has overflowed with bloodshed and explosions whose dust has never had time to settle before others have erupted; all in purportedly just causes. The quest for justice continues, and the weapons and the hatred pile up; but truth was an early casualty. The lies on behalf of which our wars have been fought and our peace treaties concluded! The lies of revolution and of counter-revolution! The lies of advertising, of news, of salesmanship, of politics! The lies of the priest in his pulpit, the professor at his podium, the journalist at his typewriter! The lie stuck like a fish-bone

in the throat of the microphone, the hand-held lies of the prowling cameraman! Ignazio Silone told me once how, when he was a member of the old Comintern, some stratagem was under discussion, and a delegate, a newcomer who had never attended before, made the extraordinary observation that if such and such a statement were to be put out, it wouldn't be true. There was a moment of dazed silence,and then everyone began to laugh. They laughed and laughed until tears ran down their cheeks and the Kremlin walls seemed to shake. The same laughter echoes in every council chamber and cabinet room, wherever two or more are gathered together to exercise authority. It is truth that has died, not God.

I often wonder how, in such circumstances, it will ever be possible to know anything at all about the people and the happenings of our time. Such masses and masses of documentation! Statistics without end, data of every kind, eye-witness accounts, miles and miles of film, video abounding. Surely out of all this, posterity, if so desiring, will be able to reconstruct us and our lives. But will they? I think of Sidney and Beatrice Webb down at Passfield patiently collecting and collating every scrap of information they could lay hands on about the Soviet regime. Travelling about the USSR to the same end. As experienced investigators, so rigorous and careful. Checking every fact, testing every hypothesis. And the result? – a monumental folly, a volume of fantasy compared with which Casanova's Memoirs, Frank Harris's even, are sober and realistic. Or I think of the messages of Our Own Correspondent, here, there and everywhere, and of all the different factors which shape them and slant them and confection them. I remember the yellow ticker-tape piling up in my office in the Washington National Press Building, and delving into it to pull out a nugget to whisk off on my own account to New York and London. Will this be much help to posterity? I doubt it. Comment is free, but news is sacred, was C. P. Scott's great dictum for *The Guardian*. Yes, but whose news?

> This Life's dim Windows of the Soul
> Distorts the Heavens from Pole to Pole
> And leads you to Believe a Lie
> When you see with, not thro', the Eye.

There never have been such adepts at seeing with, rather than through, the eye, as the purveyors of Scott's sacred news; inducing their readers, all too willingly, to believe a multitude of lies.

Or, again, I think of a camera crew on the job. Sound recordist and

cameraman umbilically linked as they back away from their commen-
tator, sedately walking and communing; their producer anxiously
hovering behind to prevent them from stumbling and falling. Moving
with a kind of *pas-de-deux* step, rather like a matador approaching his
bull. Are they holding a mirror up to nature? Cinema *verité* or *falsité*?
Where's the plastic grass? Or, as I once saw written on a can of film –
surely the perfect celluloid epitaph: 'Dawn for dusk.' The eye is the
window of the soul; film an iron-shutter, says Kafka. On the day that
Harold Wilson became Prime Minister for the first time, I happened to
be in Chicago, and stood in Michigan Avenue with a camera crew and
a microphone asking passers-by what they thought about him and our
change of government. To my great satisfaction, I was unable to find
anyone, old or young, black or white, smart or stupid, who had heard
of the event or cared anything about it. Behind where I was questioning
them, up above the *Tribune* Building, there was one of those devices
whereby news flashes by in fiery letters. Every minute or so it repeated:
DOUGLAS-HOME RESIGNS . . . HAROLD WILSON NEW BRITISH
PREMIER . . . A fine background to cut to! In Moscow when the great
purges were on, some moon-faced Intourist, trying in good liberal style
to be fair to both sides, asked one of the British newspaper correspon-
dents there – A. T. Cholerton of the *Daily Telegraph* – whether the
accusations against the Old Bolsheviks standing trial were true. Yes,
Cholerton told him, everything was true, except the facts. It fits, not
just the purges and Moscow, but the whole mid-twentieth century
scene. Perhaps some astronaut, watching from afar the final incinera-
tion of our earth, may care to write it across the stratosphere: *Everything
true except the facts.*

Yet again, supposing a wish on the part of posterity to know what
some of our great ones were really like. John F. Kennedy, say. In the
archives, trainloads of material. Photographs and profiles without end;
abundance of tape, both video and sound. We can show you him smiling,
walking, talking. On stage and off, as it were; relaxing with his family,
addressing the nation, eating, dozing, praying. We have his jokes, we
know the books he read; you can see and hear him delivering his great
speeches, or fooling with his kids. You can pretty well see him being
assassinated; you *can* see his assassin being assassinated. What more do
you want? Isn't that the man, the whole man, and nothing but the man?
Well, not quite. It's like a nightmare I once had. I was calling on some-
one I loved dearly; the door open, the kettle boiling, a chair drawn up
to the fire, a book open, spectacles laid beside it. But no one there.

Maybe upstairs. With growing anxiety I climb the stairs. Not in the bedroom, though clothes are scattered about; not in the bathroom, though it's still moist and misty from a bath recently taken. Downstairs again; really terrified now. Maybe gone to post a letter. To exercise the dog. Listening for every footstep, starting at every sound, the tension becomes unbearable, and I wake up. In the same sort of way, our methods of representation include every detail, leaving out only the person to be represented. In a sense, they're too perfect. Simulation becomes what it simulates; the image becomes the man. In Kennedy's case, even his signature was done for him by a machine which so exactly reproduced the hand signing his name that experts cannot distinguish between his real signature and the mechanical ones. In the excitement and distress of the Dallas tragedy, no one remembered to turn the machine off. So the President went on signing genial, 'personalised' letters after he was dead.

In this Sargasso Sea of fantasy and fraud, how can I or anyone else hope to swim unencumbered? How see with, not through, the eye? How take off my own motley, wash away the make-up, raise the iron shutter, put out the studio lights, silence the sound effects and put the cameras to sleep? Watch the sun rise on Sunset Boulevard, and set over Forest Lawn? Find furniture among the studio props, silence in a discotheque, love in a strip-tease? Read truth off an autocue, catch it on a screen, chase it on the wings of *Muzak*? View it in living colour with the news, hear it in living sound along the motorways? Not in the wind that rent the mountains and broke in pieces the rocks; not in the earthquake that followed, nor in the fire that followed the earthquake. In a still small voice. Not in the screeching of tyres, either, or in the grinding of brakes; not in the roar of the jets or the whistle of sirens; not in the howl of trombones, the rattle of drums or the chanting of demo voices. Again, that still small voice – if only one could catch it.

2 A Socialist Upbringing

> The world will become a heavenly commune to which men will
> bring the inmost treasures of their hearts, in which they will reserve
> for themselves not even a hope, not even the shadow of a joy, but
> will give up all for mankind. With one faith, with one desire, they
> will labour together in the sacred cause – the extinction of disease,
> the extinction of sin, the perfection of genius, the perfection of love,
> the invention of immortality, the exploration of the infinite, and the
> conquest of creation.
>
> – *The Martyrdom of Man*, by Winwood Reade

MY LIFE BEGAN in a small semi-detached house in Sanderstead, part
of the dormitory town of Croydon. This was in 1903, when there were
still traces of its village past. A drinking-trough for horses, for instance,
an ancient churchyard, and other such intimations of antiquity. But
already the tidal wave of London was sweeping over the place, so that
soon it would just be part of a single huge urban area, with no difference
between one district and another save the postal address and the name
of the railway station. In this urban conglomerate I was born and bred.
My brothers and I – we were five boys – were brought up to look with
distaste on the suburbia which was our native habitat. It was mean and
foolish, like the Pooters in *The Diary of a Nobody*; and came under the
general anathema of being *petit-bourgeois* which, in the vague Marxism
which provided our theology, signified contemptible, despicable. We
would say of someone we disliked that he was *petit-bourgeois* in precisely
the same way that middle- or upper-class boys at that time would say
he was under-bred. This attitude bred in us – or at least in me – a sort
of social schizophrenia; we were snobs in relation to our neighbours,
and anti-snobs in relation to those above and below us in the social
scale. I know that I had a dream fantasy of a 'real worker' sitting in
braces in front of a roaring fire and drinking cups of strong tea which

his missus had just prepared for him. A Hoggartian figure straight out of *Sons and Lovers*; illiterate, maybe, but gloriously so, putting to shame the literate with the pungency and grace of his utterance and ways. The salt of the earth. Likewise, of a 'real gentleman', contemptuous of the paltry hopes and timidities of suburban gentility; a Steerforth figure, or Brushwood Boy, audacious, arrogant perhaps, and too conscious of his own superiority, but still someone worth emulating, even though, at the same time, packing him off in a tumbril.

Between these two dream fantasies lay the suburban no-man's-land in which we lived. Hateful, despicable, ridiculous; little houses with preposterous names like The Elms, Chez-Nous, The Nook; with tradesmen's entrances when there was scarcely room for a tolerable front door, and mock-Tudor beams and gables. I discovered in the Blitz, rather to my surprise, that my hatred of this environment of my childhood had survived, to the point that I found myself exulting in the minuteness of the deposit left behind after the bombs had fallen. No more than little heaps of dust and debris. Gone, just like that; lacking the solidity and dignity even to make a ruin. In most of the successful writers of our time (politicians, too, for that matter; not to mention the pundits of the air and campus), coming, as they do, from the same sort of environment, similar stigmata may be detected. H. G. Wells, for instance, and his Kipps and Mr Polly. D. H. Lawrence storming out of Nottingham with his Baroness on his arm. Lucky Jim, and the wilder fantasies of Brideshead. That fearful symmetry Blake writes about, inexorably discloses itself. I think with awe of the perfection of the demonstration in, for instance, Evelyn Waugh and George Orwell; the one in his country gentleman's outfit, loud checks, overcoat sweeping the ground, grey bowler perched on large head, ear-trumpet to hand; the other in corresponding proletarian fancy-dress, corduroy trousers, not actually tied up with string, but as near as can be, choker round the neck, ancient drooping coat, hand-rolled shag cigarette. Both taken from back numbers of *Punch*. Why bother to write when the Lord provides such pictures?

My father was a small man, with wide shoulders and a frame that seemed to belong to a bigger body than his. The reason for this discrepancy between the structure and substance of him was, he told me, that as a child he had been badly and poorly fed. At the same time, being very energetic by temperament, he had always kept on the move. He had a sense of himself as being physically grotesque. 'I'm an ugly

man,' he said to me once with a kind of droll pathos. 'I've always been ugly.' It was true in a way, and yet not true. He had a quality of distinction about him; even a certain beauty, deriving from his energy and exuberance. I should explain that he often reminisced and ruminated about himself to me in a way that, in those days, certainly, was unusual. Thus I came to have an exceptionally vivid sense of him and his life. More so, in a way, than of my own. Of his moods of melancholy and self-depreciation; of his large-mouthed sensuality, his spongy pin-cushion nose, his gift of the gab, his ultimate sense of his own and everything else's intrinsic absurdity; of his abounding, irrepressible ego. Am I describing myself? As I only realised long afterwards, of all things, he wanted me to be different from him. To go to Cambridge and emerge like one of his heroes – Tawney, or Lowes Dickinson, or even Hugh Dalton. To speak down my nose as dons and Fabians did. To be as well informed as Sidney Webb, as rumbustious as Wells, as witty and rich as Shaw. Devastatingly amusing, splendidly eloquent on behalf of the down-trodden and oppressed; author, orator, statesman, seer. And all that emerged was another edition of him. So much effort and money expended just for that!

There was one terrible occasion, some dinner at the Greyhound Hotel in Croydon when I was the guest of honour. I've even got a photograph of it. Local notabilities in miscellaneous evening dress; white waistcoats showing under black coats, dubious bow ties. My father among them. Then the dreadful moment; pray silence for . . . I rose to my feet, knowing, as always, exactly what he was thinking and hoping. Witty remarks, audience convulsed; then punching home some profundities, memorable phrases reproduced in the local paper – the *Croydon Advertiser*, the *Croydon Times*. I could think of nothing to say except how I loved and respected him, what a wonderful human being he was, how much he had done for me, for Croydon, for the poor and ill-used everywhere. I plunged ever deeper into my fatal misconception, and as I went on saw he was stricken. At one point he actually ejaculated a strangled: No! I have always been touched by the way Dr Johnson went to Lichfield and stood in the market-place for a whole day as an act of penitence for lack of consideration for his bookseller father. I ought to do the same thing, in front of the Croydon Town Hall, a Betjeman-beloved neo-Gothic building of quite exceptional architectural confusion; stand there and recall that dreadful dinner, and the anguish and disappointment I inflicted on my father at it.

As he recounted his life to me, it sounded exactly like a Dickens

novel. Dickens was a great bond between us. He would read aloud bits to me; like Silas Wegg declining and falling for the edification of Mr Boffin. Doing the accents; I can hear him now – Wegg, having been told by Mr Boffin that if anything took his fancy he was to mention it, pausing majestically: 'I think I see a weal and ham pie!' How I laughed, and, for that matter, cried over the sentimental passages like the death of Dora Copperfield, which I also loved. Dickens is the true inspirer, and remains to a great extent the embodiment, of English Radicalism or Leftism; his stamp is still upon the Labour Party stalwarts, as it was upon my father. How appropriate that in the USSR his strictures on the Poor Law and other abuses of his time continue to be regarded as valid! In a sort of way they are, too. His capacity for turning on a passionate flood of righteous indignation at any time; his tears for the poor, and love of money and success; his scorn for his social superiors, and passion to be like them; the sentimentality in which all his emotions, public and private, were drenched, and the corresponding humour which so incomparably expressed what he really felt, how he really saw his fellows and the world he lived in – is not this characteristic of any of our leaders of the Left, from Lloyd George and Aneurin Bevan to Harold Wilson?

I took Dickens's novels out of the Croydon Public Library one after the other, and somehow managed to tear the pages of *Our Mutual Friend* rather badly, which was noticed when I returned the book. I awaited the awful consequences, which duly came when I noticed a letter from the Chief Librarian in my father's morning mail. He read it, frowned, taxed me with the offence, which I admitted. I had no choice. Then he went off to catch his train, and all through the day I wondered what dreadful fate would befall me. However, in the evening my father seemed particularly cheerful, and read aloud to me the reply he had sent to the Chief Librarian. It apologised on my behalf for my offence, offered to make restitution for the damage done. Then came the beautiful sentence which put the letter, as far as I was concerned, in the same class as Johnson's to Lord Chesterfield (a subsequent comparison, naturally): 'I feel sure that the damage done to the book was due, not to any spirit of wanton destructiveness on my son's part, nor even to the natural carelessness of youth, but rather to his love of the book in question, and impatience to get at its contents.' (Remembering it from so long ago, I may not have got the words exactly right, but I am sure approximately so.) He liked the words as much as I did; they came rolling lusciously off his tongue. I knew my troubles were over. Nor,

as it turned out, did my father even have to pay the Librarian any compensation.

My father was the eldest of a large family; I think nine children, but there may have been more. Their father had an undertaker's business in Penge, and was, it seemed, weak and self-indulgent, though possessed of certain social graces. He abandoned his family when my father was twelve, but reappeared from time to time. At thirteen my father left school, as you could in those days, if you were clever and passed an exam. It was the exact opposite to now when you pass an exam to be able to stay on at school. Both arrangements seem rather silly. His mother, meanwhile – a woman of strong character – set up in a second-hand furniture business in Penge High Street. I have been up and down this street trying to imagine where the shop may have been. When I asked my father how she conducted the business, he tapped the side of his nose in a very Dickensian way, winked, and said: 'She bought cheap and sold dear.' Anyway, the business enabled her to support the family. On leaving school my father took a job as an office boy with a firm of shirt manufacturers, remaining with them for the rest of his working life. He became secretary to the company, and was at one point invited to join the board if he would agree to give up his political activities. This he declined to do, and so never became rich. He told me that his salary never reached a thousand a year, but he may be said to have thriven. We never lacked for anything essential.

He contributed to his mother's household from the few shillings a week he earned as an office boy. From that time on, he once wryly remarked, he always had people dependent on him. To economise, he took what was then called the Workmen's Train from Penge to London Bridge, which went very early, but was cheaper than the ones later in the day. (What would it be called now if it existed? The Health Train, maybe. Or, more whimsically, the Early Bird Train. Or, for the ideologically alert, the Workers' Train.) It meant that he arrived an hour or so before his office opened, which he spent roaming through the City. In those days, he told me, he used to run more often than walk. Strolling through the City, as I sometimes did on a Sunday afternoon when I was working in Fleet Street, I have often imagined him darting about those streets like an excited sparrow. Between his departure on the Workmen's Train and return to Penge round about seven was a long stretch, sustained, more often than not, by nothing more substantial than buns and meat pies. His office was in New Basinghall Street off Moorgate; it was totally destroyed in the Blitz. I visited him

there when I was little older than he had been when he first started working, and can just remember, on what must have been that occasion, riding with him in a horse-drawn omnibus. His office, as I recall it, gave an impression of being dusty and murky. My father and his friend and colleague Mr Button were seated on two high stools with ledgers before them in the outer part of the office, from which doors opened into the private sanctums of the partners in the firm. Did my father ever graduate into one of these private sanctums? I rather doubt it. He had very beautiful hand-writing; not exactly copperplate, but the next best thing. Remarkably clear and regular and easy to read. I have, of course, many examples – letters, and so on – but the one I cherish most is the inscription in the first book I ever possessed. *A Pageant of English Poetry*, published by the Clarendon Press, which he gave me for Christmas 1914, when I was eleven; the year of doom.

As my father's circumstances improved, he acquired a house in Penge – with a mortgage, it goes without saying. By this means, he explained to me, he could protect his mother from the unwelcome visits of her husband. In fact, he had occasion to order him out of the house; something that afterwards he looked back on with a certain amount of remorse. I know, not only from what he said to me, but from scraps of writing that he left behind, that his attitude to his father distressed him. He felt he had been priggish. Once, he told me, he had seen his father on Victoria Station with his arm round a lady, and it had upset him considerably. After his father's death (he did not go to the funeral), this lady, or maybe another, came to see him, saying that she was his step-mother and that there were a number of half-brothers and sisters he might care to meet. He showed her the door rather harshly, saying that he only knew of one wife his father had, and that was his mother. What happened to the lady and her offspring history does not relate. With his own five children and numerous other commitments, it was impossible for him to take on a new lot, especially on such dubious credentials. All this gave me a great curiosity about my procreative undertaker grandfather whom I never saw, but the only trace of him I could ever find was an ancient dim photograph revealing a weak indeterminate face lurking behind a large blond moustache. From it I could easily imagine how appropriate a figure he would be in a funeral procession, as his profession required; top-hatted, frock-coated, sure and soft of foot, expression grave, and eyes downcast. His wife, my paternal grandmother, on the other hand – whom I also never saw – was clearly a very tough lady indeed; as she needed to be. She success-

fully brought up her nine children, though losing some on the way from tuberculosis – a family complaint, of which I also had symptoms at one stage. When she lay dying in her late fifties, my father was with her, and described to me how he went to support her, but somehow messed it up, and she fell back among her pillows muttering: 'You always were clumsy!' Again, it was so exactly the sort of thing that might have happened to me. A photograph of her shows her in a bonnet, with resolute eyes, a large decisive nose and firm mouth.

It would be possible to portray my father – certainly, he was liable to see himself so – as a victim of social injustice. He was prone to self-pity, as I have also been, though admittedly with far more justification than I. Yet even I, despite almost inconceivable good fortune, could drum up a case. How much more he, with his genuine deprivations and hardships. Obviously, nowadays he would have a quite different life. Go to a grammar school and on to the university, where he would undoubtedly have distinguished himself. Get into Parliament young enough to have a ministerial career (he was already in his sixties when he got elected for Romford in 1931); certainly in the Cabinet, maybe an outside chance of being Prime Minister. If Attlee, then any Labour Party stalwart may be considered as in the running. In any case, he would have thriven in the lush pastures between the London School of Economics, Whitehall and Westminster. There are plenty of prototypes among existing socialist brass. He would have been spared all those years of City drudgery; all that laborious learning French by himself and learning to play the piano. That strumming away at the piano, pipe in mouth, and so intent that spittle used to run along the stem, forming a great gob for whose falling I watched, fascinated! *The Flying Dutchman* played with immense vigour and verve, and a song from *Faust* which my mother used to sing in a quavering voice – 'Oh Marguerita, Oh Marguerita, still on the bough is left a leaf of gold.' I was unfortunately not with him when he died, but away on war service on some tomfool Intelligence mission; but Kitty was, and described to me how he departed this life with a broad, joyous unforgettable wink. As a Rt. Hon., D.Lit., M.A., C.H., P.C., etc. etc., we shouldn't have had the wink. I cherish it.

Each age has its special pigeonholes for sorting out lives. In the nineteenth century my father would have been type-cast as the office boy who worked his way up to be boss; in our time, as an example of gifts and abilities wasted for lack of opportunity. Now all that has been put right; look at Roy Jenkins. Well, look at him!

I remember my father most vividly and characteristically at the top of Surrey Street on a Saturday evening, where in those days there used to be a street market, with gas flares by the booths, and plenty of hucksters coaxing passers-by to take advantage of a wonderful chance to buy a gold watch for next to nothing, or a salve that would cure anything from the pox to pink eye, or shaving soap so pure and luscious that you could eat it – which the huckster then proceeded to do to prove his point, stuffing the suds into his mouth as though they were turkish delight. Meanwhile, my father had set up his little frail platform, almost like a gallows against the evening sky, and climbed on to it. He was bearded by now, having grown his beard as a result of being afflicted with a skin complaint called barber's rash which, I imagine, has now disappeared along with the cut-throat razor. The beard gave an extra dimension of drama to the scene; making a prophet of him, a voice crying in the wilderness against the soap suds man. I led the applause and the laughter, such as they were. Even at ten I knew for the most part what he would say; as well as all his jokes. They did not lose their piquancy for me because of that. I waited for them, sensed that they were coming, exploded with mirth prematurely when he was still working up to the pay-off line. 'Now ladies and gentlemen,' he would begin, addressing some ten or a dozen casual passers-by, who had paused out of curiosity to listen to him; along with myself, a couple of Labour Party stalwarts who had turned out with him, and perhaps another urchin or two – 'Now ladies and gentlemen, can you tell me this? It's His Majesty's Government, His Majesty's Navy, His Majesty's Stationery Office. His Majesty's This and His Majesty's That. Every blooming thing seems to be His Majesty's. But it's the National Debt. Why isn't that His Majesty's? We'll gladly let His Majesty have that, won't we?'

It might raise an occasional smile, but mostly the point was lost, except on me and the two stalwarts who, of course, had also heard it many times before. Undeterred, my father slogged on, abolishing poverty, illiteracy, war, inequality, every conceivable ill and injustice, and ushering in the glorious era of everlasting peace, prosperity and happiness. His voice rose, his gestures grew more intense; against the night sky, he was a gesticulating enraged shadow calling on mankind to turn away from their follies and false leaders and realise their true destiny. What a sublime prospect it seemed! How relatively easy of attainment! And yet the people in Surrey Street seemed strangely indifferent; their attention more easily held by the gold watch, the magic

salve, the edible shaving soap than by this sure prospectus for living happily ever after. Defiantly, my father, the two stalwarts and I sang 'The Red Flag' together, my small tuneless voice mixing with their deep ones, folded up his platform and made off carrying it.

On these occasions I was always uplifted, never doubting that my father was right, and that all he promised could and would come to pass, despite the seeming indifference of those he addressed. In my copy of *The Pilgrim's Progress*, much thumbed, with its coloured illustrations, Surrey Street was Vanity Fair, which, though it scorned us, would in the end come to follow the way we sign-posted. Even then I preferred Bunyan's imagery to the statistical forecasts of our ultimate triumph, showing how we would capture the borough councils, Parliament, the Government, until we were able to take over everything and everyone. Meanwhile, the co-operative societies – we were ardent co-op supporters – must in due course, since they gave back their profits to the customer, get all retail trade into their hands. Already the Croydon trams were run by the Corporation. How virtuously they glided along compared with the roistering free-enterprise buses! I should no more have thought of setting foot on a bus in those days than a strict Methodist would have thought of going into a public house. When I was sent shopping, it was taken for granted that the co-op must be my first call. Though co-op shops also had counters, and men in white coats who patted the butter into shape, and arrays of packaged goods, they were not as other shops. The coins one paid dropped into the till rather like a church offertory than a payment made and received; the bills had a picture of a wheatsheaf on them, and texts from the sayings of the Rochdale founding fathers. I remember so well that little row of shops; after the co-op, the butcher; the chemist, maybe, who also pulled out teeth for a shilling a time; the baker, who would add an extra crusty sliver of bread to make up the weight of a loaf which I munched on the way home.

My mother came from Sheffield, where her father and some of her brothers worked in the cutlery industry. My father met her while on holiday in the Isle of Man. She was staying there with some relatives, the Gadsbys, who were relatively prosperous tradesmen. They had, my mother told me – she always spoke of them with a certain awe – several jewellery shops in seaside resorts, and, having taken a fancy to her, liked her to make long stays with them, which she cheerfully did. She greatly appreciated their superior affluent circumstances and the pretty

dresses they bought her. It was an experience which much influenced her future tastes and aspirations. She told me once that her dream had been to go to church on Sunday mornings on my father's arm, he in a top hat, and we five children following behind in single file, in order of seniority, each wearing Eton collars and jackets. Alas, this dream remained unrealised; like my father's, as it would now be called, elitist one of my becoming a socialist toff, begotten by Keir Hardie out of Balliol with Toynbee Hall intervening.

How, precisely, she and my father met I never learnt, but I think it must have been some sort of a pick-up. She was extremely pretty, with very fair hair, and an expression of fathomless innocence which she retained to a considerable degree to the end of her days. Only, if you looked deep into it, far, far below the pellucid surface, you came upon something steely, tough, and even merciless, there. I imagine a Wellsian encounter, my father and the two office pals who were on holiday with him, in high spirits, and my mother flattered at being the object of the attentions of such sprightly young fellows. My father returned to Penge and New Basinghall Street in a state of extreme exaltation. Some of his early letters to my mother remain extant; they are couched in highly romantic terms, and bear unmistakable traces of his literary studies. I found them touching, and rather beautiful; to me preferable, in their implications, to contemporary arrangements which, in any case, had they prevailed then, might well have precluded my being born at all. No great catastrophe, it might be contended, and I agree; though for me, all the same, a deprivation of sorts.

My father went to Sheffield to be looked over, and gave satisfaction; my mother visited Penge, and though his mother, as appeared afterwards, had certain doubts, she kept them to herself, and gave her blessing to their union. A wedding photograph in a family album shows the bridal pair looking appropriately uplifted, though in my father's case I thought I detected just a flicker of a reservation. No mood with him was ever quite homogeneous – another trait I inherited. Their marriage lasted to the end of their days, with suitable silver and golden celebrations. When my father died my mother closed his eyes, with a certain irritation at their refusing to open again, but never accustomed herself to life without him. The bed in which they had slept side by side through so many nights had two hollows in it; with the other unoccupied, my mother lay disconsolately in hers.

Our Sheffield relations were a great source of interest and delight in our childhood. All of us at different times visited them for longer or

shorter periods, which was considered a very special treat. (The family name, by the way, was Booler; I had to dredge it out of my memory years later when I applied to join a club in Washington D.C., and was required to give the name of my maternal grandmother in order to prove, presumably, that my blood was uncontaminated by Jewish or any other alien admixture.) They were particularly kind, warmhearted, cheerful people. Each Christmas they sent us a hamper of food containing parkin, home-made pork pies and other Yorkshire delicacies. Though my mother – as she certainly believed – might be considered to have improved her circumstances by moving south and marrying my father, we always thought of the Boolers as living more comfortably than we did. Their houses warmer and cosier, with a more ample table. At the same time, they were quite definitely working-class in their ways and outlook, as we were lower-middle-class. So, in the social categories of revolutionary mystique, they were downtrodden and oppressed, and we the running dogs of the exploiters.

Looking back now, I find it curious that I never saw any disparity between the Boolers as I knew them and my dream fantasy of the noble proletarian; between my actual feelings about them and their allotted role in the great drama of revolution which I hoped with all my heart soon to see enacted – with, of course, a star part for me. I did once, it is true, ask my father how he could be sure that if, as he proposed, the proletariat were subjected to the same sort of education and style of living as our neighbours in South Croydon, and given the same little suburban houses to live in, and gardens to tend, and schools to go to, they would not just turn into *petits bourgeois* themselves, with all the stuck-up attitudes and philistine tastes we found so abhorrent? I really believe this was the only occasion on which we got anywhere near a political disagreement up to the time I left Cambridge, and probably a good deal beyond that. My father assured me that, with the right sort of education, things would not work out so, and I had to accept his word for it, though with some inward doubts. I might have cited the Boolers as a case in point, but didn't. The truth is, of course, that the whole notion of a working class with a specific political or cultural, or even spiritual, role *qua* working class is a fantasy invented by guilt-stricken renegade proletarians like D. H. Lawrence, or by renegade bourgeoisie on the run like William Morris or, for that matter, Marx and Engels themselves, or just by sociologists looking for a subject and a job. It was serving in the ranks as an ageing private in my late thirties that clinched the matter for me. I discovered then that proletarians in a barrack- or

NAAFI-hut included all the familiar types (opinionated extrovert, shy introvert, artistic, homosexual, assertive, lecherous, etc. etc.) to be found among a similar collection of bourgeoisie. I might have been back at Cambridge, and in a very short while thought I was.

I often sat up with my mother waiting for my father's return from political meetings and municipal activities in which he was heavily engaged. Most evenings he was out. There was a certain tension in the air, a sense of impending drama. She resented, I knew, my father's absence night after night, and, as I dimly understood, suspected that he did not necessarily tell her precisely where and with whom he had been. She felt excluded from all this part of his life; in his eyes, far the most important and significant part. So she sat there bolt upright in a sort of folding chair she always chose, looking severe and censorious. Even if she dozed off, her features remained set and taut. We talked little on the whole; she was not much of a conversationalist, except when reminiscing about her childhood and staying with the Gadsbys – that golden time. There was not really much to talk about from my point of view. She had read little, and even when she did read, it was very slowly, with her lips visibly moving as she spelt out the words. Writing a letter was, for her, a heavy labour – a round hand, with no punctuation, and shaky spelling. Yet I have to record that when I was away she quite often wrote to me; letters, as I should have remembered, representing so much effort on her part and, oddly, signed 'Annie', not 'your affectionate mother', or anything like that. Once when she was seriously ill in a nursing home near Bournemouth, and I went to see her, she indicated that she had something particular to say to me. I bent down my head, and at last she got it out; someone I was very interested in had in the past once occupied that house . . . someone . . . but she couldn't quite manage the name. Then she managed it – Tolstoy. Afterwards I found out that she was quite right. Tolstoy had briefly stayed in the house during a visit to England. It was only afterwards that I remembered how touching it was of her to have stored up for me this particular piece of information which she knew I should cherish. One remembers such things too late.

My mother had a way of sometimes using unexpectedly lurid phrases. Thus, at one of our evening sessions she noticed that I was apparently reading an English translation of Rousseau's *Confessions* I'd picked up from among my father's books. In point of fact, the book was far too difficult for me at that stage, and it was mere pretence on my part to be reading it. I was given to this sort of affectation, and even much later

in my life, if I was reading in public – say, in a bus or a train – I liked it to be something that would strike anyone who happened to notice as being abstruse and exotic. Later I came to love the *Confessions*, even their many lies, for some elusive quality of luminosity in them which comes out in their very style, so beautifully clear and supple. My mother, for reasons of her own, held Rousseau in the utmost abhorrence and, while indicating this to me, volunteered the information that he had been born with his blood boiling. It was an observation that greatly intrigued me, and, not understanding at all what my mother was getting at, I tried to imagine someone with his blood on the boil, bubbling and steaming like a saucepan of porridge. I was so preoccupied with this that I failed to follow my mother's subsequent remarks, and only picked up the thread when she was saying that she would rather see me, as she put it, dead at her feet than doing something or other – what I had no sort of an idea. It is a curious thing that though, as far as my reading was concerned, I was precocious, delving freely into my father's books, as far as I know, it had absolutely no effect in making me sexually precocious. My favourite book at this time, when I was about fourteen, was *The Three Musketeers*. I loved it passionately; it is the only book that, in the whole of my life, I have finished reading and then at once turned back to page one and begun again. In my edition there was a picture of d'Artagnan running away from a meeting with Milady. He is wearing only his shirt, but it did not occur to me to wonder why he should have taken off his trousers.

Even so, my mother's whole manner, and the lurid phrases she used, gave me the feeling that something unusual, frightening and in some way exciting was at issue. Without actually complaining about my father, I felt that somehow she was pointing an accusing finger at him. Once she said to me darkly that she hoped I would never know what she had had to put up with. On Sunday mornings, when my father was usually at home and, if the weather was suitable, working in the garden, this vaguely accusatory manner was liable to take a more concrete form. In a house at the back of ours, and overlooking our garden, there was a small attic window in which, my mother had managed to convince herself, a maid-servant would sit exposing herself or otherwise sending my father erotic signals. It was a preposterous notion, but so real to her that she would flit in a kind of frenzy from window to window in our house, peering out from behind the curtains and trying to catch a glimpse of the offending siren; my father, meanwhile, going on calmly planting his potatoes or hoeing between the rows of his spring onions.

My mother's expression on these occasions seemed to be quite horrifying; enflamed and enraged and somehow animal. It was my first glimpse of authentic evil, and – as always happens with evil – infected me, evil being the most infectious, and even contagious, of all sicknesses. I found myself likewise peering up at the attic window and imagining I saw there an obscenely smiling face, and two pendulous breasts hanging down like Christmas turkeys to attract my father's gaze. The only comparable incident that I have come across in contemporary fiction occurs in a novel by Iris Murdoch in which the heroine likewise mutely displays her breasts. If my mother had written a novel, it would, I fancy, have been in rather the same vein as Miss Murdoch's.

The undercurrent of suspicion running through my mother's mind frequently led to rows. My father would explode, shout with sarcastic rage: 'Take care, the servants are looking!' and go out, violently slamming the front door behind him. I dreaded these outbursts, and one of the reasons I would sit up with my mother waiting for my father's return was that I thought my presence would serve to mitigate any trouble that might arise. Even if I did go to bed, more often than not I lay awake waiting to hear his key in the lock, straining to catch the sound of their voices, to make sure they were not raised, infinitely relieved when I heard them putting out the lights and climbing upstairs to bed; one more day gone by. The precise nuances of feeling and sense of deprivation behind these rows I, of course, had no means of knowing, and should not have understood if I had known. Perhaps if my parents had been rich and more attuned to the moral dissolution of the times, they might have parted and sought other partners. I doubt if they would have gained thereby, and we children would certainly have lost. They stayed together for our sake; in any case, they were too conscientious about their financial responsibilities for others, to be in a position to do otherwise. Something for which I honour them. When I think of their companionship in old age, their interminable games of two-handed bridge, how utterly lost they would have been without one another when the Blitz made them homeless in their seventies, I marvel anew at the extraordinary strength of this bizarre institution of monogamous marriage, which goes on surviving despite the furious attacks directed against it and its own intrinsic disabilities.

Incidentally, to the best of my knowledge, my mother's suspicions about my father were quite without foundation. There was nothing he ever said to me (and we were at times exceedingly frank with one another; more so than our disparity in years might seem to permit) or

in his papers to suggest the contrary. Also, as I had occasion to see for myself when I was still quite young, he was singularly naïve in sexual matters for a man of his years and experience. It happened that we found ourselves in the spring of 1927 in Paris together. I had just come back from India, he having met me in Naples. It was a wonderful thing to find my father standing there on the quay when my boat came into Naples Harbour – my first sight of it – at dawn; his bowler hat on his head, and that look about him that I knew and loved so well, of expectancy, a boyish conviction that something wonderful was going to happen. We travelled to Paris, stopping off at Rome for two or three days. In Paris we ran into someone my father knew – some sort of a progressive travel-agent, Welsh, I fancy, with a dark chin, who asked us out for an evening to see the sights. It involved going to various brothels and lewd or blasphemous spectacles arranged for tourists. I imagine they have all long ago shut down now that rather inferior versions of the same shows are to be seen in the West End, but then they were in full swing. At one of them, when we entered, girls with nothing on except diaphanous scarves and high-heeled shoes came and perched on our knees, ordered expensive drinks, and when we left tried to haggle over the tips we gave them. Here our progressive travel-agent was useful, and soon shut them up. What preoccupied my father afterwards as we strolled down the Champs Elysées under the stars on our way back to our hotel – the Francois 1er – was that when he gave his girl a pound she put it in her shoe, though, as I pointed out, actually she had nowhere else to put it. Nonetheless, he continued to mutter to himself: 'She put it in her shoe!' as though there were any number of possible alternatives. The next day, rather shamefacedly, he asked me whether it had been my first visit to places of that kind. I assured him – not quite truthfully – that I was, if not an *habitué*, at any rate quite accustomed to them, whereupon he cheered up. Whether or not our behaviour would have come into the category my mother had in mind when she said she would sooner see me dead at her feet than guilty of it, I never knew. Nothing would have induced me to breathe a word to her about our spree.

My father's unfamiliarity with the brothel scene was the more surprising because prostitutes and prostitution played a big part in our Leftist mythology, providing us with a classic case of exploitation; of the power of money in a capitalist society to override normal human feelings, and even animal instincts. *Resurrection* was one of our classics – among the very best; and again Blake gave us the *mots justes* in his lines

about the harlot's cry from street to street weaving old England's winding sheet. They call them *filles de joies* in Paris, my father would say sarcastically, almost spitting out the words, and he liked telling a story about a man who was advised by his doctor to have a woman for health reasons. 'Then may I have your daughter?' the man says. When the doctor expostulates, he goes on: 'It has to be somebody's daughter, hasn't it?' My father delivered this pay-off line with great verve, in a tone of voice he reserved for famous retorts; for instance – also a great favourite – Voltaire's '*Je ne vois pas la nécessité.*' It is rather sad to reflect that the prostitute has gone the way of so much of our old Leftist mythology; driven out of circulation by ardent amateurs, as the armament manufacturer, or merchant of death – another great standby – has been superseded by ardent governments eager to flog their weapons, and the arrogant landowner by the arrogant bureaucrat.

What, I think, worried my mother more than any suspicion that my father was engaged in illicit amours was the notion of free love, then very current among Socialists, especially young middle-class ones. She disapproved of this strongly, and did not hesitate to say so when the subject came up, whereas my father and his friends, though most of them extremely respectable in their own lives, felt bound to accord the notion a faint gesture of sympathy. H. G. Wells in his autobiography describes making the discovery – almost with the excitement of an Archimedes – that it was possible to sleep with young progressive girls of good family without having to pay or, as was then the case, running any appreciable risk of catching venereal disease. Even the danger of pregnancy was reduced, in the sense that their families were perfectly capable of paying for an abortion, or, in the event of a baby being born, disposing of the bastard. For a time I belonged to the 1917 Club, founded to commemorate the Russian Revolution, and the scene, very appropriately, of Ramsay MacDonald's first public appearance as Labour Prime Minister in 1924, when he was greeted by a female of the locality as her Yorkshire Boy. In its somewhat dingy premises in Gerrard Street, well-spoken, good-looking girls up from the Home Counties or farther afield, who had become convinced by the *New Statesman*, or maybe some itinerant university extension lecturer, that they had nothing to lose but their virginity, were much in evidence. I once asked one of them who had fallen briefly into the hands of Wells how the first approach had been made. It was at a party, she told me, and after some preliminary conversation, Wells had whispered to her: 'Shall we go upstairs and do funny things with our bodies?' I asked her

whether the things they did had turned out to be funny. 'Not particu-
larly,' she said.

Anything like this was, of course, infinitely remote from our suburban
milieu, but even so the notion was abroad, and my mother had picked
up a tiny bat-squeak of it among the Socialist faithful in Croydon;
sensing a menace in it, hanging primarily over my father, but also to a
lesser extent over my brothers and myself. About the siren in the attic
window I had heard her mutter splenetically: 'Man-mad!' How much
more, then, some charming infants-school teacher, crammed full of
Ann Veronica and Havelock Ellis, not to mention Marie Stopes. The
whole thing was crystallised, as far as my mother was concerned, by the
Colony, a Tolstoyan settlement in the Cotswolds started by Socialists
from Croydon with whom we maintained connections. They made no
bones about it, but lived openly with one another, unmarried, and, in
principle at any rate, when they felt like it, changing their partners.
They also, incidentally, eschewed private property and the use of money,
held their goods in common, and otherwise detached themselves from
contemporary usages – all points about which my mother's feelings
were tepid compared with her attitude to their sexual *mores* which, she
considered, put them in the class of Sodom and Gomorrah, if not well
below it.

As it happened, I got to know the Colony rather well, having been
boarded out near it when I developed vague T.B. symptoms and, on
medical advice, was sent into the country for a spell. In view of his
family history, my father was naturally hyper-sensitive about anything
of the kind. I doubt if I was particularly ill, but I just remember
coughing rather a lot and feeling inordinately tired, as I still do from
time to time. As for the possibility that I might prove to be tubercular –
something that I dimly understood – it both frightened and fascinated
me. After all, Keats suffered from this complaint, which might be
regarded as among the more interesting ones. At the same time, I had a
vivid awareness, gathered from having seen relatives of my father in the
last stages of T.B., of what it was like; the high colour concentrated
round the cheek-bone, the abnormally lurid eyes, the sputum that
had to be kept for subsequent examination, the transparent skin with
fever just under the surface – like a furnace seen through a plate-glass
window.

I loved my time in the country, from the moment Miss Lidiard met
me with a pony and trap at Stroud Station, and we trotted along to the
delightful old cottage in the village of Sheepscombe where she lived

with her mother. The house made me think of David Copperfield's home before his father died, and I decided to be David there. Like, I suppose, most children, I often took the parts of characters I admired. I can remember going about for days on end as d'Artagnan, and then as Tom Sawyer – though, oddly enough, not as Huckleberry Finn, even though I admired him more than Tom. I suppose I just didn't want to *be* him. There was a large damson tree in Miss Lidiard's garden, loaded with fruit, and in the capacity of David, despite her protests below, I climbed to the very highest branches, and stripped them.

It was part of the arrangement at Sheepscombe that Miss Lidiard should give me some lessons. These went ill, and she occasionally chastised me with a cane, though I can't recall that it caused me more than passing discomfort, or any appreciable psychological distress. I was, I fear, an almost unteachable child, the reason being that I never had – or for that matter have – the slightest interest in the subjects taught at school and university, with the possible exception of scripture. Algebra, geography, physics, history even – I never wanted to learn about such subjects any more than to listen to some boring guide telling me about the Parthenon or the Sistine Chapel. As for English, the one subject I did care about – just because I so cared about it the maunderings of teachers, up to and including university ones, were somehow irrelevant. Poor Miss Lidiard! She tried her hand at arithmetic, spelling and the rivers and promontories of England without any appreciable success.

From time to time Miss Lidiard took me to visit the Colony, which was only a mile or so away. She was a gentle, reserved and rather severe lady who certainly did not approve of the Colony's ways and ideas. Her connection with it came about through Will Straughan, my father's closest friend, whom she subsequently married. Indeed, it was he who arranged for me to go to Sheepscombe. Various of his relatives had joined the Colony, and though he personally took a derisory view of everything to do with it, he continued to keep in touch with them. He was a truly enchanting human being; gentle, humorous, quixotically generous, original; somehow giving a vague impression of sadness, and yet indissolubly associated in my mind with laughter. I count such men among life's major blessings; as well as implying a strong hint of better things to come. If it is possible thus to live kindly and companionably and cheerfully in the world without any elevated mystical or philosophical insight to buoy one up; without fasting in the wilderness, or

being nailed to a cross, or speaking with tongues; just as a mortal man with other mortal men – to use Falstaff's blessed expression; why, then, surely our poor benighted human race will never wholly succumb to the follies and brutalities to which we often appear to be inexorably given. However deep the darkness, these small steady lamps continue to shine, bringing great solace.

Will Straughan's marriage to Miss Lidiard was a great success, though childless, she being, I should suppose, too old to conceive. The occasion of their nuptials remains fixed in my mind because of a remark my mother made, and the sharp retort it brought her from her mother, who was staying with us at the time. She said something to the effect that Will, after his long bachelor years, might be somewhat at a loss on his bridal night. 'Don't be a fool, Annie!' her mother sharply retorted. This maternal grandmother, left a widow shortly after my parents married, used to come down from Sheffield – whence nothing would dislodge her permanently – to look after us when my father took my mother away on holiday, which he did every year, usually abroad. Jaunts that he loved, and refused to economise over. We enjoyed our grandmother's regime, though it was more severe than her daughter's. She was a tiny, energetic lady who still wore a cap indoors, and bustled about the house, washing, brushing, polishing, cooking. For her weekly bread-making session, she put on a pair of white sleeves, and pummelled the dough with great zest. We were allowed to take the crisp overflow of the baking pans. I occasionally ran into trouble, as I had with Miss Lidiard, over answering back; an offence which has brought me rebukes and chastisement, both public and private, all my life. Once, I remember, when I had been disparaging the story of Daniel in the Lions' Den, she shut me up by remarking with great emphasis: 'If Daniel isn't true, nothing is.' I revisited Sheepscombe some years ago for the first time since I had been there as a child. In the churchyard I found the graves of Will Straughan and his wife, but the damson tree seemed to have disappeared.

Whatever Miss Lidiard might feel about our visits to the Colony, I looked forward to them enormously. The place was not much to look at – just a group of wooden huts, with a larger one for communal gatherings; but I vaguely detected something exciting, stimulating, in the air. The Colony had been started in the first years of this century, largely in response to Tolstoy's ideas. A party set out from Croydon on their bicycles, with only very little money and no agricultural experience, with the idea of settling on the land, producing all their own necessities,

and so being able to detach themselves wholly from the wicked ways and pursuits of the society around them. It was a truly heroic enterprise; the more so as most of the participants were clerks and schoolmasters and shop assistants, with absolutely no experience of fending for themselves under primitive conditions. Like Brigham Young when he first caught a glimpse of the Great Salt Lake in what is now Utah, they saw some fifty acres of rough land in the Cotswolds, and said: This is the place! The land was cheap in those days, and they acquired it by purchase; then, to demonstrate their abhorrence of the institution of property, ceremonially burnt the title deeds. It must have been a touching scene – the bonfire, the documents consigned to the flames, their exalted sentiments. Unfortunately a neighbouring farmer heard of their noble gesture and began to encroach on their land. To have resorted to the police, even if it had been practicable, was unthinkable. So, after much deliberation, they decided to use physical force to expel the intruder; which they did on the basis of a theory of detached action, whereby it is permissible to infringe a principle for the purpose of a single isolated act without thereby invalidating it. The intruding farmer was, in fact, thrown over the hedge in the presence of the assembled Colonists.

There were many such tragi-comic incidents in the years that followed; as well as quarrels, departures, jealousies, betrayals and domestic upsets. In the end, the Colonists found it necessary to re-establish their title to the land by means of squatters' rights, and then proceeded to bicker amongst themselves as to who should have which portion. Free love did not preclude the troubles of matrimony; men still tired of ageing mates and turned to younger ones. Nor did the deserted resent their abandonment any the less because they had not been shackled in the chains of matrimony. To-day, I suppose, the Colony would be called a Commune, but essentially the same hopes and desires are entertained, with the same disappointments and disillusionments lying ahead. It is a minor vexation of growing old that what seems novel and audacious to the young is stale and already discredited in the light of one's own experience.

I wandered about the Colony a year or so ago, noting how the roof of the communal meeting-place was leaking, and how weeds obscured its windows. How some of the huts were derelict and abandoned, and others that were occupied had an air of being poor and ill-tended. How the few Colonists who were still there seemed mostly old and dispirited. Back into remotest times, I reflected, this notion has existed of a Utopia,

a kingdom of heaven on earth, or heavenly city; of a little perfect community existing within the larger imperfect one of human society; from time to time finding expression, always disastrously. History is littered with the debris of extinct Colonies and Communes. The early Christians were fortunate enough to be saved from taking any such disastrous course since they enjoyed the inestimable advantage of believing that the millennium was near, which precluded them from seeking to establish a beneficent regime in this world. In the time at their disposal it was just not worth while. Perhaps the best hope of reviving the Christian religion would be to convince the Pope, the Archbishop of Canterbury and other dignitaries likewise that the world will shortly be coming to an end. A difficult undertaking, I fear, notwithstanding much evidence pointing that way.

When Miss Lidiard and I visited the Colony it was still in reasonably good shape. The leading figure among the Colonists at the time was a Czech philosopher, Francis Sedlac, who had come to the Colony originally as a fugitive from Austrian military service, and was held in great respect. Few of the Colonists could understand his philosophy, but all were prepared to esteem it. He was a tall, bearded man of decidedly imposing appearance – so much so, the Colonists would tell one with great pride, that he had once been offered the part of Christ in a Hollywood production of the Gospel story. As they did not think much of the traditional Christ, and Hollywood represented everything they considered most abhorrent, the pride they took in this offer was a little difficult to understand. Sedlac, in any case, rejected the offer. I was allowed to peep in at the great man where he sat, as I thought, playing with coloured bricks. Actually, as it turned out, he was working at his philosophy, which was based on geometrical premises. His consort at that time was a certain Nelly Shaw, an old friend of my father who occasionally visited us in Croydon. Before his marriage, my father and Nelly, we were given to understand, had gone bicycling together, when she had scandalised the neighbourhood by being one of the first ladies to appear in public in bloomers. She might be regarded, I suppose, as a forerunner of the Women's Lib movement to-day; with a harsh, resonant voice, a plump, clumsy body, and a face full of irregularities: tufts of hair, moles, pits and protuberances, the whole impression not appreciably improved by a string of large red beads that she invariably wore tightly round her neck. If my mother nourished any suspicions about her, they were, I am confident, misplaced.

The Colonists were, of course, pacifists to a man and a woman, and

Sedlac, as one who had faced persecution and exile rather than take up arms, was a hero in their eyes. Rather in the same sort of way as their like to-day are concerned about money invested in South Africa, they were exercised as to whether or not the communal funds they had accumulated should be invested in government securities, which one of them – actually, Will Straughan's sister – said would be tantamount to 'dipping it in the blood'. Sedlac, too, as a dedicated anarchist, was strongly opposed to having any truck with Treasury bonds, which he regarded with abhorrence. Altogether, he looked with disfavour on the Colony's growing prosperity, though contributing to it in a sense, as being one of the sights of the place which brought coach-loads of curious visitors from the surrounding neighbourhood to stare and buy cakes and wholemeal bread at the Colony's bakery. I was interested to find that picture postcards are still on sale in Stroud of the Colony, one of them being of Sedlac as a typical Colonist. He appears as a kind of agnostic Ecce Homo; in the style of Edward Carpenter, Walt Whitman, and all the other prophets of wind on the heath, up to and including the most distracted of them all – D. H. Lawrence. The other attraction which brought in local sightseers was the reputed nude bathing which took place at the Colony. There was, in fact, a small pool fed by a spring in which on warm days the Colonists were liable to disport themselves. Most of them, male and female alike, seemed to my childhood eyes more curious than alluring in their state of nakedness, but there were two young girls with the first bloom of adolescence upon them who caught my attention with a stab of excitement. It was my first intimation of sex, and without conscious deliberation I decided to keep it to myself. The incident must have impressed me, since I remember the names, admittedly bizarre, of the two girls in question – Elfie and Doddles.

In the Colony's early days, when the prohibition of the use of money was rigorously observed, Sedlac decided that the only way he could be sure of the safe delivery of an article he had written for a learned philosophical magazine was to take it himself to London where the magazine was published. He might, it is true, have followed the practice of some of the Colonists and put the article in the post without a stamp in the expectation that the recipient would meet the postage due. This practice greatly exasperated my father when he was the victim of it, though, loudly protesting, he would always pay up and accept the letter or package. Sedlac was above such devices and, bare-footed, with his article in his knapsack, and no money in his pocket, he set out for

London. It was mid-winter, and soon he ran into a bad snowstorm. By the time he had covered some thirty miles he was at the end of his strength – which was considerable; he was a tall man, rather the build of Bernard Shaw, whose appearance he perhaps copied more closely than that of Christ. What to do? He had reached a small village and decided to apply to the vicarage there for food and shelter. The vicar, a kindly man, sympathising with Sedlac's situation, offered him some money, which, however, Sedlac explained, he could not accept – not because it would be charity, but because he would no more possess or use money than he would heroin or any other destructive substance. For years the notion of this dialogue fascinated me, and I tried several times to reconstruct it, with Sedlac, like Lear, abandoned and alone in a stormy world where his logic was unacceptable. I saw it as a confrontation, like Dostoevsky's between the Grand Inquisitor and the returned Saviour, between the vicar and the Colonist, between the authoritarian and the anarchist; as the eternal dialogue that began when Adam, hand in hand with Eve, walked out of Paradise, and, looking back, saw the flaming sword barring his return. Likewise, mounted in the desert two thousand years ago, when the Devil, with the kingdoms of the earth in his gift, offered them to Christ, who rejected them, leaving His followers to be displaced persons for ever. I was so interested in the dialogue that I forgot to find out what happened to Sedlac, and whether his article ever reached its destination. No doubt Nelly Shaw arrived on the scene, reassuring in her red beads, and baled him out, explaining matters to the vicar in terms that were comprehensible to him.

Sedlac and Nelly are, of course, long since dead, as, I should suppose, are all the first-generation Colonists. I found a number of them, including Sedlac and Nelly, in the Minchinhampton churchyard, where an area well apart from the other dead has been allotted to them. Sedlac is described on his stone as an Hegelian, as though this might somehow bring him more into line with the susceptibilities of the Anglican authorities and the local worthies among whom he lies. It is a strange last resting-place for them. In the early days of the Colony the then Minchinhampton incumbent was particularly incensed against the Colonists for their atheism, their curious attire (at one point, some of them affected ancient Greek costume) and, above all, their attitude to the marriage tie. Especially in England, time softens everything; I have always thought that if Wilde had lived into his eighties he would probably have been made an honorary Commissioner of Scouts. Will

the Californian Communards all likewise find their way at last to
Forest Lawn? It would not surprise me.

When I returned home from Sheepscombe the family had moved into
a new house in South Croydon, built in accordance with my father's
specifications. It was semi-detached, the original intention being that
Will Straughan should live in the other half. Alas, his financial circum-
stances took a turn for the worse at this time, and he had to remain in
Sanderstead. As I learnt afterwards, he characteristically impoverished
himself in order to keep a shipping business in Leadenhall Street going
rather than sack the employees. Our house had one large combined
sitting- and dining-room on the ground floor, with a study for my
father in which he had a roll-top desk that I greatly admired. French
windows looked out on the garden and, inevitably, were fated to play a
role in my mother's operations against lickerish domestics in neighbour-
ing houses. There was one new piece of furniture which dominated the
sitting-room – a sort of old-fashioned divan with a narrow seat and tall
back, covered in red damask. It had, in fact, been in the snuggery of a
country pub, and became known to us all as the cosy corner. Nothing
could have been less appropriate in our semi-detached suburban house,
or more typical of my father. I always sat in it when I could, exchanged
my first amorous kiss on it, and found it a perfect lurking-place to avoid
being noticed or sent to bed when my father and his friends were
plotting the overthrow of the capitalist system. My mother disliked it
very much, and strongly protested when it first made its appearance.
She was out of sympathy with these occasional romantic flights my
father indulged in. Thus, on their silver wedding anniversary he
proudly appeared with a huge silver fruit salver, called, according to
him, an *épergne*, that he had bought in some second-hand shop. It was
made in the shape of a naked boy – presumably Cupid – offering a
plate of fruit; a majestic object, acquired, I imagine, from a restaurant
when it went bankrupt. I saw my mother's face fall, and as it fell all the
steam went out of my father. It was heartbreaking. I wanted to say how
I admired the salver, how it was something needed in our household,
but I knew it was no good. I just kept quiet. My father told me after-
wards that in the night he had awakened to hear my mother quietly
crying, and had thereupon opened a bottle of champagne procured for
the silver wedding occasion, in which they had toasted one another.
The next day my father turned in his *épergne* and, at my mother's
request, got instead a cutlery chest.

My father's sessions with his friends took place on Saturday evenings. They would assemble after supper, Scotch and water was provided, and they would talk far into the night. My mother soon dozed off in her folding chair, and I, lying low in the cosy corner, with a bit of luck might survive until ten or ten-thirty. Even in my bed I still strained my ears to catch what they were saying, and shared in their laughter when it came rolling up to me. They were a bizarre company of conspirators; I doubt whether, if the Lord Chief Justice or the Home Secretary had been able to listen in to them, he would have been seriously perturbed. Yet, ostensibly at any rate, their conspiracy has succeeded sooner and more efficaciously than they would have dared to hope. They looked like, and indeed were, a collection of typical lower-middle-class clerks, decently dressed, obviously thriving, and, anyone would think just from looking at them, Tory voters to a man.

Will Straughan was a regular attender, bringing his wife with him, who also was a non-participant in the conversation, though she did not, like my mother, doze off. He was not nearly as politically inclined as my father, and but for him would probably not have bothered much with politics at all. I remember how once, when Northcliffe was mentioned, he tied a piece of string round one of his fingers and drew it tight, like a man being hanged. Then there was Mr Jordan, my father's tailor, and mine when I went to Cambridge. His suits were solid rather than stylish; and he got involved in an intrigue with the girl in his shop, all the details of which were familiar to me because I heard them being recounted in a dramatic whisper by Mrs Jordan to my mother. While he was measuring me up, and the girl was taking down the measurements, I eyed her appraisingly, but without detecting in her the qualities which had so enflamed Mr Jordan. Mr Patterson, another regular attender, was a Scotsman with a sandy moustache and a gold watch that he kept in a little leather bag, carefully taking it out when he wanted to know the time, and then as carefully putting it back into its bag. In the same methodical manner he filled and lit his pipe, blowing out the smoke in rhythmic gusts through his sandy moustache. He was an accountant who subsequently became a company director and rich. There were others who came occasionally, all of the same type – men of humble origins who were making their way in the world and wanted the world's ways to be changed. They were not in any real sense revolutionaries; rather, they planned to take over the existing social and economic system and run it better and more equitably. Their arguments seemed to me irrefutable, their hopes for the future impeccable. Instead of lots

of milkcarts coming each day to each little street, there would be one; instead of money being squandered on battleships ('I'm interested in ships too,' was another of my father's open-air gambits: 'Hardships!'), it would be used for schools, hospitals, garden suburbs, and so on. Instead of railways, coalmines and industry generally being privately owned and enriching the few, they would be publicly owned and enrich us all. Listening to them in our little sitting-room seated on the cosy corner, I saw a rosy future before us if only my father and his henchmen would take over the country. Actually, I lived to see them – though not in their own persons – take over, but the rosy future continues to be elusive.

Though I did not notice it at the time, a notable absentee at these gatherings was the beneficiary of all our endeavour. I mean the worker, or, as we still called him, workman. (The change from 'workman' to 'worker' was as significant, semantically, as from 'master' to 'boss', or from 'the people' to 'the masses'.) It is true that among my father's growing number of visitors there would occasionally be one of whom my mother would say he was a workman, meaning by this, quite specifically, that he did not wear a bowler hat and a winged starched collar like my father, or polished boots, or cuff-links, or an overcoat with a velvet collar. He generally turned out, however, to be some special kind of worker, like a school caretaker or a road foreman. At Ruskin House, too, the headquarters of the local Labour Party, there were vaguely proletarian figures to be seen, but many more teachers and Quakers and ladies with private means who had been forcibly fed in suffragette days. Trotsky, in his History of the Russian Revolution, tells how a *mouzhik* was included in the Bolshevik delegation to Brest Litovsk. In his sheepskin coat and felt boots he was the admiration of all beholders, until one day, having taken a drop too much vodka, he actually started addressing the peace negotiators. Then he was speedily shut up. A worker is someone for whom everything is done as long as he keeps off stage; trade union leaders or shop stewards may have long speaking parts, but workers are for ever extras. Once, when I was conducting a television discussion on strikes, I asked for a worker to come on the programme. Our scouts searched far and wide, and at one point reported that they had found one in the neighbourhood of the Oval who would agree to appear. He turned out to be black and, in any case, failed to turn up. So we had to make do with the usual collection of notabilities from the nationalised industries and Transport House, topped up by a smattering of industrialists, civil servants, sociology dons, business

efficiency experts, MPs, Hungarian economists, and a shop steward or two with King Street affiliations. Thus, in accordance with the BBC's Charter, all sides were represented.

Though we had little or no contact with workers, we were, as it happened, vouchsafed an occasional glimpse of the prospective Labour Party Front Bench. This was because when any of them came to Croydon to speak or lecture (which happened fairly often because of Croydon's nearness to London), my father usually took the chair and invited them home for hospitality. As a child, I saw both Ramsay MacDonald and Snowden; Hugh Dalton and J. R. Clynes came for a meal, and there were numerous other lesser Fabian lights who visited us in this way and cropped up subsequently as under-secretaries and ministers without portfolio. My mother treated these occasions as she might have done a visit from the Gadsbys; got out her best silver and crockery, and put us all into our best clothes. My father was inclined to be surly, and I, as usual, taking my cue from him, also affected to regard the fuss made as foolish and unnecessary. The thing that struck me about our visitors was their enormous condescension; they felt themselves already so near the seats of authority that they had begun cultivating the appropriate style.

This was particularly true of MacDonald, who shook hands by extending two fingers, made conversation by asking fatuous questions, and engaged in little playfulnesses almost like royalty. He was still relatively coherent, but the verbal circumlocution which was to make his last public utterances totally incomprehensible had already begun to gain on him. I can remember him holding forth about reading and taking country rambles – two activities to which, ostensibly, he was much given – and the words all getting mixed up into something like 'wandering and rambling to be alone in my library'. His picturesque appearance; the loosely tied coloured tie, the tweed suit, the carefully dishevelled grey hair, the sonorous Scottish voice with the R's rolling and rumbling like thunder – all produced what would be called nowadays a good image. My father in principle detested him, but in practice was rather proud of him as billed to be the first Labour Prime Minister, and at one time contributed a small sum weekly to his support, Members of Parliament in those days not being paid. Afterwards he considered it as money very ill-spent; worse than dipping it in the blood. In little more than a decade after MacDonald's appearance in our Croydon sitting-room, he was acting as co-host with Lady Londonderry at a Londonderry House reception – far less time than it took for the

Colonists to make their peace with the Vicar of Minchinhampton and qualify for admission to his churchyard. Though MacDonald was, on any showing, a derisory figure, I am inclined to think now that he was perfectly cast as the first Labour Prime Minister; with all the right attitudes and responses – the capacity at a moment's notice to break into a discourse about the peace of the worrrld; the reassurance he provided to the middle and upper classes that any fears they might have entertained that he seriously intended to take their money or dissolve their Empire were quite groundless; his translation from the poor boy in Lossiemouth to the Prime Minister in Downing Street. It all added up, I cannot help thinking, to what we actually wanted in Ruskin House, and we got it. The really terrible thing about life is not that our dreams are unrealised but that they come true.

Our Fabian visitors were more sympathetic to my father; careless, untidy, pipe-smoking men; ladies whose bosoms floated loose instead of being laced up like my mother's, and whose hair was piled upwards like an overcharged haystack instead of being tightly curled like hers. They were, in my father's sense, cultured; had been to the university, mostly Oxford or Cambridge; had contributed to the review columns of the *New Statesman* and the *Nation* (then still separate), and maybe written books; called Lytton Strachey 'Lytton', and Keynes 'Maynard', and Shaw 'G.B.S.' They represented everything my father most admired; had effortlessly acquired what he so desperately sought. They were what he wanted to be. Those hours at City libraries when he should have been eating or playing; the poring over French irregular verbs in order to be able to have a come-back if someone on the Croydon Council (an unlikely enough eventuality, I must say) quoted a Latin tag at him! – none of that for them. They were at ease in a world from which he felt he had been excluded, and which therefore seemed the more alluring – what he saw as the world of culture. How was he to know that this culture, for which he had an almost mystical veneration, was dying, if not already dead? That a neo-Stone Age rather than a neo-Fabian one lay ahead?

My father's working day lay between the 8.05 from Croydon East to London Bridge, and the 6.05 from London Bridge to Croydon East. The morning tide took him City-wards, the evening one brought him Croydon-wards. He boasted, justifiably, that he knew the track so well that he could tell from the sound of the train's wheels precisely where he was. I quite often accompanied him to the station; up the steep hill to the Recreation Ground, by the Water Tower (the tower that, for me,

was the dark one Childe Roland came to); on past the little open-air stage and auditorium where the concert-party performed on summers' evenings (Kevin Billington in his magical way unearthed some survivors for a film he made about my childhood; creaking, groaning, a bit stiff on the lock-step, they were still able to give a suitably soulful rendering of 'I'm for ever blowing bubbles/Pretty bubbles in the air'); then the last stretch to the station with my father looking anxiously at his watch. Good-bye at the barrier, waving; he joining the throng down the slope to the platform, where I could just see him; then off to London Bridge. Over the Bridge, all of them stepping out; like a mighty army going as to work; most of them bowler-hatted, few girls in those days. Then dispersing, he to New Basinghall Street, and his high stool and his ledger. Quite often I was waiting at the barrier on his return. Train after train coming in, and a foolish dread seizing me that perhaps he never would come – anxiously scanning the faces as they came up the slope and went past the ticket collector. At last, there he was; always in the first batch, well to the fore, striding along. Only in the very last years of his time in the City did he allow himself the indulgence of a first-class season, and marched in a dignified way with the rear echelon. How delighted I was to see him! How overjoyed! Apart from one or two other rare occasions, there is no face except Kitty's I have ever picked out with such joyous relief as his, leading the field up the slope from the arrival platform at Croydon East.

From the station I quite often accompanied him to the Town Hall; down George Street and round past the fire station into Catherine Street. There was a time when I thought of the Croydon Town Hall as a kind of Duomo or Villa Borghese. Some grain of esteem for it must have survived, for I found myself vaguely regretful when I heard that there was a plan to demolish it and build a skyscraper on the site. As a special treat I was occasionally allowed to sit in the public gallery during a meeting of the Borough Council, where I followed the proceedings with breathless interest; especially, of course, when my father spoke, as he usually managed to do when I was present. For some years he was the only Labour councillor, which gave me a tremendous sense of the odds he was taking on in attacking the citadel of capitalism. I saw the Mayor in his red gown, the Town Clerk in his wig and black gown, the serried ranks of aldermen and councillors, as the hosts of the Philistines, and my father as David with his sling defying them. Politics for us consisted of this unequal combat, which nonetheless our side was destined to win. We licked down envelopes almost in our prams;

VOTE FOR MUGGERIDGE were almost the first three words we learnt to recognise. We wore red rosettes; when we were old enough we canvassed; we even appeared as a family group in my father's election address, having a family being regarded in those days, before anyone had heard of a population explosion, as a sign of civic virtue, especially in the case of a Labour candidate who might be associated by his opponents with dark reports of the nationalisation of women under the Bolsheviks in Russia.

Elections were for us like saints' days or festivals. The committee room in an empty shop, with trestle tables covered with leaflets; the windows darkened with posters; the lady helpers, mostly veterans in the cause, with grey untidy hair and cigarettes drooping from their mouths, vaguely partaking of the physical excitement which elections stir up. The endless cups of tea made on a gas-ring; the badinage with the candidate when he drops in; the interminable folding of paper and addressing of envelopes. Then the going from door to door as the evening comes on, and street lamps are lighted; Sir, Madam, I'm calling on behalf of the Labour candidate. Door slammed in your face, maybe; or some half-ribald, half-insulting remark of dismissal. Or a ding-dong argument – 'What I say is, they've got the money . . .' In any case, something a little furtive, shameful, in the way the steps come to the door in answer to one's knock; then the door opening a crack. Like making an indecent proposal – I want your vote, I want your body; love me! vote for me! Then the meetings in the school classrooms, with algebraic formulae, or other educational abracadabra still on the blackboard. Ladies and gentlemen, I'm here to-night . . .; the ladies and gentlemen not particularly responsive, apart from an occasional planted heckler. Finally, the climax: polling day, with hosts of Conservative cars, and our occasional Austin Seven. Lurking outside the polling stations with an impossible assignment to count the Labour voters; he looks like one, she looks like one – excuse me Sir, Madam. Not a seduction now, but rather the opposite; making off – Good-bye, it's been wonderful, I'll never forget, I'll call you, I'll . . . Forgetting even as the poll is declared. We're in, hurray! We're out, never mind, we'll try again.

This early grounding in electioneering has left me with an abiding interest in the pathology of universal suffrage democracy. In strange lands, where others might seek out ancient monuments, or folk music, or marriage customs, I seek out legislature, and spend enchanted hours

listening to Honourable Members of all races, colours and creeds going through the weird and increasingly meaningless rigmarole which Westminster has imposed on the rest of the world. The Lok Sabha – what a version that is, with non-violent Swamis in their white *kadi*, their spinning-wheels left at home, shouting and shaking their fists at one another. Mejlis, Dail, Cortes, Senate and House of Representatives, and all through Black Africa, where majority rule prevails and oppositions languish in gaol. Dusky faces under judicial wigs; maces where studded clubs might be more appropriate; 'On a point of order,' and other such parliamentary plainsong, intoned in Orientalised English, with the words racing musically after one another, attributable, I have often thought, to the fact that the early teachers of English in these lands were often Welsh missionaries. Likewise in the USSR I have been fortunate enough to witness the gathering of what English newspapers like to call Soviet MPs; observed their rapture as Stalin addressed them; watched the supervisory policemen timing their applause when he had finished to make sure it reached the regulation seven and a half minutes; seen how when a resolution is put to them, each hand is raised in perfect unison. This surely the final and sublime apotheosis of majority rule, of government of the people for the people by the people, which we in our small, inadequate way were trying to operate in Croydon.

My father's political activities brought us into contact with two categories of local residents whom we should probably not otherwise have known: Quakers and clergymen. Now that the Labour Party has become so integrated with the political, economic and social *status quo*, it may seem strange that a family like ours should, because of our Socialist views, have been so isolated in a suburban residential district. In the ordinary way we should never have thought of so much as nodding to the local vicar, assuming unquestioningly that he must disapprove of us as much as we of him. The Quakers were rather different; for the most part, they were Liberals and Pacifists, readers of the *Manchester Guardian* with some sympathy for our position, and in any case, dedicated rather self-consciously to taking up an ostensibly brotherly attitude towards all men, whatever their views, ways and circumstances. What in the ordinary way would have separated us from the local Quakers would have been simply their affluence. Our ones all seemed – and I think were – decidedly rich; and riches are somehow more noticeable and forbidding when combined with a self-consciously abstemious way of life and awareness that love of money is the root of all

evil. I think the rich young man who came to Jesus for guidance, and was told to sell all he had and give the proceeds to the poor, must have been a Quaker. My mother, I may add – much the most honest member of our family – liked Quakers *because* they were rich. She put them in the same category as the Gadsbys, and treated them accordingly. The rest of us took a somewhat more equivocal attitude. The Quakers were useful, certainly; they had motor-cars, for instance, and provided almost the only ones available to us at election time. They would ferry my father about from meeting to meeting, and help him out with his election expenses. At the same time, behind their backs, we used to make sly innuendos about the disparity between their wealth and their principles, and how they could scarcely be regarded as following out the precept not to lay up treasure on earth. I thought of them when I read in Wesley's Journal his cry of distress about how those he converted were made thereby industrious, abstemious and honest; virtues whose practice inevitably led to their becoming rich, and then, as he put it, all the work was to do again. My father was occasionally asked to speak at the local Friends' Meeting House, and I went with him. I noticed how his manner of speaking was slightly modified; less ranting and rumbustious, with no jokes about the National Debt or anything like that. When prayers were on he bowed his head with the others. Though he professed himself an atheist, I should not say that he was an irreligious man. In Penge he had attended a Baptist Church, though more for the ancillary activities like the Literary Society and the Mock Parliament than for the worship, I fancy.

I occasionally visited the Duncan Harrises, a Quaker household quite near us. She was a magistrate, a largish woman with a red face and faint moustache; full of good works and worthy purposes. He was appreciably smaller; a little wizened man with a limp, maybe from polio, who appeared rarely; I fancy, some sort of banker. They were obviously well off, and I observed with interest how this expressed itself even in the austerities of their way of life; the curtains in natural dyes, the bare unpolished wooden table, the oatmeal coverings of chairs and divan, the handwoven carpets and homespun dress Mrs Duncan Harris habitually wore. Wealth, like the kingdom of heaven, is within; one senses it, not so much in ostentation and luxury, as in a sort of inner gilded complacency. In Mrs Duncan Harris's case, this complacency extended to all her views and endeavour. She was a forerunner of what might be called the Good Panellist; a type as characteristic of our time as the Good Apprentice was of the Victorian age. As the Good App-

prentice's virtue met with its reward in personal success, theirs does in public esteem. They hold all the right views and espouse all the right causes – family-planning clinics, legalisation of abortion, divorce reform, raising the school age, abolition of capital punishment, support for the United Nations. I could go on and on listing their virtuous attitudes, which call for a contemporary Samuel Smiles to celebrate them. It is a litany that many misspent years of participation in BBC and other panels had made excruciatingly familiar to me. Sometimes, sleepless, in the night I hear the Good Panellist holding forth; voice rather high and tremulous but with that ineffable sense of rectitude I first detected in Mrs Duncan Harris – 'What is needed is more and *better* education . . .'

Our relations with the clergy were rather different. The fact was, we made use of them. In view of the scurrilous stories circulating about our moral attitudes (in which the Colony figured), it suited us to have a clergyman on the platform, and if he wore his clerical regalia for the occasion so much the better. My father and his friends all called themselves atheists, and greatly enjoyed making what would then pass for being blasphemous jokes about, for instance, the Virgin Birth – much, I may add, to the distress of my mother. In view of their attitude, how was it possible for them to find common ground with a beneficed clergyman whose very livelihood – to put it no higher – depended on praying to God and promoting belief in Him; and who was under a statutory obligation to recite a creed each Sunday which laid down specifically a whole series of beliefs about the deity, the incarnation, and the resurrection? Such questions may seem very naïve nowadays when we have grown used to clergymen adopting all sorts of positions, from glorifying *Playboy* magazine to detecting spiritual undertones in cults like Mau Mau. Then, however, we still had a vague notion that clergymen believed in Christianity, and upheld whatever particular version of it the denomination they belonged to based itself on. Subsequently, it has become clear that, far from this being the case, many clergymen are particularly drawn to any movement or position which denigrates the Christian religion and its founder. Having, perhaps, lost their faith, but being committed for one reason or another to their cloth, they derive great, if unconscious, satisfaction from anything that undermines the one and discredits the other.

The formula for peaceful co-existence between my father and his clerical supporters was 'making the world a better place'. Surely, one of our local clergy would say, puffing at his pipe and putting on an

expression of almost excessive amiability, while seated, to my mother's great satisfaction, I may say, in her folding-chair – surely we can agree on a programme of social betterment. More money on education, slum clearance, welfare services, and so on. That's loving our neighbour, isn't it? As for loving God – we'll see about that in due course, ha! ha! ha! This, of course, is an over-simplification, but there *was* a sort of implicit pact whereby God was left out on the understanding that my father would accept the other's credentials as a progressive. On such a basis, they could co-operate; the clergyman taking the chair at Labour Party meetings, and even standing up for 'The Red Flag', and my father in his speech referring to his good friend the Rev. so and so, and even accepting a benediction at the end of the meeting if one was offered. In Croydon at that time such an arrangement was considered highly obnoxious by most church-going people, as well as by the Marxists and other extremists among my father's supporters, but it was the way the wind was blowing. Archbishop Temple would proclaim Christianity the most materialistic of religions (like saying that vegetarianism is the most carnivorous of all diets), and the episcopal contingent in the House of Lords, if they did not line up with the agnostics and atheists in matters like divorce and the legalisation of homosexuality, came in time to accept these 'reforms' as permissible, even desirable. One ought not to have been surprised. After all, only a few centuries after Christ had been crowned with a crown of thorns his alleged representative on earth was being crowned with a gold one. Human beings have the rather endearing trait, when they falsify the record, of doing it absolutely. Has not the Labour Party done exactly the same thing to William Blake, transforming his mystical New Jerusalem into a Welfare State, and using his exquisite verses on the subject at the obsequies of party worthies, even though Blake himself believed, as he wrote on one of his Dante designs (his last commission), that Dante had made the same mistake as Swedenborg in believing that 'in this world is the Ultimate of Heaven. This is the most damnable Falsehood of Satan & his Antichrist.'

I got to know one of our tame clergymen, and quite liked him. At the same time, I found him somehow too hearty and gross; his mouth seemed somehow too red and raw, his breath too noisy as he sucked at his pipe. With his shabby-genteel rectory, its large poorly tended garden, where his wife Dorothy, in gardening gloves, worked rather hopelessly at the beds; his plain daughter learning shorthand and hoping to study at RADA, his son at a minor public school who talked unconvincingly

about backing horses and taking out girls – these were the poor whites of the bourgeoisie, and the first to leave the sinking ship. The Rev. Old Bill, looking for a better 'ole, found it, as he supposed, in the Labour Party. (Not a bad guess, as a matter of fact; Labour Prime Ministers, like any others, were prone to reward their sympathisers with preferment.) It was in such households that the crack-up of the bourgeoisie first showed; daughters turning up at the Windmill Theatre; sons among the delinquents, nature's double-agents, in the dock surprising the magistrate – 'After all the advantages you've had; a good home, a good education!' I should have expected some sociological Kinsey to work on the subject. Indeed, I might have tackled it myself, having been interested all my life in priests, clergy, monks, nuns, evangelists; any sort of professional religious or *exalté*. Perhaps I should have been one; I like to think a monk notable for his austerities, the voice of one crying in the wilderness; but more probably a tiresome Unitarian in Walsall who writes incessantly to the local paper. Anyway, the genus Intelligentsia may generally be considered as consisting of priests and religious *manqués*. The Rev. Stephen Spender, Fr Connolly, Rabbi Levin, Dom Graham Greene, Sister Brigid Brophy. It sounds right.

At week-ends and on bank holidays my father marshalled us for country walks or bicycle rides, the countryside being then easily accessible. Bicycling, and what was later called hiking, was another item in the early progressive package. There were Clarion Clubs and specially organised rambles; a love of nature was proclaimed as an enlightened alternative to religious worship, especially by healthy white-haired ladies with pink cheeks, and their weather-beaten consorts. The cult no doubt went back to Wordsworth and the Lake poets, but more immediate inspirers were Walt Whitman and Edward Carpenter, both celebrants of health and exuberance and the body beautiful, and both, as it happened, homosexual. Our copy of Whitman's *Leaves of Grass* had a splendid frontispiece of him, bearded, looking strikingly like Hemingway, and with a butterfly perched on his finger. Later, I learnt that among his effects was found a preserved butterfly with a specially fitted ring attached for fastening on his finger.

As we rode along on our bicycles with my father in the lead, he would shout back at us rapturously about the beauties of the surrounding landscape. Just look at those trees! What a view across the valley! Have you ever seen anything like the colours in the distance! His enthusiasm never flagged. My mother had given up bicycling long ago, and so did

not accompany us. She had only enjoyed it when the two of them rode a tandem together, and she could occupy the rear seat; on her own, she found riding or pushing her bicycle uphill too arduous, and free-wheeling downhill too scaring. I assented eagerly to my father's exuberant appreciation of nature, but only to please him; without truly meaning or feeling it. Then, on a particular occasion, I found I really did mean it. I can remember the occasion perfectly; it was near Chipstead, going along a lane that ran past the church, on a June evening at about seven o'clock. I expect the lane now is in the middle of a housing estate. The light of the setting sun slashed the trunks of the trees, so that they were half gilded and half in shadow. Suddenly I realised with a tremendous feeling of exultation that this golden light of the sun, this fragrance of a June evening and light rustle of leaves – the whole golden, glorious scene had some special significance in which I participated. That in its all-embracing beauty it conveyed a oneness, and that to identify oneself with this oneness, and with the spirit animating it and giving it meaning, contained the promise of ecstasy. It was a moment of great illumination. Ever afterwards I have felt lost and imprisoned when only concrete lay around me for long. Like waking up in New York, and looking out of a hotel window before the day begins. Seeing the tall grey buildings as impenetrable prison walls; the narrow streets as for monotonous, aimless prison exercise; the tops of the buildings intersecting against the remote sky as prison bars. Thus imprisoned, what is there to do but live as prisoners do on fantasies of eroticism and violence; stupefied with drugs or their own despair? I owe to, of all people, Ilya Ehrenburg, an image that I invariably turn to for deliverance from such nightmares. Speaking of Pasternak's writings during the darkest days of Stalin's oppression, Ehrenburg said he saw in them the promise that, however high and thick the concrete might be piled, however widely spread, even though it covered the whole earth, there would always be a crack, and in that crack – greenness, life.

I will not pretend that, bicycling with my father and my brothers by Chipstead Church, all, or any, of this came into my mind. At the same time, it marked a sort of turning point; thenceforth, wherever I have been, and however dismal my situation or prospect, there has been the never-failing solace of feeling earth below my feet and seeing sky above my head. Aldous Huxley in – I think – one of his later essays, makes the characteristic point that such solace is available only because nature has been tamed, and that we hug our urban sanctuaries if the alternatives are wild jungle or parched desert or roaring tornado. Ac-

tually, jungle and desert and tornado, no less than meadow and stream and gentle breezes, express what concrete hides – our own true habitat, the creation of which we are part and the creator responsible for it. It is in his inexorable separation from this habitat, in all its aspects, that the present alienation of technological man consists. The lost connection can be made in a desert or a jungle just as surely – perhaps more so – than in a landscaped garden or olive grove cultivated for centuries. Poor Huxley! – he was always looking for mystical truth in a scientific theorem; searching for a Holy Grail which turned out to be a retort; climbing up St Simon Stylites's pillar only to find himself when he got to the top in the Cavendish Laboratory. In his last years he came to believe that mystical practices and a discreet use of drugs could lead to spiritual enlightenment. Alas, those who followed this way all too often found that it led to the squalor of drug-addiction and despair.

On Sunday evenings my father read aloud to us from the plays of Shakespeare. He had a large three-volume edition illustrated with engravings. There was a companion volume of Dante's 'Inferno' with illustrations by Doré whose pages I often turned over, shivering at the plates of poor souls roasting in Hell even though I was brought up to believe that no such place existed. My father read all the parts in the Shakespeare plays, modifying his voice for the clowns and minor characters, and giving everything he'd got to Othello, Lady Macbeth or Hamlet. I doubt if he was a particularly good reader; I, anyway, found the blank verse difficult to follow, and derived little benefit from the readings, though in a way I enjoyed them; I think, again, because of the enormous zest my father put into them. My first appreciation of Shakespeare came a little later when I attended a series of special matinees for school children at the Old Vic, at which we saw most of his better-known plays. We paid sixpence for our seats, and fourpence for the journey by tram from Croydon to Waterloo; swaying and screeching our way through Streatham and Brixton on those old double-decker LCC trams whose connections with overhead electric cables on frosty days gave off clouds of sparks. I dare say the Old Vic productions were pretty rough, and the scenery scanty – I seem to recall mostly curtains – but I loved every minute of them. The star was Sybil Thorndike, who seemed to take almost every part, male and female, though she can't have played Lear; I remember her brother Russell in the role, memorable because at one of the most dramatic moments his beard came off. No doubt there have been greater actresses, but to me she has a unique

glory, because of those Old Vic performances. I was glad the other day to have an opportunity to tell her so.

My father's books consisted of six or seven shelves-full in a case with glass doors. I got to know them intimately. A stranger could have deduced from them everything my father hoped for and believed in. I, who was no stranger, saw them as the bricks out of which he had constructed his Heavenly City, to whose coming to pass his life was dedicated, and as I thought then, mine, too. Quite a number of the books are now forgotten, or remembered only for their period interest, but at the time similar collections must have existed in many a progressive household. In a way it was an odd assortment. I have mentioned Rousseau's *Confessions* and Whitman's *Leaves of Grass*, which represented the wilder flights of freedom – ostensibly, along with justice, our ultimate objective. With them, a volume of Kropotkin's *Reminiscences*. He was greatly revered among us, and always punctiliously given his title of Prince. Just about when I first turned over the pages of his *Reminiscences* he was returning to his native land in triumph; to die there shortly afterwards, and to be accorded a State funeral. As the cortège passed the Leningrad prison, his followers, incarcerated in it, shook their fists through the bars – the last anarchist demonstration ever to take place in the USSR.

Beside Kropotkin, there was the Everyman edition of *Das Kapital*. Did my father ever read it? I doubt it; I certainly didn't, and haven't. Then a collected edition of Carlyle in five brown volumes which I still possess. I felt I had a right to them because, my father told me, I was given my second name, Thomas, after Carlyle. It is a little difficult now to see how Carlyle fitted in with the others, given his loathing and contempt for representative government, his adulation of leadership as exemplified by a Frederick the Great and a Cromwell, his wild vituperative outbursts against reformers, and – as they would now be called – do-gooders. Somehow, however, the trick was done, and Carlyle given a place in the pantheon of the Left. To-day he would be seen as displaying early intimations of Fascism. I myself, whether out of satisfaction at being his namesake, or from a natural affinity, find the crusty old fellow very much to my taste; especially his curious wry humour; for instance, his account of going out to see Coleridge at Highgate – a comic masterpiece – in his Life of his friend Sterling. Standing alongside Carlyle was Ruskin's *Unto This Last*; the book that Gandhi said, along with the New Testament and Tolstoy's *Confessions*, had most

influenced him. Ruskin's socialism was, from my father's point of view, suspect, but he was held in affection for his denunciation of the sheer ugliness capitalism had created everywhere, especially in the industrial north – what we now call pollution.

In a similar vein, William Morris's *News from Nowhere* and *Earthly Paradise* (from which also Sunday evening readings were given), with their nostalgia for medieval guilds, knights in armour, and Pre-Raphael-ite ladies with long white necks; aspects of socialism which figured little in our Croydon Labour Party. The Webbs' *History of Trade Unionism*, two weighty tomes; Tawney's *Acquisitive Society, The Ragged Trousered Philanthropists*, Edward Bellamy's *Looking Backward*; socialist classics all, stood together in a solid phalanx. The last I never persevered with; on the wall of my bedroom there was a picture of a man in a field bending over a furrow which purported to illustrate it, but I never understood that either. Rather apart from the others, a Schopenhauer volume, in the Home University Library, and Heine's Autobiography, from which my father loved to quote what he regarded as sparkling *mots*, a particular favourite being a remark that the Venus di Milo had beautiful hands. This brought out with great archness and, to make sure I got the point (which I didn't), an aside explaining that the Venus di Milo had no arms. Then the famous first collection of Fabian Essays, Shaw's *Plays Pleasant and Unpleasant*, and Ibsen's Plays. Shaw was, of course, to my father the incomparable hero of our time; he treasured his acquaintance with him, and proudly displayed the correspondence they exchanged over the Boer War (including a postcard on the top of which Shaw had drawn a Union Jack), in which Shaw, ever on the side of the big battalions, supported Chamberlain, whereas my father was a pro-Boer. My own reading of his plays and their prefaces was decidedly desultory, but somehow I picked up a reference in them to Maria Bashkirtsef, who had created a sensation by disclosing in her published diary that she was prone to sexual desire – something no lady had ever before publicly admitted. This was a discovery I did not pass on to my mother, but brooded upon it, without coming to any clear conclusions as to its significance. Recently I noticed walking along the Promenade des Anglais at Nice, that the plaque to Maria on a house there where she had stayed had recently been enlarged. This seemed appropriate.

This diverse pabulum constituted my father's sacred texts, showing him the way to salvation. First, the existing structure had to be over-thrown; not with bloodshed and violence, but through persuasion and the ballot box. It was a kind of revivalism without tears; sinful men were

to be washed, but not in the blood of the Lamb; in, as it were, municipal water, with carbolic soap purveyed by the co-op. Having captured the machinery of government by means of a parliamentary majority, it would be possible to take over industry, the banks, the land etc., and operate them, not for profit, but in the public interest. So, State, producer and consumer – a new version of the Trinity; three in one and one in three – would be harmoniously related, and all impediments to the enduring health, wealth and happiness of mankind removed or, like the State in the Marxist version, allowed to wither away. All this was only, in my father's estimation, a means; the end was the Earthly Paradise, the translation of William Morris's *News from Nowhere* into *News from Somewhere*. Then Whitman's sense of abounding joy in his own and all creation's sensuality would sweep away the paltry backwaters of bourgeois morality; the horrors of industrial ugliness which Ruskin so eloquently denounced would dissolve, and die forgotten as a dream (phrases from hymns still washed about in my father's mind) as slums were transformed into garden cities, and the belching smoke of hateful furnaces into the cool elegance of electric power. As for the ferocious ravings of my namesake, Carlyle, about the pettifogging nature of modern industrial man's pursuits and expectations – all that would be corrected as he was induced to spend ever more of his increasing leisure in cultural and craft activities; in the enjoyment of music, literature and art.

It was perfectly true – a point that Will Straughan was liable to bring up at the Saturday evening gatherings – that on the present form the new citizenry might be expected to have a marked preference for dog-racing over chamber music or readings from *Paradise Lost*, but, my father would loftily point out, education would change all that. Education was, in fact, the lynchpin of the whole operation; the means whereby the Old Adam of the Saturday night booze-up, and fondness for Marie Lloyd in preference to Beatrice Webb, would be cast off, and the New Man be born as potential fodder for Third Programmes yet to come.

Very properly and logically, my father sent my brothers and me to the local elementary and secondary schools, in this differing from many Socialists of his sort who, like Lord Snow, praise the State system while preferring Eton or some lesser establishment of the same kind for their own progeny. It is something for which I personally am profoundly grateful. If I had gone even to the local grammar school – which rated as a public school of sorts – I feel sure that vanity, and a congenital and

rather lamentable passion to be liked, would have induced me to fit into the system, and I should have gone on to Cambridge, not as an outsider, but already with the requisite preliminary conditioning, emerging fully brain-washed to take my place with the new Socialist elite, the Hendersons and Greenwoods and Noel-Bakers, corresponding to the Cecils and Percys and Cavendishes in the Tory Party. From this abysmal destiny I was saved by the happy accident of going to an elementary school when, to all intents and purposes, such schools were considered to be only for the children of parents too poor and un-ambitious to look for anything better. Later, of course, this changed, with the coming to pass of comprehensive Etons like Holland Park School, specially earmarked for the progressive elite. As for my second-ary school – it had just opened and, in the conditions of the 1914–18 war, was largely staffed with a bizarre collection of aged and incompetent teachers who for one reason or another had been rejected for national service. Neither type of school was likely to make any very strong impression on the boys who went through them, and I emerged un-scathed and largely unlettered. Some years ago I returned to my old secondary school and found that it had now become a grammar school, with all the usual appurtenances in the shape of houses, prefects, blazers, a school song, and so on, and is no doubt turning out as good a crop of long-haired, pot-smoking, discotheque-frequenting youths as any other establishment of the kind. Alas, my father's vision of the intellectual, moral and aesthetic transformation this kind of education was going to bring about seemed as far from realisation as ever, if not farther.

My elementary school was in one of those stark bare buildings which successive Education Acts spawned over the country; wherever children liable under the Act were gathered together. It stood in an asphalt playground; inside, the classrooms were divided by partitions which could be pulled back to provide an assembly hall. Here we gathered in the morning for prayers and a hymn, and on Friday afternoons to sing 'Now the Day is Over' – which we did with enthusiasm since it signified two clear days of freedom ahead. This somewhat lugubrious hymn, if I happen to hear it, still awakens in me an instinctive response of delight. The headmaster presided; a grey, distinguished-looking man who spoke with great distinctness, as elementary teachers did in those days. He sounded us off with his tuning-fork. Never having been able to sing in tune, I developed a faculty for appearing to be joining in eagerly, but actually making little or no sound; a faculty that has proved useful in

all sorts of ways subsequently. For instance, in listening to long anecdotes, or expositions on how the monetary crisis can be solved. Once the late Professor Namier read me a whole front article he had written in *The Times Literary Supplement* – some three to four thousand words – in a slow deliberate voice. It was a searching test, but as he droned on, I was back in my elementary school, ostensibly singing away at the top of my voice but actually thinking of other things. After the singing, the Headmaster offered prayers; we had some difficulty with the aspirate in 'hallowed be thy name', and were sometimes required to repeat it several times before we said it to his satisfaction. I asked afterwards in class whether God was as particular about aspirates as the headmaster, and was rebuked – alas, the first of many similar occasions.

My first teacher was Miss Corke, a young girl straight from college; earnest and pretty. I did not then, of course, know, but she had become friendly with another elementary school teacher in Croydon – D. H. Lawrence – with whom she spent much of her spare time. While she was taking me through my alphabet, Lawrence was taking her through his dark unconscious. Her reminiscences of Lawrence, when I came to read them, seemed to me to give a clearer and more sympathetic picture of what he was really like than the rest of the regiment of women who ravened round him and subsequently produced their testaments. Some of his poems are addressed to her, and one of his novels – *The Trespasser* – deals with a tragic incident in her life, about which she also wrote a novel, *Neutral Ground*. Thus, an Eng. Lit. scout who wanted to could make a comparison between the incident itself, Lawrence's treatment of it and her own. I was able to persuade her to come and talk to me about Lawrence in my garden under the camera's eye. This is one of the things that television can do uniquely well – recording an experience or a relationship in the very words, and with the very gestures and expression, of the person concerned. Meeting again in such circumstances after so many years was a strange and pleasant experience; she a small white-haired lady in her eighties, but as sharp and clear as a bird, and I the person I am, in my late sixties. The June weather happened to be perfect, the garden at its best, the flowers at their brightest. Lawrence's uneasy ghost seemed to be hovering round. I still felt as I had all those years before, that I was in the presence of my teacher, whose rebukes must at all costs be avoided, and whose praise was infinitely desirable.

When the cameras had gone, and as the evening wore on, a difference of view, if not a dispute, arose between us. This concerned what human

life is about, and where we who are involved so mysteriously in this experience of living are being led. Miss Corke still took the view that mankind have their destiny in their own hands, and are passing on to new heights of understanding and achievement, with the prospect of ultimately being themselves the masters of their own universe. She even read me a passage – I must say, little to my taste – in this sense from Wells's earlier writings. I did not unkindly remind her of how totally, in *Mind at the End of its Tether*, his last work, he retreated from this position, groaning and beating his breast over, of all things, atomic fission, which, in the light of all his previous utterances and prophesies, should have been for him an occasion for great rejoicing. It was as though, on the last day, a Salvation Army band paraded with its colours flying, only to turn tail and run when the earth began to shake and the heavens to unroll like a scroll. I did, however, try and explain that this whole notion of Man climbing a mountain peak at the top of which he finds his total and definitive fulfilment is, to me, not merely absurd, but highly depressing. That, rather, as it seems to me, he is as Bunyan saw him, a pilgrim making his way through all the perils that his own appetites and wickedness create, to an ultimate enlightenment. The pilgrimage is endlessly made, from generation to generation, and from age to age, and the way is always the same way; more likely to be found by the lowly and the pure of heart than by the strong and the proud. I could see that my words impressed Miss Corke as little as her reading had me. Her preference for Darwin over Bunyan was marked.

After Miss Corke had retired to bed, I stayed awake a long time thinking of the chasm which divides those who believe in a mortal destiny, however glorious, and those who cannot find the heart to live at all, to go on from day to day, except on the basis of an immortal one. Belonging, as I do, so strongly to the latter category, the former seem to me fated, either to suppose themselves to be gods and, like Icarus, fly into the sun, there to perish, or to fall back upon their animal natures, and the Sisyphus task of maintaining a condition of permanent rut. Miss Corke's friend and would-be lover, Lawrence, straddled the two positions. With one side of him he saw with true imaginative clarity the ruinous course the world was set on – 'as if a whole social form were breaking down, and the human element swarmed within the disintegration, like maggots in cheese . . . so that it seems as though we had created a steel framework, and the whole body of society were crumbling and rotting in between'. But all he had to offer in the way of a solution were the sick phallic fantasies and perversities of quasi-impotence,

C.W.T.—E

carried in his last novel, *Lady Chatterley's Lover*, to a pitch of absurdity seldom, if ever before, equalled.

He was one of those men, tragic and gifted, who work out in themselves the conflicts and dilemmas of their time; who are themselves our own fever and pain. In Lawrence's case, his sickness became the cult of succeeding generations; Lady Chatterley, sponsored by a motley collection of writers, clerics and miscellaneous intelligentsia, was the progenitor of a torrent of porno-eroticism which her creator would have found deeply abhorrent, and incidentally so enriched her publisher in the process that his shares were quoted on the Stock Exchange as Chatterleys. It only remained for the Warden of All Souls to exercise his considerable, but dormant, scholarship in demonstrating conclusively that Mellors's own sexual fancies were distinctly abnormal, to round off a superb exercise in contemporary fatuity. When, in 1930, I heard of Lawrence's death – actually, at a cocktail party in Cairo; a quasi-literary affair of the sort that used to take place there in those pre-British Council days, in which a very little literature was served up with a lot of Levantine dressing – I found myself crying, though even then I was beginning to realise how shallow was the soil in which his thought and talent had grown and developed. It is the only occasion I can recall in which I cried over the death of a public figure unknown to me. I suppose I was unconsciously aware of how in some sense Lawrence was the prototype of us all – weaving a phallic cult out of his impotence, turning his shrill rage against the inexorable doomsday march of our time, howling down the corridors of time to produce a thin delphic echo. With his ribald seraglio of Baroness, Hon. Brett and Mabel Dodge; with Middleton Murry for John the Baptist and a sometime Bishop of Woolwich for posthumous advocate, he surely deserved my Cairene tears.

The first event in the outside world that I remember as something actually happening and involving me was the outbreak of the 1914–18 war. My father came home with a newspaper and told us. His face was grave, but what I most vividly recall is the tremendous excitement of everybody. The crowds in the streets shouting and cheering; the sense of terrific events about to happen. Contrary to what pacifists and other humane persons would like to believe, wars, when they break out, tend to be popular. They offer the illusion of an escape from the boredom which is the lot of, particularly, technological man. He will be able to make off, not shamefacedly or furtively, but as a hero; the routine of his daily life and domestic relationships will be broken, and the same-

ness of his days give place to uncertainty and drama. In August 1914 they shouted: 'Hurrah for war!'; in September 1939 they did not dare to do that after the Peace Ballot and all the talk about another war being the end of civilisation, but a lot of people may well have felt the same without letting on. How it would be in the event of yet another war fought with atomic weapons is difficult to say. It is true that the Vietnam war has been unpopular, but mainly among students, who have no routine or domestic relationships to escape from. If recruitment, instead of being among the young, had been restricted to married men of forty and upwards, I doubt whether there would have been much trouble.

Many accounts have been written of this undoubtedly momentous occasion, which will probably appear in the history books as marking the final decline of Western European dominance in the world. There was Grey with his 'They are putting out the lights . . .' (which apparently he didn't say or, if he did, meant something quite different), and Kitchener sitting behind his big moustache, and estimating, to everyone else's total incredulity, that the war would last at least five years. Leonard Woolf told me that he and the Bloomsburyites saw in the outbreak of the war the end of all their hopes, reasonable in the pre-1914 context, as he considered, for moving forward into a kindlier and better civilisation. One imagines them wailing together over those lost hopes. My father's face was grave, but he had doubtless just read in the paper that people reading the paper had grave faces. As for me, I was soon calculating that if only the war would go on for another five years I should be called up. I even, when the war had been going for two years, went with great trepidation into a recruiting office near the Town Hall and said I was seventeen, though I knew I looked, if anything, younger than my years, and my voice still had not properly broken. The recruiting sergeant, a kindly old regular with a rosette in his service hat, told me to come back with a birth certificate. My two elder brothers were soon both in the services – my eldest brother a subaltern in polished riding-boots, and the next one in the newly formed Royal Flying Corps with a tunic fastening on his shoulder like a fencing jacket and a fore-and-aft cap – and I envied them inordinately. Recruits, still in civilian clothes, were marched with a band to the railway station, and I sometimes trailed along behind them. Our school cadet corps had been revivified, and we occasionally marched through the streets to the sound of kettle drums, led by our headmaster, an unsoldierly figure who habitually wore his Sam Browne over the wrong shoulder. I myself

rose to be CSM, having developed an unexpected gift for bellowing out orders.

The outbreak of the 1914–18 war, among many other things, confronted my father and his friends with a delicate situation. They had all been pro-Boers in the Boer War, and were more or less committed to a pacifist position. One of my father's strongest points in Surrey Street was always to draw attention to what might be achieved in the way of schools and hospitals with the cost of just one dreadnought. Again, he frequently denounced war scares as a device of cunning armament manufacturers to increase the demand for their wares. General Roberts, who went about the country calling for rearmament in face of German aggression, was, if not as abhorrent as Northcliffe, a decidedly unsympathetic figure. Armament manufacturers – commonly known among us as merchants of death – were a godsend in the way of providing us with an identifiable villain; one of the great needs of the political Left being to be able to point an accusing finger at someone, or some corporate body, as being responsible for public and private wrongs and misfortunes. We spoke darkly about Vickers, Krupp, the *Comité des Forges*, above all about a certain mysterious Sir Basil Zaharoff, as being allied together to keep us all spending our money on useless armaments, to their consequent enrichment. It was one of our arguments that, if only private trading in arms were stopped, wars and war-scares would likewise automatically come to an end. How surprised we should have been to know that governments flogging arms to all and sundry would far outdo private operators, and that actually a future Labour Government would employ a representative at a very high salary to go about the world for that very purpose.

Then there was the question of Germany, greatly preferred in those days in progressive circles to France. Carlyle may have had something to do with this, and even the Prince Consort, reputed to be a progressive sort of man. Above all, there were the German Social-Democrats, respectable, God-fearing, beer- rather than wine-drinkers, who could surely be relied on to curb the sabre-rattling policies of the Kaiser and the Prussians. When in the Reichstag they voted for war credits, the bottom fell out of this whole position. At the next Saturday evening gathering, the talk went on longer, and more whisky and water was drunk than at any previous one. In the end it was decided, rather along the same lines as the Colonists when they ejected the farmer who had started nibbling away at their land, that the war must for the time being be supported in the hope that, once won, it would be possible to take

steps to prevent anything of the kind occurring again. I, listening in the cosy corner, agreed, and when, on Monday morning, on my way to school, I saw some boys throwing mud at a drawing of Kaiser Bill which had been chalked on the wall, I joined in. Being a hopelessly bad marksman, I failed to reach the target.

It was at this time that I started going to the cinema. One had opened in South Croydon. On Saturday afternoons one could get in for three-pence, and stay there till the early evening, reeling out, blinking, into the sunshine or the dusk. There was a long serial that I followed assiduously, starring Pearl White; the early Charlie Chaplin comedies were shown, and once a production of *Macbeth* by Beerbohm Tree, with Sarah Bernhardt playing Lady Macbeth. A flickering, incomprehensible film which yet stuck in my mind because of this extraordinary old woman appearing in it, by this time incapable of even standing up. In those days the cinema was in almost total darkness, broken only by the torches of the usherettes flickering like glow-worms as they showed people in and out. Every now and again, to relieve the musty, stuffy smell of the place, perfume was squirted along the rows and over our heads. A pianist tinkled away, and there was usually a singing item in which a figure on the screen appeared to be singing a song that was actually played on a gramophone. The sync frequently went awry, with the words of the song and the movements of the singer's lips not tallying. What fabulous development this presentation of moving pictures on film was to undergo! Picture palaces as fanciful as Kubla Khan's, stars whose blown-up, long-drawn-out embraces would provide erotic fantasies and dream bed-fellows for all mankind; organists, seated at their jewelled instruments, rising out of the floor; then the shadows on the screen speaking, changing from black-and-white into colour, acquiring three dimensions, to be at last piped via aerials, or dreaming spires, into private homes; a nightly spectacle effortlessly watched, with every sitting-room a Caliban's magic island, filled with sounds and sweet airs which give delight and hurt not, so that when the viewers wake – if they ever do – they cry to sleep again. The reign of the camera had begun. I cannot pretend that I was aware of the implications of my protracted Saturday afternoon communings with shadows flickering across a screen, but it is certainly true that, increasingly, when I emerged, what was outside took on the character of the pictures I had been looking at, rather than the other way round. All the world in a picture palace.

When the zeppelins, those great silver fish, came to bomb us, we

strained our eyes looking for them in the sky, heard the explosions as they dropped their bombs, then with one accord made our way to where the bombs had fallen – in this case, Brixton. Many others who had the same notion, were milling about there, looking for souvenirs; bits of bomb or shrapnel, frenziedly digging out of the wooden blocks of the roadway any fragments of metal they could find – actually, more often than not, the metal studs of motor tyres which had got embedded there. Somehow it recalled scenes I had read of in historical novels of massacres or martyrdoms in which the spectators bathed their handkerchiefs in the blood of the victims.

Or, again, Armistice Day, when with a school friend I took a bus to Woolwich, staying on at the terminus and returning in the same bus to Croydon. From the open upper-deck we watched the crowds singing, shouting, dancing, embracing, vomiting, climbing on to the tops of taxis, grabbing one another and making off to the parks. It was, to me, an eerie and disturbing, rather than a joyful, scene – those flushed animal faces, dishevelled women, hoarse voices. Perhaps at fifteen – which I then was – I should have liked to join in; at the same time, in the light of my father's hopes, I had to consider that it boded ill. Were these the future citizens of his Socialist Commonwealth? Was this what freedom meant? I found myself, as I so often have, in the position of a reluctant and indecisive prig. Then, I was too young to decide the matter one way or the other; when the next Armistice Day came round, some twenty-seven years later, too old.

At home my father attached a small Union Jack to the porch of our house. There were, of course, many other flags flying that day, but that my father should put one out was stupefying in its implications. It would scarcely have been less surprising if he had suddenly announced that he had been appointed a Governor of the Bank of England, or that he was contemplating taking Holy Orders. Union Jacks were for Conservative rallies on Empire Day, or to drape over the table at Conservative election meetings; not for us. When the National Anthem was played, we stood up as a matter of form, but in a languid way, with a deprecatory expression on our faces, indicating that the tune and the ceremonial had nothing to do with us, but belonged to the world of bearded King George V and enamelled Queen Alexandra; of prelates and judges and peers, of Lloyd George with his white locks falsely floating in the wind, and Lord Kitchener with his pointing finger; of admirals and generals and air-marshals in their glittering regalia. My father realised that the flag on our porch was something that required an

explanation, and so went on to deliver what amounted to a little formal apologia for it, with an eye cast, especially, in my direction.

In the first place, he said, he felt immeasurable relief at the ending of the war's senseless slaughter and destruction, and at the survival of my two older brothers. Then he looked forward to a new and better world. If he did not actually say one fit for heroes to live in, he might well have. We like to think that we saw through the fraudulence of the past, but actually the same false money jingles in every pocket. Furthermore, he went on, however dubious had been the purported causes of the war, and however monstrously unscrupulous its conduct, it had, willy nilly, turned into a war to end war. There must, there could, never be another; mankind would not stand for it. Already the phrase League of Nations had entered into my father's vocabulary, and thence into mine; already the Fourteen Points, and President Woodrow Wilson who propounded them, belonged to our kingdom of light. The turgid discourses of this Princeton professor were, to us, golden words, and he a knight in shining armour who could be relied on to champion righteousness. As it happened, I saw the President in the newsreel at one of my Saturday afternoon cinema visitations. He moved across the screen from his motor car to the Palace of Versailles with the quick step and in the silver rain of early movies; tall black hat jerkily raised, spectacles shining, lantern jaws opening and shutting, but no sound coming. I suppose I had expected something quite different; someone Garibaldi-like, Byronic, with shining eyes and floating hair, rather than this sober-looking professorial figure who might easily have been one of my undertaker-grandfather's men. At that moment of history he was the centre of all attention, the focus of the hopes of millions of people. It was reported that Eastern European peasants made wooden models of him before which they lit candles and prostrated themselves. If so, I hope very much that one or two exemplars remain, to be discovered by future anthropologists, if there are any. Their observations on the cult would be interesting.

Looking back, it strikes me as curious that the Russian Revolution, to the best of my recollection, made so small an impact at the Saturday evening gatherings. I should have expected it to be an occasion for great celebration, especially as my father made a sea trip to Russia shortly before the outbreak of the 1914–18 war to recover from a minor operation, and had numerous anecdotes of the police surveillance to which he was subjected there. The reason, perhaps, is that, in the war-time Press, news of the Revolution, and of the Kerensky regime which

followed, was played down, and by the time the war was over the Bolsheviks were in control. About them, Fabian Socialists like my father were extremely dubious, and with an election coming along they did not want to be identified with men who were systematically represented as murderous, anti-Christian and cynically untrustworthy. In the posters and cartoons of the time, the Bolsheviks are usually shown as bearded, piratical figures, with their hands dripping blood – visibly, if the picture happened to be in colour. Very much, in fact, as capitalists are shown in *Krokodil* to-day. Shaw, the Webbs and the other leading Fabians were likewise strongly opposed to the USSR in its early struggling days; they only began to admire it when it had hardened into an authoritarian terrorist regime. Their admiration turned to besotted adulation when Stalin took on the role, and very much the style, of the deposed Czar; only more brutally, efficiently and vaingloriously.

It should be remembered, too, that up to the outbreak of the 1914–18 war, the early Socialists assumed a continuance of the international status quo as far as Western Europe was concerned, and so took little interest in foreign affairs. In the famous first collection of Fabian Essays, not one deals with this subject. It is assumed that England will continue to be strong, rich and stable, disposing of the requisite means to introduce, constitutionally and by consent, practical socialist measures. In the shambles that followed the Versailles settlement, this assumption was rudely shattered; thenceforth the Polish Corridor, the Sudetenland, the Anschluss, the re-militarisation of the Rhineland, the Saar Plebiscite, became part of daily life; salt cellars and cutlery were arranged on the table to show that whoever controlled so-and-so dominated somewhere else. Clausewitz came to be quoted rather than Heine or Schopenhauer, and my poor father, who had put out a flag on 11th November, 1918, found himself constrained in the years that followed to pore over atlases in search of new and old frontiers. At the end of his life he ruefully reflected that, when the means to install Socialism were available, there were not enough Socialists, and when there were, if anything, too many Socialists, the means were lacking.

To me, when I got to hear more about it, the Russian Revolution seemed a glorious episode. I related it to the taking of the Bastille and all the events that followed as I had read of them in Carlyle and *A Tale of Two Cities*. The fact that both Carlyle and Dickens present, on the whole, unfavourable pictures of the French revolutionary regime did not detract from its essential glamour in my eyes; nor prevent me from believing that the October Revolution and its outcome were

similarly glamorous. A love of revolution for its own sake, quite apart from its circumstances and consequences, is part of the romantic outlook; then, as the young do now, we shouted for revolution without thinking of how, in France, it had resulted in Napoleon, the prototype for every power- and notoriety-seeking villain who has afflicted mankind subsequently; nor, of course, knowing that in Russia it would result in Stalin, one of the most blood-thirsty and obscurantist tyrants of all time. We called the Metropolitan Mounted Police Cossacks, rejoiced over early Soviet films like *Mother* and *The Battleship Potemkin*, spoke of workers' control and cadres and agitprop, and I personally decided inwardly that sooner or later I would go to Russia and throw in my lot with the new and better way of life that, I was confident, was coming to pass there. It may be that this cult of revolution for its own sake is now coming to an end, despite the vociferousness of its student practitioners. The fact that one of its most unsavoury devotees – Byron – has recently been honoured by being accorded a place in Westminster Abbey, suggests as much. What the Dean and Chapter approve to-day history will have abolished yesterday.

Now I fell in love for the first time. I happened to see Dora, a girl of about my own age, whose brother I vaguely knew, playing tennis on a public court, and instantaneously the whole of existence for me was concentrated on that one face, uniquely beautiful, as it seemed, and distinct from all other faces. At the same time, the scene itself in which I saw her was glorified and became angelic; as though the wire-netting of the court were golden mesh, the grass greener and softer than any grass ever before seen, the sound of the tennis ball against the racquets, and the laughter and shouts of the players, joyous and most wonderful. Whatever bodily stirrings accompanied these transports were merged and lost in this larger ecstasy, and I should have been outraged to think that what I felt could be reduced to the dimensions of schoolboy eroticism, with which, inevitably, I had become familiar. I was reminded quite recently of how deep-seated these feelings were when I happened by chance to see a schoolgirl wearing in her hat the same badge – an ivy leaf – as Dora had done, and found myself suddenly alerted, as though I were still constantly on the watch for it, just as I had been more than half a century before.

After our first casual encounter we spent nearly all our spare time together; often in the evening at her home. I grew very fond of her father particularly; a delightful character who called his wife 'Peach

Blossom' and was given to playing 'The Lost Chord' on his cornet. It sometimes happened that, to stay with Dora a little longer, I missed the last tram and had to walk the three miles or so home along the empty track; somehow borne up on my way; not quite fixed by gravity on the tarmac, or governed by the regular chiming of the Town Hall clock. I suppose there are few routes more intrinsically remote from Blake's notion of piping through the valley wild than from Thornton Heath, where Dora lived, to South Croydon, where I did, following the tram lines. Yet, for some reason, of all my memories of her, this one, of trudging homeward after the last tram had gone, has a special glow about it. There were, of course, quarrels and angry partings; we exasperated one another with the sexual urges we mutually aroused, and then only partially and inadequately, or not at all, satisfied. We went for country walks together, picked blackberries, talked about books and writers, and what we were going to do in the world. I even bashfully read out verses I had written addressed to her, most of which are now, mercifully, lost. I recall with shame one thing I did, which was to use some of these verses in a satirical sense in a play I wrote – *Three Flats* – that was put on by the Stage Society in 1931, and subsequently published. From time to time throughout my life, without deliberate intent, I have done such cruel things, directed often against those I cared for most.

Our youthful love belonged to the suburban setting in which we lived; to the rows of small identical houses; to the Crescents, and Rises and Avenues; to the gravel of unadopted roads, and the parks and recreation grounds and surrounding countryside into which new housing was constantly seeping, like ink on blotting-paper. In cinema darkness we sat clasped together, caught up ourselves in the silent swollen embraces and grimaces and posturings on the screen. Emerging into the lights and crowds outside, I felt vaguely uneasy and shamefaced. In the Blitz, by a strange accident, I found myself alone with Dora in a cellar after we had not seen each other for years. She by this time had been twice married, and I, too, had fully experienced what are still called in our weird jargon the facts of life. Yet we stayed side by side like grizzled adolescents, while outside the world in which we had been youthful lovers crashed and shook and burnt about us.

My going to Cambridge seems to have been almost accidental. Like most lovers of mankind, my father was inclined to be casual in making arrangements for his own family. Though my academic attainments were decidedly meagre, I somehow got myself accepted. It necessitated

passing an examination in Latin, a language I had never studied, and now know nothing of. So there must have been some sleight-of-hand. I seem to remember learning off by heart the translation of a Latin comedy which seemed to me abysmally unfunny – a premonition, maybe, of becoming editor of *Punch*. There was also, in those days, a compulsory divinity exam which I somehow managed to get through. This involved mastering Paley's *Evidences*, a long-forgotten work which purports to prove the existence of God. I cannot now remember any of the arguments, but I know they failed to convince me at the time; something I did not confide to the examiners. Finally, to go to Selwyn, an Anglican foundation, it was necessary for me to be baptised and confirmed, which none of us had been; my father as a convinced agnostic would have blushed to subject us to such a practice, though my mother would have quite liked it. I forget exactly how, but I got myself done by a bishop along with a number of others who, like myself, came into the Prayerbook category of riper years. The only thing I remember about the ceremony is that somehow at some point in it I got out of step, and that, noting this, the officiating Bishop wore a look of great irritation and ill-temper.

So, when I was seventeen, I went into residence at Selwyn College – then, officially, a public hostel, not a college at all – with the intention of reading a Natural Science Tripos. The subjects I was to take – chemistry, physics and zoology – were the only ones available at my secondary school for post-matriculation study. Thus, my choice of them was more or less unavoidable, despite the fact that I had no interest in them, and only the scantiest knowledge of them; in the case of zoology, none at all. Four years at Cambridge did little to alter this situation. I managed to scrape up a pass degree, but have never opened a book or thought about any of my three subjects from that day to this. I looked round curiously at my fellow-undergraduates. Even at Selwyn, most of them were from public or grammar schools; I must have been one of the very few secondary school specimens in my year. This was my first acquaintance, in their own native habitat, with the English middle and upper classes, whose characteristics were, I think, more noticeable at Selwyn than at more fashionable and famous establishments like King's and Trinity; in the same sort of way that a virus fighting for its existence is easier to detect and isolate than one in a lush, favourable environment. The only gentry I had known previously were the aforementioned clergy, Quakers and Fabians, all of whom might be regarded as, in a manner of speaking, class Quislings, and so not

typical. The first elucidation I had was when the Dean, in the course of an address to freshmen in the college chapel, remarked, as an aside, that none of us were likely ever to be in want, or to lack for the essential requirements for a bourgeois way of life. (He did not put it in precisely those words, but that was what he meant.) I had absorbed sufficient of my father's sense of economic insecurity, as well as of my Booler relatives' attitude to unemployment as a kind of natural catastrophe always hanging over their heads, to find this remark completely novel. It had never occurred to me that, in coming to Cambridge, I was moving into a world in which the economic hazards I had hitherto assumed to be as natural to our human condition as illness, or even death itself, just did not arise.

In South Croydon our notion of the upper classes was expressed by a notice outside a large house standing opposite ours which read: 'Oxford House School for the Sons of Gentlemen'. Now, when education has replaced institutional religion as a fount of hypocrisy and sanctimonious-ness, the very naiveté and simplicity of the notice gives it a certain charm, and even dignity. At the time, it was a constant source of derision to us, especially when we saw the Oxford House boys in their splendid caps and blazers mustered for an outing, or, in singlet and shorts, on a cross-country run. As I came to realise after the Dean's address, it was more or less true then that a boy who had been to a public school and taken a degree at Cambridge could assume that his livelihood was assured; especially as we still had an Empire on which the sun never set, as distinct from a Commonwealth on which it never rises, offering him all sorts of openings, from governorships and colonial bishoprics to affluence and a good chance of a knighthood on the banks of the Hooghly. Hence the self-assurance, and in the more ill-mannered among them arrogance, which so struck me among my fellow-undergraduates.

The converse face of this self-assurance or arrogance was the highly developed system of sycophancy which prevailed; fags required to be sycophantic to their masters, players to the captain of games, boys to prefects, prefects to their housemasters, housemaster to headmaster, and so on. I found the undiscriminating application of this sycophantic attitude of mind to anyone of note or in authority quite surprising until I got used to it. Even then I was sometimes astonished; for in-stance, to hear quite senior figures in the Foreign Office – regarded as an upper-class pasture – speak with almost breathless admiration of an Anthony Eden or an Ernest Bevin; even more absurdly, a heavily moustached Head of Chancery in an Embassy refer to Ramsay Mac-

Donald in terms which might well have seemed excessive if applied to Bismarck. In the army, again, I marvelled at the adroitness with which public-school-reared junior officers helped their brigadiers on with their overcoats compared with the clumsy efforts of us socially inferior officers to ingratiate ourselves with them. Even in the Labour Party the unlikely emergence of figures like Hugh Gaitskell, R. H. S. Crossman and Wedgwood Benn may well have been fostered by their sycophantic skills. Bertrand Russell's elder brother, when he was a member of a Labour Government, told me that he had never before been so conscious of the advantages of being an earl. I doubt, however, whether the built-in sycophancy of the upper classes can be regarded as a social asset, precisely because it is so undiscriminating. A Khrushchev attracts it as readily as a Curzon. As the Nazi régime, particularly, showed, anyone who gets into power may count upon being adulated in the upper social echelons; it is the poor whose support is difficult to attract.

The great difference I observe when I visit Cambridge nowadays is that, compared with my own time there, they are all – dons and undergraduates alike – on the run, and, as is the way with fugitives, tend to discard more than they need to make a getaway. Whereas in my time poor boys like myself were induced to copy the others – their clothes, their ways, their speech – now it is the other way round. The upper-class boys copy the poor ones, decking themselves out in a weird kind of proletarian fancy dress, and speaking in an accent which sounds like a badly rehearsed number in a satire show. They are social descenders, who display, in reverse, all the absurdities, and more, of social climbers. The most comical part of the whole thing is that when, to clinch the transformation, they adopt what they consider an appropriate ideology, it usually turns out to be a half-baked regurgitation of the Marxism and associated revolutionary notions which were fashionable at the time of the Spanish Civil War. Again, the parallel with the situation in reverse as I knew it is strikingly close. The social climber in my day felt it necessary to go to the extremes of Kiplingesque patriotic loyalty to King and Country, in precisely the same way that the social descender nowadays goes to the extremes of revolutionary disruption. It is difficult to decide which of the two attitudes is the more ludicrous; but on the whole, the latter seems to me to be the more deleterious. A ruling class may gain strength from its apes, but the forces of necessary change are weakened and discredited by jackals.

As a secondary schoolboy, I was, of course, an outsider. Public

schoolboys, whatever their particular school – from the most famous like Eton, to the most obscure – had a language of their own which I scarcely understood, games they played which I could neither play nor interest myself in, ways and attitudes which they took for granted but which were foreign to me. For instance, their acceptance of sodomy as more or less normal behaviour. When I went to Cambridge I scarcely knew what this was apart from vague references in the Bible. It was not, at any rate, in those days, a proletarian or lower-middle-class vice. The university, when I was there, was very largely a projection of public school life and *mores*, and a similar atmosphere of homosexuality tended to prevail. There was also a hangover from Wildean decadence, with aesthetes who dressed in velvet, painted their rooms in strange colours, hung Aubrey Beardsley prints on their walls, and read *Les Fleurs du Mal*. The nearest I came to being personally involved with these was when a High-Church ordinand after dinner read to me from Swinburne's *Songs Before Sunrise* in a darkened room faintly smelling of incense. I emerged unscathed.

There were also a lot of ex-service undergraduates, men some years older than the rest of us, who wore British warms and scarves, and who had served in the war. I remember them as being all, in their different ways, versions of the war books which were later to be so popular. Minor Robert Graveses, Richard Aldingtons, Ernest Hemingways, Siegfried Sassoons born to blush unseen. University ways and regulations understandably irritated them, and many of them seemed always on the point of exploding; a consequence, no doubt, of the appalling strain of their experiences in Flanders and other theatres of war, about which they were ready enough to talk on occasion, with mounting hysteria. In a way, they were tragic figures. At Selwyn a good number of them were ordinands, mostly in the Woodbine Willie, or padre, style; a version of Christianity which emerged from the 1914–18 war, enormously sincere, ardent, and at the time seemingly vital, but which subsequently, for the most part, ran into the sand. This invariably happens when it is attempted to relate a transcendental faith to an earthly hope – in this case, pacifism. Like bringing back an alpine plant from some arduous rock climb and bedding it out in a window-box. Among ordinands generally, especially at Selwyn, the ultra High-Church or Anglo-Catholic Movement was still in full swing. There was a great deal of talk about the Reserved Sacrament, Popeing (which meant going over to the Roman Church), vestments and other liturgical and ceremonial embellishments. I was taken on one occasion to breakfast

with an aged Anglican priest called Father Tooth (the 'Father' was stressed in such circles) who had once been stoned when celebrating Holy Communion in gear that was considered Romish for an Anglican service. The vestment in question, along with one of the stones heaved at him, was preserved in a glass case in his living-room. It seemed a mini-martyrdom.

Cambridge, to me, was a place of infinite tedium; of afternoon walks in a damp, misty countryside; of idle days, and foolish vanities, and spurious enthusiasms. Even now when I go there, as my train steams into the station or my car reaches the outskirts, a sense of physical and mental inertia afflicts me. It was my father who tingled with excitement at the thought of my being at Cambridge; not me. I suspect that the prestige of a university education is almost entirely due to the yearnings of those who feel they have been deprived of one, and that the present decline in its prestige comes of there being fewer and fewer who feel so deprived. Perhaps, when there are none to feel deprived, its prestige will sink to nil – one of the few benefits to be expected from the institution of free university education. It was my father who used expressions like 'my Alma Mater', or 'sporting my oak'; when he came to visit me at Cambridge he was thrilled by my rooms, the Union, dinner in hall, boating on the river; everything. If only he had gone to Cambridge instead of me! How hard he would have worked to get a first, whereas I did nothing and just managed to get a pass degree; how assiduous he would have been at the Union debates, whereas, though he paid for me to have a life subscription, I scarcely ever attended, and never once spoke. For me, the years at Cambridge were the most futile and dismal of my whole life. I look back on the self I then was with the utmost distaste – the showing off when I came to Croydon in the vacations; the getting into debt (which my father always paid with little complaining, though he could ill afford it) through buying clothes and other unnecessary things out of vanity; the fatuous imitation of a sort of person I could never be, nor ever wanted to be.

How somehow second-rate it all was! The clock at Grantchester and honey still for tea. Rupert *en beauté* to-night, as glimpsed by Lytton Strachey at Covent Garden; to be smothered in his beard, or deafened by Hugh Dalton's boom, or just transfixed by Maynard Keynes's frosty lechery. Rupert the dead poet-hero of our time. The Prince of Wales, another hero, likewise magnificently unprepared for the long littleness of life in the Boulevard Suchet. Or the even more macabre one, Lawrence of Arabia, with many a scruffy acolyte sitting cross-

legged and elfin among the unwashed-up crockery; his seemingly in-
destructible legend surviving every exposure of fraudulence and
depravity. Lectures by Quiller-Couch, notes shaking in shaky hands.
The seal The seal Wide checks and massive coloured tie to offset the
gown and mortar-board. Or Old McTaggart muttering philosophically,
and scattering anecdotes about himself with a lavish hand. In the labs,
where I was supposed to attend for long sessions, dogfish needing to be
cut up; something boiling in a retort. High up in the lecture theatre
(like, I used to think, trying to comfort myself, the Mountain in the
French Revolution) hopelessly making notes; the single piece of infor-
mation acquired there which has stayed with me being a silver-haired
professor's complaint that, having hit upon some chemical drying agent,
he patented it for making bricks out of sand, whereas someone else
used it to manufacture Cerebos Salt, and made a fortune. Poor silver
head!

On the river – Give her ten! Or watching games and yelling. Or the
university rag; requiring so little modification to become the university
demo. Or just trudging to and fro on desolate afternoons. Then in the
evening the chapel bell intruding into buttered toast, and sounding
across the darkening court. The porter in his bowler pricking the names
of those who attended evensong. Wearing a surplice; 'Dearly beloved
brethren,' spoken down the nose with a sniff at the end of each sentence,
'I pray and beseech you, as many as are here present . . .' Perhaps the
only good thing I got out of Cambridge was a certain familiarity with
the incomparable Book of Common Prayer. Then into hall for dinner.
That smell always hanging about there of stale bread and old cheese!
It must have got into the wood of the benches and tables. The clattering
plates, the passing food, the Latin grace. Perhaps it all had a meaning
once, but not for me. I found it as moribund as El Azhar, where the
Mullahs chant monotonously and unintelligibly to a little circle of
students dozing round them.

In my last year at Cambridge, through my friendship with Alec
Vidler – a friendship that has lasted all my life – I went to live at the
Oratory House. It was the headquarters of an Anglican religious order,
the Oratory of the Good Shepherd, to which Alec belonged, consisting
mostly of priests and ordinands of the Anglo-Catholic persuasion. The
offices were said during the day, periods of silence were enforced; in the
afternoons I often worked in the garden with Wilfred Knox, a rare,
sweet human being of whom I became very fond, and for whom I
sometimes acted as server when he celebrated Holy Communion. I

fell into this way of life with great contentment, enjoying its remoteness from the University, and its relative austerity as far as food and domestic comforts were concerned. Austerity has always made me happy, and its opposite, miserable. I find it strange that, knowing this, I should so often have inflicted upon myself the nausea of over-indulgence, and had to fight off the black dogs of satiety. Human beings, as Pascal points out, are peculiar in that they avidly pursue ends they know will bring them no satisfaction; gorge themselves with food which cannot nourish and with pleasures which cannot please. I am a prize example.

Living so contentedly at the Oratory House did not make me the more inclined to throw in my lot with friends like Alec and Wilfred Knox; *Lord, I disbelieve, help thou my belief* was more my cry. Despite the agnosticism of my home and upbringing, I cannot recall a time when the notion of Christ and Christianity was not enormously appealing to me, though where Peter only heard the cock crow thrice on that one tragic occasion, for me it has been over long years matutinal. I knew from a very early age – how I cannot tell – that the New Testament contained the key to how to live. I somehow knew it to be our only light in a dark world. Not just in my father's sense that Jesus himself was a good man, and his moral precepts greatly to be admired, even though his ostensible followers in the various churches ignored and perverted them. I soon saw through this, understanding that Jesus could not be turned into just a finer version of Wilberforce or William Morris or Robert Owen, into a paid-up member of the Labour Party, and potential Life Peer, without diminishing him to the point that Christianity became too trivial to be taken seriously. He was God or he was nothing.

No, what appealed to me were the wild extravagances of faith; the phrases about God's wisdom being men's foolishness, St Francis of Assisi rejoicing at being naked on the naked earth, the sublime paradoxes of *The Marriage of Heaven and Hell*. Surveying the abysmal chasm between my certainty that everything human beings tried to achieve was inadequate to the point of being farcical, that mortality itself was a kind of gargoyle joke, and my equal certainty that every moment of every day was full of enchantment and infinitely precious; that human love was the image vouchsafed us of God's love irradiating the whole universe; that, indeed, embedded in each grain of sand was eternity, to be found and explored, as geologists explored the antiquity of fossils through their markings – surveying this chasm, yawning in its vastness to the point of inducing total insanity, tearing us into schizo-

C.W.T.—F

phrenic pieces, I grasped that over it lay, as it were, a cable-bridge, frail, swaying, but passable. And this bridge, this reconciliation between the black despair of lying bound and gagged in the tiny dungeon of the ego, and soaring upwards into the white radiance of God's universal love – this bridge was the Incarnation, whose truth expresses that of the desperate need it meets. Because of our physical hunger we know there is bread; because of our spiritual hunger we know there is Christ.

I will not pretend, of course, that I saw all this then, just as I have written it down, or for that matter that I see it now as I should love to see it – as a child sees in the dawn the sure prospect of a joyous day, or reaches up for its father's hand in the sure knowledge of its loving support and guidance. Yet, then as now, I knew it, and knew it more confidently than I knew anything else; in the confusion of a wilful, opinionated and ill-trained mind, it alone was steady and luminous. Where I faltered was in establishing a connection between what I knew and the practice and dogmas of the Christian religion, even as exemplified by someone as noble and profound as Alec, or with as delicate and whimsical a spiritual perception as Wilfred. The churches altogether seemed to me part of the whole decaying social structure, the stench of whose decomposition was so strongly in my nostrils. Passing Wilfred the wine to transform into blood, the wafers to become the body of Christ, in the little Oratory House chapel, I felt perfectly at peace. As I did, saying the offices. Or ringing the Angelus for the others. Equally at peace, in the knowledge I have always had, and never wholly lost, that we are pilgrims here, with a dwelling-place elsewhere. (Never wholly lost – but sometimes the darkness falls, impenetrable, seemingly for ever!) Yet how to connect the two – the worship and the knowledge of God? This I have never solved.

Once, sweeping up dead leaves with Wilfred, he spoke of the priestly vocation. What use would I be? I asked him. His answer I found curious – that I could persuade people to do things. What things? I asked. But he left the matter there. He had this way of dropping out half sentences, fragments of jokes and innuendo, scraps of speech and thought. His brother Evoe, my predecessor but one as editor of *Punch*, though utterly different in every respect and, to me, less sympathetic, had the same way with him; so resembling his brother in this that I sometimes thought he must be there with us. Likewise, another brother, Ronnie, who, after he had become a Roman Catholic convert, was given the task of re-translating the Bible; a Via Dolorosa indeed for him, since, as the son of a Protestant Evangelical Bishop, he knew the Authorised

Version by heart. It was like asking a veteran of many Burns dinners to devise a new setting for Auld Lang Syne.

Round about the same time that I fell in love, I became acquainted with the other great fact of our earthly existence. I mean, death. Something that cannot be hidden however hard we try to persuade ourselves that we are immortal; able to replace our spare parts as they wear out, and so be kept on the road indefinitely like vintage cars; to go on having orgasms even when our flesh is dry and wizened, and our bones creak abysmally. In the end, nothing can hide the fact that this hand now tapping out these words will in a matter of at most a few years fall inert, and this mind framing the words likewise cease to function; while the words themselves over which I struggle and torment myself, be they as sublime as the sunflower weary of time, or as banal as a feature article in a travel supplement, or, more probably, something in between, matter no more to me than the *Bonjour, madame* I said this morning to an unknown lady exercising her dog.

The experience of death came suddenly, its herald being a policeman, who appeared at the door while my father was crunching his last mouthful of toast washed down with his last gulp of tea preparatory to racing for his train. When my mother opened the door to him, the policeman entered and took off his helmet, thereby at a stroke transforming himself from a portentous figure of authority into a rather appealing pink-and-white face jutting out of a blue uniform. From a whispered colloquy with my father, it appeared that my brother Stanley – the one next to me in age who served with the RFC – had met with a serious accident on his motor bicycle, which he rode daily to work, and was now in the Croydon General Hospital in a grave condition. It was decided that my mother should stay at home with her tears and fears, and my father and I made our way as quickly as possible to the hospital, passing on the way the crossroads where the accident had occurred; a place well known to me because of a crossing-sweeper there. I should suppose he was one of the last of his kind; a man with a dragging leg (I imagine he had suffered some kind of a stroke) who, while he swept his crossing, babbled away incomprehensibly to himself; something that naturally appealed to schoolboys. On this particular morning he was babbling away, as it seemed to me, more furiously than ever, which I attributed to the accident whose debris still lay about the road, including, as I thought, some traces of blood. Whether the blood was really there or not, I cannot now be sure, but whenever, afterwards, I conjured up the scene, I saw it there.

At the hospital we were shown at once to where my brother was, though we did not see him because of a screen round his bed. From behind the screen there came a curious spasmodic gurgling noise, due, as I learned afterwards, to a tube which had been inserted into his throat through which he was breathing. While I was listening to the sound with fascinated intensity, as it might be to a count-down, it became more spasmodic, and began to falter, like a top running down. Then it stopped, and I understood that my brother was dead. This was death – a gurgling noise faltering, and then stopping. I caught a glimpse of a white dead face, already drained and shrunken, and beginning to look like a skull, but with a strong resemblance to my mother which I had not noticed before. I had been intending to play tennis with Dora that morning, and so was in flannels, with a white boating blazer (to which I was only dubiously entitled), which added a touch of grotesqueness to the occasion.

On the way home my father remarked in a ruminative tone of voice: 'I'm very resilient.' It was so utterly characteristic of him that it brought tears to my eyes for the first time that morning. I knew exactly what he meant – that though he would be as grief-stricken as any other father, he would not allow this grief to prevent him from attending the next meeting of the Croydon Borough Council. After my father's remark about being resilient, we fell silent, and there came insistently into my mind the memory of an incident concerning my brother's fiancée, a luscious, bold, rather beautiful girl whom I found very appealing. Once she had come up to the little room at the top of the house where I kept my books and was supposed to study during the vacations. I must have made some sort of amorous gesture, for she looked down complacently at her legs (skirts were almost as short in those early post-war years as to-day's mini-skirts) and said: 'They're already booked,' or words to that effect. I had brooded over these words at the time, finding them crude and inelegant, but in a way exciting. Now, returning from seeing my brother die, they repeated themselves over and over as though they had some special point or significance.

At home, my father tried to comfort my mother, and I felt it necessary to go through the motions of relieving my feelings, which I did on the ample bosom of Mrs Milne, a lady who lived next door in the house that was to have been Will Straughan's. Round her mouth, as I had noticed before, were some sparse tough hairs on which particles of food were liable to get skewered – something that must have struck me forcibly, for I notice these hairs recurring several times in some sketches

for short stories that I scribbled down round about this time. The Milnes had the first motor-car I ever rode in, an Overland whose hood was put up and down with great difficulty. Its fixtures included some holes in the sides of the car into which they would put wine glasses with the stems broken off when they wanted to refresh themselves, which was rather often. It was a device which gave them great satisfaction. I never saw my dead brother's fiancée again.

I spent my last long vacation in Belgium working for Lunn's Tours. This came about through my friendship at Cambridge with Leonard Dobbs, with whom I shared rooms after I left the Oratory House. His father was a director of Lunn's, and responsible for operations on the Belgian coast. As a result of this interlude I subsequently married Leonard's sister, Kitty, and got to know Hugh Kingsmill Lunn, who became a close friend; two of the greatest blessings of my life that I owe to Leonard. He was an unusual, rather sombre man, very gifted; a brilliant skier, a scientist of exceptional promise, curious about many things, enormously argumentative, and with a propensity for carrying every thought and notion to the extremes of fantasy. At the end of his life, when he was living with Kitty and me, he devoted himself to making an enormous gramophone horn, so huge that it could not be moved from the room in which he was working on it. At one point he married a Mlle. Cantaloupe, but their union was not a success. He died in the early part of the 1939–45 war, I think with relief. Hugh Kingsmill said of him – and I am inclined to agree – that he was more lovable than likeable.

On the Belgian coast I was one of the shepherds of the Lunn flock. We met them at Ostend where they arrived, saw them to their hotels, arranged tours for them, and generally watched over their welfare. It was an occupation which, more than I realised at the time, had great bearing on things to come. In taking parties to Bruges, for instance, and addressing them on the town, its history and its art treasures, I acquired a facility for talking convincingly on a basis of very little, if any, knowledge; an accomplishment equally useful in education, journalism and television. I also learnt at an early age the great truth that the twentieth century is an age of almost inconceivable credulity, in which critical faculties are stifled by a plethora of public persuasion and information, so that, literally, anyone will believe anything. It is on this basis that our great newspapers, television and radio networks, universities and schools, churches and, above all, our great advertising agencies and all their ancillary activities in the field of public relations, are conducted.

The lesson was brought home to me by a figure of Chaste Susannah in Bruges, which, I used to say, following another Lunn's man, Louis Wilkinson, was fittingly fashioned in white alabaster. At the end of the season I was disconcerted to learn that she was in black ebony. In any case, no one ever raised the point. In later years, whenever I was troubled about some hideous misconception which had slipped into print or on to the air, I always turned for comfort to this white alabaster Chaste Susannah, never in vain. Louis Wilkinson was a writer – a novelist and literary critic – and so held in great admiration and respect by me. He had flowing auburn hair and a spade beard to match; knew the Powys family, and spoke much about them, every word of which I treasured, and as a schoolboy at Repton had written fan letters to Oscar Wilde, enclosing a photograph. Despite this daring gesture, a subsequent meeting with Wilde in Paris proved disappointing to both of them. Dining with Louis and his wife, Nan, as I sometimes did, at Blankenberg where they were staying, he always made a great fuss about the wine, praising particularly some Volnay which, he implied, was a useful aphrodisiac. Though I never liked wine or had the slightest interest in it, I used for years afterwards to repeat this panegyric of Volnay as though it was a precious piece of wine lore of my own.

After we left the Belgian coast I went to stay for a week-end with Louis and Nan at their flat in Christchurch Road, in one of the remoter regions of London. It was a fairly modest dwelling with, however, many literary trophies which held my attention – Louis's own books in their jackets, letters from Maugham, J. C. Squire and other writers, photographs of the Powys brothers. His voice was slow and ponderous, very like a clergyman's (he was, in fact, a clergyman's son), and became in time tedious. His jokes likewise palled; as when he would say that though he himself had taken no part in the war, he had given two of his boys to fight for King and Country. Nonetheless, I continued to hang on his words, though later I ridiculed him in various fictional guises. Nan was a minute creature, also a novelist, and suffering from tuberculosis. While Louis was away for some reason or other, we went for a walk together in the neighbourhood of Christchurch Road. Because of her illness she was not allowed to talk while walking, so we went along hand in hand in silence, every now and again pausing while she coughed, and then spat out the sputum into a blue bottle she had with her for the purpose. The following morning she climbed into my bed, but I was unable to appreciate this gesture owing to the looming presence of Louis who could be heard singing in his bath. A few years later I heard

that Nan had died. Long afterwards I met Louis again. He looked exactly the same except that his skin was drier and his hair more carefully combed and spread over his head. He repeated his joke about giving two of his boys to fight for King and Country, even though, by that time, another war had intervened.

Lunn's Tours, of whose operations on the Belgian coast I had this brief experience, were pioneers in what was to become an enormous industry – holidays and travel, which not only kept the Press going with its advertisements, but also provided the world of the midtwentieth century with one of its few elements of stability. International *Wagon-Lits*, it seemed, rather than the 'Internationale', united the human race. The founder and head of the firm, Sir Henry Lunn, made the discovery on which his flourishing business was based when, as a young missionary returned from India, he was given the task of organising a conference at Grindelwald for the reunion of the churches; an early essay in ecumenicalism. He found that, if a hotelier was offered an assured consignment of clients, he would reduce his charges, thus leaving a comfortable margin of profit for the entrepreneur. Applying this principle, he established, first, the Church Travellers' Club, then, at a slightly lower social level, the Free Church Touring Guild, and might have gone on to complete the social spectrum with a Workers' Travel Association. This, however, was left to other hands. He did mount higher with his Hellenic Travellers' Club and Public Schools' Alpine Sports Club, both of which catered specifically for the upper classes, and to make sure that this not only happened but was seen to happen, a number of free places were provided for peers, dons and other certified gentry. It was in the too lavish provision of these free places that the good man came to grief, his snobbishness, very creditably, proving greater than his cupidity.

I got to know him later on through Hugh Kingsmill, one of his three sons, the other two being Brian and Arnold. Hugh so disliked everything about his father that he dropped the 'Lunn' from his name. Sir Henry was, admittedly, a somewhat Pecksniffian figure, but with some redeeming traits of naïveté and absurdity. Once, going up on the train to London from Hastings, he told me that when he had persuaded some bishops to attend his Grindelwald Conference, W. T. Stead – the famous editor of the *Pall Mall Gazette* whose series, 'The Maiden Tribute of Babylon', made straight the way for many another moralistic campaigner fulminating against wickedness, and thereby advertising it – admonished him that he should now never go back to curates. When I

said that this was as though, after the conversion of St Luke, Jesus should have been instructed never to go back to fishermen, his face fell. His knighthood was a great solace, but his hopes for a peerage were disappointed. The nearest he got was to be on the list Asquith prepared of the names of those who would be recommended for peerages if their elevation proved necessary to force the passage of the Parliament Bill through the Upper House. How exasperating for them, good Radicals all, that standing up to the House of Lords did not involve their going there. I am occasionally reminded of Sir Henry when I catch a glimpse of some beach where bodies lie packed side by side roasting in the sun, or on one of the more lurid prospectuses for a fortnight at the Costa Brava, and wonder how, as a good Methodist, he would react to this outcome of his first faltering steps in the tourist business. Was it for this that he made his discovery about getting advantageous terms from the Grindelwald hoteliers when he brought together those earnest would-be reuniters of the churches – precursors of the World Council of Churches and the Vatican Council. Perhaps, after all, it was.

Mr Dobbs, Leonard's father, and my future father-in-law, was a genial Protestant Irishman who by chance had joined the crew of this Methodist brig Sir Henry sailed with such panache in the triple winds of piety, snobbishness and cash. It was he who first mentioned Kitty to me as having returned from a stay in Switzerland. The things that really happen to one, I have found, have all happened already; the other happenings – like wars, and seductions, and prizes, and going to the moon – are theatre merely. Thus, I heard of Kitty's return as I might hear of the weather forecast for a day already lived through; as something that did not need to be said because it was so obvious, and yet in its very obviousness good to hear. It is this sense, in all the true – as distinct from the theatrical – drama of our lives, that it is pre-ordained, that it not only has been and will be, but *is*, that makes us know we are immortal, and, within the smaller dimensions of imaginative literature, supports the action of coincidence – something for which a novelist like Anthony Powell is sometimes criticised, in my opinion unjustly, since coincidence is not only plausible, something that undoubtedly happens, but part of the very fabric of life itself. All our true living has already happened, and will go on happening for ever; all our true relationships already exist when we make them, and can never be broken. So, you take someone's hand, and use a name, perhaps embrace, before a hand has even been offered, or a name been given, before you have even looked in one another's faces, because that hand, that name, that

embrace are part of both; part, as Donne puts it, of the atomies of which we grow – souls whom no change can invade. There are only a few occasions on which I have felt so, and this was one of them. I saw Kitty afterwards at the villa where her family were staying, and all of us went bathing and walking over the sand-dunes. All I remember about her then is that she was wearing some sort of a red knitted jumper with patterns on it, and that she was tanned from her stay in Switzerland. During the next – and my last – term at Cambridge, she visited Leonard, and we went for a walk by the Cam. I helped her over a stile.

Somehow – I forget the precise circumstances – I had tea with Mrs Dobbs, Kitty's mother, at a café in Heyst before Kitty returned from Switzerland. She was sitting waiting for me, and I had no difficulty in spotting her. A hat decorated with artificial fruit was perched on top of her noticeably small head; she wore, as she almost invariably did, a shirt with a stiff high collar and tie of sorts; her boots were dusty, and made for comfort rather than elegance; her battered suit was cut in the style of the early part of the century, with a long coat and flowing skirt. By her side was a bag containing her painting materials, a small stool, and – though of course I did not know this at the time – some provisions of uncertain age. A large nose jutted out of a weather-beaten face; her hands were bony, with long fingers, and covered in paint; her voice, when she addressed me, was gruff and impossible to place in any of the social categories of accent and pronunciation. She might have been a gipsy beggar-woman or a duchess, or anything in between; there was no means of knowing. I greeted her, and ordered tea and cakes, which, when they came, she consumed with great zest. There was nothing she liked better than free hospitality. As I came to know later, she was a woman of almost inconceivable generosity, who would, literally, starve to give her children something they wanted. At the same time, economising was a passion with her, and she carried it to inordinate lengths; like serving horse-meat for sirloin, watering marmalade, and eschewing butter in favour of margarine, which, she said, was indistinguishable from butter, and anyway she liked it better. Her abounding hospitality led her to invite many guests to the villas and chalets and rented houses between which her family moved; her parsimony led her to provide only the same amount of food however many there might be to consume it. I suppose it could be said of her that she was one of the most maddening of human beings; certainly the most maddening I have ever known. Yet she was also, as I vaguely grasped at this first meeting with her, a kind of angel, in Blake's sense,

that she belonged directly and wholly to the great fount of life and energy, with no involvement in the systems of thought and morality and aesthetics which men create with their minds to evade living as angels in their imaginations. She had no mind; only a being. I think of her as I have often seen her, painting away to catch the last rays of the sun, immune to heat and cold, to buzzing insects as to curious spectators, utterly intent on what she saw around her, herself a part of the scene; as it might be, a bit of old creeper, or a weather-stained rock, or a tree shaken and tossed and still precariously standing on a cliff-face.

'You are a friend of my son, Leonard,' she said, and I nodded. 'I hear you have very Left-wing views.' I nodded again. 'I take my political views,' she went on, 'from my sister Beatrice Webb and the *New Statesman.*' I proceeded to try and demolish both, citing the Russian Revolution, which the Webbs at that time held in great abhorrence. She replied with 'Beatrice says . . . Sidney says . . .' It was impossible to argue with her, then, or ever. She had a way of dropping out wildly controversial statements, often chosen with great cunning to produce the maximum irritation in the person to whom they were addressed, and then, when the storm broke, of placidly repeating her original statement. We moved on to the subject of personal immortality, in which she had a passionate and abiding interest; desperately wanting there to be an after-life, but only if it were here, on the earth, with sunsets and dawns and high waves breaking against wild rocks. Dreading that there might be no immortality at all, only darkness and obliteration; or, if there were, that it would be heavenly instead of earthly, with a judgment at which she would fare ill. We went to and fro, with this subject, until it was dark. Then she abruptly got up to go, and made off, carrying her bag, with those loose-fitting boots of hers scraping the pavement as she went along.

I had no particular idea what I should do after Cambridge, except that I was committed to teach in one capacity or another. In addition to my poor pass degree, I had taken a diploma in education; yet another course of instruction of which I can remember nothing except turning over the pages of some sort of treatise on child psychology and of another volume called significantly *The Play Way*, as well as participating in various teaching demonstrations. These included a music lesson, at which, being unable to produce or recognise any musical sounds, I was at a heavy disadvantage, and giving a demonstration lesson myself, under the eye of a supervisor, on some distasteful verses by Walter de la Mare beginning: 'Three jolly gentlemen dressed in

red,/Rode their horses up to bed.' My impression was, and is, that, happily, the children had not the faintest idea of what I was talking about. Then, by chance, I heard an Anglican missionary, the Rev. W. E. S. Holland, appealing for staff for an Indian Christian college in South India, and on an impulse offered my services. I was accepted, and found myself in possession of a steamship ticket to Colombo, with general instructions to go on from there to Alwaye, in what was then Travancore, and present myself at the Union Christian College.

3 *Twilight of Empire*

The world's too little for thy tent,
A grave too big for me.
 – George Herbert

SAILING DOWN THE THAMES on a P & O liner – the SS *Morea* – on
my way to the open sea and India, I felt well content. I have always had
a great weakness for making off. Shutting a door behind me never to
open it again; disengaging myself from a sleeping figure, and tiptoeing
away, downstairs and out into the street and the grey anonymous dawn
of another day. Now I was making off, leaving everyone and everything
behind me; unpaid bills and overdrafts, actual and emotional. I had
seen little of Dora of late. We had drifted apart, largely through my
fault. The self I had become as a result of my idle, conceited years at
Cambridge was a very unalluring one. I recall with shame the falsity
and pretentiousness of letters I wrote to Dora after we became estranged.
They were even worse than Keats's to Fanny Brawne; a relationship
which greatly interested me. I was always trying to be some literary
figure or other. In the case of Keats, there were two major deficiencies
in my impersonation; I wasn't a poet and I didn't die.

My father came to see me off. He never had an engagement important
enough to stop him from being with me on any special occasion. We
walked up and down the deck together, neither of us being easy sitters,
and talked about politics. Ramsay MacDonald's first Labour Govern-
ment had taken office without a majority in the House of Commons, and
so was dependent on Liberal support. Suddenly, MacDonald, a much
hated man, especially in the 1914–18 war years, had become a popular
folk hero, with pictures of him in the papers; at Chequers wearing his
tweed knickerbocker suit, his grey curls awry in the wind, and a faraway
look in his eyes. My father's esteem for him, never very marked, was
diminishing rapidly. He feared, all too justifiably as it turned out, that

MacDonald was succumbing to what sour critics of his social ways called the aristocratic embrace. The assimilative power of the English upper classes was still formidable, enabling them to absorb into themselves alien elements; Jewish, Asian, Levantine, Negro even, not to mention a distracted Scot from Lossiemouth who went down as smoothly as an oyster. Later, as their fortunes declined at an accelerating rate, it was the other way round; the aliens absorbed them. No reference was made to where I was going, or to what conditions would be like when I got there, for the very simple reason that neither of us had looked the place up on the map, or had more than the sketchiest notion of what I should be expected to do, how I should live, or even what I was going to be paid. This was not disinterestedness, but just an engrained improvidence, to which both my father and I were prone; uncorrected, in his case, by hardships and responsibilities, and in my easier circumstances, quite unchecked. When the bell rang for visitors to leave the ship we shook hands. I cannot remember ever kissing my father, though I must have done so as a small child. As I watched him leave the ship and walk away, I was surprised, and rather disgusted with myself, to find that I felt a kind of relief at leaving him too.

The fallacy about making off, as I soon discovered, was, of course, that I remained myself; whether travelling round the Inner Circle or out to India. In this particular case, too, the SS *Morea* proved to be just a little bit of Croydon sailing over the high seas. Once again the suburban style of living proved to be the master-print of the age. I was sharing my second-class cabin with an Indian clergyman, the Rev. C. K. Jacob, who afterwards became a bishop, and in that capacity visited me when I was editor of *Punch*. I noticed that, as a bishop, he cracked his finger-joints in exactly the same way as he had when he was just a simple clergyman. After we had been at sea for some days, I became aware that my sharing a cabin with an Indian, even though he was a clergyman, aroused comment. I actually overheard one of the passengers – a man who put on white shorts after Marseilles and worked in the Army Ordnance Department – saying with considerable moral fervour that it wasn't right. Even though I knew that at Cambridge the question of Indians and Africans becoming captains of games had aroused controversy, I had not hitherto run into the Ordnance man's attitude, whereby for an Englishman to mix on intimate terms with an Indian (other than on the most intimate terms of all: viz., to sleep with Indian women, which practically all Englishmen in India did at one time or another)

was morally reprehensible. There was already a large and growing literature on the subject, I know, but for some reason I have always instinctively shied away from books about racialism, with titles like *The Clash of Colour*. Kipling I had read and enjoyed, though reading him in my home was comparable, I should suppose, with reading pornography in a Methodist one. I must, I think, have got hold of *Kim* and *The Jungle Book* at school.

Kipling has come to signify an extreme racialist attitude, but, in point of fact, the hero of *Kim* – the book of his I enjoyed most – is a little half-caste boy whose affections and loyalties are more Indian than English. Again, his brilliant short story, *Without Benefit of Clergy*, is a beautifully touching account of a love-affair between an Englishman and an Indian girl; so touching that I have always thought that it must have been partly autobiographical and may account for the curious fact that, after he left India in his twenties, Kipling never once went back there, though he was an inordinate traveller all his life. As will assuredly come in due course to be seen, he represents the only truly artistic yield of the years of the British Raj; not excepting New Delhi and *A Passage to India*. Curiously enough, it is Indians to-day who are more aware of this than Kipling's fellow-countrymen, whose judgment is twisted and distorted by excessive guilt feelings about ever having ruled over India at all, and who, in the present climate of opinion, would sooner appear as rapists than as racialists. On the recent centenary of Kipling's birth I gave a televised lecture on him to the Kipling Society. A man in the audience astonished and delighted me by claiming that Kipling was a Marxist. I have long been expecting an ecumenical pilgrimage to Marx's grave at Highgate Cemetery, led by a Salvation Army band, with the Archbishop of Canterbury well to the fore, and the Atheist International (there must be one; at any rate there's a branch at the BBC) bringing up the rear. Even in that delectable gathering, though, I had not anticipated the presence of a representative from the Kipling Society.

The effect on me of the Ordnance man's attitude was to make me spend more time in Jacob's company than I should otherwise have done. He was, truth to tell, a bit of a bore, and, had he been white, I should have seen little of him outside our cabin. As it was, I felt bound to walk up and down the deck with him, to ensure that we sat at the same table in the dining saloon, and generally to make him my bosom companion. This may well have been as tedious for him as for me, but it was imposed on us by the attitude of most of our fellow-passengers.

An exception was a piano-tuner on his way to Singapore, who also sat at our table and who behaved impeccably. I marvelled that there were sufficient pianists in Singapore to provide a livelihood for a piano-tuner, but I heard afterwards that he opened a music shop there, throve, and during the Japanese occupation behaved with great courage and charity. A weakness for the bottle, and a forlorn, lost expression I noted in his right eye, were due, it seems, to personal troubles he had been experiencing. I cannot say that anyone actually insulted Jacob; it was just an awkward atmosphere created by my sharing a cabin with him ever having been raised as an issue at all. Race is something that, like love, should never be told; never seek to tell thy race, race that never told should be . . . The Race Relations Board to-day, and the racially conscious English in India in the days of the Raj, are alike offenders in this respect.

As the voyage proceeded, I noticed a strange transformation in my fellow-passengers. They had come aboard as more or less ordinary middle- or lower-middle-class English, with perhaps, in the second class, the latter preponderating. Now they were changing, the men becoming more assertive, the ladies more la-di-da; as it were, moving farther and farther away from Bournemouth and Bexhill and nearer and nearer to Memsahib status and invitations to Government House. Luncheon was tiffin, a whisky and soda a chota peg, and instead of calling for a steward, the cry was: 'Boy!' By Port Said the change was complete; those who had topees brought them out, and those of us who hadn't went ashore and bought one at a shop called Simon Artz. I acquired an enormous white one, very heavy, such as the Marines wear, that needed to be cleaned with pipe-clay from time to time. It was a preposterous headgear, which I carried about with me but rarely put on my head, though the direst warnings were given me of what would happen if I neglected to protect my European pate from the Asian sun. This mystique of the topee was universally accepted during the Raj; it was the badge of the Sahib, and cultivated by all his imitators and aspirants, whether Anglo-Indians or westernised Indians. Among Europeans in India the belief was almost universally held that to expose their heads to the sun even for a few minutes would have disastrous consequences; I have known them, when a group photograph was being taken, keep their topees on till just before the camera was going to click, then put them under their seats, pulling them out and putting them back on their heads the moment the picture was taken. Now that the Raj is over, practically no one wears a topee, with no ill consequences. It

is an interesting example of how medical lore, like trade, follows the flag.

Wherever our ship put in now, we were met by a launch flying the Union Jack, with British officers aboard. This, of course, fitted in well with the changed personas of the passengers who, it seemed to me, almost visibly swelled with pride. For the first time I became aware of the British Empire, not just as a lot of red on the map, nor as a mystique to enthuse over or deride on Empire Day, but as a geographical and political entity. In this part of the world, it was clear, we were the lords of creation – a role which the great majority of my fellow-countrymen, from private soldiers to captains and kings with no intention of departing, found highly acceptable. The whole imperial set-up has disappeared so quickly and completely that one looks back on it now with a kind of wonder that it should ever have existed, but at the time it seemed very solidly based and durable. In the dining saloon one evening I was severely rebuked by the Ordnance man – who had blossomed more than most of them into a Burra Sahib – for saying that the British Empire, like any other, would have its day, and that its end might well be nearer than many now supposed. There was no one except the piano-tuner – who came out rather equivocally on my side – who found this proposition acceptable, on however long a view. They were one and all certain that the Empire would go on for ever; its bounds being set wider still and wider, and God who had made us mighty going on making us mightier yet, indefinitely. A view that was held at that time, I should suppose, pretty well universally on P & O boats ferrying to and fro between the Mother Country and her colonies, dependencies and dominions.

My own reaction was as predictable as that of Bunyan's Pilgrim to Vanity Fair. To my father and his friends, the Empire was a bare-faced system of exploitation, and the imperial idea additional opium of the people to supplement the dwindling soporific effect induced by religion. Though my father did once say to me that he had happened to see a British battleship come into Gibraltar Harbour, and that the sight had given him emotions of pride rather than reminding him of the old familiar equation of how many hospitals, schools and lidos the money it cost would have provided. I might easily have reacted in the same sort of way when confronted with the pomp and circumstance of imperial power, except that I was vaguely aware that its glory was already passing. There was something unconvincing about the Ordnance man as a custodian of Empire; even about the little launches as they shot

out from the shore. I sensed – or thought I did – a process of decomposition at work behind the façade of unity and strength that the Empire still presented to the world. Though ostensibly bigger and stronger than it had ever been as a result of the acquisitions of territory in the Versailles peace settlement, it was somehow shaky about the knees; a little breathless going uphill, a little trembly about the hands. Like Pavlova, when I saw her dance in *Swan Lake* in Cairo shortly before she died as magnificently turned out as ever, as accomplished as ever, but just a little tremulous when she was up on her toes and about to be whirled around by her partner.

Of course, at the time, it was no more than a vague feeling that, despite a crescendo of imperial sentiments, ranging between high-minded *Round Table* prospectuses for English-speaking orchestration, Rhodes Scholarship pieties, and Kipling doggerel; with General Smuts devising his holier than thou philosophy of Holism, and Geoffrey Dawson, alias Robinson, or vice versa, in and out of *The Times*, and Lord Beaverbrook throwing his own gilded spanner into the works – despite all this, the Empire itself was running down. As is now clear, Imperialism only arose as a doctrine when the Empire was already in decline; as it is the sick who are obsessed with their bodies, the impotent with their virility, and the faithless with their faith. In any case, whatever gloss may be attempted, the glories of imperial power are threadbare and tawdry. Hence, the pomp and circumstance. As Pascal says, judges need their wigs and robes, priests their vestments, scholars their gowns – for that matter, hippies their long hair and fancy dress; otherwise, the fraudulence of their pretentions would be all too apparent. Similarly, the British Raj needed majestic titles, and silver thrones, and ceremonial durbars. In my years of journalism – a sort of *voyeur* role – I have never seen authority that did not give off a whiff of decay, or power that was not sawdust-stuffed, or glamour without grease-paint. That White House smile! That Kremlin glower! That Downing Street you-know-you-can-trust-me look! In the immortal words of the producer to the floor-manager when one of the Nixon commercials was being recorded in the Presidential Election of 1968: 'Keep the witch-hazel handy; we can't do the sincerity bit if he's sweating.'

On those long voyages one came to accept liner life as normal. Waking in the morning to the ship's sway, watching its silver wake at night before going to bed; the stars so very near, and enveloped in darkness like velvet. Bells punctuating the day, calling one to meals; the engines endlessly chugging and churning, like time inexorably ticking away.

The walks up and down the deck, an eye perhaps alert for one of the prettier young wives on her way to join her husband; or a fiancée going to get married, with golden dreams set to the music of the Indian Love Lyrics – 'Pale hands I love, beside the Shalimar' – tinkled out on a thousand upright pianos in a thousand sitting-rooms. Matins in the first-class dining saloon, to which we second-class passengers were admitted for the occasion, and Jacob permitted to officiate in a minor capacity, surplice and hood prudently stowed in Wanted-on-Voyage luggage. Passengers getting to know one another, chatting, gossiping, amorous or quarrelsome together; and the sea all round us always, like eternity, with our little ship-encompassed world cruising through it as our little atmosphere-encompassed earth cruises through space. The past written on water by our stern, our prow nosing into the future, and no present at all.

I hate to think how many hundreds of thousands of miles this ridiculous carcass of mine has been carted about the world for one reason and another. As the years have passed, the carriers have grown faster and faster. Five weeks from Tilbury to Colombo; then five days from Delhi to London, with night-stops along the way, sometimes at mysterious desert stockades. Then flying boats following the African coast, hovering over jungle, and slithering down on to great stretches of muddy river water. Wartime flying fortresses, lying racked among the kit-bags in the fuselage. Then the stratocruisers, then the jets; faster than sound, faster than light, until our whole earth, and all its beauties and its wonders, can be encompassed in one piercing supersonic shriek. Distance annihilated, and the world with it. Bull-dozed away by the runway- and road-makers; jet-deafened, oil-drenched, smog-smothered; its inside gouged out like Prometheus's entrails. Trampled to death by stampeding travellers, consumed by curiosity's ravening eye, stung by cameras click-clicking and flashing like dragonflies. Where the rainbow ends; where the runway disappears and the motorways intersect. I cannot say that I myself derived any evident benefit from participating in this dance of death. Taj Mahal unvisited, Madura Temple with golden dome unseen, sphinx and pyramids barely noticed, Arctic splendours briefly glimpsed through a crack in a Boeing's shutter. 'We're now flying over Samarkand at a height of ... at a speed of ...' Where are you, Samarkand? What memories I must have of Peking, Celestial City! Of Katmandu where the junkies roam! Bring me my home Kine of burnished gold; bring me my transparencies of desire! Where are we now, air-hostess? Laying an extra coat of red on lips

tired with smiling, she looks at her watch. 'We'll be landing at La Guardia in . . . minutes' time.' Travel narrows the mind.

So we chugged on, through the Suez Canal, where I noticed on the left bank a train arriving at a station, and the passengers getting out to cross to the other side of the Canal to catch another train that was waiting for them there; as it might be Clapham Junction. A weird enough little group to be discovered in the desert, consisting mostly of men in suits and trilby hats, carrying briefcases, some of them with umbrellas as well. Nothing, it seemed, could stop men with briefcases making their way about the world. So far, it must be admitted, nothing has. Then on into the Red Sea, where we celebrated Christmas Day. After we had finished our Christmas dinner, the Ordnance man – a shade more portentous than usual after a bottle of champagne – made a speech in which he spoke of the various services and professions represented in our second-class saloon, finishing up with: 'Not forgetting the education corps,' meaning me. The piano-tuner, who had also drunk a lot of champagne, applauded rapturously, and shortly afterwards fell asleep. It was a relief to arrive at Colombo, say good-bye to the passengers, and go ashore.

In Colombo I stayed with some kindly missionaries, and spent most of my time wandering aimlessly about the streets; as I nearly always do when I find myself at a loose end in a strange town. Just drifting along and watching faces as they pass, one of them myself; enjoying a kind of anonymous intimacy with all the others, yet separate from them, inviolate. Such a variety of faces and expressions! Whiskers and beards sprouting, eyes hooded or smiling; faces taut or withdrawn, or – as so many are in India – full of fathomless patience which is very beautiful and touching. Sometimes a face of rare serenity, so that you want to stop and offer thanks for it there and then. Or a face stamped with a lustrous beauty; momentarily glimpsed, then gone for ever. Or a beggar's face whining and cringing, mutely exposing sores or deformities, or holding up for inspection a wizened stunted child. Then, in passing rickshaws, with bells tinkling and the pat, pat of human feet sounding, some massive bearded merchant lost in his own thoughts and stratagems. Or a topee'd clerk or official. Or a minor Memsahib on her way to the Club. The unforgettable smell of spices, cow-dung, sweating flesh; the flies, the confused shouts; the little shops like opera boxes, exuding their own smells and tinkling sounds. A shoe-maker gravely intent on his work, with wrinkled brow and meditative face, like a philosopher. A pastry-cook, shining with the heat of his oven,

arranging the delicacies he has made. A grain merchant dozing, with open sacks of rice, a shovel and scales ready to hand. A jeweller sitting, inscrutable, among his bracelets and trinkets and necklaces; as it might be some Maharajah's vizier or treasurer. A cloth-merchant with silks and brocades under his eye, quietly observant of any who come to look at them. And, as one passes, the whispered persuasion to come and buy, however seemingly hopeless the proposition. As though I should want a tortoise-shell comb to put in black silken hair! Or a little silver box for holding betel and lime!

From the moment of landing in Colombo, I was made conscious of my status as a Sahib. It was like suddenly inheriting a peerage and being addressed as My Lord. Just by virtue of being English and white, if you went to buy a ticket at a railway station, people made way for you. Similarly, in a shop. It was very insidious. At first I found it embarrassing and distasteful; then, though I continued to ridicule it, I came to count upon receiving special treatment. Finally, when for some reason it was not accorded, there was an impulse to become sulky and irritated. From that it is but a small step to shouting and insisting, as, in the days of the Raj, I saw happen often enough. Our position in India as a ruling race corrupted all concerned; soldiers – and other ranks just as much as officers, if not more so – missionaries, government officials, planters, business men, wives and children; everyone. It also corrupted the Indians, whether they kissed the rod and accepted a position of subservience, or whether they rebelled against it. Though alien rule can sometimes be more efficient and honest than self-government, it is bound ultimately to become deleterious to rulers and ruled alike. We accept bad government – we have to – but find it more bearable from our own kith and kin than from foreigners. The absurdity is to suppose that self-government, as such, is otherwise beneficent; that replacing a buffoonish colonial governor with a feathered hat by an equally buffoonish Jomo Kenyatta with a fly-switch, or white bully-boys by black ones, represents any moral or – as the World Council of Churches, that *pons asinorum* of all Christian endeavour, appears to suppose – spiritual advance. India without the Raj is, in this respect, in no way a better, or worse, place. The only essential difference is that the Sahibs are now brown instead of white.

There remained nonetheless the moral dilemmas with which life in India constantly confronted a reluctant Sahib in my time there. Take, for instance, the rickshaw. This horrible conveyance, invented, I believe, by a missionary in Japan, was often the only sort available; as I found

when I went on from Colombo to Kandy to visit Trinity College, a boys' school. When I arrived at the railway station, the rickshaw coolies surged forward; I chose one of them who seemed a shade more muscular than the others, and got gingerly, with my luggage, into his rickshaw. As he hauled me along, I watched with fascination a patch of sweat on his shirt steadily expanding, until it occupied almost the whole of his back. At the same time, I could hear him panting more and more heavily, especially as we began to climb up to Trinity College, which stands on a hill. Finally I could stand it no longer, and shouted to him to stop. He took this to mean that I was dissatisfied with the speed we were making, and quickened his pace. Thereupon I shouted louder, and managed at last to make him understand that I wanted to get down. Thenceforth, he pulled the rickshaw with my luggage in it and my white topee perched rather absurdly on top of the luggage, while I trailed along behind on foot, feeling self-consciously virtuous but also aware that a patch of sweat was forming and growing now on *my* shirt where the hot sun beat down on my back. In this way we arrived at the college, where a row immediately broke out as to how much I should pay. This was settled when my host, the acting-Principal, took the matter in hand. Thenceforth, except *in extremis*, I never took a rickshaw, which greatly annoyed the rickshaw coolies, who relied on an occasional Sahib's inflated fare to augment their meagre earnings. In Simla the situation was particularly difficult because motor-cars were forbidden there except for the Viceroy and the Commander-in-Chief (they still are restricted to two or three very senior officials), while the roads were so steep that, notoriously, the rickshaw coolies all died young of heart failure.

Once, when I was crossing the Perriar River by the ferry at Alwaye, there was a rickshaw on it, accommodating a very large Indian, with a very meagre one at the pulling end. A colleague from the College who was with me overheard someone on the ferry remark: 'Look, there's one man pulling another along. And they say there's a God!' Such remarks stay in my mind more tenaciously than speeches at the Royal Empire (now Commonwealth) Society, or fulminations against injustice and inequality, including my own, in progressive publications. I wish they didn't. My inadequacy as a sightseer is illustrated by the fact that every detail of the Kandy rickshaw ride is indelibly imprinted on my mind, to the point that now, forty-eight years later, I could draw the shape of the patch of sweat on the rickshaw coolie's back; whereas, when I visited the famous Buddhist Temple of the Tooth in Kandy, it

made so little impression on me that now I cannot remember any single thing about it.

Trinity College proved to be one of those transplanted public schools which were instituted in most parts of the Empire when it was flourishing. The boys wore blazers, played rugger, sang English songs and hymns heartily, though in fairly cracked tones because of the different scale in their own Indian music; took cold showers, and were taught to be manly and speak the truth. The idea was that thereby an elite would be produced capable of leading their countrymen in the paths of righteousness while being loyal to the Raj. Actually, such institutions tended to turn out what were known then as subversives, and subsequently as national heroes. Despite – or perhaps because of – Trinity College, Ceylon was one of the first Commonwealth countries to have a quasi-Communist government; Achimoto in Ghana, an offshoot of Trinity College, incubated Nkrumah, as Harrow did Nehru. Worthy endeavour with an interested motive nearly always results in the exact opposite of what was intended. Thus, education aimed at producing literates for industry produces illiterates for anarchy. The more motorways the more accidents, the more psychiatrists the more lunacy; hypochondria burgeons with the health service, and delinquency with remedial prisons. Evensong in Trinity College Chapel, I found, was an exact reproduction of the same service in any English public school or college. I was to live to see the situation in reverse, with white hippies in saffron robes and with shaven heads chanting *mantras* along Fifth Avenue, and Allan Ginsberg giving a rendering of 'Hare Krishna' to the accompaniment of his hand harmonium in a Chicago law court.

I had vaguely assumed that, to get to Alwaye, all I should have to do would be to go to the railway station and buy a ticket there. It turned out to be a complicated journey by boat, bus and train. A Sahib travelling third class was something of a rarity in those days, unless he belonged to the Salvation Army or some other lesser Christian sect without the law. It was pretty uncomfortable and harassing, but also oddly gay and exhilarating. The carriage packed to suffocation; everyone chattering away, and spitting on the floor; from time to time partaking of highly spiced and highly smelling refreshments, of which I was offered a taste. As a Sahib in a suit, with luggage that, by Indian standards, was munificent, I was a subject of curiosity. Where was I going? What was I doing? How much money did I earn? How many children did I have? – such questions, put in broken fragmentary English. At a venture, I said I earned one hundred rupees a month (which turned out to be just

about what I did earn at the Union Christian College, plus free accommodation); in European terms, a minuscule salary, but in Indian terms quite substantial. When I said I had no children because I was not married, they looked sympathetic. One of the difficulties of the missionaries of contraception who go about India preaching the gospel of birth-control, and distributing their coils and pessaries and pills as the early traders in Africa did coloured beads, sometimes even offering transistor radio sets in return for voluntary sterilisation, is precisely this attitude, obstinately maintained by village Indians, that children are a great blessing, and that to be sterile is to be accursed. No doubt they will learn in time as computers, television, supersonic bangs, James Bond and other intimations of civilisation reach them.

When I think of India, as I often do, it is such scenes as travelling in a third-class railway carriage that come into my mind. Or sailing with the fishermen at Cape Comorin, in a boat made just of two logs fastened together. 'Look what a strange white fish I've caught!' my boatman shouts to the others. Or going to bathe in the evenings. So many other bodies standing in the shallow river water, just letting the water lap over them; then bending down to cup it in the hands to pour it over themselves. All this to the thud, thud of clothes being beaten clean. Or waiting before dawn for a bus. Along it comes, with flickering lights, and all the passengers asleep; but still a place for me beside the driver. Off we go again, roaring and rattling along, through dark, silent villages, raising clouds of dust, barked at by dogs, driving stray cows out of our way. I sit watching for the dawn, for the first grey streaks of light in the sky. As the grey light spreads, the shapes of houses become discernible, figures stretching and yawning, the kindling of lights. And in the sky now a fabulous brightness breaking; like the beginning of the world – *Fiat Lux!* Such a golden, luminous glory! Such a beautiful coolness, faintly misty, preparing us for the leaden heat to come! Our passengers are beginning to wake up, rubbing their eyes, looking around them. Where are they? Who are they? The driver and I have a mild altercation – his lips red with betel, his eyes clouded and bloodshot from fatigue. He wants to charge me twice the normal fare; I protest, but he insists, explaining that I am sitting in the first class. Then where's the second class? I ask. Wherever you sit is first class, he counters. At this sally we both begin to laugh, and I pay up. At the next stop he brings me a glass of tea and a banana, which I gratefully accept.

They were all so poor; they all had so very little. Anyone from the

West was a sort of millionaire by comparison; even nuns and monks and vagrants. When floods came, and they had to leave their homes, they could comfortably carry all they possessed on their heads; a tin box, a mat, some cooking vessels; no more. Yet this very penury provided a kind of protection against the plastic world of the twentieth century. They had no sales potential; the siren voices recommending eating this, wearing that, urging them to consume, consume, would be wasted on their air. Their poverty immunised them against the chief sickness of the age. Perhaps it is in this that the blessedness of the poor – the least appreciated of the Beatitudes to-day – resides. In the first- and second-class railway carriages, on the other hand, in which Sahibs normally travelled, one met the other India. Indians in khaki shorts, smoking pipes and carrying briefcases stuffed with papers to read along their way; topees that sat rather low on their heads; their speech so loaded with English words and phrases ('coefficient', 'percentage', 'overall', 'output' etc. etc.) that it was possible to follow much of their conversation even when they were speaking in Malayalam or Tamil. Already proficient at the new international language of administration and business – computer-speech-to-be. They were executive material; budding survey-men, sociology-fodder. In short, men of our time.

The most convenient mode of travel in Travancore itself was by boat through the salt backwaters which, like Norwegian fjords, intersect the country. In this way I arrived at Allepey in the evening, the solitary Sahib aboard. As the Indian passengers surged ashore, and I struggled with my bags, I wondered where I should go for the night before continuing to Alwaye by train the next day. The noise, the darkness, the general air of excitement, of people arriving and being met, made it seem a rather wild and alien scene; the more so because the rickshaw coolies, when they saw me, all shouted with one accord: 'T.B.! T.B.!' At first I thought that perhaps they considered I looked tubercular, and their cry was a warning, like a leper's bell. Then I somehow understood that what they were suggesting was that they should take me to the Traveller's Bungalow which in those days was available for Europeans in places where there was no suitable local hotel. So there I was taken, and passed a comfortable night under a mosquito-net, having first been served an evening meal of curried chicken, rice and crème caramel; the almost invariable diet offered to Sahibs all over India. Subsequently, I grew very fond of sailing through the backwaters; preferably not on the regularly plying paddle-steamers, but on a hand-propelled boat, long

and graceful, with coconut matting for protection against the sun. As the boatmen poled it along, walking up and down its length, they would chant with a weird haunting rhythm which fitted their movements. It was somehow very beautiful, with coconut palms along the banks, and houses on stilts, and little villages appearing and disappearing, and children racing along and shouting. Then, at night, lying in the bottom of the boat, lulled to sleep by its motion, peeping out occasionally at the bright stars and the moon-drenched water, the night settling round one like velvet. Conscious then of being an atom of life among innumerable other atoms. Momentarily separate, like drops of spray caught in sunlight; existing separately for an instant or two, then falling back into the sea whence they came.

Alwaye, when I arrived there, turned out to be a smallish place, little more than a village, though with a large Roman Catholic college dominating the view from the railway station. Now it has become quite a centre of new industries. I was met and taken to the Union Christian College some three miles away. To get there we had to cross over the Perriar River by ferry. The College was on top of a stony hill, the stone reddish in colour, looking over the river; a cluster of buildings barely finished, in one of which, a students' hostel, I had a room furnished with a bed and a table and chair and an oil lamp. There was also a primitive shower and a lavatory of sorts. Though the term had not yet begun, some of the students were already in residence, and gathered round in a semi-circle to watch me unpack. Their steady gaze was a little unnerving, and in their white *mundus*, with their dark faces and, in the case of the Brahmins, weird hair-dos, they had a strange air, especially as they maintained total silence, only smiling when I addressed them. This, as I found out afterwards, was because they could not understand my way of speaking English, having learnt the language – in so far as they could be said to have learnt it – from Indian teachers. It turned out that I had turned up sooner than expected; Holland, who, with his newly married second wife, occupied a mission house in Alwaye, had not yet returned from his Christmas holiday; Lester Hooper, another Englishman who was joining the staff, was due to arrive in a few days' time. Thus, no arrangements in the way of setting up meals and so on for me had been made. I suppose my situation in this remote place, where, of course, it was very hot and humid, with no one I could turn to for advice as to how to settle myself in, might be regarded as somewhat disconcerting. I cannot recall that I felt it so.

My life at Alwaye soon got into a sort of routine. I had a servant, or bearer, named Kuruvella, who brought me tea early, about six o'clock. Then I would go for a swim in the river. It was rather muddy, though sometimes a strong current was flowing. Already the students would be washing and squatting about the hillside. After breakfast, classes began. My subject was English, and my sheet-anchor was a book known as Little Dowden, a brief history of English Literature by a Victorian clergyman of that name. There is, I believe, a Big Dowden, but I am happy to say I have never even had it in my hands. From Little Dowden I was able to hold forth about, say, the Lake Poets, or Milton, or Restoration comedy; indeed, on almost any theme in the Eng.Lit. rubric. Little Dowden provided not only the information but often the actual phrases I used. Thus I would say, as though it had just occurred to me: 'Dryden found English brick and left it marble.' The students would copy this down, and no doubt find some means of bringing it in, whatever the question, when they came to sit their examinations. They copied down pretty well everything I said, and afterwards learnt it by heart, so that one could actually hear them chanting it like some weird liturgy as they walked up and down – 'Dryden found English brick and left it marble . . . found English marble . . . left it brick . . .'

There were also set texts that had to be fought through, sentence by sentence, and sometimes word by word. On this basis, I went through Ruskin's *Sesame and Lilies*, *Macbeth* and *Wuthering Heights*, the last being the most painful because totally incomprehensible to the students. The sides of the classroom were open, as is the way with buildings in South India; as we droned on together, we could see the bright green paddy fields, and watch people working in them, treading round bamboo irrigation wheels which made them look like inflated daddy-long-legs, or bending in rows over the earth, singing as they worked. Looking at them from our classroom, I felt at times an almost physical anguish at being so preposterously engaged; at spending the daylight hours in so derisory a way. ' "There's nothing serious in mortality" – that means, in our mortal or earthly existence.' The students' solemn faces were staring at me, drinking in the words; then bent to write them down. ' "All is but toys: renown and grace is dead" – Macbeth is saying that, after the murder of Duncan, everything seems trivial, like playthings.' Again the dark eyes look up uncomprehendingly, the pencils scratch. ' "The wine of life is drawn, and the mere lees/Is left this vault to brag of",' I declaim: then lamely add: 'The image is taken from a cask of wine, stored in a vault, the wine being, as we say, drawn,

leaving behind the lees.' Nothing serious in mortality – I waited for them to finish their scribbling, and then continued.

Examinations, for the students, represented the climax of their studies, the point of the whole operation; having once procured the requisite qualification, they could forget for ever the sorry, tedious business of learning, whose purpose would then have been achieved. They studied past questions with feverish intensity, making use of what were called 'Made Easies'; poorly printed, paper-backed volumes on sale wherever there were institutions of higher education, which purported to contain all possible permutations and combinations in a particular subject, with a guarantee that, if thoroughly mastered, they made a pass certain. There were Made Easies to be absorbed over a three months' period before taking the examination; even, in desperate cases, over a two weeks' period. The students addressed themselves to these Made Easies as the fateful day approached, tackling them in the only way they knew – by committing them to memory. I almost got to know them myself from hearing them said over and over late into the night. Mastering the three-months' version, still more the two-weeks' one, required a prodigious effort, and there was the danger that at the examination itself the information acquired might be in too concentrated a form to be readily disgorged. Wild-eyed and desperate with the effort, unshaven, distracted, the students might have been engaged in some strange obsessive cult or debauch.

In the case of other subjects some genuine interest may have been aroused, but in mine – the study of an alien literature in an alien tongue – there was none that I was able to discern. About the worst thing the British did to India, apart from introducing a totally unsuitable and farcically inefficient Westminster-style system of universal suffrage parliamentary government, was the educational system they foisted on the country; which still, incidentally, goes on, though now the English used has departed so drastically from the original as to be almost totally incomprehensible. That may, in a way, represent an improvement, in that it precludes any possible deviation into sense. I like to think that when the Raj at last ended, among the articles hurled after the departing Sahibs were at least a few Little Dowdens, as well as an occasional copy of *Sesame and Lilies*, *The Mill on the Floss* and the *Oxford Book of English Verse*.

Most of the students were Syrian Christians, for whom the College primarily existed. The records of their Church go back to the fourth century, and they claim that it was founded by St Thomas at the

beginning of the Christian era. In the succeeding centuries it went
through all the same sort of ups and downs and schisms as the Western
churches, producing a similar crop of contending prelates – in its case,
Archimandrites and Patriarchs – and for some sixty years, during the
period of Portuguese domination, was forcibly incorporated in the
Church of Rome. This fragmentation was made worse by Christian
missionaries from many denominations in Europe and America who
found the Syrian Christians a happier hunting-ground than the Hindus
and the Moslems in other parts of India. The chief inspirer of the Union
Christian College, K. C. Chacko, hoped that it would bring together all
Syrian Christians, enabling them to find a basis for co-operation, if not
for unity. There was a single chapel at the College for all to worship in,
and under Chacko's aegis the different sectarians managed to establish
harmonious relations. He was a man of great spiritual perception, with
a high forehead, and a voice with a soft rich timbre, a sort of glow at
the heart of it. I got in the way of often sitting with him on the balcony
outside his room while he ate his evening meal, consisting, usually, of
two huge bananas. Being a sufferer from tuberculosis – a common
complaint in that humid, sultry climate – he had to live a semi-invalid
life, though a very austere one. He always worked at a desk standing up
to concentrate his attention the better. Alas, the cause he devoted him-
self to so fervently remains unrealised; the College has flourished,
certainly, in the sense that it has steadily grown bigger, and more
reputable academically, but the divisions and factions among the
Syrian Christians still persist; the rival Patriarchs and Archimandrites
bicker and contend, and, as is happening to all religions and denomina-
tions everywhere, the congregations grow smaller, and the faith of
those who still belong to them, weaker.

The students themselves, apart from a few notably pious ones, were
not much interested in Chacko's vision of Syrian Christian unity; their
primary concern being to take a degree and get into Government
employment, which at that time offered pretty well the only openings
for graduates. Before long, there were many more graduates than
openings, but still the passion for higher education continued unabated,
with the result that unemployed graduates multiplied, constituting a
natural field of recruitment for the Independence, or Swaraj, Move-
ment. Thus, the higher education facilities which the Government of
India provided, in the early days of the Raj with a view to procuring a
ready supply of cheap clerical labour (Government clerks were known

in those days as 'writers'), in practice produced the shock troops who played so important a role in bringing the Raj to an end.

I did everything in my power to stimulate the nationalist fervour of the students, seeing myself as a Garibaldi or Byron come among them to help them recover the freedom that was their birthright, and that British rule had taken from them. The cheers of students, anyway, are sweet in the ear, and easily procured, as many an aspiring politician and demagogic don has discovered. As I learnt subsequently, I was not much older than the students myself (though some of them were older than they seemed, prudent mothers, with an eye to future examinations, having quite often faked the date of birth of their offspring to give them a year or so in hand), and well primed with a romantic adulation of rebels and rebellion. I adopted Indian dress, wore *kadi* – the homespun cloth which Gandhi advocated – tortured myself by sitting cross-legged on the ground and sleeping without a mattress; risked catching hook-worm by walking barefoot, and ate Indian food off a plantain leaf with my hands, acquiring some facility at moulding rice into little balls and aiming them neatly into my mouth. I even managed to simulate certain characteristic Indian gestures; as spreading out my hands with a look of profound disgust to indicate that I did not want another helping, or shaking my head from side to side instead of nodding up and down, to signify agreement.

A visit to the College by Gandhi in the course of a tour of Travancore gave a great impetus to Swarajist sentiment among the students and staff. I went down to the railway station to see him arrive; a vast crowd, at least ten thousand strong, had already assembled there. They had trudged in on foot from surrounding villages, nearly all of them peasants; in some cases, whole families. I wondered what had drawn them, what exactly they expected to see. Their faces provided no clue; from their expressions they might just have been waiting for a train for themselves rather than for a Mahatma. Waiting, as Indians do, having no time-tables, with the utmost patience, sometimes all through the night, in the certainty that sooner or later a train would come in and take them to wherever they wanted to go. When Gandhi's train came, there was a stir; but mostly among students from the College, while a little group of local notables who had brought garlands with them took up action stations. The others remained largely impassive. Gandhi was sitting cross-legged in a third-class compartment, his curious gargoyle face showing no special awareness of the crowd and the notables and the cheers of the students. When he stepped down on to the platform

there was a concerted movement to take the dust of his feet. All those thousands of people surging forward to get near enough to him just for that, to take his dust; then tramping back the miles they had come, padding silently along the dusty village tracks. Certainly, they were not Swarajist zealots; there was little enough of that in an Indian State like Travancore, where they had scarcely heard of the British Raj by the time it was over. Nor were they uplifted by Gandhi's championship of cottage industries and hand-woven cloth; in their primitive economy, a spinning-wheel such as Gandhi recommended would have been as unattainable as a Rolls-Royce car. He drew them to him, I decided, because he gave them a feeling that they mattered; that they, too, existed in the scheme of things, and were not just helots, extras in a drama which did not concern them. This was why they saw him as a Mahatma, and took the dust of his feet.

When Gandhi caught sight of some untouchables in a sort of roped-off enclosure, he went and joined them, and started singing with them what sounded like a rather lugubrious hymn, to the obvious consternation of the notables with the garlands. Later he addressed the students in the classroom where I took them through Little Dowden. But how different a scene! He spoke very quietly, in English, of which he had a subtle and discriminating command, but the effect on the students was terrific. They jumped up and down shouting '*Mahatma Gandhi Ki Jai! Mahatma Gandhi Ki Jai!*', their eyes glowing and the dreadful inertia of our excursion through *Sesame and Lilies*, our mournful celebration of Dryden finding English brick and leaving it marble, all obliterated and forgotten. I would scarcely have known them; they were transformed. In this case, of course, it *was* nationalism that enthused them. Millions of editorial words, including my own little bucketfuls, thousands of columns of Hansard, scores of White Papers, Royal Commission Reports, Blue Books and other State documents later, their objective would be attained. The peasants who trudged in and out of Alwaye to take the dust of Gandhi's feet would be trudging in and out of polling booths to vote for yoked oxen, a lotus flower or an umbrella; the Raj would be over, the Mahatma murdered, and India free, with a national anthem, a flag, an airline, a hydro-electric project, a seat at the UN, and other appurtenances of sovereignty.

After Gandhi's visit to the College I wrote him what was, I fear, an extremely impertinent letter, in which I argued that he would be better employed in promoting the socialisation of India's economy rather than in trying to persuade his countrymen to prefer a hand-spinning wheel

to a mechanical loom. Industrialism had come to stay, and it was futile to take a Canute attitude, and try to hold it back in India; what the Indian worker needed was better living conditions and contraceptives to keep down the size of his family. Standard claptrap at the time, and still more so to-day. Gandhi replied courteously and at some length, though I thought evasively, and published the correspondence in the weekly magazine *Young India* he brought out in Ahmedabad. He also published an address I delivered in the College chapel calling on the students to rise up against the Raj, since nothing could go well for them culturally, economically or politically until they had ceased to be a subject people. Afterwards, a fellow-member of the staff whispered to me that men had served terms of imprisonment for saying less. Rather to my disappointment, the authorities either never heard of my vapourings or, if they did, decided, quite rightly, that they were of no importance, requiring no response on their part.

Gandhi's views, of course, were based on some of the same basic texts as my father's – Ruskin, Tolstoy, and the New Testament considered as a statement of ethics rather than of faith. He left out Marx, it is true, and included the *Bhagavad Gita*; but the resultant mixture was not so very different, and likewise appealed to Quakers who, when he was in England, formed a sort of non-violent bodyguard round him. At the time of the Round Table Conference I saw him in a nest of them at Friends' House. His face had changed from how I remembered it at Alwaye; it now somehow looked crafty and calculating. By this time he had become one of the *gurus* of the age, along with figures like Albert Schweitzer and Bertrand Russell (later to be joined by Che Guevara, Martin Luther King and Malcolm X) for all of whose plastic busts there was a ready sale. His bizarre turn-out – the loin-cloth, the spectacles, the watch with a large face pinned to his person – had become as familiar as Charlie Chaplin's big boots, baggy trousers and tiny bowler. Through his dominance of the Swaraj Movement he was able to impose on it, as an actual programme, the notions he had derived from Tolstoy and Ruskin and the New Testament, so that leading Swarajist desperadoes felt bound to sit at their spinning-wheels for a daily stint, wear *kadi* and profess non-violence – very unconvincingly, it must be admitted. I have myself heard Gandhi leading some of them in a barely intelligible version of 'Lead Kindly Light', his favourite hymn. Despite their ostensible adherence to similar notions, the farthest the Labour Party bosses went in this direction was to sing Blake's 'New Jerusalem' on particular occasions, and drop occasional asides to the effect that if

Christ came back to earth he'd assuredly be crucified again. One of the more bizarre consequences of the association of India and England through the Raj was that, not only Gandhi's homespun, Quakerish predilections, but the whole ideology of the British Left, came to be adopted by the Swarajists, so that when their cause triumphed this ideology automatically became the conventional wisdom of the new Indian Government and ruling class. It is true that during the struggle for independence, the example of Ireland was preponderant; I have a precious memory of a cracked rendering of 'The Wearing o' the Green' under the relentless glare of the Cawnpore sun – a companion piece to Gandhi's 'Lead Kindly Light'. When independence was achieved, however, and Nehru became the first Indian Prime Minister, it was editorials he had read in progressive publications like the *New Statesman* and the *Manchester Guardian* which provided the basis for his domestic and foreign policy. By a weird accident of history, some four hundred million Asians were thus harnessed to the confused thoughts and fluctuating loyalties of old-style English Leftists like Kingsley Martin, Harold Laski and Pethick-Lawrence. What on its home ground was regarded as being, at best, an acceptable irritant, to be pushed aside the moment a government of the Left took office, became in India the only evident alternative to the Thoughts of Chairman Mao.

In the evenings, when it was a little cooler, I usually went for a walk. The road I took, up beyond the College and in between the paddy fields, was nearly always crowded. There were cattle being driven home and a particular man I always looked for driving along a flock of geese, waving a thin, supple stick over them very delicately to keep them together; like the conductor of an orchestra. Bullock carts with sleepy drivers flicking at the bullocks, often a whole family huddled inside; solitary nondescript pedestrians, a file of women coming in from the fields moving with great grace in their coloured saris. Strange old hags with withered breasts and lined faces; an occasional bus loaded to the gills and stirring up a mighty dust; beggars, of course, dragging along elephantiasis-swollen limbs, or with bits chipped off them by leprosy, and children, and wandering cows. And a man I once saw proceeding in the most extraordinary way by falling down, reaching out his arm, marking the place, and then from there falling down again, and so on. He had, it seems, taken a vow to make his way in this manner, measuring his length in the dust, from Cape Comerin to the Himalayas. The estimated time it would take was ten years. At Alwaye he had barely started.

Everyone stared curiously at me, a Sahib walking instead of riding; especially when the monsoon rain was falling, and I took off my shirt to let it fall coolly over my bare flesh. Indian roads were like rivers, always full and always in movement; all India flowed down them, bare feet endlessly falling and stirring up dust, golden in the setting sun. My particular road delighted me, particularly as darkness suddenly fell, going oddly silent, so that you could hear somewhere or other tiny bells ringing, and voices singing; then see lights coming out one after the other. Families gathering, work over, the day done; shadowy figures squatting, very still and meditative. Later, when the full darkness had fallen, pedestrians with hurricane lamps, looking like glow-worms, sometimes carrying a lighted faggot which they swung to and fro to keep it alight, so that one saw it rhythmically flaring up and dying down as they went along. Then, quite soon, sleeping figures stretched out on mats or bare bedsteads, or just on the ground. Sleeping with a curious abandonment peculiar to Indians; utterly still, so that they can sleep tranquilly through the night on a narrow ledge, scarcely wider than themselves, with no risk of falling off.

When I got back from my walk I usually took another river bathe. There, too, stillness came with the evening; ablutions silently performed; the water silky or, if there was a moon, holding the moonlight like tangible sheets of luminosity on which one could lie like a raft. Beautiful Perriar River. This was an India I sensed, and even touched; utterly remote from Made Easies and Little Dowden; the splendid relic, as I felt, of a departed glory. Felt this with a kind of sadness, as though I knew that the vulgar destructive twentieth century was ravening near. Bulldozers on their way to bite into the ancient earth, dredgers and concrete-mixers to utilise the meandering rivers, diesel oil to belch out its exhaust over the shining backwaters, conveyor belts to disgorge plastic elegancies, replacing ancient heirloom vessels burnished and kept over the years. Wandering cows, creaky and bony and ready to chew at anything, even paper, all rounded up for extermination. Likewise, the thick-necked oxen, the sinewy fowl, the imperturbable goats. On the way, too, the family planners bringing the precious gift of fornication without tears; others bearing in their hands such delicacies as Tomato Ketchup, *Peyton Place* and after-shave lotion. Pill- and potion-makers with specifics for all ills, including political ones – in this field, remedies concocted afar; one-man-one-vote, majority rule, government of the people by the people for the people. Advertisers to unfold the secret of everlasting youth and beauty; of happiness without end, amen.

C.W.T.—H

It was all beginning even then, and somehow I sensed that this India I knew, which had miraculously survived Macaulay, Curzon and Rabindranath Tagore, was nearing its end. I felt a profound thankfulness at having known it.

I spent a lot of my time at Alwaye in the staffroom which, like the classrooms, had no sides to it. Outside, one could see the sun beating down, and if there was a breeze it blew pleasantly in. When the rains came, falling like sheets of metal, it was cooler; almost at times chilly. There would usually be one or two other staff members likewise loafing between classes, ready to gossip or chat or argue. We often took our midday meal together. Apart from teaching, I found I had plenty of leisure. Little Dowden was soon mastered, and I felt no inclination to pursue matters further. Most professional employment, in my experience, leaves one similarly unstretched, containing, as it does, a large element of camouflaged parasitism. Those lavish luncheons on someone's expense account, extending from preliminary drinks to a dreamlike return to one's desk in the late afternoon; breath brandy-laden, and flakes of smoked salmon drooping from the corners of one's mouth! That picking over of the lavish offerings of news-agency services; like walking with a plate round a well-stocked buffet, and choosing, now a slice of tasty paté, now potato salad and eggs-in-aspic! Those army headquarters in some requisitioned palace or hotel, with majors dozing before in-trays, and colonels wrestling with their claims for field-allowance! Not really, properly speaking, work; though liable to be enervating. At Alwaye there were long empty spaces of time, which passed laggardly, stretched out on a bed, or staring uncomprehendingly at a printed page, or just staring out of a window – something to which I have always been prone.

My out-of-class activities, such as they were, consisted of bringing out each term a college magazine and producing an occasional play. The magazine (I still have an issue or two) was all too typical of such publications; feebly facetious, with reports of games and other activities. Exactly in the style of any English school magazine. The plays I remember producing were James Elroy Flecker's *Hassan* and Congreve's *The Way of the World*. Looking back on these productions, the former seems the more abhorrent precisely because it was supposed to be 'Oriental' in theme and diction; the latter merely absurd – Indian students in home-made wigs trying to be Restoration gallants. I felt a kind of inner shame and rage about all this. As I dimly realised, a

people can be laid waste culturally as well as physically; not their lands but their inner life, as it were, sown with salt. This is what happened to India. An alien culture, itself exhausted, become trivial and shallow, was imposed upon them; when we went, we left behind railways, schools and universities, statues of Queen Victoria and other of our worthies, industries, an administration, a legal system; all that and much more, but set in a spiritual wasteland. We had drained the country of its true life and creativity, making of it a place of echoes and mimicry. Some four decades after these lamentable Alwaye productions, in Delhi I recorded a television interview with Nehru, and found myself irresistibly recalling them. He, too, I felt, partook of the same hollowness. A man of echoes and mimicry; the last Viceroy rather than the first leader of a liberated India. While our conversation was being recorded, one of the attendant guards fell noisily asleep, so that his snores punctuated our words as we spoke them. It seemed an appropriate accompaniment. A few months later I heard that Nehru had died.

In the evenings at Alwaye I sat with a pen in my hand and paper before me. Moisture from one's fingers was liable to smudge the ink; the lamp, no Alexandrian pharos, gave a meagre light, and buzzed with flying insects. Trying to coax out of the encircling sultry darkness, words. Oh, words! I have a folder, dim to read now in every sense, of these early efforts. They resulted in my very first earnings – fifteen rupees from the *Madras Mail* – which I sent home to signalise the occasion. My mother bought with the money a sort of tall white-metal ashtray, which she kept by her to the end, though she had long given up her very occasional cigarette. Later, to my father's great delight, I had a short sketch published in the *New Statesman*. It was in the vein of pastiche-Chekhov, very popular at that time, what with Katherine Mansfield and the Master himself appearing in the World's Classics series. The theme – an elderly elementary schoolmaster who had lost heart, felt himself a failure, etc. etc. My father wrote that, opening his *New Statesman* and finding my piece there, had kept him going.

I shared my servant, Kuruvella, with Lester Hooper. We usually took our evening meal together. He was a Harrovian; tall and thin and pale, with silky flaxen hair and, when he neglected to shave, a similarly silken beard; a meek and saintly person, with a passionate dedication to evangelical Christianity. His father was a pencil manufacturer, very comfortably off, and I imagine what is called self-made. He visited us in Alwaye, well loaded with all varieties of his commodity; large and small, hard and soft, delible and indelible, some of which I acquired. His

mother, whom I also met in England, was one of those frail powdery ladies who sit well wrapped up in chauffeur-driven limousines; so completely belonging there that one is quite surprised to see them indoors without a fur coat, or walking about in the open air. Lester and I did not have a great deal to talk about; he disapproved of my political views, and I teased him about his complaisant attitude to what is now called the Establishment. I also, I regret to say, mocked at his pieties, and tried to shock him whenever I could. I can only now remember one single remark he made to me; *à propos* Jesus chasing the money-changers out of the Temple (a favourite episode, for obvious reasons, in my father's circle), Lester said with great earnestness and, for him, emphasis, that he was quite sure that the rope Jesus took up never touched anyone. He could not bear the idea of the Son of God, like any prefect, falling back on personal chastisement to enforce obedience. After I left Alwaye, Lester stayed on, devoting himself, along with some of the students, to missionary and welfare work among the un-touchables. Some years later, I heard he had died, and when I revisited Alwaye I sought out and stood contritely by his grave in the little Christian cemetery near the mission bungalow where Holland had lived, envious in a way of his quiet resting-place.

Occasional hospitality from the Hollands made an agreeable change. It was a well-run household; Mrs Holland belonged to an affluent Bristol family with strong Tory affiliations, and injected into her husband's austere missionary ways and vaguely progressive attitudes some of the certainties and amenities which still prevailed in English middle-class life in those days – certainties and amenities which, for some reason, were always symbolised for me by a little methylated spirits burner set under a silver tea-pot to keep it hot. I think I must have seen this particular device in use at a Quaker table, or perhaps at one of our tame clergymen's, but ever afterwards thought of it as being the imprimatur of bourgeois status. Mrs Holland used such a burner and silver tea-pot. Holland himself belonged to the old evangelical tradition. His face had a sort of granitic amiability; virtue was carved into it with – given the toughness of the material – surprising delicacy and subtlety, and, of course, guaranteed durability. When he prayed, he closed his eyes tightly and spoke to God as a head-boy might to his housemaster; in strong, steady and utterly straightforward accents. This second marriage fairly late in life took him into another milieu, socially, politically, and even spiritually (Mrs Holland was inclined to be high-church); but his splendid physical and moral constitution enabled him to withstand the

shock, though leaving him beneath the surface, as I thought, a little shaken. After he retired from India he was given a City Church, once, as he proudly told me, attended by William Wilberforce. I visited him there, and was happy to find him little changed.

I sometimes went from the College to Alwaye by the river, in a little boat that I had acquired; a hollowed-out tree-trunk made into a rather primitive canoe, which I paddled along. It quite often overturned, which I didn't mind much. Once I took the Bishop of Colombo, an elegant man named Carpenter-Garnier, in it when we were both dining with the Hollands. He had got himself up in a splendid purple cassock, and I was sorely tempted to overturn the boat deliberately just to see whether the colour would run. However, I resisted the temptation, and we arrived safe and dry. Both Holland and the Bishop would have considered themselves missionaries; missionary enterprise, in those last years of the Raj, being still in full swing, with the object of actually converting the heathen and inducing them to be baptised. Nowadays, of course, this is no longer so; almost any missionary will preface any remarks he may make about his work with a statement to the effect that he by no means considers Christianity better than other faiths, and that he has learnt much from the heathen through his association with them.

In my time, apart from Holland – who was veering towards the new attitude – there were still plenty of the old-style missionaries around. One such I stayed with in Tinevelly, in South India. Besides being an evangelist, he was a doctor, and took me with him to a nearby village stricken with cholera. At first it looked as though the village was quite deserted; no one seemed to be stirring, all the huts were quiet, until my companion stationed himself by the well, and rang a bell he had with him. At its sound a few villagers dragged themselves out and gathered round him. He told them in Tamil that God had visited this misfortune upon them because of their sins; at the same time, it was also due to contaminated water, and he put some permanganate in the well to correct this. Then he went round injecting the sick with saline solution. His fearlessness and the simplicity of his faith were impressive, even though I considered it reprehensible to use the epidemic to, as it were, advertise the Christian God's power to punish. He told me how, at his dispensary, when he asked an out-patient whether his bowels had moved, the man replied, with the savage irony of the very poor, that as he had not eaten, it was scarcely to be expected that he would have anything to excrete. A similar example of this bitter wisdom in those who live on

the very edge of total destitution was provided by an official in the Punjab who told me that once he had asked a small farmer there whether he hated the Government or the money-lender more. After some thought the farmer replied that he hated the Government more, because, whereas it was to the money-lender's interest to keep him just alive so that he could go on paying off his debt, the Government didn't care whether he lived or died.

In an Indian State like Travancore the British Raj seemed very far away. The only Sahibs living in Alwaye were Holland, Lester Hooper and myself; Mrs Holland was the solitary Memsahib. There were, it is true, also two Spanish Roman Catholic priests, bearded, and invariably in their cassocks, but somehow they did not qualify. Anyway, we never had anything to do with them. At Cochin, a few miles away, there was a small cluster of Sahibs – a bank manager, some business men, or box-wallahs as they were then called, with equivalent Memsahibs, a Club and other amenities. I only once spent an evening with them, at the Club. Like every other such establishment, existing wherever two or more exiled English were gathered together east of Suez, there was a dimly lit dining-room, a bar and lounge, old tattered copies of the *Illustrated London News* and the *Tatler* lying about, lots of servants in white and red sashes and turbans, and a flavour of stale booze and vestiges of old hangovers in the air. Outside, an elaborately watered garden and tennis courts. Brooding over it all, the sense of infinite tedium which characterised all these haunts of the expatriate English in India; more especially the ones frequented by the Memsahibs, who grew pale and randy and ill-at-ease with nothing to do under the tropical sun. My evening at the Cochin Club, I gloomily recall, ended with some rather macabre drunken festivities, which involved dragging a cart through the streets and pretending it was a tumbril.

I once or twice had occasion to go to Trivandrum, the capital of Travancore, where the Maharajah had his Palace and the State Government its seat. As the ruling family were Nairs, a matriarchal community, inheritance was through the female line and, the Maharajah being a minor, effective power was exercised through the Junior Maharanee; actually, a somewhat disreputable character. The Diwan, or Prime Minister, needed to be on good terms with her; a later incumbent whom I knew, Sir C. P. Ramaswamy Iyer, achieved this in the same sort of way that Disraeli ingratiated himself with Queen Victoria – by inordinate flattery and amorous protestations. When he was in Simla seeing the Viceroy, the stability of his situation was judged by the

regularity with which the mangoes the Junior Maharanee sent him arrived. As long as they were duly dispatched it was assumed that all was well. He managed to keep in favour, with mangoes regularly arriving when he was away, right up to the transfer of power in 1949 which, considering he was well into his seventies by then, was no mean feat. He died full of years and honours in Ootacumund some years later. Incidentally, the Nairs should provide a perfect milieu for Women's Lib zealots. My memory is that the males always seemed unusually carefree and happy.

The local representative of the Raj was the British Resident; a man named Cotton, who lived in an old Dutch house with splendid wide verandas on an island in Cochin harbour. It was a delectable spot, and Cotton made the most of it. He maintained a stylish household, with a smart launch to take him to and from the mainland, and a brass band to play 'Colonel Bogey' and 'Lillibullero' on gala occasions. When he travelled to Trivandrum, all the ferries along the way were held to wait for him so that he should not have to suffer the smallest delay. On special occasions like the King-Emperor's birthday, he gave a garden-party to which even Anglo-Indians, if they were not too dark, and missionaries, if they were not too out-of-the-way, were invited. He was a man, I should have said, of considerable capacity, but indolent by nature, who preferred the remoteness from his bosses in the Political Department of the Government of India, the leisured life and the ceremonial status his post as British Resident in Cochin and Travancore provided, to more ambitious appointments which would probably have been within his reach. Two rather ravaged ladies who wore a lot of make-up and seemed always to be fatigued, to the point that they rarely managed to finish a sentence, and even long words tended to peter out before they got to the last syllable, were usually staying in the house. It was generally assumed that the younger of the two was his mistress.

It was a Somerset Maugham set-up, as I recognised subsequently; at the time I had never read any Maugham, whose works, like P. G. Wodehouse's, were considered improper in a socialist household like ours. Maugham, of course, would have made Cotton a more emphatic figure, who saved up his sea-borne copies of *The Times* to read at breakfast, and punctiliously dressed for dinner in all circumstances. The mistress would have been younger and slimmer, and have lost her heart to the Residency chauffeur, a Sikh with a black curly beard in a hair-net. The other lady would have been older, and have saved the

situation by her worldly sagacity, and a discreet gift to the Sikh on the understanding that he sought other employment. The dénouement would have been a letter to Cotton from the Viceroy's secretary informing him that he had been awarded a KBE in the Birthday Honours. When I visited Maugham at Cap Ferrat, as I sometimes did towards the end of his life, I used to think of Cotton and his household, reflecting that it was the fate of this aged pederast with his parchment face and somehow Chinese features to catch, in the portrayal of characters like Cotton, the last afterglow of Victorian romanticism. Hence the popularity of his novels and stories. He and Galsworthy, in their writings, and later on the television screen, notably celebrated a lost bourgeoisie in the century of the common man, to the delectation of one and all; especially in the USSR and its satellite countries, where the bourgeoisie, abolished in a revolution and replaced by party cadres, was particularly mourned over.

I got to know Cotton quite well. He told me that his motive in the first place for seeing me was to consider whether I might not be a suitable person to be tutor to the young Travancore Maharajah, but that after only ten minutes' conversation he realised that I would never do for the post. It gave me a momentary regret that I had not been more guarded in talking with him. All my life I have teetered between wanting to be successful and despising what constitutes success. It is a rather ridiculous posture; like making ardent advances to a woman, and then, when at last she surrenders, feeling disinclined to take advantage of her accessibility. Perhaps such a temperament, applied to public affairs, is particularly suitable for the communications business. A Thersites role. Even now, I regret to say, something of this attitude remains; like the dregs of an old passion. I still find myself avidly reading gossip paragraphs about people I have never even heard of, and following public controversies whose outcome is a matter of indifference to me. It is Dr Johnson's splendid sentences which roll one most kindly in the dust of such fatuities; for instance, his account in *Rasselas* of the old man who endeavours 'to abstract my thoughts from hopes and cares which, though reason knows them to be vain, still try to keep their old possession of the heart'.

Of course the Maharajah's court in Trivandrum was a pretty tin-pot and unimpressive affair; but then so was the Governor of Madras when I watched him come clattering into church at Ootacamund, the hill station where I spent the summer vacation, followed by his ladies and ADCs, to occupy the front pew reserved for him, Indian worshippers

being restricted to the back pews. His grey frock-coat and topper some-
how failed to suggest majesty, reminding me more of a Worshipful
Mayor than an Excellency. The Indian Princes at least had better props
and costumes; Highnesses all, and sometimes Serene ones, with their
jewels and elephants and dancing girls and dusky soft self-indulgent
faces, they belonged to the Indian scene, whereas the Governor seemed
to have strayed out of Croydon Town Hall. Both the Princes and the
Governor, had they but known it, were playing out their last act; the
one to be replaced by an Indian equivalent, though without the grey
topper; the others to linger on in their courts, the velvet upholstery
growing ever dingier and dustier, the dinner table display tattier, the
servants scruffier, the evening hours longer and the daytime ones
emptier. Cut off from their States, from India, finally from life itself;
vestigial figures, reaching back to Great Moguls, then to parchment
treaties signed, witnessed and delivered; suppliants at Durbars before
a bearded King-Emperor, a stately Queen-Empress, coming from afar;
resplendent in a Chamber of Princes, at Viceregal levees, with appro-
priate gun salutes to match their eminence. Finally discarded in con-
sequence of dishevelled MPs striding or lurching through parliamentary
lobbies, some in winged collars, with waistcoats and hanging watch-
chains, their footsteps resounding on Westminster stone under grey
Westminster skies by the grey Thames. Kingdoms all lost to shouts of
'Division! Division!'; to them an alien and incomprehensible cry; yet
full of doom. At last deprived of their only remaining prop – their
Privy Purses. So finally bereft of all authority; little lost pools
of sovereignty left behind on a barren shore by a receding tide of
history.

When, years later, we were filming in Alwaye, by a curious chance
we stayed in Cotton's Residency, now become a Kerala Government
Rest House. The fine structure of the house remained intact, and a few
pieces of furniture and old faded photographs survived from its past
glory. It was the same launch which ferried us across, but, of course,
grown shabby with the years, and lacking the smart sailors and ensign.
The grounds too were sorely neglected; though on Sundays the few
Sahibs still remaining in Cochin came over to play golf, bringing with
them their Memsahibs and their own supplies of chilled beer. Hearing
their shouted badinage, it was almost as though a ghostly garden-party
was being re-enacted; I strained my ears to catch 'Colonel Bogey' and
'Lillibullero'; and half expected Cotton's portly but elegant form (it
was thought he might perhaps wear stays) to loom into view, exuding

the absent-minded geniality, the distant joviality, the unrecognising recognition of the ceremonially great.

In Ootacamund I stayed in a house named 'Farley' which belonged to Miss Hopwood, a zealous evangelical lady of some wealth who maintained the house to accommodate missionaries on furlough. It was, for her, a labour of love, not for profit; she charged very little, and looked after us all most kindly and generously. I grew to love her, and was very happy under her roof. To me she was consistently kind, if not over-indulgent, and even sent me baskets of fruit and fresh vegetables to Alwaye, thinking that my diet was inadequate there – which I daresay it was. We knew little of her own family circumstances, but she spoke sometimes of travelling about Europe with her mother, and attending musical festivals. Music was her only 'worldly' interest; otherwise, she considered all forms of entertainment as belonging to the Devil's domain. Hymn-singing was a permissible indulgence of her taste for music, and whenever possible she threw herself into it with tremendous zest, often, in her own house, providing the accompaniment as well on a small harmonium she had. She must have been rather pretty when she was young, and even in late middle age, when I knew her, she had still a grace and charm and gaiety about her, despite her severe, if not Calvinist, religious outlook. She insisted that German theologians were responsible for the erosion of Biblical faith, and set them as a heavy debit against her love for Mozart and Beethoven and even Wagner. Her household ran smoothly under her direction; she treated the servants well, and they stayed with her. I can see her now, with her energetic step, going about the garden and in and out of the house; the chains and bracelets she was given to wearing jingling and tinkling with her movements. Always busy, always breathless, always smiling. I regret to say that I sometimes said things intended to shock her, but she invariably forgave me.

After breakfast each morning, the 'Farley' residents would get down from their chairs and kneel at them for prayers; offered by any minister or clergyman who happened to be present, or, failing one, by Miss Hopwood herself. Kneeling there amidst the relics of a hearty meal was a bizarre experience; with the fat barely congealed on the plate off which one had just scoffed bacon and egg, and one's teeth still gritted with fragments of toast and shreds of marmalade. The prayers themselves, in the evangelical style, were likewise mundane; Father, we ask thee to help so and so in his studies for an external BA degree. Or someone else to get the wherewithal to build a greatly needed extension to his Mission

Hall. Once I heard an elderly Methodist minister, attired in an old-fashioned down-turned collar and white tie, pray: Lord, we offer unto thee Miss Ogilvie's leg. Miss Ogilvie, who was present, had broken her leg; in any case rather ample of size, it seemed enormous in a plaster cast, and not, I reflected, a particularly appetising offering. It was easy to deride these simple requests, and yet there was something very touching about their particularity, which I dare say made them as acceptable in heaven as intoned pleas for peace in our time, or for the well-being of those set in authority over us. They were a sort of prosaic plainsong; heavenly actualities. If God, as we are told, has indeed counted the hairs of each head, and cannot see a sparrow fall to the ground without distress, then the particular concerns of His servants must be of concern to Him, whatever they may be.

Under Miss Hopwood's roof I met a great variety of missionaries. There were Anglican bishops who, though they might call themselves Bernard Madras or Reginald Cawnpore, were still more redolent of a cathedral close than a bathing ghat; wild American evangelists ready at the drop of a hat to show lantern slides of their work among head-hunters on the Burmese frontier; tough maiden ladies who had travelled prodigious distances in bullock carts, and lived in remote places among ferocious tribesmen; stubborn fundamentalists who had acquired immense erudition through translating the Bible into obscure vernaculars. One of these last told me that, in the case of a vernacular which had never hitherto been written, the nearest equivalent he could get to everlasting crown was a hat that will never wear out. I found them on the whole interesting and sympathetic company; much more so than other foreign residents in India who were considered, and considered themselves, intellectually and socially superior. Somehow I have always had an inner and unaccountable conviction that any religious expression of truth, however bizarre or uncouth, is more sufficing than any secular one, however elegant and intellectually brilliant. Animistic savages prostrating themselves before a painted stone have always seemed to me to be nearer the truth than any Einstein or Bertrand Russell. As it might be pigs in a crowded sty, jostling and shoving to bury their snouts in the trough; until one of them momentarily lifts his snout upwards in the air, in so doing expressing the hope of all enlightenment to come; breaking off from his guzzling to point with his lifted snout to where the angels and archangels gather round God's throne.

The Nilgiri Hills, where Ootacamund is situated, looked very beautiful from the window of my room. Miss Hopwood, who loved them and,

as I heard long afterwards, died within sight of them, gave them names from *The Pilgrim's Progress* and the Bible. As, the Delectable Mountains and Beulah. I went off with a pony and a tent to explore them; sometimes sleeping in my tent, and sometimes staying with a tea-planter glad to receive any visitor in his loneliness. They were generally rather hard-bitten men, with that aloofness which comes from being alone a great deal without any recourse like reading or listening to music by way of mitigation. A truly lonely loneliness. The coolies who worked for them, nearby in their godowns, were scarcely fellow-mortals, though they were fond of them usually, and treated them kindly; but not quite as considerately as they treated their dogs or horses, to whom they became deeply attached. If they had a native girl in to share their bed, as most of them did from time to time, it was still in the great majority of cases a purely physical, impersonal relationship. A release of sperm and sexual tensions. There would be the inevitable Club some miles away, which they would go to perhaps once a week, to play bridge or snooker, or look at the papers, or enjoy the company of the one or two Memsahibs who came in, with or without their husbands, from neighbouring estates. An evening with them at home was largely silent, with a lot of Scotch diluted with water in large tumblers consumed; faces getting redder, speech slower in the process. In one planter's house, when I was packing up to go, my host remarked how surprised he had been to notice how large a proportion of my baggage was books. The remark delighted me, though I affected to receive it deprecatingly. Actually, I have always been a great carrier of books; more, however, for show, as a kind of totem, than to read. There are books like Burton's *Anatomy of Melancholy* and Montaigne's *Essays* which I have carried about the world for years on end without ever reading a single word to this day. Johnson said he would sooner praise the novels of Congreve than read them (the reviewer's charter); similarly, there are a lot of books I'd sooner carry than read.

On my wanderings in the Nilgiris I often caught a glimpse of the plains below; yellow and sizzling, and so far, far away. It gave one a tremendous feeling of being cut off, utterly remote, from India with its noises and flies and smells and teeming population. In this aloofness and remoteness, up there among the fir trees, dark green against a piercingly blue sky, breathing the fresh mountain air, drinking the cool mountain water, bathed in the clear bright mountain sunshine, I had an overwhelming sense of being engaged in a quest. What for? I didn't know; I still don't know. Only that one has to stumble on, as I did with

my pony, aware that each corner reveals another, as each horizon opens up another. So it was borne in upon me that there never would be an arrival; there never would be a home-coming. Only, at best, a transit camp, and something seen through a glass darkly – the lineaments of a face dimly picked out, the sound of a voice whose words with much straining could just be caught, a presence towards which one could reach. No more than that. On my way back to Ootacamund I saw Miss Hopwood and some of the 'Farley' residents coming to meet me. She had brought one of her incomparable picnics, to which we sat down cheerfully together, looking across at the Delectable Mountains, clear in the bright sunlight. Before beginning to eat and drink we sang one of her favourite hymns.

Mulling over this solitary journey afterwards, I had a notion that somehow, besides questing, I was being pursued. Footsteps padding behind me; a following shadow, a Hound of Heaven, so near that I could feel the warm breath on my neck. I knew I was making for somewhere, some place of light; seeking some ultimate fulfilment in which another reborn me would extricate itself from the existing husk of a fleshly egotistic me, like a butterfly from a chrysalis. I was also in flight. Chasing and being chased; the pursuing and the pursuit, the quest and the flight, merging at last into one single immanence or luminosity. Some scribbled pencil notes that have survived finish up with the barely decipherable question: Is this God? No answer is offered.

My last months at Alwaye were marred by illness. I developed Delhi boils; little Etnas in my flesh, which went on persistently erupting. Also, I was afflicted with two kinds of worms. Unfortunately, what destroyed the one nourished the other, and vice versa. At one point in these misfortunes a local physician was brought in; a wild-looking man with heavily oiled hair and sandalwood pasted on his forehead. Rather ominously he brought with him a jam-jar of leeches which, however, to my considerable relief, he did not propose using. I cannot say that his ministrations were effective, but I did somehow manage to get well enough to resume taking my classes. Conditions at the College were, it must be admitted, rather severe for a European, and if I had stayed on, as Lester Hooper did, I should probably, like him, have died there. It might have been the better course, but I was impatient for the end of the three years I had contracted to stay; not for any reason except that, once again, I wanted to make off. In all my life I have never stayed in any job much more than three years – five at the most. It has been a kind of Bedouin existence, feeding off one oasis after another. The

things one is paid a salary for doing are never, in my experience, *serious*; never seem in the long run of any particular use to anyone. Thus I have come to think of financial rewards as purely arbitrary; like army pay which no one can foresee or understand. It is this arbitrariness, or – in the religious sense – mystery, of earnings which leads to the generally prevailing dissatisfaction with them; in the same sort of way that everyone is dissatisfied with what he pulls out of a lucky dip, irrespective of whether he has been fortunate or unfortunate.

My final departure was spoilt by an article of mine that appeared just before I left severely criticising Indian university education in general and, by implication, Alwaye in particular. The Principal, A. M. Varkey, an extremely nice man, was deeply upset, and told me that, whereas he had been looking forward to giving me a great send-off, now he had no heart for it. I was duly abashed. The curious thing is that I had no thought of the consequences of the article's appearance as I threw myself into writing it, struggling to give expression with the greatest possible emphasis to the cultural and spiritual emptiness, the intellectual and aesthetic shoddiness, of the kind of education Indian college students were getting. The same sort of thing has happened to me on numerous other occasions; I can only record, but cannot fully explain, still less justify, a propensity I recognise in myself to kick in the teeth institutions or enterprises I have served, as well as the individuals concerned in running them, at the moment of departure. This might seem to be, and has often been taken as being, deliberate treachery. If so, not consciously; rather, perhaps, a fatality arising out of an inability to follow Blake's dictum, and be a cut worm that loves the plough.

The fact that my departure from Alwaye *was* rather desultory and low-keyed did not prevent me from feeling greatly exhilarated when I found myself on my way home. The first part of the journey was by small boat on the backwaters, and I had with me Venketramen, a colleague at the Union Christian College who had become a close friend, and Mathail, a Christian sadhu or holy man, wearing the saffron robe and wandering without money or possessions from place to place, to whom I was also devoted. Their original purpose had been only to see me off at Alwaye, but then they very sweetly decided they would come with me as far as Alleppey. They needed no luggage, and felt under no necessity to inform anyone of their change of plan. I half hoped I might be able to persuade them to come on to Colombo, and even beyond, as I hated the idea of parting from them. I still had with me some examination papers to mark, which I proceeded to do in a desultory

way, throwing them away in the backwater as soon as I had finished marking them and recording the marks awarded. It seemed a satisfyingly symbolic gesture. In my ebullient mood, the candidates fared well; I believe I scarcely failed a single one.

Venketramen was a Madras Brahmin; I greatly admired the strict austerity of his way of life. He had never tasted meat or alcohol or tobacco; I never saw him in a suit, but only in a spotlessly white *mundu* and shirt. Though I often visited his house, I only once or twice caught a distant glimpse of his wife. As a strict Brahmin, he wore the holy thread, but his hair was cropped, not kept in a bun. His features were sharp, his eyes bright, and he spoke with great precision and lucidity. His subject was mathematics, but he was widely read and introduced me to the *Upanishads* and the *Bhagavad Gita*. I was utterly fascinated to get to know this completely different kind of man from any I had encountered hitherto; a product of quite a different kind of civilisation. Christianity interested him little, and the evangelistic activities at the College, such as they were, touched him not at all. I will not say that he looked down on the Syrian Christians, who were his students and colleagues, but he held aloof from them with, as it seemed to me, a touch of aristocratic disdain. In the West the association between distinction of any kind and, if not affluence, then material ease and comfort, is so close that it is difficult to imagine it in any other terms. Yet I doubt whether Venketramen spent more than a minute proportion of his in any case modest salary on himself. He had no chairs or table, only a mat; no wardrobe, no motor-car, only a very few books. I remember once saying to him, *à propos* this austerity, that Indians had no interest in preserving trophies of the past; like manuscripts, inscriptions, monuments. That they were as spartan about the past as about their own present; reducing it to the same sort of simplicities. How long can the manuscripts or monuments be preserved? he asked. A thousand years? A hundred-thousand years? A thousand-thousand years? In the end, they are dust. So what's the point? He spread out his elegant hands in a way he had.

I am temperamentally incapable of understanding anything abstractly stated. When, for instance, I read (G. E. Moore): '*When we infer that a thing did happen in the past we are in fact doing that simply on an inductive ground from the fact that we remember it . . .*'; or (Wittgenstein): '*I have two different ideas, one of ceasing to exist after death, the other of being a disembodied spirit. What's it like to have two different ideas? What is the*

criterion for one man having one idea, another man having another idea . . .', my mind shuts up; as it did when my father, as he was prone to, got on to the subject of the Categorical Imperative. Thus, I have never been able to get through any work on Hindu philosophy; I sat with the Maharishi noting how supple were his legs folded beneath him, how well tended his curly beard, how freshly and fragrantly groomed he was, but as for the discourse he treated me to – why, it might have been Professor Namier reading aloud to me that front he had written in the *Times Literary Supplement.* From my association with Venketramen, however, the times I spent with him, observing him washing and gargling his mouth, as he did punctiliously, delicately picking his rice from a plantain leaf with his quick fingers, dipping it, maybe, in curds, taking his evening bath in the river, composing himself so precisely to sleep on a narrow ledge outside his house – from all this I got a notion of Hinduism. Something, in its top flights, very beautiful; all embracing, subtle, gentle, static – above all, static. Making few demands, but few concessions too; circular, not angular; going on and on, without any drama to break the even flow. No darkening of the sun or rending of a curtain; no finishing to begin and dying to be born. No voice crying in the wilderness; rather the converse – the wilderness crying in a voice
Superficially, at any rate, no one could have been more different from Venketramen than Mathail was. He seemed to be composed of bones only, without any flesh covering them; just skin. It was rare to see him eat at all, and when he did he only pecked like a bird. He would turn up suddenly, stay a little while, and then disappear; never going anywhere in particular, or coming from anywhere in particular. I was so fond of him that I always seemed to be on the watch for him. If, when he came, you put an arm round him, it was like clutching a bundle of sticks. When I first saw an El Greco portrait, I realised how like one he was; the head shaved, the face gaunt, but with a great beauty in it. His face somehow shining, in the El Greco style, with that indomitable, inexorable Christian love; absurd, inane, if not insane, in its total refusal to exclude anyone or anything from the range of its radiance. All-inclusive to the point of idiocy; sweeping like a great searchlight across the universe, from the tiniest midge buzzing round a cow-pat to the burnished splendour of God's very throne. A sort of beatific half-wittedness in it; a fantastic strength derived from an equally fantastic weakness, an invulnerability born of being so very vulnerable. A face pared down to nothing, but that nothing, everything;

the lowliest of faces, conveying the greatest heights ever aspired to. Truly a countenance divine; eternal in time, and timely in eternity.

I felt very content in the company of these two; the happiness of our journey together glows still across the years that have passed. The sparkling water, the bright sunshine, the warm breeze; the sense of being detached from duties, responsibilities, affections even; yesterday gone, and tomorrow not yet come, and our boat propelled smoothly along; to give an extra point to my contentment, each examination paper discarded representing a defiant and final rejection of Little Dowden. We watched delightedly as the papers bobbed away on the surface of the water. Happiness is the most difficult of all things to convey. Tolstoy, I should say, comes nearest; for instance, in his description in *War and Peace* of Natasha's visit to the huntsman's house; how she and the others listened to stories, then danced, then rode back in their sledge through the frosty starlit night. With my two oddly assorted companions, gliding into the golden light of an Indian evening on my way back to Europe and home, I likewise was happy.

In Alleppey the three of us slept on the floor of a room in some sort of Christian institution with which Mathail was associated. After bathing, Venketramen sat cross-legged, still and silent, looking out at the night. Mathail's devotions were more fidgety; bowing down his head, grimacing and muttering, cracking his finger joints. The one passive, letting the Cloud of Unknowing settle about his head; the other restlessly seeking to pierce it. In either case, the Cloud remains unpierced, for 'there was never yet creature in this life, nor never yet shall be, so high ravished in contemplation and love of the Godhead, that there is not evermore a high and wonderful Cloud of Unknowing betwixt him and his God'.

As for me – I made no meditations or devotions at all, but was full of thoughts of becoming a famous author, holding audiences spellbound, seducing women. I felt like a Stendhal hero, avid for the world and what it had to offer; a true child of our time, worldly and sensual. Perhaps sensing this, Venketramen, very uncharacteristically in view of his habitual reserve, spoke to me about women and the danger they represented to someone like myself; they were ravening, he said, destructive, a coarsening and ultimately fatal addiction. His own temperament, and even physique, were so remote from anything of the kind, that his words scarcely registered; as when, his features reflecting the deep disgust he felt, he spoke of meat-eating. Mathail gave no indication of having heard what was said, but looking across at him I

C.W.T.—I

noticed a sort of half smile playing over his face. The next day I said good-bye to them affectionately, and left for Colombo. There I took a ship to Naples, where, as I have already mentioned, my father was waiting for me on the quay, his bowler firmly on his head. I was not to see India again for a decade, returning in very different circumstances; to live as a Sahib in Calcutta and Simla, never once recapturing the delight of those first magical years.

4 The Pursuit of Righteousness

The reigning Error of his Life was, that he mistook the Love for the Practice of Virtue, and was indeed not so much a Good Man as the Friend of Goodness.

– Johnson's Life of Savage

BACK IN ENGLAND, I went to stay in Birmingham with Alec Vidler, who was by this time a curate there in a parish in Small Heath. He and the other clergy, all celibates, lived in a clergy house, where I also stayed. Unmarried clerics, whatever their denomination, living together, create their own characteristic domestic interior. Austere, and, at the same time, careless; with tobacco smoke hanging about the curtains and upholstery, as well as in the lavatory, which gives an impression of being in constant use; like the crockery in a busy station buffet. No carpets, so footsteps echo up the wooden stairs and along the wooden corridors; the rustle of cassocks, and the fumes of plain cooking seeping through the service hatch; tea set ready for all and sundry in a large metal pot standing amidst an array of cups and saucers. A lot of joking, while standing in front of the fire, hands under black leather belt and black skirts billowing; in the early morning, celebrants coming and going, their faces severe and withdrawn, sometimes holding their gear; in the afternoons, a heaviness, and in the evenings an ebullience, at night vaguely heard groans and mutterings and twistings and turnings of uneasy sleepers.

The adjoining church was, of course, very high, with the little red light of the reserved Sacrament always aglow, the pungency of incense always in the air, Holy Water in good supply, and confessionals available like telephone kiosks as and when required. All this led to an acrimonious controversy with the then Bishop of Birmingham, Dr Barnes, who regarded the Eucharist as a distasteful form of magic. A sometime *Daily News* columnist, he was one of Ramsay MacDonald's clerical

appointments, another being Dr Hewlett Johnson, Dean of Canterbury, who over the years preached Stalin and him sanctified from the pulpit of the Anglican Church's senior cathedral. Thus MacDonald, least revolutionary of Socialists, all unconsciously delivered a body blow at institutional Christianity far more destructive in its consequences than all the efforts of overtly anti-Christian crusades. The best demolition work is done by such unlikely agents; bourgeois society being a Prometheus fated to gorge its own entrails. Was it not two bourgeois Jews – a typical Viennese general practitioner, and a British Museum Reading Room *enragé* – Freud and Marx – who undermined the whole basis of Western European civilisation as no avowedly insurrectionary movement ever has or could, by promoting the notion of determinism, in the one case in morals, in the other in history, thereby relieving individual men and women of all responsibility for their personal and collective behaviour?

When I was working on the *Manchester Guardian*, I met Dr Barnes, a friend of C. P. Scott. He turned out to be a rather holy-looking man. Clergymen, in my experience, tend to get holier and holier-looking as they move farther and farther away from their faith; rather in the same way that a certain type of womaniser gets more ethereal looking the more women he seduces. It must be some kind of inner adjustment mechanics, like a thermostat. There never was a more deaconal dean than Dr Hewlett Johnson when, in his gaiters and with a large cross adorning his waistcoat, he sat beaming beatifically among his church's foremost enemies. Dr Barnes's rig was also elegantly clerical, and he had a gentle, purring, exaggeratedly meek manner of addressing one. At the time I met him he was much exercised about a new telescope which had just been developed. Telescopes, he seemed to imply, were getting so powerful that before long they'd be looking into heaven itself. Then all doubts would be set at rest, and science and faith come together in one blessed consummation. When Scott died, Barnes conducted his funeral service in Manchester Cathedral. In the course of his address on that occasion he remarked that some might consider it strange that he, an Anglican bishop, should be presiding over the obsequies of a distinguished Unitarian in an Anglican cathedral; but to him it seemed the most natural thing in the world, since Scott, like himself, had been a puzzled theist. This appeared in *The Times* report as 'puzzled atheist'. It confirmed my feeling that misprints, like the foolishness of men, are the wisdom of God.

Alec, though mixed up in the controversy with his Bishop, to the

point that he stayed on in Small Heath much longer than he intended or wished in order not to give Dr Barnes the opportunity of appointing someone in his place with different theological views, was still, I felt, essentially uninvolved. He has an enviable capacity for being able thus to withdraw into some deep inward serenity of his own, and in that sanctuary, totally private and impregnable; there able to meet his God and work out the relationship between them. Without understanding precisely how this happens, or the terms arrived at, a third person can still draw strength from the resultant serenity. I regard Alec as one of the great Christians of our time, even though – perhaps because – I should have the greatest difficulty in defining just where he stands in the different theological disputes which have accompanied the steady erosion of Christian faith. To me he has been like a rock where there is always shelter, however fierce the hurricane. A lifelong comfort.

I worked in Birmingham as a supply teacher. This meant moving from school to school to replace masters on sick leave or otherwise absent. One seldom stayed long enough to get to know the staff or children in any particular school; as soon as one began to feel settled, it was time to move on. Some of the classes were enormous; I remember teaching one of sixty, with ages ranging between nine and fourteen (the then school-leaving age), and abilities ranging between average intelligence and what would now be regarded as sub-normal. It was impossible to do anything much except keep order, and that was difficult enough. No paddy fields to look out on as at Alwaye; only the asphalt playground. It was extraordinarily like a prison; an effect enhanced by the antics of the headmaster, a malignant-looking figure with a high colour, thin dark hair and a straggly moustache, who had a way of peering in at the classrooms. One would suddenly catch sight of him through the glass of the upper part of the door, or know of his presence by a sudden hush which descended on the class. His malignancy was in no way abated when he took prayers; if anything it was intensified, especially when he read some passage from the New Testament like the thirteenth chapter of Corinthians. He seemed almost to be grinding his teeth over 'faith, hope and charity', and working to a crescendo of fury when he came to: 'And the greatest of these is charity.' Even more than at my own elementary school, I found 'Now the day is over' on Friday afternoons quite magical in its promise of two days' release. I think I must have suffered more than I now remember, because even to-day, if I happen to hear that weird animal noise children make at their morning recess in a walled asphalt playground, my heart is liable to lose a beat, particularly if I then

hear a bell ringing, followed by silence, which means that soon they will be back in the classrooms. At the – as they were then unashamedly called – better class schools, my difficulty was more with the teaching itself. In a number of subjects, geography and mental arithmetic, for instance, the children were well ahead of me, as was liable to emerge all too clearly. When I got into difficulties of this kind, my usual recourse was to switch to dictation, which gave one time to collect one's thoughts, and which anyway has a kind of drama about it; first a breathless silence, and then one's voice bringing out the words to be written down, like a judge delivering a death sentence.

The post-war spirit of ebullience had now spent itself, and the depression was beginning to loom; the economists who were going to squeeze Germany till the pips squeaked were in disarray, and John Maynard Keynes, straddling King's College, Cambridge, and the Treasury, collecting modernist pictures and directorships with equal avidity, pursuing at one and the same time a passion for Duncan Grant and for inflationary economics, was coming to the fore. Lloyd George, the man of destiny of 1918, had become a ribald figure whose venerable white locks and black cloak enclosed a goatish disposition, and whose claims to be able to conquer unemployment were as dubious as had been the previous ones to make a land fit for heroes to live in. His only asset was a political fund acquired by the sale of honours during his premiership, on a tariff – according to one of the entrepreneurs in the trade, Maundy Gregory – ranging between £15,000 for a knighthood and £40,000 for a peerage. The other men of the wartime coalition were likewise in abeyance, though Churchill, with his readiness to serve in any government at any time on any terms, had, to everyone's surprise, been made Chancellor of the Exchequer by the new Conservative leader, Stanley Baldwin. At the Treasury he did all the things he afterwards denounced; returning to the Gold Standard, cutting armaments to the bone, raiding the Road Fund, etc., etc. His only point of serious difference with the new leadership proved to be the extension of self-government in India, the single item in their programme which history was to justify.

Commentators on the political scene tend in retrospect to regard the figures who emerge into prominence as totally derisory. Understandably so. It is extremely difficult, as I know from personal experience, to spend time with one or other of them without reaching the conclusion that some accomplished clown like Peter Sellers has substituted for him. Yet, in fact, those set in authority over us, whatever the means they may

have used to attain the position, whether force or fraudulence or bribery, do in some degree represent the governed. This applies to a Stalin or Hitler just as much as to a Roosevelt or Ramsay MacDonald, a Ted Heath or Nixon. It certainly applied to Baldwin, even though, at the time, I affected to regard him as a mere cardboard figure wheeled on by the bankers, industrialists and landowners whose interests he represented. His stance as a simple fellow smoking a pipe who loved England and sought to bring together hostile elements in our society, like capital and labour, went down very well. His style of oratory, seemingly artless but actually carefully concocted, was just what was wanted after a surfeit of heroics during and after the war years. He appeared as a prosaic, down-to-earth, nice man, with a prosaic, down-to-earth, nice wife, standing solidly for all the dull, serviceable virtues which seemed in the pleasure-seeking early twenties to have fallen into disrepute. Obviously, this picture of him was not true; it was what nowadays would be called his image. He was by no means the stolid, middle-of-the-road Tory and countryman he purported to be, but neurotic, treacherous and wily; temperamentally, more like his cousin Rudyard Kipling than the John Bull role assigned to him in cartoons. Yet the fact that his public image should have worked so effectively (and not only among Conservatives; my father, when he was an MP in the 1929 Parliament, thought the world of him) is itself significant, showing, as it does, the degree to which the British ruling class was already on the run, and so in need of subterfuges.

It was a relief when the summer holidays came. On an impulse I decided to go over to the Belgian coast again and see Kitty, who was, I knew, staying there with her family. I have always found that in the case of the rare things in one's life that really matter, that are truly serious, there is no deciding after weighing up the pros and cons. An inner momentum carries one along; each step seems, at the same time, both adventitious and inevitable. It is a kind of sleep-walking; or playing of a part so perfectly known that there is no conscious remembering of the lines or waiting for cues. So it happened now. I stayed with Kitty's family in their villa; one of a number recently built close to the sand-dunes. It was the same disorderly, ramshackle household I remembered from the previous occasion. Mrs Dobbs prepared the meals, such as they were; in the process getting herself covered with flour, caked with fat, sticky with sugar and burning her long leathery fingers – sores which she ignored. If the conversation was raging – which it usually was – she would emerge from her kitchen, steaming saucepan in one hand, a ladle

in the other, and join in. Her intellectual interests took precedence over all other; there were no circumstances in which she would refrain from participating in a discussion on immortality or the extent of space. Dead or alive, she was there for the kill. Over the explosive sound of a brew boiling over, in the lurid light of a roast catching fire, one would hear her proclaiming her views on the ego which affirms and the ego which denies. When at last her tumultuous chores were over, the last mouthful of horse-meat washed down by the last gulp of vinegarish *vin ordinaire*, she was off to catch the final light of the setting sun, working away with her paints and brushes as long as she could see, and even after. She did not really need to see; what she painted was the notion of a sunset, rather than anything she saw in the sky, built up from many sunsets, seen, enthused over, and painted over the years. She could do it in her sleep. When she died, she left behind her trunkfuls of paintings, all equally good, or bad, and mostly of the same subjects. The only thing she liked better than painting was having rows, of which, when the family were in residence, there were endless possibilities. Once, when I was walking with her along the *digue* at Knocke, she noticed a crowd that had gathered, all looking out to sea. Excitedly, she rushed up to one of them and asked in her nasal French: '*Qu'est ce qu'on regarde?*' When she heard it was just a passing ship, her face fell: 'I thought it was a row,' she said to me, so disappointedly.

Mr Dobbs did not stay in the villa, making the excuse that his work required him to reside at one of the hotels to which the Lunn tourists came. He was a neat, particular man, well turned out, trim and gallant. It was a strange chance which had yoked him with so wild and wayward a spouse, and I daresay he pined at times for someone more amenable and more salubrious. Yet in some ways he admired his wife, to the point of almost being awed by her; he was like, I used to think, an Irish coachman driving a particularly wild pony in a jaunting car. Tugging at the reins, cracking his whip – 'Whoa, there!' but aware that his horse, however difficult to manage, was a spirited animal, comparing favourably with more mediocre ones even though they might offer greater ease, and perhaps even pleasure, to their masters.

They had met when Mrs Dobbs was a comfortably-off widow travelling about on her own in Europe. Her first husband, by whom she had one son who was killed in the 1914–18 war, died of syphilis, contracted as a young man. She once described to me his howls for morphia in the last stages of the illness, and other horrors, with the same objectivity as she did any other experience, good or bad. Her total absence of

jealousy arose out of the same impersonality. On one occasion, she told me, her first husband, when he was away, had telegraphed to her to meet him at the railway station on his return because something terrible had happened during his absence. Greatly concerned, she met him, only to learn with relief that what was troubling him was that he had been unfaithful. 'I thought it was serious,' she blandly remarked. In worldly terms, she was totally innocent; Eve before the Fall, with no knowledge of good and evil. She made one realise how necessary the Fall was; without it, there would have been no human drama, and so no literature, no art, no suffering, no religion, no laughter, no joy, no sin and no redemption. Only camera work (towards which Mrs Dobbs's painting was reaching) and sociology (which her sister, Beatrice Webb, may be said to have invented).

The point was well illustrated by one small incident at the villa. Somehow, there had come into the house an artificial chocolate eclair, which, when you bit into it, emitted a squeak. This was tried on various visitors, with resultant hilarity, in which, however, I noticed that Mrs Dobbs did not join. When the humorous possibilities of the eclair were exhausted, she took possession of it with a view to trying it on a Belgian woman who worked for her, and who, having a large family, no husband and very little money, and being normally rather hungry herself, might be expected to bite into the eclair with genuine zest, thus, in Mrs Dobbs's estimation, giving a real point to the joke. In the Garden of Eden before the Fall, only such joking would have been permissible. Likewise, in the New Garden of Eden now taking shape, in which the twin curses of work and procreation laid on the erring Adam and Eve will be lifted – banished to computers and laboratories, and the knowledge of Good and Evil they illicitly acquired, abolished, thus restoring the innocence our first progenitors lost, and making the earth a paradise again – of a sort.

Mrs Dobbs's account of her adventures after her first husband's death, written down in a journal she kept in her nearly illegible spidery hand, meandering on and on like her speech, is full of repetitive descriptions of sunsets and mountain peaks, and banal moralising, with occasional flashes where she describes some human encounter luridly lit by that monstrous innocence of hers. Thus, in Rome she made the acquaintance of George Gissing, the dreary late-Victorian novelist, author of *New Grub Street* and *The Private Papers of Henry Ryecroft*, so beloved of Orwell, who was, he told me shortly before he died, projecting a book on him. Gissing at that time was staying in Rome, and, in the

estimation of his friend H. G. Wells, being starved to death by a French woman with whom he was co-habiting. Mrs Dobbs, whom Wells knew, seemed the heaven-sent answer to the dilemma; as a good-looking, reasonably well-off, unattached widow, she was just the person to carry Gissing off, and give him three square meals a day. Every age has its own special buffoon; as honourable a role as any of Shakespeare's Fools. My choice for this comic *Ombudsman* of our time has always been Wells. I realised that he stood alone when I read his account of a conversation he had with Stalin in the Kremlin, in the course of which, as he put it, he tried to interest him in the PEN Club; but Stalin, he observes sadly, failed to kindle, which one can well believe. Gissing, it seems, responded favourably to Wells's proposal, and made what Mrs Dobbs used to refer to as an offer. After due consideration, she turned it down, less dazzled by Gissing's literary distinction than appalled by his meagre physique and melancholy disposition. Shortly after, she met Dobbs who, though no literary figure, had none of Gissing's other disabilities. She bore him five children, of whom Kitty was the middle one, and the only girl.

Remarriage provided Mrs Dobbs with ample opportunities for indulging her taste for having rows. It was virtually impossible to contract out, since the rows were not about anything. Thus, it was no use avoiding a particular subject, or refusing to respond to a particular inflammatory observation. The row existed apart from its occasion; it was in the air like lightning, and bound to strike. A row might be ostensibly about stoking the fire, the circumference of the earth, the date of the last General Election but one, or the coastline of Alaska, but after exhausting oneself on one or other of these themes, one realised that they were as irrelevant to the fury unleashed as Lear's 'Blow, winds, and crack your cheeks! rage! blow!' to the storm that raged about his head on the Blasted Heath.

Dobbs himself was, of course, a leading belligerent, though, not being in residence, he was able to make strategic withdrawals, as it were, into neutral territory to rest and re-equip. Kitty, too, was actively engaged. She felt passionately, as I understood later, that she had to defend herself against her mother's predatory innocence, which would otherwise destroy her. Thus, on one occasion her mother told her that if she wished to have a baby without getting married, there would be no difficulty about the cost and making suitable arrangements. I had a similar breath of Eden air – only in my case, being an outsider, it was just funny rather than suffocating – when Mrs Dobbs told me that, as a

young girl, when she went out in London by herself she was followed at a respectable distance by a footman in case she needed protection. The family lived then in Kensington Palace Gardens, and her father – Richard Potter, a business man and speculator – was very rich. The arrangement, Mrs Dobbs remarked, struck her as quite derisory, since the footman was usually far more sexually attractive than anyone of her own class or acquaintance she was likely to encounter. I can quite see that, from Adam's point of view, the apple came as a blessed deliverance; the Fall was mankind's first step to heaven, and it is interesting that all the Devil's advocates, from Epicurus to Rousseau, Walt Whitman, Marx and D. H. Lawrence, want to abolish it and regain an earthly paradise.

An episode which Kitty described to me seemed to convey with particular clarity the character of her long wrestling match with her mother. The two of them had climbed Mont Salève, a hill overlooking the Lake of Geneva. Mrs Dobbs had been sketching, seated on her camp-stool, her easel set up, dipping and sometimes sucking her brushes, her unseeing eyes fixed on the Dent du Midi, whose outline she knew as perfectly as a Presbyterian minister his extempore prayers, or a television comedian his autocued patter. Overcome by the heat of the day, she lay down her brushes, and threw herself on the bare earth for a short rest. Kitty was reading, her face wearing an expression of rebellious resignation very familiar to me, and very characteristic of her. The quiet between them was broken when Mrs Dobbs let out a shriek, and said she had been bitten by an adder in her neck. Kitty made a move to kill the snake, but Mrs Dobbs told her not to hurt the innocent little creature since it had intended no harm. They were a long way from anywhere, and the only thing Kitty could think of doing was to suck the poison from her mother's neck, which she did, afterwards spitting it out. On the way home, down the steep and rough mountain track, she supported Mrs Dobbs, who occasionally passed out as the venom took effect. When they reached the bottom of the hill, Kitty wanted to take a taxi, but Mrs Dobbs would not hear of it. So they went by tram; a macabre journey, the two of them drawing many stares from the other passengers, of which Mrs Dobbs took no notice. She was always completely unconscious of other people, and what they thought; lying down, getting up, walking or eating or sleeping just when she felt inclined. I once, when we were living in Sussex, found her stretched out fast asleep on a tombstone in Battle churchyard; nor was she in the least abashed when she came to, and found me standing there and staring at her.

It somehow became understood that Kitty and I would get married. and quite soon. I cannot recall ever 'proposing' to her – something we should both have regarded as very bourgeois and conventional; terms of abuse in our vocabulary. Nor can I remember any moment of decision; or, for that matter, of indecision. Free will, in my experience, is tactical rather than strategic; in all the larger shaping of a life, there is a plan already, into which one has no choice but to fit, or contract out of living altogether. So, it was borne in upon me that Kitty and I belonged together; that somehow, to me, the shape and sense and sound of her existence in the universe would always be appreciable in every corner of it, and through all eternity. To this essential proposition all sorts of other hopes, desires, appetites, egotistic aspirations, corporeal needs and mental strivings, were attached, like subordinate clauses; sex being one of these.

Mr Dobbs was far from pleased; he considered me – and who shall blame him? – as socially and financially an undesirable match for his daughter. Mrs Dobbs, on the other hand, was delighted. I overheard her once, when the subject was under discussion, observe that I was a genius; a word which even then I regarded as derisory (still more so now), and that, as I well knew, signified, as far as she was concerned, something between Virginia Woolf and Verlaine, with Oscar Wilde hovering about in the distance. A Bloomsburyite figure with Montparnasse affiliations; boozy Augustus Johnian, bearded Laurentian, squeaky Wellsian; with broad-brimmed black hat, large floppy tie, Café Royal frequenting, Stein-Toklas admiring, James Joyce reading. A compendium of all horrors. All the same, I have to admit that, even on Mrs Dobbs's lips, the word, applied to me, gave me a secret *frisson* of demonic joy, such as, perhaps, Joan of Arc might have felt if she had overheard the Master of the King's Bedchamber remark that she bore a passing resemblance to Cleopatra.

Our union was duly registered at the Birmingham Register Office; a drab little scene in a dreary sort of place, where numerous couples were waiting about, though whether to be married or divorced or judicially separated their demeanour did not make clear. The Registrar himself made a forlorn attempt to introduce a festive note into the proceedings, and wore, I noticed, a rather better suit and a rather more colourful tie than might be expected in a civil servant of his grade. Did he, I wondered, receive a special allowance to cover this? Kitty's father, and a friend of hers named Elsie, were the only others present, and acted as witnesses. We affected to regard the occasion as of no particular im-

portance; a mere legal formality, like signing a contract for a job or a lease of a house. It was not our intention, we insisted, to put one another under any sort of obligation; we were free to do what we liked, and would only stay together as long as both of us wanted to; not a moment longer. Even so, I bought Kitty a wedding ring; a very cheap one, admittedly, made of rolled, not real, gold, but it has lasted. She wears it still. I did not have a new suit; only a grey flannel one from my Cambridge days. Kitty wore a green velveteen jacket with an accordion pleated skirt. We had very little money – certainly not more than £100, and no furniture or possessions apart from clothes and a few books. I was a little dashed, if not alarmed, when, on receiving a cheque for fifteen guineas from Sir Henry Lunn as a wedding present, Kitty at once tore it up on the ground that he was a despicable figure. This happened at St Aidan's Clergy House in the presence of the clergy, who, after we had gone, piously gathered the pieces together and managed to reconstruct the cheque. It was never, however, paid into the bank.

It was very unkind, as I now realise, not to have asked my parents, especially my father, who, as I afterwards learnt, was deeply hurt. Incredible as it seems, I just didn't think of it; though there may have been some unconscious reluctance to have him there, some sense that his presence would be awkward. Mrs Dobbs showed me a letter from her sister, Beatrice Webb, in which she wrote that she knew my father as 'a Fabian and a very worthy person, though of modest means'. Truly, there is no snobbishness like that of professing equalitarians. My father bridled at Mrs Webb's attitude: 'And to think,' he wrote in a letter to me about it, 'that I gave up a directorship!' It was indeed ironical that she, a champion of Socialist fair shares, should look down on him for the very thing – his modest means – he owed to his espousal of the same cause. All this escaped me at the time; or rather, perhaps, I deliberately averted my eyes. I was well content to be marrying into so, in Socialist terms, patrician a family; like a young Tory marrying into the Cecils or Cavendishes, though admittedly a junior branch. I think my father was well pleased, too, despite Mrs Webb's patronising attitude, the Webbs having so honoured a place among his idols.

Mr Dobbs just turned up for our wedding without being asked; looking, as always, very trim; everything about him neat and shipshape, brown shoes shining, grey moustache like a well trimmed hedge, smartly cut suit, jaunty hat. He was devoted to Kitty, and felt that, if she should change her mind at the last moment, or events took an

unexpected turn, he ought to be there to look after her interests and arrange a getaway if required. When, in the course of the ceremony, the Registrar put the crucial question, he intervened sharply, telling her in a loud voice that there was still time for her to withdraw. She just took no notice, and our union was legally sealed. It made as little impression on me as the baptism and confirmation service to get into Selwyn College. Once the matter was finally settled, Mr Dobbs put a good face on it, and gave us all luncheon with a bottle of champagne. Then he and Elsie left for London, and Kitty and I returned to our two furnished rooms and began our life together.

Marriage (whether registered or not) begins, not with setting up house, counting wedding presents, blowing kisses, looking at wedding groups, but with two bodies confronting one another like two wrestlers. To clinch and struggle and contend with one another. Rolling about, now one on top, now another; grunting, coaxing, sweating, murmuring, yelling. So the world began, with vast turbulence in the genitalia of space. Each bodily union is a microcosm of the same process; a continuation of creation, a reaching after creativity through the fusion of two beings – the flesh first; then the soul, the totality, to make a third. This achieved, peace follows; the work done, we may sleep, letting an arm grow numb rather than wake a sleeping head cushioned there. So serenely asleep after the battle, and maybe already ovum and sperm seizing the interlude to enact their own drama; the expense of passion quickening in its peaceful aftermath. We exist to continue existence; unite to be united; love in order to go on loving.

Kitty and I, after all, were children of our time. How could we be otherwise? We looked to our bodies for gratification, which we felt they owed us, and that we now owed one another. 'To our bodies turn we then, that so Weak men on love revealed may look.' It was inevitable that this pursuit should become the prevailing preoccupation, the obsessive quest, of our restless and confused generation. Sex is the only mysticism offered by materialism, whose other toys – like motor-cars and aeroplanes and moving pictures and swimming-pools and flights to the moon – soon pall. Sex pure and undefiled; without the burden of procreation, or even, ultimately, of love or identity. Just sex; jointly attained, or solitary – derived from visions, drug-infused; from spectacles, on film or glossy paper. Up and down moving stairways, with, just out of reach, legs and busts and mouths and crotches; ascending to no heights, descending to no depths, only movement upwards and down-

wards, interminably, with the trivial images of desire for ever in view, and for ever inaccessible. As enlightened readers of D. H. Lawrence and Havelock Ellis, with even a peep at Kraft-Ebbing, we looked for rarer pleasures than these. Our moving stairway, as we hoped, climbed into a paradise where ecstasy was attainable through sensation pure and undefiled. The Blessed Orgasm itself leaned out from the gold bar of heaven; and, rubber-stoppered against any adverse consequence like birth, sealed and sterilised and secured for *coitus non interruptus* that is guaranteed *non fecundus*, we pursued happiness in true twentieth-century style.

Kitty's family seemed to be bristling with lords and, if not million-aires, people who on Croydon standards were decidedly affluent. Mrs Webb told me once with quiet satisfaction that none of her brothers-in-law (except Mr Dobbs) had less than £20,000 a year, which seemed a lot. I had never made the acquaintance of a lord before, and though at the Saturday evening gatherings of my father and his friends the mere notion of titles was a subject of loud derision, they still had a certain glamour in my eyes. I found myself going out of my way to bring references to Kitty's titled relatives into my conversation, but hoped to counteract any sycophantic undertones by making the references scorn-ful rather than respectful. In this connection, I used to enjoy repeating one of my father's favourite anecdotes about how he had been mys-teriously approached as to whether one of his directors would care to have a knighthood for £10,000 – a very substantial sum in those days. After agonised consideration by the director in question, the offer was turned down. My father never found out for certain who was behind it, but had reason to suppose that the then monarch, Edward VII, who was notoriously impecunious, may have been concerned in the transaction. After all, if politicians were to enrich themselves, as, for instance, Lloyd George did, by the sale of honours, why not the sovereign, who bestowed them? I found my father's account of this affair among his papers.

The Potter clan, to which Mrs Dobbs belonged, like other plutocratic families whose wealth derived from business, tended to drift Leftwards politically; towards Radicalism, Socialism and the Labour Party, picking up peerages and knighthoods on the way. Richard Potter, the founding father, was a timber merchant who provided army huts in the Crimean War to any government that would pay for them, thereby making a fortune which he later increased by audacious speculation. As a rich man with a difficult, if not demented, wife, and a large family of spirited

daughters, he took his philosophical notions from Herbert Spencer and his moral ones from Carlyle, whom he held in the highest esteem. So much so that, according to Mrs Dobbs, when the ferocious old Sage of Chelsea went exercising along the Embankment, muttering and grimacing over his gnarled stick, her father and one or two other rich and distinguished citizens often followed at a respectful distance behind him. The scene, as she described it, took my fancy as an early example of what Tom Wolfe has so felicitously called Radical Chic, though, of course, they have subsequently found other gurus, including Stalin. As for Spencer, largely forgotten now, but famous in his day as the exponent of Creative Evolution – he was a frequent house guest. Mrs Dobbs remembered him as a little frightening in the way he playfully tumbled little girls when he took them for nature walks in the woods. According to a theory plausibly worked out by Kitty, he may well have been the original of the Mad Hatter in *Alice in Wonderland*.

The first of Kitty's titled relatives whose acquaintance I made was Lady Courtney, her Aunt Kate, who asked us to lunch in her house in Cheyne Walk. Her husband, Leonard Courtney, by this time dead, had been a Liberal stalwart, a Member of Parliament and Chairman of Committees, and a *Times* leader-writer who was raised to the Peerage after the Liberal victory of 1906. One of those men of whom everyone speaks well, and who surprise everyone by leaving rather more money when they die than might have been expected. He actively promoted a whole string of good causes – bimetallism, proportional representation, anti-imperialism, disarmament – with which I was to become all too familiar on the *Manchester Guardian*. He was fanatically devoted to the poems of Robert Browning, which he was fond of reciting to his nieces on Beachy Head, sometimes in a howling gale. Kitty recalls embroidering bedroom slippers for him as a child. I never saw him, nor even a picture of him, though there must have been many in the Cheyne Walk house, but I had a very clear impression of him as bearded, sedate, immensely solid and deliberate and full of rectitude. These great pillars of righteousness, from Wilberforce to Martin Luther King, have followed, as it were, like solemn funeral mutes the long obsequies of western civilisation; as they fell by the way, others coming forward to take their places. Now the time has nearly come for the coffin to be actually interred. Then at last their occupation will be gone for ever.

Lady Courtney herself, though by this time quite old, had the black and white colouring of the Potters, with a noticeable moustache on her upper lip, which, clearly untended, was silky rather than bristly in an

embrace. There was said to be a gipsy strain in the family; plausible enough in Lady Courtney, and in Mrs Dobbs quite noticeable, particularly in her last years. She had a great fancy for picking over things, and gathering faggots, especially on a beach; as well as for cooking over an open fire. When only an electric radiator was available, she would turn it over on its side and brew weird concoctions on it. People quite often took her for an old gipsy woman, and offered her charity, which she invariably accepted. A kind gentleman on a bus, she told me once, had given her a shilling to pay her fare, and told her to keep the change. Did you? I asked. Of course, she answered primly. Though Lady Courtney herself looked and lived like an upper-class lady, even in her one sensed a vagrant strain just under the surface. In all the Potter households I visited, this was particularly noticeable in connection with meals, which, however lavish and elegantly served, were always somehow fragmentary and furtive, as though wrapped in a newspaper and hastily gobbled. One was aware of one's hostess's eye on one as one sliced into the butter or poured out the cream. Similarly with money; Mrs Dobbs's cheques looked old and stained, as though taken out of some secret hoard under the floorboards.

In her widowhood, Lady Courtney continued to support all her husband's causes, especially peace. She was closely associated with organisations like the Women's International League for Peace and Freedom. Indeed, there was a lady from this organisation – a Miss Sheepshank – present at our luncheon. Lady Courtney had, she told us, just finished embroidering their peace banner, a white dove on a green background. After lunch, she proudly and reverently showed it to us. It was, she said, to be hung in the Chelsea Town Hall. Where is it now? I wonder. Carried into battle by Women's Lib battalions, maybe; or in some celestial museum laid beside the Stalingrad Sword. Her house was packed tight with furniture, pictures, objets d'art, ornaments, knickknacks. Until I got used to them, upper-class houses always seemed to me like antique shops by comparison with the ones I knew. So chock-a-block with things; many of them so fragile that one scarcely dared to move or stretch for fear of breaking something enormously valuable. As it happened, I witnessed the dismantling of Lady's Courtney's establishment. When she died, we were notified by Mrs Webb that she had expressed in her will a wish that every descendant of Richard Potter (she had no children of her own) should choose some memento of her from her effects. On a fixed day and time, we were all to come to Cheyne Walk and make our choice. Kitty and I went along. It was a remarkable

scene. Mrs Webb watched, hawk-eyed, over the proceedings. When we arrived, there were some hundred and fifty Richard Potter descendants roaming about the house like stampeding cattle. The niceties of polite behaviour were all laid aside; people picked up chairs and tables and brought out magnifying glasses to fix their period, carried objets d'art to the window to examine them more closely, eagerly turned over the pages of books in search of rarities. By the book-shelves I heard someone exclaim bitterly: 'They've taken away the Shelley and the Brontë first editions!' Any efforts to circumvent the conditions and make off with more than one memento were spotted by Mrs Webb, who resolutely took counter-action. By the time they had finished, the place looked like some of the interiors I remember in the 1939–45 war after a looting session. Confronted by this scene of confusion, Kitty contented herself with picking up a jewel – a little starfish, set, as we fondly hoped, in diamonds – as being easily removable and disposable. When, in subsequent hard times, we tried to flog it, it turned out to be only paste, and worth no more than ten-and-six.

In the matter of meeting Kitty's distinguished relatives, for me the big occasion, of course, was going to spend a week-end with the Webbs. I had heard them spoken of in tones of reverence by my father and his friends from my earliest years. So I approached the house they lived in at Passfield Corner with a decided feeling of awe, riding in an ancient hired car which had met us at Liphook Station. The Webbs never had a motor-car of their own. A Scottish maid – one of a pair who served Mrs Webb for many years – let us in. They were women of the utmost discretion who remained completely unaffected and uncontaminated by the procession of cranks, crackpots and egomaniacs who flowed through the house; in some mysterious way, they kept to the very end their Scottish self-containment and impregnable complacency. One of them asked Kitty, after we had returned from the USSR, whether the Five-Year Plan answered. It was a question which indicated, I thought, a very creditable scepticism in spite of the concerted insistence of their employers and most of their guests that the success of every Soviet venture must be assured.

Mrs Webb was waiting for us in the sitting-room, standing, as she so often did, with her back to the fire, and swaying slightly to and fro. So completely different from her sister Kate; frail and white, almost ghostly, by comparison with the other's solidity. She rushed at Kitty in a way the Potter women had, hurling herself upon her with a kind of avidity, as though to assure herself that Kitty was indeed there in her bodily

presence. Jewish women, I have noticed, do likewise with children; kneading their cheeks, feeling their arms and legs, fingering their ears and hair. I also was asked to implant a kiss upon Mrs Webb's cheek; an experience comparable, I imagine, with kissing the big toe of a marble saint. The thing that struck me about her at once was her beauty, so reminiscent of Kitty's. A beauty of bone rather than of flesh. She was also, as I sensed, tragic; not in any trivial way of deprivation – like losing the lover she fancied (though that had happened, as I learnt afterwards, in the person, ridiculously enough, of Joseph Chamberlain; a preposterous engraving of a man, with wooden features and a monocle, who habitually wore an orchid in his button-hole; a Birmingham industrialist and Radical turned Imperialist). Hers was some deeper tragedy, with which I felt instinctively in sympathy. To do with her restless walks along the Embankment; with her prayers, offered in a silent cavernous Westminster Abbey, but alas wrongly addressed – dead letters that were never delivered; with sleepless nights, and the longing so often expressed in her journal for the long, definitive sleep of death.

Webb came toddling in. He really was a ridiculous looking man, with tiny legs and feet, a protruding stomach, and a large head. A sort of pedestrian Toulouse-Lautrec. It was as though Mrs Webb, not being able to have her monocled giant, chose this dwarf in pince-nez instead. Such temperaments as hers always try to ridicule their own passions by making a moral tale of them; planting gargoyles where the steeple should have climbed into the sky. Webb was her gargoyle; the *reductio ad absurdum* of love and lovers; a Blue Book Abelard, or computer Casanova: Sancho Panza to their friend Shaw's Don Quixote. Maybe, I sometimes used to reflect, Shaw would have provided a compromise mate for her; something between the monocle and the pince-nez. She told me once that, the first time they were alone together, Shaw 'simply threw himself upon me'. It was something, she went on, lest I should suppose this experience had any significance in her eyes, or, for that matter in his, that he did to every woman, and she had so sternly rebuffed him that nothing of the kind ever happened again. If the thought had crossed her mind that the tall, red-bearded, pale-faced jester would have been a more diverting companion than the partner she chose, and *Plays Pleasant and Unpleasant* a more diverting *oeuvre* than the forbidding tomes the Webb partnership produced, about which she always spoke disparagingly, she took a characteristic and terrible revenge by ensuring that Shaw was married, not to one of the luscious actresses like Ellen Terry, or ad-

vanced ladies like Annie Besant that he occasionally fancied, and she so disliked (she made the word 'advanced' somehow more detestable by accentuating the second syllable and shortening the 'a'), but to Charlotte Payne-Townshend, an Irish lady of great plainness and considerable wealth. He met her at the Webbs' house; it was Mrs Webb who made the match, and resolutely cut off his retreat when he tried to make a getaway.

Mrs Webb's household rose early; before breakfast one would see her, if the weather was fine, roaming about the garden; not with the eye or step of a gardener, more in the style of a tigress pacing up and down its cage. If she caught sight of one looking out, she would pause and begin a conversation, liable to be even less discreet then than at the indoors sessions. I remember on one such occasion leaning out of the window to hear from her the most scabrous particulars of eminent Fabian Society and Labour Party figures like MacDonald and Bertrand Russell and Wells, most of whom she intensely disliked or despised. 'Poor little Wells,' she always called him. This side of her nature – curious, gossipy, scandalous – which gives piquancy to her enormous Journal, brought out all the true vivacity and charm, the audacity and insolence, in her, so muffled in the partnership with her dreary little consort and their joint enterprises, in which, in my opinion, she had little real interest, and played little real part. Certainly, her own writing, in the Journal and in her autobiographical works, is quite different in style and mood from their joint efforts.

After lunch Mrs Webb rested, and Sidney was instructed to take a walk along with any male visitors who happened to be present; ladies were expected to follow Mrs Webb's example and lie down – which did not please Kitty. Exercise was considered to be good for Sidney; though his diet was strictly controlled by Mrs Webb, and certain things like bacon and egg which he particularly appreciated denied him, he still was a hearty eater, and liable to put on weight. Once out of sight of the house, his zest for walking markedly diminished, and he usually looked round for some convenient haystack where he could take a nap. If it was hot and there were flies about, he would knot his handkerchief and wear it on his head. It was on one such occasion that he complained to me that there were no novels of business life which he had been able to discover, and asked whether I knew of any. I mentioned *Dombey and Son* and Upton Sinclair's *The Jungle*, but the suggestion was not acceptable. After a discreet interval, he would shake himself awake, get up and return to the house, quickening his step so as to arrive in a convincing

condition of breathlessness and lather. His physique facilitated this mild deception, since he easily perspired. Mrs Webb was in the habit of, as it were, issuing brief bulletins about his bodily propensities – as, 'Sidney sweats!' or, explaining the impossibility of their sharing a bedroom, 'Sidney snores!' – which he seemed to find totally inoffensive; even, perhaps, endearing.

The evening was given over to talk, and in Mrs Webb's case, to an occasional herbal cigarette; in his, a cigar. If there were several guests, Mrs Webb would arrange them hierarchically. Thus her nephew Stafford Cripps would take precedence over Kitty and me, but we would be more considered than some mousy little secretary or archivist allowed to join the company. An earl, actually Bertrand Russell's brother, who who had recently come into the Labour Movement, got better treatment than a don like Harold Laski who had been in it for years. Only in Simla in the days of the British Raj did I come across such careful *placement*. Sometimes her hierarchical arrangements were enforced at the risk of being thought rude; as in the case of the Dean of Canterbury, Dr Hewlett Johnson, who turned up after a telephone call inviting himself had given Mrs Webb the impression that it was the Archbishop who proposed a visit. The Dean was amiably but firmly put in his place. All opinions and anecdotes from our hosts were joint ones, delivered with the editorial or royal 'We'. For instance, describing a visit to Trotsky, when he was in exile on the Turkish Island of Prinkipo, Mrs Webb recalled how the sometime Soviet Commissar for War had remarked that even in England a bloody revolution would be required. 'We told him *No!*' she triumphantly concluded. While Mrs Webb regaled us with anecdotes, Sidney sat stroking his beard, with a look of sly contentment on his face; as though just being a party to such glories was enough for him. His little legs seldom reached the ground, and I wondered how it would have been possible for Mrs Webb's long, lithe body to curl up on so tiny a lap; as she claimed happened when they broke off their labours for a little – her term – 'spooning'. It seemed an impracticable proposition to me; like the angels dancing on a needlepoint which so troubled medieval schoolmen.

By the time the ancient vehicle arrived on Monday morning for the return journey, the Webbs were already at work. I once, greatly daring, peeped in at them. He was seated at a desk; as it might have been, back at the Colonial Office, where, before his marriage, he worked as a civil servant. A gnome-like amanuensis, pen strokes steady, stance assured. She was prowling about the room as, earlier, she had about the garden.

There they were, planning our future, and along lines that actually came to pass in a matter of a very few years. A weird enough pair to be so engaged, to be sure; Beauty and the Beast, twentieth-century style, I thought. Or, better, following Blake, he the mole watching the roots, she the eagle, watching the fruits; he burrowing about underground, she soaring into some wild sky of her own imagining. A two-man demolition squad, enormously effective, as it turned out; operating in their snug Hampshire home, with the two Scottish maids keeping everything ship-shape, preparing the special scones and shortcake Mrs Webb found so palatable, and everlastingly asking themselves what, if anything, answered. What the mole got out of it all was obvious; when, as Lord Passfield, he found himself sitting in the Secretary of State's chair in the Colonial Office he felt so contented that, for once, his mind lapsed into total quiescence. It was, after all, the same chair that Joseph Chamberlain had once occupied; and the mere being in it sufficed.

But what of the eagle? What did she hope to get out of it? This was a more complicated question. I got the clue, I think, the very last time I saw her, not so very long before she died. We had been quarrelling, more or less publicly, about the Soviet régime, which she had come to adulate, and I to detest, thus reversing our positions when we first met. At the same time, she continued to fascinate me, for her beauty, and for that tragic quality in her which she retained to the end; both characteristics which intensified with age. She, likewise, for some reason, went on wanting to see Kitty and me. So we still visited Passfield occasionally. On this last visit, just as we were leaving, she said she had something to show me. It turned out to be a portrait of Lenin, presented to her by the Soviet Government; as stylised and cheap, artistically speaking, as any print of a Saint of the Church or Blessed Martyr offered for sale in Lourdes. She had set the picture up as though it were a Velazquez, with special lighting coming up from below, and a fine vista for looking at it. It was vivid in its way, showing the tiny eyes, the Mongolian features, the resolute chin and cruel mouth of its subject. For her, I realised, the place was a shrine; she looked positively exalted there – uplifted, worshipful, in an almost frightening way, like someone possessed. A frail, aged bourgeois lady, wearing, as she usually did, a grey silk dress and pretty lace cap on her head, prostrating herself, metaphorically speaking, before the founding father of the twentieth-century totalitarian state, the arch-terrorist of our time! It was extraordinary and rather horrifying. Afterwards, I reflected that the two scenes I had witnessed – the Webbs at work, and Mrs Webb at prayer before her

Lenin picture – embodied the whole spirit of the age, showing her to be a true priestess and prophetess; pursuing truth through facts and arriving at fantasy, seeking deliverance through power and arriving at servitude.

I went on with my supply-teaching in Birmingham, looking forward more than ever to 'Now the day is over' on Friday afternoon, and the two days of freedom in Kitty's company that followed. In our new intimacy together, as I got to know her better, I found her companionship ever more delightful. This has continued to be so throughout our forty-odd years together; despite rows, separations, jealousies, infidelities, all the usual wear and tear of a marital relationship. Troubles which, at the time, were very agonising, sometimes desperately so, now, looked back on, seem rather trivial by comparison with the love between us that has steadily grown, like a tree, in the soil of our discontent, striking ever deeper roots, reaching ever higher into the sky.

From Mr Dobbs's point of view, with his old-fashioned Anglo-Irish views as to what constituted success in a career or socially, a son-in-law who was an elementary school supply teacher was not to be brooked. It was he, therefore, who drew my attention to an advertisement for teachers at government schools in Egypt. The salary was appreciably more than I was getting in Birmingham, the conditions of employment seemed satisfactory; what, above all, recommended the job to me was that it involved making off. One more fix with the going-away drug! I applied, and was accepted. There was not much competition, anyway; employment with the Egyptian P.I. (Public Instruction) offered no prospects in the way of advancement or pensions, and most of the applicants were very young, and from what are now called Red Brick universities, or middle-aged to elderly, with indeterminate qualifications and an air of having failed or run into trouble somewhere along the line, characters for Evelyn Waugh. Kitty and I packed up our effects, such as they were, and set off cheerfully for Minia in Upper Egypt, via Paris, Genoa, Alexandria and Cairo.

Life in Minia was rather reminiscent of India, except that the erosion of British power had proceeded farther. As the Empire ran down, the former beneficiaries – the putative colonial governors, district administrators, collectors and all the other recipients of the vast and varied patronage it offered to the middle and upper classes in its heyday – displayed a remarkable flair for knowing when to leave the sinking ship. It seems to be almost their sole surviving talent. There was a British Consul in Minia who was also district manager for a large British

cotton firm. He maintained a position of sorts, had the Royal Arms over his door and gave parties; there was even a club where local English gathered, along with Egyptians of standing like landowners and important civil servants. The local Greeks were mostly excluded as being outside the pale; we in the P.I. were accepted, but only just, our academic qualifications compensating for our lowly position as teachers under an Egyptian headmaster. Our school work was mostly no more than elementary language teaching; even then, I am doubtful if the boys learnt much from me. I stood in front of the class just as I had in Alwaye and in Birmingham, a blackboard behind me and faces before me, only vaguely aware of what I was supposed to be doing, and listening for a bell to ring, bringing my release. Kitty and I spent most of our time in one another's company; we went for walks by the Nile, and in the evenings I sat at my typewriter, expecting her to listen appreciatively to the results of my labours and bolster up my so easily sagging spirits, which she valiantly did. Occasionally, we strolled into the centre of the town where there was a rickety hotel and a Greek grocer with extraordinary protuberances on his head. The only dissipation offered was to sit at a café table and drink a cup of sweet Turkish coffee. From the window of our flat we looked across the Nile, with the desert always in view; the river running like a silver vein through strips of brilliant green vegetation, and, parallel with it, a road, a railway, and a canal. Whenever I see an Egyptian head or stone figure, I think of these parallel lines and the built-in symmetry of so narrow a land. After two terms in Minia, I was summoned to Cairo to join the staff of the university there.

In Cairo we lived in a little house on the edge of the desert in Helmia Zeytoun. For my walks I strode over the desert, where the sand was hard; sometimes in the scorching sun, sometimes, when the *hamzin* wind was blowing, breathing in dust which gritted one's nose and throat; best of all, in the evening when the sun went down, leaving the empty sky bloodshot, and dripping lurid colours on to the yellow sand. Wherever I have been – in town or country, desert or jungle, in rain or snow or ice or tropical heat, up mountains or by the sea-shore or along urban streets – I have always walked; not caring particularly about the surroundings or the conditions, often scarcely noticing them, so that for all I knew I might be in Thornton Heath or the Himalayas or Park Avenue or the Alpes Maritimes. Just pounding along, from nowhere to nowhere; sometimes with thoughts likewise pounding through my mind, sometimes not. Sometimes just vacant; unthinking, unseeing, unfeeling. In motion merely.

The university at this time was in the Zaffaran Palace; a building formerly used by the Khedive for the accommodation of his harem. In the classrooms and along the corridors there were still odd traces of the previous usage. Little frivolous twists and turns in the masonry and woodwork, fragments of marble frescoes; up in the ceilings, coloured designs and figures, now faded, and in the neglected garden a rusty disused fountain in the middle of what had once been obviously an ornamental pool. It added an extra dimension of fantasy to our disquisitions on *Antony and Cleopatra*, chosen for its topicality. Later, the university moved to new premises in Giza. The students all wore tarbooshes and suits with narrow trousers bunched up round shoes with narrow pointed toes. They seemed to be faraway, lost in some distant dream of erotic bliss; a consequence, no doubt, in the case of many of them of their addiction to hashish, widespread among the *effendi* class, and prevalent among the *fellahin*, especially the ones who had moved into the towns. The deleterious effects of this addiction were, in those days, universally taken for granted; and the Egyptian authorities, following a plan of modernisation and national revival on the general lines of Kemal Ataturk's in Turkey, spent a lot of money and effort in an attempt to stamp it out. Russell Pasha, the head policeman and the last Englishman to hold the post, was particularly active in trying to prevent hashish getting into the country, and in reducing indulgence in it. At the League of Nations, too, the suppression of the traffic in hashish was one of the few things the member states unanimously agreed about. If anyone then had suggested that all this endeavour was misplaced because hashish did little harm, and was anyway non-addictive, the suggestion would have been received with incredulity and derision. To the best of my knowledge no one at all reputable, or for that matter disreputable, ever did make such a suggestion. I had to wait forty years to hear it made, and then not just by crackpots and wild libertarians; but by respected citizens, clergymen, purported scientific investigators, and other ostensibly informed and enlightened persons. When I hear or read their apologies for hashish, I recall the Zaffaran Palace and the stupefied faces and inert minds of so many of the students there; the dreadful instances of the destructive effects of this drug on bodies and minds which any resident in the Middle East was bound to encounter. I know of no better exemplification of the death wish at the heart of our way of life than this determination to bring about the legalisation of hashish so that it may ravage the West as it has the Middle and Far East.

As at Alwaye, my duties were not arduous; the students anyway were

frequently on strike, and did not even, like the Indian students, take
their examinations seriously, let alone their studies. They were expected
to be able to follow lectures in French as well as English, and, of course,
in Arabic. My impression is that, hashish apart, only very few of them
had the faintest notion of what we lecturers were talking about. The head
of our department, successor to Robert Graves, was Bonamy Dobrée, a
fidgety, eager man with a beard (not then as popular as now among
literati) who had been a regular army officer before he became an
academic. Major professor or professor major. We became and re-
mained friends, though there has always been a certain basic dissidence
between us, due partly at any rate to his attitude to literature – Blooms-
buryite, topped up with D. H. Lawrence, with just a dash of Marx and
a good slice of Pound and Social Credit. He spoke always of T. S. Eliot
as Tom, and E. M. Forster as Morgan, and on his passport described
himself as 'man of letters'. He is another figure I have found myself
unkindly introducing in fictional guise; in Dobrée's case, a high-pitched
voice echoing along an empty street declaiming some lines from 'Lycidas',
and then breaking off to proclaim his belief in life and in living.

It was from Dobrée that I first heard of 'The Waste Land', of which
we were all going to hear and say a great deal more before we were
finished. This was at a public lecture he gave; one of those occasions at
which a few people manage to seem a lot, like a levee or reception on a
small repertory stage or in a television play. Some elegant females, ex-
pensively dressed, of indeterminate age and race, called Levantine in
those days; an Egyptian or two who had been to Oxford and looked it,
wearing club ties, tarboosh-less; some indeterminate clergy, an Arch-
deacon of Port Said, a Canon of Wadi-Halfa; a bank manager, an officer
from the garrison who read the *New Statesman*, an American missionary
in alpaca, and a sulky-looking third secretary from the British High
Commission, present under compulsion; a sprinkling of elderly, wispy
ladies who might once have been governesses, or companions, liable to
emerge mysteriously in Cairo, as in other out-of-the-way places, for
anything free and respectable and English like a lecture.

Dobrée was introduced by a French colleague, head of the Arts
Faculty, also bearded, though with a thick, black tangle contrasting
with Dobrée's tapering ginger, which he undoubtedly considered to be
Elizabethan in the style of Sir Philip Sidney or even Drake. The French,
in making cultural propaganda, always take the ball into the other court,
going on about *votre paysage ravissant, vos mosques si mémorables, vos
contributions importantes aux lettres contemporaines. . .* We play it

straight; in this case, a discourse on the Metaphysical Poets. It was in the course of delivering this discourse that Dobrée looked up, paused, and then said with great deliberation, if not defiance, that he would stake his literary reputation that the publication of Eliot's 'The Waste Land' would be considered as being on a par with that of the *Lyrical Ballads*. We, the audience, felt that some response was due, but we scarcely knew what. Should there be cheers and some cries of dissent? Should someone get up and stump out in disgust? Someone else, stand up on his chair and applaud? It seemed unkind, even philistine, to let so dramatic a challenge pass seemingly unnoticed. We shifted in our places; one or two of us half smiled, others vaguely frowned or shook their heads. Certainly Dobrée was in on a good investment, if only a short-term one. On a longer term, who can tell? In the thirties and the war years, I occasionally ran into Eliot at the Garrick Club; he was extremely amiable and polite, but, as it seemed to me, a man who was somehow blighted, dead, extinct. I wrote of him once that he was a death-rattle in the throat of a dying civilisation, for which a contributor to *The Times Literary Supplement* took me severely to task. Yet that was how I saw him – actually, several cadavers fitting into one another, like Russian dolls. A New England one, an Old England one, a Western Values one. And so on.

We often used to go swaying and clanking into Cairo from Heliopolis on the Belgian-constructed tramway which vaguely recalled Knocke, Heyst and Blankenburg. On days when riots threatened, there would be more hats than tarbooshes. Foreigners were known as *howagas*, or hat-wearers; and as they still had their own Mixed Courts, and were not subject to the Egyptian courts, it was dangerous to involve them in public disorder. Thus, a hat provided a certain immunity. Cairo gave an impression of being inflammatory. In the dry burning heat, after weeks and weeks without rain, one expected the place to catch fire; as, indeed, it did some years after I left, with most of the places I knew, like Shepheard's Hotel, burnt to the ground, though, alas, 'The Awakening of Egypt', a massive monument standing outside the railway station, remained intact. I expect it is indestructible. For the time being, however, British troops were still stationed in Cairo and Alexandria; King Fuad was on the throne, and Lord Lloyd, the High Commissioner, was the effective boss, and behaved as such. I saw him once or twice driving about in a large car flying a large Union Jack, with motor-cycle outriders; a short, pale, nervously energetic man whom I afterwards got to know, when he was head of the newly constituted British Council. He

told me that in his High Commissioner days King Fuad used quite often, literally, to weep on his shoulder. It conjured up a remarkable scene; that great swollen royal visage, with its thick, upturned moustache drawn to a point like the Kaiser's, tearful, and drooping on to Lloyd's little imperial shoulder; great sobs breaking from him, as well as a curious barking noise due to a hole in his gullet resulting from a shot fired at him by a jealous uncle. I was familiar with this barking noise, having heard it at a reception at the Royal Palace to which all professors and lecturers at the university were invited. It was so weird that a court chamberlain warned us in advance not to be surprised or disturbed if the King seemed suddenly to start barking. Even so, it came as a shock. At such receptions the regulation attire was a frock coat and tarboosh; most of us had to be content with just the tarboosh, but Dobrée, characteristically, had provided himself with an authentic frock coat with silk facings, and, with his tarboosh rakishly a little awry, looked every inch a Bey, if not a Pasha.

A favourite haunt was Old Groppi, a garden café in a courtyard with trees growing in it, and tables set under their shade or under coloured umbrellas. There, all day long sat the Pashas and Beys and Effendis consuming their tiny cups of sweet Turkish coffee, and keeping the flies at bay with their whisks; occasionally rising to greet one another with many courteous bows and gestures, but mostly, like my students, seemingly sunk in a long brooding reverie. Such a variety of faces, from dark Nubian to pale Greek, with many curious blends; as, ginger hair crowning a Bedouin head, or Negroid features contained in a pink skin. One or two, in majestic immobility, sucking at a hubble-bubble pipe; others scanning newspapers – the *Bourse Egyptienne*, *Al Ahram*, the *Egyptian Gazette*; none, as far as could be seen, engaged in any business or occupation, with appointments to keep or duties requiring their attention. Their inertia gradually became infectious, and one would likewise sit on and on, as the sun moved across the courtyard, with only the snores of a sleeping Pasha, the rhythmic gurgle of a hubble-bubble, the incursion of a newsboy, to disturb the scene's somnolence.

Once or twice a week I visited the residence of a rich Egyptian to give him lessons in English. It was well paid work, bequeathed to me by a colleague when he left Cairo. My pupil was, I should say, in his forties; rather darker than average in complexion, and usually, when I arrived in the mid-afternoon, and he opened the door to me, unshaved and in his pyjamas, though nonetheless, wearing a tarboosh, which gave an

extra touch of grotesqueness to his appearance. The house, a detached villa in its own grounds, had all its curtains drawn. Within, it was dark and rather stale smelling. There were no signs that I could discern of any other occupant, though occasionally I thought I heard footsteps, and when tea was served some hand must have prepared it and set it out on a tray, ready to be brought in. My pupil would lead me into the large sitting-room whose furniture, except for a sofa and two arm-chairs on which we sat, was permanently covered with dust-sheets. A large glass chandelier hung over us, and on the walls facing us were some hunting prints bought, I was proudly informed, at Sotheby's. I addressed my pupil in English, speaking very slowly and clearly – 'It is a warm day, but here in your house I feel delightfully cool' – but it was obvious that the poor fellow had been unable to follow. His dark liquid eyes were full of sorrow, his unshaved chin moved convulsively. Perhaps, I managed to get across to him, it might be better if we read together. He agreed, and went to fetch a book. I was full of curiosity about what it would prove to be; maybe the *Kama Sutra*, or *The Arabian Nights*. He came back with Lord Beaverbrook's *Success* in his hand, in one of those cheap editions newspapers used to give away to boost circulation. It was, I understood, a book he particularly appreciated and admired; he passed it to me reverently, as he might a rare masterpiece. So for the rest of my afternoon sessions we worked through this turgid volume, with which I became abysmally familiar. He paid me the fee for each lesson as I left, in cash, which I thankfully pocketed. Of all the numerous and varied ways I have earned money in the course of my life, this seems to me to have been about the most bizarre.

It was at this time that Kitty first became pregnant. I found the whole process utterly wonderful; her stomach gradually swelling up, and the thought that out of our fleshly gyrations, beautiful and hilarious and grotesque all in one, should come this ripening fruit, this new life partaking of us both, and breaking out of its cocoon – her womb – to exist separately in the world. I had seen death, now I was to see birth. A white stomach rounding out, and inside it something growing, moving, living. It gave a point to every touch and caress and heave and groan; like print in a foreign language, laboriously spelt over, until suddenly it says something, and one understands. How beautiful are the Magnificats, the songs of birth! How desolate and ultimately disastrous and destructive is the pursuit of Eros for its own sake! The sterile orgasm; the bow passed across the strings and no music coming, the paddle dipped in the water and no movement following.

We spent our summer holiday in Austria by the Danube, at a place called Melk. Kitty's pregnancy progressed, and I wrote a play, *Three Flats*. A lot of our time was passed in the grounds of a monastery where there were portraits of all the Austrian Emperors up to Franz Josef, whose divided beard was as familiar to me as the German Kaiser's upturned moustache. The river was full of bronzed Germans who went gliding by in their canoes, noisily singing, and somehow, despite their seeming joviality, menacing. Too well fed, too hale and hearty, too boisterous for comfort. Back in Cairo we waited for the birth, which at last showed signs of beginning. I took Kitty into a German Deaconess's Hospital, and left her there; more aware of her presence when I had left her than when we were still together. Seeing her face on the pillow; as it were, saying it over, as I might some lines of verse committed to memory. The next morning I went back to the hospital, driving myself there in an ancient Chevrolet we had acquired; seated high up, and looking out, terrified, at the swirling traffic. At the hospital, the matron told me in her broken English, grinning, almost leering, that the labour had begun. So I waited, counting the passing minutes, until a nurse came to take me to Kitty and my son, already, as I thought, wearing the expression of cool, ironic detachment combined with infinite sweetness, which characterises him to this day.

Shortly afterwards Mrs Dobbs arrived to visit us. I met her at Cairo station. The arrival of the boat train from Alexandria in those days was quite an event; uniformed men with the names of hotels on their hats – Shepheard's, Mena House, Semiramis – stood at the barrier to coax any clients they could into their buses. When Mrs Dobbs, dressed, as ever, in collar and tie, hat perched well forward on her head, long billowing skirt and boots, appeared at the barrier, not one of them made any move to procure her custom. Only an Egyptian in a dirty galabieh whispered in her ear: 'YWCA! YWCA!' She, in any case, was too earnestly in conversation with two other Egyptians she had got to know in her third-class carriage to pay any attention. 'Ah!' she said when she saw me, 'here I am!' and proceeded to introduce me to her two friends, to whom, I gathered, throughout the journey from Alexandria she had been giving particulars of her sisters Beatrice Webb and Lady Courtney. I took her bag – she never used a porter if it could possibly be avoided – and we climbed into the Chevrolet. Seated side by side on our two high perches, and picking our way through the tumultuous traffic, she at once plunged into a conversation about the pyramids, and whether it was possible, as her psychic sister Teresa (Stafford Cripps's mother) had believed, that

they contained information about the Lost Tribes of Israel. It was with reluctance that, when she saw Kitty and our son (whom we called Leonard after Kitty's brother), she switched from this subject on to more immediate personal matters.

During the days she was with us, she went off each morning with her sketching things into the desert, and sketched away through the heat of the day, returning only after sunset. She took provisions, and the inevitable Thermos with her; occasionally, she told us, one or other of the Egyptians who gathered round to watch her would make an offer for the sketch she was working on – forty or fifty piasters, which she of course accepted. Once, when she was alone, some hooligans forced her to give them the two pounds she had in her purse. About this she complained to the police, making it clear, however, that though she was prepared to try to identify the youths in question, she would only do so if she were given an undertaking that as long as they returned her two pounds they would not be punished. A parade of local bad characters was in due course arranged, which I attended with her; as they filed past, she would murmur from time to time as one of the more villainous faces came into view: 'I think it's him, but I'm not going to say so.' The result was indecisive. When the time came for her to depart for Upper Egypt, I took her to the station, where she was seized with a sudden panic as to whether she had her purse, which she kept in a body-belt round her waist. Checking involved largely undressing, which created some interest among passers-by. All was fortunately well, and she calmed down. As her train steamed out, I waved good-bye, with a sense of great relief, and also with a pang of regret. One always so wanted her to go, and then, when she had actually gone, missed that vivid crazy presence, that corncraking voice, those random, inconsequential, maddening remarks of hers.

The men in suits and tarbooshes, the Pashas and Beys and Effendis, whether somnolent in the cafés or garrulous along the streets, fly-whisks in hand, swallowing their interminable tiny cups of coffee, having their shoes shined, or their hair cut, being shaved or manicured, consuming enormous meals which left their breath onion-laden; then, replete, sucking sugar-cane, sometimes, as I have seen them, after a feast swarming into a nearby field, like stampeding cattle, grabbing canes, and there and then sucking at them – these constituted the new effective ruling class, able to bring the fellahin into the polling-booths to vote for this or that Pasha on behalf of the Wafd, the organ of Egyptian nationalism as the Congress had been of Indian nationalism. My Alwaye

sermon needed to be brushed up again; here was another people rightly struggling to be free; more work for a Byron, a Garibaldi of our time. Never in human history, it is safe to assert, have there been so many actual and potential liberators as in the last half century, and so little liberation; so many and so loud shouts for freedom, and so much enslavement.

I became absorbed in the Egyptian political scene. It would have been far more advantageous to study Arabic, or ancient monuments like the Ibn Tulun Mosque with which Cairo abounded, or the splendid Tutankamen remains in the Cairo Museum. Alas, I did none of this, but spent my time arguing about the Wafd and its then leader, Nahas Pasha, a curious, distracted, almost Ramsay MacDonald-like figure; successor to Zaglul, considered to be the founder of modern Egyptian nationalism. My indoctrination at the Saturday evening gatherings in South Croydon came into its own; I found I had a lamentable facility for translating a particular political situation into a morality play or western, with an appropriate dénouement in which the Good Guy – in the particular case in question, Nahas – triumphs, and the Bad Guy – obviously, Lord Lloyd and his Egyptian toadies, the lesser Pashas and Beys – is cast into outer darkness; with King Fuad as the saloon-keeper, who is not actually in the camp of the Bad Guy, but needs watching. Once this technique is mastered – and God knows, it's easy enough – it is possible to be a successful and instant commentator in any medium, written, spoken, visual, on any situation in any part of the world. The style – studiously reasonable, and working up to occasional outbursts of idealistic fervour and satirical spleen – comes almost of itself. Thus: 'A certain amount of street turbulence, in any case greatly exaggerated in some of the reports, should not blind us to the vitality and vision of Egyptian nationalism, or induce us to think yet again in terms of conqueror and conquered, with the inevitable consequence of struggling on for a few more years towards predictable disaster. The awakening of formerly subject peoples like the Egyptians is an essential fact of the twentieth century. . .' One could easily have produced a prototype for this kind of composition, leaving blank spaces for the name of the country, capital city and local personalities, useable at any time anywhere.

I sent off an offering in such a vein to the *Manchester Guardian*. It flew into the window of the Cross Street office like a homing pigeon, and duly appeared in the paper; attributed to 'A correspondent in Cairo', the lowliest of all appellations. I got a letter from the editor, which greatly delighted and excited me, asking for more material along the same lines.

This I gladly provided, and had the additional satisfaction of seeing myself quoted in the Cairo press. Then, to complete my happiness, I received an intimation that Arthur Ransome was coming to Cairo as *The Guardian*'s special correspondent, and would be coming to see me. Ransome, when he turned up, proved to be an amiable and attractive man, with a luxuriant blond soup-strainer moustache, a rubicund complexion, a large mouth from which more often than not a pipe protruded, and a hearty disposition. He was carelessly dressed in unseasonable tweeds, and wore a large, loosely tied coloured tie of the kind favoured in those days by middle-brow aesthetes of the C. E. Montague-J. C. Squire variety. As I came to realise subsequently, he was in a sense the epitome of all *Manchester Guardian* writers; amateurish, literary, opinionated, conceited, eccentric; immediately recognisable in any gathering of journalists, however large, by virtue of a certain self-righteousness of expression and bearing; the firm mouth and chin saying that news is sacred, the bright left eye, that comment is free. His great glamour in my eyes was that he had witnessed the Russian Revolution, and known and talked with Lenin, Trotsky, and the other leaders in the flesh. It all made him, to me, more remarkable than if he had actually been present at the Crucifixion, or accompanied Moses when he received the Ten Commandments carved on stone at God's hands. When he told me that he had actually played chess with Lenin, who proved to be rather a poor player, and with Litvinov, a much better one, I inwardly genuflected. I questioned Ransome eagerly and endlessly about his time in Russia. He went there originally to collect fairy stories; and, as I had occasion to reflect later, in addition to the traditional ones, managed to collect some of quite outstanding impact about the Revolution itself, though, ironically enough, these, like John Reed's in *Ten Days that Shook the World*, were put on the Kremlin Index in due course because they failed to make adequate mention of Stalin.

With such enthralling conversational material available, it was a wrench to switch to the matter at issue – the Pashas and their prospects. Truth to tell, neither Ransome nor I took them too seriously; with all our progressive pretensions, we had a somewhat lordly attitude to Egyptian politics and politicians, dwelling rather on their comic opera aspects. There would always, we felt, be a Pasha to form yet another government. Ransome described to me his encounters with them at the Mahomet Ali Club, where they foregathered in the evening, as well as conversations he had with Egyptian and British officials. As he talked, I could see the script being shaped for yet another version of the great morality play,

in which virtue would once more be vindicated in the overthrow of Imperialism; heroes and villains given their parts and speaking their lines. The obtuseness of British official attitudes, the brutality of British troops in action; the reasonableness of Egyptian demands, and the advantage the extremists would derive from a stubborn refusal to meet them – it all fitted into place like a Willow Pattern. The Master Myth of our time.

My aptitude in this field was so marked that Ransome recommended me to the *Guardian* as a promising recruit, and in due course I received a letter from E. T. Scott suggesting that I might like to join the editorial staff for a probationary period of three months. I believe I have never received a letter which gave me so much delight; waving it triumphantly in the air, I rushed to tell Kitty, and then to the post office to telegraph my acceptance of the offer. Whatever feelings I may have had subsequently about the high proportion of my time and energy given to journalism, I cannot claim that harsh necessity drove me into the trade. No one could have embarked upon it more hopefully or thankfully or joyously. Though, or perhaps because, I had never so much as seen a copy of *The Guardian*, I was confidently of the opinion that it was the most enlightened, disinterested and progressive newspaper in the world. To be offered a chance to join its staff and write in its columns, seemed to me the most marvellous thing that could possibly have happened.

I owed this great opportunity to Ransome, and was duly grateful. He, as it turned out, went on only one more journalistic assignment – to China. Then he retired to a house in the Lake District with his agreeable Russian wife, Jenia, said to have at one time been on Trotsky's staff. Kitty and I visited them there several times. We watched him make flies for his line, with his great solemn face bending earnestly over the coloured threads as he selected them and fastened them together; then, in his boat on Windermere, dropping the hook, dancing the fly, still with the same solemnity, and hushed silence – the beautiful solemnity of a child, though one with a large soup-strainer moustache sprouting out of a rubicund face. It was at this time that he wrote the first of his very successful children's books, *Swallows and Amazons*; a myth sans Commissars and sans Pashas; purer, sweeter, than the ones from Our Special Correspondent. Ransome never seemed to care much for children, which may well be a necessary qualification for writing successfully about and for them. Most adults like children because they are different from them; a child-like adult like Ransome dislikes them and is bored by them, precisely because he *is* like them. For that very reason, he can understand

their games and attitudes as an adult cannot, and so his writings interest them. A. A. Milne, not at all a child-like man, was just the opposite; he really liked children (as Lewis Carroll did), and so wrote about them as it were from without, as an adult. The result was that his *Winnie the Pooh* books enchanted adults, as realising their picture of children, but rarely pleased children themselves, though sometimes they pretended otherwise to ingratiate themselves with adults. I had a curious encounter with Milne soon after I became editor of *Punch*. The poor fellow was in a nursing home in Tunbridge Wells, recovering from the after-effects of a cerebral haemorrhage, and understandably in a far from amiable state of mind; especially as he had hated *Punch* for many years. My visit was rather like Sir Hugh Greene going to see Lord Reith. Or John F. Kennedy dropping in on Harry S. Truman. Christopher Robin seemed very far away.

Kitty and our son went ahead, and I followed as soon as the term was over. It was the greatest possible relief to get away from Egypt. The place, to me, had an arid feel about it; I never put out any roots there, as I had in India, or made any close friends there, or had any sense of its past – of the great civilisations which had flourished in the Valley of the Nile. It was all just an excavation site as far as I was concerned; sand and shouts, and buildings that looked like one of those international exhibitions set up quickly to seem impressive for a little while, but soon growing shabby and derelict. Yellow sandstone turrets and domes and minarets standing amidst wide expanses of yellow sand. As for the so-called cosmopolitan society to which we always referred when we said how interesting living in Cairo or Alexandria was – I had never found them particularly alluring. The rich Syrians and Greeks and hybrid French who kissed hands and rolled their Rs as though they had never been off the Champs Elysées; the expatriate English public school homosexuals, aspiring T. E. Lawrences, burnous-wearing, with dusky Arab servants – Said, Hassan – who, bringing in the drinks or serving a meal, had a sly air of intimacy, even a touch of hauteur and insolence about them. Then the anglicised locals, the Maxes and Camilles and Georges, who had their suits made in Savile Row, and bought their cigarette cases and lighters at Aspreys; whose tarbooshes sat on their heads like red rimless bowlers, and whose slang came out of early Wodehouse; whose nearly Parisian ladies in nearly Parisian gowns, olive-skinned exotic beauties, had been reared on convent culture, and given a final polish in finishing schools in Gstaad or by the Lake of Lucerne, before being posted to Cairo, Beirut and Alexandria.

The only occasion that, for me, extricates itself from the general forgetfulness was giving a lecture on Swift in Alexandria, at Victoria College, alma mater of, among others, Rudolph Hess, and spending the evening afterwards with Kavafy, a local Greek poet about whom I had read in E. M. Forster's *Pharos and Pharillon*. He was a curious little grey fragile man, who, besides being a poet, worked in an orange exporting business; a passionate lover of the English language, which he spoke fluently, having learnt it almost entirely from reading works like Milton's *Areopagitica*, Johnson's *Rasselas* and Macaulay's Essays. The result was indescribably funny and touching; such splendidly rounded phrases and sonorous words coming from so seemingly alien and frail a figure, applied indiscriminately to any subject, weighty or frivolous, which might arise.

Revisiting Cairo from time to time in the years that followed, the process of decay was evident enough. The exotic beauties had all disappeared into the pages of Lawrence Durrell's novels; Max and Camille and Georges into the seamier haunts of Paris or London or Rome, whither their fat King Farouk, in due course, likewise decamped. Even 'The Awakening of Egypt' seemed sooty and slumbering; I had to hunt for Old Groppi, and when I found it wished I hadn't, so shabby and woebegone had it become, with the few ex-Pashas and Beys still seated there beneath the trees, shadows of their former selves, too listless even to whisk away the flies or eye over the *Bourse Egyptienne*. New Groppi, or Groppi Rotunda, in Soleiman Pasha, turned into a cafeteria, and even Lappas Frères, our majestic grocery, through whose spicy twilight one could see looming up every sort of rare delicacy, as well as local cheeses and fruits and yoghurt at their pristine best – even Lappas had grown seedy and shabby and stale. Was it like this, I wondered, in Hippo in St Augustine's time, when Rome was sacked, and the tide of civilisation which had washed through all the then known world, receded, leaving stagnation and decay behind?

I took a deck passage from Alexandria to Venice on an Italian boat, munching my own provisions, washed down with chianti, and sleeping by night where I sat by day, my little luggage beside me, the bright stars above me, and the moonlight streaming down, suffusing the sea and the ship; as it seemed, the whole universe made luminous. We sailed up to the Grand Canal and into the heart of Venice at dawn. I can remember now my exhilaration at the beauty of it; the delicacy of the Campanile in that glowing rose-grey first light, and all the hopes I had. Though far

more alluring than Venice, in my thoughts, was Manchester, city of print rather than of churches, where all my future hopes were focused.

I arrived in Manchester on a Monday morning in August, 1932, and registered at the old Queen's Hotel, subsequently demolished. My instructions were to report to the *Guardian* office in Cross Street in the afternoon, so I spent the intervening time wandering about the streets of Manchester, several times passing the *Guardian* office, and staring in at a photograph in the window of the Lord Mayor of Manchester and the Lady Mayoress in their chains of office at some function or other. Also at one of some bathers on an Australian beach, the bill for the day being – all too characteristically, as I was to learn – SURF BATHING IN AUSTRALIA. The slight tang of smoke in the air was something that would always recall for me this first arrival – apart from my glamorised childhood visit to our Sheffield relatives – in the industrial North. Having read about the severe economic depression which had hit, particularly, Lancashire, I somehow expected to see queues and pinched faces and a general air of desperation. Actually, the city, matching my mood, seemed bustling and cheerful. Public reports are always misleading, and have been made more so by the camera's increasing part in them. Anyone who has had occasion, as I have, to participate in preparing compilation films about this period will know that the scanty available footage has to be arranged or doctored to produce the requisite effect. This will be easier for later periods; quasi-documentaries like *Cathy Come Home* realise the myth in terms of actuality, in the same way that, for instance, the assault on the Winter Palace in Petrograd, as presented in Eisenstein's film, has now been firmly incorporated in the documentation of the Revolution. When all the recording, compiling and documenting has been completed, it will be for ever impossible to know what happened about anyone or anything; history, in dramatising its records, abolishes itself.

Punctually at three o'clock, I presented myself at the *Guardian*'s Cross Street office, but was told that this was for receiving advertisements, not for journalists. It was, indeed, more suggestive of a travel-agency than a newspaper. The journalistic staff used a sort of stage-door at the side, much dingier than the other. Upstairs, on the editorial floor to which I was directed, things seemed pretty quiet. I was shown into the library and told to wait there. It was a long twilit room with solid-looking tomes lining the walls – mostly, as I observed, volumes of Hansard – and a bust of C. P. Scott by Epstein standing on the table.

Below me, I could feel, like a heart-beat, the steady throb of the presses turning out that day's *Manchester Evening News*; in the yard at the back of the building I had noticed the pony traps all waiting, tensed up, ready to rush away with the edition when it was ready. At once, I began to catch the fever of journalism, which even now I have not quite succeeded in shaking off; the working up each single day to a moment of climax, the frenzied effort to finish a story, sometimes actually running with copy to the stone and just getting it in; then relaxing; for good or ill, nothing more to be done about that particular edition. I suppose everyone recognises when he first finds his way to his own particular milieu or scene. The jockey-to-be first sniffing acrid stable air, his legs almost bending outwards as he sniffs; the priest-to-be catching a whiff of incense, the flash of a vestment, the throaty intonation of an exhortation or prayer – Dearly beloved brethren, I pray and beseech you . . . the palms of his hands drawing together of themselves, his eyes uplifting; the young wanton-to-be giving a lift to her gym-frock, a touch of accentuation to her budding breasts which she instinctively recognises as the tools of·her trade. So, I recognised at once my native habitat in *The Guardian* office; in the tang of printer's ink, the yeasty aroma of newsprint; curious, aged figures carrying copy, or battered trays with dregs of strong tea and the debris of chops or fried fish; the clatter of teleprinters and typewriters, and the odd zones of silence somehow existing amidst the noise, like cloisters in a railway station. Paper everywhere, underfoot, clutched, pored over, discarded, even in the lavatories, agency copy available, brooded upon before using – from Georgia news of a man of a hundred and forty who remembered Napoleon; from Montreal, of a woman who had given birth to quintuplets; from Chicago, of an explosion which had flooded the neighbouring streets with illicit liquor. Pulp to pulp – this was my line.

Minutes dragged by slowly in the library. I fastened my gaze on Epstein's Scott, noting how the bronze head seemed to be about to jump off its pedestal at me. At last I was summoned by one of the aged messengers to the presence of Ted Scott, the E.T. who had written to me, and C.P.'s son; by this time nominally his father's successor as editor. He turned out to be a man in his forties with a large noble head, a grey complexion, soft dark eyes and a smile of great sweetness; the whole impression somehow vaguely sorrowful. I liked him at once. He was sitting in a small office, like an anteroom, and after we had chatted together for a while he asked me what subjects I was interested in.

Without thinking I said India, Egypt, the Labour Party – by this time my father was MP for Romford – and education. Then he got up to take me into the adjoining office where his father, the famous C. P. Scott, was sitting at his desk staring fixedly in front of him; his eyes bright blue, his flesh rosy, his beard white and truculent; a high-minded Sir John Falstaff, looking, as the old and famous often do, a little mad.

The memory of him sitting there, as I had first seen him, vividly recurred to me when in 1950 I spent some hours at Chartwell with Churchill; by this time well into his dotage, though with another government still to form. I happened to be briefly in the chair at the *Daily Telegraph*, then serialising his War Memoirs, and it was in connection with some dispute arising over his excessive proof corrections that he had required my presence. His physical condition was vastly inferior to Scott's; flabby and puffy, and, in some indefinable way, vaguely obscene. Like an inebriated old sea lion, barking and thrashing about in shallow water. He was wearing his famous siren suit, with a zip-fastener up the front; various of his collaborators were there, familiarly sycophantic, as is the way with such people, especially the service ones. At four o'clock, in lieu of tea, a tray of highballs was brought in, and as others followed my senses began to swim. I cannot recall that the subject of the proof corrections was ever broached, except perhaps very casually. At one point Churchill took me out into the garden and showed me his goldfish and water works, and some not very distinguished paintings connected with Marlborough, that his nephew John Churchill had done on the walls of a little pavilion. Inside the house, he drew my attention to a handbill offering a reward for his capture in the Boer War. All, as I realised, a standard routine and patter; a conducted tour often provided to all sorts and conditions of visitors – for instance, Molotov, who must surely have been taken over the course, and whose wooden attention I could easily imagine.

Seated again, I raised the question of Yalta; the only incident in the late war about which I had any particular curiosity or concern. It produced a great splutter of talk about how, if he were to say what he knew, it would 'bring the United States Government down'; at that time, President Truman's second administration. I particularly remember the phrase about bringing the United States Government down because of its absurdity. Then he went on to tell me about how he had been invited to speak at a great meeting in Cologne, when he would be bound to be given the greatest reception of his life. Striding up and

down and gesticulating, he proceeded to deliver the speech he proposed to make; all about the valiant fighting qualities of the Germans, the disastrous consequences of our two wars against them, and how our two nations must henceforth walk together; their combined strength a great stabilising factor in the world. I reflected afterwards how the only thing our politicians learnt in the two world wars was to admire the Germans. It was a really ludicrous and embarrassing performance on Churchill's part, even as grasped through my highball stupor. He was at that time, I suppose, the most famous and admired man in the world. Yet I had seen him delivering himself of a rhetorical rodomontade such as one might expect to hear from some retired colonel at an Old Comrades Association dinner. Whether the proposed Cologne speech was ever actually delivered, I have no idea. I should suppose not.

Only later, going over in my mind this brief encounter with Churchill, did the comparison with C. P. Scott suggest itself. It was intrinsically implausible of course – the puffy, loose, self-indulgent, baby-smooth face of the one, and the taut, well-groomed and brushed appearance of the other. In Scott's case, the intent purposive look, the expensive tweed suit, the large loose tie, not, as might be expected, with a ring over it; the everlasting expectation that somehow Whitehall leads to Damascus. In Churchill's, a certain slackness, not exactly easy-goingness, nor even good-nature (in fact, as far as that's concerned, the reverse – something malign and disagreeable, as it seemed to me, behind the image-mask of high living, low thinking and general amiability). Ribaldry is perhaps the word; a Lear who has changed places with his Fool, but kept his blank verse. What, then, did they have in common that made my mind go back to that other occasion, two decades before? I suppose, that they had the same addiction to power which stamps itself unmistakably on all who succumb, whether they get the stuff in courts, or parliaments, or board rooms, or at mighty demos; whether in the Kremlin's obscure recesses, or exposed to millions of eyes in a television studio, or at the high altar at St Peter's. In the same sort of way promiscuity gives a greedy, hungry, coarse look at the corners of the mouth, equally in a duchess and a whore. They had different parts, of course; Churchill a poor man's Chatham, Scott a rich man's Good Samaritan; the one decked out in funny hats and uniforms, the other in sartorial righteousness; one hairless and the other bearded, one ebullient and the other dry, one a man of fraudulent rhetoric, the other of equally fraudulent principle. On different paths, but going in the same direction and making for the same destination.

Scott was very affable to me, and I tried to dazzle him with my knowledge of Indian and Egyptian politics and politicians, none of whom I had even seen, let alone met. (When, subsequently, I did see and meet them, I did not find that I gained much thereby in knowledge or in wisdom compared with when I only pretended to have seen and met them.) It was difficult to decide whether Scott was listening or not; he had the faraway air of someone preoccupied with another scene and other words than the ones being spoken. His memory by this time was very sketchy, but it required exceptional courage to risk correcting it when it seemed to have led him astray. I remember how, on one occasion, he put in the paper the obituary of someone who was still alive; only at the very last moment before the edition went to press did anyone – actually, the news-editor – manage to summon up courage to tell him. When Ted and I withdrew he was still seated at his empty desk staring in front of him. Presumably, as the evening wore on, proofs were brought in, there were telephone calls – though there was no telephone on his desk – to take, before he finally made off, riding his bicycle deliberately and sedately along the dark Manchester streets, out to Fallowfield where he lived. A majestic figure in his way; worried, maybe, about Bulgaria, whether the British Embassy should be transferred from Peking to Nanking, Lloyd George's perfidy, Asquith's somnolence, Ramsay MacDonald's confusion. So many worries, turning the pedals – O! troubled world. Pedalling along Oxford Street, into Victoria Park, then turning into his front garden; the dark silent house, a light in his study, soon the first edition specially delivered. One more to eye over anxiously. Whither Bulgaria? Nanking be of good cheer, their Excellencies are coming! Steady Lloyd George! Wake up, Asquith! Ramsay, time is running out! And so to bed.

I was allotted the task of doing a short leader on corporal punishment. Ted handed me the relevant copy with diffidence. Not much of a subject, he seemed to say, but nothing else available. Blotched teleprinted words, from the Press Association, about a headmasters' conference at which some worthy or other had pronounced himself against this barbarous custom, damaging alike to chastiser and chastised, etc., etc. I returned with the copy to the library, where, pending a perch of my own becoming available, I was to work. Anxiously, I added up the wordage of a short leader in that day's paper; it worked out at between a hundred and a hundred and fifty words. I had three hours to produce my piece. It seemed quite long, but how to begin? Were we for corporal punishment or against it? I supposed the latter, but sought confirmation.

It would not do, I decided, to ask Ted, since this would suggest to him that I was someone without principles, and also ignorant of the, no doubt, firm line already taken by *The Guardian* on the subject. So I ventured out of the library and into the corridor outside, this being, as I afterwards discovered, the seat of the editorial department, each door in it opening into a small room where a leader-writer was sitting like a broiler bird ready to lay an egg. Opening one of the doors at random, I saw a figure bent over a typewriter who turned out to be Paddy Monkhouse; a youngish man with already greying hair and a large kindly mouth; the son of A. N. Monkhouse, the literary editor. I grew to love him dearly when I got to know him. After a brief and unsatisfactory foray into Fleet Street on the *Evening Standard* (I was also on it at the time), he returned to *The Guardian*, where, as it seemed to me, the life was slowly and systematically drained out of him. This Liberal Moloch ate its children.

With great diffidence I announced myself to Paddy as a newcomer, and asked him if he would kindly tell me what was the paper's line on corporal punishment, as I had to write a leader on the subject. Without looking up, or stopping his typing, he muttered: 'The same as capital, only more so.' This had to suffice by way of a directive. I returned to the library and began my labours. Did I write or type? I cannot now remember. I fancy I must have taken a typewriter along; my handwriting has always been hopelessly illegible, I think because I can never bring myself to finish words of more than one syllable – least of all my own inordinately long name. With a shorter name I might have written more legibly.

So I began, and the words seemed to come of themselves; like lying as a child, or as a faithless lover; words pouring out of one in a circumstantially false explanation of some suspicious circumstance. The more glib, the greater the guilt. First the originating observation – *As Mr so-and-so, headmaster of such-and-such a school, justly observed at the Headmaster's Conference meeting yesterday. . . .* Then the qualifying counter-observation – *Some of his colleagues took him to task . . .* ('Taking to task' is better editorialese than 'criticised' or 'attacked', as it is better to say that Mr So-and-so's withers remain unwrung than that he is unrepentant.) Followed by a touch of facetiousness; out with the *Oxford Dictionary of Quotations! – That eminent pedagogue, Mr Wackford Squeers of Dotheboys Hall, might not agree . . .* Preparing the way for the ascent to total seriousness – *It is surely high time that this reprehensible practice were discontinued* – and working up to the moral point on which

every leader must hinge – *inflicting, as it does, quite apart from any purely physical pain or discomfiture, serious psychological damage on punisher and punished alike* . . . Finally, a note of hope, on which all good leaders must go out – *While not for one moment suggesting that punishment, as such, can be wholly dispensed with, it is greatly to be hoped that the use of the cane will be, if not abolished altogether, then reserved for only the most drastic occasions* . . . In editorialese time is always high and punishment as such.

It is painful to me now to reflect the ease with which I got into the way of using this non-language; these drooling non-sentences conveying non-thoughts, propounding non-fears and offering non-hopes. Words are as beautiful as love, and as easily betrayed. I am more penitent for my false words – for the most part, mercifully lost for ever in the Media's great slag-heaps – than for false deeds. Discussing once with Kingsmill this obliteration of language, we decided that there was no need for politicians to finish their sentences, the end being implicit in the beginning. Thus, taking the case of the then looming opening of the United Nations, the following all-purpose cues would serve for any orator:

On this historic occasion when . . .
There can be no one here present who . . .
We have just passed through an ordeal that . . .
No thinking man will underestimate the . . .
While there are many circumstances which . . .
There are solid grounds for hoping that . . .
It is surely incumbent upon all of us to . . .
While recognising the reality of . . .
No mere conflict of interest should . . .
The immeasurable strides that Science has . . .
Such is the choice that at present confronts . . .
It is idle to think that politicians can . . .
It rests with the common people to . . .
With head erect and clear purpose we . . .

For the time being, however, I was well satisfied with my first offering to *The Guardian* as I laid it on Ted Scott's desk, and returned to the library to await the outcome. Paddy Monkhouse looked in to see how I was getting on with corporal – or was it capital? – punishment. His own piece (on, if I remember correctly, footpaths in the Peak District which were threatened with closure) – being likewise finished, we repaired to the Stock Bar, a conveniently situated underground bar which the

editorial staff frequented. Standing there already were A. P. Wadsworth, a quick, eager, squeaky little man, then industrial correspondent and afterwards editor, and Kingsley Martin, who had heard of me through the Webbs. I have always thought of Kingsley as the prototype of all Leftists; Mr Lefty of our time. At this, my first encounter with him, I formed an impression which was scarcely modified in the succeeding years. Even his appearance changed little – the tousled hair greying but never thinning, the great beak of a nose like a shadow over the face, the sallow complexion which Mrs Webb, wrongly, took to be a sign of grubbiness (the grubbiness, if it existed at all, was inward). He gave an impression, not exactly of being shifty; rather, of constant mental pullalation. Like a marsh, bubbling and oozing and glistening; his very speech somehow tortured, words breaking and bubbling out of his anguish. Bred in Nonconformity, his father being one of those ministers who, in the spirit of the age, moved on from Calvin to William Morris, and then to a sight of Keir Hardie, Kingsley continued the journey to Marx, with many a detour and backward leap; as he would hover round the stone in his *New Statesman* days to insert or delete a last-moment 'not'. Indecision the very heart and soul of him; 'Shall we? Shan't we?' A man for all causes. He still had his father's pulpit manner; unction of righteousness, and, in his political leaders, the flavour of extempore prayer – Lord, we *do* beg thee to raise the school age . . . I remembered an old song I had heard; 'I am myself my own fever and pain.' Kingsley was himself our own fever and pain; he was crucified nightly (later, weekly) as the paper went to bed, and rose again from the dead when it was delivered with the milk. Every age has its own man; Medieval Man, Renaissance Man, Industrial Man, etc., etc. Ours was Kingsley – Socialist Man. At once our battle and our battlefield, our message and our medium. At the Stock Bar he was holding forth about regulations he had been endorsing for humane killing – of animals, as it happened. It might perfectly well have been men; he had a way of airily abolishing huge concourses of people, as when he considered in a leader whether or not Mao Tse-tung had been justified in liquidating some million recalcitrant Chinese.

Back in the library, I found that the proof of my leader had been laid on the table. The first galley I had ever seen, with galleys to come that would make a paper-chase round the earth's circumference. This the very first one, still damp, so that, when I tried inking in corrections, the ink spread in little rivulets. Yet somehow my morsel of newsprint with its ridiculous sentences and rivulets of ink seemed unearthly in its

wonder. My words, printed! I could scarcely contain myself; I felt up-lifted, and walking back to the Queen's Hotel through Manchester streets already emptying, I scarcely felt the pavement in the thought of all those *Guardian* readers, over the breakfast table, or swaying from side to side in crowded railway compartments, or dozing in their clubs, or strap-hanging in trams and buses, confronted with my broadside on corporal punishment. Stopped in their tracks, maybe; stunned, over-whelmed by the well-chosen, well-directed words, resolving that hence-forth the cane should be laid aside for ever. In the morning I lay in bed listening for the footsteps of the man taking round the papers; at last I heard him, rushed to the door, and there it was, the day's *Guardian*, fresh and fragrant as a newly picked rose. On the leader-page, sure enough my piece. I read it over and over – headed: 'Spare the Rod' – as though it had been some exquisite sonnet. It would be nice to feel now, and gratifying to say, that all the fatuous lucubrations of which this first one was the herald were so much waste product, preventing a more particular and lasting use of one's own verbosity. In truth, I feel about them as Falstaff did about the riff-raff he recruited to fight in the king's wars – mortal men! In my case, mortal words.

When Kitty and our son came, we moved into Kingsley's house in Didsbury while he was away. He had a special contract with the *Guardian*, much resented by Scott even though he made it, whereby he could be away from Manchester for three months in the year in order to refresh and re-fertilise his mind. Whether this purpose was in fact achieved, may be doubted; his mind always seemed to me like one of those small plots whole Indian families live off, which never lie fallow for a single instant – endlessly tramped over by buffaloes; ploughed and sown and harvested in endless succession. I stayed with him while awaiting Kitty's coming. His then wife, Olga, a spare lady with a fringe and a sharp chin who was reputedly engaged in writing fantasies, called him 'Kingly'. When we left for the office together, they would embrace warmly, she murmuring as she broke away: 'Nuffs, Kingly; nuffs!' Physically, she was fashioned very much in the style of Katherine Mansfield, a then popular model in such circles; and no doubt the fan-tasies – though I never saw one – were likewise in the Katherine Mans-field manner. (Come to that, Kingsley bore a decided resemblance to Middleton Murry, Katherine Mansfield's husband.) Warm sand trick-ling through bare cool toes; impulsive, elfin (that's the word), floor-squatting, head on one side – Do I love you? What's love? Voices crying in the wilderness to make straight the way for Virginia Woolf. To the

Lighthouse! Oh, to the Lighthouse! Long afterwards, abruptly, *à propos* of nothing, Kingsley told me how Olga came to die. They had been separated for many years; Olga drifted in and out of mental homes, weaving her fantasies therapeutically. Leaving one such mental home, carrying her suitcase, she incautiously crossed the road, and was knocked down and killed. The suitcase gave me a pang; contents scattered about the tarmac – bits of clothing, books, scribbled sheets of fantasy. To the Mortuary! Oh, to the Mortuary!

Driving from Didsbury to Cross Street with Kingsley was a hazardous business; in a car so ancient that it had no mechanical wind-screen wiper, requiring the driver when it was raining (which it usually was) to move the wiper to and fro by hand, which Kingsley did vigorously, the other hand on the steering-wheel, and, at the same time, discoursing fluently on the world situation. Poincaré, that implacable militarist, with the xenophobic French behind him, and only a few virtuous lone voices – Barbusse, Albert Thomas, Romain Rolland – protesting, the virtuous Germans, encircled by the Little Entente, malignantly kept on the edge of bankruptcy, wickedly and foolishly excluded from the comity (an editorial favourite) of nations. MacDonald's fine speeches at Geneva, but would they butter parsnips (another editorial favourite)? Kingsley had it all worked out. Later, he would have occasion to shatter this pattern of events in favour of another. The French promoted in virtue, the Germans drastically demoted, with other consequent adjustments of smaller fry like the Poles and the Czechs. It was wonderful how quickly and wholeheartedly such re-arrangments could be managed. Like a man racing after a bus, falling, picking himself up and dusting himself down, and then catching another going in the opposite direction. At the time of the Nazi-Soviet Pact, for instance, when other enlightened voices grew hoarse, were muffled and even silenced, Kingsley soon got a second wind and was off again. Similarly when Khruschev delivered his anti-Stalin broadside at the twentieth Party Congress. It was not that he was unprincipled; rather the converse. He had a super-abundance of principles; enough and to spare for all possible eventualities.

Though Kingsley was so completely tuned in to the spirit of *The Guardian*, more so than any of the rest of us, oddly enough he failed to please the Scotts, and was not a success on the paper. Quite soon after I joined, he left it to become editor of the *New Statesman*; a position in which he throve mightily. I inherited his room along the Corridor; a small cubicle with windows looking on to nothing, and a coal fire which I tended to over-stoke, generating a fug, soon laden with tobacco smoke.

Through this haze occasionally the figure of C.P. loomed up on one of his visitations. He appeared and disappeared unaccountably; the Corridor in any case was full of ghosts – for instance, a figure in a winged collar with a shining forehead, and occasionally glimpsed muttering, or passing silently by – and C.P. might well have been one of these. On one of his visitations he spoke to me about Kingsley, telling me how, almost from his very first appearance in Cross Street, he had found his physical presence distasteful; to the point that he could not bear any bodily contact with him, like shaking hands, or reading copy over his shoulder. Was this feeling, expressed so emphatically, perhaps a premonition of the moral squalor and confusion which the attitude of mind Kingsley so perfectly exemplified was bound to produce, and of which *The Guardian* would be a leading exponent, rather than a comment on his actual physical presence? Mrs Webb, in any case, reacted to him similarly, in her Journal; and so, as I had occasion to learn, did George Orwell. Once when I was lunching with him at a Greek restaurant in Percy Street he asked me to change places with him, which I cheerfully did. He explained that the reason for the change was that, from where he had been sitting, he looked straight at Kingsley lunching at an adjoining table; and the sight of so corrupt a face, he said, would spoil his luncheon. When I took his place I had to admit that I felt no particular distress at having Kingsley in vision. Was this because I was part of the same corruption? Or just that over the years the stench of it had so got into my nostrils that I didn't notice it any more.

The body comes into our moral struggles more than is commonly recognised. There is nothing out-of-the-way in Jacob's long wrestling match with his God, or in the bloody battle between Christian and Apollyon in *The Pilgrim's Progress*. Everyone with experience of mental derangement – and there are few to-day without it – will know that the sickness of the mind goes with a horrifying intensification of the body's animality; a wild animal staring out of the eyes, or dim windows of the soul, as Blake calls them. Dreadful grunts replacing human speech, froth at the corners of the mouth, and the flesh exuding smells and rankness. My own most vivid experience of the bodily implications of mental strife came in a radio session I once had with Bertrand Russell. I had spoken in praise of Christianity, and he rounded on me with unexpected ferocity, shrilly insisting that everything most cruel and destructive and wicked which had happened in the world since the end of the Roman Empire had been due to the Christian religion and its founder. I shouted back; it was an absurd and unedifying scene which nonetheless

left me physically exhausted, as though I had been engaged in a physical wrestling match. I remember still with a lively sense of horror how, as Russell's rage mounted, a flush rose up his thin white stringy neck, like a climbing thermometer, to suffuse his simian features, making of the great philosopher a flushed ape.

C.P. himself, in any case, was physically very fastidious, well scrubbed and brushed and groomed. His thoughts and attitudes were similarly hygienic, though his ear was attuned to the first tiny rustlings of the permissive tornado to come, which was to sweep *The Guardian* so notably along with it. I wrote a long leader for him one hot summer's day when there seemed no other subject, on the cult of sun-bathing, in which I quoted a line from D. H. Lawrence about the genitals of space. This he passed, though a cloud hung over our relations in the succeeding few days which suggested he may have been criticised for so doing. On one of his ghostly visitations we got on to the subject of a remark of Goethe's to the effect that women wearing spectacles put a barrier between themselves and male approaches. Yes, he said, looking knowing, he had found it so. It reminded me of Dr Johnson saying that if ever he had a harem he would dress the ladies in linen rather than silk. On another occasion, in connection with some story about racial trouble in Cardiff, we discussed whether Africans were better equipped sexually than Europeans. He had heard they were, he said. Though he was completely devoid of humour in the ordinary sense, there was a strain of impishness in him which came out from time to time; even a touch of irony – as when he remarked that printing *The Guardian* in London would be disastrous because then people would *read* it instead of just praising it. I did not venture to point out – what was, indeed, the case – that as things were, this was, with the best will in the world, impossible, because of the many misprints in the London edition.

Sometimes C.P. bicycled out to Didsbury to have tea with Kitty and me in the flat we had moved into from Kingsley's house. He was so amiable and flatteringly appreciative of my work that I should in the ordinary way have responded by liking him. Actually, I never did; I sensed something false and phoney in him – or thought I did. This feeling was heightened by my great and growing fondness for Ted, who submitted to being bullied by his father with sullen acquiescence but much inward resentment. He told me once that he had never known C.P. do any truly disinterested act in the whole of his life; everything he said and did, however ostensibly high-minded, had an interested

motive. Even his bowing out of the editorship in favour of Ted was more nominal than real; he continued in practice to hold all the strings in his hand. He represented, indeed, to a superlative degree, the great moral fallacy of our time – that collective virtue may be pursued without reference to personal behaviour. Thus he believed passionately in equality as long as he himself could enjoy the company of Oxford men who had read Greats; in security as long as he did not have to foot the bill for his own employees. His passion for freedom varied in direct ratio with the distance from Manchester of those demanding it, and he loved all mankind except those among his associates and underlings he considered to be socially or intellectually inferior. These were made all too well aware of his lofty disdain.

In our cubby holes along *The Guardian* corridor we expounded all the hopes and apprehensions this righteously exalted old man entertained for mankind. We, as it were, wrote him down nightly for the edification of his paper's readers, in words that, as we fondly believed, would reverberate round the world. Bringing cheer to Asian peasants as they followed their wooden ploughs, uplifting bearded Bedouins as they rode their camels along desert tracks; spreading enlightenment over palm and pine, over campus and conveyor-belt, wherever there were minds to think and hearts to feel. Tapping away at our typewriters on his behalf, we called upon moderate men of all shades of opinion to draw together to ensure that wiser counsels should prevail. Wars which threatened, all to be averted; wrongs which the downtrodden and oppressed suffered, all to be righted; conflicts all to be honourably resolved, and injustices all to be honourably corrected. The people of this country will never for a moment countenance, we sternly proclaimed; ourselves, the people of this country and C.P., momentarily identified; one in three and three in one, another Holy Trinity. They will recoil as one man, they will speak with one voice, they will scornfully repudiate; there was no end to the honourable capers the people of this country might be expected to cut – on our typewriter keyboards. We charted their best course, spelt out for them their finest destiny. If fingers faltered – because false sentences will never finish, sprouting clauses as profligately as gluttons stretch out their meals or spendthrifts accumulate debts – one had somehow to press on, resolutely raising the little hammers to pound out the requisite number of words. Lubricated with strong tea, fortified with buttered toast, stupefied with tobacco smoke; dog-eared press-cuttings once more turned over, past exhortations resuscitated and refurbished, shuffling along in other men's cast-off hopes, until the home-stretch

C.W.T.—M

reached at last – In this day and age surely not beyond the wit of man . . . To be hoped . . . Greatly to be hoped . . . Devoutly to be hoped . . . What, I sometimes cried out in anguish – what, oh what is to be hoped?

This is the dark night of the leader-writer, when there seems to be no wit in men in this or any other day and age; no moderate men and no shades of opinion to draw them together; nothing at all to be hoped. As with that other dark night of the soul described by St John of the Cross, for those who endure to the end, it passes, giving place at last to fulfilment and peace. Easily, smoothly, the concluding words are ejected like brushless shaving cream from a full tube – Devoutly to be hoped that resort to brute force will be eschewed . . . Self-interest in the narrower sense put aside . . . Solution hammered out at the conference table . . . On the one hand safeguards . . . on the other provides for the possibility of . . . thereby ensuring that . . . Hurrah! The job is done. Wiser counsels after all *have* prevailed, moderate men of all shades of opinion *have* drawn together. Positively glowing with the nobility of the final sentiment, I put back the cuttings in their folder and hand in my copy, to be fed in due course to the rotary machines. Soon I hear them chewing it over like giant molars.

Convivial in the Stock Bar; then in the Press Club, where, when Parliament was not sitting, the solid, dignified figure of the Honourable Member for Salford South was usually to be found. Back to the office for a last look at the news, and to pick up the first edition – pale shadow of the others to come, but still indubitably the next day's paper, whose possession the night before bestows a certain distinction; like eating strawberries out of season. Bearing it, I make my way homewards, along Oxford Street (Manchester being, with all its ostensible local glory, full of metropolitan echoes – Piccadilly, Leicester Square, etc.) and on to Didsbury. In winter more often than not, houses shrouded in mist, with only occasional dulled vagrant footsteps to be heard, and dim shadowy passing figures to be seen; in summer, long evening shadows, and occasionally, when a late story had to be waited for, the first intimations of dawn breaking across Victoria Park. At home, Kitty waiting; not pleased. Already the strife of egotistic living, of spent appetites and surreptitious actual or envisaged infidelities, charging the atmosphere with currents of rage and mutual reproach and accusation. Old rows that go on echoing in the limbo between deed and intent; lightning and thunder in the dark jungle of our human will.

Ours was the standard interior of our kind; shabby divan, three book-rows will I have there, and a flagon for the cheap chianti. A set for *Look*

Back in Anger and a hundred other like productions, assembled some two decades ahead of the Royal Court. The characters, too – we live out the plays long before their vogue upon the stage, which is why they have so often a stale *déjà vu* air about them; why, as the applause breaks, there are sour looks among those who waited for Godot years and years ago, played football on The Wasteland when its only begetter still wore a monocle and called himself Captain Eliot; who howled and howled when Ginsberg in tiny ringlets was lisping out the Torah under a Rabbi's spreading beard.

So, before going to bed, I sit surlily reading my first edition; mopping up the news like an avid eater cleaning up his plate with bread. The addiction had already gripped me. In the morning all the papers delivered, a daily pile of soggy newsprint on our doorstep; then the evenings, the Sundays, the weeklies, the monthlies. It was to be a life-long passion, only now, belatedly, beginning to wane; later, of course, to be augmented by listening and seeing. Impossible to calculate the vast expense of time and concentration on this evanescent pursuit; the equivalent, maybe, of painting twenty Sistine Chapels, or writing the Decline and Fall of several Empires. Words tapped out or scribbled or telephoned; then printed, rushed to delivery vans, trains and aeroplanes, put under door-knockers or laid beside bottles of milk, held up at break-fast tables, uncomfortably squinted at in buses and trains; by midday discarded, by tea time superseded, by evening relegated to lighting fires or wrapping fish. My own role a voyeur one; peering in through a keyhole or camera-shutter at the antics of those set in authority, and deriving therefrom some sort of perverse vicarious satisfaction, which, passed on, catered for a similar addiction in others. News an expression of the hypochondria of a sick society – like endlessly sucking at a thermometer, standing on the bathroom scales; for ever anxiously examining the tongue's colour, the breath's odour, the urine's consistency; pressing the gut for intimations of ulcer or cancer, dreading the appearance of a chancre, a gonorrhoeal emission. In a civilisation dropping to pieces, news takes some of the sting out of happenings. So, more and more of it; all day long, and often all night long, too. A sort of Newzak, corres-ponding to Muzak; instead of a melange of drooling tunes endlessly played, a melange of drooling news endlessly heard. As the motor-cars sweep along the broad highways, Newzak is absorbed; the face at the wheel, intent, almost religious and uplifted, detached from the whole mundane stationary world in this other ethereal world of perpetual motion from nowhere to nowhere, cigarette drooping, suit newly come

from the cleaners swinging to and fro on its coat-hanger like a clock's pendulum. In distant Peking, in nearby Washington D.C., in London and Paris and Rome, and everywhere, happenings, coming into view like coloured balloons. An endless succession of balloons of all colours and sizes. News.

Such was now my trade; part of the process of translating life and its meaning and significance into pictures, thereby draining it of its blood and flesh, its livingness. Surely it was not by chance that the age's essential invention in communications has been the camera. We needed it, and so invented it. Needed it to provide us with these very pictures; first stills, then moving; first black-and-white, then in living colour; first silent, then speaking; one-dimensional, two-dimensional, stereoscopic. As for the script, where my business lay – it, too, had to be what was seen *with* the eye rather than *through* it. Actualities rather than imaginings. Literature would not do, art would not do, these being through-the-eye activities. (Having no role, they were, in fact, to expire.) All that remained was pictures; the cameraman's, or the commentator's. Ultimately, a combination of both, when the deception would be complete; between the Action! and the Cut!, between the first clapper-board and the last, only fantasy.

Over and above the cotton trade, the screeching trams, the massive blackened public buildings and statues of forgotten worthies – champions of free trade, abolishers of slavery, instituters of polytechnics and public libraries; beyond the slums and the shops, the warehouses beside the stagnant Ship Canal, the clatter of occasional surviving clogs, the Midland Hotel with its majestic palm court – over and above all of them, like seraphim and cherubim high up on a white cloud in one of those vast Renaissance paintings of Creation or Transfiguration, there perched a little cluster of the culturally elect. Professors and teachers from the university, among them the massive swollen figure of Namier and the more whimsical one of A. J. P. Taylor, then his acolyte. Enlightened manufacturers' ladies with piled up hair and embroidered bodices who provided buffet and claret cup, and the presence of some distinguished visiting flautist, or bearer of good tidings from the League of Nations; even, on occasion, an Ouspensky, or Theosophist from Adyar with words to say on transmigration. The Hallé Orchestra, the Rep (then performing in a cavernous converted tram depot), *The Guardian*, of course, all provided their quota, along with an occasional museum or art gallery curator, librarian, local scribe or lady novelist from

the West Riding, Jewish or Armenian *aficionado* from Cheetham Hill (Harold Laski or Michael Arlen progenitors), rumbustious magnate with a taste for Trollope and a son at Bedales. The north country accents, muffled or defiant, seemed even then to contain a hint of migratory intentions southwards, with conquest in view; Arnold Bennett, J. B. Priestley, D. H. Lawrence beckoned, and many another cultural pilgrim would follow. Likely Lads in Eng. Lit., aspiring novelists-in-the-raw, rough but rewarding bedfellows for randy debs and girls with cultural aspirations from Girton and the Cheltenham Ladies' College, to be picked up at the Tate Gallery on a warm summer's afternoon. They, too, dramatis personae for a multitude of plays, novels, films and, above all, television documentaries yet unborn.

Kitty and I were no more than occasional frequenters of this society. For relaxation we used often to go into Derbyshire for long walks, battling our way across bleak moors and up windy hillsides, and often arguing or quarrelling as we went along; the wear and tear of two egos in two bodies laid side by side, each seeking fulfilment in the other's flesh under the watchful eye of the other's ego. It was tempting to look for answers to our dilemma, and, in exploring them, we joined in the great contemporary cacophony on the same theme. The marriage tie must not hamper or hinder us; marriage and the family were things of the past, as was jealousy, fidelity, parenthood. We abolished the lot, along with property, capitalism, money, and all other appurtenances of what we had already begun to call the Establishment, deriving the term from the Anglican Church as by law established. Having cleared away all this jungle, we should, we confidently believed, be free to live together of choice, not necessity. Finding satisfaction in one another's bodies without any sense of guilt or possessiveness; our appetites a great ecstasy rather than a great anguish, the Apostle Paul with his 'To be carnally minded is death' cast out in favour of the Apostle Lawrence with his 'To be carnally minded is life.' Phallic purification, as it were, cauterising and restoring our mind-infected flesh.

A more regular walk for me was what I called the Round; following the raised bank of a turgid stream that wound its way through a stretch of wasteland for some reason unbuilt on, just behind where we lived. It could scarcely be called country. Smoke and soot had settled upon it; the water of the stream seemed thick and lifeless, and though fishermen sometimes stood with their lines beside it, I never saw them pull anything out except old boots, and once a lady's hat. The very green of the trees and grass seemed faded and stale. In every direction, the skyline

was houses or belching chimneys; there were some adjoining allotments, heroically cultivated, and a football ground of sorts where in the school holidays and on summer evenings urchins played. The memory of this place has stayed with me more tenaciously and vividly than the Derbyshire or Cheshire countryside, or even than the Yorkshire moors or Lake District of our more ambitious outings. I must have pounded through it in all sorts of weather and temperature, some hundreds, if not thousands, of times; sometimes, in moods of special restlessness, completing the Round, and then at once beginning on it again, to the surprise of anyone who had happened to notice me on my first circumlocution. Always conscious of being incarcerated, a prisoner, the Round so pleased me, perhaps, because it was like what I imagine prison exercise to be. Not to get anywhere; always, essentially, remaining in the same place, yet moving, footstep following footstep, arms swinging, sweat accumulating, and in the mind the everlasting questions that were never answered, the everlasting desires that were never satisfied, the everlasting longings that were never realised. Curiously enough, returning to Manchester after many years, and looking for familiar landmarks which I could not find, I came upon the Round exactly as it had been. It alone survives unchanged and intact; *The Guardian* office in Cross Street has disappeared.

I habituated myself to relating my life to news as farmers do to weather. This soon became second nature, and long after the necessity was passed the habit persisted; like the man in *Rasselas* who had convinced himself that without his exertions the sun would never rise or set. We leader-writers were expected to turn up at the office in the early afternoon; one mooned around, dropped into the sub's room to see what had come in, pored over the early editions of the evening papers. At some point or other one would usually be sent for by Ted or C.P.; if not, one felt anxious and unwanted. Then, the subject of that day's leader agreed on, one would settle down to it, cuttings spread out, *Encyclopaedia Britannica* or some other relevant book or work of reference consulted, maybe even a telephone call made; though the telephone had not by any means yet come into its own as the constant instrument of daily journalism, and, in any case, on our penurious paper, its use, except for local calls, was frowned upon as an extravagance. A piece of paper fixed in the typewriter, a heading underlined – as it might be, Trouble in Panama – and off we go: 'The overthrow of Sr Farrago's (one had to be careful about Signor, Senor, Senhor; Sr was safer) Government and

replacement by a military junta (junta had a nasty sound, and could safely be applied to any régime displeasing to the *Guardian* which had an officer above the rank of major in it) under the leadership of the notorious General Fandango ('notorious' was safe enough for any Panamanian general) would seem to be a retrograde step . . . and so on, leading up to the anchor- or hinge-word 'Meanwhile'. After 'meanwhile', came, almost as a matter of course, 'it remains to be seen', the equivalent, in distant and doubtful situations, of 'it is to be hoped'. What precisely remained to be seen in Panama just then, now escapes me, but doubtless it was to do with whether the general's strong-arm men would be able to terrorise the peasants and factory workers into acquiescence, and tranquilise a population, divided between *Moderato* and *Exaltado* factions (two easily invented words betokening a deep knowledge of the subject), and notoriously subject to political instability.

Or one might have some other additional task like an editorial paragraph for the *Manchester Guardian Weekly*, remunerated at the rate of twelve-and-six a time. Or a back-page article to finish off, these being fictional pieces of about a thousand words for which one received four guineas; only three, however, if the background was derived from an expenses-paid *Guardian* assignment. Or a book review to do. I easily took to this work, which I have gone on doing more or less regularly ever since. My only steady occupation, and the only 'serious' reading that, with a very few exceptions, I have ever undertaken. I soon became versed in sampling a book here and there; like a wine-taster taking a mouthful, washing it several times round his mouth, and then spitting it out. Versed, too, in digesting a blurb (Miss So-and-so's vivid account of a relationship between a young aggressive village schoolmaster and a middle-aged recluse whose archaeologist husband thinks of nothing but his digs), in grubbing up a sentence here, a sentence there, to suggest familiarity with some unknown subject; in playing with phrases which find their way into publisher's advertisements: I could not lay it down . . . Essential reading for all students of contemporary affairs. . . . Unique contribution to . . . Alas, how easily the hack acquires his tools! In A. N. Monkhouse's absence on holiday, I even sat in as Literary Editor, and in that capacity included in the Book Page a review by myself of Mrs Catherine Carswell's book on D. H. Lawrence, *The Savage Pilgrimage*, the first of a long grisly line of female outpourings about him. In view of the fact that Mrs Carswell was a valued contributor to the *Guardian*, my closing peroration caused much indignation, within and outside the paper: 'How sick one gets of Don and John

Patrick (Mrs Carswell's husband and son)! How sick one gets of
Lawrence himself! How sick, how unutterably sick, of Mrs Carswell!'
On the whole I welcomed Monkhouses's return with relief.

I struggled on with my own writing, fitfully but ardently. To my great
surprise and delight, it was finally arranged that my play *Three Flats*
was to be produced by the Stage Society. The producer was Matthew
Forsyth, and I note in the case several names that afterwards became
well known – Barry K. Barnes, Dorice Fordred, Mary Hinton, Mar-
garet Yarde; among the extras, Anthony Quayle. I went up to London
for a dress rehearsal, and sat beside Forsyth, but was too overwhelmed
to say anything much. The play did not seem to be by me; the set – a
ground-floor flat and, above it, two adjoining first-floor ones – and the
words as I heard them spoken, were quite unfamiliar. Nor have I now
the courage to read them in the published version, of which I still
possess a copy. I went with Kitty and my father and mother to the
Sunday evening production at the Prince of Wales Theatre. It was an
occasion of delirious happiness; there were shouts for the author, and I
took a curtain with the cast. My father's pleasure was a great satis-
faction to me, and I hope it offset some at least of his disappointments.
His eyes were shining. I still had the feeling, though, that the play was
by someone else; even when I read the notices, which were reasonably
encouraging, especially *The Times*, whose dramatic critic wrote (I quote
from a faded cutting pasted in a scrapbook): 'All is vain, all is scattered
and seemingly unrelated, all is at once sad and absurd. What is the uni-
fying cause and truth? The author asks his questions with skill and
sympathy, pointing it with faultless observation, that he never permits to
become shrill ... In brief, a play distinguished by the sureness of its
detail and the economy of its writing.' I read those words over a good
many times at breakfast on the Monday morning. Subsequently I learnt
that the writer of the piece was Charles Morgan. There is always a catch in
everything. Shaw was in the audience, but my attention was focused on
the stage. He wrote a long letter to Mrs Webb about the play, which I only
saw recently. Though quite appreciative, it showed a total unawareness
of what I was getting at. This did not really surprise me, since I came
to realise that Shaw got everything wrong – Shakespeare, Caesar, the
Soviet Union, Mussolini, St Paul. He had a sparkling intelligence but a
low understanding; this enabled him to be very funny, but whenever he
was serious he was absurd. In any event, he was too encased in his own
narcissism, too remote from real life ever to do more than grimace at it

through a long-distance telescope. Once Lady Rhondda asked me to accompany her to lunch with him, but afterwards telephoned in some embarrassment to call the invitation off. When pressed, she told me that it was because I had referred to Shaw in something I had written as 'that absurd vain rich old man'. He particularly resented, she said, being called rich. It surprised me at the time that he should be so touchy; now I can see that it was understandable enough. He wanted to make a lot of money without being considered rich, as Casanova wanted to have women without being considered lecherous, or as Stalin wanted to operate a terror without being considered cruel. James Agate's notice was patronising but kindly, and advised me to change my name at once. Though Ransome had proffered similar advice, I resolutely declined to follow it.

When, a few days later, I heard from my agent, Walter Peacock, that Universal Pictures had bought an option on *Three Flats* for five hundred pounds, and that if and when they made a film based on it I should get some thousands of pounds (I can't remember how many, but it seemed a great many at the time), I thought my fortune was made. Of course they never did make a film, and though I wrote a number of other plays I never had another professionally produced. So it all came to nothing. At one point, Peacock arranged for me to meet Charles Laughton with a view to writing a play for him, and we lunched together in his hotel room in Manchester. I can't now remember what sort of play I suggested, but I know we only got to it in the last ten minutes of our luncheon. Before then, he had been telling me how, to get in the right state of mind when he was playing Al Capone in Edgar Wallace's play, *On the Spot*, he used to remember how as a schoolboy he had believed that his fingers were going to drop off as a result of masturbating. This was my only brief, and not very pleasing, encounter with the theatre and actors, though Peacock remained a friend to the end of his life. He was a curious melancholic figure, in a permanent state, as it seemed to me, of faint uncomplaining excitation by constant contact with pretty aspiring actresses anxious to please him. A sort of lovable green-room sage or oracle. He did not care much for my plays, though he did his best to get them put on. I expect he was right; my impression is that the themes were too abstract and symbolic, and the dialogue correspondingly stilted.

A mellifluous American named Constant Huntington, managing director of Putnam, the publisher of *Three Flats*, urged me to write a novel. It was my first acquaintance with the world of Henry James and

the Europeanised New Englander, beautifully dressed, elaborately courteous, enormously *slow* – in Huntington's case, this slowness accentuated by his practice of carefully masticating his food a fixed number of times, which meant that, lunching with him, one was liable to find oneself well into the celery and cheese when he had barely finished his soup. I suppose T. S. Eliot represented the last fine flower on this particular plant, unless, indeed, you count Joe Alsop, which would be to reduce the whole thing to absurdity. On one occasion Huntington took me out to lunch with Lloyd Osbourne, Robert Louis Stevenson's step-son, with whom he collaborated in writing *The Wrong Box.* I was very excited about it, and planned to get Osbourne talking about life in Samoa with his mother and step-father; alas, as has so often happened to me, I talked myself, and he barely uttered. He seemed, in any case, a rather taciturn sort of person, with a round, dull face and a rumbling American accent. All the same, it was an opportunity missed; one of many such.

The novel I wrote at Huntington's behest was called *Autumnal Face*; about an ageing dispirited suburban lady, and her longings for a more exciting, full-blooded life, but patient acquiescence in her lot; based, of course, on my Croydon memories. I wrote it in the mornings in Didsbury, between Rounds, going over it with Kitty as I went along; as I have everything I have ever done. It is dedicated to her. In the same scrapbook as the notice of *Three Flats*, there are some reviews – 'Skill and insight . . . fascinating picture . . . first novel of a genuine artist . . .' I could go on culling such choice items from an otherwise moribund expanse of print. I note with a pang that one notice in the old *Sunday Referee* has a 16 pt headline: A YOUNG NOVELIST TO WATCH. Until I looked at these notices I had forgotten that, with prophetic insight, I gave the dreary suburban family I atomised the all too apt surname of Pill!

The reception of my play and first novel, I suppose, along with whatever kudos derived from a fairly brisk start on the *Guardian*, would have qualified me to set up there and then as a professional writer, without any necessity to be on the staff of a newspaper, and undertake the writing and other chores this entailed. I cannot recall that I even considered such a thing, or claim that I was held back from dedication to letters by financial or family considerations. Kitty would not have minded – she never has minded anything of that kind; we should have rubbed along perfectly well, as later on we did. The truth is that I have no fancy for a writer's life as such; some instinct told me that in contemporary

circumstances it would prove sterile, and, ultimately, absurd. It would be Eng. Lit. and Little Dowden all over again. Living in some country retreat, by the Mediterranean if prosperous enough, or otherwise exotically situated. Coloured-shirted, sandalled, panama hatted for day-time wear, broad-brim for the evening, and maybe velvet jacketed. Puffing away at a pipe, dreaming of young girls, turning out a daily quota of words – 'Mrs Farquharson sat in the sun, a novel with uncut pages listlessly held, her neat, trim figure elegantly disposed in yellow – a colour that suited her still flaxen hair coiled round tiny, shapely ears. Would Henry speak at last when he came to dinner; just the two of them? About Angela, and all that had happened since that so strange en-counter . . . ?' Or some ferocious tirade in the Wyndham Lewis manner. Or Poundian? Or Joycean? Or, culled from Belloc, about the Faith, and Richard Coeur-de-Lion, and Thomas Aquinas? Or, perhaps worst of all, the Workers, and some champion of the down-trodden and op-pressed from Balliol, in baste shoes, who joined the hunger marchers, and reviewed the collected works of Lenin in the *Worker*, and supped at the 1917 Club with Ethel Mannin after Brecht. Or getting invited to Garsington, with a chance of catching a glimpse of Aldous Huxley, and hearing D. H. Lawrence shout across the dinner table at Bertrand Russell: 'You're all doomed!'

Kitty's and my feelings in this matter were no doubt coloured by our friendship with Gerald Bullett and his wife, whom we occasionally visited, and they us. Gerald was a fairly successful novelist, always at work on a book, with the next one already at the planning stage; this one maybe to include a touch of incest – and why not after Oedipus? A plump man with a round face, humorous eyes and sad jowls, he and his wife lived in the usual two cottages run into one, with a thatched roof – so difficult to get repaired nowadays because all the delightful village arts and crafts were dying out, but fortunately they had a man, a droll delightful old fellow who was prepared to take it on. Gerald's study was a large dark room with a lot of books lying about, mostly in their dust-jackets; he did a bit of reviewing for the T.L.S. and other literary publications, but not enough to get in the way of his creative work. His wife typed for him, very energetically; one could hear her in the morn-ings bashing away at her keyboard – like volleys of machine-gun fire. In the evenings, likewise energetically, she crocheted or knitted while the rest of us talked; only very occasionally joining in, her voice sharp and bright and cheerful. Theirs had been a runaway match; they were deeply attached to one another, kind and considerate by nature. Yet

somehow there seemed to be something weighing them down; especially him. If they had some unexpected windfall, like unexpected translation rights for one of his novels, they would launch out on a trip to the Greek Islands, or even farther afield. Their only child was at an ultra-progressive school, and Gerald was a member of the Savile Club.

He and I often went for country walks together over the downs when we were staying with them; laughing a lot as we went along, and maintaining together the fantasy that we were aloof from the ordinary world where people cashed cheques and grabbed girls, as well as a little fame, when a chance offered. All that, we implied, was outside our ken. To sustain the fantasy, we would sow our conversation with qualifying phrases like 'what's called'. Thus, we would say, 'I take it, he was what's called "in love",' or: 'I believe that, actually, she's quite comfortably off, and moves in what's called "Society"!' As 1939 approached, Gerald tended to emerge from his terra-cotta tower and write furious letters to *The Times*, or, if not accepted there, to *Time and Tide*, denouncing Neville Chamberlain in unbridled terms, or advocating World Government based on the transferred vote as a solution to all our troubles. Sometimes, so intense was his rage, he compressed it all into a postcard, as a man might express all his pent-up fury in a single expletive In the war years, he worked in the BBC, beaming programmes on Milton or Wordsworth to the Nazi-occupied countries with a view to raising their morale. In a nearby studio Orwell was doing the same sort of thing to India. I think Gerald enjoyed this work, especially when the Blitz was on; in an underground studio in Oxford Street, holding forth on *Lycidas* or the *Ode on the Intimations of Immortality*, while the Luftwaffe roared overhead and the ground shook below him. The last glimpse I had of him was when he stood in the doorway of a flat Kitty and I had in Regent's Park, on his way to the Savile Club to dine with some choice spirits – Gilbert Harding, Gerald Barry, C. P. Snow; his large moon face crumpled and woebegone as he told me that he didn't want to write any more novels; hadn't anything more to say, his act being, as he put it, played out. Like an old recitative man with a funny bowler and a nose that lit up, wanting to get off the stage. Well, he did, as it happened, because shortly afterwards he died.

I had an instinctive aversion to this role of man-of-letters, as I had to being ordained. Both roles related to things I cared greatly about, but somehow, in the existing state of affairs, neither seemed appropriate. As I see it, in the twentieth century the genius of man has gone into

science and the resultant technology, leaving the field of mysticism and imaginative art and literature almost entirely to charlatans and sick or obsessed minds. The result has been that, whereas in the last half century more progress has been made in the exploration of man's material circumstances, and in the application of the knowledge thereby gained, than in the whole of the rest of recorded time, the corresponding contribution to art and literature has been negligible and derisory. The circumstances of the age are just not conducive to such activities, and those who nonetheless pursue them tend to become unhinged or junkies or alcoholics, if not all three. This is particularly true of American practitioners; as Gore Vidal has pointed out, it is difficult to think of a single contemporary American writer of any note who is not either an alcoholic or on the way to becoming one.

In such circumstances, reporting and commenting upon contemporary happenings seemed preferable to dancing and grimacing on the grave of a dead culture. News was the raw material of this new trade, consisting of jerkily written messages torn off teleprinter machines, or long screeds, sometimes difficult to decipher, from Our Own or someone else's Correspondent. Sometimes the Correspondents themselves made an appearance; arriving, as it were, booted and spurred from distant places, and inclined to be somewhat contemptuous of editorial scribes toiling away at typewriters to produce sententious comment on the news they so heroically tore with rough strife through the iron gates of censorship and other natural and artificially imposed impediments. It was in the nature of things that they should appear to be in fancy dress; as Robert Dell from Paris, with his white gloves and cane and rakish felt hat and neat white moustache; like a seaside repertory Proust. At the Stock Bar we delighted in his tales of who was whose mistress in the Gauche Radicale, and listened attentively to how he outwitted the Quai d'Orsay, and what was said at his tête-à-têtes with Maxim Litvinov.

Then there was the Rev. C. F. Andrews, hot foot from Gandhi's ashram in Ahmedabad. Bearded, every inch a guru, with meek downcast eyes, he seemed to be saying that his heart sank when he reflected how, though well past thirty, he had still not been crucified. One could not but share his sorrow, more particularly as there now seemed little possibility of this unaccountable gap in his range of experience being rectified. He was also fond of comparing Gandhi's various appearances before the Indian courts with Christ's before Pilate. Scott leant a good deal on Andrews, whom he liked, in shaping *The Guardian*'s attitudes towards British policy in India, though curiously enough when he met

Gandhi himself, despite Andrew's mutual recommendations, he found the experience distasteful. I think perhaps they were too alike to get on well together; if Gandhi had been born of Unitarian parents in Lancashire he would almost certainly have become owner-editor of *The Guardian*, and likewise, if Scott had been born the son of a Kathiwar State Dewan, he could almost certainly have become a Mahatma. They met when Gandhi was over in London for the Indian Round Table Conference. C.P. had to fight his way to him through a posse of Quakers and even then found the Mahatma at his spinning-wheel and little inclined to talk, which was calculated to irritate him inordinately. Gandhi's meeting with Charlie Chaplin round about the same time was as successful as the one with Scott had been disastrous; the clown and the Mahatma were complementary images of the same thing, a gargoyle and a steeple in juxtaposition. I attended the official opening of the Round Table Conference by George V on behalf of *The Guardian*. It was a tremendous turn-out – Maharajahs and other Indian princes, the Aga Khan as huge as Chesterton, knights brown and white, turbans and shining pates, politicians, policemen, and even an odd member of the public vaguely curious to know what, if anything, was to happen to the brightest jewel in their sovereign's crown. Presiding was the then Prime Minister, Ramsay MacDonald, already well on the way to the condition of total incoherence and irresolution which marked the last stages of his political career. His opening address was vintage stuff, containing, as I recall, a remarkable appeal for 'the lion (I don't know which is the lion) to lie down with the lamb (I don't know which is the lamb).' It gave rise among those present to a sort of lions and lambs game, with everyone trying to decide to which category they belonged. Only King George V seemed quite certain; he, it was clear, considered himself as indubitably belonging to the lions. Despite the opening pomp and circumstances, the Conference soon got bogged down in a plethora of words, to which I contributed my quota in the shape of long messages to *The Guardian*. In making our getaway from India we laid down a vast preliminary smoke screen of words in the shelter of which we were able to make our dispositions for withdrawal.

To me, far the most interesting and impressive of the correspondents was F. A. Voigt from Germany. He did not need to dress up as a German; he was one (his family belonged to the sizeable German community in Manchester, and had a music shop there), with the raw features, desperately emphatic speech, powerful mind and ultimately

tragic disposition of the race. If Dell was a pinchbeck Proust, he was a Nietzsche; a wild swordfish put to swim in *The Guardian* aquarium among the minnows and the goldfish and the Portuguese men-of-war. I admired enormously the furious indignation with which he described the growing threat of a Nazi takeover in Germany, of the mounting terror and violence that was building up there. Unlike other correspondents, he stressed all the time the moral consequences of what was happening; showing that it was not just war that threatened, but a moral catastrophe which could engulf whatever remained of western civilisation. Voigt's strong unequivocal attitude made him an alien element in *The Guardian*'s measured columns, especially after the outbreak of war in 1939. After he left the paper, he became editor of the *Nineteenth Century and After*, providing in it almost the only free comment and criticism of Allied policy – apart from *Tribune*, under Aneurin Bevan, with George Orwell as literary editor – which stands to-day as a shining exception to the prevailing servile acceptance of Churchill's leadership in all its aspects and with all its implications. When Voigt turned the furious indignation with which he had lambasted the Nazi terror on to Stalin's, his former liberal friends and associates discovered in him a Nazi sympathiser. Another liberal newspaper, the *News Chronicle*, ran an article about the *Nineteenth Century* headed, HITLER'S FAVOURITE READING, with pictures of the Führer and Voigt looking amicably across at one another. For this, the *News Chronicle* was sued, and I was proud to appear in court to testify to Voigt's record of integrity and distinguished journalism.

The case was heard during the Blitz, and every so often an alert sounded and the court was adjourned. It was an eerie experience, but somehow I felt that the proceedings were more relevant and important than the war itself. In a sense, they *were* the war – the true war. The judge – Scrutton – conducted the case with impeccable impartiality, and I was uplifted to think that, in a world gone mad, being torn apart and destroyed by rival fanaticisms and power-maniacs, it was still possible for a case involving these passions to be dispassionately heard and justly concluded. Voigt got damages and an apology from the *News Chronicle*, and I returned to my military duties, such as they were. After the war I saw Voigt occasionally; he fell on evil days, no one wanted his work, and he found a sanctuary on *Time and Tide*, that Salvation Army shelter provided by Lady Rhondda for destitute ideologues, where I, too, in my time, was glad to take an occasional cup of hot soup. He died largely forgotten and in poor circumstances despite a charming and devoted

wife; his book *Unto Caesar*, in my opinion the most powerful and perceptive political work of our time, has long been, and to the best of my knowledge remains, out of print.

Whenever I was in London I used, of course, to look in at the House of Commons to see my father. I would wait for him in the public lobby; one of those points of intersection where rulers and ruled consort. Always crowded, with many anxious faces such as people wear before an examination; whenever they are confronted with some test of character or occasion for self-assertion. There were the usual cranks, bearded or strangely dressed, their pockets bulging with petitions, liable to mutter to themselves and make weird gestures; the women in long skirts and hats decorated with fruit and flowers, sometimes with veils – rather in the style of Mrs Dobbs. These were always interminably waiting, and one wondered if they really had any serious possibility of an appointment with an MP, or had just chosen to come there as a change from their usual haunts like the British Museum Reading Room and Hyde Park Corner and Lincoln's Inn Fields. From certain points of vantage one could see the MPs coming towards the lobby, and observe how, when they heard their names called by the policeman in attendance, they threw out their chests, and summoned up a smile, assuming a bland and jaunty air, like actors coming on the stage. So I would hear my father's name called, and it was exactly as though I were back at East Croydon Station, and had spotted him coming up the slope from the arrival platform; stepping out, ahead of the others.

We usually made for the terrace, to walk up and down there, or stare at the river; or, if the sun was shining, take tea together, and watch other MPs and their guests; just occasionally catching a glimpse of one of the great ones – a cabinet minister, a face familiar from photographs or cartoons, and now seen in the flesh; MacDonald himself, or Baldwin, or Lloyd George. Inside, whatever the season or the weather, the atmosphere always seemed dry and stale and sour. There are certain smells that remain with one – an elementary school cloakroom on a wet day; the combination of Gauloises cigarettes, urine and pungent scent which assails one's nostrils on arriving anywhere in France; a barrack-hut on waking, with one's thirteen fellow-inmates still asleep, and all the windows firmly closed. This House of Commons smell is one of them. I recall a rather similar smell in public transport vehicles in the USSR, especially on the underground. It is, I suppose, the smell of power, as in a brothel there is a smell of sex. My father liked introducing me to his

fellow-members, most of whom seemed to have little to do, and spent their time sitting around in the bars and cafés interminably talking, and listening for the division bell, which spurred them into sudden, and often unthinking, action. They had, I thought, a flaccid air; like under-exercised animals in the zoo. Even my father, most energetic of men, seemed to have lost his momentum and settled into a kind of inertia, with a predisposition for doing nothing about anything. It was particu-larly noticeable in the trade union members, the only authentically proletarian ones. They were out of condition, sagging, running to fat; their faces creased and indolent, as though they were half-drunk; as, indeed, they sometimes were. The ostensible fanatics like Maxton gave an impression of character actors who had just come out of the make-up room; the lock of hair falling over the forehead, the wild eyes and accentuated eyebrows, the ardent words soulfully spoken. Likewise the Clydesiders, the sea-green incorruptibles. Years later, from the press gallery, I happened to see one of them – David Kirkwood – introduced into the House of Lords; in his robes and floppy hat, bowing religiously at the appropriate moments in the ceremony, a fellow-peer on each side of him, and Silver-Stick-in-Waiting presiding. It was a perfect exposi-tion of the humble and meek being exalted. From Saint-Simon one gathers that things were much the same at the court of Louis XIV, from Swift that they were not dissimilar at Queen Anne's, from Djilas that very similar arrangements prevailed in Stalin's; not to mention Nebuchadnezzar, Herod and the Emperor Nero.

Journalism is, I suppose, among other things, an exploration of varieties of political experience in all their wild diversity, as William James explored varieties of religious experience. Some colonel screws a monocle into his eye and takes over a government. Or a bearded arch-bishop with a ring to kiss manoeuvres himself on to a throne. Or a black corporal breaks ranks and becomes a president. Or an obscure figure playing interminable games of chess in Geneva cafés, boring everyone, quarrelling with everyone, is suddenly whisked off to rule over a fifth of the world. Or a convention demagogue shouting and sweating and fixing, at last arrives in Connecticut Avenue, to occupy the White House and imagine that it falls to him to decide there whether or not the world is to be blown to smithereens. At fantastic levels of seeming splendour – a Viceroy moving from his law chambers to sit on a silver throne and accept the homage of maharajahs with diamonds as big as ostrich eggs stuck in their turbans. Equally at levels of infinite obscurity, as I once saw two archdeacons in gaiters sitting meekly side by side on a bench

outside the door of the patronage secretary's office at 10 Downing Street in Mr Attlee's day, waiting, presumably, to be summoned inside to hear about preferment possibilities. Helping a brigadier on with his coat, attentive in a board room; gallant to wigs and dentures elegantly mounted on scrawny flesh, as Drake and Leicester and the other Elizabethans were to the hideous old scarecrow they served – all manner of calculated obsequiousness directed to the same end. My collector's item is Brindisi after Mussolini's fall, at the Hotel Imperiale where Marshal Badoglio had formed a government under Allied auspices. What a turn-out that was! Teeming with Intelligence officers, Italian generals in enormously wide riding-breeches, hurriedly assembled diplomatic excellencies, journalists, exiled venerable anti-Fascist liberals transported from their Kensington lodgings to accept portfolios in the Marshal's cabinet after many penurious years of patient endeavour in Bush House on behalf of the Overseas Service of the BBC. All manner of personnel pushing and shoving, in the dining-room and elsewhere, with a view to restoring the Four Freedoms and other democratic blessings to Italian soil; the only notable absentees being the beneficiaries of all this – the Italian people. Unless, indeed, the Imperiale staff could be considered such, as attentive to Marshal Badoglio and his entourage now, I noticed, as they had been in the days when he was the Duce's commander-in-chief.

My father's pleasure in being an MP and in spending his evenings at Westminster was scarcely marred by public anxieties. These, in a way, sharpened the pleasure by giving the whole experience a flavour of drama. He even appended his signature to a memorandum calling for drastic action on the Government's part, drawn up by Sir Oswald Mosley, then still a Labour MP and beloved of the Left-Wing. There were furious exchanges about ever rising unemployment and cuts in the social services; all-night sessions when Honourable Members emerged dishevelled and bleary eyed, with a sense of having been engaged in a ferocious bloody battle. But with whom? About what? No one really knew. The economic blizzard, as it was called, implying that no one could do anything about it except take shelter and hope for it to pass, blew as it listed, until there came a day when MacDonald went to the Palace and returned to announce that he had resigned as Labour Prime Minister and been entrusted with a mandate to form a National Government comprising both Tories and Liberals. No item of news has ever given me quite so overwhelming a feeling of outrage mixed with incredulity as this one. All the pent up hatred of MacDonald and Snowden

and J. H. Thomas, the three leading defectors, exploded. They had gone over to the enemy, betrayed the cause, shattered the work of years in a single act of treachery.

I remembered my father telling me the last time I saw him how the members of the Parliamentary Labour Party had assembled to hear MacDonald explain the Government's policy to them. He arrived late, in full evening dress and smoking a cigar; then, waving a condescending hand, had spoken a few meaningless words – my frrriends! . . . – and hurried off to a reception given by Lady Londonderry. Now he would be able to attend as many such functions as he liked ('Tonight every duchess in London will be wanting to kiss me,' Philip Snowden quoted him as saying) in whatever rig he liked. Grinding my teeth, I saw him as the typical figure in the Soviet satirical paper *Krokodil*'s cartoons; the flunkey in some ridiculous uniform bowing and scraping to bankers carrying money-bags and noblemen wearing coronets. For the moment he and his accomplices were riding high, but, some dreadful fate must surely await them. As, indeed, it did; MacDonald, broken in health was finally turned out of office by his Tory associates, and died at sea – he, the great pacifist, brought back on a battle cruiser in a coffin draped with a Union Jack. Thomas was convicted of using budget secrets for personal enrichment, and disappeared without trace; Snowden likewise withdrew from politics, continuing to mutter to the end of his days about Free Trade, the only article of faith left to him. It was an appropriate end to the three lost leaders, each of whom, in his own way, symbolised essential elements in the Labour Party. MacDonald, the romantic elevation of the down-trodden and oppressed to cultural and intellectual heights, Thomas the jovial proletarian at ease in his own breezy way with captains and kings alike, and Snowden the canny Yorkshireman, looking after our pennies so that the exchequer's pounds could look after themselves.

When afterwards I heard from Sidney Webb the full story of what happened, the drama seemed even more appropriate. In his soft, sibilant, toneless voice he described how he and the other cabinet ministers sat in the garden at 10 Downing Street on that warm August evening waiting for a telephone call from New York to tell them whether American banking houses were prepared to put up a loan sufficient to enable the Treasury to go on supporting the pound on the gold standard. When the answer came as no, there was nothing more they could do. They just shook their heads and departed, leaving MacDonald to go to the Palace and resign. Webb, now the first, and last, the one and only,

Baron Passfield, was the perfect narrator; seated in an arm-chair, his tiny legs not reaching the ground, his goatee beard wagging, his pince-nez with their black ribbon steady on his large nose, he showed no awareness that the occasion he described had any particular momentousness. To me it seemed – and, for that matter, still seems – to mark the end of any notion that the Labour Party, or any Social Democratic party similarly constituted, can be an effective instrument of fundamental social change. Whenever, subsequently, I read or heard prospectuses of the great things a Labour Government might be expected to achieve, I remembered that little cluster of respectable-looking men in the garden at 10 Downing Street, drawing at their pipes, occasionally getting up to stretch their legs, while they waited for Wall Street to decide their fate.

Now the rage and fury at what I considered a great betrayal has long ago passed. Even the three traitors seem more absurd than villainous. One sees MacDonald as a victim of history rather than a shaper of it; a Scottish loon who found himself on the captain's deck of a sinking ship, the less able to navigate it because he had got there by insisting that it was unseaworthy. He and the others might say with General Mihailovitch: 'There is a storm in the world, and a gale and a whirlwind have carried me and my work away.' So furious a storm, so wild a gale, so fierce a whirlwind, and such featherweight men and work.

When the news came of MacDonald's betrayal and formation of a National Government, Ted was away on holiday, and W. P. Crozier, the then news editor, was in charge of the paper. He was a rather unhappy, dyspeptic man with a bright red face and a buttoned up mouth, who hated the sight of me, and found my copy highly distasteful. In Ted's absence I made no effort to come to terms with him, but just coasted along doing little or nothing. I looked on him as someone infinitely boring; a Nonconformist who had lost his faith but retained its scaffolding of self-denial. It is one thing to resolve to give up self-indulgence like drinking and smoking in order to foster and sharpen spiritual awareness, but to give them up, as Crozier had, just for abstemiousness's own sake is itself a form of self-indulgence, and a rather particularly repellent one at that. If he altered anything I wrote, it was always, as I considered, to make it more banal and flat. That scarlet face looming across a laden desk at one, those fishy hostile eyes seeking an opportunity to cause unease and embarrassment, the dreadful silence that fell as I reached round in my mind for something, anything, to say – it all was so painful that, as far as possible, I avoided ever going in to see Crozier.

An extra touch of the macabre was added because the women's page editor was often with him for consultation, leaving behind a heavy cloud of pungent scent which hung over the office like sweet smog. In my youthful arrogance I failed to notice that, though Crozier happened to think little of me, he was an exceptionally able journalist, devoted to *The Guardian*, and even to the Scotts, though, I daresay, embittered by the way he had been passed over in preference for members of the family.

Crozier's immediate impulse was to support the National Government, which he did in a leader containing the unfortunate remark that J. H. Thomas was a dab hand at preventing 'that sinking feeling' (a reference to a then famous Bovril advertisement), and so a boon to any government. In the Stock Bar that evening we raged over this piece of bad taste facetiousness. Crozier was never popular, partly because he held aloof from convivial gatherings, and seldom unbent. Now he was more unpopular than ever. Like all the dyed-in-the-wool *Guardian* men, including even Paddy Monkhouse, he was somehow stricken. Some sort of liberal lightning came down from heaven, so that they actually looked as though they had suffered a paralytic stroke; slumping along the Corridor wrapped in their own internal gloom, sometimes, as I have heard them, actually muttering to themselves. What was it that afflicted them? I suppose just the anguish of pretending – always pretending that it was possible to make virtue out of benevolence, happiness out of well-being, peace out of accommodation and freedom out of emancipation. The wish wrestling with the reality produced strain, which in turn produced despair, at last transforming the wish itself into a kind of annihilation, or death-wish.

My dislike of Crozier took the form of totemising him, constructing my own hateful image of him; making his scarlet face even more scarlet, pursing up his lips even tighter, squeezing banalities out of him like pus. In the same sort of way, Africans seek, and sometimes manage, to injure their enemies via their likeness in some crude image or picture. We who pass for being more civilised can do the same thing in our imaginations. It is a form of diabolism to which I have been prone.

When Ted returned, we all worked on him, inducing him to reverse the paper's line and show up the fraudulence of MacDonald and his National Government. The turning point was at a luncheon in Ted's house when we all held forth eloquently; one could see him yielding – as, indeed, apart from our persuasion, all his personal feelings strongly induced him to do. It was very humiliating for Crozier. Thenceforth, we thoroughly enjoyed ourselves lampooning the Government, the re-

criminatory rows inside the Labour Opposition, and the three recusants with equal zest. I have to admit that, for me, journalism is only exhilarating in opposition; I have never, happily, been in the position of having to support a government. When Mr Attlee got his huge majority in 1945, I got a job on the *Daily Telegraph*, and shortly after the Tories came back into power in 1951, I niftily transferred to *Punch*.

C.P. had played little part in these events; at last his vitality was ebbing, and in the early hours of New Year's Day, 1932, he died. One final rapturous burst of adulation and he was soon largely forgotten; or remembered only as a symbol of good, noble journalism as distinct from the sensational kind instituted by Northcliffe. 'C.P. would never have agreed to that,' people would say, shaking their heads, and recalling his refusal to allow racing news, or liquor advertising, or the publicising of the Irish Sweep in *The Guardian*. Why, in the early days, he even, it seems, on one occasion turned down a full-page advertisement for corsets, worth £260, because it showed a picture of a lady wearing the advertised product. What was conveniently forgotten was that *The Guardian* subsisted on the profits of its sister-paper, the *Manchester Evening News* (does, indeed, to this day), in whose columns racing, the Irish Sweep, liquor advertising and uncorseted bosoms got the fullest play. Every now and again someone would write in to the effect that the malicious rumour was circulating in Manchester that the great C. P. Scott had some connection with that odious sheet the *Manchester Evening News*, and might this lie please be nailed. Such letters were put on C.P.'s desk, whence they disappeared without trace. Northcliffe is alleged to have undertaken a special pilgrimage to Manchester to salute Scott as the man who had uniquely shown that truth could be made to pay. The encounter between them must have been interesting, revealing, I should imagine, that they had more in common than might superficially be supposed. If Scott had made truth pay, a lot of his truth was lies; whereas Northcliffe, in making his lies pay, sometimes told the truth. So the contest in a way evened out.

When Ted finally took over, he could not bring himself to move into his father's office and sit in his chair. I found this somehow a sombre circumstance, as boding ill for his editorship. Actually, C.P.'s office never was occupied by anyone else; when the Cross Street premises were finally evacuated in August, 1970, having been sold for demolition, it was still empty, and just as when he had last used it. Now it has finally gone, along with the whole building, and the legend of C.P. with it. The first months under Ted's editorship were among the pleasantest I have

ever spent on the staff of a newspaper. We got on very well together; he had one of those receptive minds, always ready to discuss anything and consider anything, which made working under him pleasurable. No doubt I liked it the better because he tended to lean more on me than anyone else. I even got an unsolicited pay rise; something very unusual, if not unique, on *The Guardian*. It came about because I happened to remark, unthinkingly, that with a wife and child I didn't pay any income tax. This led Ted – an expert on such matters – to look up what I was paid, and increase it quite substantially. He had to a high degree the virtue I most admire, perhaps because I so notably lack it, and, however hard I try, even now fail so miserably in my efforts to acquire it – a true humility. This was combined with a passionate honesty; a reaction, I daresay, to his father's self-centredness masquerading as disinterestedness. There are few pleasanter things in life than the companionship of a totally honest mind, which is what Ted had. This may have accounted for a certain fixed melancholy in his disposition; *The Guardian* was no place for mental honesty. An honest mind was as out of place there as a virgin in the pages of Casanova or a pregnancy in D. H. Lawrence's.

In April following his father's death Ted decided to go to the Lakes with his son Dick for some sailing. I drove up with them on the Friday evening. He had just bought a new Vauxhall car (I remember the grooves along the bonnet), and was in a particularly cheerful mood. I was to stay with some friends at Sawrey – the Spences – for the Friday and Saturday nights, returning to Manchester on Sunday because I was working that day. Ted dined with us on the Saturday evening; we all laughed a lot, and it was altogether a carefree, happy occasion. The next morning Mrs Spence drove me to Windermere, where I caught a train back to Manchester. Sunday afternoon on any newspaper is fairly drear, and *The Guardian* was no exception. News comes in laggardly, mostly from correspondents with hangovers; one turns over the Sunday papers listlessly, looking with jaundiced eyes at stories which already seem about a thousand years old. Even the arrangements for getting tea at one's desk usually don't function. I was toying with the notion of proposing yet another leader on a project for an All-India Self-Governing Federation then under consideration, when I was called to the telephone. It was Mrs Spence to tell me that Ted and Dick had been involved in a sailing accident on Lake Windermere, and that Dick had been rescued but Ted was drowned. I found some difficulty in registering what she had said; bad news transmitted on the telephone is particularly bleak and unconvincing. 'You mean it's all over; that Ted is . . .' 'Yes,' she said, in a

flat definitive voice. The time was round about five o'clock, and I realised that this would mean a crisis in the office. The first thing to do was to tell Crozier. I went into his room, and he looked up expecting me to propose a subject; I felt that the very words were shaping themselves with which he'd manage, as was his way when he was in the chair, to deflate whatever I suggested, and make it seem dubious and not worth doing. Instead, I just blurted out: 'Ted's dead!' The effect on him was instantaneous and extraordinary; I saw, or thought I saw – the impression was very strong – some strips of bright yellow come into the scarlet of his face. When he had collected himself, he asked me if I was sure. I said I was, and gave him Mrs Spence's telephone number so that he could speak to her himself. Then I went back to my room, understanding that Crozier would have to get into touch with John Scott, Ted's brother, who was the paper's business manager, and so not in the office on a Sunday evening.

It was the first time I'd felt this particular sort of shock; a numbing sense of utter desolation and lostness. I telephoned to Kitty to tell her; whenever anything happens to me, good or bad, anywhere in the world, my first impulse is to find her and tell her. She has that wonderful capacity for being neither unduly alarmed nor unkindly calm; above all not *curious*; just calm and near, and conveying without saying anything her total readiness to take any shock and share any burden. A kind of fathomless, unquestioning sympathy and support. After speaking to Kitty I just sat doing nothing; it was impossible to even think of tackling the All-India Self-Governing Federation. Then Crozier came into my room and asked me to write Ted's obituary; it seemed that nothing whatever had been done about it, and there were no cuttings. I rather fatuously asked Crozier how long it should be. It was the kind of question he was easiest with, but in this particular case he just shrugged and left me to it. Time was pressing for the first edition, and I got to work, sending the copy into Crozier sheet by sheet as I did it. All I had to help me with facts and dates was Ted's *Who's Who* entry. Crozier passed it all without altering a word – the last time this was to happen to anything I wrote for *The Guardian* until quite recently, when I did a leader-page article at the request of the present editor, Alistair Hetherington. When I came to Ted's editorship, I described with unnecessary gloating how he had drastically and courageously reversed the position first taken by the paper about the formation of MacDonald's National Government. As I worked on, I was aware of Crozier standing in the doorway of my room holding that particular sheet in his hand. He was looking dis-

tressed, and said he thought I had over-stressed the change in the paper's attitude. Without stopping typing, I said I left it to him to make any changes he considered desirable. Actually, he didn't make any changes, and nor did I. The episode, which I consider to be very discreditable, if not contemptible, on my part, sealed the hostility between us.

Otherwise, the obituary came out quite well, and I received a congratulatory letter about it from J. L. Hammond, who wrote the official life of C.P. While writing it, and after, the thought had been in my mind that somehow Ted's death was connected with his father's. People die when the momentum of their lives is spent, and C.P. had, as it were, suffocated Ted; like an old tree keeping the sun, taking all the goodness of the soil, and thereby precluding an offshoot from growing and thriving. When at last the old tree died, the other withered from the unaccustomed light and sustenance instead of burgeoning. This explained, as I thought, Ted's reluctance to sit in his father's chair; he was not strong enough to be him, and the long years of subservience prevented him from being himself. By the time he took over, he had no self to be. I felt, too, that Ted was a victim of the paper itself, succumbing where others had been maimed and stunted; fed to the rotaries, like our leaders. I tried to work all this out in a novel called *Picture Palace* about a liberal newspaper in a North country town. When it had already been sent out for review, *The Guardian* got an injunction and threatened legal proceedings, in consequence of which it was withdrawn and suppressed. The particular passage to which exception was taken described the dependence of a newspaper as high-minded as *The Guardian* on a stable companion as low-minded as the *Manchester Evening News*; a relationship I compared to someone living off the immoral earnings of his daughter. Subsequent efforts to get the novel published came to nothing; *The Guardian*'s passionate advocacy of freedom of publication did not extend to books about itself.

In the weeks that followed Ted's death my position in the office was rather curious. Crozier continued to edit the paper, and was in due course confirmed as Ted's successor, but John Scott had told him that as far as possible he should continue to follow the guidelines laid down by Ted, and that I, having been closest to Ted, was the best person to advise him on this. So for a while I was a kind of assistant editor. Crozier would come awkwardly into my room – I never went into his if I could possibly avoid it – and go through the motions of discussing with me points of policy and the choice of leaders. I suppose if I had been ambitious in that sort of way, I could have pressed home my advantage

and got into the line of succession on the paper. Actually, I had no interest in anything of the kind; the thought of working under or with Crozier was hateful to me, and anyway I was sick to death of liberalism; of drawing together with moderate men of all shades of opinion. All I wanted to do was to kick them in the teeth and be gone. This suited Crozier perfectly, and for my part, I have never found any difficulty in leaving a job, or in disengaging myself while nominally still in it.

To heighten my mood, there was the more or less total collapse of the Labour Party in the 1932 Doctor's Mandate election, which returned MacDonald and his Tory allies to power with an immense majority. My father, of course, lost his seat at Romford. I spent the last two days of the election campaign with him. It was obvious that the tide was flowing strongly against us, but he refused to succumb to low spirits, and kept up the fight to the very last moment. We went prowling the streets together trying to rally our supporters, until the polling booths closed. It was a hopeless task; hoarse-voiced, exhausted, my father still could not bring himself to pass a street corner without addressing a non-existent meeting: 'Ladies and Gentlemen...' Only a few ribald children gathered round him. It carried my mind back to those magical Surrey Street meetings, and the joke about the national debt which ought to be His Majesty's. Now, suddenly, he seemed very old and tired; no more that prophetic figure against the skyline, but shrivelled and bent. In his case, too, a storm in the world and a whirlwind had carried him and his work away. We desisted at last and repaired to a nearby committee room; the same empty shop, the same posters and slogans, the same elderly lady helpers with grey dishevelled hair and drooping cigarettes; the same cups of strong tea, the same smell of stationery, ink and gum. They affected still to be confident of victory, but we knew we had lost – as, indeed, we had, by a huge turnover of votes. It was my father's last election; the end of the road to that promised land I had so often rejoiced in on Saturday nights, securely tucked away in the tall red cosy corner in our South Croydon sitting-room.

I decided on an impulse to drive back straight away to Manchester; through the foggy night, everything muffled and misty, past the slag-heaps and the furnaces; leaving Birmingham behind me, then the Potteries, dimly glowing clusters of yellow lights that seemed to be floating on banks of cloud; across wild moorland, with no sign of a fellow-human or a human habitation. No stars, no anything; only the wind screeching and, maybe, an owl hooting, a voice wailing. Heartland of the industrial North, once pulsating with life and energy; the world's

workshop and arsenal, now sleeping under its eiderdown of mist. Or dead? When the day came, the queues would form at the Labour Exchanges, the groups gather at street corners to while away an empty day; the old red-brick factories with a hint of the chapel in their structure, standing idle and empty, their obsolete machines rusting from disuse. By the time I got to Manchester dawn was just dimly breaking; in Cross Street nothing stirring, the last edition recording MacDonald's great triumph already on its way. Would it ever revive, this birthplace of twentieth-century prosperity, this cradle of the affluent society, this technological kindergarten where the first faltering steps to an everlastingly expanding Gross National Product were taken, this beginning of the rainbow at whose end lay buried the crock of gold, the green stick, holding the secret of perpetual happiness for everyone? I thought not; it was a falling citadel, at the mercy of any marauder; the piled up debris of a greedy past, inhabited by ghosts demanding rights that were already lost and their fair share of wealth already squandered. I had resolved to go to where I thought a new age was coming to pass; to Moscow and the future of mankind. Crozier was all too ready to expedite my going; *The Guardian's* Moscow correspondent, William Henry Chamberlin, was going back to America for a lengthy stay, and I could take his place. So it was arranged.

Kitty had gone to stay with her parents in Vevey, in one of those hotels overlooking the Lake of Geneva from whose terrace Mrs Dobbs could continue to add to her collection of paintings of the Castle of Chillon. I joined her there for a short holiday before we left for Moscow. Our son was already placed at a school in Windermere where he was to stay until we were settled in Moscow and could fetch him over. It was an arrangement hateful at the time, and seems even more hateful in retrospect. On the Channel boat I ran into Arthur Henderson who had been MacDonald's Foreign Secretary. Refusing to follow him into the National Government, he had lost his seat in the recent General Election, and was now on his way to preside over the opening session of the Disarmament Conference in Geneva, having been elected President on Briand's recommendation before the electoral debacle. A former Liberal Party agent, a lay preacher, an eminently respectable figure wearing a bowler hat, a decent overcoat and suit, his face was full of woe and bewilderment. We walked up and down the deck together, and every now and again he paused, as though collecting his thoughts; took off his bowler and muttered more to himself than to me: 'The unemployed in Burnley voted against me!' It seemed like a perfect finale to all our re-

volutionary postures and hopes; our renderings of 'The Red Flag' and the 'Internationale', the canvassing, the addressing and the licking, the speaking and the cheering. All ending in one broken-hearted, bewildered little man taking off his bowler hat on a Channel steamer on his way to Geneva, as he remembered once again that the unemployed in Burnley had voted Tory.

5 *Who Whom?*

I no longer wished for a better world, because I was thinking of the
whole of creation, and in the light of this clearer discernment I had
come to see that, though the higher things are better than the lower,
the sum of all creation is better than the higher things alone.

– St Augustine

KITTY AND I were confident that going to Russia would prove to be a
definitive step, a final adventure. Our plan was, as soon as we were settled,
to fetch our son over and live there for evermore. We wanted him, we
told everyone with great emphasis, to grow up in a sane world with a
future instead of in our crazy run-down one with only a past. What we
were leaving behind, we felt, was derelict, moribund. A preposterous
Ramsay MacDonald grimacing and posturing, contemptuously retained
in office by his political adversaries for a little while longer so as to hold
up to ridicule everything the political movement which made him Prime
Minister in the first place, had ever stood for or aspired after. The de-
pression hanging like a dark cloud over the industrial North, Lancashire
especially; *The Guardian* under Crozier abysmally second-rate and flat;
another war looming, which would surely come, and complete the moral
and material destruction of the previous one. Where we were going, we
assured ourselves and one another, there was hope and exhilaration.
It was the wave of the future – a phrase even then current.

Feeling so, we sold off pretty well everything we had, making, as it
were, a bonfire of all our bourgeois trappings; my dinner-jacket, for
instance, and Kitty's only long dress, as well as some little trinkets and
oddments, and most of our books, which we considered to be bourgeois
literature of no relevance in a Workers' State. We even wound up our
bank account, taking what money we had – some two hundred pounds,
as I recall – in traveller's cheques. What possible use would a bank
account be in a country where bankers, along with industrialists, land-

lords and priests, had all been eliminated? I took particular pleasure in jettisoning our marriage lines, and my ridiculous B.A. hood and certificate; these being also, in my eyes, badges of bourgeois servitude, now to be discarded for ever. We were fully prepared to exchange our British passports for Soviet ones; indeed, we were looking forward to making the exchange. Nor did I have any anxiety about going off *The Guardian*'s pay-roll and becoming dependent on freelance earnings; the arrangement Crozier had proposed. The connection with the paper would only be useful while I was fixing myself up with a job and somewhere to live in the USSR; then, I looked forward to forgetting *The Guardian*'s very existence. Finally, to my great delight, Kitty was pregnant again, so that our next child would be born a Soviet citizen. It all seemed wonderful.

One last thing remained to be done; before sailing for Leningrad, we felt we must pay a farewell visit to Passfield to receive the blessing of the venerable couple under whose sponsorship we were venturing into the New Civilisation they had proclaimed. For us, it was the laying on of hands. 'Sidney and I,' Mrs Webb had told me, 'have become ikons in the Soviet Union.' Kitty and I hoped to participate in this sanctity they had acquired by virtue of the fact that Lenin, while a political prisoner in Siberia, had translated their *The Theory and Practice of Trade Unionism* into Russian – an example of the quality of boredom being twice blessed.

Everything at Passfield was just the same. Webb, complacently stroking his goatee beard, explained how under capitalism there might be as many as thirty or more varieties of fountain pen, whereas in the USSR we should find but one. A much more satisfactory arrangement. As he made the point, his bulbous eyes positively glowed behind the pince-nez. She, fluttering her hands like a mesmerist to shut him up, spoke about Man as consumer and Man as producer, and how under Socialism ever the twain should meet. He was seemingly delighted by the notion of reducing a plethora of pens to a single one, but she, it seemed to me, had no real interest in consuming and producing Man, and only addressed herself to the theme with the distracted over-emphasis of a sceptical Monsignor dispensing the Blessed Sacraments.

The Soviet Ambassador, Sokolnikov, and his lady came to luncheon on the Saturday, arriving in a sleek black limousine driven by an Embassy chauffeur, he doubtless being, as I came to realise later, the GPU policeman in attendance. At the time, I just marvelled at how, as my mother would have put it, wonderfully superior he was, and

wondered how he would make out with the two Scottish maids, accustomed, as they were, to capitalist subservience. Actually, I don't believe he addressed a single word to them, but just sat in the car, a still, inscrutable figure, until the time came to depart.

Sokolnikov was a pasty-faced, uneasy looking man. At one point he had been concerned with stabilising the rouble, which greatly appealed to Webb, who tried, as far as I could judge without much success, to pump him on Soviet banking. He clearly hoped to hear that the same simplification prevailed in distributing cash in the USSR as in distributing fountain pens. An important factor in the admiration of the Webbs and Shaw for the Soviet régime was what they considered to be its financial soundness and rectitude. Shaw was always going on about its budgetary surpluses in a world of deficit accounting, and the Webbs actually held some Soviet Government stock on which, they would complacently observe, the ten per cent interest was punctually paid. How far this stock represented a negotiable asset when they died, only their heirs, the Passfield Trust, and the governors of the London School of Economics, know; but it is possible to guess.

Mme Sokolnikova was livelier altogether than her spouse; a large ebullient woman, dark and hairy, who, had she been English, might well have espoused the cause of family planning, and perhaps married a clergyman. If American, I see her more as a popular novelist in the style of Mrs Parkinson Keyes; or maybe an anthropologist exploring the sexual ways of Papuans in the manner of Margaret Mead. In the circumstances of our meeting, I found her rather attractive; there is, I fear, an incipient gigolo in my make-up, and I have been conscious occasionally of an unseemly taste for public ladies like millionairesses, and female racing-motorists, politicians, and champion show-jumpers. Amy Johnson's rusty voice took my fancy in her flying days, as did Eva Peron, but not, I am happy to say, La Passionaria or the Duchess of Windsor. Mme Sokolnikova had already had one of her books – a collection of profiles of revolutionary women, including Charlotte Corday – published in England, which, by a fortunate chance, I had read and reviewed in favourable terms in *The Guardian*. It was arranged that Kitty and I should call on the Sokolnikovs in Moscow, whither they were shortly returning, to be succeeded in London by Maisky, one of those indomitable survivors the Soviet régime throws up from time to time (Ilya Ehrenburg was another), who somehow managed to survive despite all the perils and dangers of life under Stalin. By writing occasional letters to *The Times* in support of the latest version of Party

orthodoxy, Maisky even continues to have some sort of public existence, unlike more important figures like Molotov and Malenkov who, when they fall from power, get obliterated.

We did go and see the Sokolnikovs at their flat in Moscow. The Purges were looming, and there had been rumours of his arrest. The poor fellow looked very nervous and shifty, and there was a noticeable greenish tinge in his sallow face. He kept glancing anxiously over his shoulder as though at some invisible intruder. With one of the most mirthless smiles I have ever seen, he remarked over tea that, if the capitalist press was to be believed, he was languishing in Lubianka Prison. Did he look like it? he asked, getting his teeth into a chocolate eclair. Alas, he did, and I was not surprised to hear, in due course, that he had been liquidated, not even being considered important enough for rehabilitation when the climate of opinion changed under Khrushchev. She, too, disappeared for a twenty years' sentence, but to everyone's amazement reappeared, to resume her career as a woman-of-letters. Survival would seem to be the single enduring gift we humans possess, especially among the female of the species; providing the only sure foundation for Women's Lib.

After luncheon, we were joined in the course of the afternoon by Sir Stafford Cripps, another member of the Potter clan, accompanied by the chairman of his constituency (Bristol East) Labour Party, whose name Mrs Webb made little effort to discover. There was also present a grey-haired nondescript lady in sackcloth and gold chains from the Fabian Research Bureau. She must have had more audacity than her appearance suggested because she took one of Mrs Webb's herbal cigarettes and smoked it – something I had never before seen anyone do. As usual, Mrs Webb disposed us about the room like a cricket captain arranging his field, and then the conversation got under way. We began with participatory democracy, which, the Webbs insisted, was perfectly exemplified in the system of representation laid down in the Soviet Constitution. As they elaborated upon this theme, I could see that Sokolnikov was trying to say something; his lips were moving and his hands gripping the sides of his chair. By the time he managed to get the words out against the Webbs' duet – like a muted trombone and a particularly shrill flute – he was understood to say that his country made no bones about being a . . . Even then he could not bring himself to say it in English. So he tried it in French . . . a *dictature*. The word caused a stir even in French; Webb paused in mid-sentence, and then changed direction, going on to point out that, like the Roman Catholic Church,

the Soviet system was hierarchical. This parallel with the Church, equating Commissars in the Politbureau with Cardinals in the Consistory, got over any awkwardness the Ambassador's hasty remark might have occasioned.

Cripps looked delighted; he stroked his jaw as counsel do when making an advantageous point in court. *Dictature* or dictatorship, it was all one to him. How is it, Dr Johnson asked, in *Taxation no Tyranny*, that we hear the loudest yelps for liberty coming from the drivers of slaves? How indeed? One might equally well ask how it is that those with the greatest aptitude for applauding the arbitrary exercise of power are most insistent in proclaiming the virtues of freedom. Cripps went on to explain that social democracy was now discredited, that what was needed was a revolutionary dictatorship enabling the workers to take over. Mrs Webb did not fancy being lectured by a nephew, especially in terms that, if only by implication, put her among the despised Social Democrats, rather than with the proletarian elect, and anyway suggested that her ideas were behind the times. Even so, Cripps was in the category of being 'a very clever young man', and earned enough at the bar to qualify for equal billing with her successful brothers-in-law. So she left him unrebuked, and there the matter rested. Sokolnikov, having made his point about the *Dictature*, relapsed into silence, and the Webbs turned their attention to Consumers' Co-operatives, which ensured, they intoned, that the interests of the consumer were adequately safeguarded as against those of the producer and the State. Cripps scarcely seemed to be listening; his thoughts were doubtless far away – on a barricade, Red Flag in hand, leading the oppressed to revolution and freedom. Stafford Egalité.

The Sokolnikovs left in the early evening; Cripps and his local party chairman shortly afterwards. Webb soon began to doze noisily in his chair, fulfilling Mrs Webb's favourite dictum about him: 'Sidney snores!' She sat warming her hands at the fire, holding them out as though warding someone or something off. 'It's true,' she said suddenly, *à propos* of nothing, 'that in the USSR people *disappear*.' She accentuated the word, showing her teeth as she did so. Clearly, she would have been well content to promote the disappearance of tiresome people in the asme expeditious way, with no questions asked. Some of the more difficult and obscurantist figures in local government, for instance. And among trade union leaders, no lack of candidates. Yes, people *disappeared*. She looked very unearthly just then, with her white hair and white face. Very unsubstantial. It was probably, I reflected, my positively last glimpse of

her and of bourgeois life; and I wanted to fix the scene in my mind so that I should never forget it. Webb asleep in his arm-chair, grunting occasionally; the glowing fire, the sofa, the little tables and knick-knacks and photographs in silver frames. The warmth, the snugness; the wonderful insulation from what is harsh and bitter and inexorable. Those two Scottish maids sitting by *their* fire and in their own arm-chairs, but ready at any moment to spring into action, and make a hot drink or prepare a hot water-bottle. Mrs Webb hovering over it all, the genie escaped from the bottle; pronouncing a doom – that in the USSR people *disappeared*, as would we all, along with that room, that whole way of life. Set, scenery, actors and props, all due for disappearance.

On the Sunday morning the Webbs came to the front door to see us off. It was an unusual attention; except in the case of particularly important visitors, adieus took place in the sitting-room. This was a special occasion; we were going to the USSR where they were ikons. Standing side by side, she looked ridiculously tall and thin, and he squat, almost a dwarf. As the ancient limousine lurched forward to take us to the station, they waved in unison. Standing behind them, also discreetly waving, we could see the two Scottish maids. So, from this warm, snug bourgeois nest we took off on our migratory flight, saying to ourselves with the monkish author of *The Cloud of Unknowing*: 'Look now forwards, and let the backwards be.'

Sailing down the Thames again, this time with Kitty beside me, in the Soviet ship *Kooperatsia*, there was the same sweet music I remembered from when I set sail for India – a prow piercing the water; a ship's stealthily onward push as it followed its determined course. The sweet music of departure. This time I was on my way, not to tired imperial glory, but to the veritable future of mankind. Our ship's Red Flag flying proudly at the very heart of London; within sight of Westminster and Honourable Members on their terrace; within sound of their division bell and Big Ben; the Unholy City, gathered by the Thames, harbouring, without knowing it, this crimson portent of the wrath to come.

Kitty and I waited on deck as long as there was anything to see, and then explored the ship. Somehow, we expected it to be different from other ships, but apart from having a picture of Lenin and Stalin in the dining saloon where a P & O boat would have had one of King George V and Queen Mary, it seemed in no way peculiar. I even noticed that the ship's engines had been made in Glasgow. It was, in fact, a pre-Revolution ship that had been taken over by the Soviet authorities and re-

named. Our cabin was deep in the bowels; we had booked in the cheapest category, for economy's sake, and also because it seemed appropriate. The more privileged passengers in the upper regions consisted mostly of a party of miscellaneous Leftist intellectuals, or, as they were later to be called, Fellow-Travellers, on their way to see for themselves what the world's first Workers' State was really like. They recalled lectures in Croydon with my father in the chair, and visits to our house afterwards. Several were already well on the way to becoming important personages; beneficiaries of the new enlightenment, honoured, comfortably off even; in due course, persistent pundits of the air. The *Kooperatsia* echoed with their resonant, donnish-demagogic voices; their tweedy suits and coloured ties were everywhere. They had the shambling gait, the roving eye, the air of being the elect or chosen ones, which I had come to associate with those who felt they knew the answers, and could steer us aright to peace, prosperity and the everlasting brotherhood of man.

On their way to the USSR they were in a festive mood; like a cup-tie party on their way to a match, equipped with rattles, coloured scarves and favours. Each of them harbouring in his mind some special hope; of meeting Stalin, or, alternatively, of falling in with a Komsomolka, sparkling eyed, red scarf and jet black hair, dancing the *carmagnole*; above all, with very enlightened views on sex, and free and easy ways. In any case, of equipping themselves with special, authoritative knowledge which would enable them to embellish their articles and lectures, and shut up hecklers with lordly data like: Dairy produce increased last year in the Ukraine by X per cent; slightly less in White Russia, but still well above the national average of Y per cent. Or: article PQR of the Criminal Code clearly states . . . Oh, to be in Russia, now that Stalin's there.

In their dealings with the crew and the stewards they were punctilious in cultivating an egalitarian attitude; the word 'comrade' was often on their lips. What a relief it was, they seemed to be saying, not to have to cope with obsequiousness and servility on the part of the lower orders! In this new society, as most of them would shortly be tapping out on their typewriters, 'there was an agreeable absence of cap-touching. One noticed a certain confident bearing among working men and women; a new social equality divorced from a worship and evaluation of success in money terms, and from deference to the man who has won a financial position above his fellows and shows it in his habits and dress and bearing . . .'

In order to fit in with this social climate it was obviously necessary to

eschew tips, which anyway, we were given to understand, were considered gross and ill-mannered, and, especially to the younger Soviet citizens, nurtured in the régime, quite inadmissible, if not incomprehensible. To settle the matter a meeting of passengers was called, presided over by one of the intellectuals with a particularly booming voice, at which it was decided that the best procedure would be to make a collection for the crew and officers, and to spend it on books for the ship's library. This was explained to the chief steward, who, as it seemed to me, failed to kindle at the suggestion. Perhaps he dreaded, not without reason, that some at least of the books provided would be works by the present company. To clinch the matter, and to show our good will and high spirits, it was further decided to present a pageant or charade for the diversion of the crew. The subject chosen was the Genesis story of the creation, with the booming intellectual as God, and a Montessori teacher from Leeds as the serpent. Such a theme, it was calculated, would conform with the anti-religious sentiments of our audience, and show them that, however bourgeois we might seem outwardly, at heart we were as proletarian and anti-religious as they were.

When it came to the night, the performance seemed to please the players better than the audience, who for the most part sat woodenly in their seats, more bewildered than amused. God, it must be admitted, was somewhat elephantine in his antics; the serpent lacking in the deadly attractiveness which the Genesis original must be supposed to have possessed. It proved to be a *mea culpa* which quite failed to register with those for whose edification it had been intended; an unheeded act of abasement. The crew retaliated by offering a musical evening at which *Stenka Razin* and *Ochi Chornye* were sung; two songs that were to become all too familiar in the months ahead. One of the sorrows of life for a western journalist or diplomat in the USSR was the enormous repetitiveness of everything. Thus, there were veterans who had been forced to sit through *Swan Lake* on thirty or more ceremonial occasions. I myself sat through it five times; it seemed like fifty.

These fellow-passengers provided my first experience of the progressive elite from all over the world who attached themselves to the Soviet régime, resolved to believe anything they were told by its spokesmen. For the most part, they were academics and writers – the clerks of Julien Benda's *La Trahison des clercs*; all upholders of progressive causes and members of progressive organisations, constituting a sort of Brechtian ribald chorus in the drama of the twentieth century. Ready at any moment to rush on to the stage, cheering and gesticulating. The fall

guys of history; a western version of the devotees of Krishna who throw themselves under the wheels of the great Juggernaut. I was to speculate endlessly about them, rail against their credulities and imbecilities, ridicule their absurdities and denounce their servility before the naked-ness of Soviet power. The more so because I knew inwardly that I was one of them; in my heart, too, the same death-wish.

It was perhaps because such thoughts had already begun to occur to me, or, more probably, because of a certain drabness in the ship itself and in the crew, an air of oppression which seemed to hang over it and them, that somehow or other I felt less confident than I had about the Soviet régime as an answer to my own and society's problems. As we approached Leningrad my excitement at the thought of actually landing, and putting to the test all my hopes, was tinged with apprehension. This was intensified by an incident while we were at Hamburg, where we put in for a day to take on some cargo. I was loafing about on deck as the time of departure drew near when I noticed three men, arm in arm, coming up the gangway. The middle one was the ship's doctor, whose face I knew, having observed it at times rather closely as being somehow like Chekhov's. With the same kind of sparse beard, and loose, whim-sical, weak mouth; even with the same kind of spectacles fastened on the end of his long nose, and thin cigar drooping from his lips, the ash powdering his beard. There was also the fact that he was different from the crew, who all had what I came to recognise as Soviet faces; as characteristic as the equivalent American ones – rather grey and im-mobile, like lumps of stone on which features had been drawn, rather than living flesh. The doctor's face was, on the other hand, mobile and European, and would have passed unnoticed in any café in Paris or Brussels or London.

On this occasion he was obviously hopelessly drunk; his head lolled, his eyes were dead, his legs scarcely touched the ground. It was clear that without the support of his two companions he would have fallen down. They held him firmly; not tenderly, or in a comradely way, more in the manner of policemen. I had noticed them about the ship, too, as seeming not to be ordinary seamen or officers; yet obviously exercising authority. Like the Sokolnikovs' chauffeur, they were doubtless GPU men, keeping an eye on everyone's orthodoxy and correct Soviet behaviour. It seemed to me that once they had got the doctor to his berth things might go ill with him. In any case, the incident depressed me out of all proportion to its ostensible importance. I priggishly felt that Soviet ships' doctors should not go ashore and get drunk like capitalist ones. Also, there was

something Kafka-esque about the stance and relationship of the three of them which struck me as sinister; and as conflicting with the happier relationship between man and man over which we had so often cooed together at Passfield.

I had the feeling that landing at Leningrad should be different from landing anywhere else; more like the arrival of Bunyan's Pilgrim at the Heavenly City, with trumpets blowing, and shining ones waiting to welcome him. Actually, it was just like arriving anywhere; passports suspiciously examined, bags all opened and their contents gone over; then a final check to make sure that everything was in order. The custodians of entry and exit seem alike in every country and on every frontier. All the same, it was a wonderful feeling to be through the controls at last and at large in the USSR. Something I had dreamed about and longed for, and now at last it had come to pass.

Leningrad seemed a battered, shabby place, with crumbling stucco, chipped pillars, cracked masonry, paintwork in sore need of renovation; yet nonetheless somehow beautiful in the sparkling sunshine. In the streets few vehicles, on the pavement grey anonymous crowds padding endlessly along; the one constant factor throughout the USSR. I had a feeling that the place must have been lately bombarded, with only a bright shell remaining; which doubtless explains why the memory of my first glimpse of Leningrad came so vividly into my mind during the Blitz in London. Likewise, going into New York on just such a glittering day, and getting my first glimpse of the city across the Triboro Bridge, its skyscrapers, too, looked like the bombed out remains of once stately buildings arbitrarily arranged to be some weird, monstrous, luminous Stonehenge. It recalled what Brecht wrote: 'Long before the bombers appeared our cities were already uninhabitable . . . While we were still walking in our still upright cities our women were widows and our children orphans.'

In Moscow we took up our quarters in the Nova Moskovkaya Hotel, newly built for Intourists who came and went all the time. Quite often hanging about the lobby was a man named Wicksteed, vaguely known to Kitty from her Bedales schooldays. He was a Walt Whitmanesque figure, in a corduroy suit, with a high colour, an untidy beard, watery eyes, and wearing sandals, who had, it seemed, steered a course from Blake's Prophetic Books to Edward Carpenter's *Towards Democracy*, taking in Havelock Ellis and Housman (Laurence rather than A.E.) on the way, and casting many a sympathetic backwards glance in the direction of William Morris and even Ruskin. *Towards Democracy* turned

out to be, as far as he was concerned, *Towards Moscow,* and there he
stayed, sometimes with a burly Red Army soldier in tow; acting as a
sort of unofficial tourist guide, glad to get a meal in the hotel restaurant
and a drink or two in the hotel bar by way of remuneration. A bourgeois
bum in Proletaria – spare a kopek, comrade! Broken down and pathetic,
vodka-smelling, far from his native habitat of PEN Club meetings within
sound of Sloane Square, and there's wind on the Hampstead Heath,
brother; but still more sympathetic to me than the booming intellectual
playing God and the Montessori serpent.

In order to start working as *Guardian* correspondent it was necessary
to establish contact with the Press Department of the Soviet Foreign
Office, housed, it turned out, in ornate gilt and red plush quarters un-
changed from pre-Revolution days; more reminiscent in décor of the
Egyptian University, or even the Vatican, than of a Workers' State as I
had envisaged it. After a wait, I was shown into the office of the head of
the Department, a youngish-looking man named Oumansky with
crinkly hair and a lot of gold teeth. He later became Soviet Ambassador
in Washington, and was killed in an air crash on his way to Mexico, to
the undisguised joy of pretty well everyone who had worked as a news-
paper correspondent in Moscow. He greeted me affably, complimented
me on my connection with the Webbs who, he said, were held in great
honour in the USSR, and spoke of *The Guardian* in the highest terms as
being the newspaper above all others in the capitalist world which gave
a true and fair picture of Soviet conditions and achievements. He felt
sure I would maintain and enhance this reputation, and looked forward
to our continuing collaboration. The gold teeth gleamed as he summoned
up a toothy smile.

Being a newspaper correspondent in Moscow, I found, was, in itself,
easy enough. The Soviet press was the only source of news; nothing
happened or was said until it was reported in the newspapers. So, all I
had to do was to go through the papers, pick out any item that might be
interesting to readers of the *Guardian,* dish it up in a suitable form, get it
passed by the censor at the Press Department, and hand it in at the
telegraph office for dispatch. One might, if in a conscientious mood,
embellish the item a little with back references or some extra statistics,
easily procured from the Commercial Attaché at the British Embassy,
where also the Press was meticulously gone through and analysed. Or
perhaps, fancifully, sow in a little local colour, usually unobjectionable to
the censor. Blow it up a little, or render it down a little according to the
exigencies of the new situation. The original item itself was almost

certainly untrue or grotesquely distorted. One's own deviations, there-
fore, seemed to matter little; only amounting to further falsifying what
was already false.

This bizarre fantasy was very costly and elaborate and earnestly
promoted. Something gets published in *Pravda* (meaning Truth); say,
that the Soviet Union has had a bumper wheat harvest – so many poods
per hectare. (It is always preferable to use foreign measures where
possible.) There is no means of checking; the Press Department men
don't know, and anyone who does is far, far removed from the attentions
of foreign journalists. Soviet statistics have always been almost entirely
fanciful, though not the less seriously regarded for that. When the
Germans occupied Kiev in the 1939–45 war they got hold of a master
Five-Year Plan, showing what had really been produced and where.
Needless to say, it was quite different from the published figures. This
in no way affected credulity about such figures subsequently, as put out
in Russia, or even in China; any more than the repeated errors of public
opinion polls affect the seriousness with which they are received. Truly,
those who take to statistics will perish by statistics.

So we take the bumper harvest as having happened. The more
ebullient drum it up a little – 'Down in the Ukraine husky girls and
women hoisting wheat . . . Village markets flowing with eggs, fruit,
poultry, vegetables, milk and butter at prices far lower than in Mos-
cow . . .' The more sedate tone it down a little – 'The figure should be
received with some caution in the light of present Soviet imports of
grain, but without any doubt the collectivisation policy is beginning to
pay off . . .' In any case, a statistic has been planted, and makes its
appearance in tables, graphs, learned discourses, becoming part of the
world's wisdom. In the beginning was the Lie, and the Lie was made
news and dwelt among us, graceless and false.

I have a pile of the blacks of some of the messages I sent to *The
Guardian* from Moscow:

DISCOVERY ANNOUNCED BY OGPU OF COUNTER REVOLU-
TIONARY ORGANISATION IN AGRICULTURE AND STATE FARM
COMMISSARIATS PARTICULARLY IN UKRAINE NORTH CAUCA-
SUS AND WHITE RUSSIA STOP NEWSPAPER REPORT SAYS
ORGANISATION CONSISTED MOSTLY EXBOURGEOIS STATE
OFFICIALS COLON MAJORITY CONFESSED GUILTY SABOTAGE
WITH VIEW UNDERMINING SOVIET AGRICULTURAL ECONOMY
AND SPREADING FAMINE . . .

FULL DETAILS 1933 ECONOMIC PROGRAMME AND BUDGET

PUBLISHED TO-DAY AS APPROVED CENTRAL EXECUTIVE COM-
MITTEE STOP IN INDUSTRY GENERALLY GROSS INCREASE ON
LAST YEAR PRODUCTION SIXTEEN POINT FIVE PER CENT
COLON ALLOCATION THREE MILLIARD ROUBLES TRANSPORT
DEVELOPMENT AND TWO MILLIARDS AND HALF SOCIAL SER-
VICES AND HOUSING COLON STATE FARM OUTPUT PRECISELY
ESTIMATED DASH FOR INSTANCE MILLION HUNDRED AND
FIFTY THOUSAND PIGS THIS YEAR STOP ESTIMATED
REVENUE THIRTY FIVE MILLIARDS AND EXPENDITURE THIRTY
THREE MILLIARDS OF WHICH TWO AND QUARTER MILLIARDS
ON FIGHTING SERVICES . . .

To the last figure for military expenditure I added in brackets
SUGGEST TELLING THIS MARINES. The significance of the addition
escaped the censor's eye; whether it caught that of *The Guardian* chief
sub I never heard.

I was still thinking of such work as merely provisional, and it had
been on the tip of my tongue to tell Oumansky that I was not really a
foreign correspondent but a comrade who had come to the USSR to
help build Socialism. Somehow, he did not seem to be the man, nor was
the occasion apposite; he looked so like a bank manager that he put me
more in a mood to ask for an overdraft than for citizenship in the
Kingdom of Heaven on Earth. Subsequently, I could feel my resolution
ebbing away, and basic questions about the whole validity of the Soviet
régime began to arise insistently in my mind. These doubts I wrestled
with while walking round the Red Square or passing through Lenin's
tomb; a spectacle of which I never tired. The little man in his glass case,
pink head resting on a red cushion, beard carefully trimmed, small hands
clenched, finger-nails daintily manicured; the khaki tunic with its single
decoration seeming to have nothing inside it – no body; just a head, and
that empty, the brain having been removed for separate examination
and preservation. Was he not the very materialist conception of history
in person? An empty skull embalmed in a vacuum to last for ever. Made
immortal. All day long there were people filing past, mostly peasants;
they just stared at him without showing any signs of emotion, though
once I saw an old peasant woman cross herself. Heaven knows what that
signified, if anything. For a short while he shared the tomb with Stalin,
his successor. I saw Stalin there, as it happened, during his short co-
occupancy. With his thick black moustache he looked almost jovial by
comparison with Lenin. Then he was turned out, and Lenin again left
in his solitary glory.

I never missed a chance of walking round the Red Square; fascinated by the massive Kremlin buildings, so extravagant a fortress, now housing, not an anointed king or emperor, not, like the White House, an elected President, nor, like the Vatican, a Pope chosen from among a College of Cardinals, but the Dictatorship of the Proletariat. This was authority in terms of a quite new abstraction, embodying a claim far transcending Louis XIV's *L'Etat, c'est moi*. *Le peuple, c'est moi*; that's what the ruler in the Kremlin claimed for himself. All the toiling masses everywhere, their will, their purpose, their very being, embodied in this one man, who spoke and acted, and even lived, on their behalf. And everyone else – kulaks, White Guards, Black Hundreds, down to Mr Pooters of the *Diary of a Nobody*, adding up their figures, puffing at their pipes, and maybe dropping a fishing line into the water on a Sunday afternoon – must be abolished. Then, at last, when this was accomplished, history would be over, and paradise have come to earth, and the Dictatorship of the Proletariat, in the person of the man in the Kremlin, reign for evermore.

The Red Flag flying above the Kremlin was illuminated at night; a little pool of blood suspended in the darkness. This was the true image of the Revolution; the mysticism of power, equivalent of the mysticism of sex in the other part of the world. Power versus sex. What I was looking for in the USSR – liberty, equality, fraternity – was irrelevant; just as the happiness Americans were under a statutory obligation to pursue, was irrelevant. The Knout or the Phallus – in any such contest, surely the knout must win. Opposite the Kremlin the onion domes of a sometime cathedral formed weird swollen shadows against the sky. Now it had become an anti-God Museum, with a great pendulum swinging to and fro to demonstrate the force of gravity in refutation of claims made on behalf of any divinity purporting to shape our ends. There were also fossilised saints on display, once fraudulently claimed to have been miraculously preserved against the ravages of time. Was the swinging pendulum, I asked myself, more god-like than the God it confuted? And that other contemporary saint across the way, preserved in his glass case – was he less fraudulent than the fossilised saints? The whole scene seemed abstract; like one of those models set up on army intelligence courses to demonstrate how a battle should be fought. But a battle between whom? About what?

For comfort I turned, as usual, to the streets, where the endless stream of anonymous people were somehow companionable, as the pendulum god and the refrigerated saint were not. Grey-faced; as

winter came on, in padded coats and felt boots, their footfall mysteriously silent in the snow – they, too, seemed to be coming from nowhere and making for nowhere. Just drifting inscrutably along. There was little to look at in the shops except wooden cheeses and cardboard intimations of plenty to come. No neon lights, no spelt out pleasures; no whiff of flesh or snatch of music as a swing-door opened and shut. All drab and grey and restrained. And yet I had a feeling, stronger than I can possibly convey, that what was happening in Moscow must happen everywhere. That it was the focal point or pivot of the drama of our times, whose essential pattern was being shaped there. That these blank faces processing noiselessly through Moscow's blank streets were mankind processing through the twentieth century.

So it has proved to be. The Revolution has triumphed in an unexpected way, its ferment working rather through history than through the minds and hearts of men; its enemies' citadel surrendering, and the garrison opening the gates and putting out white flags, without any need for a siege or an assault. Jericho's walls tumbling down of their own decay before any trumpet sounded. So, the priests have chosen themselves to turn their churches into anti-God museums; and the image of our well-being and our plenty is shown in living colour on the television screen, like the wooden cheeses and the cardboard plenty in the Moscow shops. Above all, there were the *besprizorne*; the uncared for, or wild ones. These were children who had survived on their own, without parents or anyone else to look after them, from the famine and civil war of the twenties. Going about in packs, barely articulate or recognisably human, with pinched animal faces, tangled hair and empty eyes. I saw them in Moscow and Leningrad, clustered under bridges, lurking in railway stations, suddenly emerging like a pack of wild monkeys; then scattering and disappearing. I was to see them again in years to come on campuses anywhere between the Berlin Wall and the Pacific coast of America; waifs of plenty, spoilt children of affluence, graduate Calibans, with the same tangled hair and animal faces; likewise barely articulate, barely human.

Kitty and I continued to live in the Nova Moskovkaya, while making desultory efforts to find other accommodation. This involved visiting numerous apartment blocks where rentable rooms were allegedly available. They invariably turned out to be part of a room, with, at best, the possibility of hanging a blanket to curtain off the portion offered us, and the use of corporate cooking and washing facilities. I have often regretted

that we did not have a go at living in this way, which was how the great majority of Soviet citizens lived. With Kitty increasingly pregnant, however, and the necessity I was under to do a lot of typing, it seemed as though it would have been an impossible arrangement. Our quest did at any rate give us a notion of what housing conditions were really like in Moscow. Only important officials like the Sokolnikovs and rich writers like Ehrenburg, enjoyed the luxury of apartments to themselves. Ehrenburg's flat actually had some Impressionist paintings – otherwise banned in the USSR – hanging in it. He also had a country residence near Moscow where, when I once visited him, he showed me with great pride a plant in his greenhouse that had been presented to him by the Queen Mother of Belgium. Later, we went for a stroll, and he pointed out to me nostalgically the house in which a rich merchant named Morosov had lived, entertaining the revolutionary intelligentsia like himself there at elegant evening soirées, and arranging amateur presentations of Chekov's plays; subsequently committing suicide.

Each morning a Russian woman named Klavdia Lvovna came to give Kitty and me a Russian lesson, and to read over the newspapers with me. She was a person of indeterminate age; she might have been forty or twenty, there was no telling. In ordinary circumstances one might have taken her for a governess or lady's companion. She had a high, piping voice and the nebulous colouring and dry texture of someone who has faded without ripening. There was something very ludicrous, and even at times vaguely tragic, in her high piping voice reading over to me in halting English the turgid, portentous, and often inflammatory sentences of some *Pravda* or *Izvestia* article. Like playing 'Land of Hope and Glory' on a piccolo. Thus, she would begin: 'Comrade Stalin, addressing the Central Committee yesterday, declared that the world had never before seen so powerful and authoritarian a régime as the Soviet régime, or so powerful and authoritarian a party as our Bolshevik Party . . .' As she read one, she often faltered, appalled, and perhaps also frightened, at so unimportant and timid a person as herself getting involved in these weighty, explosive matters; then would summon up her courage and resolution to continue: 'Communists go on hunting for kulaks with beastly faces, red necks, harsh voices and guns like those on our posters; but present-day kulaks are quiet, sweet, almost holy men sitting inside collective farms as managers, secretaries, etc., leading village communists by the nose . . .'

She had to read it over again slowly while I tapped it out on my type-

writer for the delectation of *Guardian* readers. Poor Klavdia Lvovna had no concern with kulaks, whether red-necked or quiet and sweet; it was all beyond her. Her interest lay in a few old dog-eared Russian classics she had managed to keep – Gogol, Goncharov, Lermontov – and the clandestine practice of Russian Orthodox Christianity. She would not accept any money for her services, but took payment in food, which I was able to get from a special shop for diplomats and journalists where one could buy for roubles more or less anything one wanted. Later, it was abolished in favour of Torgsin shops which only accepted foreign currency or the equivalent in jewels or precious metals. Their windows were full of otherwise unobtainable foods – hams and cheeses and butter – to induce Soviet citizens to bring out their secret hoards, or solicit money from their relatives and friends abroad. When they succumbed, it quite often happened that they were arrested for hoarding or having contacts with foreigners.

When Klavdia Lvovna got to know me better she told me that the food I gave her was passed on to a nun who, though her order had long ago been dissolved, still continued to observe her vows and engage in works of charity. Somehow this nun managed to send on the food she got from Klavdia Lvovna to fellow-nuns and other religious serving sentences in labour camps. Now I feel remorse that I did not help Klavdia Lvovna more; I may even have got her into trouble by the things I wrote after I left the USSR. Unfortunately, I never liked her; there was something mousy and prim and – absurdly enough in that particular setting – even snobbish about her which irritated me. Most of the translators and secretaries of the other foreign journalists in Moscow, I may add, were cast in a very different stamp. Blousy, brassy Red geisha girls; wearing unproletarian silk stockings, bras and underwear specially imported for them by their bosses, sometimes in diplomatic bags. Reputedly easy bedfellows who compensated for their deviant capitalistic ways by reporting regularly what they saw and heard to the GPU.

The housing situation was just becoming critical for Kitty and me – we were under notice to leave the Nova Moskovkaya – when we had the good fortune to make the acquaintance of Herr Schmidt, a German business man, at a party at the French Embassy. Such parties took place at one embassy or another almost every evening, and reminded me very much of the British Raj; more or less the same guests turned up at all of them – and one had the same feeling, as in India, of being a little privileged isolated community having practically no contact with the

surrounding country and its people. Ideological sahibs. Herr Schmidt was very well turned out, gold wrist-watch on hairy wrist, sharp close-set eyes and a rather forlorn mouth lurking in the shadow of a large nose. When we told him of our difficulty in finding anywhere to live, he said that he had a dacha not far from Moscow which he only used at week-ends, and that we were welcome to stay there if we wished to while we were looking for suitable accommodation in Moscow. It seemed like a wonderful offer, and we accepted at once. Herr Schmidt kindly said that he would drive us down the next day, which he duly did, arriving at our hotel to pick us up in a smart convertible with a female beside him whom he presented as 'Die Kleine'. We never knew her by any other name; she had bleached hair, long coloured finger-nails, and a body so slender that it seemed surprising that she could, when absolutely necessary, hold herself erect. At the dacha she spent most of the time playing jazz records imported from Germany, and smoking cigarettes in a long holder. Herr Schmidt said that his wife lived in Vienna, and did not find the Russian climate suited to her. It was a set-up which would have been perfectly appropriate anywhere in the world, and Kitty and I endlessly speculated as to what business could put Herr Schmidt in so advantageous a situation. 'Chemicals,' I said, having vaguely gathered something of the sort from Herr Schmidt himself, but Kitty insisted it was just money. It was indeed the case, at that time, that foreign currency was sought after in Moscow with particular assiduity. We had not, after all, escaped from the kingdom of money. There are, I have discovered, certain constants in life which recur in all circumstances, Herr Schmidt and Die Kleine being one of them.

Herr Schmidt's dacha, which now became our home, was at Kliasma. It was a wooden house, rather like a Swiss chalet. There were other similar dachas nearby, but mostly already shut up for the winter. The pine woods round about had many long straight paths through them which I knew, as soon as I saw them, would be my walks. In among the pine trees, too, there was a large clearing obviously intended for recreational purposes, littered with cardboard slogans about building socialism. These had already begun to look rather disconsolate in the cold wind, with dead leaves swirling round them. It was a local version of the parks of culture and rest of which such a feature was made in taking tourists round Moscow, and where, despite the priggish name, on warm evenings lovers found a sanctuary though whether this usage came into the category of culture or of rest I never determined. On some days

Klavdia Lvovna came out to Kliasma, or I would go into Moscow on the electric train; preposterously crowded as all public transport was in the USSR. One just clung on where one could. I was wryly amused to find a picture of this train in a publication called *The USSR in Construction*, captioned: 'Eager Soviet Workers on their Way to the Capital'.

One way and another I managed to send off some articles and messages. The messages, of course, had to be stamped in the Press Department before the telegraph office would accept them. One took them in to be censored, like taking an essay to one's tutor at Cambridge; watching anxiously as they were read over for any frowns or hesitations, dreading to see a pencil picked up to slash something out. Later, the arrangement was changed, so that the journalists just turned in their messages, which were then processed in the Press Department and sent off without any further reference to them. It amounted to a sort of computerisation, in keeping with the exigencies of a technological society.

In my time, there were three censors, all Jews – Podolski, the most intelligent, with sad eyes and a thin pointed beard; Nehman, looking like a Rabbi, with a fringe of beard all round his face, and Ehrens, a ludicrous figure who had been in Magnetogorsk in some capacity or other, as a result of which he affected top boots and a rough pioneering manner which ill became his plump soft person. They all three disappeared into the labour camps in due course, never to be seen again. I was sorry about Podolski, who was really a very nice, intelligent, amusing man. Before the Revolution he had lived abroad, and one could even argue with him when he proposed censoring something. I remember on one occasion his shaking his head and saying to me: 'You can't say that because it's true.' It seemed like a basic twentieth-century text. I always liked to get him for my censor whenever I could; Nehman (described by Mrs Webb as 'that very clever young man') patiently and meticulously trod the Party Line. Ehrens was an oaf. The fact that they were all Jews had no particular significance. With the liquidation of the Russian bourgeoisie, Jews who had good revolutionary credentials, from Litvinov downwards, provided almost the only available personnel for Foreign Office jobs. The only non-Jew I can recall off-hand among Foreign Office personnel was a certain Fleurinski, the Chef-de-Protocol; a caricature of a pre-Revolutionary aristocrat, straight out of *Dead Souls*. He, too, was liquidated; not for being a class enemy, or a capitalist-imperialist running dog, but for pederasty when – to the great distress

of, among others, André Gide – the earlier permissive attitude was reversed, and harsh penalties re-imposed against the practice.

Articles one could sometimes send by a diplomatic bag, which, of course, eliminated all censorship. The British were not particularly helpful in this respect, but other embassies were more accommodating. It was an article sent by this means – actually about the Soviet mania for discovering sabotage and treachery on every hand – that led to my first rebuke from Oumansky. He called me to his office, and there he sat looking very grave with the offending article on his desk in front of him. This will never do, he seemed to be saying, shaking his head and showing his gold teeth; and from you of all people! Writing in the sacred columns of the *Manchester Guardian!* With the Webbs' aureole shining about your head! He found particularly offensive my remark that one could say of sabotage in the USSR what Voltaire said of God – that if it did not exist it would be necessary to invent it. Somehow bringing Voltaire, a revolutionary hero, into my squalid argument made the offence worse in his eyes. This time, he indicated, a rebuke would suffice, but if anything of the kind occurred again, more serious consequences would follow.

I swallowed the admonition as best I might. The Soviet authorities were able to control foreign newsmen almost as rigorously as they did their own. They had perforce to live and work in the USSR under the constant threat of losing their visas. If this happened, their jobs automatically came to an end, which in most cases was something they wished to avoid. Also, any foreigner resident in the USSR was vulnerable, in the sense that just going about and displaying ordinary curiosity, in Soviet terms laid one open to a plausible charge of espionage. Then again, we all changed money on the black market, likewise an offence under Soviet law. The official rate of exchange was so unrealistic that it made living costs utterly exorbitant, whereas the black market rate – in my time something like two hundred roubles to the pound – was decidedly advantageous, and easily obtainable at some of the smaller Consulates. One would come away with great wedges of notes loosely wrapped in newspaper like fried fish. Add to this that most foreign correspondents, separated from their wives, acquired a Russian mistress of one sort or another who, if not planted on them by the GPU, was bound to report their doings and transactions. This provided a ready means of exerting pressure on them. Thus, one way and another, they were not free agents, and the messages they sent had to be slanted accordingly.

Newspaper managements and broadcasting agencies have nonetheless been ready to pay out large sums of money to procure this tainted news just in order to be able to say it came from Our Own Correspondent in Moscow. The image is, as always, preferred to the reality. Looking back, I can recall only one sentence I telegraphed from Moscow which was wholly true. It may even be the only wholly true sentence ever to be telegraphed from Moscow. This was when I was temporarily standing in for the correspondent of an American news agency, and received a cable asking for the Soviet man-in-the-street's reactions to the lavish scale of entertaining in Soviet embassies abroad. Without thinking I replied: MAN-IN-STREET'S REACTION STRONG DESIRE GET NEAREST BUFFET. Podolski passed the message with a twinkle in his eye. Such twinkles, I fear, were what cost him his life.

Our life at Kliasma was very happy. Moscow and the Dictatorship of the Proletariat seemed far away; as did the little bearded latter-day saint in his glass case. The great pendulum demonstrating the force of gravity and confuting the existence of God, continued to swing monotonously, but not for us. I had started work on a novel about a liberal newspaper in the north of England (*Picture Palace*), and managed to turn out enough casual material about the USSR to feel that I was earning our keep. A very nice Volga-German woman, Lena, looked after the dacha; Herr Schmidt and Die Kleine came at week-ends, when the gramophone played, reminding us of that other cinematic world we had left behind us, which seemed even farther away than the Kremlin. We took walks in the woods, and smiled at children playing, and felt, as we hadn't in Moscow, that we were living in a country rather than a régime. Then, suddenly, Kitty got ill, developing a very high temperature.

Herr Schmidt very kindly brought a German doctor, Dr Taubkin, to see her; a little gnome-like man who looked vaguely deformed – a near hunchback, with bright eyes and a soft, purring voice. He pulled a long face over Kitty's temperature, and after his examination – very delicately done; taking a white cloth out of his bag to put over her chest while he sounded her – he said she had typhus or paratyphus, the latter being a milder, but still dangerous, form of the same virus. When he told Kitty what was the matter with her, all she wanted to know was whether the child in her womb would be harmed. Reassured on this point, she closed her eyes again. There was nothing to be done except keep her in bed, and give her lots of water to drink and occasional enemas. In any case, medicaments were rare and difficult to come by. I asked Dr Taubkin anxiously whether she should go to hospital. A look of unspeakable

horror spread over his gnomish face, and he crossed himself; otherwise making no reply. I used to recall his response to my question when I read articles by eminent doctors expatiating upon the excellence of the hospitals and public health service in the USSR.

For the next days I forgot everything except looking after Kitty. The thought that she might die filled me with desolation. All our quarrels and jealousies and harsh sayings and infidelities dissolved away; and all I saw in the universe was her flushed face, very youthful looking in its sickness, very alert and resolute, picked out as though spot-lit in the midst of an immense darkness. If she should die! A secondary terror was that I might catch the illness, and so be unable to look after her. What would happen then? Inevitably, I thought the symptoms were unmistakably developing, and secretly took my own temperature; positively dismayed, absurdly enough, to find that it was normal. Kitty's mattress was intolerably uncomfortable, so I gathered others in the dacha and piled them on it. Die Kleine, when she came at the week-end, very sweetly made no complaint about losing hers.

I slept on the floor beside Kitty's bed, waking up from time to time to look at her, taking her temperature far more often than was necessary; childishly enraged when it remained high, and equally childishly up-lifted when it dipped down. In the morning I washed her as well as I could, very gently when I came to the swollen belly, and combed her hair. For an enema we had only rather crude sunflower oil, but I managed with this, experiencing a kind of blissfulness in the process. We had with us the Everyman edition of *Shakespeare's Tragedies* (I must, in jettisoning books before we left Manchester, have given this volume a non-bourgeois imprimatur), and I read aloud to her *Hamlet* and *Cymbeline*. In the evening, when Lena was in the dacha, I took a walk in the pine woods, up and down the straight paths. For the time being all my professional journalistic interest in the régime had evaporated; how many hours people worked, their real wages, rent, rations, whether the Consumers' Co-operatives, so dear to Mrs Webb, functioned success-fully or not. My mind had momentarily stopped working in that sort of way. It just suddenly seemed to me that Russia was a beautiful place – these pine trees, dark against the snow which had now begun to fall, the sparkling stars so far, far away, the faces of the Russians I met and greeted, these also so beautiful, so clumsy and so kind. *Tovarich!* – it meant something, after all. Brother!

In the woods there was a little church, of course disused now. The fronts of such churches, like the Greek ones, are painted with bright

colours; blues bluer than the bluest sky, whites whiter than the whitest snow. Someone – heaven knows who – had painted up the one in the Kliasma woods. Standing in front of this unknown painter's handiwork, I blessed his name, feeling that I belonged to the little disused church he had embellished, and that the Kremlin with its scarlet flag and dark towers and golden spires was an alien kingdom. A kingdom of power such as the Devil had in his gift, and offered to Christ, to be declined by him in favour of the kingdom of love. I, too, must decline it, and live in the kingdom of love. This was another moment of perfect clarification, when everything fitted together in sublime symmetry; when I saw clearly the light and the darkness, freedom and servitude, the bright vistas of eternity and the prison bars of time. I went racing back over the snow to K, breathing in the dry icy air in great gulps of thankfulness.

The next day I went into Moscow in quest of a bedpan. It happened also to be the anniversary of the October Revolution, and I had a press pass for the parade in the Red Square. The only possible place where I might find a bedpan, Herr Schmidt had told me, was in the commission shops; a sort of Soviet version of pawn shops, where the relics of the old Russian bourgeoisie brought their family treasures – ikons, pieces of furniture, books, stamp collections, Czarist medals even, anything that could possibly have a value – to exchange them for money to pay taxes and procure necessities. They were a great haunt of visiting Intourists, especially Americans, who eagerly poked about, looking for a bargain – Rasputin's breviary, a sometime duchess's fan, an ikon from some ancient monastery in remote Turkistan, to be carried away across the Atlantic and proudly displayed alongside wedding groups and college graduation trophies. The commission shops were recognised as capitalistic enclaves, their interiors dusty and shadowy as befitted such alien establishments in a Workers' State. They were tolerated as a means of relieving Intourists of their Valuta – that magical incantation for foreign currency, breathed in one's ear at restaurants or when making a theatre booking, like an Ave Maria, to find out whether one proposed to pay in real or ersatz money.

When my turn came to be attended to, it was obvious that the shopman assumed I was a seller rather than a buyer. He asked me arrogantly what I wanted, clearly anxious to hurry on to the more agreeable and rewarding business of Valuta transactions. The mistake doubtless arose as a result of my appearance, which did not at all suggest an affluent foreigner. I was wearing a short black leather jacket with a fur collar bought in an army surplus store in Manchester, dating back, as I was

told, to General Ironside's force at Archangel at the time of the Allied Intervention in 1918. It was not a stylish or elegant garment. When I explained in my halting Russian that I wanted a bedpan for a sick wife, and that I would pay sterling, his interest kindled a little, and he produced a porcelain object which, if not exactly a bedpan, could be made to serve the same purpose. It was wrapped up for me in an old issue of *Pravda*; I paid in Valuta, and we parted amicably.

I went on to visit Cholerton, who at that time was still *News Chronicle* correspondent, before he joined the *Daily Telegraph*. He was far and away the nicest and most intelligent of the foreign journalists in Moscow, habitually stretched out on a couch, having a lung infection which made him subject to sudden temperatures; often with a bottle of red Caucasian wine beside him. He had a way of lining up bottles in the morning for the day's consumption. With his untidy beard, incessant conversation, wide-ranging, inconstant but scintillating mind, he was the very image of the Russian intellectual as portrayed by Dostoevsky. I once asked Podolski why, in view of the fact that Cholerton never bothered to hide his loathing and contempt for the Soviet régime, he was on the whole so tolerantly regarded, and always given his re-entry visa, when other ostensibly far more sympathetic reporters were persecuted and expelled. They were indulgent towards him, Podolski explained, because they liked him. He reminded them irresistibly of the good old days of their exile, when they lived penuriously in Geneva or London, arguing and quarrelling together, in and out of the British Museum Library, playing chess in cafés, bringing out obscure revolutionary sheets, splitting and re-splitting into ever smaller factions over minute doctrinal differences. Ah, too happy, happy times! Podolski seemed to be saying. I could see that Cholerton fitted perfectly into the scene, and that his detestation of of the régime somehow expressed theirs. He, as it were, hated it on their behalf, and so his presence was comforting. When they had all been shot by Stalin, this consideration no longer applied, and Cholerton's visa was at last withdrawn. He finally decamped to the Riviera, that last refuge of rebellious hearts, where I have continued to visit him from time to time, always with delight.

His household in Moscow consisted of a very sweet Russian wife, Katerina Georgevna, and their little daughter Katya, a sharp-tongued, aggressive secretary, Natalia Dmitrievna, who looked after his affairs, and numerous domestics and hangers-on. I felt happier there than anywhere else. He lived in an ordinary ramshackle Soviet apartment house, but his free-ranging intelligence, unpackaged in the ideologies of the age,

irradiated the shabby room; as did a set of Stations of the Cross by some Ukrainian peasant artist he had somehow acquired. I remember them as being very beautiful in their strength and simplicity. He had neither the temperament nor the inclination to be a journalist; least of all for the *News Chronicle*, a sort of poor man's *Guardian*, which he abominated. If anything, he was a don (actually, a sometime fellow of King's College, Cambridge), with all the special donnish qualities of indolence and intellectual arrogance. His flat was littered with books; mostly paper-covered French editions in which he would forage from time to time, picking one up and opening it to read a few pages. Through him I first became acquainted with Taine's *Origines de la France Contemporaine*, from which I derived great enjoyment and enlightenment. How, in any case, could he be expected to provide nourishment for *News Chronicle* readers? With my experience of *The Guardian*, I, alas, knew the form all too exactly, and was happy to oblige occasionally on his behalf. His true spiritual home was Paris in the early twenties; he had flown to the USSR on the wings of the Gauche Radicale, not the Fabians, with Léon Blum and Marc Chagall for his ikon rather than Sidney and Beatrice Webb. It was the sheer philistinism of the régime that appalled him; its total humourlessness, its abysmal taste, its dreadful buildings, its flat, heavy representational paintings of Lenin and Stalin, like portraits of Lord Mayors in Manchester Town Hall; the long-winded cant and dull hatred which hung like an oppressive cloud over it. Reacting against this philistinism, by a quirk of history, he who had walked about Montmartre in a wide black hat, and looked on Hemingway and Joyce and the Shakespeare Bookshop, became almost the last voice to be heard in Moscow, if not in the world, expounding bourgeois virtues. The ultimate champions of a civilisation in dissolution, the Casabiancas who stand on its burning deck when all but they have fled, are, by the nature of the case, a weird lot, and Cholerton among the weirdest.

We went together to the Red Square for the parade, rather tipsy, and I still resolutely clasping my bedpan wrapped in an old edition of *Pravda*. As we approached the press stand, holding out our passes, one of the many security guards insisted on examining my parcel, no doubt supposing it to be a bomb. He was quite astonished when he saw what it was, and handed it back to me with a polite bow. From the press stand one looked straight across at the top of Lenin's Mausoleum where the Dictatorship of the Proletariat were standing; Stalin in the middle, with Kalinin on one side of him and Voroshilov on the other, and the rest carefully graded. They looked like a row of pygmies perched up there;

little clockwork manikins who might at any moment disport themselves
when their mechanism was released, jerkily raising their hats and kicking
their legs in unison, but for the moment completely still.

The Red Square was densely packed; there, the Proletariat, and up
on the Mausoleum, the Dictatorship. How were the two connected? As
Lenin so succinctly posed the question: Who whom? The scene seemed
pure fantasy; I couldn't believe in it. Not even as the mighty procession
rolled past; the gymnasts, the troops, the bands, the armoured vehicles,
the dashing cavalry. I wanted to raise my bedpan in the air in a special
salute of my own; particularly when I noticed a little group of vaguely
familiar faces behind a banner emblazoned CPGB; they, too, paying
their tribute to the great Dictatorship of the Proletariat. We who are
nothing shall be all; he hath put down the mighty from their seats, and
hath exalted the humble and meek – it was the everlasting theme of
revolution, here exemplified in all its majesty and fatuity.

I was so taken with the point that I turned to Cholerton to make it,
but by mistake addressed a little red-faced buttoned-up Frenchman
who turned out to be the correspondent of *Le Temps* – a Corsican
named Luciani. He shrugged and agreed. On the stand next to ours
were the diplomatic corps; the ambassadors all arrayed in astrakhan
collars and fur hats, of varying size and splendour; the service attachés in
their uniforms, which, in that setting, had a decidedly comic opera air
about them, as though they had lately been fetched out of the property
box and dusted down for the occasion. Altogether, they looked a non-
descript, and even rather sinister lot assembled there, and so completely
separate that they might have been seated together in a commodious
tumbril which at any moment would begin to roll.

In the cold air, the Caucasian wine I had consumed with Cholerton
began to wear off; he, too, looked somewhat pinched and abstracted,
wondering, I daresay, what, if anything, could be gleaned for the *News
Chronicle* from the turn-out:

TO-DAY FIFTEENTH ANNIVERSARY BOLSHEVIK OCTOBER RE-
VOLUTION MARSHAL VOROSHILOV STANDING NEXT STALIN
WITH REST POLITBUREAU TOOK SALUTE MASSIVE MILITARY
TURNOUT AMID SCENES GREAT ENTHUSIASM . . .

'An unforgettable experience,' I heard a voice say. It was Lord Marley,
a recently created Labour peer who had come over with us on the
Kooperatsia, his face full of rapture. The Montessori teacher said she
wished the accent had been somewhat less military, but the enthusiasm
of the people was infectious. If only we had something like that at home!

A nearby American warmly agreed. He was wearing a button which bore the legend '3%'. The notion, he explained, came from Professor Einstein, who had said that if three per cent of mankind were against war there never could again be one. He hoped in Moscow to recruit Stalin into the programme, which would mean, he figured, the involvement of the whole Soviet population.

I arrived back in Kliasma triumphantly bearing my bedpan, to find Kitty much better and sitting up and ready to laugh over my adventures. The sense of relief drove away all the fears that had been haunting me – only £90 left of our travellers' cheques, and very little money coming in; the impossibility of settling in the USSR as we had planned, or of going on being a foreign correspondent in Moscow, indeed, of working for *The Guardian* at all; the need to find somewhere for Kitty to have her baby, as well as a job for me. All these dilemmas seemed of no account in the light of her returned health and smile. A local woman doctor who visited her from time to time came in that evening, found that her temperature was normal for the first time since her illness began, and shared in our rejoicing. She was a cheerful amiable soul, the best type of Soviet product; simple, capable and pleasant looking, with a warm bright face. We managed to converse in a mixture of Russian and German. Her equipment struck me as primitive. For instance, her stethoscope was like a little wooden trumpet, and she had no drugs of any kind, not even aspirins. One of her favourite treatments, called *banki*, which she insisted on administering on this last visit, consisted of warming up a lot of little glass pots and then affixing them to Kitty's back. As they cooled, they sucked up the flesh, giving excruciating pain, and, allegedly, easing the bronchial tubes. The whole process was so bizarre that we couldn't help laughing, which, of course, made the pain all the greater.

This so painful laughter was the sign for me that Kitty was now alive. What an ecstatic experience to see someone greatly loved who has been languishing and dying thus come to life again! Blood moving through the veins and arteries, like traffic after a stoppage; nourishment again taken, gulped down greedily, each mouthful desperately needed, and preparing the way for the next, no less desperately needed. Likewise, air greedily breathed in. Talk returning, and laughter; even irritability – all manifestations of life. Like Lazarus raised from the dead. Even in plants this is wonderful; watering and easing the earth to coax some drooping, famished plant to lift its head and stand upright. Each morning's awakening similarly a miracle; beautiful to observe, especially in a child. Eyes slowly opening; consciousness coming back into them, chasing

away the dreams, and focusing on the new day beginning; stretching, coughing, scratching, making ready. So, this preposterous laughter of ours, making the little *banki* jars quiver and shake, to poor Kitty's greater anguish, was particularly joyous as an outward and visible manifestation of her recovery. She was, after all, alive; the graph was upwards, not downwards; our journey was not over, the road stretched onwards.

Along the straight paths through the pine trees I tried afterwards to sort it out in my mind. How suffering, rather than pleasure, should be the sacrament of love. The imperfection of the flesh so much more crucial than its imagined perfection; the transports of tending it in sickness far transcending those of coupling with it in health. A contradiction, a mystery. Peeping in through a broken window of the little church with the newly painted front, I saw that it was used now for storing tools, as well as some of the fallen slogans from the nearby clearing, neatly piled for use the following summer. Yet at the back where the altar had been there was still the faint outline of a cross to be seen. Another statement of the same proposition. In its survival I read the promise that somehow this image of enlightenment through suffering, this assertion of the everlasting supremacy of the gospel of love over the gospel of power, would never be obliterated, however dimly and obscurely traced now, and however seemingly triumphant the forces opposed to it might seem to be.

By the time Kitty was really better we were able to move back to Moscow, where we occupied the flat of William Henry Chamberlin and his wife Sonia in the Borisoglebski Pereulok during their absence on leave. Chamberlin was the staff correspondent of the *Christian Science Monitor* and also worked as a stringer for *The Guardian*. He was a short, podgy, highly intelligent, droll man who neither drank nor smoked, his only form of self-indulgence being eating chocolate. As he read or ruminated, he chewed steadily, reckoning to consume his own weight annually. Perhaps because of this, he came increasingly to resemble a figure of the Buddha. Originally, he came to the USSR on a wave of pacifist-progressive sentiment, but soon soured on the régime, working off his resentment in little odd digs and innuendoes delivered on a wide front. Each week, for instance, he cut out of the *Manchester Guardian Weekly* an advertisement for a private mental home, posting it off to the public figure he considered most in need of it. One week he would send it to Mrs Eleanor Roosevelt, another to Rabindranath Tagore, always

choosing the recipient with the utmost care in the light of his or her current attitudes and pronouncements. I was glad to know that one had been dispatched to the up-and-coming Anthony Eden, and another to Bertrand Russell. Chamberlin, and more particularly Sonia – a Russian Jewess by origin – had every intention of staying in the USSR for some time to come, and very cleverly used his complaisant coverage in *The Guardian* to offset any sharp criticism of the régime he might essay in the *Monitor*. By playing off one against the other he managed to achieve the delicate balancing act of keeping on his feet in the USSR without becoming its committed stooge. Thus, when readers of the *Monitor* learnt from him that agricultural production was sagging alarmingly, the hearts of readers of *The Guardian* were uplifted by the news that the policy of collectivisation was producing undoubted results in the Siberian heartlands. This kept Oumansky happy, since he believed – no doubt correctly – that the USSR got the better of the bargain, *The Guardian* being a far more influential organ than the *Monitor*. After my floundering efforts in Chamberlin's absence to provide a less inhibited service from Moscow, Crozier was delighted to have Chamberlin back and resume the old arrangement. Substituting for Chamberlin on the *Monitor* presented its own special difficulties. For instance, I was given to understand that the subject of death was considered to be unsuitable in its columns. Unhappily, at the time, nearly all the stories out of Moscow were about humans and animals dying, and the various possible synonyms – like 'fell' – scarcely seemed appropriate. I did not fancy cabling Boston to the effect that x thousand kulaks had fallen as a result of the party instruction to liquidate them. Or that y thousand livestock had fallen, having been eaten by famished moujiks in the famine conditions induced by collectivisation.

The house in Borisoglebsky where we took up our quarters was an old-fashioned pre-Revolution one, and the Chamberlins' flat had a large tiled stove in it of the kind that occurs in so many of Tolstoy's and other Russian stories. I used to imagine Oblomov's servant Zachar curled up on top of it. We very soon got used to living there, so that we might have been back in Didsbury. Revolutions, like wars, upset things far less than might be superficially supposed. As the very word 'revolution' implies, they have a way of ending up where they began. Most days I would go to the Press Department, just as I had to the Cross Street *Guardian* office. There one met one's colleagues, also waiting for the attentions of Podolski or Nehman or Ehrens. The older hands knew the form per-

fectly, and brought in copy that passed easily through the censor's scrutiny. Newcomers might sometimes argue against the exigencies of censorship, and even shout and bang the table, indignant over excisions in what they supposed to be straight reporting. They had to learn that in the Soviet Union – as, later, everywhere – happenings occur exclusively on communication media, never in life. It is put out by *Tass*, therefore it is. Or, it has been shown on television, therefore it is. It amounts to the same thing.

The most notable activist among the press corps was Ralph Barnes, an earnest eager American reporter who kept us all on our toes. He used to pad about the streets of Moscow in rubber shoes hoping to come upon some newsworthy person or event, and endlessly apply for interviews with Stalin, which were rarely accorded, mostly to eminent visitors like H. G. Wells, and even then settled, if not drafted, in advance. When, as happened from time to time, Barnes disappeared from Moscow, there was great apprehension among the other correspondents. Where had he gone? What was he up to? On one such occasion he pulled off a coup of stupendous proportions, which made him the envy of all his colleagues. He went down to Georgia and managed to interview Stalin's mother, actually getting a photograph of her wearing an old-fashioned peasant dress, seated in the porch of her modest, but spotlessly clean cottage; like any American mum in Michigan or Minnesota. She was, as he put it, a little old lady in black, inordinately proud of her famous son in the Kremlin, her Soso. The story had a sensational success, and was widely reproduced. Later, doubts were cast on whether the lady in question really was Stalin's mother, or someone dressed up for the part. By that time, anyway, who cared? Her appearance in Barnes's story coincided, certainly, with a campaign mounted in the Soviet Press to show that Stalin was human – on any showing quite a sizeable undertaking. Nothing, however, could detract from the splendour of the scoop, which continued to have a special place in Moscow newspaper mythology.

Another coup Barnes pulled off, less noticed at the time but intrinsically more remarkable, was to procure an interview with someone who purported to be fairly high up in the GPU. In the course of their conversation, Barnes put to him the naïve but fundamental question: Why is it that in the USSR innocent people get arrested? The GPU man, it seems, fairly shook with laughter at this, to the point that it was quite a while before he could get his answer out. Of course we arrest innocent people, he said at last in effect; otherwise, no one would be frightened. If people are only arrested for specific misdemeanours, all

the others feel safe, and so are ripe for treason. Probably without meaning to, he expounded the central doctrine of every terror, as well as of all dictatorial government, so brilliantly exemplified by Orwell in *Nineteen Eighty-Four*, and, more imaginatively, in Kafka's *The Trial.* By making justice subjective and arbitrary, every citizen can be plausibly arrested and charged at any time, with the result that they live in a permanent state of incipient guilt and fear; really feeling themselves to be miserable offenders, not just in the eyes of God, but of their earthly rulers as well. Hence the so easily procured confessions, which do not need to be invented or extorted, but truly come from the heart.

In those days foreign journalists were vouchsafed some contact with lower echelon Soviet bosses, besides an occasional sight of the top ones; even of the boss of the bosses, Stalin himself. He would walk into view on a platform, or appear in a box at the Opera House, or at the topmost end of a reception, always to the accompaniment of protracted cheers that were precisely timed by the GPU men in attendance. Their duration steadily increased, and at the time of Stalin's death had reached a minimum of seven and a half minutes. It was a preview of the studio audience. Sometimes, again, one would catch a glimpse of the back of his head, with its thick neck, as his heavily escorted car shot past, going to or from the Kremlin.

The receptions, whatever their occasion, were invariable. There would be a long table loaded with food and drink beside which officials would cluster like foraging bees, eating as hard as they could, and sometimes, when no one was looking, surreptitiously pocketing something portable to take home for their dear ones. A regular attender at these functions was Borodin, who at one time had played an important role in the execution of Soviet policy in China. Now, in semi-disgrace, he had been made, of all things, editor of the *Moscow Daily News*, an English language propaganda sheet published in Moscow. The unfortunate man had on his staff some ebullient English and American Communist and Communist-leaning girls of quite exceptional horror. When I read of his inevitable eventual arrest and disappearance, I thought that perhaps there might have been a tiny element of relief as he was taken off to Lubianka in the thought that he would no longer have to cope with these unspeakable harridans. At the reception he would sit alone, quietly drinking champagne and chain smoking, wearing an expression of oriental vacancy.

Another fairly frequent attender was Radek, a vivacious quick-speaking man with a beard like Nehman's, who might easily in other

circumstances have been taken for a Rabbi. The first time I saw him he was the centre of an attentive group of sycophantic listeners, to whom, puffing away at his curved Meerschaum pipe, he held forth eloquently. At his subsequent appearances they dwindled, until he, like Borodin, sat alone. Then he, too, disappeared, to reappear in court to explain how, during his days as an active revolutionary in Germany, he was recruited into the British Intelligence Service, which he thenceforth faithfully served. The last article of his that Klavdia Lvovna translated for me was in the vein of the new spirit of nationalism ordained by Stalin, and described how, when he was in the arms of his mistress, he found himself speaking in his native patois, rather than in the Russian or German he used in his writings and public addresses.

Sometimes, too, Gorki was wheeled in, if he happened to be in Moscow rather than in the Italian villa the Soviet Government allowed him to keep. He looked like some extraordinary old performing seal, scarcely aware of what was going on around him, or of who anyone was. To me, he was an awesome figure because he had known Tolstoy and written so beautifully about him. I even made an effort on one occasion to get into conversation with him, but it was fruitless. The eyes were asleep; he was dozing behind his walrus moustache. In the end I usually gravitated to the side of D. N. Mirsky, a former prince in Czarist days, with whom I had a vague acquaintance in England. He was always invited to Moscow receptions to show any foreigners present that a prince could survive unhurt under a dictatorship of the proletariat. 'Look at him!' Oumansky would say, flashing his gold teeth. 'A prince! Just imagine!' Mirsky always turned up, I think largely for the free champagne. He was a great drinker, and not too well provided with money. In any case he only earned roubles – by writing articles in the *Literaturnaya Gazeta* tearing to pieces contemporary English writers like D. H. Lawrence, T. S. Eliot and Aldous Huxley, to whom, in conversation, he would always refer as 'Poor Lawrence!' 'Poor Tom!' 'Poor Aldous!' I found this sympathetic. In the civil war he had fought with the Whites, afterwards living as an exile in Paris, and associating himself there with the most extreme reactionary views. Then, he came to London, where, inevitably, he became a professor, and was commissioned to produce a book on Lenin. In the course of working on it, he came to see his subject as an enlightened saviour rather than, as heretofore, a degraded villain. So he changed from being a prince to being a comrade: a transformation which was celebrated on the dust-jacket of

one of those yellow-covered, left-wing books of the period by showing his title struck through with a red line. When I outlined his career to Luciani, the *Temps* correspondent, he observed sourly that Mirsky had pulled off the unusual feat of managing to be a parasite under three régimes – as a prince under Czarism, as a professor under Capitalism, and as an *homme-de-lettres* under Communism. It was a just saying, but all the same I liked Mirsky.

He sometimes visited Kitty and me in our Borisoglebsky flat to take a bath; an amenity not available where he lived. I used to chat with him while he dried himself; his body white and tender like a boy's, and the old battered, bearded head, so ravaged and decayed, with its rotting teeth, seeming not to belong to it; like an old worn hood on a new motor-car. All the wear and tear of living seemed to have gone into the head, leaving the rest of his body fresh and new. Once, chatting in this way, and feeling totally isolated and secure – the bathroom having no windows, and being filled with steam, so that we might have been in some remote cave, or just floating about in space – I ventured, on an impulse, to ask him if he really believed the awful plays shown in Moscow theatres (apart from the Stanislavsky productions, which, after all, belonged essentially to the pre-Revolution period) were any good; Stalin and his unsightly gang, great leaders and seers; the unspeakable buildings, fine architecture; the new Socialist cities, other than instant slums, the empty slogans mechanically bawled, the dogma of a new religion; the stale Marxist notions, superficial in themselves, and even then misunderstood or deliberately distorted, the messages of the future.

Mirsky went on drying himself slowly and deliberately, as though anxious to delay as long as possible covering up his body and leaving only his stained head exposed. Then he turned on me in one of his sudden furies, telling me that I was a fool who understood nothing. Plays and people and buildings and slogans and ideas, he said, didn't matter in the least.

What did matter, then? I asked him. Now he stopped drying altogether, and just looked scornfully at me. What mattered was that what was happening in the USSR *had* to happen. That forces, interacting, produced a resultant force, which was irresistible. He might have been a Hebrew prophet, Jeremiah or Isaiah, proclaiming: Thus saith the Lord! Or Calvin preaching to the predestined the inevitability of their predestined salvation or damnation. Or Beethoven with his *Es Muss Sein*. When all the cant was put aside, I reflected, this was why all those

ribald nondescript intellectuals so assiduously and cravenly followed their sour, Georgian Pied Piper – because in his wake they were among the Elect, and could count on salvation. They were ahead of history; propagandists for a victory which had yet to be won. Who Whom? – yes; but for ever Who!

One evening Mirsky took me along to a party at a sort of hostel where foreign writers were lodged. It was in honour of a Soviet writer whose play – *Cement* – had just been produced with great critical acclaim but little convincing audience enthusiasm. The guest of honour was a little man in top boots with a youthful lined face, like a jockey's. Whenever anyone spoke to him, he bowed, but said nothing. A group of Soviet poets in embroidered shirts stood round him like a bodyguard, who also bowed in unison when anyone greeted him, and, if he ventured a remark on his own account, gave it their respectful attention, or, if it was meant to be funny, fell into paroxysms of laughter; picked up by other guests, so that it echoed and re-echoed through the room. Again, there was a long table loaded with food and plentiful supplies of gaseous Soviet champagne, of which Mirsky partook lavishly. Drink made him more sombre and silent than usual; he sat looking balefully across at Elsa, the companion of the French poet Louis Aragon, for whom he had conceived a strong passion. She was, indeed, very beautiful.

At a certain point in the proceedings Aragon stood up and announced that he had just received a message from Paris that the members of the French Surrealist Movement had joined the Communist Party *en bloc*. At the news of this addition to the ranks of the World Proletariat there was a burst of cheering, in which, I noticed, Mirsky did not participate. This was doubtless due more to resentment over Aragon's favoured position *vis-à-vis* Elsa than to any scepticism about the importance of his announcement. Aragon read aloud an adulatory poem in *vers libres* that he had lately written about the French Communist Party, rolling out the words with immense gusto, his arms outstretched against the wall as though he was being crucified.

Leaving Mirsky's side, I wandered about the party rather disconsolately, trying to find someone to talk to. There were one or two American writers present of whose works, although apparently they sold in millions in the USSR, I had never heard, and quite a few Poles and East Europeans, some of them wearing decorated skull-caps. The only fellow-Englishman I came across was a man in top boots and a belted shirt who had, he told me, just come back from Baku, where he had been helping with the direction of a film reconstructing an incident

at the end of the 1914–18 war when British forces executed a number of Soviet Commissars who had fallen into their hands. One of his tasks had been to teach the extras playing the part of the British troops to sing 'Tipperary', which had really been quite difficult; they had to learn the words phonetically, and he himself had been pretty shaky on the tune. He was deadly serious about his curious assignment.

Soon after this encounter I slipped away; there seemed no point in trying to stir up Mirsky, whose eyes by this time were quite glassy, and who had fallen into a deep trance. I walked briskly home, through the now almost deserted streets, near the Pushkin Memorial passing a bearded man in a sheepskin coat who was stretched out asleep or dead in the snow. Footsteps had made a detour round him; I followed them.

Mirsky never discussed with me how he felt about having returned to the USSR as a Soviet citizen. It was obviously an act of great imprudence, and it was clear that he disliked living in Moscow, and having to associate with other Soviet penmen. In London his position had been quite comfortable; as a crossed-out prince he had an assured social position both in upper-class and intelligentsia circles, besides being welcome at working-class gatherings. Even – perhaps particularly – the Communists were glad to have a prince with them on the plinth in Trafalgar Square when they assembled there. In Moscow he was completely at the mercy of the authorities. I don't, of course, know whether he ever meditated trying to escape, but once, when we happened to be looking at a map together, his finger moved to Batum, on the Turkish frontier, and stayed there. I never heard for certain what happened to him, but know that he was arrested and taken off, either to be executed or to die in a labour camp. The ostensible cause of his fall from favour was, it seems, an article he had written on the occasion of the centenary of Pushkin's death in 1937. Following what he supposed to be the Party Line, he wrote of Pushkin as a court lackey and toady. Alas for him, the Line had changed, and Pushkin had been reinstated as a national hero. So, as it turned out, Mirsky was liquidated for denigrating Pushkin – a delectable example of Fearful Symmetry, whose cruel whimsicality may well have appealed to his own savage temperament. When I heard how his fall had come about, I recalled Luciani's remark about him; of his three essays in parasitism, it was the last that had proved the most hazardous and exacting.

I saw Kitty off at Moscow station to go back to England to have our baby by herself. It was one of many partings which all seem hateful to me now; at the time my feelings were more mixed. I remember very

vividly her face at the window as the train steamed away. Smiling and serene, as though she would be back in the evening. Actually, she was leaving with practically no money, and no certainty as to when, how, or even if, we should all be together again; with a baby due in two to three months, and only a dubious prospect of staying with my mother. Again and again I have been made aware of this rare quality of courage in her, taking refuge myself, with my easily failing heart, within the sanctuary it offers. I expect I should have gone with her; she never once asked me to, and I never thought of going. My callousness in such situations – a callousness the more abhorrent for being often quite unconscious – is something I look back on with particular disgust.

When the rear-lamp of the train had finally disappeared, I turned and walked away with Strang, of the British Embassy, whose wife had left for London on the same train. He was a diligent and kindly *fonctionnaire*, who later became head of the Foreign Office, serving sedately through the troubled appeasement years. Neville Chamberlain put him in the ignominious position of having to go through the motions of negotiating an Anglo-Soviet Treaty while Stalin was busily extorting the maximum loot from lining up with Hitler. He gave me a lift in his embassy car, and I tried to improve the occasion by questioning him about British policy towards the USSR. Without seeming to do so, he managed to evade my questions; like an experienced waiter managing not to catch the eye of a customer clamouring for attention. How fascinating they are; these gentle, diligent, honest souls, carefully buttoned and tailored, who somehow follow the twentieth century's Gadarene way without ever losing their breath or becoming dishevelled! For ever Jeeves, to an increasingly demented Bertie Wooster.

Shortly after Kitty's departure Sonia Chamberlin returned to Moscow without William Henry, and for some weeks we took our meals together in the Borisoglebsky apartment. Apart from this, I saw little of her, usually withdrawing to my own room as soon as I decently could to get on with my novel, or write articles and news stories for *The Guardian*. I also spent a lot of time with Cholerton, and roaming the streets. It is the kind of existence I have always fallen into very easily when relieved of the necessity to be in such a place, and to do thus and thus at such a time. Sonia was a low-built solid little woman with clumsy features and the shades of the ghetto still about her. There was also a strong flavour of Brooklyn, topped up with cultural and social aspirations, which took

the form of wanting to have a salon frequented by professors and writers and musicians; people she regarded as having intellectual or artistic distinction.

In Moscow she was well placed to assemble a creditable salon; though no Madame du Deffand, a warmed house and modest refreshments were a big draw, and she had no difficulty in attracting to her evening parties quite an impressive collection of the more old-fashioned sort of Russian intelligentsia who had somehow managed to survive into the Stalin era, along with an occasional first or second secretary from one of the embassies, and itinerant European or American writers who happened to be in town. Rather like Cholerton (who perhaps for that reason did not find her sympathetic), she was another unexpected Casabianca, standing on the burning deck of the good ship *Bourgeoisie*. I caught a last glimpse of her in 1969, when she came to see us with William Henry, wearing, I noticed, white laced-up kid boots of the kind to be seen in old pictures of Baden Baden at the turn of the century. This was her period, and not even the Russian Revolution could deflect her from living in it. Soon after her visit to us I heard that she had died. William Henry did not wait long to follow. Theirs had been a very close partnership; I remember how, when the *Christian Science Monitor* arrived in his absence, she would point to some headline above his by-line likely to please Oumansky, and say, glowing with warm tenderness: 'He's thinking of me.' When he finally left the USSR, William Henry compensated for such indulgent marital signals by becoming an ardent supporter of Senator McCarthy and a regular contributor to the *Wall Street Journal*.

The battered, broken fragments of pre-Revolution Moscow intelligentsia who gathered at Sonia's salon had an apologetic air about them, as though saying: We quite recognise that in a manner of speaking we have a measure of responsibility for what has happened. But is it, when you come to think about it, such a calamity as might at first sight appear? After all, it *has* meant free universal education, and the emancipation of women, and birth control, hasn't it? Perhaps after a bit, when things have got into their stride, some of the harsher aspects will be softened, and we'll have proportional representation with the transferred vote, and a branch of the PEN Club here in Moscow, and available copies of the *Times Literary Supplement*, the *New Statesman* and *The New Republic*. My old *Guardian* editorials came wanly alive in them. They went on hoping, greatly hoping; the very last moderate men of all shades of opinion to draw together in the USSR. Eating tiny sweet cakes and

sipping coffee in little cups at Sonia's salon, they were back twenty years before, when they talked about workers' control, and nationalising the land, and female suffrage; about making the past a *tabula rasa*, with no property, no family, and then the State would wither away, leaving labour to organise itself. They heard themselves proclaiming it all, in voices younger and more confident than their present apologetic whispers. *Tabula rasa* indeed; so it had come to pass. A clean slate, and they the first to be wiped off it. A lady with a raw face and little tufts of stiff black hair growing out of it began to talk about Chekhov. 'She knew him,' the other murmured. 'She's going to talk about Chekhov. It'll be such an interesting evening.'

Alexander Woolcott, a *New Yorker* mandarin who had looked in, suddenly gave his attention to what was being said. He saw a splendid piece in this, whimsically reporting how, at such a dingy, unappetising gathering in Moscow, new vivid reminiscence of the famous Russian playwright had been recounted. Mentally, he began to make notes of the scene; the old house, in what had doubtless once been a superior residential suburb; dark, musty passages, pieces of carpet and cloth draped over the walls, chairs and tables all likewise covered. A dusty, muffled, stale old house, and these people part of the dust and the staleness themselves. Ideological waifs and strays – he liked that phrase. He was a well-covered man himself, with a wide expanse of face, gleaming spectacles, and a camel-hair coat and fur hat hanging in the hall ready for when he went out. Clearing his throat noisily to attract full attention, he enjoyed telling them how that morning, when he stood on the steps of the Metropole Hotel where he was staying, a passer-by had come up to him and just gently passed his hand over his camel-hair coat, following the curve of his ample stomach, by way of a salute to his *en-bon-point*, his well-being, his affluence. The others laughed, but uneasily; they felt they were themselves rather in the position of the passer-by. They, too, metaphorically speaking, had been stroking Woolcott's stomach, so beautifully moulded, mounted and arrayed. The warmth of the flat, the talk, the refreshments, all brought them momentarily to life; like hibernating flies in sudden heat. When they put on their outdoor clothes, their shabby old coats and galoshes and nondescript knitted balaclavas, and went out into the street, they died again, creeping away to their holes.

For these residual ageing progressives who had not even been considered worth liquidating, the visits to Moscow of famous foreign intel-

lectuals were gala occasions. Long-standing household gods come among them, whom they might even have known personally in the past; fraternal delegates at some conference or convention at which a Harold Laski or a Bernard Shaw or an Albert Thomas had been among the speakers. The fact that this link existed nourished the hope that it might somehow be possible actually to exchange a word with one or other of them, recalling past acquaintanceship. In practice, of course, it never happened. How could the distinguished visitors be expected to remember the last time they had seen these dismal relics of the past, when they, too, wore carelessly elegant suits, and had their hair in fine disarray; maybe with pince-nez like Webb's on a black ribbon; or even a monocle, like his fellow-Fabian, Hubert Bland? When, instead of creeping about apologetically in old balaclavas, they likewise stood on a platform, waving their hands in the air and proclaiming the coming of the great day when the workers would seize power, and mankind live happily ever after? Nor were to-day's distinguished visitors likely to reflect that, come another revolution or two, they might find themselves in their turn seedy citizens of a workers' paradise, with no return first-class ticket in their pockets to take them back to capitalist exploitation in London or Paris or New York whenever they had a mind.

For resident foreign journalists in Moscow the arrival of the distinguished visitors was also a gala occasion, for a different reason. They provided us with our best – almost our only – comic relief. For instance, when we heard Shaw, accompanied by Lady Astor (who was photographed cutting his hair), declare that he was delighted to find there was no food shortage in the USSR. Or Laski singing the praises of Stalin's new Soviet constitution. Or Julian Huxley describing how a 'German town-planning expert was travelling over the huge Siberian spaces in a special train with a staff of assistants, stopping every now and again to lay down the broad outlines of a future city, and then pushing on, leaving the details to be filled in by architects and engineers who remained behind.' Or – a collector's item – Maurice Hindus describing a young man at the reception desk of a Soviet home for reformed prostitutes who 'wears a modern suit of clothes, complete with collar and tie, and, what is more astonishing, spats.' 'Communist though he is,' he adds of this worthy, 'he deems it essential to keep up as presentable an appearance as the scanty supplies in the Moscow haberdashery shops permit.' Hindus, an American of Russian-Jewish extraction with black curly hair and a winning smile, wrote best-selling books in such a vein (*Red Bread, Humanity Uprooted*) about the Soviet régime. Future historians

may well comment that the road to world revolution is paved with best-sellers.

We used to run a little contest among ourselves to see who could produce the most striking example of credulity among this fine flower of our western intelligentsia. Persuading church dignitaries to feel at home in an anti-God museum was too easy to count. So was taking lawyers into the People's Courts. The Webbs, too, were for beginners only. I got an honourable mention by persuading Lord Marley that the queueing at food shops was permitted by the authorities because it provided a means of inducing the workers to take a rest when otherwise their zeal for completing the Five-Year Plan in record time was such that they would keep at it all the time, but no marks for floating a story that Soviet citizens were being asked to send in human hair – any sort – for making of felt boots. It seemed that this had actually happened. A correspondent the *Neue Freie Presse* was commended for inducing the French Premier, Herriot, to believe, when he visited the USSR, that the milk shortage there was due to the large amounts allocated to nursing mothers. Cholerton, rightly, received the *Grand Prix* when, overhearing an eminent British jurist ask Oumansky whether Habeas Corpus operated in the USSR, he broke in to tell him, to his complete satisfaction, that, whatever might be the case with Habeas Corpus, the authorities strictly adhered to Habeas Cadaver.

I have never forgotten these visitors, or ceased to marvel at them, at how they have gone on from strength to strength, continuing to lighten our darkness, and to guide, counsel and instruct us; on occasion, momentarily abashed, but always ready to pick themselves up, put on their cardboard helmets, mount Rosinante, and go galloping off on yet another foray on behalf of the down-trodden and oppressed. They are unquestionably one of the wonders of the age, and I shall treasure till I die as a blessed memory the spectacle of them travelling with radiant optimism through a famished countryside, wandering in happy bands about squalid, over-crowded towns, listening with unshakeable faith to the fatuous patter of carefully trained and indoctrinated guides, repeating like schoolchildren a multiplication table, the bogus statistics and mindless slogans endlessly intoned to them. There, I would think, an earnest office-holder in some local branch of the League of Nations Union, there a godly Quaker who once had tea with Gandhi, there an inveigher against the Means Test and the Blasphemy Laws, there a staunch upholder of free speech and human rights, there an indomitable preventer of cruelty to animals; there scarred and worthy veterans of a

hundred battles for truth, freedom and justice – all, all chanting the praises of Stalin and his Dictatorship of the Proletariat. It was as though a vegetarian society had come out with a passionate plea for cannibalism, or Hitler had been nominated posthumously for the Nobel Peace Prize.

When William Henry returned, I moved out of his Borisoglebsky apartment and took up residence in the National Hotel. The decor was in heavy marble and gilt, rather like the stations in the Moscow underground, then under construction, and to become a tourist show-place. Once, sitting with Mirsky in the hotel lounge, I remarked upon its excruciating taste. Yes, he agreed, it was pretty ghastly, but it expressed the sense of what a luxury hotel should be like in the mind of someone who had only stared in at one through plate-glass windows from the cold, inhospitable street outside. This, he said, was the key to all the régime's artistic products – the long turgid novels, the lifeless portraits and landscapes in oils, the gruesome People's neo-Gothic architecture, the leaden conservatory concerts and creaking ballet. Culturally, it was all of a piece. There is no surer way of preserving the worst aspects of bourgeois style than liquidating the bourgeoisie; whatever else Stalin may, or may not, have done, he assuredly made Russia safe for the Forsyte Saga.

The ceremonial opening of the Dneprostroi Dam, to which all foreign journalists were invited, provided a welcome opportunity to get away from Moscow. A special train was laid on for us, consisting entirely of ancient international wagons-lits, in which we were allotted berths. There was also, of course, a restaurant car. In over-heated carriages, with vodka flowing freely, gossiping and laughing, we rolled southwards, looking vaguely out of the windows at the passing countryside, which gradually, as we progressed, grew less wintry, more sunny and salubrious. For the most part the small stations we rattled through were cleared of people, but sometimes there were some bedraggled looking peasants clustered together on the platform. Noticing one such cluster, a large German correspondent carelessly threw out of the window a leg of chicken he had been gnawing at. There was a concerted move to pick it up. The gesture and the response have stayed with me through the intervening years like stigmata.

It seemed somehow symbolic of our whole situation that we, the reporters, should thus be coursing so cosily through this vast country that was our territory. Seeing, and yet not seeing. In it, and yet inexorably isolated and insulated; as it might be in a television control-room, and

looking down at a distant studio; faces, gestures and words there transmitted to us in recorded sounds and pictures. In the restaurant car a game of poker was in progress, round which a little group of spectators had gathered, including Ehrens, a keen player himself. With no deadlines to meet, no possibility of cabling, we could take it easy. Whatever happened would be a non-happening because unrecorded by us. I looked out of the window as night fell; such a beautiful countryside, luminous in the winter sunshine. The countryside of *War and Peace*, of *Oblomov*, of *Dead Souls*. I knew it as though I had lived in it all my life. What, after all, could Stalin and his henchmen do to it? It would surely outlast and outshine them. I had a notion even that I might live to go about in it cheerfully and freely, as in Sussex or Provence. Forty years later, this has not yet come to pass. Still, I do not despair, though there are now not many more years to go.

I was joined by an Englishman in shorts who carried his luggage in a rucksack, and was preparing material for a series of articles in the *New Leader*, then the organ of the Independent Labour Party. He was a nondescript sort of person, with a small black moustache, not as young as he looked or as old as he felt, who had been to prison as a conscientious objector in the war. It was easy to imagine him, at some ILP summer school, holding forth in his gritty, insistent voice about how, in the USSR, there were other motives than greed as the mainspring of action, nobler ideals to fight for than country or empire (not that he advocated violence in any circumstances; he meant mental fight, in the sense of striving after, seeking earnestly to attain); new standards of value, a new relationship between man and man. Now he had begun to wonder. There seemed to be a lot of violence about. Was all the talk about the Three Letters (a pseudonym used in conversation to avoid mentioning the dreaded GPU) justified and true? He was, I could see, troubled in spirit; like an evangelical clergyman who has suddenly been smitten with doubts about the Thirty-Nine Articles; with the same look of mute suffering in his eyes.

'Being actually in the USSR,' he said, 'drives one back to first principles, doesn't it?' Cholerton, who was standing nearby, said he thought it drove one back rather to last principles. Louis Fischer, correspondent of the American *Nation*, then chipped in to say that one mustn't expect too much; after all, the great experiment had only been going for fifteen years. We must give them time. Fischer was a sallow, ponderous, inordinately earnest man, dear to Oumansky as one who had never once through the years veered from virtuously following the Party Line.

Later, at the time of the Nazi-Soviet Pact, he did veer, quite drastically, afterwards turning for solace to Gandhi; a port in a storm for many an ideological wanderer. If the Mahatma had been present, I should have referred the troubled Englishman to him; as he wasn't, I told him to try Wicksteed who was, as being the next best thing. Wicksteed generally managed to attach himself to jaunts like the Dneprostroi one, if only to partake of the plentiful hospitality. I saw the two of them later in earnest conversation. I doubt if Fischer's defection, when at last it came, much troubled the Soviet authorities. His usefulness by that time was largely exhausted, and they might have reflected with Dryden that they had lost a villain, and his new patrons gained a fool.

I shared my compartment with a charming Bulgarian named Andreychin whom I had met at one of Sonia's salons. As we lay in our berths we talked together through much of the night. With the blinds up, we could look out of the window at a countryside now bathed in moonlight, most wonderfully still and serene, with just an occasional little cluster of lights coming into view and then disappearing. Andreychin had lived in America, where he had been a member of the International Workers of the World (the Wobblies). Describing to me with great zest and delight the antics they got up to with a view to undermining the economy of the State, he spoke of it all as though it had been an undergraduate frolic in his golden youth; something so delightful and gay and blameless that he could not hope ever again to recapture its spirit. Occasionally he broke out into one of their Wobblie songs, as it might have been a boating or a drinking song at some festive campus fraternity gathering, rather than a call to workers to rise up in their might and fury, and death to all bosses. He had been deported at the time of the Sacco-Vanizetti affair, making for the USSR, and remaining there ever since. Already he had done one stint in a labour camp.

But surely, I said, what you were striving after in America you've got here. Yes, he replied, doubtfully; it must be so. All the same, what would he not give to be back with the Wobblies in Detroit, engaged in bringing about the dissolution of the capitalist system! In the great purges of the middle thirties I heard that he had been given a further ten years' sentence. Then, to everyone's amazement, he turned up in Paris in 1946 as an interpreter with the Bulgarian delegation at the peace negotiations. He had lost most of his hair and all his teeth at the labour camp – tougher this time, he said, than at his first stretch – but was still liable to break into his Wobblie songs over a bottle in the evening. His

western friends would have been glad to persuade him to stay in Paris, but he insisted on returning to Sofia, where in due course he was disposed of, like all the others, with a bullet in the back of his head. Did he give one more rendering of his Wobblie songs as they took him off? It would be nice to think so.

The next morning we arrived at Kharkov, now, instead of Kiev, the capital of the Ukraine. We were played into the station by a band; as it struck up the 'Internationale' in honour of Kalinin, nominally the head of State, who was travelling with us, everyone stood to attention, though in our Press carriages, where there was a general atmosphere of hangover, somewhat laxly. Kalinin was a small thin man with a wispy beard; so innocuous that, almost alone of Stalin's closer colleagues, he died unpurged. In the legend he was said to be a peasant, but I thought he had a decided resemblance to Sidney Webb – not by any means the same thing. Oumansky was waiting for us to take us to breakfast, wearing a cloth cap, breeches and top boots, which made him look woebegone; like a child at a Christmas party who has put on a cowboy outfit, and feels uneasily half aware that it isn't quite making the hoped for impression.

I was confronted with a similar sartorial surprise in the Ukraine when I accompanied Harold Macmillan there in 1959. In view of the fact that a visit to a collective farm was included in his itinerary, he arrayed himself for his arrival at Kiev in a plus-fours ensemble of the kind still considered appropriate for opening Conservative garden fêtes in the Home Counties. At the station he was met by local dignitaries, and delivered a speech which one of his staff had prepared about how in the twelfth century an English monarch had espoused a Ukrainian princess, and how ever since relations between the two countries had been particularly warm and cordial. On such occasions the ostensible Soviet public in attendance have in front of them a solid phalanx of policemen in issue civilian suits, with wide trousers, and plenty of room under the armpits for whatever they might wish to lodge there. I scrutinised the granite faces of some of these worthies to see whether there was any reaction to the British Prime Minister's remarks, and in one or two I thought I detected a faint flickering of the eyelids expressive of surprise, wonder, and maybe an impulse to laugh. That Christmas, greatly to my surprise, I got a telegram from the Soviet satirical magazine, *Krokodil*, asking me to let them have an account of the funniest thing that in my estimation had happened during the current year. In reply, I sent off a description of Macmillan in Kiev, but the editor wrote back very

politely to the effect that, though he personally thought my piece decidedly funny, his magazine circulated among the broad masses, who held Macmillan in the highest esteem and therefore would not be amused. It might have been Crozier.

After breakfast Oumansky took us to see some newly constructed factories. We traipsed rather disconsolately through them after him, to a barrage of incomprehensible and unbelievable statistics. If any of us allowed our attention to wander or lingered behind, Louis Fischer took it upon himself to round us up. 'Come on! It creates such a bad impression if we don't seem interested.' A man from the *Chicago Daily News* muttered under his breath that he *wasn't* interested anyway. Where's the colour? Where's the human interest? he groaned. Visiting factories and listening to statistics – unless of course, one happens to be a specialist, and even then, readers aren't – is one of the major miseries of reporting in Communist counties. There is no getting out of it; unavailing to say, as I did when I was in China, that I was uninterested in heavy, or for that matter light, industry, that I was perfectly ready to take on trust the giant strides made in the way of industrial development, and only interested in things like clergymen and co-education. It made no difference; the dreadful ritual was inescapable. I imagine that pilgrims in the Middle Ages were likewise required to go on all fours through the Catacombs, and make their reverent but uncomfortable way to remote desert shrines.

Our special train arrived at Dneprostroi late at night, and Oumansky suggested that we should go at once and look at the dam and the hydroelectric station. He was, one could see, already excited himself. So, we piled into motor cars (in those days all the official Soviet cars were Ford Lincolns), and there it was; looking like a huge theatrical set, with searchlights flashing, sirens sounding, and written across the sky in letters of fire: ELECTRICITY PLUS SOVIET POWER EQUALS COMMUNISM. A sort of Red Broadway. In the river below a great swirl and rush of water; at the dam, soldiers on sentry-go, their bayonets gleaming as they marched to and fro. Accompanying us there was a retired American colonel with several tremulous chins and a southern accent, who had directed some of the construction. He, too, was uplifted. 'It looks great,' he murmured. 'Great!' Louis Fischer warmly agreed, going on to ask: 'How have you found working here, Colonel?' 'That's been great, too,' the other answered, adding, half to himself: 'No labour trouble!' Everyone knew what he meant; prisoners on forced labour had been available

as and when required. Fischer hurriedly changed the subject, moving on to the safer territory of how many kilowatts were being generated, and what volume of water the dam contained.

Oumansky climbed on to a little knoll and took off his cloth cap; he looked very Napoleonic standing there, and I almost expected him to tuck his hand into his overcoat in Napoleon's favourite gesture. The noise, the flashing lights, the movement; the sense of something immense that was reined in, controlled; power concentrated into a switch that anyone's fingers – his – could turn on and off; enormous wheels and turbines turning; silently, precisely revolving – all this went to his head. 'You see, gentlemen, what we have done,' he shouted at us, and went on to recite to us the tale of achievement – the largest hydro-electric station in the world; the world's record for cement-pouring, more electricity being generated than ever before in one single place; the whole thing finished in under four years, and now fully operative. 'Who,' he concluded, 'dare talk now of an interesting experiment?' Louis Fischer also took off his hat; it seemed the right thing to do, and he hoped the rest of us would follow his example. Actually none of us did. The ILP man certainly would have followed suit, except that, despite the freezing cold, he had no hat, though for some reason he had put on his rucksack to come to the dam. Fischer made up for our lack of response by a short formal speech: 'Mr Oumansky, we, representatives of many nations and many newspapers, would like you to know . . .'

The next morning Kalinin stood with the other notables on a raised platform and addressed a large audience assembled in an amphitheatre consisting mostly of delegations with banners and bands. Every so often one or other of these bands would play the 'Internationale', whereupon everyone would rise to their feet. Kalinin, with photographers hovering round him like insects with protruding eyes, delivered a speech which droned on and on, echoed and re-echoed by a series of loud-speakers, so that his words seemed to be chasing after each other across the amphitheatre. There was no response to them anyway; only an occasional rumble of drilled applause, and an occasional outburst of the 'Internationale'. He was followed by Henri Barbusse, author of *Le Feu*, a cadaverous looking Frenchman who spluttered over his words and waved his arms helplessly in the air as he spoke. It was impossible to hear what he said, but certain words and phrases came sizzling out of him; like *la Paix, la France, une journée inoubliable pour la classe ouvrière*. 'I see a vision,' he shrieked in his vibrant French, moisture glistening like dew on his moustache, 'of the toiling masses everywhere looking up from

their misery and degradation, with hope in their eyes because of what you have achieved in your great workers' republic under the mighty leadership of Comrade Stalin.' Luciani aptly described him as *un homme décomposé*, and, indeed, his decomposition was such that one almost expected him to fall to pieces with the very vehemence of his oratory in so frail a body.

Compared with the night before, all the fire and mysticism of the occasion seemed absent; it needed the search-lights piercing the darkness, the letters of fire, the sentries and the sound of the swirling water, to provide a proper setting. Even Oumansky seemed subdued and dejected; the interminable speeches had a debilitating effect which not even the Commissar for Heavy Industry (Cholerton called him the Commissar for Heavy Income), an enormous Georgian named Ordshonikidze, was able to overcome. Cold and dispirited, we returned to our train, glad when it started on the return journey to Moscow.

Back in Moscow I felt at a loose end. My enthusiasm for dredging up items from the Soviet press with Klavdia Lvovna's help, had greatly abated. I spent more and more time tramping about the streets, or talking with Cholerton. My novel about *The Guardian* which I had sent off with Kitty was not, I now heard, acceptable to the publisher, who wrote complimentary things about it, but said the risk of legal action was too great to take. So I did not even get the £50 advance on which I had been counting. In the evenings I made a round of the theatres, often accompanied by Katerina Georgevna, whom I liked more and more. Her great simplicity of character and goodness shone in her face, making her beautiful. I have always loved such qualities and those who have them, and, contrariwise, been attracted sensually by those who lack them – who are egotistic and greedy and faithless. This is why happiness through the senses, even when I have sought it, has always seemed to me a vain pursuit, and also why, I suppose, I am often called a Manichee. No statement could possibly be, to me, more self-evidently true than St Paul's when he says that to be carnally minded is death, and to be spiritually minded life and peace. Unfortunately, I have wasted too much of my life in the death-camp of carnality.

Katerina Georgevna, in any case, was a delightful companion. She loved Russian drama and gave me the feel of it as no professional critic could. It was part of her life, something she treasured to keep alive a past that had been historically abolished. Thus, for instance, at a mar-

vellous production of *Dead Souls* at the Moscow Art Theatre, then still
being directed by Stanislavsky, she, as it were, introduced me to each of
the characters, so that I knew them and can remember them perfectly
to this day, even though I could not follow the dialogue. Afterwards, she
gave me a set of postcard representations of them which I have kept
carefully to this day and I have gone on reading Gogol's masterpiece
from time to time; along with Don Quixote, Gulliver, Rabelais, Candide
and Falstaff. In the interval we followed the pleasant Russian custom
of joining the procession winding round and round the foyer,
watching the others as they were watching us, and talking about
the play.

One comment of Katerina Georgevna's that sticks in my mind was
made about *The Cherry Orchard*. After agreeing with me about the
excellence of the production, she added: 'But all the same, I couldn't
see what they were bothering about. They had plenty to eat.' As a child
she had been through the famine and the Civil War, and the memory
was so searing that the sorrows and deprivations of Chekhov's characters
failed to register. It was indeed a superb production, I think the best I
have ever seen, and the first to be put on in Moscow since the Revolu-
tion. Up to then, Chekhov's plays had been banned as ideologically
unsound and decadent. So, for the Art Theatre, and for Stanislavsky
personally, it was a great occasion; the theatre's reputation had been
built on Chekhov, and there was still a sea-gull on its curtain. Chekhov's
widow, Knipper, played the lead, and the whole cast, down to the smal-
lest part, perfectly recreated a society so rootless and without values that
a revolution seemed scarcely necessary to bring about its destruction.
The end was almost insupportable – the steel teeth of a saw biting into
a tree-trunk; the downfall of a way of life, if not of a civilisation.
Chekhov only foresaw the downfall, but this audience had lived through
it. Many of them were in floods of tears, all were deeply moved; as was
Katerina Georgevna despite her comment about the cast having plenty
to eat; as, indeed, was I, despite my valuta origins and prospects.

We occasionally visited the other Moscow theatres – the Tairov, the
Mayerhold, the Vakhtangov – but without caring much for them. After
the Art Theatre, they all seemed rather spurious though, as can now be
seen, making straight the way for Peter Brook, Peter Hall and other
illuminati of the Arts Council. Their directors all in due course came to
grief at Stalin's hands, as did Eisenstein, whose films, like *Mother* and
The Battleship Potemkin, were part of the holy writ of all good Leftists.
In the end, it was Stanislavsky alone who was given the Order of the

Red Banner and allowed to die in his bed. He, bourgeois of the bourgeois, flaunting to the end his soft black hat set rakishly on white locks, his astrakhan collar and flowing tie, as though he had just stepped out of the Hotel de Paris in Monte Carlo. The only production other than a Stanislavsky one which sticks in my mind is *Die Dreigroschenoper*, put on by the Moscow Judische Art Theatre, long since liquidated. It was my first acquaintance with Brecht.

Our stories from Moscow were increasingly concerned with the agricultural situation, which even the Soviet newspapers were featuring in, for them, a big way. In the circumstances, I decided that the best thing to do would be to have a go at visiting the agricultural areas in the Ukraine and the Caucasus by myself. Nowadays this would be quite impossible, since foreign journalists, like diplomats, have to get special authorisation to travel. Then, one could still, in theory at any rate, buy a railway ticket like anyone else. The odds were, of course, that one would be picked up at some point, but before this happened there was a chance of arriving unheralded somewhere, and talking to people other than under the shadow of the GPU. Actually, in my experience the Soviet security arrangements, once you get, as it were, off the moving stairway, are by no means as ruthlessly efficient as is commonly supposed. At a time when I had been persistently refused a visa to go to the USSR I happened to find myself in Peking, and on an impulse went into the Soviet Embassy there, and asked for a transit visa to stop off in Moscow on my way back to London. My passport was politely stamped, and handed back to me then and there; I stopped off in Moscow for ten days or so, without, as far as I could judge, my presence attracting any interest or attention.

Even so, I doubt if I should have had the perseverance or courage to join the immensely long queues always waiting in front of the ticket office at Moscow Station. Happily for me, Natalia Dmitrievna took me under her wing, and by dint of pushing, shouting and seeming to be important, made her way to the top of the queue, and procured the requisite return ticket to Rostov, with the possibility of getting off the train anywhere along the way.

The evening before I left there was a party at the British Embassy to which I went. Owing to the debourgeoisation of my wardrobe before leaving for the USSR, I had no appropriate clothes for such an occasion, and felt very self-conscious in a light grey suit, decidedly shabby, the only one I had. The ambassador was a man named Sir Esmond Ovey, a suave figure with brushed back grey hair and a small trimmed mous-

tache. When I told him how my sartorial inadequacy had come about, he thought it very funny, and went on through the evening telling everyone he spoke to why I was so inappropriately dressed. I expect I deserved this. The only thing I can remember about Ovey is that he had a plan for solving the unemployment problem which on various occasions he tried to explain to me, no doubt calculating that *The Guardian* would be the ideal medium for launching such a proposal. Unfortunately, I never got the hang of it, maybe through my own inattention, or because he never managed to finish his exposition. So the plan must, I fear, have died with him. After Moscow, he was posted to Brussels.

On this occasion I managed to escape from his clutches quite quickly, and withdrew to a sofa where I found myself sitting between Anna Louise Strong and Walter Duranty, the *New York Times* correspondent. Miss Strong was an enormous woman with a very red face, a lot of white hair, and an expression of stupidity so overwhelming that it amounted to a kind of strange beauty. When in years to come I embarked on that Via Dolorosa, the American lecture circuit, I was constantly reminded of her; looking down on my audience from the podium, I saw row upon row of Anna Louises, as eagerly waiting for some crumbs of enlightenment from me as she did from Oumansky, or Borodin (under whom she worked on the *Moscow Daily News*), or the great Stalin himself. She had been around in Moscow from shortly after the Revolution, and allegedly, finding herself once in a car with Trotsky, the great man put his hand on her knee in what might have been taken as an amorous gesture. Whether because of this past anti-Stalinist deviation, or for some other reason, in the stormy days of the cold war even she got arrested; an item of news which, I regret to say, like Oumansky's fatal accident, gave great satisfaction among former newspaper correspondents in Moscow. Some of them even sent congratulatory telegrams signalising the glad tidings. Her incarceration proved to be brief – I imagine that even in Lubianka, her presence was burdensome – and she ended her days in Peking, where she was accorded a State funeral. A triumph of sheer staying power.

Duranty, a little sharp-witted energetic man, was a much more controversial person; I should say there was more talk about him in Moscow than anyone else, certainly among foreigners. By origin he was an Englishman from Liverpool, which probably means he was Irish; a conclusion supported by his proneness to hint at aristocratic connections and classical learning, of which, I must say, he produced little evidence. One of his legs had been amputated after a train accident, but he was

very agile at getting about with an artificial one. His household, where I visited him once or twice, included a Russian woman named Katya, by whom I believe he had a son. I always enjoyed his company; there was something vigorous, vivacious, preposterous, about his unscrupulousness which made his persistent lying somehow absorbing. I suppose no one – not even Louis Fischer – followed the Party Line, every shift and change, as assiduously as he did. In Oumansky's eyes he was perfect, and was constantly held up to the rest of us as an example of what we should be.

It, of course, suited his material interests thus to write everything the Soviet authorities wanted him to – that collectivisation of agriculture was working well, with no famine conditions anywhere; that the purges were justified, the confessions genuine, and the judicial procedure impeccable. Because of these acquiescent attitudes – so ludicrously false that they were a subject of derision among the other correspondents, and even Podolski had been known to make jokes about them – Duranty never had any trouble getting a visa, or a house, or interviews with whomever he wanted. His subservience to the Party Line was so complete that it was even rumoured that he was being blackmailed by the Soviet authorities. Yet I do not myself think he was just a simple crook; in some strange way, his upholding of the Soviet régime was, besides being materially advantageous, a response to some need of his nature. Not, I hasten to add, because he believed in the Revolution, or in its beneficial consequences to Russia or to mankind – anything like that. Quite the contrary; I think he despised all that sort of apologetics, indulged in by Fischer and still more by Anna Louise Strong, more than anyone.

No, he admired Stalin and the régime precisely because they were so strong and ruthless. 'I put my money on Stalin,' was one of his favourite sayings. It was the sheer power generated that appealed to him; he was always remarking on how big Russia was, how numerous Russians were. Thus, for instance, in this last conversation I was ever to have with him, we got on to the subject of the agricultural situation and the famine. He admitted there was an appalling food shortage, if not a famine (something, incidentally, no one could have deduced from his messages to the *New York Times*, which were in an exactly contrary sense), but, he said, banging the sides of the sofa, remember that you can't make omelettes without cracking eggs – another favourite saying. They'll win, he went on; they're bound to win. If necessary, they'll harness the peasants to the ploughs, but I tell you they'll get the harvest

in and feed the people that matter. The people that mattered were the men in the Kremlin and all their underlings; the men in the factories and the armed forces; us, too, the elite. The others were just serfs; reserves of the proletariat, as Stalin called them. Some would die, surely, perhaps even quite a lot; but there were enough and to spare in all conscience. It might have been a Burra Sahib talking about the natives.

I had the feeling, listening to this outburst, that in thus justifying Soviet brutality and ruthlessness, Duranty was in some way getting his own back for being small, and losing a leg, and not having the aristocratic lineage and classical education he claimed to have. This is probably, in the end, the only real basis of the appeal of such régimes as Stalin's, and later Hitler's; they compensate for weakness and inadequacy. It is also why their particular ideologies – *Mein Kampf, Das Kapital, The Thoughts of Chairman Mao* – are, in themselves, of no significance. Duranty was a little browbeaten boy looking up admiringly at a big bully. By the same token, if the *New York Times* went on all those years giving great prominence to Duranty's messages, building him and them up when they were so evidently nonsensically untrue, to the point that he came to be accepted as the great Russian expert in America, and played a major part in shaping President Roosevelt's policies *vis-à-vis* the USSR – this was not, we may be sure, because the *Times* was deceived. Rather, because it wanted to be so deceived, and Duranty provided the requisite deception material. Since his time, there have been a whole succession of others fulfilling the same role – in Cuba, in Vietnam, in Latin America. It is an addiction, and in such cases there is never any lack of hands to push in the needle and give the fix. Just as the intelligentsia have been foremost in the struggle to abolish intelligence, so the great organs of capitalism like the *New York Times* have spared no expense or effort to ensure that capitalism will not survive.

My journey to Rostov remains in my mind as a nightmare memory. The worn railway compartment, with glasses of tea endlessly served; other passengers coming and going, mostly party officials (who else could afford to travel first-class?), very companionable and amiable and ready to listen to my rudimentary Russian, but shutting up at once if I brought up the subject of what was going on outside. Then, their faces stony and expressionless again. Men in leather coats with briefcases, sucking at cigarettes, clearly used to giving orders and to being treated with deference in the Forestry Department, or the Audit Department,

or I daresay in the GPU Department, but that also were unmentionable. The restaurant car, likewise cosy, with meals pleasantly served and plenty of vodka. There, too, the outside pleasantly remote, except for one intrusion; a bearded moujik in a padded coat, very drunk and wild looking, suddenly appeared, shouting out something – some sort of protest, I suppose, but I couldn't understand what. He was quickly disposed of; frog-marched out, still protesting.

It was tempting not to get down at any stations along the way as I had planned, but just to continue in the train. By comparison with its warmth and snugness, the stations looked very uninviting. I had no contacts, no transport, nowhere to go; the moment one arranged these amenities, one was back in Oumansky's charge. However, I did break my journey several times, and can never forget what I saw. It was not just a famine. No one, alas, news-gathering about the world in our time can fail to have seen quite a lot of famine. In India, in Berlin, in Africa – people picking over garbage, scrabbling about in rubble, maybe in their desperation cannibalising one another; swollen or skeletal, with huge stomachs suspended between bony arms and ribs, and heads that, while still alive, are already skulls. This particular famine was planned and deliberate; not due to any natural catastrophe like failure of rain, or cyclone, or flooding. An administrative famine brought about by the forced collectivisation of agriculture; an assault on the countryside by party *apparatchiks* – the very men I'd been chatting so amiably with in the train – supported by strong-arm squads from the military and the police.

As I wrote in *The Guardian*, in the course of three articles of mine that appeared on 25, 27 and 28 March, 1933: 'To say that there is famine in some of the most fertile parts of Russia is to say much less than the truth; there is not only famine, but a state of war, a military occupation.' The articles were held up to follow a series by Voigt on the Terror in the Polish Ukraine, and were run side by side with another series by him on the Nazi Terror, by way, I imagine, of neutralising some of their effect. In them I tried to describe it all – the abandoned villages, the absence of livestock, neglected fields; everywhere famished, frightened people and intimations of coercion, soldiers about the place, and hard-faced men in long overcoats. One particularly remarkable scene I stumbled on by chance at a railway station in the grey early morning; peasants with their hands tied behind them being loaded into cattle trucks at gun-point (this, incidentally, was the nearest I came to being in trouble myself; I was angrily told to make off, which I hurriedly did, fortunately without having to disclose myself as a foreign journalist); all so

silent and mysterious and horrible in the half-light, like some macabre ballet.

Reading the articles over again, they seem very inadequate in conveying the horror of it all, which far surpassed just the human misery. *Rien de plus dangereux,* Taine writes, *qu'une idée générale dans des cerveaux étroits et vides.* Stalin's collectivisation of agriculture was just such a general idea in a narrow empty mind, pursued to the uttermost limit, without reference to any other consideration, whether of individual or collective humanity. To be oppressed by an individual tyrant is terrible enough; by an enraged deity, as the Old Testament tells us, even more terrible; but Taine is right when he contends that the worst of all fates is to be oppressed by a general idea. This was the fate of the Russian peasants, as it is, increasingly, the fate of us all in the twentieth century.

As it happened, no other foreign journalist had been into the famine areas in the USSR except under official auspices and supervision, so my account was by way of being exclusive. This brought me no kudos, and many accusations of being a liar, in *The Guardian* correspondence columns and elsewhere. I had to wait for Khruschev – who surely knew the truth if anyone did, having been himself one of the chief terrorists in the Ukraine – for official confirmation. Indeed, according to him, my account was considerably under-stated. If the matter is a subject of controversy hereafter, a powerful voice on the other side will be Duranty's, highlighted in the *New York Times,* insisting on those granaries overflowing with grain, those apple-cheeked dairymaids and plump contented cows, not to mention Shaw and all the other distinguished visitors who testified that there was not, and could not be, a food shortage in the USSR. I doubt if even Khruschev's testimony, let alone mine, will weigh against such honourable and distinguished witnesses.

In Kiev, where I found myself on a Sunday morning, on an impulse I turned into a church where a service was in progress. It was packed tight, but I managed to squeeze myself against a pillar whence I could survey the congregation and look up at the altar. Young and old, peasants and townsmen, parents and children, even a few in uniform – it was a variegated assembly. The bearded priests, swinging their incense, intoning their prayers, seemed very remote and far away. Never before or since have I participated in such worship; the sense conveyed of turning to God in great affliction was overpowering. Though I could

not, of course, follow the service, I knew from Klavdia Lvovna little bits of it; for instance, where the congregation say there is no help for them save from God. What intense feeling they put into these words! In their minds, I knew, as in mine, was a picture of those desolate abandoned villages, of the hunger and the hopelessness, of the cattle trucks being loaded with humans in the dawn light. Where were they to turn for help? Not to the Kremlin, and the Dictatorship of the Proletariat, certainly; nor to the forces of progress and democracy and enlightenment in the West. Honourable and Right Honourable Members had nothing to offer; *Gauche Radicale* unforthcoming, free press Duranty's pulpit. Every possible human agency found wanting. So, only God remained, and to God they turned with a passion, a dedication, a humility, impossible to convey. They took me with them; I felt closer to God then than I ever had before, or am likely to again.

From Rostov I went to visit a German agricultural concession in the Kuban district of the North Caucasus, which had rather surprisingly survived from the early post-war years. It was like going abroad. Everything was completely different; the fields, the cowsheds, the piggeries, all in perfect order. I found it difficult to believe I was still in the USSR. A Bavarian in a green knickerbocker suit with a feather in his hat showed me round. Sensing, perhaps, that my attention was flagging, he asked me whether I was really interested in *Landwirtschaft*. I replied that I had to admit to being no specialist, but that I could not fail to notice how conditions in the concession contrasted with those outside. He agreed, and said that in consequence of the famine conditions all round them, they had been faced with a constant stream of famished peasants looking for work and food. In the evening I sat with him and a number of other Germans, all of them healthy and jovial and friendly and hospitable. While we were talking, one of them brought out a map, showing me just where the concession was situated, and going on to point out, *à propos* of nothing, how large the USSR was, and how rich agriculturally and in minerals. There was something vaguely ominous and menacing as his strong, short forefinger went moving about the map. Then someone turned on the radio, managing to get a German transmission. The news was that Hitler had become Chancellor. I had not been following the papers for some time, so it took me by surprise. 'How terrible!' I said, or something like that, expecting them to agree. They were, after all, professional people, agricultural experts, technicians; the sort of Germans, one assumed, who would find Hitler and his Nazis ridiculous and abhorrent. On the contrary, I could see that

they were delighted. It was a good thing, they said; no doubt they and their class would once again lose everything they had, as had happened before; but this time Germany would recover her strength and resume her history. I had little inclination to argue, and, pleading tiredness, retired to bed. After I had gone they would, I felt sure, let their exaltation have free play; shaking hands, slapping one another on the back, drinking toasts. Late at night, I heard them, shouting and singing uproariously. Thenceforth, I never doubted that another war was inescapable.

When I got back to Moscow I found a telegram from Kitty telling me that we had another son. I managed to telephone to her, and we agreed that they should not come to Moscow. She told me that a chalet in Switzerland was available to us if we would run it as a guest-house for the Workers' Travel Association, a Labour Party tourist-agency with which my father was associated. It seemed a perfect solution, and we arranged delightedly all four of us now, to meet in Montreux. There seemed nothing left for me to do except write my articles about my visit to the Ukraine and the Caucasus, which I proceeded to do, getting them off by diplomatic bag unseen by Oumansky. When they were published, I should, I knew, have my visa withdrawn.

As it turned out, there was one last story to cover. The news got around in Moscow that some British engineers working on construction projects for the Metropolitan-Vickers Electrical Company in the USSR had been arrested, and were to be charged with sabotage and espionage, the chief of them being Allan Monkhouse, Paddy's cousin. I made use of this relationship in telephoning cryptic messages to *The Guardian* in the hope of thereby evading the censorship. Our first efforts to get news out by the usual channels met with a blank refusal. At the Press Department they said no arrests had taken place, and denied all knowledge of police raids on Metro-Vickers premises. In our fury and disgust at thus being deprived of our legitimate sustenance, we did something unprecedented, and late at night invaded the home of the censor on duty – who happened to be Ehrens. It was a cosy enough little apartment, with a wedding group in a silver frame, and crimson plush curtains, and a sofa with two round salmon-pink cushions on it, and a souvenir from Berne in the shape of a Swiss peasant doll. Ehrens appeared, to let us in, wearing pyjamas and a short embroidered coat with frogs, rather like a bandsman's tunic. We crowded in angrily, as though we were an insurrection; banging the table, shouting. The collectivisation famine, the Terror and the Purge, the Torgsin shops and the long queues outside the food shops

– all this, with some effort, we could take in our stride. But to be denied a story bound to get front-page treatment everywhere! That was too much. Poor Ehrens, too, was really troubled. What would the neighbours think? A GPU visitation? He pleaded with us to withdraw while he telephoned, which we did, standing in the passage outside until he had finished. Then he called us back to say that the bare facts of the arrests having been made could be telegraphed, and nothing more. We grudgingly and grumblingly accepted this meagre concession. I felt rather a Judas myself in the knowledge that, as I thought, my cryptic telephone call to Paddy Monkhouse some hours before would have given *The Guardian* an exclusive story. I need not have worried; only a drastically cut and sub-edited version of my coverage of the Metro-Vickers story appeared in the paper.

Later, Allan Monkhouse was released on bail, and we were called to the British Embassy to meet him. He turned out to be a quiet, solid sort of man who patiently answered questions of the kind that journalists, especially Americans, ask – How old was he? Married? Any children? How long in Russia? – to gain time before putting the serious ones they know won't be answered anyway. Like a juggler desultorily bouncing his little balls preparatory to getting them all into the air at the same time. It was a gentle enough curtain-raiser to what followed – the great Purge of the thirties mounted by Stalin; one of the most gruesome and macabre happenings even of our time, involving, according to Robert Conquest's careful estimate in his book *The Great Terror*, some twenty million souls.

In itself, the Metro-Vickers affair was rather a minor episode in this protracted *grand-guignol*, but it attracted a great deal of attention outside the USSR because of the appearance of foreign nationals among the accused. The brightly-lit court, the mechanically repeated confessions, the spectators baying in unison for the death penalty, the ravings and howlings of the Public Prosecutor, formerly Krylenko, and now Andrey Vyshinsky, subsequently eloquent Soviet spokesman at the UN – it was all to become part of twentieth-century folk-lore. Spreading in different versions throughout the world; to Leipzig for the Reichstag Fire Trial, to Nüremberg and Tokyo for the War Crimes Tribunals, to Washington for the Un-American Activities Committee, etc., etc., until it seemed that history itself had become a trial, at which, in Cholerton's words, everything was true except the facts. All the world's a trial, and all the men and women in the dock; Who whom? boiling down to Who's trying Whom?

Even now it is difficult to grasp the magnitude of what happened; a stupendous horror film conceived in the narrow, suspicious mind of Stalin, and produced and directed by him, in which every single Soviet citizen, from the Baltic to Vladivostok, willy-nilly participated, whether as extras, or with speaking parts. In Moscow one sensed the omnipresent fear in frightened, furtive eyes; sniffed the sour body-smell it gave out, which still, after all these years, remains with me. The endless interrogations; interrogators themselves in time interrogated, until no one knew who was confessing what to whom, who were the judges and who the accused. A fearsome morality play in which it had to be interminably demonstrated that, the system being perfect, as were all who had been submitted to the great baptism of the Revolution, any imperfection, whether in the system, or in individual beneficiaries of it, could only be due to malign stratagems, saboteurs, wreckers; to plots and subornings and conspiracies engineered by the powers of darkness – capitalists, imperialists, colonialists and their running dogs.

And how could the denizens of this dark, sub-human underworld find the strength to impede and frustrate the working out of Lenin-Stalin's revolutionary purpose? Only, obviously, when their efforts were reinforced by the very Revolution-makers themselves; all the Old Bolsheviks, who, one after the other, were required to make their public acts of penitence, beating their breasts, confessing their sins and misdemeanours, and receiving at the hands of a firing squad their just quittance. So the Revolution consumed its own children, reaching even outside its boundaries, and striking down a Trotsky in far-off Mexico. Power has its own mysticism of violence, symbolised in the USSR by what Stalin called the 'Flaming Sword of the Proletariat'; wielded on his behalf by the secret police, ever changing the initials of their name (Cheka, GPU, NKVD, KGB), one boss succeeding another (Dzerzhinsky, Jagoda, Yezhov, Beria; dreaded names until, in their turn, the purgers were purged), yet always remaining the same. As God's Flaming Sword was set at the entrance to the Garden of Eden to keep out the fallen children of men, so Stalin's barred the fallen children of the Revolution from his paradise. There was no need to set up a counter-revolution in the USSR; Stalin was his own counter-revolution.

As my increasingly hostile attitude to the régime became more apparent, my reception in the Press Department was correspondingly cold and hostile. Lost for ever now was my position of favourite son, as a protégé of the Blessed Webbs, and contributor to the beneficent columns of the

Manchester Guardian. I was the more surprised, therefore, to receive an invitation to dine with Oumansky, which, of course, I readily accepted. The occasion was set for the evening before my departure from Moscow, and the place the Spirodonovka, a former rich merchant's house which had been requisitioned intact, to be used for government hospitality, with all the furniture, décor, and other fittings kept just as they were. Such invitations were very rarely accorded to foreign journalists; not even to the tamest (in Soviet Double-Speak, most objective), like Louis Fischer or Duranty; least of all, one would have thought, to someone like myself who had proved, in the régime's terms, unreliable and unhelpful. Those that are not against us are for us, Podolski once remarked, smirking over some statement by an Anglican dignitary to the effect that if Christ were alive to-day he would probably be a communist. Even on that basis, I was an enemy now. Why, then, the invitation to dinner? Was it that Oumansky had some notion of plucking a brand from the burning? Or, at any rate, of moderating excesses of hostility I might indulge in on leaving the USSR? Or was it just that he saw a chance of having a good dinner for once? If so, a very human calculation. Or – an outside possibility – that he genuinely wanted to make a gesture of friendship before we parted, probably not to see one another ever again? An unspoken recognition on his part that my changed attitude represented a genuinely reached conclusion, not an interested calculation? Some support was given to this possibility by a remark he made to me; he had, he said, formed the impression when I first came to the USSR that I believed in nothing, whereas I went away believing in something. Yes, but in what? He didn't say, and I didn't know – then. Poor Oumansky, he was a sort of Soviet version of Maupassant's hero, Bel-Ami. It would be nice to think that the invitation was some sort of friendly gesture.

Oumansky was waiting for me at Spirodonovka when I arrived. He showed me over the house, which, he explained, had been built by a rich merchant; in very bad taste, of course, he added, but still use could be made of it. I followed him from room to room; tall, dimly lighted rooms, heavy with coloured marble; a décor of gold fleurs-de-lys on a blue background, with frail gilt candelabra hung from the ceiling. Oumansky, I could see, loved the house, and took great delight in showing it off – more so, perhaps, than in showing off the Dneprostroi Dam. The only other guest was Nehman, who had brought his photograph album to show me. We sat looking at it side by side on one of the delicate gold and blue sofas; so delicate that I half expected it to break under our weight

and movements. There were a lot of snapshots of Nehman, his wife, and their little son wearing a sailor suit, on a Black Sea beach. I duly admired them. Then the three of us went into dinner.

The table was set for us in the centre of a black and white Japanese room, with many mirrors reflecting an endless series of Oumansky, Nehman and me. We sat underneath a massive candelabrum whose light shone down on us; again, a preview of television locations-to-be. The light, as it seemed, brought the confused pattern on the walls to life, so that it looked as though it was in perpetual motion; rippling and pulsating like a surface of dark water in a wind. Passfield had been, as I supposed, my last glimpse of snug bourgeois life; this was to be my last glimpse of proletarian life, and I wanted similarly to imprint the scene on my mind. As course followed course, and drink followed drink, my senses began to dissolve. I felt myself becoming absorbed into the Japanese room; the rippling, pulsating walls were closing in on me, as in an Edgar Allan Poe story; the mirrors revealed a long, long corridor along which I trudged, with no end in sight. The figure of Oumansky loomed up across the table, misty and remote. There was a question that I desperately wanted to put to him, but every time I got it into suitable shape, somehow or other he was off on another tack.

My question was, of course: Who whom? The only question to put concerning matters of power; all the other related ones, like justice, equality, freedom, representation, and so on, being diversionary. 'Yes, but look here, Oumansky, Who whom?' Did I actually say it, or only mutter it into my glass? Or just envisage saying it? I can't be sure – I was rather drunk by this time – but I do remember Oumansky going on about how, when the Provisional Government of Kerensky fell, the power passed to the broad masses, whence, via the first Congress of Soviets it found its way to the Dictatorship of the Proletariat, and, under the inspired leadership of Comrade Stalin and the Communist Party...

Did I then rudely interrupt with: 'No, but seriously, Oumansky, Who whom?' I doubt it, but something must have happened, for I swear that Oumansky's dissertation, as it were, changed gear. He dropped his voice to take on a more confidential note, explaining how the broad masses are like children; they need a father, a dictatorship of themselves; a force that is them, but that, working apart from them, makes it possible for everything to be subordinated to their interests. Any other force must, by its very nature, deceive and enslave them. It alone...

Perhaps he did say something of this sort, but it can't surely be true

that, as I seemed to remember in my fuddled mind the following day, I once more interrupted, this time to say, pleadingly: 'Please, Oumansky; Who whom?', to which he replied, whispering softly, so that not even Nehman sitting with us could hear, but I just could: 'I they!'

It was time, anyway, for me to go. Oumansky and Nehman came to the door to see me off, as the Webbs and the two Scottish maids had at Passfield. As I walked unsteadily away, I could hear Oumansky say: 'Good-bye and *bonne chance!*' He liked speaking French; it befitted a diplomat, as it did his pre-Revolution prototype. '*Bonne chance* to you!' I shouted back over my shoulder. Before returning to my hotel I took a few turns round the Red Square. The place was deserted except for the soldiers with fixed bayonets on duty outside Lenin's tomb. I walked briskly; breathing in the icy air cleared my head. Suddenly, I thought I noticed a change in the wind that was blowing against my face. It seemed to be touched with warmth and fragrance, as though spring was already beginning. An extraordinary feeling of happiness welled up in me. Soon the river would thaw, the earth be green again. Thus it had happened a million times before, thus it would happen a million times again. Nothing could prevent it – the sudden, unexpected coming of spring. I filled my lungs ravenously.

I left the USSR via Riga, then the capital of an independent Latvia, breaking my journey at Leningrad, where, on an impulse, having some hours to spare, I decided to go and look for Dostoevsky's grave. It was by no means an easy quest. I found the cemetery where he was buried easily enough, but when I asked where his grave was, no one seemed prepared to give me any information other than pointing vaguely. At last, after much laborious spelling out of the names on tombstones, I did manage to locate it. The grave and the monument had a neglected, untended appearance, which was not really surprising since, following Lenin's view, the Party Line had pronounced anathema upon Dostoevsky as a reactionary who had rejected and ridiculed the very notion of progress and of Socialism. I wondered if anyone else had come there of late to do him reverence. Anyway, I was glad to take off my hat and stand for a while in silence, honouring his memory in the strange circumstances which had befallen his country – circumstances he had so uncannily prophesied in *The Possessed*, the book that of all others had been most in my mind during my time in the USSR.

What a scene it must have been, I reflected, at that very place when he died some half century before! What a turn-out of the great and the celebrated! He who, in his famous Pushkin Memorial speech, had pro-

claimed the great destiny of the Slav peoples to overthrow the corrupt, decadent civilisation of the West, and bring to pass a new, glorious era of Christendom reborn! Who had so brilliantly and devastatingly exposed the vain hopes and destructive purposes of the liberal mind, and, in the character of Raskolnikov, created its very prototype. Who, when he spoke of how now Russians must look to their roads southwards, had every general jumping in the air until his medals shook; every archbishop dancing about, his tall black hat askew. I could see it all, the carriages waiting, the exquisite ladies in veils, the splendid vestments of the officiating priests. And now just me!

But wait a minute. Go forward another forty years, to 1971, the 150th anniversary of Dostoevsky's birth, and lo! it turns out that Lenin put Dostoevsky only second to Tolstoy in a list he prepared of the greatest Russian writers, and that the judgement that 'Dostoevsky could not be in accord with our epoch was one of the errors of our young society, those errors which, in their own time, had their own truth and logic.' (Let other Mirskys, scavenging with their pens, watch out!) With the Great Soviet Encyclopaedia also suitably adjusted, there could well be another turn-out no less brilliant. As for the grave I found so neglected – it would surprise me if by this time it had not been refurbished.

Among several pieces I wrote about the USSR which never got published was one entitled 'Red Imperialism', in which I argued that the cause of liberating the toiling masses could lend itself just as well to Dostoevsky's brand of Slav imperialism as the notion of liberating Christians from the Ottoman yoke. In those days, with the worthy Litvinov advocating total disarmament whenever he had a chance, and every pacifist and internationalist cause sure of a warm endorsement in Moscow, my suggestion seemed too absurd. To-day, no one would print the piece because it would seem too banal. When I read in the documents from the archives of the German Foreign Office published in 1948 of the conversations between Hitler and Molotov relating to the Nazi-Soviet Pact, I realised that Dostoevsky would have found in Stalin's emissary an exponent of his views far more resolute and unscrupulous than any Czar; and one no less concerned than he was about roads going southwards.

Walking away, I noticed another funeral in progress; the coffin lifted off a red hearse, and the little group of mourners raising their hats while it was lowered into the grave. Some were in tears, and there was the same embarrassed expression on the faces of the less involved that one

sees at all funerals. One of their number delivered a short exhortation, to which the others listened impassively. Dust to dust; or, in this case, a comrade who had faithfully followed Lenin's way, now departing. It was soon over, and the mourners dispersed, leaving the grave-diggers to fill in the grave.

There were not many passengers on the train to Riga. As we approached the Latvian-Soviet frontier, all of us with one accord went into the corridor to stare at the soldiers in their long grey great-coats, red stars on their caps, guarding it. Then, when we were safely in Latvian territory, we all began spontaneously to laugh and shout and shake our fists at the sentries. We were out, we were free. It was one of the strangest demonstrations of the kind I have ever been involved in. Subsequently, I have seen many Soviet frontiers, with barbed-wire, and land-mines, and dogs; with armed sentries in watch-towers ready to shoot on sight, like prison guards. All designed, not so much to bar people from coming in, as to prevent those inside from getting out. How strange, I have often reflected, that a régime which needs thus to pen up its citizens should nonetheless be able to make itself seem desirable to admirers outside. As though the purpose in taking the Bastille should have been to gain admission there and do a stretch.

The buffet at Riga Station seemed momentarily like paradise; the crisp rolls and butter, the piles of fruit, the luscious cheeses and succulent ham – who could ever believe in such plenty? My euphoria soon passed. Man cannot live by buffets alone, and the angels in this paradise were puffy, pasty men carrying briefcases instead of harps, with their beatitudes securely tucked away in wallets in their hip-pockets. On my way to Berlin, where I proposed stopping off for two days, my spirits steadily fell. I was, I felt, returning on my tracks; going deeper and deeper back into the bourgeois world I thought I had discarded for ever. Its very affluence made it the more abhorrent; I was a prodigal son puking over his fatted calf.

In Berlin the Nazi storm-troopers were out in the streets marking Jewish shops, and beating up their owners and anyone else who displeased them. Mostly not quite young; burly in their brown shirts, with incipient paunches filling out their breeches. The females likewise in brown, with blond plaits and pink cheeks, but also inclined to be outsize; more like women policemen than Rhine maidens. The city was hushed; like a theatre when the lights have been lowered preparatory to the curtain going up. Its glossy porn was still on display, and the transvestite shows still running; but the steam had gone out of it all.

To paraphrase Grey's alleged famous observation, they were shutting down the sex-supermarkets all over Germany, but we should, alas, see them opened again in our time. As for the then hippy model, the *Wandervögel*, in decorated braces, twanging their *Lauten*, and going ever *weiter im Blau*, further into the Blue – they had all become Hitler-jugend, and were marching and saluting and shouting in unison.

Always gloomy, Berlin seemed now under a permanent thunder cloud, a place of doom. I was not to see it again until 1945, when it was just an expanse of rubble, with occasional jagged fragments of buildings rising stark against the sky. If one looked carefully one could see that people were actually living in the rubble, having carved out for themselves little caves and cubby holes for dwellings, where they carried on commerce of a kind, with, for currency, cigarettes and spam, as well as their own bodies, if negotiable. I was reminded of the scene in the first pictures from the moon. Then, ten years later, back again, and this time I was amazed to find that a magical city of glass and lights, a Disney Deutschland, was rapidly rising; cafés crowded with solid citizens smoking cigars, sipping cognac; glossy porn back in the kiosks, *Schlag* back in the coffee, transvestites back in business. A city reborn. Or was it all done with mirrors? I am not certain even now.

I wrote to Crozier: 'From the way you've cut my messages about the Metro-Vickers affair, I realise that you don't want to know what's going on in Russia, or to let your readers know. If it had been an oppressed minority, or subject people valiantly struggling to be free, that would have been another matter. Then any amount of outspokenness, any amount of honesty.' I went on to describe the scene in Berlin, and the Nazis beating up Jewish shops, and everyone with his story of murder and folly, and concluded: 'It's silly to say the Brown Terror is worse than the Red Terror. They're both horrible. They're both Terrors. I watched the Nazis march along *Unter den Linden* and realised – of course, they're Komsomols, the same people, the same faces. It's the same show.' David Ayerst quotes this correspondence in his book on *The Guardian*, and says it read 'like a letter to end all communication'. So it did; I was finished with moderate men of all shades of opinion for evermore.

Montreux Station in the very early morning waiting for Kitty seemed about as far away from the USSR and Oumansky, from Berlin and the storm-troopers out in the streets, as it was possible to be. The coffee so hot and fragrant, the rolls so crisp, the butter so creamy; the waiter so

obliging, his hair so sleek and black, his face so sallow, his coat so fresh and spotlessly white. Everything and everyone so solid and so durable. Even Kitty's train, roaring in exactly on time, was part of the omnipresent orderliness. There is always a dread on such occasions that somehow the rendezvous will not be kept; that arrangements which seemed so precise will somehow have gone awry. So one studies the gathering faces with mounting anxiety; every sort of face showing up except the particular one in question, until, at last, there it is; unmistakable, unique, infinitely dear. Waving to Kitty in the distance when I see her, holding one son's hand and another son in her arms, a Shakespearean tag comes into my mind: 'Hang there like fruit, dear heart, till the tree rot.' What is love but a face, instantly recognisable in a sea of faces? A spotlight rather than a panning shot? This in contradistinction to power, which is a matter of numbers, of crowd scenes. I heard of an inscription on a stone set up in North Africa which reads: 'I, the captain of a Legion of Rome, have learnt and pondered this truth, that there are in life but two things, love and power, and no man can have both.' Some twenty centuries later, I append my own amen.

We extravagantly hired a car to take us to Rossinière, where our chalet was, climbing up the still snow-covered valley under a blue sky and in bright sunshine. I took stock of our new son, very robust and hearty, and renewed my acquaintance with the older one, who even then had the air of slight aloofness and detachment, of being vaguely surprised at finding himself in so strange a place as this world, and in the strange company it offers, which characterises those who from the beginning walk with God. There we were, reunited, in the seemingly secure peace and security of the Canton de Vaud, with the rumblings of the wrath to come that I had unmistakably heard, well out of earshot. It was a moment of great happiness; as though, having found each other, we should never again be separated. As though, having found a blue sky, there would be no more grey ones; breathing in this fresh, clear mountain air, no more smog.

Such moments of happiness, looked back on, shine like beacons, lighting up past time, and making it glow with a great glory. Recollecting them, I want to jump up and shout aloud in gratitude at having been allowed to live in this world, sharing with all its creatures the blessed gift of life. Alienation is to be isolated and imprisoned in the tiny dark dungeon of the ego; happiness to find the world a home and mankind a family, to see our earth as a nest snugly perched in the universe, and all its creatures as fellow-participants in the warmth and security it offers. Its

very components, the very twigs and mud of which it is made, likewise participating. Then, indeed, all the world in a grain of sand, eternity in an hour, infinity grasped in one's hand. So, such moments of happiness comprehend a larger ecstasy, and our human loves reach out into the furthermost limits of time and space, and beyond, expressing the lovingness that is at the heart of all creation. Curiously enough, of all people, it was of Karl Marx I thought as we rode joyously up to Rossinière; recalling how in one of his letters he describes to his wife the longing he has to return to Paris, where the family were then living, after one of his interminable quarrelsome conferences, and how the only lasting and satisfying joy he knows is to be with them and see around him their dear familiar faces. The memory of this letter stayed with me, I suppose, because of the contrast it offers with the efforts made in his name to promote the happiness of all mankind; in the result, so desolating, so bloody and so futile. Poor old Jewish enragé, whose furious indignation was to rumble and echo through the world for years to come – he, too, gratefully flying back to his nest.

Our chalet – called the Chalet de la Colline – turned out to be rather a large one which had only lately been completed. It seemed that the Englishman who had built it ran out of money, and the Workers' Travel Association took it over to run as a guest-house. Happily, none of the guests were due to arrive for some little while, and we had it to ourselves. There was a marvellous view up the valley, and the owner had left behind quite a good library, including *A la recherche du temps perdu*, which I settled down to read slowly and systematically. For Kitty, it was old territory. She was born at Château d'Oêx, the next place to Rossinière; at the Pension Rosat, still presided over by Madame Rosat, a stern, ageless lady. We went to pay our respects to her, and she remembered Mrs Dobbs well, saying of her, I thought with great acumen: '*Elle est très intellectuelle; elle voyage beaucoup.*' It just about summed her up. Most afternoons we walked a mile or so up the valley and then back. As the snow melted, the spring flowers, no less white, came out to take its place.

There are always ideal circumstances for reading any book, which should, perhaps, be indicated on the dust-jacket, along with particulars of the author and the subject. Rossinière was ideal for reading Proust, and whenever I think of Charlus or Swann or Odette or Albertine, the road up the valley to Château d'Oêx, and the flowers, and the cow-bells sounding as the cattle were taken to the mountain pasture, come

into my mind. I quite enjoyed the book, but not overwhelmingly; not at all as I did, for instance, Pascal and Constant and La Fontaine when I came to read them. The long maundering sentences, the prevailing flavour of snobbishness and perversity, of a sick mind at work, detracted from my enjoyment, even though I had to recognise the book's genius of a kind. Its great appeal to intelligentsia of all denominations, who have praised it inordinately, has been due, I suspect, to Proust's being yet another celebrant of a lost bourgeoisie. I should never be surprised to find a televised version of *À la recherche du temps perdu* enjoying as great and widespread a success as *The Forsyte Saga*, especially in the communist countries and Japan. The great literary quest of the twentieth century has been for writers with authentic *avant garde* credentials and strongly conservative, if not reactionary, predilections. Proust filled this role perfectly. So did Yeats and Pound, both of whom were overtly fascist in tendency; in Pound's case, in practice as well. Eliot, D. H. Lawrence, Hemingway, Aldous Huxley, too, and even Orwell in his odd way, came into this category. Most of the political heroes of our time have been of the Left, from Rosa Luxemburg to Che Guevara, and most of the literary ones of the Right. A two-way *Trahison des Clercs*, or double-Judas act.

Apart from Proust, my mind was endlessly preoccupied with thoughts of the Soviet régime. I felt furious about the whole experience, as though I had been personally cheated, and poured out my righteous indignation and hurt vanity in a series of articles as bitter and satirical as I knew how to make them. They probably struck most readers as being just angry. Clearly, I could not offer them to *The Guardian*, and so, going to the other extreme, I sent them to the old *Morning Post*, long since extinct, but in its day a reputable Tory newspaper of the extreme Right. The editor accepted five of them, rejecting two – the one about Red Imperialism, and another giving an account of how foreign journalists working in the USSR are induced to toe the Party Line. Subsequently, I tried this latter piece on *The Times*, where it was likewise rejected, even though at that time the paper had no correspondent in Moscow, and relied on the reports of a man named Urch in Riga. Anyone who had the curiosity to look up Urch's dispatches would find that they maintained a high level of accuracy and reliability; certainly by comparison with Duranty's, so prominently displayed in the columns of the *New York Times*. Again one marvels at the almost mystical importance attached to the location of a news-gatherer as distinct from the truthfulness of the news sent.

I was paid five guineas each for the five articles accepted by the *Morning Post*. It was not much, but in those days twenty-five guineas sufficed to keep us going in food for quite a while in Rossinière. In the Leftist legend of the thirties it is usually assumed that attacking the Soviet régime was made temptingly lucrative, whereas supporting it involved penury and perhaps martyrdom. For the most part, precisely the opposite was the case; most of the best-selling writers about the USSR were strongly favourable (for instance, Maurice Hindus, Dr Hewlett Johnson and the Webbs, whose *Soviet Communism: A New Civilisation?* had a very large sale, especially when, as Stalin got into his stride as the master-terrorist of the age, they dropped the question mark from the title – a vast and mercifully forgotten literature of Soviet adulation, all very profitable to its progenitors), whereas antagonistic works were difficult to get published and sure to be knocked or ignored. Even *Animal Farm*, one of the few undoubted works of genius of our time, was rejected by fourteen publishers on the ground that it was too hostile to the Soviet régime, before being accepted. One of the rejectors was T. S. Eliot on behalf of Faber & Faber.

The *Morning Post* articles attracted a certain amount of attention. Arthur Schlesinger told me, when he was working on his book, *The Age of Roosevelt*, that Henry Wallace used them as an argument against recognising the USSR when the matter was under consideration by the Roosevelt Administration. As he was Secretary of Agriculture and one of the President's inner circle of advisers at the time, he may even have had some effect. I was rather glad to be abroad and inaccessible when the articles appeared. Inevitably, they aroused the interest of organisations and individuals belonging to the wilder shores of international politics, such as ultra-royalist Russian exiles, and various brands of Ukrainian nationalists and separatists; curious societies and organisations with elaborate letter-heads dedicated to restoring lost cultures and recovering lost lands. I had no wish to get mixed up in such company, and kept on trying to explain, whenever an opportunity offered, that disliking the Soviet régime did not imply any particular liking for its predecessors or possible successors, or even a wish that the October Revolution had not happened.

It was the memory of my anxieties at this time which first drew me to George Orwell, who went through a similar experience as a result of the publication of his articles about his experiences during the Spanish Civil War, in which he exposed the monstrous hypocrisy and chicanery of

Communist policy in Catalonia. The articles were rejected out of hand by the *New Statesman*, and appeared finally in the *New English Weekly*, the rather obscure organ of the Social Credit Movement. When I got to know him, we often discussed how difficult it is, in an ideologically polarised society like ours, to take up any position without being automatically assumed to hold all the views and attitudes associated with it. Like voting the ticket in an American election, when by just pressing one button support is automatically accorded to a whole string of candidates for all sorts of offices. Thus to attack the Soviet or the Spanish Republican régime was automatically to support their Fascist or Nazi opponents; to expose the fatuities of the liberal mind, to commend the authoritarian one. Orwell's devastating exposure of the pursuit of power through revolution in *Animal Farm*, and of the maintenance of power for power's own sake in *1984*, was intended to show, with the desperate intensity of an utterly honest mind, that the world of the mid-twentieth century was moving towards a collectivised way of life, whose only truth would be slogans, whose only duty would be conformity and whose only morality would be power. Admittedly, the pioneer and first exemplar in this field was the USSR, but the trend, as was to become increasingly apparent, was universal. It was not by chance that he took the BBC as his model for the Ministry of Truth in *1984*; his picture of a continuing state of war whose aims and even location are largely unknown, has come to pass in Vietnam, and television has become Big Brother's provenance, if not his kingdom, just as he foresaw. All my own conclusions as a result of my time in the USSR pointed in exactly the same direction.

Soon the clients started arriving at the Chalet de la Colline, which was just as well; our money was again running out, and it was only when we had clients in residence that we could get any from the Workers' Travel Association – whose name, incidentally, soon became an embarrassment, and had to be used only as initials, proving once more that the more workers are cracked up and adulated in the abstract the less anyone wants to be categorised as a worker in practice. The clients, in any case, proved to be mostly school-teachers and accountants, with an occasional civil servant, though there was one authentic worker, a railwayman accompanied by his wife, of whom we all made a tremendous fuss to show how un-class conscious we were. As it happened, they were both as nice as could be, and managed with great ease to find congenial places to take a quiet glass of wine in the neighbourhood of Rossinière. Mrs

C.W.T.—8

Dobbs also came to stay with us, engaging in some clandestine marketing of her paintings with the clients. Sometimes she accompanied me on my afternoon walk, talking all the way about such matters as whether there was a devil, and the prospects for all creation in due course becoming one. She had a way of shuffling and scraping her feet as she went along which produced a sandpaper effect by way of background to the rasp of her voice, thereby making the envisaged oneness of all somehow less alluring than might otherwise have been the case. One thought with relief of the aeons and aeons of time that must pass before this happy consummation would be realised.

We spent in all some three months in Rossinière, during which time I finished a book about my experiences in the USSR, later published as *Winter In Moscow*. As with the *Morning Post* articles, I wrote in a mood of anger, which I find rather absurd now; not so much because the anger was, in itself, unjustified, as because getting angry about human affairs is as ridiculous as losing one's temper when an air flight is delayed, or in a traffic jam. The only parts of the book I find tolerable are the humorous passages; laughter being a great prophylactic which disinfects anger as it does lechery and all other passions. When *Winter In Moscow* came out, it enjoyed a certain vogue among old Moscow hands like Chip Bohlen, Bill Stoneman and William Henry Chamberlin, who prided themselves on having a glossary of the real people behind my fictitious names. Cholerton said of it that it was the great anti-cant Bible of the USSR, which pleased me very much, but in actual fact it achieved nothing in the way of clearing up misconceptions and propaganda lies; people continued to regard as an open question whether there was forced labour in the USSR, and whether the confessions of the Old Bolsheviks to have worked for the British Secret Service, etc., etc., were genuine. Shaw's picture of Stalin as the Good Fabian, and Dr Hewlett Johnson's of him as building the Kingdom of Christ, continued to carry more conviction than mine of a bloodthirsty tyrant of unusual ferocity even by Russian standards. People, after all, believe lies, not because they are plausibly presented, but because they want to believe them. So, their credulity is unshakeable.

Sitting at my typewriter in the mornings, and tramping about the Canton de Vaud in the afternoons, I tried desperately hard to sort out my thoughts and emotions following the total reversal, in the light of what I had seen and understood in the USSR, of everything I had hitherto hoped for and believed. It was not just a disillusionment with

segmentsegment...

the Russian Revolution as such; that, after all, was something that had happened, a historical event like any other, with causes and consequences which could be explored and evaluated. No more, for that matter, with the Soviet régime as such, which, with all its cruelties and privations, was a way of life like any other, endurable to the Russian people as being in their historical tradition. Anyway, an essentially *Russian* way of life rather than a Marxist one. Requiring, therefore, the move to Moscow from elegant Europeanised Petrograd-Leningrad – something that Dostoevsky, and Tolstoy, too, would have heartily endorsed. Requiring, also, for Red Czar a Georgian bandit like Stalin, not one of his Old Bolshevik colleagues like Trotsky or Bukharin or Zinoviev or Radek; mostly Jewish, 'rootless cosmopolitans', as they were later to be contemptuously dubbed when Stalin swung the Russians back to their traditional and habitual anti-semitism. These, Stalin decided (and he may well, from his own point of view, have been right), were better dead. And dead in the most humiliating way – beating their breasts, and abjectly apologising for doing things they couldn't possibly have done, being where they couldn't possibly have been, keeping assignations they couldn't possibly have kept.

All this likewise indubitably belonged to history, and would have to be historically assessed; like the Murder of the Innocents, or the Black Death, or the Battle of Paschendaele. But there was something else; a monumental death-wish, an immense destructive force loosed in the world which was going to sweep over everything and everyone, laying them flat; burning, killing, obliterating, until nothing was left. Those German agronomes in their green uniform suits with feathers in their hats – they had their part to play. So had the paunchy Brown-Shirts, and the matronly blonde maidens painting swastikas on the windows of Jewish shops. So had the credulous armies of the just, listening open-mouthed to Intourist patter, or seeking reassurance from a boozy sandalled Wicksteed. Wise old Shaw, high-minded old Barbusse, the venerable Webbs, Gide the pure in heart and Picasso the impure, down to poor little teachers, crazed clergymen and millionaires, drivelling dons and very special correspondents like Duranty, all resolved, come what might, to believe anything, however preposterous, to overlook anything, however villainous, to approve anything, however obscurantist and brutally authoritarian, in order to be able to preserve intact the confident expectation that one of the most thorough-going, ruthless and bloody tyrannies ever to exist on earth could be relied on to champion human freedom, the brotherhood of man, and all the other good liberal

causes to which they had dedicated their lives. All resolved, in other words, to abolish themselves and their world, the rest of us with it. Nor have I from that time ever had the faintest expectation that, in earthly terms, anything could be salvaged; that any earthly battle could be won, or earthly solution found. It has all just been sleep-walking to the end of the night.

Chronicle II:

THE INFERNAL GROVE

Till I turn from Female Love,
And root up the Infernal Grove,
I shall never worthy be
To step into Eternity.

—Blake

FOR MY EVER-DEAR CHILDREN:
LEONARD, JOHN AND VALENTINE,
AND THE OTHER THREE THAT HAVE
COME TO US THROUGH THEM:
SYLVIA, ANNE AND GERRIT-JAN

6 *The Iron Gates*

Let us roll all our strength and all
Our Sweetness up into one ball,
And tear our pleasures with rough strife
Through the iron gates of life
 – Andrew Marvell

O! dreadful is the check – intense the agony –
When the ear begins to hear, and the eye begins to see;
When the pulse begins to throb, the brain to think again;
The soul to feel the flesh, and the flesh to feel the chain.
 – Emily Brontë

A passionate tumultuous age will overthrow everything, pull every-
thing down; but a revolutionary age that is at the same time reflective
and passionless leaves everything standing but cunningly empties it
of significance.
 – Kierkegaard

IN THE AUTUMN of 1933 I came to Geneva from Rosinière, where I
had been staying after my Moscow adventure, to take a temporary job
at the International Labour Office, then part of the now defunct League
of Nations. Kitty and the two children and I had a small apartment in
the Rue de Lausanne overlooking the Lake and the Jardin des Anglais.
The stern, forbidding Kremlin seemed far away, with its Red Flag
endlessly flying; by night arc-lit to make a pool of blood in the surround-
ing darkness. As were also the brown-shirted bully-boys and braided
embonpoint maidens roaming the streets of Berlin in search of cowering
Jewish shopkeepers. It was a snug little retreat, tucked away among
mountains; more like a stage-set or a willow-pattern than an actual
place, with steamers puffing to and fro across the Lake, and pretty
Renaissance-style houses, their gardens reaching down to the Lake

shore, recalling Mme de Staël, with her tall, red-headed Benjamin Constant in attendance, and their interminable rhythm of meals and talk and talk and meals. Then, as now, a great storm raged beyond the snow-capped mountains, standing guard like majestic sentries; their heads rosy at dawn, shining white by day, and in the evening scarlet. I comforted myself by recalling the many honourable precedents for thus taking refuge in this particular sanctuary. For instance, Rousseau wearing Armenian dress and seated at his crochet work; or Voltaire, an earlier version of Bernard Shaw, growing rich and famous by shocking and thrilling those for whom the tumbrils were already waiting. As today there are the millionaire colonists of Gstad, and the lords of show business scattered about the cantons where the Inland Revenue men cease from troubling and the wealthy are at rest.

It was through David Blelloch that I came to hear of the ILO job, and thanks to his kind offices that I got it; he being the son-in-law of Robert Dell, *Guardian* Paris correspondent during my time in Manchester, who had now been transferred to Geneva to report the doings of the League of Nations. I used to run into Dell there from time to time; still gloved, cane in hand, shoes of patent leather, soft hat rakishly tilted, reminiscing about Anatole France and the villainies of the Quai d'Orsay. Employment of some kind I urgently needed, as once again I had practically no money. So I was greatly beholden to Blelloch and his wife Sylvia, who were uniformly kind and generous to Kitty and me while we were in Geneva.

The ILO, brain-child of Albert Thomas its first Director-General, was set up at the same time as the League of Nations in the mood of ebullience which followed the 1914–18 war, the intention being to reinforce the League's machinery for safeguarding international peace by equivalent machinery for promoting social justice, on a basis of fair wages and humane working conditions. Alas, despite Albert Thomas's valiant efforts and ardent oratory, as little progress seemed to have been made towards the realisation of social justice as of peace. By the time I arrived on the scene, Thomas was dead, and his place had been taken by an English don and sometime civil servant named Harold Butler, who accorded me a brief interview when I took up my temporary post. He had to a marked degree the curious, disconcerting way dons had in those days, when one was supposed to be conversing with them, of seeming to have dozed off and to be muttering in their sleep.

The section of the ILO to which I was posted had overflowed from the newly constructed main building into a temporary structure in the

grounds, and was engaged in preparing a survey of co-operative movements throughout the world. It was to assist in this work that I had been appointed. The head of the section was a tiny, pedantic Frenchman, M. Prosper, with a large moustache that seemed quite out of proportion with the rest of him; like the luxuriant bushes you sometimes find sprouting out of a minute crack in a rock face. I never discovered that he had any particular interest in co-operative movements; any more, for that matter, than I had myself. This, despite lingering memories of going shopping for my mother at the Croydon Co-op, and of the confidence of my father and his friends that a retail trader whose profits were distributed as divi to the customers must ultimately put out of business competitors who kept them for themselves.

When asked to pronounce upon some point of policy or principle in connection with the work of his section, M. Prosper invariably retreated behind his moustache, and exclaimed in a voice that was quite remarkably deep and resonant for so tiny a frame: *'J'ai mes règles, j'ai mes règles!'* What these rules were, who had drafted them, and to what end, no one was ever able to find out. Contrasting with his laodicean attitude to co-operative movements, even in his native France, let alone in China or Peru, was the relentless concern with which he followed anything to do with the ILO's internal organisation; more particularly, promotions, salary scales and superannuation arrangements. When these were under consideration, he would become enormously vehement and excited, waving his arms about, and injecting into his voice a note of passionate concern, which, as things turned out, met with its just reward. I like to think of M. Prosper living out his days comfortably in some agreeable spot in Provence, noting with quiet satisfaction that his monthly cheque, drawn on the Banque de Genève, maintains its value in a shifting world. I only once encountered him outside the office, and that was in the Rue de Lausanne, just when I was turning into the apartment block where we lived. 'Ah!' he said to me, with, as I thought, a note of accusation in that deep voice of his, *'vous avez planté votre tente'*. It made me feel quite uneasy, as though he had caught me out in some nefarious enterprise, and I tried to reassure him by muttering confusedly: *'Mais non, Monsieur, nous sommes seulement des locataires'*. He gave me a distant, condescending nod, and passed on, presumably to some tent of his own, where Madame Prosper awaited him, maybe some children, shouting, as he hove in sight, *'Voilà Papa!'*; a dog barking, a *grandmère* serenely smiling, a servant laying the table – just like the Bontemps family from whose doings I learnt my first French words and grammar.

There were some six or seven of us in his department engaged in preparing the survey of co-operative movements. The only one of my colleagues who made much impression on me was H, a Lithuanian Jewess, with whom I spent a lot of my time talking. She had contracted polio as a child, and now needed to wear metal braces; because of her condition, walking painfully and slowly with two sticks. Everything she did required an enormous effort, which somehow resulted in the upper part of her becoming magnified. Her head and bust were a caricaturist's drawing, the face being particularly huge and swollen, yet in its own way, beautiful – like one of those lurid flowers that grow in stony wildernesses. After Kitty and I returned to London, she came and stayed with us there, and I took her round sight-seeing – something I hate anyway. She was avid to go everywhere and see everything. Her audacious refusal to accept the limitations of her crippled state drove her to undertake the most difficult operations. She went traipsing through Hampton Court and the Tower of London, climbed up into the dome of St Paul's, and, shaking and straining over her two sticks, and dragging along her two helpless legs, got on and off moving-stairways and made her way onto the tops of buses. I admired, and in a way loved her, and yet was also horrified by her, and glad when her visit came to an end.

Inevitably, however we might begin, much of our talk had a way of veering towards the Soviet regime, with which, as a Lithuanian, she was all too familiar. Although we heaped obloquy in unison on the GPU, the forced labour camps, and all the other horrors, I sensed in her a certain reservation, as though deep down in her heart, despite everything, she nourished an unquenchable expectation that somehow the socialist hopes she had invested in the Russian Revolution would be, if not realised in the USSR, made more realisable by what was happening there. In the unacknowledged world-wide civil war that was going on then – still is, for that matter – cutting across all existing loyalties, all accepted values and codes of behaviour, H was on one side and I on the other, and, ultimately, as I well knew, nothing could change either of our allegiances. Not even, in her case, such incidents as when, during the operation of the Nazi–Soviet Pact, at the Brest-Litovsk Bridge – Margaret Buber-Neumann has described the scene – the GPU handed over to the Gestapo, German-Jewish Communists who had taken refuge in the USSR, with Soviet and Nazi officers jointly checking the lists. Nor, in my case, the realisation that, as grows ever more obvious to me, what is still called our free way of life turns out to be neither free nor a way of life; safeguarding nothing that makes it

worth defending, and with no future prospects that make it worth protracting.

After H's visit to us in London, I never saw or heard of her again until I happened to read the Royal Commission Report on the Canadian Spy Case resulting from the defection of Gouzenko, a cipher-clerk in the Soviet Embassy in Ottawa. One of the names Gouzenko handed over of Soviet agents operating in Canada was H's. It seemed that she had been sent to Montreal by the ILO, and there, no doubt partly through pressure on her family in Lithuania, by this time incorporated into the USSR, induced to perform minor espionage services in a Soviet spy ring. So, in the end, her true allegiance did come out. I wonder if mine ever will. Or if I really have one.

In our temporary building where we toiled on M. Prosper's behalf it used to get very hot owing to an uncontrollable heating system, and this made me sleepy. From time to time a trolley brought in tea or coffee and biscuits. I used to long for its coming, as I had for the tea-tray when I was wrestling in my room in the *Guardian* office with a leader; maybe one on this very ILO – an institution held in high esteem in Cross Street. The biscuits, when they came, were all stamped with the initials BIT (Bureau International de Travail), which some-how made them like sacerdotal wafers; if so, presumably munched in remembrance of the lantern-jawed Princetonian, Woodrow Wilson.

I cannot pretend that I threw myself with much zest into collecting and collating data about co-operative movements. For one thing, the information came exclusively from government sources, and was therefore highly suspect. Some of it, indeed, was manifestly absurd, suggesting, as it did, that co-operative enterprises were more numerous and advanced in countries like Cuba and Afghanistan than in France and Switzerland. When I raised this point with M. Prosper, he rather crossly remarked that it was not our business to question the genuine-ness of the data provided for us by member States; our business was to present it, as clearly and cogently as possible. So, with these dubious bricks, we constructed our great statistical edifice. When I left, it was still far from completion. Perhaps even to this day it exists somewhere or other as a work of reference, to be quoted from, or used in arguing a thesis or making a case. Cholerton's famous comment on the Moscow Trials – that everything about them was true except the facts – might well be applied to it; as, indeed, to much of the output of the League and its affiliates. I well remember a senior official coming one evening into the canteen, and telling me with the utmost satisfaction that eight years

of earnest endeavour had just been brought to a successful conclusion. So, it was a gala-day for him. It seemed that he had been engaged in drafting a Convention banning the employment of women in mines, and at last, with only two member States – Poland and India – entering a reservation, his draft had been unanimously approved. It came out afterwards that Poland and India were the only two countries among those adhering to the Convention in which women did work in mines.

As the winter came on, chill winds began to blow, mists to gather, so that we were often quite shut in, with even the Lake lost to view. Nonetheless, I doggedly took my walks along the Quai Woodrow Wilson, noting League delegates and their hangers-on similarly bent. Men in overcoats with astrakhan collars, sometimes cigar-smoking, or talking vehemently; maybe arm-in-arm with a single companion, or in groups, gesticulating, pausing to spread out their arms as though making some dramatic point. The solitaries often trying to open their newspapers in the wind – *Journal de Genève*, *Gazette de Lausanne* – a quick, anxious peek preliminary to subsequent more particular study. More important ones with a plain-clothes man or two trotting behind to ensure that no harm should befall them, or maybe a secretary or PA respectfully in attendance in case some need should arise for their services.

Occasionally, a face was vaguely recognisable. As Briand, somnolent-eyed, heavily moustached, nicotine-stained, or his opposite number, Laval, sallow complexion and white tie contrasting; the two of them like figures in a weather-gauge, one going in as the other comes out. Or Politis, Titulescu, Benès – names to conjure with in their day, but who remembers them now? Or fat little Litvinov waddling along to propose once more the total disarmament of one and all, unconditionally and for ever; in his train, three or four GPU men, with wide trousers, and bulges under their arms, and little, dry, expressionless eyes. Or Arthur Henderson in his bowler, still presiding over the Disarmament Conference to which Litvinov's proposal would be put, and still wearing that lost look I had noticed when I ran into him on a channel steamer just after the Labour holocaust of 1932. Or the then British Foreign Secretary, Sir John Simon, reptilian, a snake in snake's clothing if ever there was one, with Strang – whom I had known in Moscow – at his elbow, so that a distant greeting could be exchanged, and, for adjoint, a newcomer to the international scene, none other than young Anthony Eden, a spring in his step, a song in his heart, moustache likewise vibrant, homburg-hatted (headgear, as his fame increased, to be named

after him), *ce jeune homme extraordinaire qui aime tant la paix*, as the French newspapers referred to him. Who could then have foreseen the stormy course that lay ahead for him? From glory to glory; the Foreign Office, the War Office, and finally Downing Street, and then that weird withdrawal to the Jamaican Bondhouse, Goldeneye, and, reappearance as a ghostly earl or belted ghost. And, finally – was it really he? Looking out across the Lake from a hotel balcony in the early morning? That grey straggling moustache, those floating locks and flashing eyes, that air of woebegone self-satisfaction – was it, could it be . . . ? Yes, it was. None other than our Prime Minister, the Rt Hon. Ramsay MacDonald. 'Good-morning, sir,' I said as cheerfully as possible. In return he gave me one of his slow, lugubrious looks, and then delivered himself of a characteristic line: 'The day is for the wurruld, but the morrrning is for myself!' I left him to enjoy his own morning in preparation for the world's day.

The League of Nations in those days focused the hopes of the enlightened everywhere; all eyes were upon it in the confident expectation that it would succeed in making war as obsolete as duelling, and armed forces as unnecessary to nations as wearing a sword had become to individual citizens. In some mysterious way, just willing this would bring it to pass; by renouncing armaments, nationalistic policies and other works of the evil one, good would triumph, and peace reign for evermore. Sooner or later, everyone who was anyone came to Geneva to celebrate this new era of universal peace that was being inaugurated there. As well as the delegates themselves and their suites, there were innumerable campaigners of one sort and another, male and female, clerical and lay, young and old; all with some notion to publicise, some pet solution to offer, some organisation to promote. They gathered in droves, fanning out through the city, and settling in hotels and pensions, from the Lakeside ones down to tiny obscure back-street establishments. Ferocious ladies with moustaches, clergymen with black leather patches on the elbows of their jackets or cassocks and smelling of tobacco smoke, mad admirals who knew where to find the lost tribes of Israel, and scarcely saner generals who deduced prophetic warnings from the measurements of the pyramids; but one and all believers in the League's historic role to deliver mankind painlessly and inexpensively from the curse of war to the great advantage of all concerned.

What a time that was for Geneva! Not since Calvin has the spotlight of history so shone on it; and, of course, with the spotlight, came the world's newspapermen, their favourite haunt being the Café Bavaria,

whose walls were lined with appropriate cartoons in deference to this special clientele. Thither they came, hot-foot from Berlin or Paris or London or New York, their stringers respectfully in attendance, with stories to write, expense accounts to draw on – *Garçon, encore des scotchs!* I occasionally dropped into the Bavaria myself to join an acquaintance for a drink, breaking off my researches into co-operative movements and my talks with H to get the feel again of news-gathering and the news-gatherers. More often than not, there would be present one or other of the famous American special correspondents – John Gunther, Vincent Sheean, Negley Farson, H. R. Knickerbocker – who in those days roamed the world, and would touch down at Geneva from time to time to cover a meeting of the League Council or Assembly, or in the vague expectation that even the Disarmament Conference as it meandered on, like Charles II taking an unconscionable time in dying, might yet yield a story. There was always the possibility, too, of something actually happening; as when Herr Greiser, President of the Danzig Senate, cocked a snook at the League delegates, or when the German delegates scornfully withdrew from the Disarmament Conference, leading the President, Arthur Henderson, to remark, on being asked what his reaction was, that it was 'a bit awkward'.

They were the knight-errants of our time; rescuers of nations in distress, champions of the downtrodden and oppressed, who smote the offending dragons hip and thigh with breathless words rattled off on their typewriters, and, later, caparisoned, cap-a-pie, cantered more sedately, but no less lucratively, round the lecture circuits. Above the tobacco smoke and the clatter of glasses, words and phrases resounded. Civilian bombing. . . . Would they be able to re-phrase the resolution to make it acceptable to the Great Powers? . . . Drafters hard at work . . . Eden optimistic and sees light at the end of the tunnel. . . . Even Briand awake and optimistic. . . . Even Sir John Simon wearing a frosty smile. . . . Begins: HOPE RISING GENEVA LEAGUE CIRCLES RESOLUTION NOW DRAFTING BANNING CIVILIAN BOMBING UNCONDITIONALLY RECEIVING QUASI-UNANIMOUS SUPPORT MORE. In the warmth of the Bavaria, three or four *fines* under my belt, I joined in the talk with a sense of being at the hub of events. Here, one knew what was happening; felt the world's pulse, and listened to its heartbeat. Here, as the *Guardian* would have put it, 'a new way of conducting international relations was being forged; quiet reasonable discussion round a table instead of bluster and gun-boats. Nor should the clownish gesture of a Herr Greiser be taken too seriously, and certainly not

allowed to jeopardise the promising prospects for a wide-ranging peaceful settlement. . . .'

Outside, breathing in the cold damp air, the glow I had felt in the Café Bavaria soon wore off. News, like sensuality, is a passing excitement; perhaps the ultimate fantasy of all. A shadow's shadow, the scenario of the film of the play of the book. TRIUMPH FOR MR EDEN . . . DISCOURS MAGNIFIQUE DE M. BRIAND VAUT À LA FRANCE UNE JOURNÉE INOUBLIABLE . . . STRONG SUPPORT FOR POLITIS-TITULESCU COMPROMISE RESOLUTION. . . . Such items flashed round the world, shouted down telephones, set up by compositors, tapped out on teleprinters, subbed and digested and commented upon. Seemingly so momentous, and so soon cold. Who is Briand? What next Politis? Whither Titulescu? And the League itself? What was it but another Tower of Babel, climbing inanely into the sky? Through the mist I could just see the outline of the great new Palais de Nations, then under construction. Cedars from Lebanon, marble from Italy, precious metals from the Andes; contributions of one sort and another from every corner of the globe. A Palace of the Nations as stupendous as Kubla Khan's in Xanadu.

Alas, as it turned out, barely was the Palais des Nations completed and ready to be occupied than the second world war was ready to begin. While Hitler's panzers were actually roaring into Poland from the west, and Stalin's divisions lumbering in to meet them from the east, the League was in session in its new premises, discussing – the codification of level-crossing signs. At the time I remember feeling a sort of relief. At least there would be no more compromise resolutions, whether devised by MM. Politis and Titulescu or anyone else; no more triumphs for Mr Eden, or magnificent discourses by M. Briand. How wrong I was! Another Tower of Babel, taller, more tower-like and more babulous, would spring up in Manhattan, to outdo the League many times over in the irrelevance of its proceedings, the ambiguity of its resolutions and the confusion of its purposes. What will they be discussing there, I ask myself, when the guided missiles begin to fly?

By this time, Kitty and the children had gone back to London to set up house in preparation for my return, and I had told M. Prosper that the tent I had planted I now proposed to roll up and be gone. He kindly provided me with a testimonial to the effect that I had performed my duties with diligence and conscientiousness. It was, I fear, even less deserved than such statements usually are; my contribution to the massive report on co-operative movements throughout the world having

been minute, and shaky at that. My last days in Geneva were solitary and morose, and largely spent pounding along beside the Lake, which seemed particularly leaden and ill-omened on those dark winter days. It, too, had I but known it, had a future destiny as the last hiding place of the world's hoarded gold, deposited there in fear as, in my time, its hoarded peace had been deposited there in hope.

As a place of pilgrimage, Geneva lacked the melodrama of Moscow; its cult more fatuous than sinister. Yet, just as, pounding round the Red Square, I endlessly asked myself how it came about that the choicest spirits of the age – all the gurus and dancing dervishes of enlightenment – prostrated themselves before a brutish tyrant like Stalin, so, pounding along the Quai Woodrow Wilson, I kept wondering what Pied Piper had been able to lead them to the shores of this sullen Lake, confidently expecting to find there Tennyson's Parliament of Man and Federation of the World. In both cases, as it seemed to me, the significant thing was the ready acceptance of fantasy as reality; even a predilection in favour of fantasy, and a corresponding abhorrence of reality. Why?

It was the question of questions; confronting it, I could only wail and lament by the Lake shore, cursing its dark waters, its chill mists, its icy winds, as I remembered my own readiness to take to the plastic wings of fantasy; to listen with Caliban to the sounds and sweet airs which give delight and hurt not, so that when we wake – but we never do – we cry to sleep again. All I could claim – so miniscule a claim – was that I knew, had always known, would always know, that the alternative reality existed, and that, all too desultorily and faithlessly, I had looked for it, aware that the quest was the only true and serious purpose life held. Trying to tear it out of the sky, or out of other flesh; searching for it in grains of sand, and on the stony tops of mountains. Pursuing and pursued, stumbling on as it breathed down my neck, and chasing after it as it disappeared from view; crying for mercy as I waited for it to pounce, shouting myself hoarse as I tried to call it back – like a shipwrecked man shouting hopelessly after a distant ship. Glimpsing for an instant the fearful symmetry, the mystery and the meaning of things; then, the vision lost, as it seemed, for ever, and I left stranded. Borne down by the mountains, sightless in the darkness, chilled as though the Lake water flowed in my veins.

Coming back to London, it seemed as though I had been away for years; actually only for eighteen months. Everything looked differently to me;

especially the assumption on which I had lived from my earliest years, that such and such changes, brought about peacefully through the ballot-box, or drastically through some sort of revolutionary process, would transform human life; making it brotherly, prosperous and just, instead of, as it had always been, and still was for most people, full of poverty, exploitation and conflict. I no longer believed this, nor ever would again. The essential quality of our lives, as I now understood, was a factor, not so much of how we lived, but of why we lived. It was our values, not our production processes, or our laws, or our social relationships, that governed our existence.

This conclusion was by no means as clear-cut then as it subsequently became. I still felt rather dazed, like a clergyman from under whom the mât of orthodoxy has been pulled. Also – quite unreasonably, I admit, in view of the way I had written and spoken about them – I was upset at having become a kind of moral leper in the eyes of old friends and acquaintances like Kingsley Martin and other former *Guardian* colleagues. I was still in the happy position of not receiving press-cuttings, but when *Winter in Moscow* was published, soon after my return from Geneva, I found myself called a liar and a renegade in most publications of the Left. In the case of the *New Statesman* I was foolish enough to send in a letter of self-vindication and protest, but, needless to say, it was not published. It was only when Khrushchev, in his famous speech at the twentieth Party Congress, disclosed the full magnitude of the calamity the forced collectivisation of agriculture had brought about in the USSR, that what I had reported received official confirmation. No one, however, apologised for having called me a slanderer and running dog of Capitalism, or thought any the less of Shaw, the Webbs and all the others who had so ardently and indignantly denied there had been a calamity at all.

Kitty, with her usual skill, had set up in a modest flat in Parliament Hill Fields, but it involved sharing a staircase and various other domestic arrangements, which, with two small children, presented difficulties. Shortly after my arrival on the scene, the landlord asked us to go. Kitty, in any case, was six months pregnant, and in no condition for house-hunting with practically no money. Asking the *Guardian* for a testimonial would have involved approaching Crozier – something that was infinitely repugnant to me. I had, it is true, the good M. Prosper's one but, not surprisingly, it failed to register in Fleet Street. From Geneva I had written to *The Times* to know if there was any chance of being taken on, but received an answer from Barrington Ward which

held out little hope. A similar feeler put out to the BBC likewise met with no response. Altogether we were in a mess.

This was a low point in my fortunes; not just materially, but in every sense. I saw no prospect of making a living as a free-lance writer; the articles I wrote and submitted to various publications all came back to me. *Winter in Moscow*, it is true, was reprinted in England, and published in America; but the financial results of this were relatively meagre, and the professional consequences disastrous. Most of the minor patronage in the world of journalism and communications, even in the early thirties, was in the hands of lib-leftists to whom I was now anathema, while in Conservative eyes I was, rightly, suspect. In a rather self-pitying note I jotted down at this time, I described how isolated I felt myself to be, and how I knew that henceforth I should always be so; whereas, to get along in the world, it was necessary to support a ticket, whether Left, Right or Centre. One could love the Soviet Union and detest the British Raj, or vice versa; but to hate both, and for the same reasons – which was my case – was not permissible. So, when I called on the editor of the *Morning Post*, H. A. Gwynne, who had published my articles on my time in the USSR, I found him most friendly and charming but, on the subject of a job, evasive. Similarly, Gerald Barry, then still editor of the *Week-End Review*, and later of the *News Chronicle*. This was to be increasingly an age of polarised loyalties. A review I wrote for the *Spectator*, which predicted the eclipse of liberalism as a moral and political irrelevance, was returned as being inadmissible in its columns; likewise an article submitted to *The Times* about the impossibility of functioning as a conscientious and honest journalist in the conditions imposed by the Soviet authorities.

I had finished my novel, *Picture Palace*, about the *Guardian*, and the publishers of *Winter in Moscow*, Eyre & Spottiswoode, had accepted it for publication. At the same time, out of the blue, Jonathan Cape asked me to write a book about Samuel Butler, the author of *Erewhon* and *The Way of All Flesh*, to appear on the centenary of his birth. The proposal was made over a meal at the Etoile in Charlotte Street; an excellent restaurant that I never enter nowadays, if I can possibly avoid it, because, for me, it is haunted by the ghosts of the books I haven't written and the contracts I haven't fulfilled. Between the hors d'œuvres and the cheese, I hear them incessantly groaning and rattling their (or maybe my) chains. Cape, a tall, solid man with a muddy complexion and ill-fitting false teeth, had originally been a travelling book salesman, but, branching out as a publisher himself, had been remarkably successful.

He enjoyed the great advantage of rarely reading his books, having, in Richard Garnett, a chief reader who read them on his behalf with great acumen. This left him free to estimate their possibilities in other, more subtle ways; holding and weighing them in his hand, turning over their pages, perhaps even smelling them or nibbling at the end-papers. I imagine that a successful picture-dealer operates similarly; Cape was a sort of Duveen, with Garnett as his Berenson. His first bold venture was to publish *Arabia Deserta*, which was an immediate success, and put him in the way of taking over T. E. Lawrence as a literary property. Another great coup was a collected edition of Mary Webb, which he launched to coincide with a speech in praise of her works by the then Prime Minister, Stanley Baldwin, about which Cape had prior knowledge from Tom Jones, the trusted counsellor of a whole series of Prime Ministers. A real relish would come into Cape's voice as he described how he went round from publisher to publisher buying up the rights in Mary Webb's hitherto unsuccessful novels for quite small sums in preparation for his own collected edition, which in the end sold something like a million copies. When he came to this part of the narrative, he would observe: 'Money talks!' Cape, certainly, made it talk, if not sing.

In his innocence – often a quality of worldly success, as sophistication is of worldly failure – he took it for granted that I should admire Butler's works, and find his character and personality congenial. I encouraged him in this view, though actually I knew next to nothing about Butler, and was only very scantily conversant with his works. It was agreed between us that I should take on the book, and appropriate financial arrangements were made. From Cape's point of view, the project ended badly; the more I explored Butler's life and outlook, the less I liked him. By the time I had finished, the result could not but be unacceptable to Cape, as the publisher of Butler's collected works, as well as of Festing Jones's adulatory biography, and much other Butleriana. In the end, another publisher took over my book. I consider it a great compliment that nonetheless Cape several times approached me subsequently with a view to getting me on his list. Perhaps, after all, he shared my feelings about Butler more than he cared to say.

The last time I saw him, we lunched together alone in his flat in Bedford Square, shortly before the outbreak of the 1939–45 war. He was extremely indignant about the state of the world, which he attributed largely to H. G. Wells, one of whose books he had lately published with a substantial advance which had not, as of then, been earned. He

told me how he had approached Wells and demanded an explanation, not so much of the book's poor sales, as of all the fraudulent hopes Wells had held out for the future as a result of the discoveries of science and the alleged enlargement of human understanding. The thought of this encounter appealed to me greatly, even though, not surprisingly, it failed to provide Cape with any satisfaction. He also complained bitterly about women novelists, who, he said, were either hideously unattractive but considered their publisher owed them a pass, or so alluring that if he offered one he was liable to be repulsed. My impression is that he was more often in the latter than the former case.

With the Butler book to do, and *Picture Palace* coming out, this was another point in my life when I might have plausibly given up journalism and settled down to be a writer. It was lucky I didn't, because, shortly after my novel had been sent out for review, I received an intimation from the publisher that the *Guardian* had applied for an injunction and threatened an action for libel, which, he explained, could only be fought if I was prepared to put up at once several thousand pounds to cover costs. Otherwise, a settlement would have to be made, necessarily involving the withdrawal of the book. As I had no money at all, only an overdraft, and no possibility of laying hands on any, the publisher's proposal was purely a formality, as he, I am sure, knew; and a settlement was duly reached, whereby the book was withdrawn and all existing copies destroyed. I kept one myself, which I still have; and I believe one or two others are extant. Otherwise, the novel, along with all the work I had put into it and the hopes I had invested in it, was sunk without trace. This was the heaviest blow I ever received as a writer, and it came just when I was least equipped, financially or in any other way, to withstand it. At the time I raged inwardly at the *Guardian's* – as it seemed to me – contemptible hypocrisy in thus bringing about the suppression of a book, which, though critical of itself, could not, by any stretch of the imagination, be said seriously to damage it commercially – the ground of its complaint. Even now, I have to admit, if my eye happens to fall on some ardent protest in its columns against a move to ban an obscene publication or entertainment, on the ground that any infringement of the right of self-expression is indefensible, I remember – more, I hope, with a grin than a groan – how little such considerations weighed when it was a question of preventing the publication of *Picture Palace*.

The situation was saved for me, financially speaking, by noticing, in the Situations Vacant column in *The Times*, that applications were in-

vited for the post of assistant-editor of the *Calcutta Statesman*. I applied
at once, though in a somewhat desultory way, and, to my great surprise,
was appointed, at what seemed to me a princely salary. My feelings
about this sudden prosperity were mixed. In matters like money and
sex, in which the ego is heavily engaged, no satisfaction is attainable;
what one wants is to be both rich *and* poor, to be Don Juan *and* St
Francis at one and the same time – which cannot be managed. Kitty
and I found a pleasant little Regency house in Grove Terrace, over-
looking Hampstead Heath, and there I was to leave her once more; now
with three children, my daughter Valentine having got herself born
with reasonable ease and celerity. Next to Kitty herself, she is the per-
son I have most loved and watched over in this world.

Before leaving for Calcutta, I was required to wait upon Lord
Reading, a former Viceroy and Lord Chief Justice, who acted as gen-
eral adviser to the financial trust which owned the *Statesman*. His office
was in a large building at Blackfriars, on the Embankment. I found him
seated at a desk with nothing on it, looking immensely old and Jewish
and worldly. The very texture of his face was like a parchment deed
made out in his favour; with his beak of a nose, a flourishing signature,
and his tight red mouth, the seal. Actually, as I soon discovered, he was
in a mood of jubilation, and for a strange reason. Gandhi had been going
through one of his occasional phases of unpopularity because of a clash
with Hindu orthodoxy – the same thing that led ultimately to his as-
sassination – and that very day it had been reported in the papers that he
had been stoned by fellow-Indians. Nothing could have pleased Reading
more. When he had been Viceroy, the stones were all thrown at him on
Gandhi's behalf; now they were being thrown at Gandhi. His parchment
face was positively beaming, and, if not actually rubbing his hands
together, he seemed to be on the point of doing so. So overpowering
was his delight at the turn of events that I wondered if he really remem-
bered the purpose of my being there in his office, apart from a vague
awareness that it had something to do with my going to India. Anyway,
we talked briefly about my own, scarcely Viceregal, time in Travancore,
and I mentioned that Gandhi had visited Alwaye when I was there.
This set him off, and again he was far away, watching the grotesque
little figure in the loincloth, the hostile crowd pushing towards him, the
stones falling round him; instead of the everlasting '*Mahatma Gandhi
ki jai*' which had so often assailed his ears (though only distantly, as he
sat secure in his Viceregal carriage), this time, angry, derisory shouts.
It was, in his eyes, a delectable reversal of fortune. When he got up to

shake hands and indicate that my audience was over, I was quite surprised to find that he was wearing an ordinary lounge suit. I had all along been seeing him in buckskin breeches and a gilded coat shining with orders and decorations. A secretary took me to lunch in a canteen in the basement; he told me that Reading had recently been married for the second time, to a lady a good deal younger than himself. She had particularly instructed him, the secretary said, to see that her celebrated husband did not eat oysters – a difficult assignment because he was greatly addicted to them.

Another call I was required to make before leaving for Calcutta was on the then Secretary of State for India, Sir Samuel Hoare. He received me at the India office, very suave and genial. Reading looked back on Viceregal days; Hoare perhaps saw himself as one day becoming Viceroy. Meanwhile, the Reforms! He was for them heart and soul; and, indeed, piloted them through the House of Commons with skill and subtlety, warmly cheered on from Printing House Square and Cross Street, for once in unison. He asked me to write to him from time to time about how things were going at the Indian end, which I gladly undertook to do. Face still Quakerish, but with worldly accretions, Hoare's Bank intervening between the Society of Friends and Rt Hon. Hon., Gallant and Learned ones in the House of Commons; neatly attired, sleek, with white kid tops to his boots, he felt himself to be in charge of India's destiny. In that same office of his, seated at that selfsame desk, had not successive Secretaries of State settled the affairs of India and its hundreds of millions of inhabitants, far, far away though they might be. As I tried to point out in our correspondence, duly engaged in when I got to India, things were different now. He might push the tiller this way or that, but the ship would not respond. Surely, it couldn't be quite as bad as that, he wrote back. But couldn't it? All that grinding of Parliamentary mills; all those divisions, sometimes through the night; the flushed faces and dishevelled hair, Churchill on his feet, papers waved – Here! Here! Shame! Resign! At last, *le roy le veult*. A triumph for the Secretary of State, *The Times* and the *Guardian* intoned, and a tribute to his patience and persistence. Even so, when the hour struck, the Raj fell, like others before it, and what had happened, or was to happen, in Westminster and Whitehall had little or no bearing on the manner of its falling, or on the sequel.

How different was my journey to India and arrival in Calcutta this time, from the previous occasion ten years before! On the boat, *Viceroy of India*, and the train from Bombay to Calcutta, I travelled, of course,

first-class. Now I had become a Burra Sahib indeed, however much I might try, conversationally and in my attitude of mind, to pretend otherwise. This was gratifying to my conceit, but otherwise a source of wretchedness, which was crystallised in an incident, trivial in itself, which nonetheless made a deep impression on me. A missionary who was travelling second-class on the same boat, and who had known me when I was at Alwaye, sought me out for a chat. We greeted one another affectionately, and then, after we had exchanged a few words, he looked at me strangely and said: 'You've changed, you're quite different.' I knew exactly what he meant, but I tried to pass his remark off facetiously; saying something about being older, though not wiser. Shortly afterwards, he got up abruptly and left me. I never saw him again, but what he said stayed with me.

The year I spent in Calcutta was easily the most melancholy of my life. For once I kept a diary regularly, which I find now so full of misery and self-pity as to be barely readable. I lived in a flat above the *Statesman* office with a man named Wordsworth – he claimed to be some sort of descendant of the poet – who was acting-editor of the paper when I arrived. He had been in the Indian Educational Service; then had moved over to journalism. A short, plump, pasty man, who had all the correct liberal views and attitudes of mind; believing, for instance, that it would be possible, through constitutional changes, to transform the British Raj peaceably into a Westminster-style self-governing democracy. Also that the League of Nations, given the proper support, might be relied on to keep the peace while remedying Germany's legitimate grievances. And so on. I must have been a disagreeable member of the household. His soft persistence in upholding such views led me to go out of my way to pour scorn and ridicule on them, as well as on all his heroes, like Anthony Eden, Noel Baker, Robert Cecil and Gilbert Murray.

Among some old papers I kept from this time in Calcutta, I came across a leader I had written when Wordsworth was in the chair, heavily scored by his editorial pencil. It was headed 'Towards A Repetition of 1914', and began: 'It is interesting to look back and see how, little by little, Germany has shuffled out of the Treaty of Versailles,' and goes on to point out that this process did not begin with Hitler and the Nazis, nor was it a consequence of the harsh treatment Germany suffered at the hands of the Allies; it started before the Treaty was even concluded. 'No sooner, that is to say, was the war over than Germany began to prepare for another.' This sentence was deleted, and Hitler given a 'Herr'. Thereafter, when his name occurred, it was usually replaced by

'the Nazis', as though to indicate that there was a distinction between him and his followers. I was not allowed to say that there were plenty of people, including the Foreign Secretary, 'who appear to think that, although Germany has just publicly repudiated one treaty, peace may be safeguarded by persuading her to sign another'. Nor that trying to coax Germany back into the League of Nations in the hope that thereby European security might be safeguarded, was like sending a criminal who has broken all the laws in one country, into another where the laws were different, in the expectation that there he would be law-abiding. Even in my concluding sentence: 'While Sir John Simon tries to soothe Hitler back to Geneva, and Mr Anthony Eden carries his load of well-worn platitudes from one capital to another, everything is being prepared for the final stage – a repetition of 1914, only worse', 'platitudes' is altered to 'arguments'. This old, dog-eared leader with its rash of heavy pencilled deletions, is, in its tiny way, an historical document, providing, as it does, a true image of the spirit of appeasement which had already captivated so many of the righteous and the enlightened, like Wordsworth. I cannot now remember whether or not, as editorially amended, it ever appeared in the paper; if it did, it would have made no conceivable difference to anyone or anything, even though the concluding prediction was to come true, and more than true, before five years had passed.

Over my desk there was a large fan, which, turning, scattered the papers on my desk, and blew the sheet in my typewriter back on itself, with disastrous consequences to my typing. On the other hand, to turn the fan off left me sitting with a stagnant mind in stagnant air. So, I was always turning it on and off; as I did, likewise, such thoughts as I could muster – two parallel processes. It was the period when some White Paper, or Blue Book, or Royal Commission Report relating to India was always coming out. Since they were all accorded editorial treatment, they needed to be studied, analysed, criticised, even though they had little, if any, relevance to the actual existing situation – a tottering Imperial Power confronted with a rising tide of nationalism, still attached to the bizarre figure of Gandhi, but with other Indian leaders – mostly western-educated, like Nehru, and Moslem zealots like Jinnah – increasingly taking a hand. It seemed obvious to me that there could only be one outcome; the British would have to go. Yet they themselves, in their clubs and offices, at their mah-jong and bridge tables, on their polo-grounds and tennis-courts, were serenely convinced that, with some adjustments here and there, the Raj, in one form or another,

would go on for centuries yet. A favourite saying among them was that, if the British left, within six months the Indians would be down on their knees begging them to come back. It seems almost inconceivable now, but this was seriously believed. Certainly, I cannot recall meeting a single British business man or government official, soldier or even missionary, who would have considered it possible that the Raj was to end before the twentieth century had half run its course.

This made it difficult to talk seriously with them about the Raj and its outcome; still more to write seriously about it in the *Statesman*, which was the organ of British business interests, particularly in Bengal, and largely dependent on them for its very substantial advertising revenue. So I just did what I had to do, without bothering too much about it. Bored in a way, and yet not bored; for instance, finding something vivid and captivating in the scene each night when the paper was going to press. The humid heat hanging over everything, muffling sounds and smudging galleys; the strange chant of the proof-readers, in which stock prices, cricket scores, and even at times maybe words of my own, were all mixed up, and addressed, as it seemed, to some deity. But who? Their Excellencies? Sun Life? BP? Perhaps returning after dinner, rather tipsy, cigar-smoking, white dinner-jacketed, to drop into the subs' room to see if there was any news. There, inscrutable faces, and such a variety of heads; some of them shaved, wholly or partially, maybe with a shaved strip down the middle like an airport runway; others tousled, turbaned, with or without buns, bent over copy or Linotype machines. Despite the noise and the chatter, like the night itself, all so still. Anglo-Indian girls, rather beautiful and hopeless, beautiful in their hopelessness – Ivy, Gladys, Renee; barely contained in their dresses. Down below, the rotaries, recently installed, pounding away; they, too, leaving intact that brooding stillness, heavy and fathomless. Holding a galley in my hand to look at it – 'Before any forward step can be taken, terrorism must stop; that is the first condition . . .'; damp patches marking where I had held it, the ink running. When we were filming *Twilight of Empire*, I turned over the pages of bound volumes of the *Statesman* covering the time that I worked on it, and read out sentences as empty and as turgid. Did I write them? Honesty compelled me to admit that I might have.

The greatest alleviation of my dismal life in Calcutta was a friendship I had with four Indians. It started with Shahid Suhrawardy, who had heard of my coming to Calcutta from Hugh Kingsmill's brother, Brian Lunn, and so he sought me out. I liked him at once. He had the virtues

of his faults; heavily pock-marked, a great fantasist, reputedly a dedicated womaniser, and belonging to one of the leading Moslem families in Bengal. The adventure of his life had been to go to Russia, where he fell in with a theatrical company and became the lover of the leading lady. Though he was separated from her, he continued to send her a substantial part of his salary as Professor of Fine Arts at Calcutta University; a post that made little demands on his time and energies, there being few students, and they not particularly diligent, and no arts, fine or otherwise. Through Shahid I met the others – Sudhindranath Datta, a Bengali poet who had been Rabindranath Tagore's secretary, Apurbo Chanda, a large, jovial man, a civil servant, at that time Calcutta's acting Director of Education, and Tulsi Goswami, a rich landowner and Congress politician. Sudhin was the most elegant and cultivated of them, and the one I came in the end to know and love best; Tulsi the most dazzling, whose wearing of *kadi*, or homespun cloth, as a good follower of Gandhi, did not prevent him from looking like a dandy and living a life of great extravagance and self-indulgence; Chanda large, cheerful and amicable.

We met often, and at least once a week dined together, either at one of their houses, or in a restaurant – often a Chinese one because Shahid had romantic notions about China; sometimes in the Bengal Club, of which I was now a member. This necessitated having a private room, Indians not being allowed in the club dining-room. I must say, as I often told them, they missed nothing by being excluded; but even so it was vaguely embarrassing. It seems extraordinary now that such absurd arrangements were maintained almost up to the end of the Raj.

The motive of the Calcutta Sahibs and their Memsahibs for thus guarding their exclusivity so jealously was social rather than racial or political. Service in India, whether in Government, commerce or even as a missionary, provided, in its day, a ready means of instant social climbing. It was perfectly possible to acquire an upper-class way of life, with servants, playing polo, changing for dinner and other intimations of gentility in a single generation. Furthermore, a socially aspiring Sahib, by sending his progeny to public schools, could ensure that they took this changed status for granted, and so were firmly integrated into the upper classes from the beginning. This was one of the attractions of Empire for its lowlier devotees, and maybe, too, why its loss has tended to produce revolutionary impulses among those who would have been its beneficiaries – the Brushwood Boys with nowhere to go, the Sanderses without a River, the Bulldog Drummonds hopelessly studying the classified advertisements in the *Daily Telegraph*.

On my first visit to India none of this arose, but in Calcutta it did. I used to go riding in the early morning on the Maidan, or out at the Jodhpur Club. Being up on a horse is a great assertion of social distinction – being a knight rather than a pawn; the riding schools flourish with the gossip-columns. Fortunately for me, by some special mercy, whenever I have been caught up in knightly fancies, something has always happened to make me look ridiculous. Don Quixote rather than Sir Galahad has been my prototype. Thus, riding in the Maidan one morning, my horse ran away with me; pounding along, I noticed a little compact group of horsemen, one of whom detached himself, and came racing after me. As my horse lost its momentum – due to fatigue rather than to anything I did – he caught up with me, and angrily asked me whether I realised that I had galloped past His Excellency, the Governor. I said I hadn't realised it, but even if I had I shouldn't have been able to do anything because my horse had run away me. Whereupon, he muttered something about how riders as incompetent as I obviously was, ought not to be allowed to use the Maidan; and anyway not to let it happen again. The governor in question was none other than Sir John Anderson, a portentous civil servant who subsequently became Churchill's Home Secretary in the war, and gave his name to an air-raid shelter, ending up as Viscount Waverley.

Some fifteen years later, when I was a newspaper correspondent in Washington, Walter Bell, the then British Ambassador, Lord Inverchapel's PA, telephoned to say that they had Lord Waverley staying at the Embassy, and could I possibly arrange some sort of journalistic party for him. This was duly done. In the course of the evening I mentioned the incident on the Maidan in Calcutta, but it did not please him; however it was told, it presupposed a certain pomposity on his part. I did not add that it cured me for ever of feeling important on a horse. In appearance, he was more like a bronze statue of a man than a man and might, in the ordinary way, have expected to figure on one in the streets of Calcutta. The cities of the Empire used to be full of such statues of British soldiers and administrators. Now they have mostly been removed, the few left standing, forgotten and neglected, for the birds to use; one or two of the very famous – a General Gordon, a Kitchener – sent home at great expense. The process of change has been speeding up so fast that already some of their indigenous successors have fallen out of favour and likewise been removed – for instance, Nkrumah in Accra. History is written in statues as well as in blood.

My four Indian friends were, of course, all nationalists, or *Swarajists*,

though Tulsi was the only practising militant. At the same time, in education and tastes, and even habits, they were completely Anglicised. Indeed, it was I who often found myself arguing most strongly against the cultural and spiritual consequences of the Raj, and insisting that it would only truly come to an end if it were pulled up by the roots, not just sliced off. Otherwise the white Sahibs would be dismissed, only to be replaced by brown ones. Sudhin alone really agreed with me about this; he felt differently, perhaps, because Bengali was his true language and medium of expression, whereas, in the case of the others, it was English. Shahid regarded himself, anyway, as a cosmopolitan; in Europe he spoke nostalgically about the sensual delights offered by Oriental women, and in India he was in raptures over the pleasures he had experienced in the arms of European ones. *Kharma Sutra* abroad, *Fanny Hill* at home. Tulsi, who had made a runaway marriage with the daughter of the only Indian peer, Lord Sinha, was by upbringing and temperament an aristocrat, and seemingly perfectly at ease in all circumstances; Chanda likewise, by virtue of the sheer ebullience of his nature.

Yet in all of them I sensed an undercurrent of melancholy, corresponding to my own. This was especially true of Sudhin; but Shahid, too, despite his outward show of being a contented sensualist, looked tired and lost when his face fell into repose. In Tulsi's case, he drank excessively, and, in the end, self-destructively, to evade thoughts that might sadden him; and even Chanda was liable to fall unaccountably into long silences. Deep inside them they knew that this western culture they had so brilliantly acquired, this very English language they spoke so fluently and idiomatically, and, in Sudhin's case with great artistry, these ancient seats of learning (they had all been at Oxford or Cambridge) where they had been so proud to be alumni that it had all seen its best days, and was now in a decline, and they with it. Though in a sense I was in the same case, it was at least a home-produced gold brick that I was landed with; whereas, what they had acquired at such great trouble and expense was an imported product. Sudhin called the elegant fragment of autobiography he left behind him '*The Twilight World*'. No one has described this no-man's-land between a dying Indian culture and a debased western one more subtly and delicately than he. It was the habitat of all my four friends, and, in somewhat different terms, my own. A twilight growing ever darker.

We went on a visit together to Santiniketan, the *ashram* founded by Rabindranath Tagore; it, too, a confluence of cultural streams. William Morris knights-at-arms, on elephants instead of white horses; there's

shade under the banion tree, brother; arrows of non-desire building a garden city in India's dry and dusty land. In the morning we were awakened by acolytes singing under our windows, and in the evening we sat at the Poet's feet, listening, along with the other *ashram* residents, to an address by him. He was a majestic figure with a long silky beard, robed rather than dressed, hair parted in the middle – a sort of ethereal Rasputin; a steeple to Gandhi's gargoyle. The two of them represented the poles of Indian nationalism; Poet and Mahatma, with Miss Slade, an admiral's daughter, shuttling between them. A German lady, spectacled, head shaved, and wearing a saffron robe, continued to spin as the Poet exhorted us to turn away from western materialism. I preferred her in saffron to dirndl.

My four friends looked forward to Indian Independence, but also, in their different ways, consciously or unconsciously, dreaded it. Even Tulsi, who for a time was actually a Congress Minister in the Bengal Government, and who would certainly have given everything he had – including his life – for the Swarajist cause, as I well knew, kept hidden deep down in his heart some reservations. Our parts in history are allotted, not chosen; and theirs belonged to the Raj, which they hated, rather than to the Swaraj, whose coming to pass they sought. Curiously enough, the one who in worldly terms throve most when Independence came was Shahid, who cared least about it. As a Moslem, western-educated and with some academic distinction, he had a rarity value in the newly constituted Pakistan, and was made chairman of the Civil Service Commission responsible for appointments to government posts. I met him briefly when he occupied this position, and he complained wryly that, though he could appoint others, himself he could not appoint. In time, he must somehow have overcome this difficulty, because he was posted as Ambassador to Madrid; a congenial appointment, Spain being a country he liked, and, as he was happy to find, harbouring few Pakistani nationals, which made his duties correspondingly unexacting. I saw him several times during this period; he had grown very deaf, but his face had come to wear an expression of great serenity and benevolence. Soon after he retired and returned to Karachi, I heard that he had died.

The other three were less fortunate. Tulsi ran through his fortune, and his health collapsed. Once when I happened to be passing through Calcutta, Sudhin took me to see him. We found that he had recently suffered a stroke, which had partially paralysed him, and made it difficult for him to speak. As we sat with him, he was struggling to say something, which turned out to be that he was distressed I should see

him in so poor a state. I tried to tell him – I hope so much that I succeeded – that it was a joy to me to see him always. This was true. Even then, a dying man, something of the charm, the gaiety and profligacy, which had so captivated me when we first met, still remained. I knew I should never see him again, and was glad of an opportunity to say good-bye. He died a few weeks later. Sudhin himself, as a Bengali poet and writer of the highest reputation, might have been expected to thrive in post-Raj India. Instead, he chose to make himself partially an exile, and went with his wife, Rajeshwiri, an accomplished singer and musician, on a protracted foreign tour. I saw him several times in the course of it, but had the feeling even then that he was taking a last look at the places and people and things he cared most about. I thought I detected something muted in him; a smiling disregard for the projects – in his case, among others, a definitive biography of Tagore – the world always heaps in the laps of those with no zest to undertake them. Back in Calcutta, one night he just died. As for Chanda – in the last conversation I had with him, in one of the Calcutta clubs some years after India had become independent, he complained bitterly about the dreadful people who, under the Nehru Raj, managed to get themselves elected as members; for all the world like some ferocious Indian Colonel Blimp. Now he, too, has died and I alone remain.

Though I was nominally living in Calcutta, I was not really living there at all. It was extraordinary how, as a Sahib in India, this could be done. For instance, I had a car with a driver, and he drove me wherever I wanted to go, from door to door; the shops and restaurants and cinemas and clubs frequented by Sahibs were clean and orderly, insulated from the teeming town. In the crowded streets, my driver would sound his hooter persistently, and a way would be opened before us; shadowy figures melting away, gibbering and grimacing. If, as I sometimes did, I walked through the bazaar, I might actually rub shoulders with fellow-pedestrians, but if they saw it was a Sahib, as likely as not they would draw aside. Again, if I showed interest in a particular shop, the shop-keeper would drop whatever he was doing, leave any customer he happened to be serving, to attend to my requirements. Though such treatment in some ways appealed to my vanity and egotism, it was a hateful feeling to be thus cut off from the life and people of the city. Sometimes I would stand on the balcony of the flat above the *Statesman* office, and look down at the street below – Chowringee – envious of passers-by pushing and elbowing their way along the pavement, the road likewise packed with jostling vehicles, trams and cars and rickshaws and

bicycles all mixed up. Below me, the noise of an Indian street, with its jabber and bells and shouts; and I up above there, cut off from it all, isolated in the absurdity of the additional caste the English had created in India, over-topping all the others.

On one occasion I did get involved, and then too nearly for my taste. Driving me to a dinner party for which I was rather late, my driver ran a man over. I felt the jerk as it happened. The driver naturally stopped the car, and at once a crowd began to gather; faces peering in at me angrily through the windows, shaking their fists, shouting, suddenly wild and furious. There were no policemen about, and no one, as far as I could see, had sent for an ambulance. Was there even one available for such lowly casualties? I began to wonder what was going to happen, when my driver, with great presence of mind, got out of the car, picked up the injured – or, for all I knew, dead – man, deposited him beside the driving-seat, and drove off as fast as he could go to the nearest hospital. It all happened so quickly that there was no time for the crowd to react. A few stones came hurtling after us, that was all. At the hospital, the man was taken to the emergency ward to be examined, and I trailed along, thinking that perhaps, as a Sahib, I might be able to get him attended to more quickly. I felt particularly absurd in my dinner jacket; the more so because, in order not to get any blood on it, I kept well away from the injured man. Everywhere bodies were stretched out, overflowing from the wards into the corridors. It was difficult to avoid treading on them. To my great relief, it appeared that my man had suffered no serious injury, and was only shaken. While I was arranging matters for him – inevitably producing some money, the only thing I had to give; rupees, pieces of paper, too easily earned, with the King-Emperor's head on them – another emergency case was brought in. This time, it was a man who had cut his throat.

I shuddered at the gaping hole in his neck; at the blood, and his grey, inert face. Who was he? No one seemed to know, or to care much either. All I wanted to do was to get away. Back to my dinner party, a drink, talk, spoons dipping into soup, servants in red cummerbunds passing round plates of food and bottles of wine – a scene calculated to put out of sight and mind this other one of sprawling bodies, and the man with the gashed throat who was too inconsequential even to have a name, or arouse curiosity as to why he should have cut a gaping hole in his wind-pipe; his single gesture of defiance against a world which seemed indifferent whether he lived or died.

At our dinner-table conversation I mentioned the incident, giving

rise to a number of sage observations. Calcutta medical services very inadequate, traffic control deplorable; anyway life held cheap in the East – look at the way they treat animals! – in contradistinction to the West, where the individual was valued. Yes, admittedly in the recent war there'd been retrogression, but that wasn't going to happen again. We were learning; hence the League of Nations. What about transmigration? Maybe my man hoped to have a better break in another incarnation; to be born in Croydon, say, instead of Calcutta, and pass matriculation, and take books out of the public library. In Calcutta we'd reduced infant mortality, certainly, which, of course, was a good thing – no one was going to deny that – but led to the other difficulty; too many people, my man being one of the surplus. So it went on through the evening, until it was time to call for our cars and go; but I still hadn't managed to exorcise that other scene in the hospital. Even years afterwards, when I was back in Calcutta with Mother Teresa, it came back more vividly than ever. I could not but contrast my attitude with hers; not just in the sense that we moved in opposite directions – she to where the poor and afflicted were, and I away from them. It was in her response to them that the true contrast lay; she seeing in each sorrowing, suffering human being, neither a body surplus to a population norm, nor a waste product, but the image of a sorrowing, suffering Saviour, so that in solacing them she had the inestimable honour and joy of solacing him. A *Via Dolorosa* that was also a *Via Gloriosa*.

In my office, I worked more often at Samuel Butler than on contributions to the *Statesman*'s editorial columns. I daresay the conditions under which I wrote about him – with the fan churning up the stagnant, humid air, and my stagnant mind needing to be churned up likewise if it was to function at all – affected my view of him and his books. Sentences came laboriously, and the very physical effort of typing left me limp and exhausted. Visitors occasionally dropped in, breaking the thread of my thoughts; mostly Indians, who had a disconcerting way of sitting on and on in total silence. There was, for instance, B, a barrister-at-law who had been at Harrow and Oxford. His ostensible purpose was to collect a book for review (books, even new ones, soon had a damp, musty smell in Bengal's humid climate), but, as he put it, he'd just pushed his head through the door to say Salaam. His appearance still bore some traces of Inns of Court formality – alpaca jacket, winged collar, watch-chain, but with the lost eyes, weak mouth and sometimes tremulous hands of a drunkard. He had legal tales to tell – repartee of a Birkenhead, eloquence of a Patrick Hastings, skill of a Birkett. 'My *guru*,' he said to me once,

'is Hilaire Belloc.' It was almost unbearably poignant; after all, B was our creation.

In such circumstances, I saw Butler more luridly than I might otherwise have done, as symbolising everything I most abhorred. In my estimation, the poor fellow might have drafted the League of Nations Covenant, been a founder-member of the Fabian Society and a Friend of the Soviet Union, instead of holding strongly conservative views about everything except homosexuality and patricide; he being homosexual himself, and hating his father for persistently refusing to die and leave him his money. Like Columbus stumbling upon America when he thought he was finding a route to India, Butler, all unconsciously blazed a trail which many have subsequently followed. Thus, through *The Way of All Flesh*, published posthumously, he helped to make it as fashionable to detest parents as formerly it had been to revere them. His sentimental, timid homosexuality likewise went down well among the enlightened; as also did his profound respect for money as the source of all happiness, and the condition of personal freedom. 'No gold, no Holy Ghost' he jotted down in one of his grotesquely over-praised Notebooks.

Excoriating Butler through leaden Bengal afternoons and evenings, seated under a fan; breaking off to cope with the Report of the Joint Select Parliamentary Committee on Indian Constitutional Reform ('A state paper of the highest importance whose language is adequate to the gravity of the scene . . .'); then back to Butler, and his weekly visits to a French lady in Handel Street, whom he shared with his friend and future biographer, Festing Jones, though on different days – in the circumstances, I consider it quite a feat that the book was somehow finished and dispatched to the publisher. A good part of the credit was due to Kitty, who patiently went through the Butler papers, lodged with Geoffrey Keynes, the brother of Maynard; copying out for me what she thought would be of interest or significance, and doing it so skilfully that pretty well every scrap of material she sent me was usable. I had been to see Keynes and his fellow literary executor before leaving for India, and found him a fussy, finicky man, with whom I should have found it difficult to deal. Needless to say, when he read my book he hated it, and I half-feared that there would be a repetition of what happened with *Picture Palace*. It was within his power to prevent publication because of my use of copyright material. However, though less liberal in principle than the *Guardian*, to my great relief he behaved more liberally, and contented himself with just expressing his own personal distaste and disapproval.

It was from Mr Cathie, Butler's servant, whom I met shortly before leaving for India, that I got the details of the visits Butler and Festing Jones paid to Handel Street each week. Cathie was a respectable-looking man in a dark suit, stiff collar and shirt-front, who had set up in a grocery business after Butler's death, and who proved to be a true disciple of his late master by at once raising the question of remuneration. We agreed on a fiver in advance, to be followed by another at the end of our confabulations. 'The Governor,' he told me, 'would go every Wednesday afternoon. "Oh, bother, Alfred," he'd say. "It's Wednesday today, and I've got to go to Handel Street." He'd leave about two-thirty and be back by five, walking both ways.' Jones, it appeared, went on Thursdays, but how long he stayed, and whether he, too, walked both ways, Mr Cathie did not know, or particularly care. 'He was always crying,' he said of Jones, whom he obviously disliked. Of the French lady herself, he said that she was dark and large, a fine-looking woman, whom the Governor had picked up one evening at Islington. He and Jones paid her a pound a week each, including their holidays. While they were away, Mr Cathie handed over the money in person, and, as he put it, took her out once or twice himself. Rightly or wrongly, the impression I formed was that on these occasions he considered himself to have been more than the equal of the other two together.

Their hearts, anyway, whatever may have been the case with their bodies, were not in Handel Street, but with a Swiss youth named Hans Faesch, a lock of whose hair they wore, turn and turn about, in a locket suspended from their watch-chains. Together, they saw Hans off from Holborn Viaduct Station when he went to Singapore. Butler celebrated the occasion with some verses beginning:

> Out, out, into the night,
> With the wind bitter north-east and the sea rough.
> You have a racking cough and your lungs are weak,
> But out, out into the night you go.
> So guide you and guard you, Heaven, and fare you well.

which he considered to be 'the best thing I ever wrote'. He sent the verses to the *Spectator* for publication, but later withdrew them because, as he wrote to Hans, 'things have happened in England which make Jones and me decide not to publish them even anonymously'. On Butler's copy of this letter there is a note to the effect that the event in question was the trial of Oscar Wilde. Just before we separated, and after he had received his second fiver, Mr Cathie paused to remark: 'There's one man I didn't care for. Now what's his name? I've got it –

Bern*ard* Shaw [accentuating the second syllable of 'Bernard']. I didn't care for the way he spoke at the Erewhon Dinner. Not at all. And the Governor didn't care for him either. "He's a beast," he said when he came back from seeing him. "He's a beast!" ' Mr Cathie departed chuckling. After being thus briefed by Mr Cathie, I visited Handel Street with Hugh Kingsmill and Hesketh Pearson to identify the house. While we were there, Kingsmill drew so hilarious a picture of these weird transactions, including the French lady's imagined comparison between M. Mercredi and M. Jeudi, and a recitation of 'Out, out, out into the night', that by the time he had finished, Hesketh and I were holding onto lamp-posts, helpless with laughter.

My book on Butler, when it appeared, offended all the critics, E. M. Forster called it a cross-patch of a book, and Desmond McCarthy, the reigning pundit at the time, devoted two whole articles in the *Sunday Times* to demolishing it. Needless to say, the Butler cult has continued unabated, and even to this day Mr Cathie's Governor is held up as a Voltarian exploder of Victorian humbug and complacency; whereas, in point of fact, he was himself – if there is such a thing – the quintessential Victorian. It is curious how often the cult figure turns out, on investigation, to be the antithesis of the cult he is supposed to have initiated. Who, for instance, would have disliked *O! Calcutta* more than D. H. Lawrence? Or Stalinism more than Karl Marx?

By this time, the editor of the *Statesman*, Arthur Moore, had returned from leave. He had only lately been appointed to the editorship, after his predecessor, Alfred Watson, had been shot at by a Bengal terrorist for some articles that Moore had written. It was a rather embarrassing basis for inheriting the position, especially as Watson would have been well content to stay on. However, the proprietors considered this would be imprudent, and so Watson returned to London, where he frequented the National Liberal Club and was knighted. Moore had worked for *The Times* as correspondent in Persia, and very much belonged to that tradition. In happier circumstances he might well have been offered the throne of Albania, or have sent long delayed messages from Mecca or Tibet, or trudged through Outer Mongolia. As it was, he had turned up in Calcutta, where his mercurial temperament took him from the out-and-out imperialist position which might have cost Watson his life, and did cost him his job, to one of close affinity with the Swarajists. He was a gifted, unstable, Northern Irishman, fated to make a mess of his career, not through being too rigid – which is one way of doing it – but through being too flexible – which is another. I noticed that Europeans

living in India either grow duskier or whiter; Moore was in the latter category. Belieing his political views, he grew whiter and whiter, the impression being intensified when, after he left the *Statesman*, he stayed on in Delhi and grew a black beard. Towards the end of his life he fell on evil days, and came to see me once about some project or other. I received him sympathetically, but, I regret to say, offered no effective help.

Kitty came to Calcutta for a short visit at Christmas. It was an unhappy time for both of us, and the nearest our marriage came to breaking up. Just before she left, we found ourselves briefly at one again, and, after she had gone, I sent her a long telegram saying that nothing could ever part us – as, indeed, has proved to be the case. Of all the memories I have to confront, the most hateful are occasions such as this, when I racked my mind to think of words which would hurt and allusions which would stir up bitterness. If there were any possibility of unsaying anything – which, of course, there isn't – this is what I should most wish unsaid. The immediate cause of strife was, inevitably, infidelities. I think of them with a kind of wonder. Can I really have been so obsessed by a relationship which made so little lasting impression that now I have difficulty in recalling the person concerned? Did I really wait like that, with my heart furiously beating, for a telephone call? Ring a door bell, and listen with such a concentration of excitement to approaching footsteps? Scribble notes so ardently? Tear open others received so eagerly? In the consequent pin-pointing of emotion and desire, feel the warmth of the sun on my back, breathe in the fragrance of jasmine in a garden, with sharpened senses? Aware, as never before, of the bright colours and silken texture of a sari, and the touch of fingers so soft and supple that they might have been boneless. Overwhelmed likewise by the sudden onslaught of night, velvety black, dancing with fire-flies; the stars themselves so near and bright that one of them might be a tiny jewel fixed in a nostril, and, at the same time, so distant that they seemed to be beyond the furthest limits of space, in the eternity that sensuality cannot reach? Was it really so?

Don Juan, more even than Raskolnikov, is the hero of our time; his impersonation, our most gruelling servitude, the quest for his Unholy Grail our most tortuous journey. He is everywhere – on the motorways in his GB-ed car, at cocktail parties recce-ing the company; a huntsman in a game-reserve. Once, in a Stockholm roof café, the people I was with happened to mention that one of the waiters – a Canadian named Harry – was in the habit each evening of picking on one of the customers to come home

with him. They pointed him out to me; like the other waiters, wearing a sort of smartly cut red hunting jacket, and weaving his way among the tables while holding aloft his tray loaded with bottles and glasses. Examining him curiously, I noticed that his face had a rapt, almost mystical expression, as though his thoughts were far removed from the mundane business of serving drinks and collecting tips; at the same time, full of the ineffable sadness that comes of seeking the attainable. A People's Byron; the egotist persisting in his egotism to the point of becoming disinterested; the carnal so ardently pursued that it becomes a kind of spirituality. Looking more closely, I saw that he was older than I had thought. There were wrinkles, a certain thinning, and even perhaps greying, of the hair; a dry parchment look about the flesh. Did he always, I asked, manage to pull off his evening conquest? Nearly always, I was told, but there might be occasional evenings when something went awry – when he made the wrong choice, or when he or the chosen one happened to be out of sorts. The pale Scandinavian light – it was summer and the days scarcely ended – hung over the scene, adding a macabre unearthly touch.

Who can be expected to look for a God when there isn't one? Or for perfection when there is nothing beyond the ticking of the clocks. What is to be done but play the Crucifixion backwards, and reverse the Logos – in the beginning was the flesh, and the flesh became Word? Celluloid the only recourse – moving pictures, presenting between Action! and Cut!, the seven ages of lechery. The pimply schoolboy creeping willingly into his sex-instruction classes; then the youthful, zestful sex-instructed lover. After him, the grown man, bearded like the pard, twin-slitted coat, motel habitué, with contraceptives to hand, stoking up nature's fires with bottled ones; followed by the seasoned veteran, round bellied, full of wise saws and modern instances culled from his Bond, his Clockwork Orange, his Last Tango. Finally, the lean and slippered pantaloon, with spectacles on nose, squinting into his TV screen; and last scene of all, a second childishness and mere oblivion, sans teeth, sans taste, sans everything; even – the ultimate desolation – sans telly.

Moore disliked the views I expressed in my leaders no less than Wordsworth did. So it was a great relief to us all three when it was decided that I should go to Simla and represent the paper during the summer months when the Government of India functioned there. My four friends saw me off at Calcutta Station; we were never to be all five together again.

The train pulling out of the station, gave me an enormous sense of relief. For most of the fifteen months I had spent in Calcutta, I felt ill, dispirited, melancholy. Apart from somehow staggering through the Butler book, my time had been wasted and my mind vacuous. At last I was on the move again; and movement can seem a substitute for being. Like tops, we spin ever faster in order to be still. I stopped off in Delhi for a couple of days. India's new capital was then still in process of construction; the only deliberate architectural monument the Raj left behind it. The foundation-stone was laid by King George V in a cemetery by mistake, and Clemenceau provided the perfect benediction when he said that, of the six ruined capitals round about the same site, the Raj's would provide the most magnificent ruin of all. Even this is doubtful. The princes were never to take their places in the splendid Chamber of Princes designed for them, and it was in the garden of the Commander-in-Chief's residence that, two decades later, smelling the roses still blooming there, I waited to record a television interview with Jawaharlal Nehru, ruler over an independent India.

It was exhilarating to be in the little train climbing up into the mountains to Simla; the air getting appreciably cooler and fresher all the time, and bringing the travelling Sahibs visibly to life. To the handful of English who manned the highest administrative posts, it seemed, even at this late hour, the most natural thing in the world that the government of some four hundred million souls should thus be transferred to a little mountain eyrie, so far away and so inaccessible. They found the hot weather oppressive in the plains; therefore, the whole lumbering administration must follow them to higher altitudes where they would be more comfortable. It was like moving a general headquarters in a war. Whole convoys of lorries carrying files and other documents, whole train-loads of clerks and minor personnel; then the heads of departments, the staff-officers, and finally the Viceroy himself, at this time Lord Willingdon, and his Vicereine, along with their little court – their Comptroller-of-the-Household, their ADC's and secretaries, valets and maids – to take up their residence in Viceregal Lodge, a hill-station version of an English country house.

Simla, at any rate, was an authentic English production; designed by Sahibs for Sahibs, without reference to any other consideration – not even Maharajahs. If, in the future, it is desired (something extremely improbable) to preserve some genuine memorial of British rule in India, then Simla is the place which really conveys what it was like; and, mysteriously, still does. The church, whose dilapidated state is not

apparent in the distance; the Mall, along which the Sahibs and their ladies took an airing on Sunday afternoons, with a band-stand where an army band entertained them with appropriate music as they strolled up and down, the ladies with parasols, the gentlemen in large white topees. There were separate houses for the more important officials, allotted in accordance with their status, their name and department indicated on a board at the gate, so that everyone knew who and what everyone was, from members of the Viceroy's Council downwards. On the Mall, a little theatre where plays were produced, and Kipling once acted – Gilbert and Sullivan, Pinero, Barrie, and, more daringly, Noël Coward. Then Viceregal Lodge itself, with a special guard of Sikhs, their black curly beards in nets to keep them tidy, and Wildflower Hall, built by Lord Kitchener when he was Commander-in-Chief, some little distance away from Simla, just far enough to make a pleasant ride and to feel like a rival seat of authority.

Journalists follow authority as sharks do a liner, hoping to feed off the waste it discharges, with perhaps someone occasionally falling overboard to make a meal, and once in a way the whole ship going down and providing a positive feast. There was a little band of us swimming along in the wake of the Government of India – Sandy Inglis, representing *The Times*, and Jim Barnes, Reuter's man, as well, of course, as any number of representatives of Indian newspapers and news-agencies. Public relations, as we know it today, was in its infancy, but already the Government of India had its spokesman, whom we constantly pursued for hand-outs and leakages, and to arrange interviews. Among other useful services, he made a point of mastering the first names of Indians who were going to be knighted, so that on the very day the Honours List came out, he had them pat – Sir Shrinivasa, Sir Rahimtoolah, Sir Girja. It was, in any case, a glad day for one and all. Indian politicians and civil servants were even more avid for honours than their English opposite numbers, and the distribution of knighthoods and lesser decorations, down to MBE's, was followed with breathless interest; so much so, that equivalent post-Raj honours have had to be devised.

Sandy Inglis and his wife Jean became great friends of mine. He was a shrewd, hard-working Scot, who toiled away at producing turn-over articles and news stories about the Reforms, packed tight with information, and full of sober hope for the future. Naturally, he deplored my disparagement of the very idea that the Raj could reform itself in any way that would be acceptable to the Swarajists. The Raj, I vociferously insisted, would either have to re-establish itself on an authoritarian

basis – which was virtually inconceivable – or wind itself up, while pretending that power was being gradually and lawfully transferred to Indian hands with a view to creating an All-India democracy on Westminster lines.

We often argued about this, mostly good-naturedly, but sometimes acrimoniously. I have never really been able to understand how anyone can believe in the possibility of compromise in matters of power, which is an absolutist passion, and felt the same incredulity in Simla about the proposed constitutional reforms as I did in Geneva about the League and the ILO as instruments for promoting international and industrial peace. Sandy, on the other hand, faithfully read and digested all the relevant documents, and patiently listened to the various officials concerned as they interminably explained what they were at and what they hoped to achieve. Extreme attitudes are often an excuse for laziness; if the apocalypse is just round the corner, why bother with what is to be done today or tomorrow? All the same, in this particular case it would seem that I lost nothing by avoiding an avalanche of irrelevant words, written and spoken, and that Sandy's heroic labours to reduce them to some sort of sense were a barren pursuit. There never was to be any genuine constitutional reform; only a constitutional debacle, celebrated by Mr Attlee, the Prime Minister responsible, by a visit to the cinema. Or so his then Press Officer, Philip Jordan, told me. I like to think of the little man sitting in the three-and-six-pennies on the day the Bill making India and Pakistan independent states became law, and the Raj was finally wound up. Poor Sandy deserved better than that.

Jim Barnes, the other English journalist in Simla, was the exact antithesis of Sandy – a fanatical admirer of Mussolini and pro-Fascist. A man with a violent temperament, to the point at times of seeming a little mad. He had just come from reporting the Italian conquest of Abyssinia for Reuter's. I never read any of his by-lined dispatches, but it would surprise me if they were notable for impartiality and objectivity. He used to stride up and down the room gesticulating and bellowing about Eden, and the rottenness of British policy, and the feebleness of the Raj. Sometimes I went riding with him; he sat heavily on his horse, and on one occasion, when it persistently refused to canter, I heard him shouting into its ear: 'You're my slave, you've got to do what I say!' His Italian wife was more measured in her attitude to Mussolini than he was, and just accepted her husband's tantrums as an incidental affliction. Once I went to Mass with her, and on the way back, à propos of nothing, she said to me: 'Perhaps one day God will

take pity on you.' Barnes's father had been in the ICS, finishing up as Governor of Burma; his mother had died when quite young in Quetta, and was buried in the cemetery there, like many other Sahib's wives, and he was brought up by his Strachey grandmother in Italy. The poor fellow never managed to sort himself out, and spent the 1939–45 war in Italy, where, like Ezra Pound, he broadcast anti-Allied propaganda, though, unlike Pound, he had no admirers or defenders in the victor's camp. After the war, he hid in a monastery, where it would be nice to think he found the peace which had hitherto eluded him. Through his brother, George Barnes, for a while Broadcasting House's Director of the Spoken Word (that inimitable title which only a Sir William Haley could have invented), and then Director of BBC Television, I was about to get a friendly message to him. Later, I heard that he had died.

I doubt if any government has ever existed so cut off from the governed as the Government of India nestling among the Himalayas in Simla. Up there, we might read of rioting, or famines in the plains below, or – as happened when I was in Simla – of a ferocious earthquake in Quetta but these disasters were far, far away, and scarcely impinged on us. For researchers into the nature of government, Simla provided a unique opportunity for studying one in isolation; examining it, as it were, under the microscope; without any confusing involvement in side issues, such as people, or demagogy, or armed forces, or taxes. It was government pure and undefiled; endlessly minuting and circulating files, which, like time itself, had neither beginning nor end, but just were. I grew familiar with the various government departments, trudging, as I had to, from one to the other to find out what, if anything, they were at. All housed in identical wooden structures, with broad verandahs, it was impossible to distinguish Finance from Home, or Political from Defence, except that, in the case of the last, instead of a peon in red and gold dozing at each office door, there would be a sepoy in khaki drill. Typewriters hard at work, Indian clerks and minor officials clustered together like bees in a hive, the senior officials still mostly Sahibs, and, at the centre of it all, the Queen Bee, or member of the Viceroy's Council, responsible for the department in question.

Mooning about in these departments, waiting to see someone I didn't want to see in order to ask him questions I didn't want answered, I used sometimes to think of India as I knew it. The dusty roads, the teeming bazaars, the lurid paddy fields, the sluggish rivers, the women carrying water from the well in pitchers on their heads, the brown bodies sweating in the sun as they followed behind the lumbering oxen and steered their

wooden ploughs; the innumerable villages, and feet endlessly padding – little processions, a man leading, then a woman with a baby on her back, and a child barely able to walk, clutching her hand, other children trailing behind. Everywhere people; washing, sleeping, chanting, buying, selling, giving birth, suckling, living, dying. Where was the connection between them and this typewriter fusillade, these dozing peons, the clerks, the Sahibs, the Members of the Viceroy's Council? Power only exists in so far as it connects the government and the governed; the gap between them has to be spanned, whether by demagogy, or the long lashes of whips and barrels of guns, or lies shouted or borne on the waves of sound and light, or magical incantations and emanations, or, as is more commonly the case, by some combination of all or some of them. In the case of Anglo-India, the gap had widened to the point that it was no longer spannable. Governors and governed were like two jagged coastlines, with a torrential sea running between them, and no ferry-boats plying, overhead telephone lines all down, under-water cables all broken; the machinery of government still ostensibly functioning, but like a main-line station with no passengers, a supermarket with no customers.

The focus of all attention in Simla, political, social, administrative, was, of course, Viceregal Lodge; whether ladies aspiring to appear, suitably arrayed, in the highest circles, or their spouses with an eye on promotion and the increments and honours that went therewith, or just anyone, white, brown or mottled, buzzing round the honey-pot of authority in the vague expectation that something sweet-tasting might be sucked out of it. Those embossed invitation cards – Their Excellencies request the pleasure . . . – how precious and sought-after they were! Their Excellencies never, or only rarely, in very exceptional circumstances, requested in vain. My turn came round. Encased in starched shirt and tails, conscious of lines being crossed at the back of my white waistcoat, embossed card in hand, I sat in a rickshaw propelled by four coolies trotting along like ponies, two in front and two behind; knowing, but trying to forget, that Simla rickshaw coolies all die young from enlarged hearts through trotting up and down hills at so high an altitude.

Anyway, there was no alternative; only the Viceroy and the Commander-in-Chief being allowed motor-cars in Simla. Who, in his senses, would care to arrive on foot, hot and dishevelled, for a dinner party at Viceregal Lodge? Certainly not I. So, on we trot, past the turbaned, bearded sentries, who spring to attention, and up to the main entrance where ADC's are waiting to speed guests on their way to join the

glittering throng. Unglittering myself, without one single tiny medal, I fall into conversation with a resplendent Guards officer named Codrington, lightly ginger, with pale eyes, who has been trying, he tells me, to upgrade the military music provided by adding a touch of Purcel and summer a'coming in to the usual Colonel Bogey-ish repertoire. The ADC's shepherded us into some sort of a line, the band struck up the National Anthem, two folding doors were ceremonially opened, and in came Their Excellencies, who proceeded slowly down the line to greet their guests; the names of any doubtful ones whispered into their ears, the ladies courtseying, and the gentlemen bowing low. When my turn came, I, too, bowed: 'I've heard of you,' the Viceroy said, a touch of grimness in his voice. It seemed better than nothing. The Vicereine, a large, zestful lady with a red sash, wore a permanent unvarying smile which beamed upon one and all. He, on the other hand, was slight and frail, like a Max Beerbohm drawing, and studded with gleaming stars and orders. I examined him closely. After all, at any rate in theory, he was one of the world's great potentates; absolute ruler over more souls than any other ruler extant. Even so, he gave out no emanation of authority, but might have been, at a casual glance, a chairman of some board or other, or a City Alderman, or, for that matter, what he really was – an amiable back-bench Conservative MP. Even a Maharajah in his train, with a great jewel in his turban and a self-indulgent face, seemed more like a ruler than the Viceroy. Should I have felt the same if it had been Curzon instead of Willingdon? I asked myself. Probably not. But then Curzon's power over his hundreds of millions of subjects was, to some extent at any rate, real, whereas Willingdon's existed only to the degree that he didn't exercise it. This office, the Viceroyalty, the only one under the British Crown carrying with it the trappings and pomp and circumstance of a Sultan or Caliph, aspired after by so many politicians, drab little men in black coats and spongebag trousers who saw themselves in those splendid robes, seated on a silver throne and presiding over Durbars of inconceivable magnificence – its glory had already departed.

We dined to music which bore little trace of Captain Codrington's efforts to amend it, and afterwards waited to be summoned to Their Excellencies. I was guided first to Lady Willingdon, where she sat giving out waves of energy and enthusiasm. She wished, she said, that they were staying on for another ten years. I put on an expression, I hoped convincingly, of one who wished likewise. What about our successors? she asked. I murmured 'Linlithgow,' with as much journalistic

knowingness as I could summon up. 'He's terribly pompous,' she said. I agreed heartily. 'Look at John Anderson,' she went on, 'and how he's changed!' How? I wanted to ask, but at this point an ADC hove in sight to take me away and over to the Viceroy. It was somewhat unusual, I was given to understand afterwards, to be moved straight from her square to his, and was duly flattered.

Willingdon, when I got to him, looked tremendously like an old beau in a Restoration comedy; I half expected him to take a pinch of snuff and flick his handkerchief. People were inclined to think that India was difficult to govern, he began, but he'd found it almost ridiculously easy. You just had to be nice to these fellers, and they responded. Such, at least, had been his experience. He doubted if there was in all the world an easier country to govern than India. In the circumstances, it was a pretty extraordinary statement, and, while I was digesting it, he went on to say that he believed in Providence; otherwise, he'd never have been able to carry on. Then, looking sidelong at me, he added: 'You won't believe in that, I suppose.' Before I could elucidate my own attitude to Providence, my replacement had arrived; a man with a goatee beard who had some sort of connection with the *Round Table* and South Africa. I saw the Viceroy moistening his lips from a glass of water in preparation for another conversation.

Walking back to the Cecil Hotel where I was staying – I was happy not to need a rickshaw for the return journey – I kept going over in my mind what the Viceroy had said about India being so easy a country to govern, and those fellers (meaning, presumably, Indian politicians of one sort and another, from Gandhi and Nehru to the latest batch of Indian knights and CIE's) being so responsive to niceness. It was one of the little vignettes which mark out history like a surveyor's white posts; the last Viceroy but three, up there in the Raj's mountain retreat, his guests around him, his ADC's at his elbow, his rumbustious lady within hailing distance, the band playing Elgar by way of a compromise between Captain Codrington and Colonel Bogey – this grey fragile-looking old gentleman telling me how easy he had found governing India and managing those fellers within so short a time of the Raj's total collapse.

I had several other meetings with Willingdon in his office in the way of duty as the *Statesman*'s man in Simla. His amiability, and a certain shrewdness acquired through the years as a politician and proconsul (he had been Governor-General in Canada in addition to his service in India), made him easy to talk to, but he never really said anything about

anything. As Viceroy, he was content just to coast along. Indeed, there was nothing much else he could do. The only matter that cropped up about which he seemed to have strong feelings was the reputation of his predecessor, Lord Irwin – later Lord Halifax, and Chamberlain's Foreign Secretary. It annoyed him to think that, though Irwin's Viceroyalty had been full of trouble and violence, including the incursion of Afridi tribesmen, he passed in the public estimation for being the better man of the two of them. His method of denigrating Irwin was to begin by flattering him; he was, he said, a very great and high-minded gentleman (something, incidentally, that no one was likely to say of Willingdon, however admirable he might otherwise seem), but he had not found India, as Willingdon had, an easy country to govern; nor had he managed to get along with those fellers despite his sanctimonious exchanges with Gandhi. Why, then, such a high reputation?

To comfort him I developed on the spur of the moment a theory, often propounded subsequently – that to succeed pre-eminently in English public life it is necessary to conform either to the popular image of a bookie or of a clergyman; Churchill being a perfect example of the former, Halifax of the latter. Willingdon liked this notion, and we successfully applied it to a number of other public personages. As a matter of fact, I felt very much on Willingdon's side in his attitude to his predecessor; sentimentally virtuous people like Lord Halifax and Mrs Roosevelt do far more harm in the world than recognisable villains. Solzhenitsyn has provided the perfect parable on this theme with his description of Mrs Roosevelt's conducted visit to a labour camp where he was doing time. The estimable lady, who spawned the moral platitudes of the contemporary liberal wisdom as effortlessly and plenteously as the most prolific salmon, was easily persuaded that the camp in question was a humanely conducted institution for curing the criminally inclined. A truly wicked woman would have been ashamed to be so callous and so gullible.

The only member of Willingdon's Government I got to know well and like was P. J. Grigg, the Finance Member. We began – as almost everyone did in dealing with P.J. – with a ferocious row; in my case, over some articles I had written in the *Statesman* about India's fiscal policy, which, I argued at some length, was subordinated to British interests. After a slanging match between the two of us, we became friends, and remained so to the end of P.J.'s life. He was a strange, irascible, infinitely kind man, who from humble origins had risen to be a senior civil servant, and then was sent to India, where he had political

responsibilities for which he had little aptitude, and administrative ones at which he was superbly competent. Life induced in him a more or less permanent condition or irritation, which he vented on anyone who happened to be around; especially his wife Gertrude, a stately lady, daughter of a bishop, who loved him dearly and proudly, and accepted his strictures with equanimity, while quietly working away at translating books into braille. She looked rather like a pantomime dame herself, and together they put up a wonderful comic turn. To P.J.'s great credit, the various prizes he had worked for – his professional advancement, his KGB, his familiarity with the great (he had been private secretary to both Lloyd George and Churchill), his easy financial circumstances, his directorships, his wine cellar and library and other such amenities – failed to give him any lasting satisfaction. To the end of his days he was looking for something else, but never, I think, found it; anyway, dying still irascible. Thinking of him – and of myself, for that matter – I draw comfort from Pascal's saying that to look for God is to find Him. In the Indian Legislature P.J. sat on the Government front bench in the style of the masters he had served in Whitehall; red-faced, feet up, ostentatiously sleeping through vituperative sessions – a second-string touring company performance.

After a spurt with the articles on fiscal policy which had so enraged P.J., I soon lost interest in the Simla scene, of which I was supposed to provide the *Statesman* with a day-by-day report. My communications to the Calcutta office grew ever shorter and more occasional, as did my responses to queries from London, where I had one or two stringer connections. One, I remember, asked for the reactions of Indians to the announcement of Linlithgow's appointment as Viceroy. It reminded me of the time in Moscow when I was asked for the reactions of the Soviet toiling masses to the lavish scale of entertaining in USSR embassies, and I had replied that the only ascertainable reaction was a desire to get near the buffet. In the case of Indian reactions to Linlithgow's appointment, there just weren't any; not even imaginable ones. So there was nothing for it but to fall back on quotations from the English-language Press, culling a few sentences where I could – 'If the New Viceroy will but see the need to speed up drastically progress to Indian self-government, then Indians, we are sure, will take him to their hearts . . .' Somehow, the idea of Indians taking Linlithgow to their hearts appealed to me.

My detachment from news-gatherings in Simla became total when I got to know Amrita Sher-Gil, an artist now generally considered to be

the outstanding one of modern India. There is a room in the Delhi Art Gallery dedicated to her work, including a portrait she did of me. It was one of those obsessive relationships which for a while occupy one's whole being; then come to an end as suddenly as they begin. In the context of a life, a sort of play within a play. Her father was a Sikh nobleman, Sardar Umrai Singh, and her mother a red-haired solidly built Hungarian lady named Antoinette. I have no idea how they met, but their union gave an impression of being discrodant; he, Tolstoyan in his views and ways, ascetic, aloof, scholarly, and she a somewhat earthy person, who, when she played the piano – which she did a lot – seemed to be tearing greedily at the notes with her short, stubby fingers, the many rings on them knocking against the keyboard. Usually she wore European clothes – what used to be called gowns rather than dresses, with flounces and frills and billowing skirts; but when she appeared in a sari, as she sometimes did, she looked ungainly, her bare feet splaying out like trotters. They lived in a house at Summer Hill, just outside Simla, where I was a constant visitor. Amrita had her studio there, and I sat for her; or rather lolled on a sofa, sometimes reading, or just watching with fascination the animal intensity of her concentration, making her short of breath, with beads of sweat appearing on the faint moustache on her upper lip. It was this animality which she somehow transferred to the colours as she mixed them and splashed them on her canvas.

She was ten years younger than I, born in Budapest in 1913, and when she was seven came with her parents and her younger sister, Indira, to Simla, where she went to school. Then she studied art in Paris. When she spoke English, it had the Anglo-Indian lilt (called chee-chee in the days of the Raj); when French, it came straight from the *Ecole des Beaux Arts*. She habitually wore richly coloured saris with heavy gold or silver edging; and her face was Indian in its perfect symmetry, which she accentuated by painting – quite gratuitously, of course – a caste-mark in the centre of her forehead. The expression, however, lacked the characteristic softness of an Indian woman's face; Heavily made up, the lips loaded with red as her person was with jewellery – ear-rings, bangles, bracelets, necklaces, like gilded manacles – it was hard, self-contained, at times arrogant.

Even more than in my four friends in Calcutta, I sensed in her an inner conflict, which in her case was manifested in the disharmony of her parents. Her father, though smaller, more shrivelled, than Tolstoy, actually looked like him, with a similar beard and loose belted shirt, and

displaying the same sort of petulance when assailed by distaste for what he considered to be the unduly luxurious manner in which the household was conducted. If, say, he were offered a pastry at tea-time, he would reject it with positive disgust, muttering: 'No, I won't take, I won't take!' Mme Sher-Gil's whole style of living – bourgeois Viennese in the days of the Austro-Hungarian Empire, transplanted to Simla, of all unlikely places – was displeasing to him. If the Sardar's displeasure became too marked, she resorted to her piano, getting going on a Richard Strauss or Liszt number; pounding away at the keyboard, head nodding, foot furiously pressing and releasing the pedal. He would then withdraw to the roof, where he spent much of his time engaged in abstruse calculations, and, by night, assiduously studying the stars through a telescope. I occasionally joined him there. Up on the roof by night, he was a wild-looking figure; hair and beard dishevelled in the wind, peering intently through his telescope as though he hoped thereby to get nearer to the stars and their celestial music, and further away from the Hungarian Dances whose strains reached him even there.

A similar disharmony was apparent in Amrita's painting. Her subjects were nearly all Indian; many of them peasants working in the fields, executed in the destructive twentieth-century style of the west – a mixture of something faint and dying and rather beautiful, and something furiously disintegrating. Rosewater and raw spirit. In the former mood, she sometimes seemed infinitely sad; in the latter, self-assertive, morally vacuous, even rather vulgar. Despite all the time I passed in her company, and our ostensible intimacy, I never felt that I got to know her. Or was it that there was really no one to know? In any case, she had built a wall between herself and the world, behind which she lurked, brooding on some secret of her own, or perhaps despairing; her sensuality being just fire signals that she sent up from her solitude to indicate where she was to any passing stranger. She often dined with me at the Cecil Hotel, where her appearance in the dining-room always created a marked impression. This I liked. In relations between the sexes, there is a strong element of exhibitionism. The pleasure of her company – and also at times the fatigue – lay in her vivid, forceful, direct reactions to life; the moral equivalent of her taste for steaks that were almost raw, and curries that were almost on fire. When she achieved, as she sometimes did, some sort of weird amalgam of the bearded Tolstoyan star-gazer and the red-haired pianist pounding away at her keyboard, she was very appealing. Often we talked on and on, with her rickshaw waiting outside the hotel – a smart yellow-painted

one, with four coolies in a sort of livery to match; a characteristic Mme Sher-Gil touch. Then, at last, I would see her to it, and, rather than separate, walk beside it for a mile or so, still going on talking against the padding of the coolies' bare feet. Afterwards, walking back alone, smelling the pine trees and breathing in the cold mountain air.

As I had more or less severed all communication with the *Statesman*, and never went to any press-conferences or put in an appearance at any of the Government Departments, my position in Simla became rather ridiculous. Salvation came in the shape of a telegram out of the blue from Percy Cudlipp, editor of the *Evening Standard*, offering me a job on the Londoner's Diary at twenty pounds a week. I at once wired off accepting the offer, sent a letter of resignation to Moore in Calcutta, and with great thankfulness let Kitty know that I was coming home. Amrita saw me off at Simla Station in the very early morning – a great concession on her part, she being a late riser. We walked up and down the platform until the little mountain train blew its whistle to indicate it was starting, when I got in. Through the window she said we'd had some *beaux moments* together, which was true. I waved as long as she was in sight, knowing I should never see her again. In 1941, when she was still only 27, she died suddenly in Lahore. Then I heard that her mother had committed suicide. Somehow, neither Mme Sher-Gil's suicide nor Amrita's early death surprised me; I had always been aware of an aura of tragedy hanging over them.

Thirty years later, I was in Simla again with Kevin Billington when we were filming *Twilight of Empire*. By an extraordinary coincidence, Viceregal Lodge was just then being emptied of its contents – furniture, carpets, pictures, all loaded into vans to be taken away. So, in a sense, I saw with my own eyes the final dismantling of the Raj. When we came to film, little remained in the big reception hall except three silver thrones on which the Viceroy, the Vicereine and the Governor of the Punjab used to sit on ceremonial occasions. I sat on the Viceroy's throne, and tried to reconstruct the scene there as it had existed, and as I had known it, so short a while ago in time, yet already so infinitely remote – the bustling throng, the frail Viceroy in his grey frock-coat, the resplendent Indian Princes, the bearded Sikhs and sly old Dewans, and officers in all their regimental glory. All over now, and almost forgotten; soon to be wholly so. In the evening I went for a walk to Summer Hill, and looked for the Sher-Gil's house, but couldn't find it. It, too, seemed to have disappeared.

*

Back in London, I soon got in the way of going each day to and from the *Evening Standard* office in Shoe Lane, off Fleet Street. I have invariably felt about everything I have had to do for a living that I have been doing it always, and, equally, that I shall stop doing it tomorrow. Two seemingly incompatible states of mind – like free will and determinism – which nonetheless, in my experience, easily co-exist. I travelled up each morning by tram, from Kentish Town, via Gray's Inn Road, to Holborn; a form of urban transport that appealed to me, perhaps because of childhood memories of the virtues of municipal enterprise, and of similar tram rides to the Old Vic for the special matinees of Shakespeare productions put on for elementary schoolchildren.

The *Evening Standard*, a Beaverbrook newspaper, was produced in a single large room, the idea being that thereby the whole operation of bringing it out would be integrated and co-operative. Whether this aim was realised is doubtful, but at least the arrangement accustomed me to working in conditions of noise and disorder. The only person missing was the most essential – Beaverbrook himself, who never came to the office, but nonetheless managed to maintain from afar his close control of how the paper was run, and of everything that went into it. The single department which resisted the process of *gleichshaltung* was the Women's Page, which fought a last-ditch battle to maintain its seclusion, and obstinately went on functioning in what looked like a little hut amidst the encircling chaos. Inside it, two stern unbending ladies continued to deal magisterially with readers' queries about such matters as too large pores and the appearance of hair in untoward places. Their resistance was finally broken when one night, in their absence, their little hut was razed to the ground. Arriving the next morning and finding it gone, they had no recourse but to sit among us, which they surlily did.

In our Londoner's Diary corner, Bruce Lockhart reigned as a quasi-independent satrap. Having a direct line to Beaverbrook, he could treat with the editor, Percy Cudlipp, more or less as an equal; as well as with Captain Wardell, Beaverbrook's man on the premises. I once heard Bruce, on the telephone to Beaverbrook, call him 'Tich'; but the word was pronounced so softly and respectfully that it might have been some honorific title like 'Your Eminence' or 'Your Grace'. In matters of sycophancy, as of virtue, it is the spirit, not the letter, that counts. The Captain, as we all called Wardell, had an office upstairs, though what his precise functions were I never knew. He had a patch over one eye and high social connections, and as one of Beaverbrook's familiars was

treated with considerable awe and respect. His eye, it seemed, had been injured in a hunting accident, and in his day paragraphs about hunting and related matters were frequent in the Diary. In his upstairs office he gave regular luncheon parties, to which I was occasionally invited. At them, one would meet such figures as Brendan Bracken, Beverley Baxter, Bob Boothby, and other such kulaks of journalism, politics and finance.

Bruce Lockhart himself was a cheerful, amiable Scot, who had been the first unofficial British agent in the USSR; an adventurous time for him, described in his book *Memoirs of a British Agent*. In the end, he was exchanged for Litvinov; a swap which might be considered, in worldly terms, advantageous to the Soviet side, but humanly speaking, I should have said we were the gainers. Bruce was on good terms with the Soviet Embassy, perhaps as the *de facto* donor of their Commissar for Foreign Affairs, and drolly complained on one occasion that paragraphs I put in the paper led to the discontinuance of his annual present of caviare. He and Lord Castlerosse were the two wild ones, *avec peur et avec reproche*, in Beaverbrook's little court, who brought to it a flavour of high living and society gossip; as Aneurin Bevan and Michael Foot did of Radical thinking and political gossip, enabling Beaverbrook to enjoy vicariously the sensation of being a rake and a rebel without jeopardising either his social or financial standing. When, as sometimes happened, the money-lenders closed in on Bruce and Castlerosse, they turned to their master for help. It was accorded with some ostensible grumbling, but, I suspect, much inward satisfaction. Beaverbrook felt he was subsidising their lubricity and general extravagance, in the same sort of way that Balzac's miser, Père Goriot, delighted in setting up his fashionable daughters in luxurious circumstances. Giving money away was a means of attaching people to himself; a kind of Devil's sacrament – 'This is my money . . .' At Christmas-time his smart lady friends could count on receiving a cheque, and Lord Ismay told me that when, in the 1939–45 war, he joined Churchill's *apparat*, the first thing Beaverbrook did was to offer him money, which, however, he prudently declined, realising instinctively that it would involve a dangerous servitude. Aneurin Bevan, too, told me that at one point Beaverbrook wanted to take him on to his payroll at a large figure, but, like Ismay, he saw the danger, and turned the offer down, contenting himself with drinking champagne at Beaverbrook's table and enjoying the company he met there – a strange taste for so fervid and sharp a mind. Money was really the only thing Beaverbrook believed in or cared about; it was the source of such power

as he exercised, both within the organisation of his newspapers and in the larger world of politics. It was also the reason that, in the end, despite the huge circulations he commanded, and his intimacies with the leading politicians of his time, his influence was negligible. Money is a fragile power base to operate from, and can no more procure lasting influence than sensual pleasure can lasting affection.

Even *in absentia*, Beaverbrook's presence hung over the *Evening Standard* office as intensively as C. P. Scott's had over the *Guardian* office in Manchester. It was not just that he telephoned directives to particular individuals – though this, of course, happened; in the case, for instance, of the ill-starred leader-writer. One would see this unfortunate with the receiver glued to his ear, and a look of anguish on his face, desperately trying to grasp and stamp on his mind each word Beaverbrook uttered. Even when Cudlipp installed some sort of primitive dictaphone, things were not much easier. Out of curiosity, I listened to one or two of these recordings, and all one could hear distinctly was a raucous Canadian voice saying at regular intervals: 'You've gotta say.' When I left the *Evening Standard* I tried to take a few specimens away with me; I thought they would be nice to play over at one of those gatherings – like the Newspaper Proprietors' Association, or the English-Speaking Union – when *Areopagitica* is quoted, and our free press extolled. Alas, I found that, on Beaverbrook's orders, they had all been destroyed. After all, he was not a fool. More effective than such direct interventions was the mood he managed to create in his staff, whereby, instinctively or deliberately, they angled everything they wrote to please him; echoing what they took as being his thoughts, views and prejudices. This applied to correspondents abroad working for Beaverbrook newspapers just as much as to the home staff. Once I asked Milton Shulman what public he had in mind when he wrote his theatre and television criticism for the *Evening Standard*. He replied with singular honesty that he wrote with one little old reader in mind – Beaverbrook.

The essential difference between Scott's control of the *Guardian* and Beaverbrook's of his papers was that Scott had views and attitudes which, however distasteful, were fairly consistent, and could be cogently expounded; whereas Beaverbrook, when you got down to it, really had no views at all, but only prejudices, moods, sudden likes and dislikes, which his newspapers had to keep abreast of and reflect; in their news columns, as in their features and editorials. Overnight, he might reverse a previously held position as a result of a conversation, or of something

he had read or heard. Or he might have a row with one of his children, and in the heat of it start a campaign for higher death-duties; or fail to ingratiate himself with some high-born lady and, to work off his irritation, mount a ferocious attack on class distinctions. Equally, if the approach proved successful, we might find ourselves adulating the lady in question, as being notable for beauty, wit and concern for the commonweal. Working for Scott was like waltzing with some sedate old dowager at a mayoral reception in Manchester; for Beaverbrook, like taking the floor in a night-club in the early hours of the morning, when everyone is more or less drunk.

Beaverbrook's affections were as unstable as his views, and he greatly enjoyed playing off one of his familiars against another. He might, for instance, instruct Bruce Lockart to review adversely a novel by his friend Arnold Bennett, and then, when Bennett complained, shake his head over the impossibility of controlling his subordinates. One of his best coups in this *genre* – which, I must say, I greatly enjoyed – was to punish Rothermere's *Daily Mail* for having acquired at great expense exclusive rights in Dickens's *Life of Christ* by publishing Thomas Wright's disclosures about Dickens's affair with Ellen Ternan. His pet aversions – for instance, in those days, John Reith and the BBC – were relatively steady; it was as much as anyone's job was worth to let a favourable word about them get into the paper. In other cases, his feelings fluctuated, and one had to make sure, before going into print, how the barometer stood. Happily for me, I was not considered of sufficient standing or reliability to be entrusted with promoting any of his political campaigns, and so was spared the humiliating task of trying to make sense of intrinsic absurdities like Empire Free Trade. On the Diary we were concerned more with personalities than politics, and there are few in public life at whom it is not a pleasure to take an occasional swipe. In this respect, the job suited me well enough.

Underneath Beaverbrook's vagaries and inconsistencies, however, one soon came to detect a strain of cunning and self-interest. Thus, our policy was to be cheerful and hopeful; everything was going well, prosperity reigned, and would steadily expand; the war that everyone was talking about and expecting, just wasn't going to happen. Such a view, of course, was good for advertising, and reassuring for Beaverbrook himself. He read and believed his own papers, even though they were fashioned specifically to convey all his favourite fantasies. When they told him there was not going to be a war, he having instructed them so to do, he felt reassured, and assumed, I daresay with reason, that

advertisers would react likewise. The true doom of the Media barons at all levels is to believe the Media, thereby infallibly encompassing their own ultimate destruction.

Another strand in the web of fantasy we wove on Beaverbrook's behalf was religiosity. Something of his early Calvinist upbringing lingered about him; he was not quite sure that there might not be such a thing as everlasting damnation, and if there should be, then, clearly, he would be a likely candidate. An evening with his cronies was liable to end with a hymn-singing session, and his book about Christ – *The Divine Propagandist* – is another essay in reassurance; this time against hell fire rather than another war. Jesus, he concludes, was a cheerful, sociable soul, who, as the parable of the talents shows, believed in investing money shrewdly and making a killing on the Stock Exchange when a good opportunity presented itself. Any suggestion that he was inclined to take a poor view of man's earthly circumstances represents, Beaverbrook insists, a distortion of his teaching; as does the literal interpretation of those parts of the Sermon on the Mount which deal with non-resistance, the suffering of persecution gladly, and the doctrine of turning the other cheek. An antidote to such error was provided in the *Evening Standard* by Dean Inge's weekly articles which, Beaverbrook considered, took a decently realistic view of the Christian message, while upholding something he clung to with particular tenacity – the sure hope of immortality. One of Inge's articles on this theme was advertised on our vans with the bill: IS THERE AN AFTER-LIFE? SEE TOMORROW'S EVENING STANDARD. Beaverbrook, as it seemed to me, was a perfect example of the validity of the Faust myth; he really did believe he had sold his soul to the Devil, and was terrified of having to settle the account.

The basic policy laid down for us was to write always on the assumption that our readers were a notch or two higher in the social scale than was actually the case. In the columns of the Londoner's Diary, they had all been to public schools, played rugby football rather than soccer, changed for dinner, went to the Private Showing of the Royal Academy and to gala occasions at Covent Garden, read the novels of Evelyn Waugh, and liked Shaw's plays for serious theatre-going and Noel Coward's for relaxation, attended the better-known race-meetings, especially Ascot, ski-ed, motored, and knew their way about the Riviera and the Rue de Rivoli. They might even hunt – but this was a shade beyond our reach, and only included out of deference to the Captain. Such a picture of themselves was comforting as they commuted between Purley and London Bridge, and alleviated the tedium of trimming their

privet hedges on Saturday afternoons, or holidaying *en famille* at the seaside in the summer.

Working on the Diary, we divided the various portfolios between us. Thus, Bruce Lockhart handled diplomats and diplomacy – ambassadorial postings, Excellencies turning up in London from distant places looking bronzed and fit, anecdotes about diplomatic bags and linguistic misunderstandings; anything like that. He also had the first bite at the Honours' List, when it appeared, speculating on such matters as what titles the ennobled were going to take, and what coats-of-arms they might be expected to adopt. Here, Garter or one of his underlings at the College of Arms was invaluable. Bruce would arrive in the morning bursting with what he had heard the evening before at this or that party – so-and-so tipped for such a job – and had a quick eye for pointers in the morning papers. As when he spotted in *The Times* Personal Columns that a dog had been lost near Churt. Could it be Lloyd George's? A few telephone calls – we all spent most of our time telephoning – elicited the fact that it was, and Bruce, his eyes sparkling, led that day's Diary with the story of how the self-same littler terrier which had once disgraced itself by biting the Italian Prime Minister, Sr Orlando, during negotiations at Rapallo, was now at large in Surrey.

Politics rested largely in the hands of Randolph Churchill, who, to the considerable awe of the rest of us, could telephone almost anyone without fear of a rebuff. That you, Bobbity? Duff? Fruity? Bob? Rab? There was also, of course, his father, to whom he could always turn, and who contributed a highly paid weekly article to the *Evening Standard*; in those days, very much out of things, and, I thought from a fleeting glimpse I had of him, showing it. I have always been fascinated to note how indelibly worldly success and failure write themselves in a person's appearance; the one keeping the trousers pressed, linen fresh, shaves clean, and the other, almost over-night, bagging the trousers, fraying cuffs, leaving tufts of hair and dried gobbets of blood on the chin. Randolph still had about him some of the glow of his youthful promise, when he was called – alas, only by the first Lord Rothermere – England's young man of destiny. In the succeeding years I saw him from time to time, and so was able to observe his rogue-elephant course; growing obese and grey and feebly thunderous, though never quite losing some quality of, if not originality, unexpectedness, which almost amounted to it. Perhaps it was fitting that his days should end enmeshed in what was to be an interminable biography of the father whom he had so assiduously emulated, and even copied, and in whose shadow he had been fated always to live. I

wrote his obituary in *The Times* – the only one I have ever done, or been asked to do. It would have seemed an unlikely eventuality in our Diary days.

The portfolio of cultural affairs was in the hands of Patrick Balfour, son of a Scottish judge and peer; a versatile writer who, in the course of many assignments, collaborated with the Duke of Windsor, which at one point involved their sharing a forlorn Thermos of tea on the steps of the Duke's sometime residence, Fort Belvedere. It was he who attended art shows, went to the ballet, knew Beverley Nichols, Somerset Maugham and Evelyn Waugh, and even frequented publishers' cocktail parties – the equivalent, in gossip-writing terms, of slumming. John Betjeman, the film critic when I first joined the paper, helped out with architectural and ecclesiastical news, especially clerical appointments. There was also a strange, red-faced, rather tragic figure with dyed black hair named Philip Page who had been in his day a well-known theatre critic, but now just sat around contributing occasional paragraphs to the Diary. His harmless vanity was to have known everyone intimately, but it was noticeable that, whenever this knowledge was put to the test of providing a paragraph, it needed heavy reinforcement from the cuttings – those envelopes, bulky or scanty according to the estimated eminence of the subject, containing whatever fragments of information had appeared about them in the press. Footprints of a kind in the sands of time. When the subject died, the word 'dead' was scrawled across the envelope; a necessary precaution, in Page's case particularly; he was all too prone to turn in a paragraph about having run into Beerbohm Tree, or Lily Langtry looking prettier than ever, at the Trocadero.

Page had one of those rich, port wine voices you seldom hear nowadays, and in all weathers wore a bowler hat and an overcoat with a velvet collar. He alone of us all believed in what we were doing; seeing each Diary paragraph as a sacrificial offering laid on the altar of social rectitude. When King George V died, I found him in tears, staring at a half-crown piece, which, as he said, was the man's picture. It was a testing time for us all, instructions having been handed down by the Captain from Beaverbrook that until the royal funeral had taken place every paragraph in the Diary must deal with the nation's bereavement. This meant, in all, some 120 paragraphs. I remember wrestling with a couple myself about a tapestry that Queen Mary had been working on at the time of her husband's death. It was heavy going – for me, I mean; though doubtless for her, too.

Literary paragraphs were turned in by Howard Spring, the book

critic; a former *Guardian* star-reporter, with an adoring wife whose praises of him, Neville Cardus once remarked, would have been excessive even if he had been Shakespeare. In the course of reporting an Empire Free Trade meeting in Manchester for the *Guardian*, Spring referred to Beaverbrook as a pedlar of nightmares. Crozier, ever timid, thought this rather strong, and altered 'nightmares' to 'dreams', thereby procuring Spring an immediate offer of a job on the *Evening Standard* at a greatly increased salary, which he accepted. Later, as a successful popular novelist, he became a pedlar of dreams on his own account.

The real pillar of the Diary, and, to me, far the most sympathetic person connected with it, was Leslie Marsh, who, in effect, edited it. He was a strange, sad, infinitely lovable man who had drifted into journalism, like so many others, because it seemed to be vaguely connected with writing, and, at the same time, offered regular wages. Like an aspiring actress who joins the Bluebell Girls. At one point he tried to break away, and turned to hedging and ditching for a living, but family responsibilities brought him back to Shoe Lane. His distaste for the Diary was very great. If one asked him whether he had enough paragraphs, he would never admit to more than: 'I can fill'; if one sought his help in finding a subject, more often than not his only response would be: 'Have you looked at the stiffs?' I used to say that he was like Augustus Moddle in *Martin Chuzzlewit*, who spoke for all the poetically disappointed when he wrote to Miss Pecksniff: 'I love another. She is Another's. Everything appears to be somebody else's.' When I went to *Punch*, the first thing I did was to ask Leslie to join the staff, which, to my great joy, he did. When I left, he was still there; the only truly useful contribution I made to the magazine's well-being.

My own role in the production of the Diary, as the latest arrival, was to deal with unconsidered trifles like sudden deaths, a book that needed to be hurriedly gutted for some morsel of gossip, or the appointment of a new headmaster at one of the lesser public schools like Lancing or Repton. Also, I was considered as something of an expert on the Labour Party alternative Establishment that was taking shape, and whose gossip potentialities were beginning to be apparent. Kitty's family – Stafford Cripps, the Webbs, the Booths, Lord Parmoor – were an important element in this. Windsor, Eton and King's contributed Dr Dalton; Winchester's offering – Crossman, Gaitskell, Jay – were already in the pipe-line. At the London School of Economics they were gathering for the harvest; from the high-tables and senior common rooms the

word was passed down that Labour could wear a mortar-board as well as a cap. Nor was the Church behind-hand, with Archbishop Temple ready to add an eight-hour day and public ownership of the means of production to the other Beatitudes, and his Dean in Canterbury, Dr Hewlett Johnson, already preaching in the Cathedral that Stalin was busily engaged in building the Kingdom of Christ. The Services and the Law likewise offered their quota, and as for literature – with Shaw, Wells, Bertrand Russell and a large Bloomsbury contingent to the fore, why should lesser pens hold back? Well might an old-timer like George Lansbury rub his eyes over so gilt-edged a recruitment, but from a gossip-writer's point of view, it was gravy.

My political prognostications were less fortunate. For instance, I remember writing a paragraph when Major Attlee (as he was then always called) was elected leader of the Labour Parliamentary party, to the effect that the appointment must be considered purely a stop-gap arrangement. So obscure and light-weight a figure, I contended, would never make an effective leader of the Opposition, let alone a Prime Minister. I thought of this when I happened to run into him in the lavatory of the Reform Club shortly before he died. He was on his way to some sort of banquet, in full evening dress, every inch an earl, his tiny frame borne down by the weight of hardware upon it, his eyes glazed, his face skull-like; but indubitably no stop-gap. Our paths vaguely crossed in the sense that we had the same lecture agent in America – the redoubtable Mr Colston Leigh, and were liable to pass one another like ships in the night at Cincinnati, Ohio, or Denver, Colorado. His form, I was told, was splendid except for his propensity to fall asleep; the local worthy collecting him at his hotel was quite likely to find the Earl tucked up and fast asleep in bed, and even when delivered onto the platform he sometimes dropped off during the chairman's intro-ductory remarks. Once awakened, however, he would advance to the podium, and deliver a flawless, if somewhat abbreviated, address on the ardours and practice of government.

Our hours on the Diary were short. We were expected to arrive round about ten o'clock; the Diary went to press at half past twelve, and in those days was seldom changed between the afternoon editions. With so many of us working on it, two, or at most three, paragraphs was our daily stint. Quite often one made no contribution at all. Every Friday, at the accountant's office on the ground floor, we collected our pay in cash, mine being four white, crinkly five-pound notes. It was, on any showing, good money for very little work. In theory, it is true, we were

expected to spend our afternoons and evenings roaming the town, making contacts, picking up useful information, attending social occasions – cocktail parties, dinner parties, receptions, first nights, even hunt balls. Randolph, of course, was in great demand among hostesses, and Patrick Balfour had his own special milieu where paragraph-fodder was plentiful; but I personally never sallied forth or attended anything on the Diary's behalf. Appearing in it was considered in those days very good publicity, and all sorts of people, from debutantes to authors and Intelligence agents (in the last category, one who used to bring two mastiffs with him when he visited the office) were after us in the hope of planting something, or, at any rate, just getting a mention.

The easier course, from my point of view, was to rely on the cuttings and my own inventiveness. I found that no objections were ever raised so long as what appeared in the Diary ministered to the subject's self-esteem; not even to purported quotations given in direct speech. Dr Johnson had the same experience when he was producing reports of parliamentary debates without ever going near the Houses of Parliament. Indeed, he gave the job up when he discovered that the fictitious speeches he attributed to Noble Lords and Honourable Members were being taken as true. Journalism has moved a long way since his time, and I must say it never occurred to me to feel any qualms when my imaginary conversations passed unchallenged. At times there might be carping over trivialities; as when, as a matter of routine, I said of a newly ennobled Scottish peer that his grandfather had been a poor crofter, and he wrote in to deny that this was so. Honour was satisfied when I made the necessary correction by stating in a subsequent paragraph that his grandfather had been a rich crofter. On another occasion I chanced my arm by remarking of an up-and-coming politician that he was very fond of music, and never missed a symphony concert if he could help it. Afterwards, I heard from someone who knew him that he was tone-deaf, but by that time my paragraph had got into the cuttings, and a lover of music he will now remain for all time.

Occasionally, a Beaverbrook-sponsored paragraph would come my way, marked with the word 'must'. One, I remember, consisted of a scribbled, garbled quotation about many aspiring but few succeeding, which was to be applied to animadverting upon how rarely politicians who move over from Westminster to the City make good there. The point was clear enough; Beaverbrook had acquired a huge fortune, but been a relative failure in politics, and so wanted to read in the Londoner's Diary – a favourite feature – that making money was a more difficult

pursuit than politics. My own researches, such as they were, failed to provide much support for this proposition; and I turned to what was for all of us in all circumstances a last resort – Bonar Law, who had made no particular mark either as Prime Minister or tycoon, and could therefore be said to have tipped the balance either way. What was more important, he was highly esteemed by Beaverbrook, who, when Bonar Law was on his death bed and worrying over some falling copper shares, is said to have bought them in to keep the price up, thereby enabling his friend to die in piece. Another 'must' paragraph entrusted to me was to point out that the bronchial complaint of which Sir James Barrie was reported to be dying, was known as 'old man's friend' because it was so painless. Again, the reason was clear; Beaverbrook an asthmatic, expected to die of a similar complaint, and wanted to be reassured that it made for an easy death by reading it in the Diary. Harley Street was unresponsive when asked to provide confirmation, but the Diary nevertheless made the point, and kept its little old reader happy.

This well-paid and unexacting servitude to Beaverbrook's wayward fancies and malign purposes was more spiritually burdensome than might have been supposed. There was a steady and insidious process of corruption going on all the time, which I could observe working in others, and, in moments of candour, in myself. Underneath all the buffoonery, I detected a whiff of sulphur; a transposing of values, whereby whatever was most base was elevated, and the only acceptable measure of anyone and anything was money, the only pursuit worth considering, worldly success. My own part in the Beaverbrook circus was, happily for me, only a minor and insignificant one. Even so, it became increasingly distasteful, and I decided to take a chance, and spend the remaining time before the next war began engaged in my own pursuits rather than Beaverbrook's.

Almost the last two tasks I was given on the *Evening Standard* might have been specially designed to confirm me in taking this decision. The first was to provide some copy for a page of advertisements on behalf of various charities, the editorial space available being carefully marked out to correspond exactly with the amount of advertising space taken. Thus, Distressed Gentlefolk might have three lines, the Salvation Army five, Dr Barnado's Homes eight, and so on. The other task was to take note of a book called *Metropolitan Man* by Robert Sinclair without distressing our readers by drawing their attention to disagreeable data about their urban environment. As the book consisted almost entirely of such data, it was a difficult if not impossible, assignment.

When I pointed this out to Percy Cudlipp, he quite agreed, but still insisted that the Beaverbrook directive to keep everyone cheerful must stand. It seemed time to hand in my notice, which I did, knowing I should miss the four five-pound notes on Fridays, but nothing else.

As it happens, I was employed by the *Evening Standard* again some twenty-five years later, when Charles Wintour was editor, to write a weekly book article. This arrangement was terminated, and my place taken by Michael Foot, when an, I must admit unsympathetic, account by me of the Beaverbrook cult in New Brunswick appeared in the Canadian magazine *Maclean's*. This is the only occasion in my life when I have been actually fired. In the course of my visit to Fredericton, New Brunswick's capital, I ran into the Captain, who has a suite in the Lord Beaverbrook Hotel where I was staying. We spent an evening together, in the course of which he described to me how, on Beaverbrook's advice, he had taken over the local newspaper, the *Gleaner*, whose publisher and editor-in-chief he now was. For some reason, spread about his room, he had a lot of new camera equipment, including a lens, which from time to time he extended, until it reached a truly enormous length; then appeared to be squinting at me through it. After dinner, we stepped across to take a look at an exhibition of ultra-modern art – Beaverbrook's latest benefaction to Fredericton. The Captain, I could see, cared as little for the pictures as I did, but he characteristically comforted himself by observing that, if experts like Kenneth Clark approved of them and millionaires like Beaverbrook bought them, they must be good. It seemed a *non sequitur* to me.

Strolling about in Fredericton, and surveying all the different intimations of Beaverbrook's connection with the place – the bronze statue in the centre of the town, the Beaverbrook Art Gallery, the Beaverbrook Birdbath, the Beaverbrook Theatre, the Beaverbrook Reading Room, the Lord Beaverbrook Hotel – I wondered what would be the outcome of this deliberate pre-humous creation of a shrine and a cult. Would it, perhaps, be oblivion just the same? – and this not so much because of Beaverbrook's intrinsic insignificance, as the insignificance, as it would turn out, of the historical setting in which he had gone to such pains and expense to make a place for himself. After buying up all those papers – Bonar Law's, Lloyd George's, H. G. Wells's even; after all that suborning of people, and faking of the record; after piecing it all so carefully together – then to find that, after all, it signified nothing. Deserving, at

most, one tiny little footnote rather than large tomes – would not that
be something?

We found a house in the country at Whatlington, near Battle, which cost
eight hundred pounds – a sum that we could just manage with the aid of
a mortgage. It was quite large, and had been unoccupied for some con-
siderable time. As we discovered after we had moved in, it had quite
recently been the scene of a rather disagreeable suicide; and this, added
to the fact that it had once been a village shop, reduced its desirability,
and so brought down the price. The suicide didn't trouble us, any more
than the shop. In fact, as far as the latter was concerned, if it had been
practicable we might well have opened up business again. Having disposed
of our house in London, we moved in with our, now, four children –
our youngest son, Charles, having lately arrived on the scene. It was a
fairly austere existence; water came from a well which had to be pumped
by hand, and drinking water from a spring some little distance away.
Each day I fetched two bucketsful. Bathing was done in a small metal
bath in front of the kitchen stove; there was no heating apart from fires,
and, of course, we had no car. The nearest shopping-centre was Battle,
some two miles away; and we would usually walk or cycle in and out.
My only regular income was five guineas a week for doing a weekly
column on novels in the *Daily Telegraph*. A parcel of five would arrive
on Mondays, and my copy had to be sent off on the following Friday.
It gave me a distaste for new novels in dust-jackets which I feel to this
day – for Mr A who can spin a rollicking yarn, for Miss B who so subtly
explores the relationship between a housemaster's wife and one of the
prefects, Mr C who writes with a fine zestful bawdiness reminiscent of
Tom Jones. I used to put off opening the parcel when it came as long as I
dared, and even then it took me quite a time before I could nerve myself
to read even the blurbs – as far as I got in some cases, I regret to say;
but then I would comfort myself by remembering Dr Johnson's saying
about the novels of Congreve, that he would sooner praise them than
read them. Gerald Gould, who had been in the business much longer
than I, had reached the point that his weekly quota of volumes used to
be passed to him through a hatch; after which he could be heard groan-
ing and beating his head against the wall. Other odd jobs turned up. For
instance, I ghosted part of the translation of Caulaincourt's *Memoirs*
at thirty shillings a thousand words, and contributed two items, at
fifteen guineas each, to a book of Fifty Famous Crimes given away by
the *Daily Herald* to boost circulation. My subjects were a French

maniac who murdered his entire family for the insurance money, and a sordid affair of poisoning in Penge. Kingsmill, who also contributed two items, with singular obstinacy tried to get hold of a copy of the book, but was finally defeated, even though he tracked down a barge loaded with them on its way to Manchester.

I also did quite a lot of work for Lady Rhondda's *Time & Tide*; a feminist organ, largely staffed and written by women. Lady Rhondda, plump and curly, was the daughter of a coal magnate who had been Food-Controller in the 1914–18 war. She and her father were on the *Lusitania* when it was torpedoed in 1915, and she wrote a very good description of the adventure. It appears that she found herself in the water holding onto a spar, at the other end of which there was a man likewise holding on. She says that she and this man looked at one another, whereupon he unaccountably disappeared. Somehow, I understood why; working for *Time & Tide* was rather like holding onto a spar with Lady Rhondda at the other end. All the same, she was very kind to me, and let me write what I liked. I particularly appreciated her literary editor and friend, Theodora Bosanquet, who had been Henry James's secretary when he was living in Rye; a salty, hearty lady who wore well-cut tweed suits and good shoes with flat heels. She and Lady Rhondda shared a house in Surrey and a flat overlooking St James's Park; both establishments being so luxurious that they were almost uncomfortable – the cream too rich to eat, the peaches too soft and large to bite into, the beds too downy to fall asleep in.

The three years I spent in Whatlington waiting for the war, despite financial anxieties and stringencies, were the happiest I had known. Our children were beginning to emerge as separate people whom I could get to know; Kitty was well content, as she always is when they are near, and the ardours of house-keeping are heavy. When we are staying in France I have the greatest difficulty in stopping her joining the women at the communal village washing place, scrubbing away in cold water. The routine of my day was the one that has best suited me always; waking up early, working through the morning, walking or gardening in the afternoon, working again in the early evening, and lolling about and talking until bedtime; with no contractural job to bother about, no fixed obligations to fulfil, no forms to public entertainment to sit through – least of all the cinema, about which I have always nourished a secret distaste and dread, today amply justified. Above all, the scene I looked out on as I worked was the one I most love – the English country-side.

The happiness of this time was enormously enhanced by my friendship with Hugh Kingsmill, who lived nearby in Hastings with his wife Dorothy and their three children. Most weeks we met two or three times, either in Hastings or Whatlington, and often had long conversations on the telephone. It is impossible for me to convey the delight his companionship gave me, or what I owe to him for the enormous enhancement of living I derived from the stimulation of his mind and imagination. There is scarcely a book I care about which is not, as I turn over its pages, evocative of him, to the point that even now, a quarter of a century since his death, I positively hear his voice commenting on it, and feel, welling up in me, the wonderful laughter that was never far out of reach, whatever the matter under consideration might be. For someone like myself, among the walking-wounded from the ideological conflicts of the age, he was the perfect physician, simply because he was himself totally uninvolved in them. In some mysterious way, he managed to remain uncontaminated and unbrainwashed in an age that specialised in both processes. When, under financial stress – a chronic condition with him – he took on doing a book about D. H. Lawrence, he used to read aloud to me with a kind of wonder dialogue from Lawrence's novels (for instance, the exchange between Mellors and Lady Chatterley's father, Sir Malcolm Reid, the Royal Academician – 'Sir Malcolm gave a little squirting laugh, and became Scotch and lewd . . . ! "How was the going, eh? Good, my boy, what? . . . My daughter, chip off the old block, what? . . . You warmed her up, oh, you warmed her up, I can see that. . . . A gamekeeper, eh, my boy! Bloody good poacher, if you ask me. Ha-ha!" '), as though asking: is it conceivable that this should be regarded as human speech arising out of a human relationship? It was very refreshing and very funny.

Similarly, he never for one second entertained any hope or expectation that the various political prospectuses, from Left to Right, for making an earthly paradise, were realisable, or conducive to any lasting good for mankind. All such expectations he dismissed as Dawnism; and no one has ever stated more clearly than he the fallacy of the collective remedies for our ills that Dawnists so ardently recommend, when he wrote in his Introduction to *The Poisoned Crown*: 'What is divine in man is elusive and impalpable, and he is easily tempted to embody it in a concrete form – a church, a country, a social system, a leader – so that he may realise it with less effort and serve it with more profit. Yet the attempt to externalise the kingdom of heaven in a temporal shape must end in disaster. It cannot be created by charters or constitu-

tions nor established by arms. Those who seek for it alone will reach it together, and those who seek it in company will perish by themselves.' Such an attitude struck Orwell, with his mania for categories, as Neo-Toryism; and in his 'Notes on Nationalism' he worked out a Neo-Tory *apparat* which included, as well as Kingsmill, Wyndham Lewis, T. S. Eliot, Evelyn Waugh and myself. After the war, I brought Kingsmill and Orwell together, and they got on quite well. Recalling the meeting, Kingsmill said that Orwell reminded him of a gate swinging on a rusty hinge. I saw what he meant.

Either I would bicycle into Hastings to see Kingsmill, or he would take the bus to Battle, and I would set out to meet him along the road from Battle to Whatlington, delighted when I first caught a glimpse of his solid figure in the distance and heard his shouted greetings: 'Hullo! old man! Hullo!' He walked with a rolling gait, rather like a sailor's; always hatless, his head exceptionally large, his already grey hair (he was fourteen years older than I was), sparse and dishevelled, his complexion ruddy. Even when he was full of troubles – as was all too often the case – he invariably gave an impression of immense cheerfulness. All his complaints were addressed to the phenomenal world, which he saw as only the shadow of another greater reality. 'Poor old mankind,' I would sometimes hear him mutter, as he might affectionately about some friend who had run into a lamp-post or fallen down a man-hole. Even his money difficulties, pressing though they were, came into the category of the phenomenal world; and when there was no post, as on a Sunday or Bank Holiday, to bring him bills or solicitor's letters, ceased to worry him. It was only a surface worry, though a persistent one. He had the foolish habit, based on his incorrigible hopefulness, of sending post-dated cheques in settlement of bills, and was very amused when the recipient of one of these wrote back asking for 'something liquid'. Another time, we noticed, in a grocer's shop in Hastings that the ham was recommended as being 'mild and cured'. It was, Kingsmill said, the condition we should all aspire after.

Sometimes, when he just had to lay hands on some ready money, he would make a foray on London, travelling up grandly from Hastings in a first-class carriage with the pass Sir Henry Lunn, his father, still had from his tourist-tycoon days. This pass, I may add, was in pretty constant use one way and another; I was even given an occasional run with it myself. Once in London, Kingsmill would survey the possibilities; like a general looking over the terrain for an attack on enemy positions. He might decide to descend upon some unwary publisher with a proposal

for an anthology; he always had ideas for several floating about in his mind, and could knock them off in no time, without recourse to libraries, from his well-stocked, retentive memory. Or there was the office of the *New English Review*, edited by his friend Douglas Jerrold, whose literary editor Kingsmill then was. There would surely be some review copies of books lying about there, which could be glanced over, and then disposed of to our friend and benefactor, Thomas Gaston, in the Strand. On one heroic occasion, nothing else offering, he made his way into Bernard Shaw's flat in Whitehall Court – he had a faint acquaintanceship with him – and said boldly that he needed money. As Kingsmill described the scene to me, Shaw was sitting there, bolt upright, and giving an odd impression of being made of cotton-wool. He just leant forward stiffly, took out his cheque-book, and gave Kingsmill a cheque for ten pounds; as it were, in full and complete settlement of his obligations as an affluent author to an impecunious one. Kingsmill wished afterwards that he had stood out for fifteen.

A joint venture we were involved in was to describe a series of literary pilgrimages for a short-lived *New Yorker*-type magazine, *Night & Day*, at the suggestion of Graham Greene, its literary editor. The two I remember best were to Paris to see Wordsworth's great-great-grand-daughter, Mme Blanchet, a direct descendent of his illegitimate daughter, Caroline, by Annette Vallon; and to Wimpole Street at dawn to commemorate Tennyson's dawn visit to No 67, where, shortly before Hallam died, the two of them had spent a happy time together. Mme Blanchet showed us a copy of the *Lyrical Ballads* sent to Annette by Wordsworth, and a number of documents in which Wordsworth's name occurred – for instance, Caroline's birth and marriage certificates – usually as M. Williams of Rydalmount near Kendal. As usual, the legend proved to be the exact antithesis of the truth; far from Annette being a revolutionary influence against which Wordsworth turned when he became respectable and Poet Laureate, she was a strong royalist, decorated for her services by Louis XVIII after the restoration of the monarchy, and greatly concerned to get Caroline respectably married, which she succeeded in doing, without, I regret to say, any substantial help from M. Williams of Rydalmount. We spent the night before our dawn visit to Wimpole Street at a nearby Turkish Bath, talking about Tennyson as we sweated on adjoining stone slabs, and then were kneaded, thumped, soaped and sluiced under the masseur's hands. The scene in Wimpole Street, when we got there, all too exactly fitted the lines from *In Memoriam* that Kingsmill quoted:

He is not here; but far away,
The noise of life begins again,
And ghastly thro' the drizzling rain
On the bald street breaks the blank day.

I also did a joint piece for *Night & Day* with Graham Greene – on a one-day trip to the Continent. We took off from Margate, where we spent some time in Dreamland, being particularly struck with the easy way some Air Force cadets picked up girls.

Once, in the British Museum (a place I always pass with a shudder, remembering the hours I have spent in the Library looking up things I didn't want to know) Kingsmill and I overheard a conversation between two attendants in blue uniforms. One asked the other where so-and-so – obviously another attendant – was; and the first replied; 'Oh, he's in the Illuminated', meaning, of course, the Illuminated Manuscripts Room. Thenceforth, we adopted the term, the Illuminated being the world of the imagination, as Wordsworth's Sunless Land was the world of the will. Kingsmill saw the imagination and the will as contending impulses, and he liked to recall an inscription on a stone found in North Africa: 'I, the Captain of a Legion of Rome, serving in the desert of Libya, have learnt and pondered this truth: "There are in life but two things, Love and Power, and no one has both." ' The will was the dynamo of action and the fuel of lust; the imagination, the way to ecstasy and the fount of love. To live in the will was to be imprisoned in the dark dungeon of the ego; the imagination was a window, to look out of, and dream of escaping. On the one hand, the men of the will – Caesar, Cromwell, Napoleon, Hitler and Stalin; on the other, the men of the imagination – Jesus, St Francis, Blake, Bonhoeffer and Solzhenitzyn. The will belongs to time, the imagination projects time into eternity. When Jesus rejected the Devil's offer of the kingdoms of the earth, he turned away from the will; on the Cross he died in the will; the Resurrection was his rebirth in the imagination.

All this is worked out very beautifully in Kingsmill's too little known novel, *The Fall*, in which his hero, having fallen and cracked his skull, comes to in the Illuminated. Thus, this Fall is the opposite of the one in *Genesis* – from the will into the imagination, rather than the other way round. A sort of Paradise Regained. The original of Kingsmill's hero was his younger brother, Brian, who also lived in Hastings, and who actually did fall from the top of a bus and crack his skull, afterwards giving intimations of being in the Illuminated, as well as, from time to time, having rather violent spasms. He was a highly eccentric, lovable

character who lodged with the widow of a naval petty officer named Mrs Pitcher, in a house that had formerly belonged to an undertaker and monumental mason, and still had tombstones and immortelles lying about in the garden. One of the local sights was to see him early every morning run down to the sea for a swim, wearing the white shorts of the late Petty Officer Pitcher. After his accident he went for a time into the local hospital, where Kingsmill and I visited him. In view of his occasional violent spasms two male nurses sat with him, one on each side of his bed. Our arrival was the signal for them to go for a break, and Kingsmill and I were left looking at one another rather uneasily across Brian's inert body, which, to our great relief, continued to be inert until the male nurses returned. When he came out of hospital, Brian had an enormous piece of plaster down the middle of his large bald dome of a head where it had been cracked. The effect, when he suddenly took off his hat, as he frequently did, especially in saloon bars, was sensational.

It was at this time, doubtless owing to my companionship with Kingsmill, that I began consciously to have mystical experiences, and have gone on having them ever since, though sometimes, when I have been particularly caught up in egotistic or sensual pursuits, only at very long intervals. The first intimation is, quite simply, that time stops, or rather one escapes from time. Then all creation is seen in its oneness; with each part of it, from the tiniest insect or blade of grass, to the vastnesses of space, with the stars and comets riding through them, visibly related to every other part. One sublime harmony, with no place for the discordancies of hatred and the ego's shrill demands; the death of death, since each note in the harmony exists harmoniously for ever. Peace that is no one else's strife, sufficiency that is no one else's famine, well-being that is no one else's sickness. Flesh still, mind still, leaving the soul free to experience the inconceivable joy of seeing beyond the Iron Gates, to where the Creator watches over his creation.

I can remember three such experiences during my time in Whatlington. On the first occasion I was standing with Kingsmill on the cliffs, just outside Hastings, and looking down on the Old Town. It was an autumn evening, slightly misty and very still, with a sharp chill in the air. From the chimneys below, wreaths of smoke were rising into the sky; from each particular chimney, pale smoke, briefly separate, then becoming indistinct, and, finally, lost to view; merging into the grey, gathering evening. I was suddenly spellbound, as though this was a vision of the Last Day, and the wreaths of smoke, souls, leaving their bodies to rise heavenwards and become part of eternity. At the same time,

I felt full of an inexpressible tenderness for these fellow-humans, sending up smoke-signals to me from their separate hearths, and an inexpressible joy at sharing with them a common destiny.

The second occasion was at harvest-time, and I was standing on a little hill that overlooked our house. It was quite late – about eleven o'clock; there was a full moon, and the fields' abundance filled the air, almost visibly, like a mist of fruitfulness. Behind me stood Whatlington Church, small and very ancient, making a shadow in the moonlight, beyond which there was a massive yew tree, and grave-stones all around standing in lush grass. I suppose for a thousand years and more past, anyone standing on that little hill would have surveyed the self-same scene. I felt myself being incorporated into it, until I no longer existed, except as a voice in a choir of innumerable voices, swelling a chorus of gratitude for the gift of life, of sharing in its plentitude, of experiencing its joys and its afflictions, and treading its ordained path, from the womb where I was shaped, to a grave under that yew tree where I hoped to lie. Some ancestral memory formed on my lips the words *Gloria in excelsis Deo*.

The third experience was the most dramatic, and made the deepest impression. Kitty was in hospital, on the danger-list, and I was told by the surgeon who had operated on her that she had only a very small chance of surviving. It was a cruelly anxious time from every point of view. Each day, arranging for someone to be with the children, I went and sat with her. She was fighting to live, her face pared down to a skull, her body a yellow skeleton. Whilst I was there, the doctor came in and said that in the night she had lost a lot of blood, and desperately needed a blood-transfusion – it was before the days of bottled plasma. Wouldn't I do for a donor? I asked, with a sudden access of hope. My blood-count was taken, and to my infinite relief proved satisfactory; and there and then, by a procedure that would seem grotesquely primitive nowadays, I was joined to her by a tube with a pump in the middle, so that I could actually watch the blood being pumped out of me into her. 'Don't stint yourself for blood,' I said to the pathologist, a man named Barlow, perhaps partly to be theatrical, but also feeling it. Never in all our life together, had I so completely and perfectly and joyously experienced love's fulfilment as on that moment. As my blood, systematically, to the pump's rhythm, pumped into Kitty's veins, bringing life visibly into her face, my blood pouring into her to keep her alive, my life reinforcing hers, for the first time I truly understood what love meant.

I tried to put some of the fruit of these experiences into a short book I wrote at this time called *In A Valley of This Restless Mind*, but failed to make myself clear, at any rate to reviewers. A gratifying exception was Evelyn Waugh, who wrote a long and perceptive review in the *Spectator*. Otherwise, the book was a total failure. My main occupation during the period of waiting for the war to begin was writing *The Thirties*, a survey of the decade now coming to an end, commissioned by Hamish Hamilton. I managed to acquire *The Times* for the whole ten-year period, and stacked the issues in piles on the floor of my study, so that I was, literally, walled in by my material. In addition, I carried in my head echoes and memories of the events I had reported or commented on as a journalist; while, at the same time, of course, the drama was unfolding from day to day – the Spanish Civil War ending, the Abdication, the Anschluss, the invasion of Czechoslovakia, and Chamberlain's grotesque essays in international statesmanship. I wrote the book knowing what the end would be; from Ramsay MacDonald's formation of a National Government, everything happened with the inevitability of a play – the tragi-comedy of our time. Each character had his part, and came on the stage precisely on cue; scene followed scene, moving towards a pre-ordained climax, which was to fall exactly pat, some two months before the decade's end.

The summer of 1939 happened to be an unusually beautiful one, and I somehow knew – I think we all did – that the passing hours were particularly precious; golden hours unlikely to recur. Kingsmill and I went on meeting as often as possible. Sometimes, when he came to Whatlington, I would walk with him to catch his bus at Battle, and then he would decide to walk part of the way back to Whatlington with me. So we would perambulate up and down the road, talking and laughing into the night, as though the talk and the laughter might soon be running out, and we must grab them while we might. Often Hesketh Pearson, a close friend of Kingsmill who became a friend of mine, was with us on these occasions.

When news came of the conclusion of the Nazi–Soviet Pact, I knew, of course, that the waiting was over. In a way, I had been expecting such a development; never losing an opportunity to say that Bolshevism and National Socialism were the same thing, except that one was a Slav version and the other Teutonic. Why should they not come together, then? My first reaction to the actual line-up between them was a fearful joy. I thought with glee of the confusion in the office of the *Daily Worker*, where they had to get out a leader saying that the holy war

against Hitler they had been demanding so vociferously must now be regarded as an imperialist one, and at all costs prevented from happening. Of the distress in Cross Street, Bouverie Street and Long Acre, that there should now be so mighty a hole in the common front against Fascism they had been advocating. Of the sadness in Printing House Square that, after all, Stalin was not going to come forward as civilisation's resolute defender, and take the Houses of Parliament, the Bank of England, Black Rod, and for that matter *The Times* itself, all under his wing. Of the desolation in Great Turnstile; of the Left Book Club volumes in their yellow dust-jackets being silently removed from windows in Henrietta Street, and, perhaps, even the Dean of Canterbury having a momentary doubt as to whether Stalin really would go on building the Kingdom of Christ now that he had aligned himself with Hitler. For a minute, in my delight, I thought that apologists for the Soviet regime among the Western intelligentsia were confounded for ever; and then, of course, I realised – not so. In a little while, they would recover their breath at the *Daily Worker*; in Cross Street, Bouverie Street and Long Acre, be tapping away again as confidently as ever; joy returning to Great Turnstile, the Dean recovering his nerve, and the Henrietta Street windows filling again. Like alcoholics after taking the cure – never another drop; well, just a taste perhaps, and then, before you could say knife, back on the meths. Meanwhile, there was the war.

7 *Grinning Honour*

Soft! Who are you? Sir Walter Blunt:- there's honour for you! . . .
I like not such grinning honour as Sir Walter hath: give me life;
which I can save, so; if not, honour came unlook'd for, and there's
an end.
 – Falstaff

Even wars, then, are waged with peace as their object, even when
they are waged by those who are concerned to exercise their warlike
prowess, either in command or in the actual fighting. Hence it is an
established fact that peace is the desired end of war. For every man is
in quest of peace even in waging war, whereas no one is in quest of
war when making peace. In fact, even when men wish a present state
of peace to be disturbed they do so not because they hate peace, but
because they desire the present peace to be exchanged for one that suits
their wishes. Thus their desire is not that there should not be peace
but that it should be the kind of peace they wish for.
 – Augustine's *City of God*

AS NEARLY ALWAYS HAPPENS with long-awaited excitements, war,
when at last it came, proved an anticlimax. After all the apocalyptic
warnings delivered on so many solemn occasions from so many solemn
throats, we confidently expected the sky to darken, Big Ben to be silenced,
and destruction to fall about us with sheets of flame and mighty roarings
as of a tempest. It was all to come, but not yet. What happened immedi-
ately was that, on a bright September Sunday morning, an old man's
quavering, angry voice was heard on the radio, rising to shrill heights as
he told us that we were at war fighting against all the evil things in the
world and for all the good ones. Through the open window we saw our
stand-in parson, the Rev. Browell, making his way along the road with

great deliberation, and repeating at intervals, to no one in particular: 'We're in God's hands, we're in God's hands.' He had a bustling, purposeful air about him, like a teacher marshalling his charges. Alas, it seemed as though we were in Neville Chamberlain's hands rather than in God's, or even the Rev. Browell's. In my mind's eye I saw Chamberlain at the microphone, in black cutaway coat, with winged collar, and adam's apple throbbing convulsively above it; as forlorn at this moment of defeat as he had been vainglorious at his corresponding moment of triumph, waving in the air his piece of paper signed by Hitler, and prattling of peace with honour.

As Chamberlain's tremulous words died away, the sirens sounded, and the silver barrage balloons rose into the clear sky, riding on the wings of this most unmelodious melody which was to be our theme song for some years to come. I saw Kitty look round with her special vigilant air to take stock of where the children were and what they were at. I myself tried, without much conviction, to summon up a suitable expression of *gravitas*; as of a man resolved to do his duty come what might. As I have invariably found on occasions of public drama, I felt nothing more than a sense of suppressed excitement; I was curious about what was going to happen rather than appalled. Some deficiency in my mental make-up or metabolism prevents me from reacting otherwise; but for that very reason I feel bound to look preternaturally solemn, and strike an attitude of overwhelming concern. Just as, at a funeral, the mourners who care least about the deceased put on an outward appearance of being the most stricken.

We had all been talking about war for, literally, years past. It would be the end of civilisation – this without considering whether any civilisation still existed to be ended. Our cities would be razed to the ground in the twinkling of an eye; the bombers must always get through, there being no defence against aerial bombardment. Many thus held forth with great vigour and authority at dinner tables, in clubs and railway carriages; as did leading articles, sermons in St Martin's-in-the-Fields and other enlightened pulpits, after-dinner speeches at gatherings like the League of Nations Union and the Peace Pledge Union; wherever two or more were gathered together who felt they had the true interests of mankind at heart. Books appeared interminably on the subject, with lurid blurbs – usually in yellow dust-jackets; films were made about it, garden fêtes dedicated to it, tiny tots lisped out rhymes about it. All agreed that another war was unthinkable, unspeakable, inconceivable, and must at all costs be averted; coming forward in large numbers to

vote against it in a Peace Ballot – resolved, and carried unanimously: That we will not countenance another war.

Well, now this other war had come. The sirens had sounded, the barrage balloons had risen, the hospitals had been cleared for the hosts of expected casualties, and the cardboard coffins manufactured in bulk in view of the anticipated shortage of wooden ones. We awaited the apocalypse, and nothing happened; like children shutting our eyes after a lightning flash in the expectation of a big bang to follow, and then cautiously opening them again to find everything precisely as it had been before. It was oddly exasperating. Not just to retired colonels irritably mowing their lawns in the Home Counties, and dreaming of adding to their campaign medals; of taking out their Sam Brownes once more, polishing them up and adjusting them to their enlarged girths. Not just to men of my generation who had missed out on the 1914–18 war, and saw a chance of getting into this one by the skin of their teeth; catching up on all the excitement, danger and fun that had eluded them on the previous occasion – the war books they hadn't written, the girls they hadn't slept with on some hilariously desperate forty-eight hours' leave from the trenches, the shell-shock they hadn't had, the decorations for valour they hadn't received and then contemptuously returned to show how they despised decorations and those who awarded them. Even the conscientious objectors had been looking forward eagerly to conscientiously objecting. Now it looked as though this so often predicted war to end all peace was going to prove as illusory as the peace to end all war.

On the Monday following the declaration of war I announced to Kitty that I was off to join the army. She did not, as I half expected she would, reproach me, but just accepted what was, given my age, circumstances and family responsibilities, an intrinsically imprudent, foolish and egotistic thing to do. The inducement was certainly not an access of patriotism; neither then, nor at any time subsequently, did I suppose that the war, however it turned out, could have other than ruinous consequences for all concerned, especially for England. The alternative to Hitler, as I well knew, was Stalin; and it was impossible to damage Hitler without helping Stalin, or *vice-versa*. So all the evil things which, according to Chamberlain, we were to fight against – dictatorship, bad faith, intolerance, persecution of the weak etc., etc. – must, whatever happened, get a boost. As, indeed, it has turned out.

The nearest recruiting office was at Maidstone, and when I got there I found quite a queue had already formed, consisting mostly of aspiring

combatants, like myself, well on the way to middle-age. Conscription was already in force, so there was no occasion for the real cannon-fodder – between eighteen and twenty-one – to come along. The scene was very different from the beginning of the 1914–18 war, with all its hysteria, frantic outbursts of patriotism and distribution of white feathers. Everything was noticeably subdued; more in the style of a Labour Exchange in a period of economic depression than of a recruiting office at the beginning of a war. No A. E. Housman-esque bucolic sergeant with ribbons in his cap, all agog to inveigle a likely lad into accepting the King's Shilling. No likely lads, for that matter, or silver shillings; no band playing or flags flying. Just the eternal questionnaire – name, age, address, married or single, educational qualifications, religion, any record of VD, epilepsy or other disability? These the ice-floes, from one to the other of which we must nowadays jump; whether in seeking employment, getting married, exercising the franchise, or going to war.

There was only one man in the queue who seemed outwardly excited. He was, I should say, in his fifties; with snow-white hair, a battered rubicund face and broken teeth. Suddenly he began to gesticulate, and shout that he wanted to do something with his life. He may well have been drunk, but anyway was quite beside himself, to the point that a policeman who was keeping an eye on the queue led him gently away, still gesticulating and shouting. Did he, I wonder, manage to do something with his life as a result of participating in the war? Or, for that matter, with his death? I rather doubt it; this particular war offering few possibilities of the kind in either case. The rest of us kept our thoughts to ourselves; remaining silent, if not morose, as we moved slowly forward with the queue. When my turn came, I filled in my form, and learnt that only specialists were being called up for the moment, and that, anyway, journalists of my age-group were classified as in a reserved occupation. So, wouldn't I do better at my typewriter?

I returned home feeling rather foolish, more particularly as I had taken a small suitcase with me of essential requirements with the idea that I might be sent straight off to a military depot. To relieve my feelings I wrote to Lord Lloyd, whom I vaguely knew, to ask if he would exert his influence to get me taken on as an Air Force pilot or rear-gunner; and when Beaverbrook and Brendan Bracken became Ministers, I likewise applied to them in the same sense. Needless to say, in each case I got only a polite brush-off. One or two middle-aged men disposing of more influence than I did – Sir Arnold Wilson, for instance – managed to get taken on as rear-gunners, and were duly killed; but there was

no possible basis for my expecting such preferential treatment. I cannot pretend that it was heroism which prompted me in making these appeals; though possibly a desire to *seem* a hero – a very different thing – played its part. The armed forces, as I subsequently discovered, were overflowing with aspiring 1914–18 war heroes – mute inglorious T. E. Lawrences, meticulously scruffy and insubordinate; Rupert Brookes with beautiful profiles, and poems scribbled down on army memo-pads with indelible pencils; Siegfried Sassoons ready at the drop of a hat to canter off the hunting field and into battle; clergymen who had become padres, damning God under their breath as they booked a double-room at the Regent Palace Hotel; HELLO, TO ALL THAT! from up and coming Robert Graveses.

The first days of the war were, for me, full of discontent and irritability. Everything that was supposed to come to an end when hostilities began looked like going on for ever. I had to get off my review of five novels as usual, posting it at the very last moment in the same old way; my overdraft still stood, and the piles of copies of *The Times* in my study reminded me that there was still some way to go yet if I was to finish my survey of the Thirties by the end of the year. The siren-trumpet had sounded, but the walls of Jericho, shaky as they were, refused to fall down. Moreover, such outward manifestations of war as there were had a decided air of *déjà vu*; with the old sets, the old lines, and the old cast, most of whom were decidedly shaky and creaky by this time, but could still manage to get through their parts – just. So tatty a show, to be kept going, required a truly seasoned and outstanding impresario. Before long, one would be coming along, equipped with funny hats, siren suit, cigar, and, above all, rhetoric to fill the empty spaces of our hopes and resolution with portentous words – a blended brew of Macaulay, Gibbon, and the Authorised Version of the Bible, which, like Horlicks, could be taken at bed time to ward off night starvation.

About this time, I got a request from a publisher to undertake a new version of Ian Hay's *The First Hundred Thousand*, published in 1915, about the British Expeditionary Force in France. He must have meant pounds, Kingsmill said when I told him. Thinking about it – the advance proposed was substantial – I could not bring myself to relish the project. It would inevitably mean dishing the war up as some sort of a crusade, whereas I saw it as an act of self-destructive desperation on the part of all concerned. Even the most resourceful columnists and leader-writers had run into grave difficulties in avoiding, as they clearly

felt they must, the semantics of the 1914–18 war. Thus, an article in the *News Chronicle* was headed: 'Making the World Safe for Go-Aheads to Live In'. 'Go-Aheads' seemed a shabby synonym for 'heroes'. How could I expect to do better? Turning over a few pages of Ian Hay's book convinced me of the hopelessness of the task. *The Last Hundred Thousand* would be more in my style, I decided, and declined the offer. The only basis I could discover for my own zeal to participate in the war was the sort of consideration which induced the Russian anarchist, Bakunin, when he saw some men setting fire to a house, to leap out of his carriage and lend a hand, without bothering to find out who they were and what was their purpose. When, after the war, I was a member of the Garrick Club for some years, I used sometimes to see Ian Hay there; a tall, lantern-jawed, elusive-looking man. I never managed to summon up the courage to tell him that I had been chosen, but declined, to pick up in the second world war the torch he had carried in the first. I felt it might upset him.

My distress at having to go on reviewing novels was relieved when I received a note from the literary editor of the *Daily Telegraph* saying that, in the light of the war situation, it was unlikely that sufficient works of fiction would be forthcoming to support a weekly feature, and that in any case the space would be required for copy relating to the national emergency. My joy at this deliverance was very great. Bunyan's Pilgrim did not climb out of the Slough of Despond more eagerly than I did out of this fictional slough in which I had been immersed, resolved never to fall into anything of the kind again. It is one of the few resolutions I have approximately kept.

By the same post as the letter telling me that my weekly column of novel reviews was no longer wanted, came another offering me a post in the newly established Ministry of Information. I felt bound to accept this, having now no regular income of any kind. It meant being in London during the week, and only coming home for week-ends. As things turned out, I was not to live with my family again, except for odd week-ends and periods of leave, till the end of the war; leaving Kitty to keep our home together, look after the children and see to their schooling in very difficult circumstances. I did this, not under compulsion, not from any genuine sense of duty, but just out of vanity and foolish bravado; ultimately, I suppose, because I wanted to get away on my own, and behave as I liked. Something that wars make permissible, practicable and even praiseworthy.

The hurriedly improvised Ministry of Information had been set up

in the new London University building in Bloomsbury, where there were still intimations of its academic function; scientific formulae scrawled on blackboards, the whiff of chemicals and dead dog-fish in the laboratories, and even a tattered old gown hanging in one of the lavatories. When I presented myself, I found the place teeming with people, all moving about energetically and purposefully; like an airport. Some were in uniform, most carried brief-cases; dispatch-riders roared up to the entrance on their motor-cycles, and then, after a brief wait, roared away again, the only familiar sight being the commissionaires in blue, who spring up from an apparently inexhaustible supply whenever and wherever a new Ministry is instituted.

The department I was attached to was responsible for producing, for use all over the world, feature articles calculated to raise enthusiasm for the Allied cause. Leader-writing on the *Guardian*, the counterfeit words with which I was required to juggle – like 'freedom', 'democracy', 'self-determination' – had died on me.

Resurrecting them now into some sort of pallid existence for use as counters in a war that persistently refused to begin, was an uninspiring task. As it happens, under the auspices of the BBC, Orwell was similarly engaged, his special territory being India and South-East Asia. We often used to talk about this when I got to know him. From a studio deep under Oxford Street, he beamed at listeners in Cawnpore, Kuala Lumpur and Rangoon – assuming, of course, that there were any – *Areopagitica*, *The Wasteland* read by the author in person, and other gems of Western culture, with a view to enthusing them for the Allied cause. When I delicately suggested that this may well have failed to hit its target, the absurdity of the enterprise struck him anew, and he began to chuckle; a dry, rusty, growly sort of chuckle, deep in his throat, very characteristic of him and very endearing.

Graham Greene, who had also joined the Ministry of Information wartime staff, as characteristically took a highly professional view of what was expected of us, coolly exploring the possibility of throwing stigmata and other miraculous occurrences into the battle for the mind in Latin America to sway it in our favour. In the way of duty, he also had access to a file of letters from successful writers like Hugh Walpole, Michael Arlen and Godfrey Winn offering their pens for King and Country. Dipping into this gave us much pleasure. He was staying near the Ministry in a little mews flat where I spent an occasional evening with him, the invariable supper dish being sausages, then still available. Whatever his circumstances, he has this facility for seeming always to be in

lodgings, and living from hand to mouth. Spiritually, and even physic-
ally, he is one of nature's displaced persons. Soon after his house on
Clapham Common had been totally demolished in the Blitz, I happened
to run into him. There was no one in the house at the time, his family
having moved into the country, and he gave an impression of being well
content with its disappearance. Now, at last, he seemed to be saying, he
was homeless, *de facto* as well as *de jure*.

At the Ministry I was given a desk in a room for two, with, on the
door, the word 'Editorial'. No one was ever able to explain what, if
anything, this signified. My stable-companion was a pale, staid figure
named Palmer from the League of Nations Secretariat. We neither of us
had much to do, but when I girded against this, Palmer gently rebuked
me. Such, he said, had been his lot on the League Secretariat for years
past. He had grown used to it, and saw no reason why I should not in
time come to do likewise. It was a perfectly permissible and acceptable
way of life. Palmer had, indeed, as I saw, developed in himself a sort of
Buddhistic power of contemplation as he sat at his desk staring in front
of him; expenditure of energy being reserved for things like getting
stationery, paper-clips and other clerical impedimenta together, taking
control of the opening and shutting of our window, and seeing that his
blotter was changed from time to time, and supplies of ink replenished.
What thoughts and aspirations were in his mind during these pro-
tracted periods of contemplation I had no means of knowing, but he had,
I gathered, a special interest in Eng. Lit., and had written a book or two
in that field. He also collaborated with another League official, Hilary
St George Saunders, in writing thrillers under a joint pseudonym.

Sometimes he spoke of Saunders, whom I vaguely knew, and saw
occasionally after the war when he had become librarian at the House of
Commons; executing his responsibilities as provider and distributor of
books to Hon. Members with great aplomb. Palmer clearly held Saunders
in considerable awe as a man with sparkling gifts born to shine in a
world to which he, Palmer, could not aspire. Mixed with his veneration,
I thought I detected a strain of envy, and perhaps resentment. The
relationship between the two, yoked so strangely in the production of
thrillers, fascinated me, and I tried to explore it in a novel of my own
(*Affairs of the Heart*), in which two similarly dissimilar collaborators
devise a plot whose only possible outcome is for one of them to murder
the other, which he duly does, the single clue being the manuscript of
the last novel they were working on together. The result, alas, was
unsatisfactory, though published, and, for some inscrutable reason,

translated into Italian and Mexican. I came across the Italian edition – *Affari di Cuore* – once in a Milan bookshop, standing, blameless, on a shelf of porn; on the cover of the Mexican edition – *Deseo Y Muerte* – I am described as '*el genio del Humor Negro*', an undeserved compliment.

The days passed at the Ministry of Information very much as they had at the International Labour Office. There were even tea trolleys and biscuits, but not stamped MOI as the others had been BIT. R. H. S. Crossman was in an adjoining office, and we spent much time talking together. It was then that for the first time I became acquainted with one of the most versatile, engaging, and irresponsible of contemporary minds. My impressions at the time were only confirmed when, years later, we were together, along with Peter Thorneycroft, on a weekly television programme which involved endless talk on and off the screen. Whatever position Crossman took up was defended with vigour and panache, though he was quite likely, on another occasion, to demolish it with equal vigour and panache. He left the Ministry of Information at about the same time as I did, moving over to a secret organisation where he found himself more sympathetically engaged in devising and disseminating Black Propaganda to Germany, using for the purpose admitted lies instead of, as at the Ministry, disguised ones. His great ambition in life, he told me once, had been to become editor of the *New Statesman* or Foreign Secretary; the first of these objectives he, somewhat belatedly, achieved, but his performance at it suggests that it is just as well for all of us that the other has eluded him.

Apart from the barrage balloons, which had now become part of the London skyline, and posters exhorting us, among other things, to Save for the Brave, the only evident sign of the war was the black-out. As the winter came on, by the afternoon when it was time to leave the Ministry and my communings with Palmer and Crossman, darkness had fallen over London, unrelieved by street lamps. Buses and cars crept silently along with only two tiny points of light to mark their extremities; the people in the streets no more than passing shadows, everything hushed and subdued, like Moscow when the snow had fallen. I preferred to grope my way on foot through the black-out to Chelsea, where I was staying in a house in Bramerton Street, rather than trying to get onto public transport. From Gower Street via St Martin's Lane, to Trafalgar Square, up the Mall by Buckingham Palace, past the tall houses in Eaton Square, and on to Sloane Square, King's Road, and Chelsea Town Hall – these were my land-marks, but I often lost my way, suddenly finding myself by the Embankment, and once almost walking

into the Albert Hall. Muffled in an overcoat, umbrella up when it was raining, sometimes choking over yellow fog, I had a wonderful sense of being cut off and alone in a lost world. Along King's Road the prostitutes signalled with torches, little quick flashes indicating their presence; rather sweetly, as I thought. Thus groping my way about blacked-out London, a phrase took shape in my mind: Lost in the darkness of change. I said it over and over to myself, like some incantation momentarily crystallising our human condition.

The house in Bramerton Street had been kindly lent me by Gerald Reitlinger, who had managed to get into an anti-aircraft battery manned almost entirely by Twenties figures like himself. It must have been one of the most bizarre British Army units ever to be mustered, whose personnel were trapanned, not, like the early East India Company's troops, in the back streets and stews of Bristol and Liverpool, but in the Café Royal, the Gargoyle Club, the Cave of Harmony and the Fitzroy Tavern. In his private's uniform, especially fitted in Savile Row, Gerald at last realised his lifelong dream of merging himself in the English social scene, instead of, like Satan, going solitarily to and fro in the world and up and down in it. Never can there have been so ardent and battle-worthy a recruit. If Hitler had only struck then and there, without a doubt his euphoria would have carried him into performing deeds of valour deserving of the highest praise and decorations. Alas, during the period of the phoney war, his morale gradually subsided, and he finished up going round lecturing to the troops, a civilian again. When, once, I asked him what he lectured about, he was evasive, and I was never fortunate enough to come across anyone who had heard him. His Bramerton Street establishment was littered with Twenties bric-à-brac; his easel stood in its place with a half-finished Impression-istic canvas still on it, the *Week-End Book* was placed by the bedside, and, over supper, his housekeeper, Mrs Gray, provided anecdotes of glittering figures like Constant Lambert, and even Augustus John, who had at different times visited the house. Outside, the darkness of change, inside the past; but where was the present? It eluded me then, and still does. Perhaps there is no such thing; an imaginary point where the past and future intersect. Or, as Pascal puts it: '*Le passé et le présent sont nos moyens; le seul avenir est nôtre fin.*'

The Ministry was presided over during the first months of the war by a Scottish judge, Lord Macmillan; a man with a thin, precise face and judicial style of speaking, who seemed as far removed from his opposite number on the enemy side, Dr Goebbels, as any run-of-the-mill

Archbishop of Canterbury from John the Baptist. We were required to take a similarly judicial attitude in our articles, eschewing bellicosity, and appealing rather to reason and enlightened self-interest. Germany's shortage of molybdenum, we argued, would infallibly bring the Nazi hordes to a halt; their supplies of rubber and petroleum products were running out, with no possibility of replenishing them, so their cause could be considered as good as lost. Towards putative allies of Germany whom we wished to coax over to our side, we were likewise supple and conciliatory. The Turkey of Kemal Ataturk might not be, in the technical sense, a one-man-one-vote democracy, but it was unquestionably progressive, and responsive to majority opinion; and even the USSR, despite having carved up Poland with Hitler, and mounted an unprovoked attack on Finland, might be considered as forward-looking, and so on the side of peace and freedom.

My *Guardian* training held me in good stead in meeting these requirements. At times, it almost seemed as though I were back in Cross Street, so reminiscent of my time there were the editorial specifications, as well as the earnest, sometimes heated, talk in the canteen about war strategy and aims, and the problems peace would pose when it came. Not to mention the people – those unmistakable voices, eager, throaty, tumultuous; that untidy hair, those keen, ardent, somehow ravening, eyes, with a core of calculation, like a drunk pulling himself together to count his change. How reminiscent they were of old *Guardian* colleagues! Indeed, many of them *were* old *Guardian* colleagues. Then the knowingness about this and that, and here and there – how things were up on the Burmese frontier, how the tribesmen were feeling in the Upper Nile, what they were at in the shanty towns of Brazil or on the shores of Lake Chad. A stage army of the just; in and out of Broadcasting House, on and off the campuses, marching triumphantly down Cross Street, fanning out through the USSR's wide open spaces, massing for the duration in the Ministry of Information, with ABCA (the Army Bureau of Current Affairs) to take the overspill, and, when the war was over, UNESCO providing a home from home, Chatham House a sanctuary. Indestructible, inexorable, sometimes reported missing, possibly dead, but always reappearing sooner or later behind the microphones, before the cameras. Do the panel think . . . ? They do, they do! Thinkers all!

The only tangible evidence I saw that any of the pieces I wrote while at the Ministry ever got published was a smudgy cutting from a Ceylon newspaper of an article under my by-line, headed 'Eternal Vigilance', and animadverting upon the cost and uses of liberty. Otherwise, it may

be assumed that my offerings, though doubtless circulated to press attachés in the relevant countries, found no takers. Meanwhile, the Ministry visibly grew and grew; new departments being born almost daily, and old ones expanded. For instance, the religious department, with which I had occasional transactions, gathered in ever more personnel, including a miscellaneous collection of Roman Catholic lay intellectuals, a Jesuit or two, as well as a representative atheist. Palmer and I continued in the the seclusion of our office; he working steadily, I gathered, at some literary study, and I, fitfully, at the closing chapters of *The Thirties*. It was in these circumstances that I received a paper calling upon me to present myself at Mytchett Hutments, Ash Vale, with a view to joining the Field Security Police. I had almost forgotten that, after my abortive attempt to join up, I wrote a short satirical account in the *Daily Telegraph* of how, in this war, unlike the last, places in the armed forces were as difficult to come by as tickets for the Royal Enclosure at Ascot or invitations to the Lord Mayor's Banquet. It drew a rejoinder from a Lt-Colonel asking me whether I was bluffing or seriously wanted to join the army; if the latter, what was the matter with this new formation, the FSP, which had been advertising for linguists in the daily press? I replied that I was not bluffing, and asked nothing better than to be called to the colours in any capacity. The summons to Mytchett was the delayed response.

It was, I confess, with a sinking heart that I turned in my railway warrant at Waterloo station, and got in return a ticket to Ash Vale; especially as, the day before, I had been offered a higher post at the Ministry, which would have meant a substantial rise in salary and allowances. As usual, I inwardly equivocated, half hoping that I might be turned down for the FSP on health grounds, or because of my atrocious accent when I spoke French, the only foreign language I could claim to know; and then, thinking of the Ministry, its thronging corridors, its fraudulent output, the resonant voices prophesying peace against the rat-tat-tat of typewriters; Bloomsbury within and all about me – thinking of all this, I longed to make my escape, even though only into a barrack-square.

As the train approached Ash Vale I became aware of the Aldershot countryside, with its air of having been endlessly tramped over in heavy boots; like a chicken run, denuded of vegetation, bare and untidy. Mytchett Hutments, too, when I reached them, stood out bleakly among pine trees, very much recalling the picture I had formed in my mind of a Soviet labour camp. I might even then, I thought, turn tail

and run back to my typewriter. In the end, I just surrendered myself to
the process of becoming a soldier; filled in yet another prodigious form,
stripped for the purpose of being medically examined, wandered about
naked holding a phial of my urine; then swore on a dog-eared Bible to
fight loyally for King and Country as and when required. Thus the
matter was settled; the Ministry of Information knew me no more, and
I became a private, acting unpaid lance-corporal, in the shortly-to-be-
formed Intelligence Corps.

My medical category was low, C3, but I was subsequently able to
persuade a drunken MO in a lax moment to alter this to A1, which I
considered, I really think correctly, to be a truer description of my
physical condition. Had the category stood, I should never have been
sent abroad, and probably have remained at the depot for the rest of
the war – a fate almost more awful than staying at the Ministry of
Information. Battle-dress was still not on issue, and we were provided
with riding breeches, puttees, peaked caps, and tunics with high collars
and brass buttons; gear that I found it difficult to manage and to muster.
On the first evening, when I arrayed myself in it as best I could, having
acquired a bed in a barrack hut – one of fifteen – I felt, as I so often
have, that I had acted impulsively, and landed myself in a ridiculous
position. There were still some final pages of *The Thirties* to write; my
pay and family allowances as an unpaid lance-corporal would make
Kitty's circumstances even more straitened than heretofore, and I saw
little prospect of shining in my new profession of arms. I thought with
positive nostalgia of the room in the Ministry I shared with Palmer. Ah!
if only I could get back there, would I not throw myself with renewed
fervour into an appeal, even to the islanders of Fiji, or the head-hunters
of Borneo, to rally to the Allied cause in defence of freedom and democ-
racy. Alas, there was no escape route from Mytchett back to Blooms-
bury now; once again I had kicked down the ladder on which I might
have made a getaway. In the event, I managed to get the last pages of
The Thirties written, seated on my bed in the barrack hut, with a pad in
my lap, and they were by no means the poorest in the book. In the bar-
rack hut, too, I got the news that *The Thirties* was a Book Society choice,
and autographed the requisite number of title-pages in an edition on
special paper, to the accompaniment of much good-natured derision on
the part of my fellow-occupants.

Mytchett, the depot of the Corps of Military Police, or Red Caps, was
run on very strict lines. Smartness was called for, saluting was vigorous
and imperative, any carelessness in dress or slouching or lounging was

anathema. The NCO's, and particularly the warrant officers, yelled out orders with thunderous emphasis, tucked their swagger-sticks under their arms, pounded the pavement with their boots, and larded their speech with swear-words and obscenities like any sociologist, underground newspaper, or alternative culture exponent today. When for a short while I became a warrant officer myself, I found, rather to my surprise, that I could emulate these old pros in volume of voice if nothing else; shouting out 'Squad, Abbbbout turn!', or 'Staand eas y!' as to the manner born. My performance was so unexpected that it attracted attention; a little crowd would gather to hear me at it, drawn, I suppose, by the ludicrous disparity between what I looked like, and perhaps was, and what I was doing. Or did my accomplishment in this field, like Dr Johnson's in emulating a bargee's vocabulary of abuse, which so dazzled Boswell, point to a potential loud-mouthed bully under my skin? I have sometimes thought so.

It was while I was putting up this impersonation of an old-style warrant officer that an incident occurred which, once and for all, demolished any military fantasies I may have entertained. It seemed that an important officer from the War Office was coming to Mytchett on some undisclosed but urgent mission, and I was instructed to meet him at Ash Vale station. It was, I felt, an important occasion. I pressed my tunic and trousers with loving care, polished up the crown on my sleeve till it shone like the morning sun, worked on the toes of my army boots with a hot spoon to give them a comparable glory. Thus resplendent, I awaited the officer's arrival on the station platform, and, when I saw him get down from a first-class carriage, gave him a thunderous salute, which he nonchalantly returned. Then I took his bag and saw him into an army car, seating myself beside the driver. In the driving mirror I studied the face of our distinguished visitor. He was young, I decided, to be so important a personage, with a sensitive, vaguely melancholic countenance. As I went on looking at him, it struck me that there was something familiar about his features, and all at once it dawned on me that I knew him. He was Edward Crankshaw, a neighbour of ours in the country, whom we had seen occasionally and liked; a gifted writer, and subsequently the *Observer's* Kremlinologist – the equivalent in our time of a Delphic Oracle, deducing our present fortunes and future prospects, not from a chicken's entrails, but from the turgid columns of *Pravda, Izvestia* and other Soviet publications.

Crankshaw, as he told me afterwards, had been going through the same motions of penetrating my disguise, and our mutual recognition

was instantaneous. We began to laugh long and helplessly. He had been thinking that, after all, the old depot sweats like this sergeant-major who had met him at Ash Vale Station so smartly turned out, were still the fine flower of the regular army, and I that this brilliant young captain from the War Office was really more like an intellectual in uniform than the conventional notion of a staff officer. We laughed and laughed at the deception we had all unconsciously practiced on one another. Somehow, thenceforth, I was never again able to take my military duties, such as they were, quite seriously; like other exercises of the will, they required dressing up and histrionic skills to be convincing. The learned judge in his ermine, the erudite professor in his gown, the holy priest in his vestments, the anointed monarch with his crown and orbs, and I, impersonating a sergeant-major with shining boots and buttons.

The FSP were an alien element at Mytchett, and regarded by the native Red Caps with an implacable detestation. An advertisement for linguists such as had brought us together there, was calculated to assemble as sorry a company in their eyes as could possibly be imagined; ranging between carpet-sellers from Baghdad and modern language teachers in grammar schools and colleges, with a stray expert on Bengali or Sanskrit, or pimp from Marseilles or Beirut; as well as tourist agency men, unfrocked priests who had lived irregularly in Venice and Rome, and contraceptive salesmen who had roamed the world. Our appearance in uniform was even more derisory than when we first arrived among them as civilians; trimming and tidying us up only served to accentuate our disorderly bearing and ways. To add to the comedy, our own reaction to the situation in which we found ourselves tended to become. more military than the MP's themselves. We saluted on all possible occasions, we polished our buttons and our boots with an obsessive assiduity, we dropped out 'Sirs' when talking to officers and NCO's in wild profusion, and when called upon to step forward to receive our pay or a leave-pass we made such a clatter that the very floor-boards groaned. All this, far from endearing us to the Mytchett regulars, made us even more repellent, especially as promotion came to us, from their point of view, with dazzling rapidity. We moved up from being unpaid lance-corporals, to sergeants and sergeant-majors, almost overnight, as more and more Field Security sections were mustered. I well remember with what distaste the MP's looked at me on the first day I walked between the hutments with a crown on my arm. Then, when I became an officer some months later, all was changed. Hostility turned into amiability; I found myself quite a favourite when I condescended to

visit the sergeants' mess, being regarded as a card, an odd fellow who said preposterous things but needed to be cherished and protected.

Apart from the drill, being given injections, assembling and setting out our kit in accordance with a set pattern (something I never properly mastered), and keeping our quarters spick and span, to the point of polishing the floor until it was like a skating-rink, and arranging the pebbles outside our hut into an elegant mosaic, there was the course in Security Intelligence. This consisted of a series of lectures given by officers and NCO Instructors on how Intelligence was collected, and how those collecting it on behalf of the enemy might be circumvented. The syllabus was based exclusively on 1914–18 War practice, and even to our inexpert minds had an air of irrelevance. For instance, there was the *Dames Blanches* organisation set up in Brussels, which consisted of Belgian ladies who counted the carriages of troop trains rumbling past as they knitted at their windows, thus providing material for making an estimate of the forces the Germans were moving up to the front. Another theme was how to set up an informer network, taking account of the fact that barbers and taxi-drivers were normally garrulous by nature, and could be tapped for information, which, however, must be accepted with some reserve. We were expected to follow the scripts provided with scrupulous exactitude, which, when I became an instructor, I faithfully did, in the process becoming quite attached to them, as I had when I was at Cambridge to the Latin grace in hall and other ceremonial incantations. To the best of my knowledge, they continued to serve right through the war. Whenever I ran into anyone from Field Security I always asked if the *Dames Blanches* were still going strong at the depot, and learnt with relief that they were. Also that the playlet about how an enemy agent was detected by finding among his toilet accessories a tell-tale ball-pointed pen for writing in invisible ink, was still being performed with great panache for successive courses.

The war itself seemed even more remote at Mytchett than it had at the Ministry of Information, despite our drilling, our uniforms, our military status, and the blood-curdling tales we were regaled with about the dreadful things that happened to Intelligence personnel who fell into enemy hands. We seldom spoke about the war, and our training soon became an end in itself rather than a preparation for subsequent action in the field. Occasionally, an officer or other rank who had been in France with the British Expeditionary Force visited us and spoke about trench life, and the unsympathetic attitude of the French civilian population; the general assumption being that the Maginot Line was

impregnable, and that the Germans, with their dwindling supplies of essential war material, were bound to collapse and surrender before so very long. When I asked once what would happen if the attack came, not on the Maginot Line, but on some other relatively undefended part of the Franco-Belgian frontier, the question was brushed aside. Military expertise, I soon discovered, was even more dogmatic and immune to criticism than other kinds. Later on in the war, when I was on an Intelligence course at Matlock Hydro, an officer came especially from the War Office to give us an account of the defences of Singapore. He unrolled a map of the Malay Peninsula, and, waving his pointer about over it, demonstrated conclusively that no land force would ever be able to make its way through such jungle terrain. At that very moment, while he was speaking, the Japanese were moving swiftly down the peninsula to Singapore, which fell a few days later. The Hydro seemed a perfect shrine for such outmoded military lore; with its odour of hot baths, hot drinks and decaying flesh. A nearby chemist told me that when the inmates were evacuated to make way for our Intelligence courses, several of them died on the way to the station, and, subsequently, an occasional corpse of someone left behind was found in one of the remoter rooms.

Our life at Mytchett was really rather a happy one; we were cut off, alike, from civilian responsibilities and from the hazards of war. Our chief preoccupations were to keep our buttons and boots bright, our tunics pressed so that we made a good show on parade; to climb the ladder of promotion as expeditiously as possible, and to ingratiate ourselves with the CO and his officers in whose hands lay our future posting; as well as with the NCO's who allocated fatigues and handed out leave passes and stores. I, as an instructor, had also the lectures to consider, including one of my own on propaganda, in which I drew on journalistic experience, trying to present myself as an old, hard-boiled Fleet Street hand. Delivering them, I sometimes imagined myself back in Alwaye, and looking out of the window, half expected to see paddy fields and brown figures chanting as they trod round their bamboo irrigation wheels; instead, a squad being drilled on asphalt – 'Left, right! Left, right! Abbbbout turn!' It seems as though all my life I have been holding forth and looking out of windows; though, I venture to hope, rarely quite as irrelevantly as at Mytchett.

For those of my generation, it was a kind of charade of the war we had missed. We spent our evenings in local pubs, or made our way to Aldershot, clattering through its blacked-out streets; pushing open faintly lit

doors into public bars, there to join other troops stoically drinking draught beer. The very songs we sang belonged to the last war – 'Pack Up Your Troubles', 'It's a Long Way to Tipperary'; the ENSA entertainers who occasionally visited us were getting on in years, and groaned over their dance routine as I did over my PT. Most week-ends I had a pass to go home, made out 'for the purpose of going to Battle', this being the nearest station to Whatlington; the only soldier in the British Army so bent, I used to boast. There, with Kitty and the children, I tried to play the part of a warrior taking his ease. It was not very convincing.

In the dark cavernous space of Waterloo Station, on my way back to Mytchett, I resumed my place as a member of the armed forces; a greying NCO somewhat abashed to be wearing a CMP badge pending the issue of a newly designed I Corps one. We were packed tight in railway compartments, dimly lit with blue electric bulbs, cigarettes glowing in the darkness; in our identical khaki, mostly silent and ruminative, except for an occasional snore or grunt. At Ash Vale, our contingent got off the train, and, in twos and threes, or solitarily, tramped to Mytchett; boots echoing up the hill, past the guard room and the sentry, on to my barrack hut, tiptoeing in, the other fourteen all tucked up and asleep. Undressing by torch-light, shining it across at my neighbours, their faces quite gentle, and even innocent, in repose, with the strange poignancy of sleeping men. One with part of a cigarette behind his ear, ready for the first morning puff; all the defensiveness and defiance dissolved in sleep, a rehearsal for death and its peace. I felt a great tenderness towards them; brothers-in-arms, except that we hadn't been issued with any arms.

I became an officer in May 1940. Having ordered a uniform and the necessary kit in Aldershot, I now went into the shop to put it on; entering as a company sergeant-major and emerging a lieutenant. As I arrayed myself, garment by garment, a feeling of melancholy, almost of despair, assailed me. It was rather like arriving at Montreux from Moscow; another imagined escape from bourgeois life had proved illusory, and I found myself infallibly back among the saloon-bar folk. I suppose everyone who has straddled the classes, moving from dinner to luncheon and from supper to dinner, from Saturday evening to daily morning bathing, from strong Indian to weak China tea, from weekly currency notes and coins in a little envelope to a monthly cheque paid into a bank account, is in some senses subject to such fantasies, which seem now to have quite taken possession of the middle- and upper-class young, who

array themselves in tattered clothes, eschew bathing altogether, and live by Oscar Wilde's dictum that work is the curse of the drinking (in their case, pot-smoking) classes. Yet it is true that I greatly enjoyed the relationship of full and free equality which being an other rank involved, and regretted becoming an officer, having a batman, drinking too many pink gins in an ante-room before going to dine in a mess, and other intimations of commissioned status.

At Mytchett, depot life was, for us, the war. The nearest we got to being belligerents was to array ourselves in battle-dress, worn by officers and other ranks alike; the only outward sign of commissioned rank, apart from pips on the shoulder-straps, being the wearing of a collar and tie. I came in for some disapproving words in the mess when I developed the theory that we liked wearing battle-dress because, in case of a revolution or other upheaval, we could button up our tunics, take off our insignia of rank, and no one would know we were officers. In the event, it worked the other way round, as King George VI appears to have foreseen. P. J. Grigg told me that, when he was Secretary of State for War, the only point the King ever raised with him with any seriousness was the dangerous possibility that other ranks might take to wearing collars and ties with battle-dress; as, in due course, they did, thereby equalising upwards and all looking like officers.

Matters of dress, I found, loomed large at Mytchett, especially among the regulars. I was for a time in a barrack hut with several guardsmen, and marvelled at how prima-donnaish they were about their appearance, cavorting and twisting in front of a mirror when they had been issued with a new stripe or other embellishment, to see how it looked. They devoted as many hours to bulling themselves up as any society beauty, and felt very deprived if they missed their afternoon nap. They were like society beauties, too, in the attitude, humorous and at the same time complaisant, which they adopted to the amorous advances their splendid appearance brought them, whether from lonely females who, despite rationing, could produce a tasty supper, or – as, according to their own account, was more often the case – love-sick pederasts; this being a recognised hazard of guard duty at Buckingham Palace.

As spring turned to summer, the war suddenly began. Even in Mytchett we became aware of the Norwegian campaign, of Chamberlain's replacement by Churchill, and then of the triumphant sweep of the *Wehrmacht* through Holland and Belgium and on to Paris and the Channel ports, until it suddenly occurred to us that there seemed no particular reason why the momentum thus achieved should not carry them

across the Channel. At our mess in the evenings we listened to the BBC's news bulletins, wearing grave faces at news of further German advances, and ardently discussing afterwards where a stand might be expected, and how the Allied disasters could be reversed. Mixed with the *angst* that news of disasters brought, was also a queer subterranean satisfaction; I think there is in most people, underlying their ostensible passion to win a war, a secret passion to lose it. The same thing applies to seduction. We also listened to Churchill's broadcasts, which, of course, had an electric effect, and were heard in an awed hush by one and all. I personally found the broadcasts somehow distasteful and embarrassing, especially as, from the beginning, they came to be imitated to a tiresome degree, so that practically everyone, in retailing any sort of anecdote or reminiscence about Churchill, copied his phraseology and tone of voice. I naturally hid these feelings, but sometimes they came out in some chance remark or derisory reference, which offended my fellow-officers. I think, on the whole, that their hostility was justified; it was necessary at that time to accept the validity of Churchillian rhetoric, which to me recalled the last sentences of Scott Fitzgerald's *The Great Gatsby* – a favourite novel – about beating on, 'boats against the current, borne back ceaselessly into the past'.

It was at this time that our depot was transferred from Mytchett to Sheerness, in the Isle of Sheppey, where, as it turned out, we constituted almost the only military force – if such we could be called – available to combat a German landing should one be attempted at what seemed to be, from a casual glance at the map, a rather vulnerable point in the Thames Estuary. To provide us with the means to carry out our role we were issued with rifles and twelve rounds of ammunition apiece, none of which, however, could be fired by way of practice to familiarise us with our weapons because of shortage of supplies. At night we prowled along the coast, steel-helmeted, battle-dressed, and shouldering our rifles; speaking only in whispers, looking out intently across the mud flats for signs of grey advancing figures, and to the estuary beyond for the dark shapes of approaching boats.

Our officer in charge was Captain Partridge, a bulky schoolmaster wearing 1914–18 campaign ribbons. He was carrying field-glasses, which in the circumstances could not be of much use, and a map-case which he occasionally examined by the light of a small torch. There were frequent alarms and alerts; once we thought we heard aircraft overhead, and Captain Partridge told us to throw ourselves on the ground, which we did with alacrity, my rifle, to my great shame, going off in the

process. This caused near panic; everyone thought the invasion had begun. One lance-corporal insisted that he heard church bells ringing – the agreed signal that the invader had arrived – another that he clearly saw the outline of a boat approaching the shore. It was a case, Captain Partridge explained, of fighting to the last man and last round of ammunition; which in my case would now be the eleventh round instead of the twelfth.

While the troops prepared themselves for the desperate encounter which lay ahead, Captain Partridge spoke to me in whispers about the hopes he had entertained when, at the end of the last war, he had started on his teaching career. How he had tried to make the boys see the need for a kinder, juster way of life; Christian, but not in any narrow sectarian sense. And how he had really made some progress, getting, for instance, T. S. Eliot – later, he confidently expected, Dylan Thomas, and perhaps even D. H. Lawrence, but one had to proceed with discretion – included in the school syllabus, and birdwatching and country walks accepted as an alternative to compulsory games for those so minded. Such changes were not, he went on, in themselves particularly drastic, but all moves in the right direction. Now he felt that his work had all been undone; he did not think he would survive this second war in one lifetime, and was not even sure he wanted to. His voice droned on; I was conscious of his massive physical presence, the forlorn expanse of face under the steel helmet, so grieved and troubled. All I could do was murmur vague noises of agreement and understanding, hoping that the Germans would soon land and bring his anguish to a summary end. The night, however, was stiller than ever; no church bells were ringing, and the boat we had seen turned out to belong to a clandestine fisherman plying his trade despite security regulations. In the event, Captain Partridge lived on to continue after the war his work of enlightenment at one of the smaller public schools.

As it happened, the war did intrude visibly into Sheerness in the shape of French troops, fugitives from across the Channel, who arrived there in a state of great demoralisation. They were in all manner of uniforms, from all sorts of regiments; white and black and Moroccan. Some of them had weapons, which we took off them; all of them were exhausted, bewildered and disgruntled, grumbling and muttering about the absence of Allied air power to counteract the *Luftwaffe*, which, they said, dive-bombed them without respite. I felt very sorry for them so lost-looking and demoralised. Soldiers in such circumstances look particularly wretched, I suppose because one associates them with

marching in formation and being smartly and identically attired; when their discipline breaks down they seem more disorderly than any civilian rabble. We looked at them with pity, and they looked at us surlily; as the ally who had failed them, whose immunity from attack had been procured at their expense, '*Où est le Royal Air Force?*' they kept asking savagely, rolling the 'R' in 'Royal', as though we had personally, for our own selfish ends, hidden it somewhere. Our first thought was to hand them cigarettes – that currency of the lost – which they looked at curiously; then lit, and gratefully sucked in the smoke.

As good security men, we had, of course, to take account of the possibility that enemy agents might have been infiltrated with them, and made a move to examine their documents, which, when they reluctantly produced them, turned out to be for the most part crumpled grubby bits of paper bearing a smudged photograph which told us nothing. Carried away, I even attempted to rally them with a sort of sub-Churchillian address in my bad French, about how the struggle against the Nazis had only just begun, and how the defeat we had suffered in France was but a minor set-back in a war in which the triumph of freedom, etc., etc., was assured. It got me back into an editorialising vein; I was, metaphorically speaking, tapping away at my typewriter again. In any case, my words notably failed to break the sullen discontent reflected in the faces of my audience, and I can only suppose that, fortunately for me and for them, they understood not a word of what I said. When I had finished, we marched them back to our depot, trying to maintain as jaunty a pace as possible, and on arrival sat them down for a meal. One of the French officers drew me aside to say that arrangements should be made for *les noirs* to eat and sleep and wash separately. I passed this embarrassing request to the camp commandant for him to deal with as he thought fit.

When, some months later, I had occasion to visit the French troops temporarily housed in Olympia, I found that some of them were from the Sheerness contingent. They had spruced up a bit, but still looked forlorn, despite a group of local girls who had gathered to stare appreciatively at them. I asked one or two about General de Gaulle, and whether they proposed to join the Free French, but they only shrugged and made non-committal remarks. Most of them, I heard afterwards, opted for repatriation. A thing I noticed about the war was how the lowlier participants usually seemed reluctant to join in if they could possibly avoid it; quite contrary to what might be supposed from the history books. The weapons collected at Sheerness made a sizeable pile,

consisting of a great variety of guns and side-arms; some of them ancient enough to be regarded as antiques. I took for myself a small Belgian automatic, which thenceforth I always carried, fully loaded, in the breast-pocket of my tunic with a vague notion that in the times that lay ahead it might be as well to be armed. As things turned out, I never once fired it.

I had long been pressing to be posted to a unit, having wearied considerably of lecturing at the depot about the *Dames Blanches*. The CO, when I put this to him, said he could not sacrifice his tools, of which I was one; but at last he was persuaded, and I was posted to GHQ Home Forces, then located at Kneller Hall, in London, where military bands are trained. The last course in which I participated included an officer whose large soup-strainer moustache at once caught my eye. It was matched by Mongolian features which made him look rather like Maxim Gorky. I turned up his papers and found that he had been a classics don in Sydney, Australia, and that his name was Enoch Powell. The moustache, I subsequently learnt from him, was due to a passion he then had for Nietzsche, who had cultivated a similar one. I remembered noticing it in a picture I had seen of Nietzsche, painted in Venice when he was quite mad and on his death-bed; crying out on the last evening of his life, as he saw through his window the sun sinking in wild Turneresque colours into the Grand Canal: 'Good-bye sun! Good-bye, sun!' It was obvious at once that Powell was a very unusual man; isolated, as I later came to realise, in the terrible seriousness and intensity of a sense of destiny. This, for the time being, took the form of determining to be a brigadier in the Operations Branch, which he readily achieved, functioning with great success in this capacity at GHQ Middle-East in Cairo. Later, there were differences about Allied strategy which resulted in his withdrawing to India, where he discovered the British Raj just at the time of its final dissolution. He returned to London after the war resolved to become a Tory MP and save the Raj, succeeding brilliantly in the first objective, and inevitably failing in the other.

Kneller Hall, when I arrived there with my FS Section – myself and batman-driver in a small Austin car, the rest of the section on motor-cycles – was in a state of considerable confusion. Music-stands and other gear and regalia for training military bands were still about the place; a war-room had been hastily improvised, and arrangements

generally made for the effective functioning of a supreme headquarters in a beleaguered country likely soon to be invaded. At the mess in the evening I was dazzled by the array of senior officers, booted and spurred, their leather all aglow, their breasts bright with decorations and campaign ribbons, their grizzled locks and white moustaches neatly trimmed. Never before had I consorted with such military eminence, and I felt very lowly, by contrast, in my sober tunic, ribbonless, with its general service buttons and meagre two pips. After dinner we listened to the nine o'clock news which told, in as unalarming a way as possible, of more Allied military reverses. I felt that the minds of the listeners were mostly far away from the silky voice of the news-reader; dreaming of their in-trays, of transport, of establishments and allowances and orders of the day. It was a Sunday evening, and so, after the news came the succession of national anthems of occupied countries, to which almost daily a new one seemed to be added. They caused a faint stirring in the mess; some of the officers, I daresay, had been military attachés, and had an instinctive impulse to rise to their feet; others put down their glasses and held their cigars or cigarettes out of sight. To me, this mustering of the defeated had a macabre fascination, and I was quite disappointed when it came to an end. Someone at Broadcasting House, it seemed, had the notion of including Abyssinia, about whose national anthem there was considerable uncertainty. After one false start which upset the exiled Emperor himself – at this time resident in Bath – it was decided to drop the whole procedure.

Feeling very out of things, I wandered about the Headquarters until I found an officer with red tabs and black buttons gloomily trying to plot the latest order of battle on a large survey-map spread out on a table. He had a collection of coloured wools which he stretched out between pins to mark enemy positions in accordance with the situation reports which a signals orderly brought in from time to time. I watched him, fascinated, for a while, and then was drawn into lending him a hand, and soon became quite absorbed, not so much with the war situation as such, as with the coloured wools; one colour indicating a Panzer Division, others Artillery batteries, reserve troops, observation posts, and so on. We worked away assiduously, only very occasionally exchanging a word or two. He plotted the positions and I arranged the wools. Things were moving at such a rate that I soon got left behind; so much so that, finally, he exploded at my ineptitude. What in the hell did I think I was doing? The whole thing was now in a frightful mess! I could find no better excuse than to blurt out: 'I'm sorry, sir, but there's no more wool'

– which was, as a matter of fact, true. We had used it all up, and there seemed as much chance of procuring a further supply as of stemming the German advance. I thought it the course of prudence to slip away, hoping that some more competent IO than I would appear on the scene; retiring, literally, to my tent.

It was the only time in all the war that I was under canvas. Owing to the shortage of accommodation in Kneller Hall, tents had been erected in the grounds, and I was allotted one of them. It gave me a great feeling of satisfaction to be thus accommodated – the grass floor, the canvas bed and wash-basin, the sound of the ropes straining in the wind, the fresh smell of the night. Shortly afterwards, the whole Headquarters moved to larger premises at St Paul's School, Hammersmith; a red brick, rather murky building evacuated by the school at the beginning of the war, and now demolished. My FS Section was accommodated in a semi-detached house nearby; we set up an office, with a telephone, a box covered with an army blanket for a desk, on the wall a map of Hammersmith and district, a file and other clerical accoutrements to hand. It was the invariable set-up for an army office; only the maps differed from place to place.

I was billetted myself in another semi-detached house in an adjoining street, along with an elderly major in the Ordnance Corps; a desiccated man with a sallow face who had served for some twenty years in India. Though the ordinary washing facilities were available, including a gas geyser, I was surprised to find that he used camp equipment in his own room. On my way back from the bathroom I would catch a glimpse of him crouching over a canvas wash-basin with a cut-throat razor in his hand. In this way, as I later discovered, he was able to claim field allowance, which otherwise, if he had made use of the house's facilities, would have been disallowed. The lady who ran the house, providing us with an ample breakfast each morning, joined me in finding the major's behaviour bizarre, but I think in her heart she preferred him to me. He conformed more to her notion of an officer and a gentleman, whereas my irregular, and sometimes dissolute ways, though she looked on them tolerantly at the time, induced in her a strong feeling of disapproval and resentment which later became apparent.

The excitement of expecting an imminent invasion soon wore off, and GHQ Home Forces, like Mytchett, developed its own routine and tranquillity. On warm afternoons the playing field at the back of the school buildings was littered with sun-bathing figures; in the smaller class-rooms, four majors would be sitting with in- and out-trays before

them, in the larger ones, two lieutenant-colonels, and in the more commodious staff-rooms and masters' studies, a single full colonel or brigadier. I never penetrated to the Commander-in-Chief's office, but probably he occupied the Headmaster's quarters. The laboratories and lecture-theatres were turned over to Signals and squads of ATS pounding away at typewriters. Thus the Headquarters might be said to be in full swing. My only personal part was being on the roster of duty officers, which involved, when my turn came round, sleeping in a cubicle beside a white telephone that would ring in the event of a German landing anywhere. It would then be my responsibility to alert the Headquarters, which would at once spring into action, dispatching a division here, a division there, mounting special security guards on various key points like Broadcasting House and the London Telephone Exchange, transferring essential personnel to a tunnel which had been specially dug at Virginia Water to be an emergency operations centre, and generally getting ready to cope with an invasion in accordance with a prepared plan. Perhaps fortunately, these arrangements were never put to the test. On my duty nights I always hoped the white telephone would ring, and tucked up with a book, fully expecting that if it did ring I should hear Churchill's voice at the other end. Alas, it remained obstinately silent; except once, when to my great delight it rang. I rushed to pick it up, only to hear a drunken voice asking for a taxi.

I find it difficult, looking back, to recall what regular duties I had, if any. The administration of my FS section was in the capable hands of my sergeant-major, a middle-aged man named Laversuch who had spent a lot of his life in Africa. He subsequently became an officer, and was instrumental, as I heard, in hijacking a German ship off the African coast. Our section was supposed to be responsible for securing the Headquarters from the incursions of enemy agents who might pry out its secrets or subvert its personnel. This gave us a free hand to do almost anything and go almost anywhere. If we went drinking in pubs, it was to keep a look-out for suspicious characters; if we picked up girls, it was to probe their intentions in frequenting the locality. A fellow-officer told me of how, on a pub-crawl, ostensibly a security reconnaissance, he got drunk, and, as was his way when in such a condition, pretended to be a foreigner, using strange gestures and speaking with a broken accent. The next day, badly hung over, he was sent a report of the movements of a suspicious foreigner, and told to check up on them. Tracing the suspect's movements from pub to pub, it slowly dawned on him he was following himself the night before. When he told me of his

adventure, to comfort him I said that it was what we were all doing all
the time – keeping ourselves under close surveillance. This was what
security was all about. In a similar vein, another FS officer, idly
thumbing over the Security List – a top-secret document containing the
names of all subjects who were to be at once apprehended if they tried
to get into or out of the country – found he was in it.

The officer at Headquarters to whom I had to report was Colonel
Ross-Atkinson, an Irishman, I should say in his late fifties, with jet-black
hair, a high colour, a large pointed nose, bandy legs from much sitting
on a horse, and a kind heart. I grew very fond of him. He had been a
regular soldier, and took a severely realistic view of his own and our
side's prospects in the war. Occasionally, he lost his temper with my
nihilistic views, and bawled me out, but something in him, despite his
Burke's Landed Gentry credentials, responded to them. He had arrived
in his own way at somewhat the same conclusion as I had about the future
prospects of the British Empire, and his attitude to Churchill was well
this side of idolatry. I ferried him about a lot in my little FS car, which
saved him from getting one from the pool. He would ask me about
things like homosexuality and Bernard Shaw and Stafford Cripps; in
return, I learnt from him the bivouac attitude to army life that seasoned
regular soldiers like himself had. How you must always, as it were, live
off the land, taking advantage of every opportunity to scrounge and
draw allowances. How the nearer you could get to the top command the
better, because that was the fount of promotion and decorations; the
dispenser of good billets of every kind.

Through driving him around and picking him up, I became familiar
with his ways and circle of friends. His club was, of course, White's; he
consorted with rich men, bankers and the like, and a certain number of
fashionable ladies, somewhat faded and getting on in years. Also with
racing people and old army cronies. When I called for him I used to be
asked in, and had the feeling that I was being shown off; something, I
regret to say, to which I have always been all too ready to respond; in
life, as on the television screen. The high point of our relationship was
reached in the Blitz, when the house of two of his lady friends was bombed
so badly that they had to remove themselves, just as they were, in their
night-dresses, to a nearby flat. The colonel was informed of their dis-
tress by telephone, and we went along together in my car to their
bombed-out house to see what, if anything, could be salvaged. The
fire-engines were there, and air-raid wardens and the police, but, with
our GHQ Home Forces credentials, we were able to make our way

in, and, groping about in the smoke and dust, managed to collect together an approximate wardrobe for the two ladies, including stockings, bras and underwear. Our emergence, bearing these various garments over our arms, obviously surprised and amused the onlookers; the more so as the colonel had thoughtlessly disposed of one of the ladies hats by putting it on his head.

Life at GHQ Home Forces was, if anything, more a matter of coasting along than at Mytchett, where at least I had drills and lectures to attend, buttons to clean, and various fatigues to undergo. The only occasion that Colonel Ross-Atkinson asked me to do anything that presented any serious complexities was quite early on, when he handed me a paper reporting how the car of the C-in-C, General Ironside, was often seen standing outside a house in Holland Park, some of whose occupants were alleged to have dubious political associations. Would I, he said, make an investigation; taking care, for obvious reasons, to be infinitely cautious and tactful. I, of course, realised that this was a potentially explosive assignment; the more so because Ironside was reputed to have had in the past associations with allegedly Fascist organisations. Such investigations as could be made, generally supported the original report, though it looked as though the general's interest in the house was personal rather than political. In any case, I felt vaguely shocked that, in the circumstances, he should be able to find time for his often quite lengthy expeditions to Holland Park. Though all too often irresponsible and self-indulgent myself, I have found it easy to be censorious about others.

What to do? It seemed to me quite futile to put in a report to Colonel Ross-Atkinson which would only embarrass him, and, anyway, was unlikely to result in any action being taken. The mere fact that he entrusted me with such a report suggested to me that he hoped I would do something about it on my own account; like one of those off-the-record confidential disclosures which are made to journalists with a view to their being leaked. I consulted my friend Bobby Barclay – we had been at Mytchett together – and he suggested we should pass on the story to his step-father, Sir Robert Vansittart, at the Foreign Office, to take whatever action he thought fit. After all, Bobby pointed out, it *was* the Commander-in-Chief who was concerned, and we *were* expecting to be invaded by the Nazis at any moment. With much trepidation I agreed, and an appointment was made with Vansittart for the following day. We went along to the Foreign Office together in the early afternoon, sent in our names, and sat on a bench on one of the

landings on the large ornate stairway waiting to be summoned; rather conscious – at least I was – of being stared at by clerks and messengers passing to and fro with files in their hands. It must have been one of the very few places in London where there seemed to be no signs at all of war; everything, as far as I could judge, being just as it had always been.

Vansittart, when we were admitted to his presence, looked very much a part of the place; seasoned and solid himself, with gleaming brass fittings. Having quarrelled with Chamberlain over his Munich policy, he had been made special adviser on foreign affairs, which meant, of course, that no one took his advice, and he exerted no influence at all, while still having a large office and all the appurtenances of dignity and authority. When Churchill replaced Chamberlain, he fully expected to be brought into the Government to reward him for all the services he had performed for the new Prime Minister in his days in the wilderness; but the telephone did not ring for him. How many there were – John Reith among them – thus waiting for a call that never came!

I told Vansittart about the Holland Park affair, explaining to him why I considered it right to put the information in the hands of someone outside GHQ Home Forces who had personal access to the Government. Vansittart made no comment and took no note; just stared across his desk at us, a monocle in one eye; in his blank gaze all the past comprehended – Victorian–Edwardian, limited editions, epigrams fashioned, restaurant table looking out on the Danube and an orchestra playing Chopin and Richard Strauss, boots with trees in them, velvet smoking-jacket. A whole décor – embossed notepaper, 'My dearest love', leisure hours given over to literary pursuits: 'Lady Eleanor's boudoir. "The Count, my lady, left the flowers with a note." Opens, reads . . .' All this in a gaze directed at Bobby and me, not exactly vacant, but – how shall I put it? – stolid, wooden, impassive; like a heathen idol receiving the prayers and oblations of worshippers. On our way back to Hammersmith I felt uneasy, as though I had betrayed a confidence or behaved dishonourably. Bobby, on the other hand, seemed particularly cheerful; the more so the next day, when the evening paper had a banner-headline: IRONSIDE SACKED. I comforted myself by reflecting that it was inconceivable things should have moved so quickly just on the strength of our little scrap of information; that at most it would only have served to give an additional push to a position that was going to topple anyway, and that, however it was brought about, the replacement of Ironside by Sir Alan Brooke, who succeeded him, was on any showing advantageous to the war effort.

I never found out exactly what happened, and when after the war I saw Vansittart occasionally, I preferred not to question him further, I remember that it was a relief to read that Ironside had been made a field-marshal and raised to the peerage. When I went abroad in the war I left behind in a sealed package an account of the whole episode, imagining that it had some historical importance. Journalism conditions one to this magnification of transient occasions; rushing to the stone to get in a new lead – X RESIGNS, Y APPOINTED; bawling it down a telephone after an anguished wait for the connection; furiously tapping it out on a teleprinter, just in time, with luck, to make the edition. All expense of shame in a waste of spirit. So short a time afterwards – who was X, and what did he resign from? Who Y, and what was he appointed to? When he retired, Vansittart lived in a large house at Denham, where Kitty and I were occasionally invited to lunch. On winter days a large wood fire failed to keep the house warm, and the butler distributed rugs. We all sat under them, listening to Vansittart as he reminisced about his diplomatic days, which [also] seemed very far away and long ago.

Apart from thus helping to unseat the Commander-in-Chief, my days at GHQ Home Forces were uneventful. To while away the time I quite often played chess with one of my lance-corporals named Felix Fenston, who was partly Irish and partly Jewish; very quick-witted and eager to please. Once, while we were thus engaged, the telephone rang; it was another lance-corporal telephoning to say that he had caught a deserter, and what should he do with him? Without looking up from our game – which, incidentally, Fenston won, as he almost invariably did – I said: 'Let him go!' The episode got repeated and embroidered upon, and was thought to be rather funny. Recalling it now, it occurs to me that officers have been, perfectly properly, court-martialled for lesser misdemeanours than airily telling an NCO to release a deserter unconditionally. Nor can I claim, in justification, that I acted as I did out of sympathy with deserters, or because I considered the punishment liable to be meted out to them was excessive. It is just that I have always been prone, and am still, to what is called, I seem to remember from a court case I once followed, in psychiatric jargon, *la belle indifférence*. It would be comforting to relate this aberration to a preoccupation with spiritual considerations; to an awareness that, as Augustine puts it in *The City of God*, 'our good (whose end the philosophers jangled about) is nothing but to adhere to Him, and by his intellectual and incorporeal embrace our soul grows great with all virtue and perfection'. Alas, I

fear it is primarily due to a sort of callousness and irresponsibility, more egotistic than other-worldly.

After I left GHQ Home Forces I heard from Fenston – he always addressed me as 'Muggers', which was another unofficerly procedure – from time to time. In one of his letters he told me of how he had been involved in a bad accident when he was riding his motor-cycle, which resulted in his having his leg amputated and being discharged from the army. Then I heard nothing more till after the war, when I got a note asking if I would dine with him one evening. It was from an address in Hill Street, and I vaguely wondered how Fenston came to be living in so select and expensive a neighbourhood, thinking perhaps it might be office premises, or even that he had a caretaker's job. When I went along, however, the mansion was in full swing, with waiters in tail-coats and white gloves on every landing, and pink champagne flowing freely. It seemed that it had been the Duke of Devonshire's residence, which Fenston had recently acquired. Later, when we sat talking, he explained how he had become a millionaire. It was terribly simple, he said, with noticeable irritation, as though this very simplicity was a mean trick, depriving him of the true satisfaction of acquiring riches. There he was in war-time London, with no job, a meagre disability pension, no prospects. All alone. Thus situated, an idea of dazzling, almost ridiculous, simplicity seized him. London was full of bombed-out sites which in the then circumstances had practically no value. If the war was won, they would recover their value anyway, and more; if lost, the question did not arise. In mundane terms, it recalled Pascal's famous wager. Why not, then, somehow raise some money and acquire a site or two? Then use them as collateral to raise more money, and so *ad infinitum*. By the war's end he was, like Gogol's hero in *Dead Souls*, on paper at any rate, a large property-owner. Thereafter, it was easy to become a property-developer and millionaire. By this stage in his recital he was almost shaking with rage to think that he, a sort of genius, should have had to bend to such paltry devices, when he could have done things so much more difficult, requiring so much greater audacity and imagination.

I saw him afterwards from time to time, but at very long intervals. He was always pressing for a meeting, almost embarrassingly. 'Muggers, I wish you'd promise to lunch with me every week', he'd say. I think my presence somehow comforted him; I being a fairly obscure journalist, by no means well off, and so reassuring him that, by comparison with me, he had scored by becoming a millionaire, and acquiring all the hangers-on, male and female, that went therewith. He was always trying to dazzle

me, too, with tales of big-game shooting in Kenya and India, of his financial deals and his country estate. Or producing smart people at his table. This culminated in a dinner party to meet Princess Alexandra and her husband, Angus Ogilvy. Paul Getty, a lugubrious figure reputed to be the richest man in the world, was another guest. After he had seen the Princess off, Fenston did a strange thing; he went pounding down the great stairway he had just come up, jumping ferociously from step to step, until he got to the bottom, sweating and triumphant. With his artificial leg and heavy build, the effect was frightening; he might so easily have fallen and killed himself. I took it to be a demonstration, primarily for my benefit, of his strength and virility despite his disability and millionaire status. Some months later I read in the papers that he had suffered a heart attack; then that he had died. It gave me a pang to think I had only responded to his showing off by my own kind of showing off; not trying to meet him on some other basis – stretching out a hand and receiving a hand.

The Blitz, when it came, gave a sort of focus to our existence at GHQ Home Forces. It started on a bright summer's Sunday afternoon. I was standing on Camden Hill with Andreas Mayor, son of Kitty's cousin, Beatrice Mayor, then serving with the Royal Fusiliers, of whom I became very fond and saw often. He was tall and sallow, with large, dark, molten eyes, full of a gentle, inert melancholy; wonderfully aware of all the subtleties and delights of life and art and literature, but also standing apart; aesthetically rather than spiritually detached. An onlooker by temperament rather than by choice, a true anchorite; but of the library, not the desert. There was a loud hum in the clear sky, and we looked up to see a lot of planes in close formation going by; not realising at first that they were enemy ones. Then came explosions and the sound of ack-ack, and a thick cloud of smoke rising in the East End, where the docks were. 'It has begun,' Andreas said in a quiet, almost complacent, voice.

Thenceforth, the Blitz was a nightly occurrence. I nearly always went out when it was on; often with Andreas, occasionally with Graham Greene. This was not out of bravado, or a wish to be killed; just an instinctive movement towards where the noise was loudest, as people on a seaside beach gather where the throng is greatest. Also, there was something rather wonderful about London in the Blitz, with no street lights, no traffic and no pedestrians to speak of; just an empty, dark city, torn with great explosions, racked with ack-ack fire, lit with lurid flames, acrid smoke, its air full of the dust of fallen buildings. I remember

particularly Regent's Park on a moonlit night, full of the fragrance of the rose gardens; the Nash Terraces, perfectly blacked-out, not a sign of a light anywhere, white stately shapes waiting to be toppled over – as they duly were, crumbling into rubble like melting snow. Andreas and I watched the great fires in the City and Fleet Street from St James's Park. It was a great illumination, a mighty holocaust; the end of everything, surely. Threadneedle Street no more; likewise Cheapside and Moorgate which my father's feet had trodden day by day for forty years. The *Evening Standard*, the *Daily Express* – would they appear again? Even Printing House Square in jeopardy; even at Broadcasting House the suave recital of news interrupted by a muffled sound of an explosion in the building's very bowels. I felt a terrible joy and exaltation at the sight and sound and taste and smell of all this destruction; at the lurid sky, the pall of smoke, the faces of bystanders wildly lit in the flames. Goebbels, in one of his broadcasts, accused us of glorying obscenely in London's demolition. He had a point, but what he failed to understand was that we had destroyed our city already before the *Luftwaffe* delivered their bombs; what was burning was no more than the dry residual shell.

Andreas and I made our way to the Temple on foot, treading over firemen's hoses, and ducking when things fell about us; though he, noticing a fire bomb fall nearby, was liable to murmur in a disappointed voice: 'Oh, it's missed us!' Just as someone, looking out of a window, and seeing the postman pass without a rat-a-tat at the door, murmurs: 'Oh, there's nothing for us!' The Inner Temple was a smouldering ruin, the Round Church largely gone, but we managed to get into the Library, awash with water. The two of us all alone there, the sodden shelves at our disposal, a trolley of books ready loaded for distribution, but never to be distributed. Andreas mourned for the books, tenderly picking up one or two to see whether the damage was reparable, but I was thinking only of the lawyers; red-faced, heavy-jowled, with great beaks of noses, wigs on their heads or carried in boxes, gowns over their arms, their white bibs fluttering in the wind – 'I put it to you . . .', 'Tell My Lord what you were doing . . .' Forensic, otiose, watch-chains reposing on substantial stomachs; their haunts, too, laid low.

The Blitz was a kind of protracted debauch, with the shape of orderly living shattered, all restraints removed, barriers non-existent. It gave one the same feeling a debauch did, of, as it were, floating loose; of having slipped one's moorings. Once, in an access of folly, I drove round and round Piccadilly Circus the wrong way to celebrate the absence of all other traffic. Restaurants were often almost empty; it was possible,

for instance, to dine at the Café Royal – still with marble-topped tables and red-plush seats – when there were no more than a dozen or so other patrons present, the five or six waiters on duty scurrying to and fro as though engaged in a game of musical chairs, and the music about to stop at any moment. From time to time, some shattering explosion nearby made the walls shake and the tables rattle and the windows crumble. Even at the much-boosted Windmill Theatre there would be just a handful of dedicated addicts in the auditorium, gazing balefully at the nudes; rather pinched and ravaged in the footlights' glare, yet still bound by law to keep absolutely still. Almost the only stillness to be found in all London those nights.

I went once with Graham Greene. The spectacle appealed to him for its tattiness and seediness; the guise in which he most likes the Devil's offerings to be presented. He explained how the *cognoscenti* knew just where to sit to get the best view, and how, as the front rows cleared, spectators at the back pressed forward to take their places; wave upon wave, like an attacking army. For expeditions in the Blitz, he made a special act of penitence and other appropriate liturgical preparations in case death came upon him unawares. It made me feel uneasy, and even envious; like travelling in a first-class railway carriage with a first-class ticket-holder when one only has a third-class ticket oneself. I imagined Graham being carried away to paradise, and I left behind in purgatory, or worse. Ever since I have known him, he has seemed to me to possess some special quality of aloofness and detachment from the passions he so concerns himself about in his novels, and, for that matter, in his life. If you come upon him unawares – as I sometimes have, catching a glimpse of him from the top of a bus, or walking in or out of Albany, where we both for a time resided – an expression in his face of isolation from everything and everyone around him, makes it seem almost as though he were blind. One almost expects him to have a white stick, and to need a friendly guiding hand to see him across the road. I once without thinking said of him that he was a saint trying unsuccessfully to be a sinner, and I a sinner trying equally unsuccessfully to be a saint. The remark, which was widely quoted, annoyed him, not so much because it credited him with being a saint (a role for which he has no taste), as because of my pretentions to be a sinner. What sort of sinner are you? he asked scornfully, as though I had claimed some quite undeserved achievement or beatitude.

By day, with my FS section, I explored the previous night's destruction, having somehow persuaded myself that this was one of our duties.

I doubt very much if it really was. The police reports of where the bombs had fallen came to Colonel Ross-Atkinson's office, and we plotted them on a map and checked on them; driving out to remote suburbs where whole rows of frail houses had been obliterated – Crescents and Avenues and Gardens reduced, literally, to handfuls of dust. Just vanishing overnight; their scanty remains, like cremated corpses, scattered to the wind. Jerry-built and Jerry-demolished. Or we would go to the main-line stations to see how they had fared, finding them often deserted and immobilised; great cavernous spaces with no trains, no passengers, no porters, no luggage; silent except for our own echoing footsteps. St Pancras, King's Cross, Euston – somehow, with all the hazards, these massive ungainly structures were surviving, seemingly indestructible. Contrary to the old song, echoed by T. S. Eliot, London Bridge was not yet falling down.

Waking in the night, it seemed as though the Book of Revelations had veritably come to pass. All the sky alight, and rent with furious sounds, the earth itself visibly shaking and groaning; missiles flying through the air, and occasional screams heard, followed by explosions. Then, momentarily, silence, as though for all eternity; actually, for a few seconds only. On one such turbulent evening Andreas took me to a party. So familiar a scene – glass in hand, hum of talk, eyes roving; in this case, mostly *Horizon* folk, like its editor, Cyril Connolly, unquiet in their graves. Nothing seemed changed, except that Stephen Spender, towering like a Snow King above the others, had a fireman's hat in his hand. Someone was playing a piano, the notes competing with the ack-ack din outside – 'Thank you, Natasha, for that beautiful music!' It was, it seemed, a new composition by Benjamin Britten, whose production, Raymond Mortimer said, was the most important event that had happened in the world for some considerable time. This was spoken *sotto voce*, and, at the same time, a little defiantly, as though uniformed men-at-arms like Andreas and me could scarcely be expected to understand; we no doubt supposed that the Battle of Britain, or Churchill's broadcasts, or the Atlantic Charter – some event of that kind – was what really mattered.

Another place Andreas took me to was a basement flat in Bentinck Street, belonging to Lord Rothschild, where Andreas's sister, Tess – who was subsequently to marry Rothschild – was then staying. Above was the office of the *Practitioner*, in whose boardroom we lingered, seated, lordly, on leather chairs, and staring at the magazine's splendidly bound volumes, before venturing below. There, we found another

gathering of displaced intellectuals; but more prosperous, more socially secure and successful, than the *Horizon* ones – John Strachey, J. D. Bernal, Anthony Blunt, Guy Burgess, a whole revolutionary *Who's Who*. It was the only time I ever met Burgess; and he gave me a feeling, such as I have never had from anyone else, of being morally afflicted in some way. His very physical presence was, to me, malodorous and sinister; as though he had some consuming illness – like the galloping consumption whose symptoms I had seen in my father's brothers and cousins, or leprosy as I remembered it in India. The impression fitted in well enough with his subsequent adventures; as did this millionaire's nest altogether, so well set up, providing, among other amenities, special rubber bones to bite on if the stress of the Blitz became too hard to bear. Sheltering so distinguished a company – Cabinet Minister-to-be, honoured Guru of the Extreme Left-to-be, Connoisseur Extraordinary-to-be, and other notabilities, all in a sense grouped round Burgess; Etonian mudlark and sick toast of a sick society, as beloved along Foreign Office corridors, in the quads and the clubs, as in the pubs among the pimps and ponces and street pick-ups, with their high voices and peroxide hair. A true hero of our time, who was to end his days in Moscow; permitted even there, for services rendered, to find the male company he needed. Now gone to Stalin's bosom; hip before hipsters, Rolling before the Stones, acid-head before LSD. There was not so much a conspiracy gathered round him as just decay and dissolution. It was the end of a class, of a way of life; something that would be written about in history books, like Gibbon on Heliogabalus, with wonder and perhaps hilarity, but still tinged with sadness, as all endings are.

It was about this time that I attended, on Colonel Ross-Atkinson's instructions, the trial in camera at the Old Bailey on security charges of an American diplomat, Tyler Kent, and Anna Volkov, a Russian lady whose father, Admiral Volkov, had been the last naval attaché at the Imperial Russian Embassy. When the Revolution happened, the admiral stayed in London, and in due course he and his daughter ran a sort of tea-shop-cum-restaurant in Kensington which for a time enjoyed a certain vogue. There was no really valid reason for my presence at the Old Bailey, but each day I gave Colonel Ross-Atkinson a new thrilling instalment of how things were going, which he greatly appreciated; especially any episodes reflecting on MI5's handling of the case – of which there was no lack. I think at some point he must have been reprimanded for allowing me to attend the trial at all, for quite suddenly he became unusually insistent that any record I made of the proceedings

should be scrupulously destroyed. As I made no record, there was nothing to destroy.

Anna Volkov, as I remember her in the dock, was short, compact, and, though still quite young, already white-haired; Kent, one of those intensely gentlemanly Americans who wear well-cut tailor-made suits, with waistcoat and watch-chain, drink wine instead of high-balls, and easily become furiously indignant. They always strike me as being somehow a little mad. A tour of duty in Moscow had given him a maniacally hostile attitude towards the Soviet regime, and an extra hatred of Roosevelt and his policies, besides fortifying his anti-semitism. Thus, between him and Anna there was much common ground; while her aristocratic origins doubtless gave her an extra glamour in his eyes. Kent, it appeared, had been removing whole suitcases-full of secret documents from the United States Embassy, then presided over by Ambassador Joseph Kennedy, founding-father of the clan. He showed some of them to Anna, who passed on any that seemed of interest, via the Roumanian Embassy, to Lord Haw-Haw (William Joyce) as material for his broadcasts from Berlin. The Italian and German Intelligence Services also got a sight of them. I became quite absorbed in the case, snatching a quick snack at a pub opposite the Old Bailey in order to be back in court in time to miss none of the proceedings. The fact that every now and again the sirens sounded, and one and all – Judge, Learned Counsel, prisoners, witnesses – repaired to underground cellars to await the All Clear, only added to the drama. Outside, such sound and fury; inside, the Judge with his wheezy dispassionateness, doodling or listening with closed eyes to interminable cross-examinations. A strange, remote, barely human figure; glasses on beaked nose, layers of wig and folds of cloth about his withered person, fingers tapping, or scribbling down a word or two.

At one point a whole contingent of internees under Regulation 18b were summoned from the Isle of Man to testify on behalf of the defence that they had no knowledge of the two defendants, or of what they were at. Distraught women in battered fur coats, blonde hair whitening and dishevelled, make-up running; men in tweed jackets to their knees, leather-patched, frayed club ties, suede shoes; Sir Oswald Mosley himself, bearded at this time, his suit crumpled, speaking with the vibrant voice of a wronged man who asked only to be allowed to join his regiment in the battle-line to fight for King and Country. Also, Captain Ramsay, a Scottish Member of Parliament – for Peebles – with a passing resemblance to Neville Chamberlain. A letter of his was read out in

which he referred to 'those two lovely ships' (*Scharnhorst* and *Gneisenau*), and how sad it would be if anything untoward happened to them. This brought a prodding finger from the prosecuting Attorney General, Sir William Jowitt. Was this a way to speak about two enemy warships? With the benighted innocence of the crazed, Ramsay said that when he wrote the letter it still seemed possible that the war, though declared, would never get going; in which case the loss of the ships would have been a pity. It was part of Hitler's weird genius thus to be able to persuade a lost bourgeoisie and their treasonable clerks in attendance, that he intended them no ill. Stalin performed a similar feat with a lost intelligentsia. Ramsay and the others were a woebegone procession indeed, as, one after the other, they held up a Bible and swore to tell the truth, the whole truth and nothing but the truth, while outside their erstwhile heroes and putative allies tried to blow the Old Bailey, along with all the rest of London town, including them, to smithereens.

In the end, Anna Volkov got ten years' penal servitude and Tyler Kent seven. When his sentence had been pronounced, Kent made an indignant protest, pointing out that he had acted throughout as a patriotic American anxious to keep his country out of a ruinous war. This was doubtless genuine enough, and if his illicit disclosure of secret papers had been Leftwards instead of Rightwards directed, he would have found himself, like Daniel Ellsberg, numbered among the contemporary saints, and appeared on post-Christendom's most notable stained-glass window – the cover of *Time* magazine. In such circumstances, too, he would have had many vociferous champions, in the press and the legislatures and the pulpits, to denounce the harsh punishment meted out to him. Even at the court proceedings themselves, despite their being in camera, what had really troubled Kent was slurred over – the exchanges between Roosevelt and Churchill when he was First Lord of the Admiralty, sent via the United States Embassy, and by-passing Chamberlain, the Prime Minister, which conveyed such classified information as the siting of minefields and the clear lanes for Allied shipping; evidently designed, Kent considered, to manœuvre America into becoming a belligerent. He professed to be outraged by so devious and unconstitutional a procedure, which, he contended, entitled him to leak what was happening, even though, as it turned out, he thereby ensured that the Italian Government was made privy to the highly un-neutral relations subsisting between the President and the First Lord, and so was given an extra pretext, when the time came, for declaring war on the Allies. As we know from Ciano's *Diaries*, Mussolini had

made up his mind to declare war anyway, and may be assumed to have decided exactly how and when, on a basis of calculations of his own. It is a favourite illusion that historical events would not have happened but for such and such a disclosure, or might have been prevented by some skilful *démarche* here or *pronunciamento* there. There never need have been a Nazi–Soviet Pact if only someone more important than Strang had gone to Moscow to negotiate with Stalin! Italy never would have joined in the war as a belligerent of sorts if only Tyler Kent and Anna Volkov between them had not let the Duce know that Roosevelt and Churchill were hand-in-glove! Journalists and diplomats, even historians, thrive on such fantasies; I have, in the exercise of my profession, aired many, not one of which had the slightest validity.

The Blitz became a sort of apocalyptic *son et lumière*; a nightly spectacle widely appreciated. When it began, with sirens sounding the alert, everyone scattered – to air-raid shelters if they had one, or to cellars and basements, or to special little nests under tables or stairs; wherever they might hope to have some sense of security, real or illusory. A few, in places like the Dorchester, tucked up in beds arranged in the basement, resplendent in dressing gowns and negligées; many others repaired to the nearest Underground station, where they bedded down on the platforms and along the draughty corridors, apparently oblivious to the roar of the trains, coming and going, and to the passengers passing. Then, surfacing at dawn; a strange sight – grey dishevelled figures carrying blankets, sometimes draped in them, emerging in the pale light from below ground. Like a Brueghel painting of Resurrection Day – predestinated souls rising from their graves. I saw them so on several occasions, when returning myself from hazily dissolute adventures; in that moment of rare lucidity between the end of the night and day's leaden hand on one's shoulder. Long after the Blitz was over, the night-time Underground habitués continued to sleep there, preferring these public beds to their private ones. Finally, they had to be dislodged by force; otherwise, they might be sleeping there still.

I drove about everywhere in the little camouflaged Austin car I had as a Field Security Officer. It gave me great immunity; no one ever asked me who I was, or what I was about. Once, by mistake, I attached myself to a procession of cars which turned out to be a Royal cavalcade, with King George VI leading in his Daimler. I came to just in time to avoid driving into Buckingham Palace. My car and my time at GHQ Home Forces, as it happened, came to an end simultaneously. On the evening of the day that Colonel Ross-Atkinson told me I had been transferred to

5 Corps Headquarters near Salisbury, I imprudently went on a round of night clubs with a fellow-officer. By about our third port-of-call I had lost track of where I was, and even of who I was. My companion at some point disappeared, and after what seemed like a long time I found myself at the wheel of my car trying to go somewhere. As I drove along I was aware that the dawn was breaking, and in its first light I glimpsed vaguely familiar buildings; like Admiralty Arch and the Houses of Parliament, some of which recurred as I proceeded on my way, still no nearer to my elusive destination. My progress was abruptly terminated when I ran into a lamp-post on a traffic island at Blackfriars Bridge. The shock brought me sufficiently to my senses to make me aware that I was in no condition to account for myself. Already the traffic over the bridge was beginning. I managed to extricate myself from the car, and, shaking some of the glass out of my hair, hailed a passing cab which delivered me at my billet in Hammersmith. There I had a bath and went to bed. I have Fenston to thank for never hearing anything further about the wrecked car. When its discovery was reported by the police to our FS office, Fenston took the call, and in a truly masterful way managed so to arrange matters that the wrecked machine was removed to a REME station, where it disappeared without trace forever. It has to be admitted that such debauches have occurred from time to time in my life. I look back on them now with distaste rather than remorse.

Five Corps HQ was situated in Longford Castle, the seat of the Earl of Radnor, a mile or so from Salisbury; a large mansion partitioned off into offices for the various branches of the Headquarters. I was given a perch in one of these under the heading I(b), or Security Intelligence. After St Paul's School, the scene was familiar enough; repeated in numerous other castles and mansions throughout the West country, including the seat of the Earl of Pembroke at nearby Wilton, hallowed in my eyes because Shakespeare was supposed to have played Adam in a production of *As You Like It* in the grounds. The war familiarised us with these stately homes, which, when it was over, were to become places of pilgrimage for Welfare State citizens and destinations for motorists with nowhere to go. It was almost like getting into Debrett.

On my arrival at Longford Castle I noticed displayed about the place curious notices asking: 'Are you 100% Full of Binge?' They represented, as it turned out, my first acquaintance with General Montgomery, or Monty as he was even then universally known, who had devised them, being at that time GOC 5 Corps. The use – or misuse – of the word

'binge' was highly characteristic. Even this initial whiff of his presence gave me strongly the feeling that he was the man of the hour. It is something at once detectable, to those accustomed to picking up the scent; an aptness of a particular ego or temperament for dealing with a particular set of circumstances. With his schoolboy mind and ebullience, his wierd idiom, his exhibitionism and love of dressing with punctilious informality, his flair for publicity and eye on the main chance, Monty seemed just right for the war we were engaged in. After one of our Corps exercises (which consisted, for me, in wandering about looking hopelessly for map references I never could find), we would all be assembled in the largest cinema in Bournemouth. Then, not exactly to the roll of drums, but with a spotlight playing upon him, Monty would appear on stage, pointer in hand; a tiny figure, ferret-faced, a huge map displayed behind him over which his shadow flitted. In a curious intonation, more schoolmasterish than military, with a touch of evangelical clergyman thrown in, he would go over the exercise, making jokes as he went along; obsequiously laughed at by the senior officers in the front rows, arousing ribald cries from the NCO's at the back, and in the middle regions, where the majors and the captains sat, myself among them, little response. It was in its way a brilliant performance, delivered without a note, ad-libbed throughout. When I became a television practitioner, I recalled the scene, realising that Monty was an instinctive camera-soldier; as was also Rommel, his opposite number. The Western Desert provided an ideal location up and down which the two of them could chase one another; like those much-trodden-over stretches of sand and battered rocks just outside Los Angeles where a thousand Westerns have been shot.

After the war, when I was working on the *Daily Telegraph*, I got to know Monty quite well through P. J. Grigg, the two having been closely associated when Grigg was Secretary of State for War. Despite his obvious faults – the showing off, the ungenerous attitude to fellow-generals like Eisenhower and Alexander – there was something engaging and very endearing about him. I don't understand warfare well enough to know if, in Liddell Hart terms, he must be considered a great general or not, but he certainly won victories – which is, after all, the essential qualification, as Lincoln remarked when someone complained to him about Grant's drunkenness. His way of looking at things was so entirely his own, even at times so comical, that his company could be highly enjoyable. There was a clown inside him struggling to be heard; his very overweening egotism being part of the act. I visited him once or

twice at his Hampshire Mill, where he lives with his old Command Caravan to hand, just as it was, maps and all, when he directed operations from it in the Western Desert; as well as all his different trophies – the freedoms of cities, the honorary degrees, the portraits. One of these was by none other than General Eisenhower – no Valesquez, certainly, but recognisable. Such treasures displayed, like the rows and rows of ribbons on his army tunic; gaudy cankers of a troubled world.

Once, when I was on the point of leaving for Singapore to do some articles on the Communist insurrection in Malaya, he summoned me to Paris for a briefing, which, as a matter of fact, proved most useful. There was no time to pack a bag; I just rushed to the airport, caught a plane, and at Orly found a car waiting to take me out to Fontainebleau, where Monty had a chateau provided for him as NATO Deputy-Supreme Allied Commander, Europe. When I arrived at the chateau he was warming in front of a large open fire a pair of flannel pyjamas that he proposed to lend me. It was long past his bedtime, I knew, which made the scene all the more touching. Also, he had a drink ready, though, of course, he never took one himself. At once we began to talk about Malaya. Monty had a report on the situation there by the then Colonial Secretary, Oliver Lyttelton, not yet published, which he gave me to read when I went to bed. There must, I knew, be something particular on his mind, and it soon became clear that he was considering whether to go to Malaya himself and deal faithfully with the Communist guerrillas. I knew from Grigg that he had long entertained the fantasy of being called upon in the post-war years to become England's Man of Destiny – the politicians all shown up as having no capacity for real leadership, no master-plan. Then a cry going up: Monty! He saved us in the war, leading a victorious army from El Alamein to Berlin. Let Monty now take over on the home front, with equally beneficial results. Would Malaya, perhaps, prove a stepping-stone to the realisation of this dream? That's what was in his mind.

The dream never was going to be realised, of course; his glory had faded, along with the circumstances which brought it to pass. As phantom Deputy-Supremo of a phantom army, his strangely concocted phraseology – knocking them for six, a dog's breakfast; 'Over the Rhine, then, let us go, and good hunting to you all on the other side', no longer pulled. Nor did his black beret with its two badges, and other sartorial eccentricities. They were an old comedian's useless props. Better stay where he was in his chateau, with a plane to carry him to and from his Mill, along with bottles of wine and cheeses to regale his guests. Over

the Channel, then, let us go. . . . In the event, it was Templer who went to Malaya. At breakfast the next morning a youthful ADC provided a résumé of the news, which he did, blushing and stuttering, like a shy sixth form boy reading the lessons in chapel. Before I left to catch my plane to London, Monty took me for a stroll, delighted when anyone seemed to recognise him – 'Vive Montgomery!'

I was on leave with Kitty and the children at Whatlington in June 1941, when Hitler invaded the USSR, and we listened together to Churchill's speech announcing that all possible aid would be provided to the Soviet Government. The following December, in the officers' mess at 5 Corps, I heard a BBC announcer report that the Japanese had attacked Pearl Harbor, automatically bringing the United States into the war. 'That settles it; we're bound to win now,' an officer remarked complacently. Each of these occasions gave me a leaden feeling of apprehension rather than of jubilation; history, as it seemed to me, was a ferocious current inexorably bearing us on to rapids whose roar could already be heard. I thought of the men in the Kremlin as I remembered them; the grey, hard faces grouped around Stalin, the greyest and hardest of all. They were now the liberators, bearing aloft the banner of freedom and justice and enlightenment. Even so, I cannot claim to have foreseen the wilder ironies – the Nuremburg judges, a Soviet one among them, solemnly condemning the Germans for partitioning Poland and making use of forced labour; that ribald trio, Churchill, his fur hat awry, the dying Roosevelt in his cloak, Stalin inscrutable behind his moustache and slit eyes, settling between them, as they supposed, the world's future; Vyshinsky's venomous rhetoric translated from the Moscow court-room, where it was directed against old Bolshevik colleagues, to the vapid deliberations of the UN about national sovereignty and the right of self-determination. All this lay ahead, but still I envisaged already the awful perversion of words and meanings that would soon be upon us. On sleepless nights read, and even wrote, in my mind, the leaders in the *Guardian* and *The Times* about our great ally with whom we looked forward to collaborating in making a just, free, and above all peaceful, world in the years to come. Heard the speeches at banquets; Churchillian rhetoric about his old comrade-in-arms, Marshal Stalin, whose word was as good as his bond; generals rising in their places, all a-glitter with medals, to toast the feats of the great Red Army in defending European civilisation and its free institutions against the barbarian Nazi hordes. It was an unappetising but inescapable prospect.

At 5 Corps I spent my time going from one office to another, turning over papers, initialling them, and speeding them on their way. Or getting on my motor-cycle and liaising with other headquarters – at Wilton, or Sherbone, or Blandford, or as far away as Taunton. Roaring across Salisbury Plain, and, on arrival, like a dispatch-rider with important papers to deliver, jumping off my machine; a little dazed from the wind and the sun, goggles removed. Then, opening the door of a Nissen hut, standing at attention, a tremendous salute, to find confronting me the identical scene I had left behind – officers seated at trestle-tables, ordnance maps covered with talcum and marked with coloured crayons, orderlies coming and going, antique typewriters tapping. How are things? Later, off to the mess for a drink; some idle chatter about anything that might be happening – promotions, transfers, gossip, even the war. In the evening light, roaring back across Salisbury Plain on the return journey; remembering Hazlitt lying on his back there, thinking how happy his life had been, despite *Libor Amoris* and other troubles. Mine, too, inexpressibly happy; even then, battle-dressed, on an army motor-cycle, the wind in my face, ostensibly engaged in a war. Back at 5 Corps, dutifully full of Monty's binge, I was in time to bath, change, and appear in the mess for dinner. Another day had passed.

Other officers at the Headquarters, including Intelligence officers like myself, were obviously busy and anxious; hurrying back to their offices when meals ended, impatient at being held in casual talk. From Monty downwards, there was a sense of urgency; of things to do and not enough time to get them done. What were they all at? I often wondered, but never properly discovered. There were, of course, a few specific duties. For instance, each week – a particular notion of Monty's – all the officers at the Headquarters were required to go on a run along a carefully marked-out course, with the Chaplain at the end to take our names to make sure there were no defaulters. Presumably, Monty chose the Chaplain for this task as being a man of integrity, with little to occupy his time. One or two of us found the run too strenuous for our years and training, and managed to join the runners at a later stage in the course, thereby arriving in relatively good shape at the finishing-post. It was remarkable to see some of the senior officers, too conscientious to adopt any such deception, puffing and blowing as though about to expire, all with a view to pleasing Monty, who occasionally joined the Chaplain to watch late arrivals.

Another task that fell to the Intelligence Branch, in which I participated, was to make a dummy of a German soldier with all the appropriate

badges and insignia, and stand him outside the mess so that officers
coming and going could familiarise themselves with him. Having set him
up more or less correctly, I felt an irresistible impulse to make him
wounded and bloody; with his arm in a home-made sling, and a blood-
stained bandage round his head. Then, warming to the work, I put him
on a crutch, and finally amputated one of his legs. It was another of the
occasions when I did something which caused almost universal offence,
without any deliberate intention, or even awareness, of so doing. It
culminated in the BGS, Gerald Templer, shouting at me furiously:
'Take that horrible thing away', which I duly did. There was no high-
minded intention, let me add, to express a loathing of war by drawing
my fellow-officers' attention dramatically to what it signified; Templer
and the others, in any case, knew much better than I what war was like.
Doubtless, this was why they were so annoyed.

Templer was a dashing figure. He wore superbly polished boots, and
a great-coat which almost swept the ground; had a sallow, lean face,
with a moustache so thin as to be barely perceptible, and spoke in sharp,
clipped words. Once, for no apparent reason, he showed me a letter he
had received from Claire Luce, whom he had met in the early part of the
war, when stationed in France with the BEF. I saw him as a character
in *Le Rouge et le Noir* dedicated to the profession of arms, a d'Artagnan
(my old hero) of the twentieth century, and found him correspond-
ingly attractive. Though I received much kindness at his hands, he was
unmistakably relieved when, in due course, I disappeared into the limbo
of MI6, the wartime version of the Secret Service. Among his fellow-
officers after dinner in the mess he would sometimes engage in the
strange horse-play which often characterised these gatherings. I found it
a curious spectacle – grizzled veterans who had served in distant parts of
the Empire, tanned and scarred and covered with medals and decora-
tions, now leaping and prancing about like undergraduates on Boat-race
Night. Belabouring one another with rolls of paper: on one occasion,
aiming potatoes through a cardboard partition, on the other side of
which, all unknown to them, a number of valuable pictures had been
stowed away, through one of which – a Romney – a potato passed,
leaving a gash in the bottom of the canvas. This, as may be imagined,
caused quite a rumpus, and an expert had to be fetched from London at
considerable expense to repair the damage.

While I was at 5 Corps I did an attachment with a Motor Recon-
naissance unit at Hinton St Mary nearby. They were nearly all young,
eager officers, and I greatly enjoyed my time with them. The house

where the unit was stationed belonged to G. H. L. Fox Pitt-Rivers who had been interned under Regulation 18b for his pro-Hitler attitudes, and in his library there was an elegantly bound presentation copy of *Mein Kampf*, which was occasionally taken out and looked at, almost reverentially; then put back, without ever being damaged or mutilated. I found this bizarre, but rather endearing. The house was in excellent condition, Pitt-Rivers being, as I gathered, very rich. Despite wartime stringencies, the extensive grounds were all maintained, and there was a neat little theatre which Pitt-Rivers had constructed for his wife, an actress. Someone told me that she used as her stage-name, Mary Hinton, after the place, and then I remembered with a pang that she had taken the part of one of the frustrated young women in my play, *Three Flats*, at its Stage Society production at the Prince of Wales Theatre in 1931.

When I got back to 5 Corps I wrote to the commanding officer at Hinton St Mary to say how happy I'd been there, and to ask if there was a chance of my joining the unit, which, of course, there wasn't. It was yet another of my fatuous endeavours to become a belligerent soldier. Soon after this futile *démarche*, I got a mysterious communication to the effect that I was to present myself at an address in London with a view to being considered for special Intelligence duties. The summons was a consequence of a plot long before hatched with Graham Greene, whose sister, Liza, worked for someone important in the Secret Service. We hoped that she would recommend us both to her boss as suitable overseas representatives, and be able to pull the requisite strings to get us accepted. I had almost forgotten we ever entertained such a plan when the summons came. When I reported the matter to Templer, he said he envied me, which might even have been true. Though he was so dyed-in-the-wool a regimental soldier, I think he had a secret taste for the more nefarious aspects of warfare. I went to London for my interview, which turned out to be with a writer of thrillers named Williams, whom I met at his club, the Savage; a man with bushy eyebrows, and, I seem to remember, like his best-known character, a club foot. His brother, Douglas Williams, was a colleague of mine on the *Daily Telegraph*. Writers of thrillers tend to gravitate to the Secret Service as surely as the mentally unstable become psychiatrists, or the impotent pornographers. Williams spoke darkly of the dangers involved in a service in which, by the nature of the case, a blown agent had to be discarded. After a year as IO at a corps headquarters, I said, this held no terrors for me. To my great satisfaction, shortly afterwards I heard that I had been accepted.

I might have said of my duties at 5 Corps, as Gibbon did of his as one
of the Lords Commissioners of Trade, that they were not intolerably
severe, but, unlike him, I was temperamentally incapable of enjoying
the many days and weeks of repose that, as he mentions so complacently,
they permitted. Thus, it was an enormous relief to be departing. What
remained with me from the experience was the delight of travelling freely
and pointlessly about one of the most beautiful parts of England, and
visiting its ancient towns – Sherborne, Wincanton, Dorchester, Yeovil,
Shaftesbury – all, in the war-time absence of traffic, tranquil and alluring.
I particularly appreciated the different views of Salisbury Cathedral
from whichever direction one approached the town, and, in moments of
distress, have turned to the memory of its grey steeple reaching so
exquisitely into the sky, never in vain. As, for instance, on an American
lecture-tour, at some cinema on a week-day morning in the fastnesses of
Oregon or North Dakota; several hundred chattering, perfumed, blue-
rinsed ladies assembled before me. Or in Los Angeles, facing row upon
row of tousled UCLA students, with only breasts or whiskers to
signify their sex, and that sometimes indeterminately. On such grievous
occasions, the cathedral and its steeple have delivered me from despair.

During most of my stay at 5 Corps I lodged with a number of other
officers in an agreeable house, The Moat, about half way between Long-
ford Castle and Salisbury. My room-mate, Victor Stiebel, our camou-
flage officer, was in private life an eminent dressmaker. His profession,
as he explained to me, provided a natural training in camouflage;
especially in coping with some of his more eminent clients. Sharing a
room with him brought great advantages in the way of extra comforts.
He managed, for instance, to ensure that in cold weather we always had
a bright fire, and that our morning tea came punctually; and he even,
on occasion, had a hot-water bottle put in his bed. His own appearance
was magnificent – splendid pale riding breeches and top-boots that
shone even more brightly than Templer's. He and the BGS, inciden-
tally, were on excellent terms, and used to swop stories about Noel
Coward. I began by regarding Stiebel as a somewhat ridiculous figure,
but through our companionship and the long talks we had, I came to
realise that he was a person of unusual sensitivity and perceptiveness;
particularly apparent when he spoke about South Africa, where he had
spent his childhood. In his later years he developed some sort of para-
lytic complaint, which he bore with great fortitude.

Our association at 5 Corps was brought to an end when the APM, a
Northern Irishman named McNally, who was also Mess President, had

me turned out of the house. It was my talk, he said, which had caused the trouble; there had been complaints. When I pressed him to tell me what particular things I'd said which were considered offensive, he refused to be drawn; it wasn't anything specific, he went on, just how I talked, the whole tenor. People couldn't stand it. I ought, I suppose, to have been annoyed, and even perhaps to have taken the matter to the Corps Commander; made an issue of it, demanded an explanation. But I knew I was leaving soon, and it didn't seem worth while. In any case, McNally looked so abashed and troubled himself that I felt quite sorry for him. He had drawn me aside to talk under the stairs where no one would see us or overhear us. I have never found any difficulty in understanding how irritating I can be to other people; perhaps because I so often irritate myself. So I affected to be magnanimous; in police terms – I imagine that he belonged to the Royal Ulster Constabulary – I agreed to go quietly, and moved over to the Castle for my short remaining time. That was the end of 5 Corps for me. I ran into them once or twice in Italy afterwards, recognising the Viking ship which was the Corps sign; but never with any particular cordiality.

8 *On Secret Service*

But vain the Sword and vain the Bow,
They never can work War's overthrow.
— Blake

Only when a man has become so unhappy, or has grasped the misery
of this existence so profoundly that he can truly say, 'For me life is
worthless;' only then can life have worth in the highest degree.
— Kierkegaard

MY INSTRUCTIONS were to present myself at an office in Broadway,
opposite St James's underground station, which I duly did. As a reader
of *Ashenden* I was naturally excited at the prospect of entering the
portals of the world-famous British Secret Service (or SIS as it was
usually called), though I assumed that at this first preliminary encounter
I should not be admitted to the actual headquarters, but only to some
shadow set-up, or façade, used to try out aspirants before definitely
taking them on. I may add that everyone I saw and everything that
happened seemed to support such an assumption. It was only later that
I came to realise I had been in contact, not with a hurriedly improvised
dummy, but the real thing. While I was awaiting my own clearance at
the main entrance, I was able to observe the people coming and going.
A good proportion of them were in the services, with the Navy pre-
ponderating. I only saw one, as I thought, false beard – a luxuriant
tangled growth, whose wearer turned out, on closer acquaintance, to be
a former trade-unionist and Marxist, allegedly from the boiler-makers'
union. He was responsible for providing expert guidance in industrial
matters; and his beard, he assured me, was genuine, though he admitted
that he had allowed it to proliferate since joining SIS, as he had also
his use of strong language, and tendency to bang the table to emphasise
a point. The last glimpse I had of him was towards the end of the war,

in the Athenaeum Club dining-room, where he was holding forth noisily to some abashed-looking Americans, including a three-star general.

My contact, to whose office I was led, turned out to be an agreeable man named Leslie Nicholson, who had been, I learnt afterwards, a Secret Service agent himself in Riga. His manner was gentle, amiable and helpful; more in the style of a Bertie Wooster, I decided, than of a spy-master as popularly conceived. He told me that various stations were being opened up in Africa, and that the intention was to send Graham Greene to Freetown and me to Lourenço Marques in Mozambique. I said that nothing could suit me better, implying that Lourenço Marques was a place I had always been interested in and wanted to visit, though in point of fact I had never before heard of it, and had no idea where it was. My ready acquiescence, I think, pleased Nicholson, who might otherwise have had to look up where Lourenço Marques was himself, and answer questions about its climatic conditions, port facilities, population, and so on. As it was, we could agree on my departure there without either of us being unduly troubled about the whys and wherefores. When, a few days later, we dined together at Boodles, Nicholson's club, we talked, as I recall, about everything under the sun except Mozambique. I did, in point of fact, read up the entry in the *Encyclopaedia Britannica* on Mozambique, and learnt – it is the solitary fact remaining with me – that Gladstone could have bought it off the Portuguese for a million pounds, but decided the price was too high. His parsimony was ill-judged; it would have been a good buy, Delagoa Bay providing an excellent harbour, which Durban notably lacks.

My first task, as now an MI6 officer, was to get myself, notionally, transformed into a civilian. For this purpose I was handed a passport stamped to indicate that I had lately landed in the UK, and giving my address as St Ermin's Hotel. To form some idea of my place of residence I dropped in there for a drink, finding the lounge dim and quiet, suggestive of conferences to promote world governments, family planning, or the practice of eurythmics. My instructions were to go with my passport to Caxton Hall, and apply for a civilian identity card, explaining, if asked why I had not got one, that I had recently arrived at Liverpool from extensive travels abroad, and was expecting to leave the UK again at any moment for further travels. I was also instructed to memorise the number in the left-hand top corner of the form of application for an identity card, and to apply for an emergency ration card. Waiting my turn in the queue, I was seized with anxiety. Supposing they asked me the name of the ship on which I had arrived at Liverpool,

what should I say? Or questioned me about the places I had been to abroad, and how long I had stayed in them? Or asked for details of my projected departure and subsequent travels. My story, as it seemed to me, was full of obvious pitfalls. And how should I ever memorise that number in the left-hand top corner when I find it impossible to remember the registration number of a car, even when I have been driving about in it for years? By the time my turn came, I was in a state of nerves which must have seemed highly suspicious in the light of my threadbare story, tremulously recounted. To my great relief, no questions were asked, the man behind the *guichet* positively winking as he handed me my identity card and emergency ration book. As for the number I was supposed to memorise – I forgot all about it, and no one ever asked me for it.

It might well be wondered – as, indeed, I wondered at the time myself – what was the point of this exercise in mystery when it would have been as easy to procure an identity card and emergency ration card for me as it had been to procure a passport. To ask such a question is to fail to understand the whole character of secret Intelligence, one of whose basic precepts is that nothing should ever be done simply if there are devious ways of doing it. With old hands it becomes second nature, for instance, to communicate in code, and to use an accommodation address, for perfectly innocuous communications; to prefer a cache in a potting-shed to a normal letter-box, and a diplomatic bag to a suitcase for carrying blameless personal effects. Kim Philby's American wife, until she got used to it, and came to regard it as a harmless eccentricity, was astonished when he sent her loving messages on tiny fragments of tissue paper, which, as he explained, could comfortably be swallowed if this should be required in the interest of security. As it happened, the address of the Broadway office and the names of most of its leading occupants had been given out on the German radio quite early on in the war following an incident when two SIS representatives at The Hague fell into enemy hands. This made no difference to security arrangements; the Chief, at the time Sir Stuart Menzies, was still known as 'C' even in the internal telephone directory, and all other blown symbols and aliases were scrupulously maintained. Again, in coded messages, countries had always to be referred to by symbols – Germany, for instance, was 'Twelve-land'. The practice was scrupulously observed throughout the war even though, on one festive occasion at an Istanbul hotel, when the orchestra played the German national anthem, the staff of the German embassy stood to attention and sang as one man: '*Zwölfte-land, Zwölfte-land, uber alles!*' Outside 'C' 's office a blue light

shone, like a dispensary or a police-station; the sense of secrecy was so great that, walking by it, one instinctively tiptoed. Secrecy is as essential to Intelligence as vestments and incense to a Mass, or darkness to a Spiritualist seance, and must at all costs be maintained, quite irrespective of whether or not it serves any purpose.

The two captured Secret Service men at The Hague – both slightly parodying what they purported to be; with monocle, trimmed grey moustache, club tie, touch of the Raj, whence, in fact they came – had imagined themselves to be in touch with a group of dissident Germans, including a general, who were anxious to get rid of Hitler and call off the war in return for an honourable peace. What excitement in Broadway as the messages from The Hague came in! Passed Most Secretly from hand to hand, until they reached the Prime Minister, Neville Chamberlain himself, and his Foreign Secretary, Lord Halifax. Full approval was given to keep the contact going; finally, for a meeting face to face at Venlo, a drab little place on the Dutch–German border. There, alas, it turned out that the so prized contact was not with a dissident general at all, but with the Gestapo; and one more dream that the doom which had come upon us could be averted – the last Munich – blew up in the faces of the dreamers. One of the captured men, Payne Best, was in custody for a time with Dietrich Bonhoeffer, and went with him on the last journey, in April 1945, to the East German village of Schonberg, participating on a bright Sunday morning in the service Bonhoeffer conducted there, which concluded with the singing of *Eine Feste Burg ist unser Gott*. Almost immediately afterwards, Bonhoeffer was taken away to be executed. Before leaving, he entrusted Best with a message for Dr Bell, the Bishop of Chichester, to tell him that the 'victory of our universal brotherhood, rising above all national interests, is certain'. Thus, for Best, from the total fantasy of Venlo to the total reality of Schonberg; from darkness to light – the full circle.

Becoming a civilian again, by means that struck me as grotesquely devious, after my so strenuous efforts to be a soldier; discarding my uniform when I had first put it on with such a sense of drama, was like washing off the make-up for the last time, turning in props and costume, when a play's run is ended. My MI6 indoctrination comprised visiting its various branches and affiliates. First, Section Five, responsible for counter-espionage abroad, under whose auspices I should largely be operating; located at that time at St Albans. It was here that I came across Kim Philby; not, as he recalled, for the first time. We had met before, when I was working on the *Evening Standard*, at the office of the

Review of Reviews, a magazine started by W. T. Stead, and subsequently reborn in De Witt Wallace's *Reader's Digest*; a golden Phoenix indeed. The then editor, Wilfrid Hindle, introduced me to Philby; a dark shy young man just down from Cambridge, and, as Hindle whispered, son of the well-known Arabist, St John Philby. Even on this brief encounter I noticed his stutter, which was liable to become truly agonising, his lips moving convulsively and his hands clawing the air as he tried to get words out. It was more like some kind of a fit than just a speech impediment. Shortly afterwards, the *Review of Reviews* finally collapsed, and Hindle, as I heard, went into the Foreign Office, which of course meant into SIS. Perhaps he was already in it when he tried, from a journalistic point of view very unconvincingly, to make a go of the *Review of Reviews*, and either recruited Philby or had him planted on him. Since Philby, according to his own account, had by this time started working for Soviet Intelligence, this would have meant that his career as a double-agent had already begun when I first met him.

Philby's was undoubtedly the dominating presence at St Albans. Felix Cowgill, the head of Section Five, a kindly, conscientious, nervous man, by comparison made only a dim impression. He had the sallow face and withdrawn tired air that came of long years of service in India – in his case, with the police. Quite a number of the senior personnel in MI5 and MI6 in the days of the Raj were similarly drawn from retired members of the equivalent Indian services, which provided, as it was considered, valuable experience in dealing with matters like espionage and subversion, which arose only rarely and exotically at home; men of the kind, incidentally, under whom Philby's namesake, Kipling's Kim, worked – and against the Russians. Philby, on the other hand, gave an impression of great energy and determination, which in some mysterious way his stutter only seemed to enhance. After his defection to Moscow many of those who had known him spoke of his irresistible charm and magnetism. The prevailing impression I had was of a kind of boyishness, even naïveté. As I think of him now, in Moscow, in what must be rather melancholy circumstances, no doubt turning to the vodka bottle for solace; studying cricket scores in old copies of *The Times*, managing to get supplies of Players cigarettes sent over from London, and listening clandestinely, whenever possible, to the Overseas Service at the BBC, I see him rather as a boy-scout who lost his way than as the cool, calculating player of a long-drawn-out traitor's role, which, I am sure, is how he would like to see himself.

In the office he habitually wore an old army officer's tunic of his

father's in the 1914–18 war; an indication, I assumed, of how much he would have wished to be a combatant soldier, this being precluded, presumably, because of his stutter. Also, of his undoubted filial admiration for his father, at that time interned in the Isle of Man under Regulation 18b, along with some of the weird figures I had seen at the Tyler Kent–Anna Volkov trial. Philby senior's incarceration resulted from some, as it turned out, ill-considered advice he gave to his friend King Ibn Saud of Arabia to keep out of the war, which, he insisted, Hitler was bound to win. Had Philby succeeded in becoming a combatant soldier, he would almost certainly have got himself killed; the violence one sensed in his temperament would have found full expression in actual fighting and killing. As it was, he had to exercise this side of his nature through the often infantile plots and stratagems his Section Five work involved, as well as by his ultimate stupendous double-cross. In a letter I had from Ben Gurion after I had recorded a television interview with him at the kibbutz where he was living in retirement near Beersheba, he remarked of Philby: 'I knew his father; he was not a nice man. The father became a Moslem, so why should not the son become a Communist?' It summed the situation up neatly and succinctly, I thought.

Philby was not a person who, at the time, particularly interested me; but inevitably, when he became notorious and much written about, I found myself looking back meticulously on early impressions, refurbishing dim memories and resurrecting lost ones. The legend that emerged about him was of a patrician charmer who received advancement, and escaped retribution, because he had been to the right school and spoke with the right accent. A sort of espionage Raffles; a Bond in reverse, whose brilliance and audacity made him, at once, the Secret Service's favourite son and the master-spy of the age. As far as his accent was concerned, it was totally muffled by that appalling stutter; he might have been speaking broad cockney, Glaswegian Scottish or stage Yorkshire, but no one would ever have have known, so strangled and malformed were the words that finally emerged from his tormented mouth. His tastes, habits and attire might, I suppose, be regarded as characteristic of the wilder reaches of the contemporary public school product, though the drinking, on any showing, was excessive and indiscriminate. His friends and cronies, in so far as I met them, were far from being, in the conventional sense, upper-class, but rather oddities; often disreputable, like Burgess, about whom Philby always spoke in adulatory terms. There was, too, a Jewish antique-dealer who may have been as erudite and fascinating as Philby implied, but who by no stretch

of the imagination could be considered as figuring in the old-boy network that was supposed to have operated so faithfully on his behalf. I should have said myself that he was as little in the style of a Steerforth of our time as is Chairman Mao or Germaine Greer.

Since Philby's defection became public, I have often tried to work out in my mind what were its origins. His own *Apologia Pro Defecto Suo* tells us less than nothing; in any case, emanating, as it did, from Moscow, and therefore requiring the Kremlin's imprimatur, it cannot but be as worthless as any similar recantation at the time of the Inquisition. Conversations with him, as far as I remember them, provide no clue. He rarely spoke about politics, though one assumed he took the vaguely Leftish position fashionable among the bourgeois intelligentsia of his generation. Far stronger in him than anything of this kind, as it seemed to me, was his romantic veneration for buccaneers and buccaneering, whatever the ideological basis – if any – might be. Boozers, womanisers, violence in all its manifestations, recklessness however directed, he found irresistible. Hence his, and many others', otherwise unaccountable love for Burgess, and tolerance of his preposterous and unlovely ways. On this showing, he would have been more at home among Nazi bully-boys than the pedantic terrorists of the USSR. He actually said to me once that Goebbels was someone he felt he could have worked with. At the time of his defection a group photograph in which he appeared was published; taken at a dinner given by one of those societies which existed in the thirties to promote Anglo-German fellowship – the Nazi equivalent of organisations like the Society for Promoting Cultural Relations with the USSR.

Philby at this dinner, we have been told, was building up his cover. But was he? I think it far more likely that he attended it as a genuine member. His admiration, if not veneration, for his father would have pointed in this direction. I have always myself believed that he joined up with the Soviet *apparat* at a much later date; when it was clear that the USSR was to be in the victor's camp. In other words, he and the other gilt-edged defectors, actual and potential, were more toadies than rebels; aware that a new giant had arisen in the world with whom they wished to make their number in good time. Another contingent was at the same time moving westwards across the Atlantic to shelter under America's wing. None of them had much regard for the displaced giant, our poor old Britannia, who had come staggering into the ring for one more round, mouthing old rhetoric, wearing old braid, flaunting old medals, waving old banners. Burgess at least had the honesty to admit

that it was this very feebleness which induced him to offer his allegiance elsewhere. According to his friend Goronwy Rees, his rage, for instance, when the British Raj was abjectly wound up, knew no bounds. In any case, had Philby been a convinced Marxist or sentimental friend of the Soviet Union rather than just Old Kim looking for a better 'ole, he would, we may be sure, long ago have – as Mrs Webb would have put it – disappeared, along with Spanish Civil War veterans and other revolutionary heroes who made the mistake of returning to the Soviet Fatherland in Stalinist times.

My instructions at St Albans were to familiarise myself with the working of Section Five, and generally – a favourite expression at that time – put myself in the picture. This involved going from room to room and from desk to desk, and listening to particular officers explaining what they were at; whether directing and supervising the operations of agents in the field, devising and planting deception material, or co-operating with other counter-Intelligence agencies connected with the various Allied governments-in-exile like the Poles and the Czechs, or with the French, whether Pétainist, Gaullist or nondescript. They had obviously had occasion to do this explaining many times before, and had developed a standard dissertation; in the case of the service personnel, especially the military, delivered to a regular rhythm that runs right through the forces, from sergeant-instructors explaining the working of an internal combustion engine, to chiefs-of-staff respectfully putting a Secretary of State or Prime Minister into the picture of some impending offensive. The civilians were different; more like advertising executives (which some of them, in fact, were); persuasive and plausible in expounding a carefully prepared sales campaign with the aid of graphs and tables and coloured diagrams. My old facility for seeming to listen attentively without hearing anything, again held me in good stead. Though my thoughts were usually far away, I still managed to ask a question or two, betokening interest and attention, though, at the end of it all, I was little nearer putting myself in the picture, or even knowing what the picture was supposed to be.

There was also a fair amount of paper to look at, the prize exhibit here being the yield of cracked enemy ciphers; especially, in my case, material relating to Mozambique, which, I must say, held my rapt attention. These messages from enemy sources had the rarity value of Dead Sea Scrolls, and had to be handled accordingly. Their circulation was rigorously restricted; very few hands touched them or eyes rested upon them. By virtue of just knowing about them, I automatically came

into the category of those who must in no circumstances fall into enemy hands for fear that, under interrogation or torture, I might be induced to disclose my knowledge, whereupon the enemy cipher would be changed, and all the work of cracking it need to be done again. Thus, henceforth it became a positive duty, rather than just a negative inclination, to keep well away from the enemy. At the same time, being privy to this source of high-grade and impeccable information about the enemy's plans and intentions gave me a new sense of importance. I might be a mere captain, but now I could look with condescension at brigadiers, and even generals, conscious that, as far as what was called 'the overall Intelligence picture' was concerned, I was likely to be more in it than they were. This sense of importance, of cherishing secrets beyond the ken of ordinary mortals, was characteristic of SIS personnel at all levels; particularly the females, who, however careless they might be about their chastity, guarded their security with implacable resolution. So much so that a party of them arriving in Cairo were unable to find anyone to whom they felt able to disclose the nature of their mission, and in the end had to be sent home.

Cracked cipher material was, indeed, as things turned out, the staple product of MI6, and provided the basis for most of its effective activities. The old procedures, like the setting up of agents, the suborning of informants, the sending of messages written in invisible ink, the masquerading, the dressing-up, the secret transmitters, and the examining of the contents of wastepaper-baskets, all turned out to be largely cover for this other source; as one might keep some old-established business in rare books going in order to be able, under cover of it, to do a thriving trade in pornography and erotica. As 'C' quickly saw, he never need fear criticism or cuts in his budget as long as he could drop in on the Prime Minister at breakfast time with some tasty item of Intelligence – the enemy's latest operational orders, say, or a full report of one of the meetings between Hitler and Mussolini immediately after it had happened – whose authenticity he could vouch for without being too particular as to its source.

The establishment which produced this precious material was located at Bletchley, in a manor house in which I spent some days familiarising myself with the place, its staff, its output and manner of working. As might be supposed, in view of the business in hand, the staff were a curious mixture of mathematicians, dons of various kinds, chess and crossword maestros, an odd musician or two, and numerous wireless telegraphy experts. Not surprisingly, Andreas joined them before the

war was over, and proved one of their most capable practitioners. On a superficial glance, it might have been taken to be a Fabian summer-school, or – a more ancient model – one of those reading parties Victorians were so fond of organising in the long vacation, in the Lake District, or further afield, in Switzerland or Italy, when they all grew bored together over unreadable books instead of separately. Perhaps, even, some kind of public affairs forum or seminar of the kind which, in the post-war years, were to be clandestinely financed by the CIA; dealing, say, with Whither Europe? or: After Fascism, What? or: South-East Asia – a New Look?

Each day after luncheon when the weather was propitious the cipher-crackers played rounders on the manor house lawn, assuming the quasi-serious manner dons affect when engaged in activities likely to be regarded as frivolous or insignificant in comparison with their weightier studies. Thus they would dispute some point about the game with the same fervour as they might the question of free-will or determinism, or whether the world began with a big bang or a process of continuing creation. Shaking their heads ponderously, sucking air noisily into their noses between words – 'I thought mine was the surer stroke,' or: 'I can assert without fear of contradiction that my right foot was already . . .' The females, too, were mostly donnish; either dons' molls, with solemnly pretty faces, studiously amorous or amorously studious according to their temperaments or the exigencies of the occasion; or themselves academics, grey, untidy, rough and hairy and spluttering – Asia Minor excavators, experts on Beowulf and Anglo-Saxon, delvers into folklore and marriage customs. Instinctively, I relapsed into my Cambridge state of mind, and thought how long the afternoon was bound to be, how interminable the wait for tea. Intelligence services in wartime naturally look to senior common rooms and high tables for recruits, and not in vain; a don-watcher in any of the theatres of war might hope sooner or later, if he was patient enough, to catch a glimpse of a Major Trevor-Roper, a Captain Ayer, a Lt-Colonel Rothschild, and in far-off Washington, DC, of an Isaiah Berlin, a John Foster, among the numerous attachés.

My instructress at Bletchley was an elderly lady who had been ciphering all her life at different embassies throughout the world. I noticed she was suffering from codist's thumb, the thumb she used for turning over the pages of the code-book having become slightly deformed through the years, with a consequent protective thickening of the skin, like Koestler's midwife toad. In all her extensive travels, what she most

vividly remembered was not famous sights like the Taj Mahal or the Chinese Wall, but occasions when ciphering changes had been introduced – at Teheran we started on one-time pads; at Kabul we tried out the new machines. Under her kind and patient guidance I was able to grasp more or less how I should cipher and de-cipher messages myself, but I never became proficient. I was billeted at another country house nearby, where technical staff resided. On the first evening, after dinner, a hunt was organised, led by a plump wing-commander blowing on a horn; we followed him up and down stairs, in and out of rooms, shouting Tally Ho! and other appropriate cries. What we were supposed to be hunting I never discovered; unless it was a pretty WAAF girl, who fell to our chief huntsman, the wing-commander.

My tour of instruction ended with a short course in invisible inks and their use. This took place in a house in Hans Crescent, so innocent-looking outside, with its trim curtains and array of milk bottles by the front door, that I thought I must have mistaken the address. However, when I rang the bell, sure enough a Signals NCO opened the door, and, when I had established my identity, took me upstairs to where my instructor awaited me. He was a sad-looking man with a large rubicund face, thinning black hair and short fingers. Another old SIS professional, as it turned out, who obviously felt he had come down in the world in being relegated to expounding the mysteries of writing in invisible inks to such as me – as though some county cricketer had been put to selling cricket bats in a toy shop. He had his array of ball-pointed pens, his various substances and liquids, a small collapsible stove for heating the paper, thereby bringing out any invisible writing on it, and other appropriate gear, amidst which he sat like some weird, doleful alchemist. My lesson went on through the afternoon and into the evening. First mixing my inks, the simplest being milk, and, at a pinch, wine; then solutions of various chemical substances, among them a well-known brand of headache tablets which had the advantage – besides being, as I discovered, an excellent hangover specific – that it could be carried in one's luggage without arousing suspicion. And, finally, what my instructor referred to primly as BS, meaning bird shit.

This last required some special explanation; it could, he said, be used when all else failed, and worked well, but procuring a supply was not as easy as might be supposed. For instance, he once had to fall back on it when he was stationed at The Hague, and had imagined that crumbs spread out on his little balcony would bring a goodly number of

sparrows along that might be relied on to leave behind a supply of BS. Not so; the birds duly arrived and ate the crumbs, but, whether because they were constipated, or out of delicacy, there were no droppings. In the end, he explained to me, he had to take a walk in a public park – which, fortunately, was spacious – and when he saw traces of BS, he dropped his handkerchief as though by chance, and scooped the BS up. His dolefulness became almost unbearable as I pictured him walking mournfully about questing for BS, and I tried to cheer him up by expressing unbounded admiration for the brilliant stratagem he had devised, which, I said, I was sure would prove invaluable in Mozambique. He nodded, I thought without much conviction, and expressed some doubts as to whether the sort of birds found there would prove suitable donors.

Having dealt with the inks, we moved on to practise writing with them, using a ball-pointed pen very lightly so as not to mark the paper. I was very ham-fisted at this, and, holding up one of my productions to the light to show that the indentations I had made were clearly visible, my instructor shook his ponderous head over me, as much as to say: 'You'll never make a spy at this rate.' I tried again, this time with better results, and we then tackled the process of heating the paper to develop the writing on it. This, also, my instructor said, required great care; not using too much heat, which would burn up the paper before it could be read, or too little to bring out the writing at all. We toiled away, scarcely noticing that by this time it was dark outside. Maybe, I reflected, he had a family awaiting him. Or lived alone, feeding the birds for company, but now disinterestedly, without any thought of benefiting from their visitations. I'd come again, I said, if he was dissatisfied with the standard I had attained; no, he replied, I'd done well enough, though from the tone of his voice I felt he'd known better students. Sitting with him there and looking out on the still blacked-out square, not a light showing, the absurdity of what we had been doing struck me with such passionate intensity that I had great difficulty in not blurting it out to him.

What were we at? What was it all about? How had we been induced, two grown men not totally incapable of making some contribution, however lowly, to human existence – how had we been induced to spend our time thus? He and I, strangers, but also fellow-humans. And not just us. Bletchley, where those donnish heads were bent over ciphers, wrestling to get at their meaning as though they contained the key to life's secrets, instead of just the trivialities and fatuities which constitute far the greater part of all Intelligence traffic. 'C' in his office with

his blue light shining, the Prime Minister in Downing Street, Hitler in his Chancellery, Stalin in his Kremlin; armies marching and counter-marching, maps earnestly studied, planes flying, bombs falling, U-boats prowling, convoys sailing. The whole vast panoply of war, down to this room in Hans Crescent where I had been learning how to fabricate and write in invisible ink. The intensity of my mood seemed to have spread to my instructor, for now he looked thoughtful, as though some urgent question were racking his mind, too – perhaps as to whether history itself might not be recorded in invisible ink; our very lives, not just, as Raleigh put it, writ on, but also with, water! As I went through the door I turned and shouted to him: 'I'll remember BS.' So, as it happens, I have; when I have forgotten so much else.

It now only remained to pay my respects to 'C' before venturing into the field on his behalf, and to shake the hand of the head of Passport Control, whose parish took in Section Five personnel posted to neutral countries in the same sort of way that the Bishop of Gibraltar's see takes in Siberia. There was also a man in the Foreign Office whose 'friends' we purported to be for the purpose of being allowed to make use of diplomatic bags to communicate with our headquarters in London. He, however, accepted us as friends without requiring, or even, I should suppose, wanting, to make our personal acquaintance. The head of Passport Control, I found, kept his office in a permanently twilit condition, with the curtains closely drawn, in order to counteract as far as possible the extraordinary colour of his face – a rich purple fading into pale blue, or thickening into a murky black, due, it was said, to his having been given the wrong injection by a doctor who combined attending to SIS's medical requirements with being on call at the Savoy Hotel. Despite this weird pigmentation, he turned out to be particularly agreeable, and, after an amicable chat, we duly shook hands, and I took my leave.

The visit to 'C' was more exacting. Just penetrating beyond the blue light that shone outside his room, required a special effort; I had a feeling that perhaps I ought to wait for it to turn amber before entering. Overcoming this hesitation, I made my way into an inner sanctum where I found two sedate, middle-aged secretaries who gave an immediate impression of being exceptionally well-bred. Readers of the Bond books will recognise the scene, but, of course, glamorised in Fleming's version; the secretaries more alluring, 'C' more steely, the office more daunting. I once, long after the war had ended, dined in a private room at the Garrick Club with a company that included both the then reigning

'C' and Fleming. It was like dining with Sherlock Holmes and Watson, or, perhaps better, with Don Quixote and Sancho Panza.

The 'C' of my day, Sir Stuart Menzies, was a regular officer in a Scottish regiment; sandy-haired, liable to be kilted, with a soft handshake and an air of indolence, belied by a glint of cunning in his brown eyes. His predecessor had been an admiral, the then practice being to alternate the office between the two services. We chatted together about Mozambique, he having obviously been briefed from the same source as I had acquired whatever knowledge I had of the place – the *Encyclopaedia Britannica*. On such occasions as this, I always find myself torn between a desire to please and resentment at so desiring, and have to confess to never having worked out a basis for harmonising the two states of mind. The interview with 'C' was brief; after a few desultory questions, he got up to indicate that it was over, and wished me well in Mozambique. I only saw him once again. This was in his hotel room in Paris shortly after the Liberation, when he was in full uniform as a major-general; booted and spurred. With us was Paiolle, head of the French *Securité Militaire*, whose liaison officer I had been. 'C' was much impressed by the punctilious way Paiolle packed cushions round the telephone in the room to counteract any possible listening device, even though – or perhaps because – his countrymen were again in charge in their capital city.

Before finally taking off, I had a few days' leave, which of course I spent at Whatlington with Kitty and the children. It was the only place I ever wanted to be, and the place I was constantly leaving; my heart was there, but my body was restless and nomadic. Kitty and the children were with me always, yet easily forgotten in the foolish, and often vainglorious, if not squalid, preoccupations of the moment. The saddest thing to me, in looking back on my life, has been to recall, not so much the wickedness I have been involved in, the cruel and selfish and egotistic things I have done, the hurt I have inflicted on those I loved – although all that's painful enough. What hurts most is the preference I have so often shown for what is inferior, tenth-rate, when the first-rate was there for the having. Like a man who goes shopping, and comes back with cardboard shoes when he might have had leather, with dried fruit when he might have had fresh, with processed cheese when he might have had cheddar, with paper flowers when the primroses were out. 'Nothing is so beautiful and wonderful, nothing is so continually fresh and surprising, so full of sweet and perpetual ecstasy as the good,' Simone Weil writes. 'No desert is so dreary, monotonous and boring

as evil.' True; but, as she goes on to point out, with fantasy it is the other way round – 'Fictional good is boring and flat, while fictional evil is varied and intriguing, attractive, profound, and full of charm.' Alas, so much of my life has been spent pursuing this fictional good, and forgetful of the other, the real good, that is ever inspiring, ever renewed, making us, again to quote Simone Weil, 'grow wings to overcome gravity'.

The days at Whatlington passed quickly and happily, even though the situation was intrinsically absurd. Here was I, notionally, going to the wars, but actually to Lisbon; a destination I was not supposed to divulge. I could scarcely, in the circumstances, take a brave stance, gathering my wife and children to me, as I remembered my eldest brother doing to us when he went off to France in the 1914–18 war. The drama, in so far as there was one, was all on their side; if there was any danger, it was they, with the possibility of more daylight raids, who had to confront it, not I, who was making for a neutral country where there was neither rationing nor blackout. How, then, should I conduct myself? Though it was true that I was going away for an uncertain time to an uncertain future, that I was under orders, and even if I had wanted to, could not have remained with them, I still felt ill-at-ease, a deserter, running away from my responsibilities rather than to them. Looking back I feel this more than ever; the loss was inestimable, the gain, to me or to the war effort, negligible. All that I can be grateful for is that, despite my shallow departure, thanks to Kitty our little bark remained afloat, and remains so still.

Leaving for Lisbon in 1942 had a special character of its own, even for someone as departure-prone as I was. One slipped surreptitiously away in a flying boat from Poole Harbour without any of the usual distractions – being seen off, finding things to say up to the last moment while looking round anxiously for one's luggage, and listening with half an ear to the loud-speaker for the announcement of departure and the gate to make for. Everything silent and clandestine. It was like a premature demobilisation. Now in civilian clothes again; more than that, with every trace of military accoutrements scrupulously removed from my luggage lest prying neutral eyes should detect them and ask awkward questions – though this was probably an imaginary danger; it may be doubted whether the Portuguese authorities cared much either way about camouflaged service men, whatever their nationality or allegiance, passing through Lisbon. On my brand-new passport my profession was given, for the one and only time in all my life, as a government official;

at the earliest possible moment, I had it crossed out and 'journalist' written in. The other passengers were as inscrutable as I tried to look; some of them probably also serving officers, and maybe on Intelligence missions, too. There were one or two whom I took to be genuine diplomats, British and foreign, and a sprinkling of business men in well-preserved suits, and carrying brief-cases, which they opened on their laps as soon as they settled in their seats in the plane, for the purpose of scribbling notes and studying figures and diagrams. We were silent together, fearful of giving ourselves away; heedful of Fougasse's little drawings of Hitler as an eavesdropper. It all added to our sense of self-importance; clandestinity being a form of vanity, as abstemiousness can be a form of self-indulgence.

In any case, the mere fact of being allowed to depart to a neutral country – which seemed so infinitely remote in beleaguered Britain that it was like going to another world rather than just abroad – was in itself a kind of distinction. We were a little group of the elect for whom, for one reason or another, the drawbridge was raised for an instant, and then at once lowered again. It gave me a feeling of being on some high-priority mission, though in point of fact I had only the vaguest notion of where I was going and what was expected of me. Also, of stepping into the unknown; rather alarmingly in our case, since a plane on the Lisbon run had recently been shot down, allegedly because one of the passengers was the film actor, Leslie Howard, and so much fuss was made about him that the Germans thought he might be Churchill travelling incognito. We looked at one another anxiously to see whether there were any among us about whom a similar mistake might be made; relieved to find there weren't. Our silence continued throughout the flight; scarcely a word spoken. All of us, I daresay, were thinking of that other flight, with the false Churchill aboard, which fell into the sea with no survivors; and those of us on Intelligence missions, doubtless going over the planned masquerade that lay ahead, like actors rehearsing their parts. In my case, it involved presenting myself as a member of the Consular Service, and seeking a visa to go to Lourenço Marques and take up my post as vice-consul there. *En poste* – the expression came into my mind; one of the particles of knowingness which accumulate over the years through the practice of journalism, like *matériel*, or collateral, or Bushido; intimations of a bogus expertise.

Lisbon, with all its lights, seemed after two years of blackout like a celestial vision when we landed there by night. For the first day or so I just wandered about the streets, marvelling at the shops, the restaurants

with their interminable menus, the smart women and cafés sprawling over the pavements; all the affluence and bustle of a city not at war. Was this how we, too, should one day live again? Or was it all done with mirrors? I couldn't be sure: I'm not sure even now. With escudos in my pocket, I wanted to buy something, and stared in at the goods displayed, tormented by indecision. Likewise, as to which restaurant to go and eat in; irresolutely studying the menus, and in the end munching a sandwich washed down with coffee. There were two almost adjoining shops exhibiting Nazi and British propaganda pictures and publications; oddly resembling one another, like different brands of the same commodity – Coca and Pepsi Cola. Then all those wax figures beauteously arrayed in the shop windows! By night the cabarets, the dancing lights, the bursts of jazz music coming through half-opened doors! Pleasure stalking the streets, with many trailing it, I a forlorn straggler. Magically, the war had disappeared; hey, presto! – gone. The only thing I could find to buy was a coat which I saw in the window of an obscure tailoring establishment, billed as late of Savile Row, and displaying some sort of royal coat-of-arms. It was made of drill, very strong; originally, I should suppose, ordered by some retired British officer resident in Lisbon, and for some reason never collected by him. It gave me good service over many years.

Having spent my statutory period of careless living to put any enemy counter-espionage agents who might have noticed my arrival off the scent, I presented myself at the British Embassy, where I was expected, and directed to the relevant department. These SIS corners of British Embassies, of which I got to know quite a number before the war was over, all had a character of their own. They were different from the other departments, like Chancery, or Trade, or Information; more free-and-easy – men in shirt-sleeves, their feet up on their desks, a lot of coming and going, and strange visitors. The old Secret Service professionals, it is true, tended to look more like diplomats than diplomats did, and were given to spats and monocles long after they passed out of fashion among the regulars. The prevailing fashion among the wartime MI6 intake, on the other hand, was to aim at being as unlike the conventional idea of a diplomat as possible; slouching about in sweaters and grey flannel trousers, drinking in bars and cafés and low dives rather than at diplomatic cocktail parties and receptions, boasting of their underworld acquaintances and liaisons. Philby, in this sense, may be taken as the prototype of them all, and was, indeed, in the eyes of many of them, a model to be copied.

It seemed there was nothing for me to do but wait for the Portuguese Foreign Office to accept my credentials and grant me a visa to Lourenço Marques. This might well, it was explained to me, take time. When the war was going badly for us – as just then – the Portuguese authorities fell over themselves trying to please the Axis Powers; when our prospects looked up, they were ready to do us an occasional favour. I may add that things went on like this throughout the war. For instance, I noticed that the number and standing of Portuguese officials who would show up for a garden party at the British Consulate-General in Lourenço Marques bore an exact relation to the latest communiqués from North Africa and the other fronts; until, finally, when Hitler's body had been consigned to the flames outside his Berlin bunker, Portugal resumed her role as our oldest ally, and the Consul-General might expect the Lourenço Marques élite to turn out in the same strength for the Queen's Birthday as they previously had for Hitler's.

While waiting for my visa, my colleagues told me, I should employ myself in studying the language, and familiarising myself with the Salazar regime, and its colonial policy. It seemed an unexacting assignment, and markedly unlike the role I had imagined for myself when I first thought of participating in the war. Having settled these matters, we all went off to lunch together at the Avish Hotel, notable as being the residence of Mr Calouste Gulbenkian, then reputed to be the richest man in the world.

It was one of those twilit, enormously expensive, old-fashioned, restaurants which have continued to function in places like Lisbon and Monte Carlo and St Moritz, seemingly unperturbed by the many convulsions taking place around them; the ageing waiters in their shabby black suits continuing to carve and pour and serve with sad serenity, refusing to be put out by a changing world, and looking with the same coldly indifferent eye at young girls wearing elegant shorts as at old dusty dowagers mumbling and muttering over their toasted tea-cakes. Other Intelligence Services, my companions told me, were well represented. The Germans were seated at a nearby table entertaining a bronzed film star who had been holidaying in Estoril; there was a solitary Vichy colonel covered with decorations, eyed contemptuously by a noisy party of Gaullists, and three Italians in earnest conversation. Also, a White Russian with a sallow boy friend and a lot of gold teeth, who, it seemed, was on everyone's books. The war was clearly raging in the Avish. While I was hearing these and other piquant details of the various belligerents present, Mr Gulbenkian came into the restaurant. He was preceded by

412 *The Infernal Grove*

his secretary and followed by a valet; two waiters approached as he took his place at a slightly raised table reserved for him. All eyes were upon him. He lunched alone, the secretary and the valet seating themselves at another table within reach, in case at any time their services might be required; his face sallow and expressionless, the movements of his hands the minimum required to get food and drink to his mouth, the mastication barely perceptible. Was he not, I reflected, a totem figure? Some cherished image which like the king in chess, needed to be protected and sustained, or the game was lost.

Mr Gulbenkian did not linger long over his luncheon, and after his departure we, too, got up to go; my companions back to the Embassy and their counter-espionage, I to stroll in the sunshine. What with the wine and the talk and a general sense of well-being, I found myself not quite touching down on the pavement; borne along on a wave of contentment in which the white jangling trams, the passing faces, the flowers that I seemed to see everywhere, and snatches of music I kept hearing, presumably from some café orchestra, were all comprised. A posting to the Lisbon Front was certainly an agreeable change from other forms of war service I had experienced; it was difficult to believe that only a little way away the war was still in full swing. What was it really about anyway? *Lebensraum?* Defending Mother Russia? Unconditional surrender? Roosevelt's Four Freedoms? Ah, how easily it might have happened that I had to handle them! At the *Guardian* office in Cross Street, asking: What's our line on Freedom from Want?, and being told: The same as from Fear, only more so. At the Ministry of Information, labouring to show that, despite appearances to the contrary, Stalin must be regarded as a doughty champion of Freedom of Worship and of Speech; as one burning to deliver mankind from fear. It would have been heavy going; I was glad to have missed it, and to be strolling about in Lisbon, sans blackout, sans rationing, sans Blitz, sans war, thinking almost affectionately of Mr Gulbenkian; a war aim in himself – five per cent without end, amen?

I managed to arrange to leave my hotel and become a lodger in a modest Portuguese household. It was an agreeable change. The way of life in a hotel is, to me, the most hateful there is. And the more expensive, the more desolating. Those restless, unnecessary trips up and down in the lift; the constant visits to Reception to see if there are any letters when none are expected; the effort to find something on the menu one wants to eat, and then, having ordered it, to eat it! It is not surprising that residents often throw themselves out of upper-floor windows –

I have toyed with the idea myself – or are found dead in their beds of a surfeit of barbiturates. The first meal I sat down to with my Portuguese family, with a plate of their soup before me, I almost wept for thankfulness. Through practising Portuguese with them I managed to learn a little, and acquired a certain facility at reading the language from spelling out the newspapers, which I did seated at café tables, the newspapers conveniently fixed to bamboo frames. I also started reading *Don Quixote* in Portuguese, and a sermon that took my fancy because it was addressed to the fishes; these creatures, the preacher contended, being specially beloved of God, since the flood He sent to punish men, benefited them. Thus, unlike the inhabitants of Lisbon, they might perhaps heed his words.

The head of the household I was staying in was a retired shop-keeper, some eighty years old and diabetic; his wife, also old, a little plump woman who served him with his food, watching him closely while he was eating it, as though to note his reaction to each mouthful. For servant they had a huge Negress from Cap Verde, always smiling and cheerful, who put great splashes of rouge on her black cheeks, where they stood out like British colonies in the old Empire maps, used when I was at school, in which I first saw the shape of the world. She brought me my morning tea, and I used to long for her to come and dissipate – as she invariably did – the sleepless hours' deposit of *angst*. My Portuguese teacher, who also sometimes took meals with us, was an enthusiast for Esperanto; a little man in a black suit, with a wife to match. I occasionally passed an evening with them, and we argued, he in his scanty English, I in my even scantier Portuguese, about the efficacy of Esperanto as a counter-irritant to the Tower of Babel. He turned out to be a reader of *Time and Tide*, who thought *Punch* was funny, and the *Guardian* the greatest newspaper in the world.

From time to time I dropped into the Embassy to collect mail and some money, and also to find out if there was any news of my visa for Mozambique. There never was, and I really believe I might have spent the entire war quietly studying Portuguese. Wars scatter many forgotten men about the world, and I looked like being one of them. A letter from Kitty brought me the news that my father had died. She described the scene in her incomparable way. How his angina had got worse, and he had taken to his bed; then had gone to hospital, where she visited him regularly with my mother. Towards the end he rallied, sitting up suddenly with the old animation in his face – that expression I knew so well, compounded of unquenchable high spirits, a shrewd appraisal of

how the world works, and a not so shrewd hope that somehow it might be drastically rearranged in accordance with his heart's desire, topped up with a Cockney cheekiness which advancing years and venerability quite failed to extinguish. He told me once that it was only because his beard got white and his eyes grew dim that he came to behave more sedately; he never *felt* any differently in himself. Sitting up and seeing my mother's tears falling, he turned on her one of his splendid grins, and then with a wink slipped out of bed, and offered her his arm. 'Come on, Annie,' he whispered gaily, 'we're off to the Greyhound!', and swaggered down the passage with her. It was, Kitty wrote, a glorious wink; knowing and joyous and infinitely reassuring. On their last visit he lay in a coma, and my mother, irritated that she could get no sign of recognition from him, tried to turn back his eyelids. 'It's me, Annie,' she said sharply, as though that was bound to bring him back to life. This time it didn't work; there was no response.

Even though I knew my father's life was moving towards its end, I still felt very sad not to have been with him when he died, more particularly because my absence was due to my being in Lisbon, where I had nothing particular to do but wait for a visa. If I had been engaged in some enormously hazardous secret operation requiring my presence abroad, I might have felt differently. As it was, there was really no good reason why I should not have been at his side, which would, I knew, have brought him comfort. His partiality for me, and irrational pride in me, survived all the follies I engaged in and disappointments I caused him. His presence seemed very near, and once more I was waiting at East Croydon station, anxiously scanning the commuters' faces as they came off the trains; catching sight of him at last, well to the fore. An indomitable figure, striding out, bowler hat a shade too large, somewhat low down on his ears; wearing the City's livery, yet so evidently not of it. So evidently a man on his own, a man apart; serving parties and movements and causes loyally and ardently, but without ever being wholly committed to them. Hence, perhaps, his relative isolation at the end of his days. No place reserved for him in the pantheon of the rebels; like the Abbey for the Webbs, or the Miserden churchyard for the Whiteway colonists. Just some family and a few friends at his funeral, which Kitty organised; then forgetfulness. When, after the war, we set up a stone to mark his burial place in the graveyard of the little church at Whatlington, I asked my eldest son, Leonard, what should be written on it, and he suggested, 'A good man, and a just', after Joseph of Arimathea, who was also a councillor. It seemed exactly right. There is

an empty space beside him under the same tree where I hope to lie.

As the days got hotter I moved out to a small pension at Estoril in order to be nearer the sea, bathing daily and going for walks along the coast. In the pension I made the acquaintance of a Russian lady, Mme Sazanov, also staying there, with her son Dmitry. She belonged to the family of a well-known Russian diplomat of the same name, and had left Russia at the time of the Revolution. Now she managed to eke out a precarious livelihood for herself and her son by writing travel books. Hence her presence in Portugal, where, in collaboration with the state tourist organisation, she was engaged in preparing some sort of guidebook. In talking to me about it, she grew lyrical on the subject of *le folklore Portugais* (we usually spoke in French, which she knew better than English, having, she explained, been accustomed to speak the language as a young girl in Petrograd), of *la dance folklorique et les chants folkloriques* which so enchanted her. With her thickly coiled nebulous hair, and general impression of having been kept for a long time in a damp cupboard, and so in need of airing, she reminded me very much of the clientele at Sonia Chamberlin's salon in the Borisoglebsky Periulok. It was another example of how revolutions change things much less than might be supposed; if Mme Sazanov had remained in Russia, and managed not to get killed by one side or the other, her life would have been very much what it was as an exile. Only, she would have been staying by the Black Sea instead of in Estoril, and writing, doubtless in an equally *folklorique* vein, about workers' holiday resorts.

Dmitry was what used to be called simple; with a gentle face and disposition. He took the greatest possible delight in all sounds and sights when we went for walks together. In his eyes Mme Sazanov had the genius of a Mme de Staël combined with the mystical insights of a St Teresa of Avila; he listened, enthralled, to her long reminiscences, however many times he had heard them before, and never seemed to tire of her company. She likewise showed no impatience over his sometimes vagrant thoughts and meandering talk and movements. He hoped, he told me, to be an aviator. One evening he arranged chessmen on the table to illustrate the Russian Front; the Queen, Leningrad, the King, Moscow. Another time he came up to my room with *des petites choses qui peuvent vous interesser*, which turned out to be a collection of British and Gaullist propaganda. It was very beautiful to see Dmitry and Mme Sazanov together, and easily compensated for the tedium one sometimes felt as she ground remorselessly on about the glories of Portugal's

historical past and enlightened present. A favourite remark of Dmitry's, which he might repeat several times in the course of an evening, was: '*Je suis plein d'enthousiasme, Monsieur*'; on the other hand, small misfortunes were liable to upset him unduly – as when he came to breakfast, having cut himself shaving, and kept muttering: '*C'est affreux! C'est affreux!*'

On one occasion, when the three of us went on an expedition to Cascais along the coast, we saw the fishing fleet being blessed, with the wives of the fishermen going from ship to ship carrying candles and singing ancient songs. The occasion unleashed in Mme Sazanov a great flood of *folklorique* enthusiasm, but Dmitry just fell on his knees, completely captivated by the scene. I hovered uneasily between the two of them; taking the shock of Mme Sazanov's massive bombardment, and enchanted by the light shining in Dmitry's face. It was the same scene, as I learnt subsequently, that led Simone Weil, in a moment of great illumination, to conclude, 'that christianity is pre-eminently the religion of slaves, that slaves cannot help belonging to it, and I among them'. A thought that has often echoed in my heart.

A day or so after our visit to Cascais I got an urgent call to the Embassy, where I was informed that at last my visa had been granted, and I must present myself at the Foreign Office to collect it. I was beholden for this, not to the Ambassador or other senior figures in the Embassy who allegedly made representations on my behalf, but to Rita Winsor, an energetic, kindly and resourceful member of our Section Five Lisbon contingent, who managed to propel the relevant Portuguese official into action. One of the few useful things I learnt in the course of my five years of war service was that one gets little help at the top in any organisation, but only in the lower reaches; the favours of brigadiers are rare and fragile, it is the sergeants, especially in the Quartermaster's branch, who have it in their power to attend to one's practical needs. The same principle applies in civilian life. At the Foreign Office I duly received my visa, written in red ink – *Bon para Lourenço Marques* – and dated 9 May 1942. Now, at last, I could book a passage on a Portuguese boat and be off. I still occasionally, I may add, get a letter from Dmitry in his spidery writing. The last one told me, sadly but not despairingly, that Mme Sazanov had died.

I sailed from Lisbon in the Portugese liner *Colonial*, with, in my charge, some six or seven large sealed diplomatic bags to be handed to the British representative at the various ports-of-call on the way to Lobito, where I was to disembark. My instructions were to keep these

bags always in sight to ensure that they were not tampered with, it being the easiest thing in the world to run a hot knife through the seal, thereby opening them up for inspection. Or, for that matter, to X-ray them. Resultant discoveries, as I understood from experienced SIS practitioners, were sometimes curious – as, black market articles like bottles of scotch, lingerie and silk stockings, as well as supplies of contraceptives, porn, and, in the case of one particular ambassador, tennis balls and a set of new uniforms for his flunkeys. A man from the Lisbon Embassy handed over the diplomatic bags to me on the quay, whereupon they were at once whisked off by the porters with my luggage. I thought despairingly that I had lost them before my journey had even begun, especially when I found my luggage safely deposited in my cabin, but no sign of the bags. Later, I discovered them in the hold with the not-wanted-on-voyage luggage, and was able to peep in at them from time to time to make sure that they were still there – the best I could do to ensure their inviolability. This sense of the sanctity of diplomatic bags did not long survive my becoming HM's vice-consul in Lourenço Marques, and consequent familiarity with them. I soon got into the way of travelling about carrying my own private diplomatic bag, in which I kept my liquor and other personal accessories secure against the prying eyes of customs and security men. It was a convenience which I sorely missed when my brief and lowly tenure of diplomatic status came to an end.

The departure of the *Colonial* was noisy and emotional, with many tender farewells and passionate embraces; handkerchiefs continued to be waved till the shore was lost to view. Most of the passengers were military or administrative officers posted to the colonies, and leaving their families or sweethearts behind; though there were some wives and children on the ship. As we drew away from the dock, I waved with the others, pretending to myself that one or other of the dark-haired girls was weeping so profusely at my departure. We sailed down the coast of Africa with all our lights blazing, occasionally catching a glimpse of darkened, furtive belligerent vessels. Once we even thought we saw a submarine, but with our name and neutral status so brightly illuminated, felt no qualms. I soon fell in with two other non-Portuguese passengers, and spent most of my time with them. One was a French naval officer on his way to Tokyo to take up the post of naval attaché there; the other a Swiss diplomat, also on his way to Tokyo to join the Swiss Embassy, whose responsibilities had been greatly expanded through having to act on behalf of all the Allied Powers when they broke off diplomatic

relations with the Japanese. They were extraordinarily different; the French naval officer stern, austere, with closely cropped hair and sparing with his words, which, however, when he did speak, were uttered with great intensity, and the Swiss, extrovert, cheerful, verbose and good-natured.

The three of us carried on a marathon discussion, specifically about the war, but generally about the state of the world and future prospects; interrupted when we put in at the Portuguese colonies along our way – Madeira, Guinea, Cap Verde, San Tomé – and then resumed when we found ourselves on the high seas again. Walking up and down the deck, in the bar and the dining-saloon, seated in deck-chairs or leaning over the side of the ship, we talked and talked. At first the naval attaché was sullen and ill-disposed to me, obviously with Mers-el-Kebir in mind, though he never once mentioned it; but gradually he melted, and though he continued to be reticent and taciturn, began to give us occasional glimpses of his real feelings and attitudes. I became completely absorbed in this running conversation, to the point of forgetting that I, unlike the other two, was an actual participant in the war. Anyone listening would have formed the impression that the Swiss was the only one who truly hoped for and believed in an Allied victory, that the Frenchman entertained some expectation that a stalemate of sorts might develop, and that I saw only disaster and confusion ahead whatever the war's outcome might be.

The truth is, I never could shake off the feeling that the war was 'theatre'; like my mother's antics when jealousy afflicted her, or my own tantrums when I succumbed to any of the rages of the will. For that matter, like history itself – a kind of running soap-opera whose actors and script-writers change, but whose essential theme remains the same. I think the Swiss was vaguely shocked by my attitude; between the naval attaché and me, on the other hand, a certain sympathy developed, and when I got to Lourenço Marques I found a long affectionate letter from him, written in his neat hand and couched in his stately French, expressing the pleasure he had taken in our companionship and talk. I sent the letter back to London with the suggestion that perhaps he might be approached as a useful contact when he took up his post in Tokyo. My true motive – rather a shabby one, I fear – was precautionary, in case the Swiss repeated some of the things I had said. In such a case, the letter would have enabled me to claim that I was playing a part with a view to getting on good terms with the naval attaché. In Intelligence stratagems there is always a built-in emergency exit; like

those iron staircases in case of fire that one sees outside brownstone houses in New York. I never saw the naval attaché again, but always asked about him when an opportunity offered. In this way I heard that after the war he had joined a religious order with a particularly strict rule; then that he had died. I wish I had kept his letter.

At each port-of-call I was met for the handing over of diplomatic bags, about whose arrival in my charge advance advice had been given. I handed them over as though I had kept them in sight throughout the voyage, but this subterfuge was quite unnecessary. Taking a drink with a local consul, I learnt that the bags contained, for the most part, material from the Ministry of Information, which could scarcely be considered top secret. There might even have been one of my articles, written while I was at the Ministry, on defending our free way of life, though whether this would have gone down particularly well in, say, Säo Tomé, where we saw prisoners chained together and working under an armed guard, may be doubted. My two friends and I regarded the Portuguese Empire as *opéra bouffe*, and noted how run-down the colonies we visited seemed to be. How surprised we should have been to know that the British and French Empires, which still in 1942 seemed quite substantial structures, were shortly going to drop to pieces and disappear, while the Portuguese Empire remained more or less on its feet. In the last century attempts were made to devise a means of giving away the Portuguese colonies – to the Germans, for instance, to keep them quiet – but as it turned out, by a strange quirk of history, they were fated to be the last to survive. It was a sort of *misère* result, with the weakest and most decrepit player scooping the pool – such as it was.

For me, the voyage ended at Lobito, in Angola, where I was to take the train to Elizabethville in the Belgian Congo, and from thence a plane to Nairobi where 'C' 's man in East Africa was stationed. I had farewell drinks with my friends the Swiss diplomat and the French naval attaché, and then stood waving on the quay as the *Colonial* was gently unloosed and moved away in the evening light. It gave me a pang – something familiar disappearing, and I left standing alone as darkness suddenly came down. The British Consul in Lobito arranged my tickets and saw me off on the train which left only once a week – a modest three or four carriages and dining-car, puffing and rattling across the vast spaces of Africa, stirring up the dust, frightening the cattle, and causing a momentary stir of activity and excitement at its various stopping places, where any local Europeans, or near-Europeans, were liable to assemble and stare at the train and its passengers, seeing

in them their only link with what they conceived to be their own world, as distinct from this dark Africa where they were fated to live. I liked thus being cut off from everyone and everything; on my own, for ever moving, and through a countryside which never seemed to change – dry and dusty and interminable. Soon I found myself wishing that the journey would never end. It seemed like a way of life, to keep moving; just as, at the Ministry of Information, it had seemed like a way of life to keep still, and at Mytchett to keep drilling. I spent most of my time looking out of the window at the huge dusty vistas as we rattled along; watching the sun rise murkily and set gaudily, and in between ride relentlessly across the glaring, empty sky, with only an occasional herdsman or shepherd to be seen, his black limbs graceful and at ease, as though even then confident of being the ultimate inheritor when the storm raging in the world at last subsided.

After a while, in the restaurant car we started chatting together. There was a little farmer, a doctor, and a veterinary surgeon – a huge man with a large impassive face who illustrated all his remarks with appropriate actions. For instance, when he was arguing that men were unequal because they had different tastes, he showed this individual driving a car, that one drinking, and that other saying his prayers. At one station a priest got in who was carrying a pastoral staff to be delivered to his bishop. He showed it to us, gleaming and jewelled, and we much admired it. As each passenger arrived at his destination, he said good-bye to those of us who were continuing on the train, until, at the Angola frontier I alone remained. The last to get down was the doctor, who bought me a present of a basket of fruit, which he handed to me when he said good-bye.

At the frontier there was a long wait, and I was entertained by some missionaries, who turned out to be Plymouth Brethren – an elderly man, his two daughters and some ladies. We sat round a table drinking tea together and talking about God and the Bible. 'If the Bible is lies,' the elderly man said at one point, 'then we've lived on lies for two thousand years.' I assured him earnestly that I didn't think it was lies – most certainly not. We stayed together till the train left at midnight, walking up and down the platform affectionately, and going on talking. The thought occurred to me then: Suppose I stay with them here, and go no further! But, of course, when the guard's whistle blew, I got back in the train, as I always have. An old steam train, naturally, that slowly picked up speed; so I could lean out of the window and wave to them for quite a time, where I saw them standing with their lanterns in the

darkness and waving back. My compartment, when I returned to it, seemed quite desolate. I remember my encounter with the missionaries on the Angola–Congo frontier so very vividly, and even now with a kind of anguish.

Whatever I might wish, the train rolled inexorably on to Elizabethville, and I had to leave the little home my compartment had become and grapple with getting a plane on to Nairobi. For me, the town had a familiar air, being so very like Heliopolis where Kitty and I had lived while I was teaching at Cairo University. Both Elizabethville and Heliopolis were Belgian built; even the tramway bore an uncanny resemblance to the one I used to take to Abbasiah. The European shops were full of all the things like whisky and cigarettes and silk stockings unobtainable in England, the reason being that the Congo's copper production was of great importance, and it was considered essential to keep the local producers in good heart. The Belgians who ran the place looked very large and self-confident and pink in their khaki drill. With ancestral memories of Roger Casement, King Leopold I and E. D. Morel, I looked for signs of brutishness in them, and, as it seemed to me, not in vain.

'C' 's man in Nairobi turned out to be a kindly avuncular figure whose attitude to me was rather like that of a bishop briefing a curate for work in some distant and possibly hazardous mission field. In the pre-war years he had been stationed in Cairo, and told me that, dating back to the time I was resident there, my name appeared in his card-index of subversives and undesirables. He and his Russian wife were very kind to me, and took me to the club, which still retained something of its smart-set character, but was beginning to look a little faded and worn; as, even more so, was Government House, where I was invited to stay because of my friendship with Arthur Dawe, an Under-Secretary at the Colonial Office. It always fascinates me to observe how what is to happen reveals itself in advance; so that though politicians may make speeches proclaiming that we shall never yield here or cede there, their words are belied in peeling paint and fallen tiles and patches of damp. In Government Houses I have visited shortly before the regimes they represented have collapsed, there has always been a musty smell of decay; a premonition that a change of tenancy is imminent.

I felt this very strongly in Nairobi, even though ostensibly Government House was in full swing, with all the usual appurtenances – a car with a flag flying, black soldiers who sprang to attention and presented arms whenever I went in or out, a respectful servant to lay out my clothes

and an attentive A.D.C. who led me to His Excellency as and when required, meanwhile ready to engage in polite conversation for an indefinite period. The Governor was a Pickwickian figure; a civil servant translated from his Colonial Office desk to the glories of being an Excellency. These posts, in the last stages of the British Empire, began to be relinquished to civil servants, presumably as a solatium, or maybe just because no one else wanted them. The Governor's wife, on the other hand, had rather a savage look, I thought, as though she might have been more at home among the Kikuyu. Over dinner, served majestically by waiters in gold and red, in Raj style, the Governor remarked that an indication of our present lack of belief in ourselves and our civilisation was that we no longer attempted to make our African and Asian subjects like ourselves, but insisted that they were better as they were. Later in the evening, when we were chatting together, he developed the theme.

There were, he said, three things that had held the Empire together – the military security it offered, the economic advantages it provided, and the institution of the Monarchy. The first could scarcely be expected to survive our military reverses, even though in the end we were technically victorious; the second had been dissipated in the enormous expenditure of two world wars; the third was a matter of sentiment, notoriously fickle and fragile. A young secretary who was with us interjected that, on the contrary, wonderful new prospects were opening up of an Empire based, not on fear, but on genuine collaboration and mutual good will. His words seemed to come from far away; I had written them long before in the columns of the *Guardian*. It was obvious that the Governor thought the game was up, and obviously he was right. What he could not have foreseen was that the preposterous frontiers the colonial powers had drawn when they carved up Africa would come to demarcate independent sovereign states, ruled over by black African demagogue-dictators, each with a flag, an airline, a hydro-electric project and a seat at the United Nations; the conduct of whose affairs would provide a rich, and often cruel, burlesque of the institutions and practices of the governments which had initially brought them into existence.

A flying-boat carried me down the African coast, and at last I arrived at my destination, Lourenço Marques. My first impression was of a rather run-down Mediterranean resort, with bathing beaches, picture postcards, souvenirs, cafés, restaurants, and, at night, cabarets and casinos; except that the sun was hotter and the air more humid. I

stayed at the Polana Hotel, overlooking the sea, and only lately completed. The idea of the Portuguese authorities was to attract clients with money to spend from Johannesburg and other cities in the neighbouring Union of South Africa by offering a style of living and of entertainment more 'continental' in character than was permissible in the Union under the aegis of the zealots of the Dutch Reformed Church. This worked even in war-time, and there was a steady influx of South Africans looking for a gamble, and even an occasional clandestine visit to a brothel.

Both my opposite numbers – the Italian Consul-General, Campini, and the German Consul-General, Leopold Wertz – also lodged at the Polana Hotel, so I was able to examine them at my leisure in the hotel restaurant, where, like me, they came for meals. Campini was a large ebullient man, who obviously tried to look as like his Duce as possible; wearing a cloak whenever an occasion offered, and given to using extravagant gestures and rhetorical flourishes. Wertz, on the other hand, was not at all like Hitler or any of his henchmen; unless it was Ribbentrop, who, as Foreign Minister, was his ostensible boss, and to whom he might have been said to bear a passing resemblance. He had the youthfulness common among Germans of his type; blond and pink and spectacled and earnest. I had occasion later on to read some of his letters home, which a friendly purser on the Portuguese ship carrying the mail gave me a sight of before sailing. They were addressed to his mother; very affectionate and filial, if not sentimental, written in a rather formless hand sprawling across page after page. After the war I also read some of his official dispatches made available from captured *Abwehr* archives. They, too, were decidedly verbose, and in them I appeared as a ruthless intrepid spy-master, with a chain of agents extending over the whole of Southern Africa, whom he, Wertz, was able nonetheless ultimately to pulverise. Diplomats and Intelligence agents, in my experience, are even bigger liars than journalists, and the historians who try to reconstruct the past out of their records are, for the most part, dealing in fantasy.

If, as sometimes inevitably happened, I bumped into Campini or Wertz, or passed through a door at the same time, we bowed politely, but never spoke. Or we might meet in the lavatory, there, too, maintaining a coolly distant manner. Yet, of course, we were conscious of one another, living, as we were, under the same roof, eating the same meals, sharing the same servants; not to mention bribing the same local officials and police officers. Espionage and counter-espionage, as far as the Portuguese were concerned, made good their war-time losses on

tourism; we secret agents represented an invisible import, if not a capital gain. It was altogether a curious relationship I had with Campini and Wertz; a kind of wordless intimacy. Even now I feel as though, if I ever ran into one of them, it would be as an old acquaintance – 'My dear fellow, how are you?'

Ledger, the British Consul-General, a kindly low-keyed man, treated me handsomely, though it was obvious that he had considerable scepticism about my supposed duties, and disliked handing out money to me even though it did not affect his own careful accounting. The other members of the staff likewise regarded me as a kind of pampered interloper whose activities were not to be taken seriously. I had a room to myself in the Consulate-General, and there I sat, with my typewriter, and a safe, in which I kept my code-book, my invisible inks and my cash, my general assignment being to try and stop the enemy from getting information about our convoys sailing to North Africa up the Mozambique Channel, where they were being torpedoed by German submarines. This was happening on a large scale, greatly assisted by the ease with which a message could be sent from Durban to Lourenço Marques giving details of Allied shipping passing through the port. The task was daunting, and I scarcely knew where to begin, seeing I had no local contacts, and my knowledge of Portuguese was sketchy to say the least. To while away the time I deciphered a long telegram which had come for me via Ledger. It was a laborious business, and the kind of thing I have always been bad at. First, one had to subtract from the groups of numbers in the telegram corresponding groups from a so-called one-time pad; then to look up what the resultant groups signified in the code book. Any mistake in the subtraction, or, even worse, in the groups subtracted, threw the whole thing out. I toiled away at it, getting into terrible muddles and having to begin again, but finally managed to disentangle the message in an approximately legible form.

It came from Philby, as I knew from the style, and provided a résumé of the espionage scene in Lourenço Marques in the light of Wertz's and Campini's latest telegrams. All their traffic was being intercepted and cracked at Bletchley; so I had the inestimable advantage of knowing just what they were up to – like having access to the answers at the end of the book in an arithmetic test. This benefit was available to Montgomery fighting the Battle of North Africa just as much as to me fighting the Battle of Lourenço Marques. It also meant, of course, that my activities showed in the Wertz–Campini traffic, so that any bluff, or any pretence practised on my own account without reference to London was

bound to become known there at once. Nonetheless, to show at all in the
Bletchley material was considered in MI6 circles to be an enviable
distinction; exactly like having a leader quoted in the foreign press in
my *Guardian* days. The Philby directive suggested that it might be a
good idea to concentrate on infiltrating the Campini *apparat* rather than
the Wertz one, since the personality of Campini, to judge from his
boastful, high-flown style, seemed the more vulnerable of the two.

That evening at dinner at the Polana Hotel I looked across at Cam-
pini's table – where they seemed to be in a particularly festive mood –
wondering how I could hope to plant an informer among them, or
otherwise get at their secrets. Signora Campini, for instance – what
about her? Might she be approachable? A short, compact lady, not
particularly beautiful, but quite vivacious looking, and about a third of
Campini's bulk. I began to think of her almost amorously, and after
dinner, when the Italian party went for a stroll in the cool moonlight,
followed at a distance, only, however, catching vague echoes of their
voices and their laughter. I sent a longish message to London, ciphering
with anguish late into the night. It announced my arrival and establish-
ment at the Consulate-General, and gave an account of how things were
at the Polana Hotel; as it were, setting up the board and beginning to
arrange my pieces.

Like Brighton rock, a war spells out the same word wherever you bite
into it; on the various fronts, from Stalingrad to the Polana Hotel, the
same essential line-up. Only the scale varies; not the dramatis personae.
Wertz and Campini, Führer and Duce – what's the difference? Lipski,
a Polish diplomat, told me once that when he saw the accused at
Nuremberg he could not believe they were the same men he had
treated with so deferentially in Berlin. That shambling figure, surely not
Ribbentrop; that woebegone clown couldn't be Goering. But they were;
it was just that they had changed their positions on the board, moving
from an attacking position, to a defensive one, and then to surrender.

So, the drama of the war was played out on the Polana Front as on
any other, though it has to be admitted that actual hostilities occurred
but rarely. On one occasion, a South African lurched as though by
accident into Campini, and a fracas of sorts followed; on another, after
a drunken party, someone went round muddling up all the Axis boots
and shoes put out in the corridor for cleaning. There was also an ugly
scene about which particular radio station should be turned on for
the news, to the point that the management decreed that the public
transmission of broadcast news bulletins, from whatever source, was

forbidden. Naturally, we all believed that our rooms were bugged and our bags searched; and I occasionally prowled about the hotel corridors and peered in through windows, though the only discovery I made was that Dr Wertz wore a hair-net in the privacy of his room – an interesting, but scarcely significant, item of intelligence. It piqued me slightly to observe that when visitors from South Africa arrived in the hotel it was always Wertz and Campini they wanted pointed out to them, never me. However, I comforted myself with the thought that, in war, the enemy enjoys the advantage of being glamorous; like other men's wives.

It was through the good offices of Ledger that I recruited my first sub-agent; Camille, a Polish Jew who had managed to escape from the Gestapo and make his way to Lourenço Marques, where he subsisted largely on bridge, which he played extremely well. He came to see me often. Through his bridge-playing he had a large circle of acquaintances among Portuguese officials, including the police; and in his long conversations with me – in French, which he spoke with rather a thick accent – he always presented himself as a sort of *chevalier* or dashing cavalry officer, who, through the fortunes of war, found himself in strange, if not disreputable, company, towards whom his attitude was one of tolerant condescension, as I, a fellow *chevalier*, would readily understand. It is the measure of his essential decency, and of my fondness for him, that we maintained this fiction intact to the end of our relationship, despite the fact that money passed hands, and sometimes led to wrangling which could easily have become acrimonious, and that sometimes the information he passed to me likewise partook of the fantasy which governed so much of his life in Lourenço Marques. I can see him now – the close-cropped hair, the jaunty appearance, the carefully pressed linen suit that had seen better days and white shoes always meticulously pipe-clayed, the cane, the ravaged face liable to carry an afternooon shadow even in the morning, and, above all, the eyes peering out from this ensemble anxiously, courageously, and with a touch of sheer consternation.

Quite early on in our acquaintanceship he brought to see me one of the more senior police officers in Lourenço Marques – Inspector Y. From his colour and bearing the inspector seemed to be decidedly a local product; as, indeed, were a good proportion of the officials in Mozambique. The Portuguese, I found, had no colour prejudice as such. Any resident in their colonies who acquired money and was generous in handing it out to his betters; who adopted a name like Costa da Silva, went to Mass regularly, and generally conducted himself

in a responsible, respectable way, became automatically socially accept-
able. The pawn got through to the back row more easily than in other
African colonies. I used to think because of this, that, had I been a
black African, I should have preferred to live under Portuguese rule,
despite its brutality, incompetence and corruption, than under that of
any of the other colonial Powers; certainly than under the rule of
Afrikaners in the Union of South Africa across the border.

Camille had given his police inspector friend a great build-up before
bringing him to see me – '*Vous savez, un homme très intelligent, très
cultivé, très fin. Franchement, je m'étonne; même en comparaison avec les
cercles intellectuelles les plus estimeés de Varsovie. Un homme exceptionnel.*'
He lingered over the syllables of this last word – *ex-cep-tion-nel.*
Inspector Y did not, at first glance, live up to this panegyric. He had one
of those bashed-in faces which look as though lumps have fallen off
them here and there; like a plaster bust which has been left exposed to
the weather. As he spoke only a few words of French and English, I had
no means of appreciating his wit and learning, so highly praised by
Camille. Despite linguistic difficulties, I managed to convey to him the
suggestion that if, in the course of his duties, he came across anything
that might be of interest to the British Consulate-General, I should be
most grateful if he would communicate it to me via our mutual and
esteemed friend Camille. The suggestion was well received; something
in the nature of a smile broke across the waste-land of the inspector's
face, followed by a pause in which we all three looked at one another,
aware that we had reached the heart of the matter.

Diffidently – it was my first bribe; later, I became brazen enough –
I produced from the drawer of my desk an envelope in which I had put
some hundred escudo notes, and mentioned that, no doubt, certain
expenses would arise in connection with the assignment the inspector
had so graciously undertaken which I hoped he would allow me to
defray. Thereupon, I passed the envelope to Camille to pass on to his
friend. Camille opened it, took out the notes and counted them, with the
other's eyes closely upon him. I noticed in the Inspector's face, as he
watched Camille counting the notes, a faint but unmistakable look of
dissatisfaction; a barely discernible shake of the head, a touch of cold-
ness breaking in on the amiability he had previously displayed. It would
not do. Camille, as ever, master of the situation, very courteously asked
permission to enter into a private colloquy with me. Drawing me aside,
he said in an undertone that his friend was too polite (*trop gentleman*) to
say so, but the amount I had handed over was quite inadequate. Wertz,

in such a case, paid at least three times as much; Campini even more, *et même les Japonais, bien plus*. As I well knew, he went on, he never cared to discuss money with me; the subject was highly distasteful to him. Where money was concerned he was *un enfant nouveau né*. Even so, in this particular case, his honour was involved, and he must ask me to increase the amount paid to his friend, even if it had to be deducted from his own paltry honorarium. I suggested another three hundred escudos; his lips soundlessly formed the word *cinq*, and *cinq* it was. I should add that Camille's notion that he disliked discussing money was scarcely in accord with the facts; we discussed little else, invariably to the disadvantage of HM's Government and the British taxpayer. Having settled the matter of the escudos, Camille and his friend departed, with many courtesies, leaving me to work out a telegram to London announcing the new recruit to my *apparat*, and seeking approval for the rate we had settled on for the job. I anticipated no difficulties.

I found that bribing, which inevitably played a large part in my Lourenço Marques activities, had as many subtleties and diversities as seduction. Thus, in certain circumstances the passing of money had to be engineered in such a way that it seemed to happen of itself, which, in seduction terms, was the equivalent of lolling or reaching out an arm as though by accident. Alternatively, there were occasions in which one yelled or banged the desk, insisting that not a cent more would be forthcoming. This might be compared with violent assault. It is interesting, incidentally, as bearing on the close relation between the two activities, that the same word is used for both – to pass money or to make a pass. I became quite an adept as time went on, knowing just when to show the colour of my (or rather HMG's) money, and how much was needed to provide the necessary incentive in this or that case. In Intelligence operations, money is an essential ingredient; even where other motives arise – as patriotism or ideological affiliations – money, however little, or its equivalent, must be dropped in, like a touch of bitter in a mint julep, to validate the deal. Only when money has passed is the mystical union fully established; it's money that makes Intelligence go round. And money, as it were, on trust. For obvious reasons, I couldn't ask Inspector Y for a receipt. In bribery there are no accounts; only good, or, more often, bad, faith.

As it turned out, Inspector Y proved to be well worth his pay. In numerous operations his help was invaluable. Thus, when we arranged for some South African troops interned in Mozambique to be taken into Swaziland, then British territory, the good man was able to ensure that

there were no traffic hold-ups or other misadventures along the way. The troops in question had been torpedoed off the Mozambique coast, the troop-ship transporting them to North Africa sunk without trace in a sea infested with sharks. At the Consulate-General we heard of the catastrophe, and I went along with the rest of the staff to receive the survivors when they came ashore, wet and shivering and bewildered; some of them, especially the lascars, babbling incomprehensibly, and letting out strange anguished howls which merged with the cries of the scavenger birds the scene had attracted. It was an eerie spectacle; a moonless night, pitch-black, the sea stormy, and, apart from our flickering lights, only the white of the breakers to be seen as they came roaring in. The survivors, as belligerents landing in a neutral country, had to be interned by the Mozambique authorities, and were put in the *Assistencia Publica,* a place of such squalid horror that even rebellious seamen planning to desert in Lourenço Marques, after a sight of it, returned meekly to their ships and the boatswain's whistle.

I managed to get a message to the interned South Africans that, if they would arrange to take a stroll along the road to the Swaziland frontier on a particular Sunday afternoon, I'd hope to have some cars going in the same direction that would stop and give them a lift. First, I tried the South African business community resident in Lourenço Marques to see if any of their cars would be available, but none were. They feared trouble with the authorities which might damage their business. In the end, it was the taxi-drivers of Lourenço Marques who saved the day; especially one of them who brought in the others – a little man with a big mouth strikingly like Lord Beaverbrook, and known thenceforth by the name. Happily, he knew nothing of the original; otherwise, as I told him, he might well have been tempted to sue me in the courts for defamation. Some ten of them happened to drive their taxis in the direction of Swaziland on the afternoon in question, and loaded up with the interned troops, depositing them at the frontier some fifty miles away where I had arranged for them to be admitted. In no time they were in Mbabane, the capital of Swaziland, and thence whisked away to Johannesburg and home. The taxi-drivers would accept no more money than the normal fare, though the risk they ran was far greater than the South African business men would have had to face. It is true, of course, that, thanks to Inspector Y, the risk was far less than they supposed, but I doubt if they knew this. I really believe they would have done the job for nothing, so delighted were they to have a chance of serving the Allied cause. Thenceforth, they were all

my firm friends. Years later, when I was banned from entering the Union of South Africa, the story of the escape of the interned soldiers was resurrected in the South African press. I was happy to learn that some of those who took the Swaziland road had survived the war, and remembered their deliverance from the *Assistencia Publica*.

Another episode in which Inspector Y's part was even more useful concerned a local resident known to be an organiser and collector of shipping intelligence for Campini. He, too, we decided, should be given a trip to Swaziland. The problem was to ensure that he took a drive in that direction on a specific evening and at a specific time. As it turned out, we were able to arrange a stratagem on the best Hollywood lines. Our man, it appeared, was enamoured of a white South African girl dancer, who, however, had so far repelled his advances. At the same time, she very much wanted a return visa to Johannesburg, this having hitherto been withheld on the ground that her way of life in Lourenço Marques was immoral. As so often happens, Afrikaners tend to combine tolerance of collective wickedness, as embodied in the vile doctrine of *apartheid*, with particular squeamishness in matters of personal behaviour. Similarly, the privately immoral are often the loudest in protestations of public virtue. Hence the insistence in the New Testament that a balance must be struck and maintained between our duty to God and to our neighbour.

The girl came to see me, and I encouraged her to tell me about her life in Lourenço Marques and wish to go home. She was rather pretty in a dusky way; like so many ostensibly white South Africans, probably by no means of pure European stock. Financially, I remarked, she had presumably not been doing too badly. She nodded; there was plenty of money about; but the Portuguese! She pulled a face; the bars and cabarets of Johannesburg, she said in effect, were scarcely Cheltenham Ladies' College, but by comparison with their Mozambique equivalents, delectable. Anyway, she was sick of being passed around from hand to hand, with everyone wanting the same thing and wanting it at once. Like so-and-so, I said, mentioning the man we proposed to kidnap. Yes, like him, she agreed readily. Then we got down to business. We wanted this man, for reasons she could easily guess, somewhere on British territory where he could be questioned. Would she help to get him there? All she had to do was to induce him to go for a drive along a particular road at a particular time. In return I'd guarantee to do everything possible to overcome the difficulty about her visa. It was a very dishonest proposition on my part. I had no reason to suppose that

I could persuade the South African Consul-General in Lourenço Marques – who certainly had no great liking for me – to change his attitude towards allowing her to return to Johannesburg, and I deliberately let her form the impression that I could pull strings on her behalf in high quarters, which was, of course, quite nonsensical. I hadn't even referred the project to London for approval, as I was bound to do before embarking on anything of the kind. It was extremely unlikely that approval would be given, at least without a whole lot of questions being asked, and consequent delays. I found very early on in Lourenço Marques that it was better to act first and ask afterwards. If the action was successful, everyone was delighted; if not, there was bound to be trouble anyway, irrespective of whether or not prior approval had been sought.

Rather to my surprise, the girl readily agreed, and we went ahead. She duly induced her aspiring paramour to take her for a drive; Inspector Y stopped the car at the agreed place, where another car was waiting, and our man was expeditiously transferred into it, and then driven to Mbabane, where I lost sight of him. Later, I vaguely heard that he had been taken to England for interrogation, and spent the rest of the war there. Fortunately, when he arrived in Mbabane he had notes of Allied shipping movements in his pocket. His disappearance from Lourenço Marques created a minor sensation, and was widely attributed to financial difficulties. It was said that the accounts of his business were in disarray. I was tempted to claim this as a piece of deliberate deception on our part, but in fact it came about naturally, which is always the best kind of deception. The girl behaved impeccably, and said nothing to anyone about what had happened, which made me more than ever ashamed about my shabby bargain with her. Intelligence work necessarily involves such cheating, lying and betraying, which is why it has so deleterious an effect on the character. I never met anyone professionally engaged in it whom I should care to trust in any capacity.

In due course I nerved myself to approach the South African Consul-General about the girl, trying to make him believe that my interest was due to a personal infatuation. I overdid it, of course, dwelling on the girl's desire to make a fresh start, and on the essential purity and goodness of her nature. The Consul-General had one of those lean, dry antipodean faces – he was Australian by origin – and seemed unimpressed by my apologia. After I had finished, he brought up the subject of the kidnapped man, and asked me if I had any views on it. I said I hadn't, apart from vaguely hearing that he was in financial difficulties. 'I think

you did it,' the Consul-General said quietly. I let that pass, and got up to go. A few days later, to my great relief, I had a scribbled note from the girl saying that she now had permission to return to Johannesburg, and thanking me. I sent her some flowers. By a happy chance, Inspector Y was put in charge of the police investigation of the missing man, and he looked in to tell me how his enquiries were going. It was the only occasion during our acquaintanceship that I knew him to laugh heartily. He laughed and laughed, and I handed him an extra envelope.

It was curious how quickly I became used to this weird business in which I engaged. Going each morning to the Consulate-General, opening my mail, telegrams deciphered now, happily, not by me but by an expert elderly Scottish lady, Miss Stewart, sent from London for the purpose; in- and out-trays, telephone calls, visitors, appointments, all the usual procedures of office work. Back to the Polana Hotel for lunch, and a glimpse of Campini and Wertz, or, if they were absent, speculation as to where they were. In the afternoon, a stroll by the sea, and then back to the office till the evening when there were liable to be social occasions. The various consulates celebrated their national days, like embassies; receptions were held, uniforms worn, gossip exchanged, just as though Lourenço Marques were an important capital, and no war raging throughout the world. For news I was dependent on the local newspaper, which I spelled out each morning, and on a cyclo-styled sheet issued by the Consulate-General. It was thus that I learnt of the Battle of Stalingrad, and of the continuing triumph of Japanese arms. Far, far away these momentous events were taking place, but we on our African coast, in tropical heat and humidity, dozy and amorous and scandal-mongering, went our way; for us, the struggle symbolised by Campini in his cloak, Wertz in his shorts, and me, contending to-gether. Occasionally I relieved my feelings by despatching a message to Graham Greene in Freetown; it, too, scrupulously coded with one-time pads, as though most secret, and replied to in similar style.

Occasionally, too, I would find some reason for visiting South Africa; driving there, dusty mile after dusty mile, or, when it rained, churning and floundering through mud. After green Swaziland, the parched Veldt, where I came upon little Boer townships and villages; strangely silent and deserted, almost as though unoccupied, until I suc-ceeded in knocking up some large, somnolent inn-keeper who, with slow sulky movements, produced beer and a hunk of bread and cheese, gazing suspiciously the while. A weird survival, as it seemed to me; some

brontosaurus from another age, lumbering, barely articulate, brutal in a slow kind of way, but also lost, dazed, as though involved in a bewildering situation beyond his understanding, yet stubbornly resolved to stay as he was because there was no alternative. Brobdingnagian, towering, brooding, but with some valid relationship to this country where fate had put him; blindly resolved to live out his destiny there to the end, whatever it might be. The black Africans serving him, working his land, digging out his gold and his diamonds, seemed utterly subservient; yet beneath their oppression, strangely enough, I thought I detected a sort of patient confidence and satisfaction; almost a quite joy, that the future was theirs. All they had to do was to wait – which they were well accustomed to, and good at.

It is one of those situations in the world which everyone, consciously or unconsciously, recognises as being somehow crucial; more so than others seemingly more momentous. In South Africa itself this sense of momentousness is made more poignant by the very fascination of the countryside itself – something Alan Paton has conveyed beautifully and vividly in his writings. What is happening there, I realised, is not just a political squabble, a matter of ins and outs; but rather a great drama, in whose working out the Afrikaners, the ostensible villains, have their own peculiar nobility, as the black Africans, the present victims, their own special exaltation. It may even be, I sometimes speculated, that this land is earmarked to be the scene of the last battle between our expiring civilisation and the up-and-coming barbarism threatening it. By an accident of history and geography, the Afrikaners have been cut off from the demoralising currents of the twentieth century, and in their isolation have been able to go on believing in themselves as a people chosen by God to maintain and defend the beliefs and ways of their forebears; to see themselves as the guardians of Christendom in a dark continent. Despite the, in contemporary terms, lunacy, and even criminality, that such an attitude has led to, it has a great fascination; even those who find it most abhorrent and scandalous are still held by it. In the American Deep South there is plenty of anger and fear, but in South Africa there is something else – this weird, distorted, grotesque, in its own way, heroic attitude of the Afrikaner, defying, not just contemporary anti-racialist principles, not just the propositions and hypocrisies of the conventional liberal attitudes and the World Council of Churches, but history itself. Dull, sullen, paunchy men, obstinately, stupidly, standing up to the currents which have swept aside in our time ancient dynasties and social orders, and reduced to rubble and

despair so many proud cities and citadels which, only a few short years
ago, seemed strong and rich and enduring.

I usually arrived at Johannesburg after nightfall; the city ablaze with
lights, headlights bearing down on this rough Babylon prospering so
mightily, gold being no less needed to fight wars than men and machines.
So, every effort made; backs straining and bending, sweat pouring over
dusky faces, furnaces glowing, winches turning, to extract the last
yellow ounce to forge into ingots to stock bank vaults and Treasuries.
I had seen some of the requisite labour being recruited in Mozambique.
Good biceps, a fine chest expansion, straight legs and solid thighs; all
this surveyed and felt by the recruiters, like a cattleman at a market.
He'll do! Now, in Johannesburg, the recruited to be seen, wild looking,
separated from tribe, home and family, and in their own way likewise
engaged in the feverish quest for gold. On Saturday nights when they
received their pay, rolling about drunk in the streets, with notices
warning white motorists – Beware, Natives! lest they should run them
down like straying dogs or cats. A wild feverish city, awash with new
red wine and raw brandy; a place of violence, with more to come –
smelling already of the blood that must flow. A city of gold and blood;
yellow and red.

On one such occasion, I went on to Cape Town, where there was an
MI5 man to liaise with; MI6 not being permitted to operate in a British
Dominion, as South Africa then, of course, still was. Through this
MI5 man I made the acquaintance of Brigadier P, a South African who
was a strong and avowed Anglophil; a genial host and interesting talker.
At the time he was dealing with the case of Robey Leibrandt, which had
made a considerable stir in South Africa, and even caused some ripples
in Lourenço Marques; Leibrandt being a German agent who had been
despatched from a U-boat in a rubber dinghy to land on the South
African coast. This he succeeded in doing, and in setting up some sort of
radio transmission, but he was fairly soon caught. The man primarily
responsible for turning him in, and whose evidence was essential in the
forthcoming court proceedings, was, Brigadier P told me, lurking in the
top storey of the Post Office building. Would I like to come and see
him? I said I would, and the Brigadier took me along. Never have I
seen a man so scared. He had an armed guard watching over him night
and day, and nothing would induce him to venture out-of-doors, where
he considered, Brigadier P believed with reason, that he was bound to be
murdered. By way of camouflage, he was in the process of growing an
enormous moustache, and so eager was he for the protection he hoped

this foliage would afford him that he seemed to be fostering its growth, strand by strand, like an assiduous gardener. Was it not, I remarked to Brigadier P, a strange case for a man to be in who had apprehended an enemy agent in time of war? He shrugged significantly, and agreed that, to anyone who did not know South Africa, it doubtless did seem strange. I should have paid more heed to the object lesson he had kindly arranged for me. Afterwards, I heard that the man, by this time his moustache having reached stupendous proportions, was taken under the most stringent security conditions to give evidence for the prosecution at Leibrandt's trial, and then whisked off to some distant place where the fury of the Afrikaner nationalists at what he had done could not reach him. Leibrandt was sentenced to a term of imprisonment, of which he served some five years, and then was predictably released when Dr Malan became Prime Minister. I vaguely heard that he set up as a butcher, and now is dead.

In Lourenço Marques I acquired another informant, Serge; a small, eager Jew from somewhere in Eastern Europe. One of those veterans of persecution who had somehow made his way across half the world, hiding, scurrying to and fro, changing his name and documentation from time to time; an expert on identity papers, in and out of prison, settling for a while – in Constantinople, in Beirut, in Alexandria, then on the run again. Any hat he wore a shade too large, clothes with some remote stylishness of their own, a cut about them, shoes pointed and perforated. It was his face I loved; so full of knowingness and woe and wistfulness. What battered endurance and heroism traced in it! He would come in to see me two or three times a week; sitting in front of my desk, occasionally gesticulating or getting up to illustrate a point – this person and that who'd turned up, gossip he'd heard, conversations he'd listened to. India-rubber features screwing up, the suspicion of a wink – '*J'ai joué la comédie avec lui*'; his favourite saying, perhaps because life had so often played the tragedy with him. He'd done everything, but had no trade or profession; with the traditional Jewish veneration for learning still in him, he occasionally picked up a book, but was only vaguely literate. A polyglot if ever there was one, with snatches of every language under the sun, including German, which he knew quite well, but would not speak if he could possibly avoid it. We spoke in French, with occasional English words breaking in. With me, he never once played the comedy; I treasure his memory.

It was thanks to Serge that I became involved in what proved to be, in MI6 terms, the most successful of my Lourenço Marques operations.

In one of his *tours d'horison* he mentioned that he had made the acquaintance of a Greek sailor who told him that the captain of his ship was working for the Axis, and had a rendezvous with a German U-boat operating in the Mozambique Channel, for the purpose of handing over stores and equipment. It fitted exactly with a rather obscure reference in my latest dollop of Bletchley material to a Greek boat Wertz was to keep a special look-out for. There was only one place, Serge told me, where we could be sure of running into his man, and that was the oldest established and best-known Lourenço Marques brothel, invariably referred to as Marie's Place after the proprietress, herself a veteran in the business. He mentioned this establishment with a certain diffidence, having, as I well knew, a wholly undeserved respect for me as someone removed from the sordid necessities to which such as he were subject. Sometimes, in our conversations, I sought to disabuse him of this notion, trying to explain that I considered his life to be heroic compared with mine, and his instincts purer and more disinterested, but it was no use; he continued to see me as a creature living on a different plane. As far as visiting Marie's Place was concerned, I was able to convince him that, in the course of duty, I was ready to present myself there or anywhere else, however unsavoury, at any time. He said he would alert me, and there we left the matter for the time being. I may add that of course I gave Serge money from time to time, and of course he took it, but he never once raised the question of the amount or counted it in my presence, or came to me – as every other agent I ever had, did – with some hard luck story requiring an additional sum urgently.

The very next day I got a message from Serge to meet him that evening at a café near the waterfront. He was looking more dapper than usual; wearing an old-fashioned boater with a coloured ribbon of a kind still worn when I was an undergraduate, which he had acquired somewhere or other in the course of his wanderings. We went together to Marie's Place, where, in the old style, a red light was shining over the heavy front door, corresponding, I decided, to 'C' 's blue one. We rang, and a grating opened, and a face peered out. On recognising Serge, we were at once admitted – something that embarrassed him a little, and led him subsequently to explain at some length how it was only since working on my behalf that he had become a frequenter of Marie's Place, which was so very useful for making contacts and picking up gossip. The old-fashioned appearance of the exterior was matched within – heavy plush curtains, deep dusty divans similarly covered, with brocaded cushions; little mother-of-pearl tables, a large leopard-skin rug with a

snarling head, and the whole bathed in heavy, all-pervasive perfume. There are two interiors which scarcely seem to have changed through the centuries – brothels and the anterooms of ecclesiastical dignitaries, both expressing, in their heavy hangings and upholstery, a certain continuity, a relationship with what is changeless in us and our lives; in the one case, sensual, in the other, spiritual. Serge and I sat down side by side on one of the divans, and presently Mme Marie herself swept in; an ageless lady, with a curled blonde wig, pendulous ear-rings, and much jewellery gleaming and jingling about her person; a large bosom amply displayed, a voluminous dress of red satin, and at the heart of all this infra-structure, a gaunt, bony, lavishly rouged face. It was said that she had arrived at Lourenço Marques some sixty years before from Marseilles to join the present establishment, becoming in due course the patron and enormously rich. There was always a reigning gigolo, the current incumbent being a young Tunisian named Mustapha.

Yes, Mme Marie told us, the young man we were interested in was expected that evening, and it was Monique who would entertain him. Monique, it seemed, had got to know him quite well, and could tell us more about him. At the moment she was working (somehow it went even better in French – *pour l'instant, elle travaille*), but – looking at her little jewelled wristwatch – she should be free soon. Meanwhile, could she offer us a glass of champagne. This was brought in on a tray by a negro boy in a red coat and turban, While we waited, sipping it, clients came in and were attended to – mostly South Africans, fairly tipsy and on a spree, one or two obvious sailors very drunk, and a local Portuguese, immensely respectable-looking, who took off his glasses and carefully wiped the lenses before going upstairs. At one point Camille's friend, Inspector Y, put his head in through the door, saw me, and, with an expression half leering and half astonishment, at once withdrew. When, later, I referred jocosely to our encounter, thinking this the course of prudence, he went to great pains to explain that inspecting the *maisons de tolérance* was one of his more disagreeable duties.

In due course Monique appeared, unruffled by her recent labours. Incidentally, we saw the clients come in, but not go out – there was another exit. So I never knew on whose behalf Monique had been working. She turned out to be an exceptionally amiable woman, well, even heavily, built, rough featured, with a pleasant smile and smooth, cheerful voice; my idea, to the life, of Oblomov's wife. Yes, she knew our Greek quite well; a nice boy, but young, naïve, inexperienced – the last slightly accentuated. He had told her about the goings-on on his ship,

and she had considered them important enough to pass on to Serge. If there was any way she could help further we had only to mention it; she would do anything – but anything – against the Nazis. No idle boast, as I had occasion to learn later. Now she must go; the Greek might arrive at any minute, and she would not wish him to find her with us. It was not so much a matter of security as of etiquette, of delicacy. I could quite see why. If we talked all four together, she and the Greek, at a certain point, would have to leave us, or be left by us, and we should know why, and they would know that we knew, which would be inelegant, and, in any case, possibly add to the difficulties of his lack of experience.

As it happened, the Greek arrived immediately after she left us. He was extraordinarily beautiful; one of those faces you still find among modern Greeks whose features exactly recall the broken statues in Ephesus or Corinth. Yes, they could easily take over the ship; the first officer was wholly on our side. All that was required was that I should arrange for them to be able to sail the ship into Durban after they had disposed of the captain and the one or two members of the crew on whom he could count. 'Dispose?' I asked. He smiled. That was optional; they could be thrown to the sharks, or, alternatively, secured and handed over to the Durban authorities. It was obvious where his own preference lay, but I opted for the latter course. He promised to bring the first officer to see me at the Consulate-General the following morning, there being a certain amount of urgency as they were due to sail in forty-eight hours' time. On this note we parted, leaving him with Monique.

I found myself greatly excited by this venture. Everything about it seemed wonderful – cast, plot, *mise-en-scène*. Serge was equally delighted; for the first time I saw him truly excited. His only disappointment was that the sharks were not to be fed, but I argued that what could be got out of the captured men would be more useful than killing them, and anyway I could guarantee that they would be immobilised for the rest of the war. This had to satisfy him, but I could see he was thinking of the extermination camps, and of all it had cost him to have to dodge and run across half the world. My argument, anyway, was specious; it was extremely improbable that anything of importance could be got out of the captain. He and his associates could be thrown to the sharks with impunity; no one would ever know or care. I chose to have them kept alive, even though they had been engaged in fuelling and provisioning the U-boats that were sinking our convoys in the Mozambique Channel. This, not out of humanitarian or pacifist

sentiments – I read without undue perturbation of the saturation bombing of German cities – but because I could see in my mind's eye their bodies being thrown overboard, hear their cries, observe the shadows of the sharks as they gathered, and the blood staining the water after they pounced.

It was rather absurd, I admit, when one of the great holocausts of history was taking place, to fret like this, one way or the other, about the fate of a Greek captain and a sailor or two. Yet I did fret. Why rob Serge of a taste of legitimate vengeance? I asked myself. This tiny drama – what was it by comparison with the global one being enacted? Well, the difference was that in the tiny drama I had a part to play, lines to speak, whereas in the other I was only an extra; part of a crowd scene, shouting obediently Hosanna! or Crucify him! according to the exigencies of a script I had no hand in writing. So the Greek lived, and I knew that I was a fraudulent belligerent, with no passion like Serge for victory and vengeance – the same thing, really; no sense of being engaged in a life and death struggle against the powers of darkness. If I had been truly honest, in the light of this realisation I should have turned in my Mozambique assignment and returned home to grow potatoes in Whatlington. Instead, I threw myself with renewed zest into our plot, spending half the night ciphering a long message to London about what we proposed to do, and meeting the first officer the next morning, as arranged, to work out the final details with him. To my great satisfaction I was able to get from him the precise bearings of where the projected rendezvous with the German U-boat was to take place, and telegraphed this information, along with the ship's probable time of arrival at Durban, to Cape Town for transmission to Naval Intelligence.

In the event, everything happened according to plan; the ship duly arrived at Durban with the captain locked up in his cabin and his associates likewise secured, and I had every reason to hope that the rendezvous would be effectively kept. A long message from London indicated that at last they had realised there that the ship I had been telegraphing about and the one Wertz was being urged to keep an eye on, were one and the same. There was also some criticism of the procedures I had employed, especially my communicating direct with Naval Intelligence rather than through them. I could afford to take a light-hearted view of these strictures because, shortly after receiving them, I had a congratulatory telegram from 'C'; considered in the Service a rare and precious accolade. I never knew for sure whether I

could claim to have contributed towards reducing by one the submarines operating in the Mozambique Channel, or heard what happened to the Greeks, pro or contra, but the operation enhanced my standing in MI6.

Thenceforth Monique and Marie's Place became part of the Lourenço Marques scene for me. Oddly enough, in retrospect, they seem the only homely – if I dare use the word – aspect of the whole adventure. There was a down-to-earth quality about the establishment which was very appealing. As for Monique herself – she, as I came to see, had some truly admirable qualities, partly due, perhaps, to her very profession, which served to canalise into workaday channels emotions and desires which otherwise can become unduly pretentious, overstrained and ultimately even destructive and demented. The only point on which we differed, was over whether or not she should knife one or other of the visiting Germans to whom, when they visited Marie's place, she was liable to be allotted. It would be so easy, she insisted, and showed me just how it could be done when the German, however husky, might be expected to be quiescent. She did not accept my arguments against such an action, but she bowed to them.

I am happy to think now that my last word of her related to an episode in which she was at her most sublime. A small black box she left at the Consulate-General was found to contain charts, a log-book and a code-book belonging to a British ship's captain who had recently put in to Lourenço Marques. It appeared that the captain had brought the box ashore with him for security, got drunk and gone along to Marie's Place, where he had been handed over to Monique. In view of his condition, she thought it more prudent to take the box off him for safe-keeping, and the following day, not knowing where or how she could find the captain, thought it best to bring it to the Consulate-General to be returned to him. Without any question, she could have got for it from Wertz or Campini a sum that, to her, would have been a fortune. Equally certainly, she knew that this was so, but never, I am sure, for a moment even considered such a possibility.

One late afternoon, sitting in the Polana lounge, I noticed a young woman, obviously Portuguese, come into the hotel and speak to the clerk at the reception desk. Something about the way she moved, some special ease or grace in her, at once held my attention, and without thinking what I was doing, I went up to her and said, 'Hullo!' It was a risky thing to do; she might easily have responded in a way that

would have been highly embarrassing for me – by being angry, or complaining to the clerk, or just ignoring me. There were all kinds of possibilities. As it was, she smiled, and returned my greeting. Her beauty was even more striking near to than I had supposed; with her large dark eyes and hair, and the sallow complexion that went with them. Also – though this was more apparent later, when I got to know her – some quality permeating her whole being that I can only describe as the innocence which comes of accepting life in its totality, all it has to offer, to the mind, the body and the soul. When she had gone I risked asking the clerk who she was. The wife of a local German business man, he told me, who might be described as the Gauleiter of the German community resident in Lourenço Marques; adding that she and her husband were moving into the hotel in a day or so. This information added a professional dimension to a personal inclination.

Thenceforth, I was, of course, on the look-out for her; saw her arrive with her luggage, and managed to make a rendezvous for that evening, at the end of the hotel terrace overlooking the sea, where it was dark and unfrequented. I stationed myself at the end of the terrace – much too early, it goes without saying. In the dining-room I had noticed she was seated at Wertz's table, so that, in addition to the excitement of meeting her, was the thought, that she would be coming, as it were, hot-foot from the company of my chief antagonist. I dreaded that someone else might choose that particular evening to be on the terrace, and resented every footstep I heard that was not hers. At last she came, with a characteristic swinging gait she had that I got to know well and recognise at once. It is always easy to talk to someone with whom one is going to become intimate; the future casts its shadow backwards, and there is no explaining to be done, even though there is everything to explain. A stumbling, awkward first encounter rarely ripens into intimacy. The first thing I learnt was her name – Anna. We talked about the war; she was much more sanguine than I about the Eastern Front, and absolutely certain that the *Wehrmacht* would be routed. She easily guessed that I was wondering how she could feel so when she was married to a Gauleiter. Their marriage, anyway, she said, was breaking up; hence the move to the hotel, where, in fact, they occupied separate rooms and rarely saw each other. As for Wertz – she detested him because he was a Nazi.

All this came out, not perhaps in the course of our first talk, but certainly in the early days of our acquaintanceship. She told me, too, of another German, Johann von X, a refugee, whom she loved and hoped

to marry, and would like me to get to know. He had come to Africa as
a fugitive from the Nazis; had been interned in Rhodesia, then escaped
and made his way to Lourenço Marques, where they had met. I had
to consider, of course, whether the attitude she took might not be a plant
on her part to lull me into confiding in her, to the point when I might
perhaps be pulled into the German network, or at any rate exposed.
The delight of her company, the charm of her full, rich voice and
occasional misuse of English (which she had learnt at a school in South
Africa), especially slang; the sheer pleasure of being with her on those
warm Lourenço Marques evenings, on the terrace, or, as sometimes
happened, I in my car, driving slowly along until I saw her, a vigorous,
striding shadow – how, in such circumstances, could I possibly suspect
her of engaging in deliberate deception. As it turned out, my instinct was
correct; in all her dealings with me she was never other than straight-
forward and truthful. All the same, I had to cover myself by reporting
the contact to London, giving her a code name, and seeking authorisa-
tion for going on seeing her. It was as well I did this; an Englishman
staying in the hotel who had spotted us together on the terrace sent the
Consul-General a letter complaining of my behaviour. Ledger showed
the letter to me before sending it on to the Consular Department of the
Foreign Office. So I was able to forestall it.

The gap between my relationship with Anna as presented in my
Intelligence reports, and as it actually existed when we were together,
was so wide that it amounted to a sort of schizophrenia; being two people
in one, and at times getting confused between them. Double agents
quite often go off their heads, and I can easily see why. They begin to
doubt both their identities, or imagine a whole multiplicity; one fitting
into another, like those dolls which get smaller and smaller, until,
right at the centre – nothing. In this particular case, the situation was
greatly eased by the inclusion of Anna's friend Johann in our relation-
ship. He was a highly intelligent and perceptive person of whom I also
got very fond, and so somehow, as it were, completed the circuit;
whereas before there had been open wires sparking and spluttering,
with the risk of a fuse at any moment, now the current flowed smoothly.

The first time we picked him up in the car we went for a picnic by
a rock pool some miles away. I had brought provisions and a bottle of
drambuie, which for some reason, though I did not particularly like it,
became our regular drink. It was a perfect moonlit evening, warm and
still. I realised when I saw Johann that I had noticed him about in
Lourenço Marques; a tall striking figure one could scarcely miss, with

fair hair, blue eyes and the standard sabre cut down his face. At one point I saw him on the beach directing a fat German dentist named Dr Schwab in some reducing exercises. We often laughed about this. He spoke English well, but with a characteristic lilting German intonation. In his own style he was decidedly handsome, so that he and Anna made an impressive pair; he so blond, she so dark. Their intimacy was strong and deep; they were wrapped up in one another, two castaways who had found a sanctuary together. Though, alas, I am very prone to jealousy, even in the most ridiculous circumstances, so that I can find myself feeling jealous of two total strangers who, maybe in a railway carriage or some other public place, seem totally preoccupied with one another, to the exclusion of anyone else who may be present, including myself – nonetheless, being with Johann and Anna on our outing together, I had not a single twinge, save once, and then only momentarily. This was when Anna turned to Johann to shelter her while she got into her bathing suit, I having meanwhile tactfully jumped into the pool and started splashing about in it. After our swim we ate our provisions, drank our drambuie, and talked and talked, covered with a blanket because the night air began to get fresh. Finally, we dozed off, for how long I can't be sure, but I know that when I awoke I had a curious sensation of not knowing which of us was which; of our being inextricably mixed up together. The sensation lasted, I suppose, for no more than a few seconds; then it passed, and we got back into the car and returned to Lourenço Marques.

Soon, by the operation of Parkinson's Law, the staff in Lourenço Marques began to grow. First to arrive on the scene, as I have mentioned, was Miss Stewart, to take over the ciphering and re-ciphering. Her arrival was a great relief; though I improved a little with practice, the one-time pads continued to baffle me, and I would sweat and groan over them far into the night. Now I just had to type out a message and hand it over to Miss Stewart, and await her ciphered version of any that arrived. One ill consequence, I fear, was that, lacking the restraining influence of having to encipher messages myself, I became ever more verbose. Happily, all this paper has now, as I understand, been destroyed, though, ironically enough, not its counterpart, the *Abwehr* records, which were captured by the Americans, and have been carefully microfilmed and stored in Washington. If, by some infinitely remote chance, anyone in the future wants to know what went on in the way of counter-espionage in Lourenço Marques during the 1939–45 war, it will be Wertz's version, not mine, that will be available. Indeed,

this may be said already to have happened in Ladislas Farago's *The Game of the Foxes*, which leans heavily, if not exclusively, on the *Abwehr* records in purportedly recounting the story of German espionage in the 1939–45 war.

Soon after Miss Stewart's arrival there took place in Lourenço Marques a diplomatic exchange which led to a further accretion of staff. Two ships sailed in, one bearing Allied diplomats from South-East Asia, and the other Japanese diplomats from Europe and America. They then exchanged passengers for the return voyages. Journalists arrived to cover the event, among them some old acquaintances amazed at my vice-consular impersonation, and I had the task of organising a press-conference at the Consulate-General at which the British Ambassador from Tokyo delivered a kind of diplomatic incantation; like a monsignor splashing holy water over a missile site. My chief interest in the occasion was meeting the various Secret Service and related personnel who had managed to get in on the exchange. They all came clandestinely and severally to see me in my office (were Wertz and Campini similarly invaded? I never found out) to collect money, send messages to London, and generally establish themselves as being again in circulation. I tried, before they came, to guess which of the passengers might turn out to be in SIS, but failed in every case save one – that of Steptoe. He, I decided, when I first set eyes upon him, was every inch a Secret Serviceman, and so, sure enough, he was. I took an instant liking to him, and persuaded him to stay behind in Lourenço Marques with me.

He was a little cock-sparrow of a man, with a bristling moustache, a high voice, a monocle and a lot of suits, ties, hats and shoes despite the fact that he had been in internment since Japan came into the war. A real pro, I felt, to whom every encounter, however innocent, was clandestine, every letter – even bills – needed to be tested for invisible ink, and everyone near him, in a café or restaurant, in a railway carriage, or just happening to pause in his vicinity to light a cigarette or do up a shoelace, was keeping him under surveillance. He carefully burnt every communication he received that could possibly be regarded as in any way compromising; not just content to set fire to them and leave them to be consumed by the flames, but watching the ash to make sure it mouldered into undecipherable dust. I never actually saw him eat any paper, but he told me – and I entirely believed him – that before the Japanese came to take him into custody, he swallowed his code book, page by page, from A to Z, and was just settling down to consume his

one-time pad when he was arrested. He was never, drunk or sober, forgetful for an instant of the burden of secrets that he carried; a treasure trove that he felt the enemy were longing to take off him. By some miracle, he told me, the Japanese failed to avail themselves of the opportunity which his being in their custody provided, but he was ready with all manner of ingenious false confessions if they had pulled off his toenails, roasted the soles of his feet, or otherwise exerted themselves to wrest his secrets from him. Ironically enough, one of his fellow-passengers on the exchange, a blameless British Council representative, a brilliant Japanese scholar with a Japanese wife, who subsequently became *The Times* correspondent in Tokyo, did get the full treatment, the Japanese doubtless calculating that no government would finance and support the activities the British Council engaged in without some ulterior motive. Steptoe, on the other hand, would have struck them as a purely Wodehousean figure of no security interest – the Japanese being, as Wodehouse himself told me, among his most avid readers.

Steptoe's feeling that he represented a prize any enemy Intelligence service would give their eyes to have at their disposition, was not abated by the failure of the Japanese to try to extort his secrets from him. The Germans, he felt sure, would know better, and when at one point it was suggested that he might return to London via Lisbon, travelling there on a Portuguese boat, he indignantly rejected the suggestion. Without a doubt, he said, the boat would be intercepted by a German submarine, and he would be taken aboard to be delivered into the hands of the Gestapo. One imagined the signal going out from Berlin: 'Calling all U-boats, get Steptoe at all costs.'

Apart from these harmless eccentricities, which, I found, he shared with most old SIS hands, Steptoe was a cheerful companion, and in many ways a sagacious counsellor. For one thing, he knew the Secret Service through and through; how it worked and the people who ran it. Every trade has its own particular style and gibberish, and he was a master-hand at letting fall the technical terms of espionage (letter-box, chicken-feed, cover, etc., etc.) thereby giving an impression of effortless expertise. He would come and sit with me in my office at the Consulate-General and read all my telegrams, offering occasional suggestions, which I invariably accepted, for making them seem more authoritative. I soon introduced him to Anna whom he treated with great gallantry, and later to Johann. To both of them he conformed much more closely to their idea of a typical Englishman than I did. Occasionally, we

gathered clandestinely in his room, when he would make a great point of turning on his radio as loudly as possible to counteract any hidden microphones or eavesdroppers. Once, when we were shouting to one another against this noise, we suddenly realised that God Save The King was being played on the radio to mark the end of that day's Overseas Service of the BBC. As it resounded through the room at full blast, Steptoe out of habit half rose from his seat to stand to attention, I just shifted uneasily in mine, and the other two looked on the ground. If there had been an enemy agent peeping in at us through the keyhole, I wondered what he would have made of the scene.

During the period of the diplomatic exchange Campini gave a great dinner in the Polana Hotel to the Japanese diplomats, at which I was able to take a peep. The Italian Consul himself was holding forth, with many Mussolini-like gestures, his words being translated into English as he went along by a member of his staff, there being, presumably, no one available who could translate them into Japanese. The interpreter knew English only imperfectly, so that he stumbled along behind Campini's flowery eloquence, with occasional words and phrases – 'Victory . . . Pluto-democracies . . . Eastern Front . . . Bolshevisms finally trampled in the dust . . .' emerging comprehensibly. It was, however, the faces of the Japanese that held my attention; they seemed frozen in their wonderment, like a moving picture that has suddenly stopped. When at the end they came to applaud, they clapped their hands together mechanically, as though they were little toys which had been wound up to perform this gesture. I was reminded irresistibly of their faces when, after the war, I attended a few sessions of the Japanese War Guilt Trials in Tokyo. General Tojo and his fellow war-criminals wore precisely similar expressions as they listened to numerous translations of the pleas of the various Allied prosecuting counsel, turgidly expatiating upon the evils of tyranny and its guilty instruments in true Lockean style – something between an Eisenhower Inaugural and Laurence Olivier delivering Lincoln's Gettysburg Address. Remembering that the trials had been going on already for two years, that counsel were paid by the day, and no end was in sight, I could not but feel a pang of sympathy with General Tojo and the others, submitted, as it seemed to me, to a protracted refinement of torture. The returning Japanese diplomats got off more lightly in Lourenço Marques, but, as I could see, they, too, suffered.

I, also, had my troubles; a telegram from London required me urgently to screen the Polish citizens from the Far East involved in the

diplomatic exchange. The Poles in question turned out to be a party of orthodox Polish Jews who, for some unexplained reason, the Japanese had seen fit to send along with the diplomats. No one knew their names, they had no papers, and during the voyage, it seemed, had kept to themselves, preparing their own food in accordance with their particular dietary requirements, and scrupulously performing the various requisite ceremonies. 'Screening' was a term which had come into great vogue; if someone had been screened, his loyalty and reliability were considered to be impeccable. It was the security equivalent of a medical smear. Actually, as it turned out, Philby and most of the other defectors had all been repeatedly screened, which did not seem to have incommoded them in any way. To have screened my Polish Jews with any degree of exactitude would have taken a whole array of screeners several years, even assuming it was possible at all. I telegraphed back that such investigations as I was able to make gave them a clean bill, and they were shipped to Tanganyika. How they fared there, I never heard.

Another arrival at Lourenço Marques was Hunt, or to give him his full name, Huntington Harris, an enormously tall American who belonged to the Office of Strategic Services (OSS), the first essay of the United States Government in the field of espionage, later to burgeon into the ever-proliferating CIA. They came among us, these aspiring American spy-masters, like innocent girls from a finishing-school anxious to learn the seasoned demi-mondaine ways of old practitioners – in this case, the legendary British Secret Service. Most of the early arrivals were Yale or Harvard dons, who imagined themselves writing Ashenden-type stories when the war was over; in the case of the chestier ones, Hemingway-esque ones. Or they might be the offspring of Senators or Congressmen, adept at looking after their own. Or unsoldierly sons of generals, or the un-nautical offspring of admirals Or advantageously connected in some way with the State Department or the *New York Times*. Or just, like Hunt, unmilitary by temperament, while belonging to rich patrician families. In any case, indubitably an élite corps, presided over by 'Wild Bill' Donovan, a corporation lawyer and friend of Roosevelt. Alas, the period of tutelage lasted all too short a time. The first feeling of awe and respect soon evaporated; and it turned out that the finishing school products had learnt all the tricks and devices of the old practitioners in no time at all, and were operating on their own, sustained by lavish supplies of money whose reckless dispensing sent up the accepted tariff of bribes to astronomical proportions everywhere, making even the cost of trivial services like getting

charladies to go through wastepaper baskets quite exorbitant. As for the police – once the OSS appeared on the scene, it cost as much to suborn an assistant inspector, or even a mere sergeant, as would once have sufficed to buy up the whole force.

I got over this difficulty in Lourenço Marques by simply co-operating with Hunt. He was, in any case, a pleasant companion, with a dry drawling wit, and his extra supplies of cash made it possible to gladden the hearts of Camille and Serge, not to mention Inspector Y. We found a convenient residence that we could share, rather on the outskirts of Lourenço Marques, with a garage that had a door into the house through which visitors could pass without being noticed. Johann often visited us in this way; he had a cat-like facility for suddenly appearing out of nowhere. On the whole we lived amicably enough together, though at times Hunt's good nature was severely strained. For instance, once when Johann was driving my car and got into some sort of trouble with the police, it was necessary for Hunt, as the only available person as tall as Johann, to insist that the police were mistaken, and that it was he, not Johann, who had been at the wheel. For some reason which now escapes me, to support this dissimulation, it was necessary for Hunt to grow a beard, which he heroically did.

Then there was Nero, a huge man with a shaved head who was working for SOE, a sabotage organisation set up by Dr Dalton at the Ministry of Economic Warfare. Though SOE and MI6 were nominally on the same side in the war, they were, generally speaking, more abhorrent to one another than the *Abwehr* was to either of them. Fortunately, however, I was soon on the best of terms with Nero and his family, consisting of Andrée, his French wife, and Susie and Anne, their two daughters, of all of whom I became very fond. Susie had long yellow hair, and Andrée herself was one of those well-educated French women who manage to be intelligent without becoming like Simone de Beauvoir. She and Nero had met in Alexandria, where Andrée was a teacher and Nero a business man, some twenty years older than she. I really had – and, for that matter, have – no clear idea of what, if anything, Nero was up to; but his household was, for me, one of the bright spots in Lourenço Marques, and I spent many happy hours there, talking, laughing and planning impossible operations – such as taking over a German ship immobilised in Lourenço Marques harbour. Life did not smile on Nero after the war; he got a job as starter on the race-track at Heliopolis – the one that Kitty and I looked out over from our flat when we lived there. Then, when all the English had to leave

Egypt, he came to see me at *Punch*, and a little later I heard he had died. I wish now that I had tried harder to help him.

Johann continued to interest me, as a person and as a phenomenon of our time. He was ten years my junior; an artistocrat, born into the war of 1914–18, and growing up in the period of famine, inflation, unemployment and corruption which followed. When he was still quite young he joined the Nazis, and rose rapidly in the party hierarchy, though from early on he began to have doubts. Perhaps because of his mood of uneasiness, he took on a crazy mission in Austria which involved organising an attempt on the life of a minister in the Austrian Government with a view to creating a condition of political confusion. This, it was hoped, would seem to justify German intervention, leading, of course, to the Anschluss. An alternative plan was to assassinate Von Papen, then the German Ambassador in Vienna, but this laudable project was abandoned. Anyway, Johann's mission failed, and he was arrested, being later exchanged for an Austrian – von Strachwitz, an ultra-conservative Catholic who abominated the Nazis, and who had fallen foul of the authorities in Munich and been arrested there. On his release, Johann found himself quite disenchanted with the Nazis; indeed, in actual danger from them. So he made off to Africa, to Dar-es-Salaam, and what was then Tanganyika, where there was still a quite large German community. When the 1939–45 war broke out he was interned in Rhodesia as an enemy alien, but escaped, and made his way to Mozambique, the nearest neutral territory.

It was a strange experience, in the middle of a ferocious war, thus becoming intimate with someone like Johann, who, for instance, when we talked about Himmler, could draw on personal experience of working with and knowing him. It would be easy for me to claim that I culti-vated his acquaintance solely for Intelligence purposes, and had to choke back my moral indignation at his past association with the Nazis' evil deeds and purposes. This, however, would be quite untrue. I greatly enjoyed his company, and grew to like him very much. It would be equally untrue for me now to say that Philby's double-cross fills me with abhorrence. If I were to run into him, I should, I am sure, pass as agreeable an evening with him as ever I did in the days when we were both in Section Five. I have never been able to relate my feelings about people as individuals to my reactions to their public attitudes and behaviour, whether approving or disapproving – something that has often got me into trouble.

Johann and I played chess together, went for expeditions with Anna,

talked incessantly about our plans and hopes and fears for the future. He had a great love of wild animals and places, and was quite at his best in this setting. I think he had come to care little for human beings, having seen them at their degraded worst, and been cheated or captivated into participating in their degradation. With wild animals he was more at ease, holding in his hands a lion cub or baby alligator with great tenderness. Shakespearean tags easily come into my mind, and of him I found myself saying under my breath: 'Timon will to the woods, and there shall find / The unkindest beast more kinder than mankind.' Ironically enough, in our discussions it was Johann who took the liberal, hopeful view of the war's outcome, I who insisted that whoever won or lost – and we assumed, of course, that the American–Russian–British alliance would win – our civilisation had seen its best days, and that we must expect another Dark Age. We even exchanged some letters on the subject, which I still possess; their faded typescript – jejune thoughts are all that remain of many hours of ardent disputation.

By various means, we got to know that Wertz was sending a man into South Africa with funds at his disposal, to make contact with pro-Axis elements there. I knew the man in question by sight; a rather lost-looking soul, often to be seen mooning about, who never seemed to have anything much to do, and was regarded as something of a joke by his fellow-Germans in Lourenço Marques. We even were able to trace in advertisements in a South African newspaper oblique announcements of his coming, and Bletchley provided confirmation. So I decided the best thing to do was to go myself to alert the police in Johannesburg, who should be able to pick him up fairly easily, and find out who his contacts were. It might, I calculated excitedly, put them in the way of infiltrating, and ultimately exposing, the whole enemy set-up in South Africa. Passing through Swaziland, I looked in on Captain T, the head of the police there, who was very co-operative and sympathetic. For instance, he had been most helpful over speeding the shipwrecked South African troops on their way home. Somehow I had the feeling that he wasn't quite as enthusiastic about the project as I was, but still he responded sufficiently to confirm my opinion that my mission was well worth undertaking.

There had been heavy rain, and the mud roads were a morass, with no proper surface at all. My car slithered about in a most alarming manner, and several times I thought I had got hopelessly bogged down. However, at last I reached Johannesburg, where I registered at my hotel,

had a bath and a meal, and then went round to police headquarters, taking with me under my arm a file we had compiled in Lourenço Marques, containing all the relevant information. As it happened, the Commissioner was away, but an assistant received me most affably. I remember him as a large dark man, rather handsome, in a smart uniform; not at all like an Afrikaner in appearance. He might even have been Jewish. After compliments and pleasantries, he put on a serious air and asked me just what I wanted of him. As clearly and succinctly as I could, using my documents where necessary, I told him how this emissary of Wertz's, whom I could identify, was crossing into the Union illegally, probably on his way now, with contacts to make and money to hand over. I know pretty well the route he'd take; so couldn't we go after him and get him? The other listened to me attentively; he was sitting on the side of his desk, one leg, very smart and shapely in its tight blue trousers, swinging to and fro, the boot brightly polished, gleaming. Suddenly he began to laugh, positively to shake with laughter. Naturally I looked surprised. The leg stopped swinging; then, glancing at me quizzically, but by no means unsympathetically, he asked me if I realised that there was scarcely a homestead between the Swaziland frontier and Johannesburg that wouldn't be proud to hide Wertz's man, feed him and see him on his way. Did I see the point? I did, of course. He went on to tell me how, an evening or so before, they had been tipped off that a meeting of the Ossewa Brandwag, an extreme nationalist organisation, was taking place at such a house at such a time. So a man had been sent along to see what was afoot. Sure enough, a lot of people had turned up at the house in question, and the man had taken the numbers of their cars. When, back at police headquarters, these were checked, they were found to include the registration number of the then Minister of Justice's car. Again he asked me if I saw the point, and again I said I had. Very well, then, would I come and join them for a drink? This I did; indeed, for several drinks.

When I left the police headquarters, I was feeling very sore and depressed, but worse was to come. The following morning, strolling about the town, I actually *saw* Wertz's man. He was quite unmistakable, looking very lost and forlorn; in blue shorts, too large for him, and unseasonable in the chilly weather. The heavy, German climbing boots that he was wearing over thin socks were likewise inappropriate. From the look of him, I should say he had just arrived at Johannesburg, and had not yet had time to get his bearings. Obviously, I should have done something about him in spite of my discouragement at police

headquarters. But what? I just stared at him. Whether or not he spotted me, I have no means of knowing, but while I was staring he disappeared. Afterwards, miserably going over the incident in my mind, I decided I should have grabbed him myself; or at any rate shouted and pointed at him so that people gathered round. But just to do nothing! It was inexcusable.

That afternoon I drove to Pretoria, and on the way saw a car skid and crash. As it turned over, legs were waving in the air; like an insect on its back. For a minute I was the only person present, and got out of my car to approach the overturned one, again with no clear notion of what I should do. The waving legs were subsiding; now with only an occasional faint twitch, and soon they were entirely motionless. Fortunately, others arrived on the scene, more capable than I; a doctor and an ambulance were procured, and I drove on to Pretoria more subdued than ever. There I called at Army Headquarters to see an officer I knew in the Intelligence Branch. He was in a Nissen hut, the set-up so like 5 Corps that I almost forgot myself and gave a noisy salute on entering. I told him the whole story of what had happened, only omitting my abortive encounter with Wertz's man that morning. I cannot say that he seemed particularly surprised. When, after the war, Dr Malan became Prime Minister, I was interested to read in *The Times* that one of the first acts of the new Government was to raid this particular office and remove some documents. I think I know what they were, and may even have made a tiny contribution to them myself.

When I got back to Lourenço Marques, feeling very dispirited, I was disconcerted to find that my house was in a state of great confusion, as though it had been burgled. Then I remembered that the burglary had been arranged with Johann to offset any suspicion that he might be responsible for tipping us off about Wertz's emissary to South Africa. As now Wertz would never know that we had been tipped off, I reflected bitterly, the burglary was unnecessary. The only pleasing feature of it was that, among documents left around for Johann to find and pass on to Wertz, was a bogus memorandum, purportedly addressed to me, to the effect that very little information of late seemed to have been coming from Campini, and asking whether it was worth while going on making substantial payments to him. This malign suggestion seems to have registered in Wertz's mind.

From South Africa I was summoned to Cairo to discuss the possibility of using our contacts in Lourenço Marques for the purpose of disseminating deception material. The officer I had to see was Peter

Fleming, whom I had vaguely known for a number of years. We were both staying in Shepherds Hotel, and met in his room, where he was still unpacking, looking, even more than usually, like a beautifully polished piece of furniture – a tallboy, say, or grandfather clock. While he was talking, he absent-mindedly picked up one of his bush-shirts, and touched the crown on its shoulder-strap very gently; like a jeweller picking up and handling some rare stone. He told me that his boss, Colonel Dudley-Clark, would shortly be arriving in Cairo, having, as he put it, God-high priority. He repeated this expression 'God-high priority' several times, as though it established Dudley-Clark's eminence, and the importance attached to his deception activities, which were, as a matter of fact, extremely successful, especially at the time of the Normandy landings. When he finally appeared – by no means as soon as his God-high priority might have led one to expect – he turned out to be a sharp little man with bright, quick eyes, who easily explained to me what he wanted put about in Lourenço Marques – rumours of imaginary Allied plans for invading the continent to put the enemy off the scent of the actual intention to land in Normandy. In this field, too, the results of one's labours, if any, could be monitored at Bletchley, where the injection of the deception virus showed, and then the degree to which it had taken in the enemy's blood stream and nervous system. All Intelligence roads seemed to end in this rather drab little town, hitherto only known as a railway junction; that ritual game of rounders turned out to be a masque of victory.

I spent my time in Cairo wandering about, and trying, without much success, to find old haunts and old acquaintances. The town was full of troops; and GHQ Middle East itself – within whose perimeter an MI6 contingent was installed – covered a large area. There were still a few British civilians to be seen. I overheard one of them at the Gazira Club complaining about the influx of war-time officers as honorary members. The next time I went to Cairo, shortly after the disastrous Suez venture, British nationals were being treated like displaced persons, and Shepherds Hotel, where Peter Fleming and I waited for Dudley-Clark to descend on his God-high priority, had been razed to the ground.

For the moment, however, our position seemed solid enough. The threat of an Axis occupation – which at one point led shopkeepers to lay in stocks of German and Italian bunting – had receded, and over my morning tea I read in the *Egyptian Gazette* the exhilarating headline: AFRIKA KORPS IN FULL RETREAT. An additional satisfaction for me

personally was that it meant my job in Lourenço Marques, such as it was, must now be considered over, since troopships would once more be able to use the Mediterranean instead of going round the Cape and up the Mozambique Channel. This knowledge made me more than ever bored and restless when I got back to Lourenço Marques. In every job I have ever had the same thing has always happened – after an energetic start, I have lost interest in it, and spent my time coasting along and waiting to make off. This, I may add, excludes writing, which, as far as I am concerned, is not a job at all, but a necessity; like breathing, or circulating one's blood.

It was in this lack-lustre mood at the end of my time in Lourenço Marques that I became involved in an adventure, at once foolish, squalid and heart-rending. It concerned Hélène, a dancer at a night-club in Lourenço Marques called the Café Penguin. Serge brought her to lunch with the idea that she might be useful, speaking, as she did, French, Spanish, and Portuguese, and having, by the nature of her profession, many contacts among local officials and visiting shady characters. She was, as I learnt afterwards, partly Greek, but had lived and worked in Portugal and Spain; her face, with its large nose and small chin, reminded me vaguely of one of those Egyptian heads in the Cairo Museum. Her voice was rather hoarse, her clothes cheap-looking and flashy; but there was something bright and brave about her that I found appealing.

We spoke over lunch, I remember, sententiously about how people's attitudes towards one changed with one's material situation, and how rare was affection which was wholly disinterested. She obviously enjoyed herself, and promised to come again and prepare a Spanish meal for us. This proved difficult to arrange, and in the end I took her to lunch at Costa da Sol, a restaurant by the sea. Again, our conversation was inclined to be sententious; and without much conviction, since I was thinking of getting away from Lourenço Marques at the earliest possible moment. I broached the question of her keeping her eyes and ears open on my behalf at the Café Penguin. To this, she eagerly agreed. Out in the sunshine, she looked very made up, with black glistening hair; and her coquetry seemed excessive, if not professional. I felt ill-at-ease, and even a little ashamed, to be seen in her company. Then one evening by chance I went with Hunt to the Café Penguin. It was quite a small place; some tables, mostly occupied, a tired orchestra, upstairs a gambling casino, a few faded taxi-girls, lights turned down for the dancing. At about midnight the cabaret began. First a

young Spanish girl singing, strutting about, exposing her youthfulness; then Hélène, vigorous with her castanets, and much applauded. Afterwards she came and sat at our table, and at 2 a.m., when the orchestra stopped, I took her home, Hunt having already left. In the car, inevitably, being rather drunk, I made a lurch in her direction. She was astonished, truly astonished: '*J'avais beaucoup de considération pour vous*,' she said in a flat, sad voice. It was not exactly a reproach; much worse than that. No words ever spoken to me, I think, have echoed more wretchedly in my ears, and made me feel more sick with myself.

After this, I went to the Penguin quite often, though I hated the place. Alcohol helped me through the evening till 2 a.m. Hélène, I found, was really two people. She was by nature rather sad and melancholic, liable to say that her life was a *futilité*, or: '*Je ne suis pas une femme pour un quart d'heure*,' or, when I asked her why she was crying: '*Je n'ai pas le droit de pleurer*.' Then, when other people were around, she would assume her professionally gay manner, with the exaggerated coquetry, the too elaborate smile and the too studied gesture. I liked her best when she talked about her own life; about her difficulties with the proprietor of the Penguin, in arranging a new dance, or in insisting on her position as an *artiste* as distinct from a *papillon* or taxi-girl. Once we went into the country on a Sunday, when she wore blue trousers, a red blouse and an enormous straw hat with ribbons. The effect was somehow indescribably poignant. On the way back she sang little Spanish songs, all sad; then when we got to my house and she heard voices upstairs, she at once put on her other manner, becoming a shepherdess in a bawdy French farce.

On one occasion she showed that she had strong nerves. We were driving along a straight road with trees planted on each side, and suddenly the car got totally out of control, lurched across the road, just missed running straight into one of the trees; then came to a standstill. Hélène was perfectly calm, more so than I was. It turned out that a vital part in the steering apparatus had been removed, and as I, very foolishly, had been going to a garage run by an Italian, it was reasonable to assume that Campini was responsible. When, after Italy's collapse, he was interrogated at length, he described how he used to see me going for my morning swim, and had a strong compulsion then to run me over himself. Another time, on an impulse, I took Hélène upstairs to the gambling – something I have always intensely disliked, as the pornography of cupidity – and won three centos straight off, to the great

annoyance of the proprietor. I gave them to her, and she stowed them away on her person with great satisfaction.

It was now that the absurdity, the futility, the degradation of how I had been living seized me with irresistible force. The fact that my activities were nominally related to the conduct of war, and might even be interpreted as having been, within their own preposterous terms of reference, effective, even successful and deserving of commendation, only made them the more distasteful to me. One particular night, after returning from the Penguin, I lay on my bed full of stale liquor and despair; alone in the house, and, as it seemed, utterly alone, not just in Lourenço Marques, in Africa, in the world. Alone in the universe, in eternity, with no glimmer of light in the prevailing blackness; no human voice I could hope to hear, or human heart I could hope to reach; no God to whom I could turn, or Saviour to take my hand. Elsewhere, on battlefields men were killing and dying. I envied them; it was a solution and a solace of sorts. After all, the only bearable thing about war is the killing and the dying. That is its point. In the Blitz, with, as I thought, London falling about my ears, I had felt a kind of contentment; here in this remote forgotten corner of the world, I fell into the final abyss of despair. Deprived of war's only solace – death, given and received, it came into my mind that there was, after all, one death I could still procure. My own. I decided to kill myself.

It was before the days of barbiturates; otherwise, I should have certainly swallowed a bottle of them then and there, and not be writing these words. The notion of blowing my brains out – apart from the fact that the only weapon I had was the little pistol acquired at Sheerness when the fugitive French troops arrived there; a shaky and unreliable instrument for this or any other purpose – had the disadvantage, that, so dying, my children could not but know that their father had taken his own life in this particularly squalid way. I decided that the best thing to do was to drown myself. Somewhere I had read that drowning was like falling asleep in the sea. So, I would make of my death one last morning bathe; these bathes being, I reflected, with unctuous misery, the only part of my life in Lourenço Marques that had remained uncontaminated. It was all ridiculously easy. I put on my clothes, got into my car and drove to the sea shore, leaving no notes because I wanted my death to seem like an accident. It was known that I often bathed at unseasonable hours, so there would be nothing out-of-the-way in my having decided to take a dip in the middle of the night, swum out too far, and been unable to get back, with no possibility of being heard

when I cried out for help. A telegram to Kitty from Ledger; deeply regret, etc., etc.; grief in Whatlington, but not shame; the end of a relationship, which had been full of separations and betrayals, but also of joy and intimacy. Basically, however, constructed out of the rubble of a broken-down way of life. A shanty structure built on a bomb site, with no foundations, and, at best, no more than a corrugated iron roof.

All the same, at this moment of anguish that I believed to be my last, it was of Kitty, and Kitty alone, that I thought; wondering about her, caring about her, and about no one and nothing else. (The children, also; but only as part of her.) 'Only death will part us,' she had said to me on the night before I left for Lisbon; and now the death I proposed to find would fulfil her words. She was not so much someone I loved as part of me; we had been grafted together to become one. Nothing could alter this; not even my cowardly decision to end a life I could no longer endure. Our union was more, infinitely more, than the means sought to unite us. The clumsy gropings after unity of the flesh – licking the earth, as Pascal calls it; the even more ridiculous gropings after unity of mind, a Sidney and a Beatrice Webb laboriously assembling their facts, jointly stating their conclusions. Perhaps most preposterous of all, the gropings after unity of the spirit; two upturned faces marvelling in unison at the Sistine Chapel, tapping their feet in unison and wagging their heads to Beethoven's Ninth, Brecht, their amour, wit and wisdom of Shaw their edification, Karl Marx and the Brothers their loadstar and their mirth. Such was not the union I had defaced, but something infinitely more profound and enduring. From the depths of the trough into which I had fallen, my soul cried to depart.

I drove to the furthest point along the coast road, some six miles from Lourenço Marques, and there got out of the car and undressed. The lights were still on in Peter's Café and Costa da Sol. As the tide was far out, I had to wade on and on before there was enough water to swim in. So this was the end of my life, my last little while on earth. I kept on trying to think of the French word for 'drown'. Everything seemed to me unreal – had there been a single moment in my life when I had truly lived? Everything false – love, hate, happiness, despair, all equally false. Even this dying seemed false. Was it me, wading on to the open sea? Was it really happening? The bottom I trod on was muddy now, the water creeping up and cold, the air damp. At last there was enough water to swim in. I started swimming, the dark water churning white as my arms beat through it. Soon I was out of my depth,

and still swam on. Now I felt easy, now it was settled. Looking back I could scarcely see the shore; only the lights of Peter's Café and Costa da Sol, far, far, away. I began to tremble, all my body trembled; I went under the water, trembling, came up again and reposed myself as though on a bed. I could sleep on this watery mattress, sleep. Then, suddenly, without thinking or deciding, I started swimming back to shore. I was very tired, and kept feeling if I was in my depth again, and wasn't; I shouted foolishly for help, and kept my eyes fixed on the lights of Peter's Café and the Costa da Sol.

They were the lights of the world; they were the lights of my home, my habitat, where I belonged. I must reach them. There followed an overwhelming joy such as I had never experienced before; an ecstasy. In some mysterious way it became clear to me that there was no darkness, only the possibility of losing sight of a light which shone eternally; that our clumsy appetites are no more than the blind reaching of a newly born child after the teat through which to suck the milk of life; that our sufferings, our affliction, are part of a drama – an essential, even an ecstatic, part – endlessly revolving round the two great propositions of good and evil, of light and darkness. A brief interlude, an incarnation, reaching back into the beginning of time, and forward into an ultimate fulfilment in the universal spirit of love which informs, animates, illuminates all creation, from the tiniest particle of insentient matter to the radiance of God's very throne.

Now I felt the bottom, and began to wade laboriously back to the shore, reaching it by the estuary of a river, a long way away from where I had first gone into the sea. All round me was deep black mud, through which, shaking with cold, I floundered, until, by luck more than any sense of direction, I saw my car where I had left it. Even at the time I realised, and realise now ever more clearly, that this floundering was a sort of parable. Plodding and floundering on through the black deep mud, but never again without hope; thenceforth always knowing, deep in my heart, remembering even when I forgot, that it was not by chance or for nothing that the lights of Peter's Café and Costa da Sol had called me back. That I, too, had something I must try to say and be, until the time came for God to put me to sleep, as I had tried, in my own fatuous and sinful wilfulness, to put myself to sleep in the sea off Lourenço Marques. When, finally, I reached my car and my clothes, the morning was just breaking; the black African sky just beginning to be tinged with grey. I breathed in the dawn air, greedily; after all, I was still alive.

Though I scarcely realised it at the time and subsequently only very slowly and dimly, this episode represented for me one of those deep changes which take place in our lives; as, for instance, in adolescence, only more drastic and fundamental. A kind of spiritual adolescence, whereby, thenceforth, all my values and pursuits and hopes were going to undergo a total transformation – from the carnal towards the spiritual; from the immediate, the now, towards the everlasting, the eternal. In a tiny dark dungeon of the ego, chained and manacled, I had glimpsed a glimmer of light coming in through a barred window high above me. It was the light of Peter's Café and Costa da Sol calling me back to earth, my mortal home; it was the grey light of morning heralding another day as I floundered and struggled through the black mud; it was the light of the world. The bars of the window, as I looked more closely, took on the form of a Cross.

The next day I took the precaution of reporting to London, giving the impression that I had gone through the motions of trying to drown myself as a deliberate ruse to delude Wertz into thinking I had completely lost heart. In the end I began to wonder whether, after all, it *had* been a ruse. In all deception, whether of governments, or demagogues, or press lords, or media pundits, or advertisers, down to little con-men and columnists and street-corner *exaltés* – the ultimate doom is that the deceiver comes to believe his own deceits. Wertz heard from Johann what had happened, and duly sent a long message on my suicide attempt, which he attributed to despair at my inability to measure up to him in Intelligence work. It was in this message that he so exaggerated the importance of my position in the Allied Intelligence network in East Africa in order to enhance his own achievement in laying me low. Graham Greene, who was back in London now, and dealing with my telegrams, as well as seeing the Wertz intercepts, minuted that he was sceptical about my explanation of the suicide attempt, and considered it to have been genuine. With his novelist's eye, he understood.

When I left Lourenço Marques for good, Nero's daughter, Susie, was allowed to come with me in the launch that took passengers out to the flying-boat. So the last thing I saw as we climbed into the sky was her long yellow hair. When we got to Kampala, in Uganda, I was afflicted with acute abdominal pains, and rushed to hospital for an emergency appendix operation. I rather doubt if this was really necessary. Indeed, when I was under the anaesthetic, before it had fully taken effect, I overheard two doctors talking in Scottish accents, and

one of them was saying to the other that the operation seemed rather precipitate, but they might as well go ahead now. Illness, in my experience, is often a device for opting out for a while. Even so, according to the doctor who cut me open, my appendix was in poor shape. I only stayed in the hospital five days, and then managed to get on a Belgian plane to Lagos. What I remember most about Kampala hospital is how gentle the African nurses were, with their smiling faces and clumsy, kindly hands.

At Lagos I was met and taken to an SOE establishment there, being still rather weak and inactive. A seat had been booked for me on a plane to England the next day, but a colonel with a wooden leg claimed priority, and took my place. This priority game was played in all the transit camps; junior officers whose places were constantly being pre-empted by majors and colonels and brigadiers, were liable to be stuck in one of them for weeks at a time. One saw them, unshaved, wild-eyed, rushing out in packs whenever a plane landed or took off, in case some last-minute cancellation left a seat vacant. I felt pretty annoyed myself with the one-legged colonel, until I learnt that the plane in which he had taken my place ran into the mountains round Shannon Airport and crashed with no survivors. As Kitty had been alerted that I was on this plane, when I did turn up it was as one risen from the dead. My welcome would, I am sure, have been warm in any case, but in the circumstances it was positively ecstatic, and added to my own wonderful sense of homecoming; of being in contact with something real and lasting after my fantasy life in Lourenço Marques. It was tempting to regard my ejection from the crashed plane as a kind of miracle (as, when he was serving in the army in the Civil War, Bunyan did his replacement by another soldier, who was subsequently killed in a siege; this being, incidentally, his only reference to the Civil War in all his writings), but on reflection such a view seemed disrespectful to the memory of the one-legged colonel, who would certainly see the incident in a different light.

9 *The Victor's Camp*

... Justice, that fugitive from the Victor's camp.

— Simone Weil

When truth conquers with the help of 10,000 yelling men – even supposing that that which is victorious is truth; with the forms and manner of the victory a far greater untruth is victorious.

— Kierkegaard

AFTER SOME SICK-LEAVE, I reported back to Section Five, now installed in Ryder Street in premises that were subsequently to house the *Economist*; an appropriate succession. Everything seemed very much the same as it had been at St Albans, with Philby more than ever the dominant personage. He still, when working at his desk, wore his father's old 1914-18 war officer's tunic, and still had his same little circle of ardent admirers. My performance in Lourenço Marques – which looked so much better in the telegrams than when actually happening – was considered to have been impressive, and earned me a certain prestige, but I never felt other than an outsider when I was with Philby and his friends. They were altogether more serious than I was about our plans and stratagems, and found my derisory attitude towards SIS, and refusal to accept the USSR as the one just Power engaged in the war, particularly distasteful.

Occasionally quite sharp arguments developed. I cannot recall that Philby ever joined in these, save once – and that might have been significant. It arose out of someone complaining very bitterly that invaluable intelligence from Bletchley relating to the enemy order of battle and operations on the Eastern Front was being withheld from the Russians for fear that they might compromise the source. I argued that such caution was legitimate, especially in view of the way the Russians had passed on to the Germans everything they knew about us and our

intentions during the period of the Nazi–Soviet Pact. Another similar occasion for treachery might arise, and we were right to guard against it. In any case, Stalin was bound to disbelieve anything coming officially from the Allies, and assume it to be provocation; as he had when Stafford Cripps, as British Ambassador in Moscow, informed him – correctly, as it turned out – of the date and place he must expect a German attack on the USSR. This line of talk for once infuriated Philby, who spluttered and shouted that we were in duty bound to do everything within our power, whatever it might be, to support the Red Army, including risking – if there was a risk – the security of the Bletchley material.

It occurred to me afterwards, when Philby's double-cross was officially admitted, that it might have been this particular issue, on which he felt so strongly, that first involved him in illicitly handing over documents to the Russians. Giving them intercepts relating to the Eastern Front was something he would certainly have considered it to be perfectly proper and honourable to do, and from this start he could easily have got fully enmeshed. We shall probably never know for sure, but I find the possibility more plausible than that he was specifically a Soviet agent – on the books, as it were – from his undergraduate days. In any case, if he had been a fully fledged Soviet agent at the time, it is reasonable to assume that he would have been supplying the Russians with Bletchley material anyway, and so would have kept out of any dispute about the rights and wrongs of so doing. Incidentally, I learnt from Alexander Foote, who had been the radio operator in the famous Lucy Ring in Switzerland, that, in fact, Stalin *was* getting the requisite Bletchley material. It was being sent to him via the Lucy Ring; acquired, purportedly, from sources in the German High Command. This, given its detail and invariable accuracy, was quite inconceivable. It could, in fact, only have come from Bletchley. I found it highly appropriate that Stalin could only be persuaded to believe in the reliability of Allied Intelligence if it reached him from an undercover network on a dubious channel.

I got to know Foote after the war, when he was working as a clerk at the Ministry of Agriculture and Fisheries, then located in Regent's Park near where I was living. He used to drop in for a chat on his way home; a large stolid-looking Yorkshireman, who could be very funny about his time in the USSR and the training in espionage methods that he was given – no less fatuous, I was relieved to learn, than our own essays in the same field. He went there in the first place as a drop-out of the

depression years and a Communist sympathiser, and then managed to get himself trained for a foreign espionage mission with a view to being sent abroad. By this means, in due course he got to Berlin, where he re-defected. When the 1939-45 war began he made his way to Switzerland, to be taken on there by the Lucy Ring. No one could have been less like the popular idea of a secret agent – he was much more like an insurance agent, or possibly a professional cricketer – but he had developed a taste for clandestinity, and found his overt life with Ag. and Fish. very tedious.

Philby had lately moved into a new smart house in Chelsea, which was still being decorated when I visited him there. Given wartime conditions, it struck me as surprisingly luxurious, and knowing that his pay would scarcely extend to such a style of living, I assumed – wrongly as it turned out – that his wife Eileen must have private means. I should perhaps point out that all SIS salaries were supposed to be a closely guarded secret, kept even from the Inland Revenue men by making them tax-free. Actually, of course, we all knew what everyone else got. Looking back, it seems clear that at some point Philby's income must have been substantially augmented from Soviet sources – something that would certainly have played a part in his suborning. He was by nature generous, extravagant and hospitable, and so liable to be impecunious and in dire need of money. The Russians were adept at taking advantage of such personal situations.

In his new home, with his wife and children round him, he seemed particularly cheerful and well content, but I thought I detected a shadow over Eileen's face from time to time. I heard afterwards that she had some sort of mental collapse, which may well have been due to getting an inkling of what her husband was up to. I always found her especially sympathetic; if only because, in the rather exotic company in which Philby habitually moved, she seemed as alien and vaguely uneasy as I felt. When I said how nice the house was, and how pleasant for them all to be settled there together, Philby told me that Eileen and the children, like other MI6 families in London, were shortly moving into the country. It seemed that the Bletchley material clearly indicated some new devastating development in the German air offensive – as it turned out, the use of V weapons. It strikes me as curious now that I cannot recall making any use of this information myself; either to alert Kitty and our friends, or just to show off by dropping dark hints about what lay ahead.

Trevor Wilson was already in Algiers, having gone there when the

Allied landings took place in November 1942. It was decided that I should join him and take over liaison duties with the *Securité Militaire*, whose head was Commandant Paiolle. While waiting to leave for Algiers, I spent my time fraternising with the French, and getting to know the various warring factions, ranging between straight Vichyist and straight Gaullist, all with supporters and patrons in SIS, SOE, and OSS, to whom they could look for money, supplies and patronage. One of the most ardent Vichyist supporters in SIS was Claude Dansey, a veteran of many intrigues, and by this time at odds with most of his fellow-Broadway *apparatchiks*. He summoned me to come and see him, for no reason that I could discover except that he wanted to have a look at me. We sat for a half an hour or so, staring at one another across his desk, and exchanging banalities. I carried away an impression of a grey, tired, angry face; an adroit player in a game whose rules had been changed beyond recognition.

Personally, I felt drawn to the Gaullists from the beginning; I found Jacques Soustelle, de Gaulle's Intelligence chief – a brilliant anthropologist who had been Assistant Director of the *Musée de l'Homme* in Paris in his twenties – more interesting and easier to talk to than his rivals, most of whom were professionals, and very military in their bearing and attitudes. Also, I felt sure the Gaullists would win in the long run anyway. The other factions had no leader who could compare with de Gaulle; the alternatives produced by Churchill and Roosevelt – Weygand, Giraud – being derisory. The first glimpse I had of de Gaulle in the flesh was in the lift in the Connaught Hotel where he was staying. I was struck at once by the woebegoneness of his expression; but more like a clown's than a martyr's. The face of a man born to lead a lost cause, with the additional sorrow that it would ostensibly triumph.

The London Gaullists proved, on closer acquaintance, to be a curious collection of zealots and adventurers, some, like Passy (de Wavrin), belonging to the extreme Right, others, like Soustelle, to the Left, with all sorts of variants – devout Catholics and anti-clericals, civil servants, admirals and professors (whose numbers noticeably augmented as the Gaullist cause prospered), and other miscellaneous hangers-on – united only in their devotion and allegiance to their aloof, ungainly leader, with whom most of them had barely exchanged a word, and whose very names he was liable to confuse. I went in and out of their various offices, dotted about in the region of St James's Street, lunched with them at the Écu de France, where most days a row of *képis* was to be seen in the

cloak-room; had talks with them at Ryder Street, and briefed myself by reading Section Five's own collection of their communications at home and abroad – a field which Bletchley in no wise neglected. It is sad now to reflect that the person of them all I should most like to have known – Simone Weil – was at that very time sitting in one of their offices preparing the document, subsequently published as *The Need for Roots* (*Enracinement*), which made so profound an impression on me.

When, through my friend Richard Rees – now alas dead – I first became acquainted with Simone Weil's life, it was this part, in London with the Gaullists, that I found most poignant, doubtless because I was so familiar with the scene, and thus could the more readily imagine her reactions. She managed to get to London under the auspices of André Philippe and Maurice Schumann, and hoped to be dropped in occupied France to join the Resistance. This, of course was quite impossible, if only because of her noticeably Jewish appearance. Her temperament, also, unfitted her; as Soustelle (who was with her at the famous *École Normale Supérieure*) remarked to me once, her kingdom was not of this world, whereas the Resistance was. I think she must have suffered, too, through what would have struck her as the essentially worldly, if not frivolous, attitude most of the Gaullists had towards what she thought of as their sacred mission to liberate France. De Gaulle himself said of her: '*Elle est folle*', as in a sense she was, but with the madness that St Paul commended to the first Christians. In the end, she was bitterly disillusioned with the Gaullists and Gaullism, and actually wrote a letter resigning her post. Her passionate sense of identification with the French in their suffering led her to insist that she must eat no more than would have been available to her in France, where by this time, in theory at any rate, rationing was very strict. The result was that she in effect starved herself to death. I cannot help feeling that, in taking this decision, the row of *képis* in the Écu de France, may well have been in her mind.

The Gaullists had not known what to do with her, and so had given her the task of considering the various moral and social problems that would arise when France's Liberation was achieved. Few of them read, and none heeded, her brilliantly perceptive analysis of the dilemmas the post-Liberation situation would present, but it may well prove to be the case, when the final accounting is made, that *The Need for Roots* will be seen to represent the only lasting achievement attributable to the Gaullist presence in London. Simone Weil's death took place at a

sanatorium in Ashford, the coroner's verdict being that it was suicide. Thinking about this long afterwards by the stone that marks her burial place, it occurred to me that it was perhaps a special mercy, to spare her the agony she would undoubtedly have suffered at the spectacle of what actually happened when France was, *soi disant*, liberated. She was quite on her own when she died, so was buried in a pauper's grave, thus achieving in death what she had so ardently sought in life – identification with the poorest and lowliest of her fellow-humans.

Algiers, when I got there, was teeming; like a boom town when oil has been struck or gold discovered. Everyone moving about eagerly and energetically, talking, gesticulating; many varied uniforms, male and female, to be seen. In the hot summer nights, with the stars bright in the sky, no one wanted to go to bed. I joined the throng myself, drifting along with the others; an officer again, in khaki drill, a crown on my shoulder, having been advanced one notch on resuming military status. From HM's Vice-Consul to major. There I stayed, a major to the end; it sounded better in French – *mon commandant*. What particularly excited us all was that Algiers seemed so unmistakably French, with policemen in blue carrying white truncheons, blowing whistles and directing traffic, just as if they were in the Place de la Concorde; with cafés sprawling onto the pavements, and waiters in white coats sweating profusely as they miraculously steered trays of drinks to those who had ordered them, and, above all, that composite smell of *gaulloise* tobacco smoke, cheap scent and *pissoirs* which still, across half a century now, carries me back to the first time I stepped off a Channel steamer and found myself on French soil. Algiers was a half-way house to France.

The SIS contingent had established themselves in a large Arab house high up above Algiers, presided over by a handsome naval captain in a white uniform with a row of interesting looking ribbons. There, the spy-masters lived together, operating into Italy, Jugoslavia, Greece and adjacent territories. Our Section Five office was downtown, in the Rue Charras; a busy street, more in keeping with Trevor Wilson's temperament, to which noise and confusion were congenial. He was a short, unaccountable man with a toothbrush moustache, who had been a bank-manager in France; knew the language perfectly, but spoke it in a strange muttering whisper, with his head bent down, and usually a cigarette in his mouth which got affixed to his upper or lower lip, wagging with his words. In this manner he would carry on a running monologue, only partially comprehensible, and whether in English or

French barely discernible; in any case, broken up by sudden furious exclamations, as: 'Where's that fool Brent?' – Brent being our long-suffering driver. Nonetheless, he managed to get inside the skin of our French associates in a unique way; something for which having to decide, in his capacity as bank manager, whether or not to grant an overdraft to some peasant farmer or small tradesman or industrialist, doubtless provided an inestimable training. Take him for all in all, he was about the ablest Intelligence officer I met in the war, with an instinctive flair for the work, including all the deceits and double-crosses involved.

His own opinions were fanatically held and frenetically expounded. He leant, if anywhere, in the direction of Maurras and the *Action Française*, which did not, incidentally, prevent him from being on the best of terms with Philby, whom he enormously admired and endlessly praised; one fanaticism, in my experience, finding another congenial, irrespective of its ideology. At this time, he was violently anti-Gaullist, to the point that if, driving about in Algiers, he happened to see the General, solitary and sedate, in the back of his car, he would actually shake his fist and shout abusively: 'Look at him! Look at him!' He correspondingly admired de Gaulle's rival, General Giraud, who enjoyed the support of the Allies; the Americans in particular. Algiers was plastered with posters displaying a message from Giraud: UN SEUL BUT: LA VICTOIRE! I myself felt instinctively, but did not say, that Giraud hadn't a chance; especially after I saw a photograph of the two generals shaking hands in the presence of Roosevelt and Churchill – like a seal and a hippopotamus nibbling the same bun under the eyes of their keepers at the Zoo. It was, indeed, soon after this fraternisation that Giraud just seemed to fade away.

Even Trevor Wilson's laughter was extreme; something would amuse him, and he would return to it again and again, laughing more hysterically each time. Once, for instance, someone remarked that Chinese sages were in the habit of cultivating a single strand of hair on their chins, till it grew to an inordinate length. This so took Trevor Wilson's fancy, that he almost exploded with mirth; I quite expected him to have a go at the fashion himself. His loves were as strong as his hates, and he handed over Paiolle – whom he revered – to me, as though dealing with him must be regarded as a sacred trust. We went along together to the *Sécurité Militaire*, then housed in some army hutments on the outskirts of Algiers; rather like Mytchett. The form in seeing Paiolle was invariable; on being admitted to his office by his adjutant, one

saluted, with a '*mes respects, mon commandant*', and then shook hands. Commandant to commandant. First, causal observations were exchanged, followed by the business in hand – usually relating to a communication from London based on Bletchley material (which Paiolle was supposed to know nothing about, but did), pointing to a suspect, or requiring an investigation to be undertaken. This dealt with, more casual talk followed, and perhaps a drink, or lunch in the mess. One way and another, I saw a lot of Paiolle, and got to like him very much, but never to know him well, or to find talking to him easy, as I did with Soustelle. He was through and through a professional soldier, a St Cyr product; of a type I imagine to be now virtually obsolete in France. A dignified, handsome man; in all ways honourable and correct. The Gaullists were very hostile to him, and but for his close relations with us might easily have got him out: '*Le Général a voulu le saquer,*' Passy said to me once, *à propos* Paiolle. As it was, he managed to hold on; ultimately accepting the inevitable and serving under Soustelle.

Thenceforth I spent much time at the *Securité Militaire*, getting to know the other officers, and sometimes passing an evening with them in their *popotte*; which I was able to manage, but with nothing like Trevor Wilson's ease and panache. For one thing I lacked his capacity to drink vast quantities of what Paiolle called fire-water – very new brandy, the only liquor in good supply in Algiers just then. The aching boredom of some of these evenings weighed heavily upon me; especially the French dirty stories, which I found even longer and less funny than their English equivalents, and the marching songs which they had sung as cadets, and managed still to bellow out despite swelling stomachs and thinning hair.

Paiolle took me on a tour of North Africa, visiting units of the French army whose morale, reportedly shaky, he wanted to check. I was strongly reminded of the situation in India, though, as it turned out, the French had before them an even longer weariness to endure than had the upholders of the Raj, while their rule was being defended in order to be liquidated. The young officers were very touching; wondering what had gone wrong, and why their dedication and enthusiasm, and the – as they thought – loyalty of their Zouaves, seemed to count for nothing. The only really cheerful unit we visited was the Foreign Legion, consisting mostly of Germans, who, it appeared, were perfectly content to be ranged against their fellow-countrymen, though, had they wished to, by the terms of their enlistment, they could have contracted out when France declared war on Germany. I heard one of the legion-

aries singing a song as he polished his equipment, whose words continued to echo in my mind.'

Il y a des pierres dans toutes les routes
Il y a des femmes dans tous les chemins.

We drove along the coast road; pine trees and blue sky on one side of us, and the blue Mediterranean on the other. In Fez we stayed in the Citadel, in the middle of the town, guests of the then commander, a general with one arm. After dinner he and Paiolle went into the garden, walking up and down in earnest conversation. I watched them from my bedroom window, the distorted shadow cast by the one-armed general in the bright moonlight exaggerating his infirmity. While watching them, I heard a trumpet sounding the Last Post, announcing to the troops in the Citadel that the day was over.

Other people's empires tend to seem more tolerable than one's own, and in this last view I had of French North Africa I was reminded of stories and films which had excited me as a child rather than of the tirades of my father and his friends against the villainies of colonialism. The immediate impact and the colourfulness was stronger than the sense of outrage at the exploitation involved. Driving along, Paiolle and I talked about the assassination of Admiral Darlan in December 1942, which fell so conveniently for all concerned (perhaps even including Darlan himself, who may well have felt himself at the end of the road), that many assumed it must have been planned, with the assassin, a young royalist named Bonnier de la Chapelle, a conscious or unconscious instrument. More probably, he was just, as I gathered from Paiolle, allowed to go about his business; like Van der Lubbe when he set fire to the Reichstag, or like Lee Oswald when he fired at President Kennedy in Dallas. History, like wood, has a grain in it which determines how it splits; and those in authority, besides trying to shape and direct events, sometimes find it more convenient just to let them happen.

A bearded British Council man kindly took me to tea with André Gide, who was staying in Algiers as the guest of a professor in the Rue Michelet. He had been wandering about in North Africa – a milieu that he found very much to his taste – and after the Allied landings, came to Algiers to, as it were, adjust himself to the new phase of Liberation that was obviously on the way. The adjustment was necessary because, from a Gaullist point of view, his comportment during the occupation had been somewhat equivocal. For me, it was an exciting visit even though I had not read much Gide – only *Si le Grain ne*

Meurt, and his two books on the USSR, the one highly adulatory and the other as highly critical. The fact that he was a famous writer was quite enough to make me feel more uplifted, as I climbed the steps to the apartment he was staying in, than if I had been about to make the acquaintance, at one and the same time, of General Eisenhower, President Roosevelt and King Farouk of Egypt. We found Gide sitting by an open window, and looking down at the Rue Michelet, up and down which GI's were endlessly passing, rolling their buttocks inside their tight uniform trousers in a way which is very characteristic of North Americans – so much so that even strangers settled briefly among them soon acquire it. For Gide, the spectacle, for obvious reasons, held a special attraction. I was aware at once of his grey, coldly luminous face; almost priestly in style – an impression enhanced by a skull-cap that he wore. But priestly on the Devil's side; the sanctity somehow foetid, the luminosity unearthly without being heavenly – studio lighting rather than light, an effect. Nonetheless, there was something enchanting about his words, as he chose them and used them, the timbre of his voice; so clear and so true, like the bells of those little Swiss churches sounding out on a Sunday morning in the chill mountain air.

At this time Gide was preparing his translation of *Hamlet*, and we discussed it briefly – translating being, for writers in ideological distress, a ready recourse; for instance, Pasternak, who also turned to Shakespeare. Gide was puzzling over some of the more obscure phrases – 'a bare bodkin', I seem to remember – but I was unable to offer any help. Then he described how he had been trying to meet John Steinbeck, whose work he greatly admired, and who was in Algiers as a war correspondent. Whenever he managed to get hold of him, Gide said, he was drunk. He had tried at different times – in the evening, at lunch-time, and finally at breakfast; but always with the same result – *Il etait soûl.* There was something very funny in this picture of the great Gide making sudden forays by day and by night to find Steinbeck sober; always without success.

I had a strong sense of something evil in Gide; not just in the way everyone has evil in them, but in a particular concentration that can be eerily attractive as well as repellent. This prevented me from truly appreciating his company. It was like being in some very beautiful place – say, the Duomo in Florence, or in Chartres Cathedral – when the drains have gone wrong. An exhalation from him hit me in a similar way. To believe in evil today is not considered permissible, or,

if evil is allowed to exist, it tends to be elevated, as having some inherent creativity, beauty, joyousness, of its own. Yet what I saw in Gide was the terrible desolation of evil, the total alienation from the principle of goodness in all creation; he seemed to be imprisoned in darkness, like someone waking in a strange room, and looking in vain for a switch or a door or a window.

Inevitably, the subject of the USSR cropped up between us. Gide said that not being allowed to visit Russia any more was like a physical deprivation to him, he so longed to be there. I could understand this; quite irrespective of the Soviet regime, there is something about the people and the countryside, something in the very air one breathes, that exerts a tremendous pull. The impression I had was that Gide now regretted the break with the Soviet authorities that the publication of his second book about the USSR had caused, and looked back nostalgically on his first visit, when he was treated as an honoured guest, like any Bernard Shaw or Henri Barbusse. His disillusionment, in any case, seems to have resulted rather from the changed attitude to pederasty in the USSR, making its practice a penal offence, as it had been before the Revolution, than from any outraged sense of the injustice, inequality and cruelty Soviet rule involved for its ostensible beneficiaries. I was tempted to pass on to him something the British Consul-General in Algiers had told me. He had been instructed to present to Bogomolov, head of the Russian Mission, a list of Soviet nationals who had found their way to Algeria, and ask him what he wanted done about them. Bogomolov took a pencil and ticked the names of those who were forty and under. When the Consul-General asked what should be done about the others, he just shrugged expressively. So Alaric, King of the Visigoths, might have shrugged if someone had asked what should be done about the old and the sick when Rome was sacked.

The only person I had ever met who knew Gide was Alfred Douglas, and it was on the tip of my tongue to mention him to see how Gide would react; but I desisted, vaguely remembering all the rows and charges and counter-charges that had accompanied the notorious visit Wilde, Douglas and Gide paid to Algiers in 1895. Hugh Kingsmill and Hesketh Pearson took me to see Douglas towards the end of his life, when he was living in a small villa in Hove, and in the habit of taking his evening stroll along the promenade. Other local residents might well have been surprised if they had known who was in their midst. By this time he was a small shrivelled-up man with a large bulbous

nose. As though to accentuate the disappearance of the beauty Wilde
had so extravagantly praised, the walls of his little sitting-room were
covered with portraits of himself as a young man; blazered, straw-
hatted, exquisite. It was a narcissus room; the Dorian Gray story
come to life. Douglas was still very indignant about Gide's scabrous
account of their Algiers adventures. He told us how Robert Harborough
Sherrard, Wilde's romantic champion, was in the habit of insisting, to
refute Gide, that anyway Arab boys were not available in Algiers; but
Douglas added softly: 'They are, you know; they are!' I didn't feel
capable of conveying this scene to Gide, and, in any case, it would
scarcely have been appreciated. We left him back at his window,
watching the GI liberators rolling their buttocks up and down the
Rue Michelet, and maybe meditating another foray to find Steinbeck
sober. When I thought of his grey, cold face, and his exquisite words
rising out of it, like a clear spring out of stony ground, it seemed more
than ever fitting that the Devil should be a fallen angel.

This same bearded British Council man persuaded me to give a
public lecture in French. The moment I had agreed to do it, actuated,
no doubt, more by vanity than good-nature, the prospect of actually
standing up and holding forth in French became a nightmare, which,
every time I contemplated it, filled me with panic fear. However,
thanks to the kindly assiduous help of Bobby Barclay, who, fortunately
for me, was in Algiers, I managed to produce a text, and to stumble
through it without breaking down. The audience carried me back to
my Cairo days; even in war-time Algiers there were nooks and crevices
where devotees of culture lurked, ready to sally forth when a suitable
occasion offered; as well as a certain number of Anglo-French and
American *littérateurs* who had begun to gather in the wake of the
advancing Allied forces, like white penguins behind a plough. The
theme of my address (the text has, I am thankful to think, long since
disappeared) was my joy as an Englishman at being in Algiers, where
I felt nearer to France than ever I had since the war began, and how I
had been going over in my mind all the different reasons, seldom
expressed but deeply felt, that France meant so much to us on our side
of what Churchill had called our moat. It might have been Charles
Morgan or André Maurois speaking. I must have laid it on pretty
thick because there was positive acclaim at the end, and I found myself
for a day or so in some social demand. I am always surprised when
anything I do is well received. Also disconcerted, since, I can never
manage, ultimately, to persuade myself that what is applauded is ever

any good. In this particular case, my predilection received abundant verification.

At our MI6 establishment up on the hill I was particularly taken with one of the faces. It was older and more mature than the others, more, properly speaking, a face; like some ancient manuscript, creased and smudged, rather than mint-fresh off the rotary presses, and done in tens, if not hundreds, of thousands of exemplars. The name he went by – Adrian Hunter – was obviously a *nom de guerre*; and I learnt later, when we had become intimate, that he was none other than the von Strachwitz who had been exchanged for Johann following his abortive assassination attempt in Austria. After being thus exchanged, Adrian just managed to get away from Vienna before the *Anschluss*, and made for London, where he allowed himself to be recruited by SIS, being convinced that the Nazis meant war, and nothing but war. We spent many of our evenings talking together, and laughing – in my case, jeering – at the young spy-masters, who, with a seemingly infallible instinct, supported, supplied and financed the Communist guerrillas who were already preparing their own offensive to follow the final overthrow of the Nazis. When our war was won, theirs would begin. At one end of the scale, Adrian insisted, Roosevelt and Churchill did everything in their power to ensure that, when Germany finally collapsed, Stalin easily occupied and dominated the countries adjoining his frontiers, and, at the other, our young spy-masters showed a like determination so to arrange matters that, in countries further away, he was presented with a well-armed, well-financed and well-organised underground army.

To someone like Adrian, with his deep-seated Catholicism and sense of history, it all seemed crystal clear. He himself worked in the MI6 Jugoslav Section, where the others, much younger than he was, and Philby-like in their ways and attitude of mind, automatically assumed, for instance, that Mihailovitch must be dropped and Tito adopted as our man in Yugoslavia. Why? Adrian asked. Only because Mihailovitch was on our side, whereas Tito hated and despised everything we purported to stand for and believe in. We sat talking in this strain, looking down on the lights of Algiers, and on the Mediterranean beyond – the same coast from which Augustine in Hippo had watched the collapse of Rome as we were now watching the collapse of Christendom. Adrian's face, with its ironical creases and wrinkles, its tired eyes, which yet, behind their tiredness, held an impregnable serenity, was like a veritable map of what we were talking about.

Another favourite theme of Adrian's was of how the Allied strategists had unaccountably failed to push against the door Mussolini's fall left open. Here, of course, he was thinking of his Austria, and of how, as we both knew from Bletchley, the *Abwehr* actually withdrew from Italy when Mussolini was deposed, assuming that all was up; then, when nothing happened, drifted back, dumbfounded. The long, slow campaign up the peninsula was delayed still further when the Americans insisted on transferring all available troops from the Italian front to reinforce an operation into Southern France; surely one of the most bizarre in history, being against no one and serving no purpose – unless it was Stalin's. I went with Paiolle to Bastia in Corsica to watch the convoy leave – a majestic sight, if we hadn't known, from the empty order of battle, that there were no troops to oppose a landing and no military or strategic gain in effecting one. Not even Adrian in his darkest mood of prophesy foresaw the final *dénouement*, when the Anglo-American forces checked their advance, standing by while the Red Army occupied the countries of Eastern and Central Europe, never to be dislodged thence in our time. It is a curious and little noticed fact of history that it is the strong, not the weak, who are most prone to surrender, and that usually before they are even called upon so to do.

Adrian remained a friend till his death. After the war, he returned to live in Vienna, where he edited a magazine which provided a platform for his own conservative view, in matters ecclesiastical as well as political. On his visits to London we always met. On one of these occasions, he described to me how, late one evening in Vienna, he had happened to take a tram going in his direction. At one of its stops a drunk Red Army soldier had got on, and when he found that the tram would not be passing what was then the Soviet Zone, he pulled out a pistol and forced the driver to alter his route. Adrian just sat where he was, smiling drily to himself at being thus confronted with the brave new world that lay ahead, until, the Russian having been put down, the tram resumed its regular route. It was another parable to which I should have paid more heed.

Such considerations scarcely arose in AFHQ (Allied Forces Headquarters), packed tight in the Hotel St Georges, where General Eisenhower reigned supreme. It was laid down that every staff post might be filled by a matching Anglo-American pair, so that instead of one colonel, two majors and four captains, there would be two colonels, four majors and eight captains, with the requisite in- and out-trays and

other impediments. It seemed a cumbersome and expensive way of promoting Anglo-American understanding. To my great delight, I found Colonel Ross-Atkinson still at his old post in charge of what was now called Counter-Intelligence. His matching American had, I thought, a somewhat puzzled air, but they seemed to be on cordial terms. I dined with him one evening in his mess, and found that he was more prone than ever to fall asleep; but he still had the same rough, shrewd way of judging everyone and everything which I liked so much, and determination to stay with the Headquarters caravanserai till the end – as he succeeded in doing.

My only business with him now was to bring him occasionally a Bletchley intercept of special Security interest. This I had to do by hand, showing it to him, and then taking it away. Once, having shown him one of these intercepts – about enemy intimations of a forth-coming meeting between Roosevelt and Churchill – we got talking, and I forgot all about it. Back in the Rue Charras, I hunted through my brief-case and pockets, and there was no sign of it. Had I dropped the piece of paper somewhere? Or left it on Colonel Ross-Atkinson's desk? This was a hope, and I rushed back to the Hotel St Georges to find that his desk was bare and that he had gone to lunch. So I sat in his office waiting for his return, and woefully speculating on what was likely to happen to me. Should I be shot? Or just sent to the Glass-house? Or court-martialled and disgraced? To have lost a Bletchley intercept, thereby jeopardising the whole invaluable cipher-cracking operation, was the most serious offence I could possibly have com-mitted. When Colonel Ross-Atkinson returned, I explained my plight, and he was extremely sympathetic. We considered all the different possibilities, and when and to whom the loss should be reported. While we were thus talking, his clerk came in with a pile of papers, on the top of them being the lost intercept. It seemed that I had absent-mindedly put it in the out-tray while the Colonel and I were talking, and that it had been automatically circulated to various Headquarters branches, in none of which had it made any particular impression. This was vaguely disconcerting, considering the importance we attached to such material; but anyway the intercept was back, to my intense relief.

A regular duty I had was to attend a weekly conference on security matters presided over by Duff Cooper, who had arrived in Algiers as special emissary to de Gaulle's Provisional Government – which is what his CFLN (*Comité Français de Libération Nationale*) had now become. I used to look forward to this, as I liked Duff Cooper and

admired his book on Talleyrand. The matters which came up for discussion at our meetings cannot have been very weighty, because I am unable now to remember one single item. I also grew fond of the Foreign Office official in attendance, Patrick Reilly, who has one of those wonderfully steady, clear minds I so admire, doubtless because my own is so unsteady and prone to obfuscation. These two favourites of mine – Duff Cooper and Reilly – both had, relatively speaking, disappointing careers; whereas the other governmental personage in Algiers – Harold Macmillan – who always struck me as a parody of a Conservative politician in a novel by Trollope, became Prime Minister.

It was at a picnic party given by the Duff Coopers (Lady Diana had joined him in Algiers) that I caught my only war-time glimpse of Evelyn Waugh. He had recently been involved, along with Randolph Churchill, in an air accident on their way to Jugoslavia, and looked a little shaken. I had the feeling that his uniform was not as smart as it was meant to be; likewise his moustache, which readers of his brilliant war trilogy will remember. Altogether, he seemed dispirited. We sat for a while side by side on a bench, and I recalled gratefully the very generous notice he had written in the *Spectator* of my book *In A Valley of This Restless Mind*. I knew that what I wrote and said afterwards disappointed him; in another notice, he spoke of the promise of 'serious interests' which had not been fulfilled.

Thereafter, on the few occasions that we met, it was always a matter, as Serge would have put it, of *Jouant la comédie*. For instance, at a literary luncheon for the publication of *The Ordeal of Gilbert Pinfold*, over which I presided, words I intended as homage to a writer and a book I greatly admired, turned into a meandering, facetious discourse, while Waugh himself engaged in a pantomime act with an ear-trumpet he then affected. Similarly, without any conscious intention on my part, a note of acrimony always seemed to come into anything I wrote about him – even his obituary. When I became editor of *Punch* he wrote me a gratifying letter saying that my appointment could be revolutionary in its consequences; but here, too, the results that followed were distasteful to him, and I declined to publish an article of his which I considered to be libellous.

Now that Waugh is dead, I greatly regret that I made no serious attempt to overcome our mutual antagonism. Probably I should have failed, but I wish I had tried. Most of his friends and admirers regarded him as a superb clown, or as a brilliant trafficker in nostalgia; but I saw him as like Bernanos, 'between the Angel of light and the Angel

of darkness, looking at each in turn with the same enraged hunger for the absolute.' His true charity comes out in some letters he wrote to George Orwell in his last illness which I have read; perfectly phrased in their consideration for someone in affliction, despite the fact that, ostensibly at any rate, he and Orwell were, temperamentally, and in many of their opinions and aspirations, as opposed as any two writers could possibly be. I was given a last chance when he was staying in a rather dismal hotel in Menton, near Roquebrune, where Kitty and I had rented a villa. We used to see him sitting, as it seemed, disconsolately, in the lounge with a book in his hand. I had then an almost overpowering longing to go up and speak to him, and twice drafted a letter proposing a meeting, but in each case resisted the impulse through a cowardly fear of being repulsed or made to look foolish. When I heard the following Easter that he had died, I felt quite stricken; not just because he was so talented a writer and satirist, but because there would now never be another opportunity in this world to gather strength and courage from him for the lost battles that lie ahead.

I came into contact with his ghost in curious circumstances some years later. The Soviet writer, Anatole Kuznetsov, had sought asylum in England, and was staying with Waugh's mother-in-law, Mary Herbert, and her son Auberon Herbert, a long-standing and dear friend of mine. I was asked to interview Kuznetsov for BBC Television, and it was necessary to find a more or less clandestine location for fear that the KGB might seek a chance of organising his murder, as had happened in the case of other distinguished fugitives from the USSR. Evelyn Waugh's widow, Laura, kindly offered their house, and there we all duly assembled – cameraman, sound-recordist, David Floyd to be interpreter, Tony Smith and Peter Chafer as joint producers, and, of course, Kuznetsov himself.

It was a scene that the late owner of the house would scarcely have relished, but its piquancy on his premises would surely not have escaped him; and from the beginning I was conscious of his presence. Kuznetsov, as it turned out, was all too typically a Soviet product, with granite features, broad trousers, gold teeth and a fathomless conceit of himself. However hard we tried, it proved impossible to get him to assume the role of a literary Nureyev – which was greatly to his credit. Every time we took our eyes off him he raced over to a hired car that we had, got behind the wheel, and, never having driven before, began pulling the levers and releasing the brake, until the vehicle started moving, and he disappeared round a bend in the drive, to the great

concern, particularly, of the MI5 men who were keeping an eye on the proceedings. In the house itself – a huge Victorian mansion with furniture to match – there was in the dining-room a bust of Waugh on whose head his war-time army cap had been placed; I thought I caught an ironical smile flitting about the mouth from time to time. We spent our evenings in Mary Herbert's house, with Auberon and Kuznetsov, who there seemed like an intruder into Brideshead; or, alternatively, to have been given an extra part written into a Soviet version of the *Forsyte Saga*.

Far the most interesting aspect, to me, of Intelligence operations was providing appropriate material (known as chicken feed) for transmission by enemy agents who had been turned round – that is, induced to go on functioning under control. This needed to be very carefully and subtly concocted; on the one hand, sufficiently high grade to impress their *Abwehr* masters, thereby building up their reputation; on the other, not so high grade that it gave away anything of major importance to us. Then, at the required moment, they could be used for deception purposes, at the risk, if necessary, of being blown. Fortunately for us all, Sir John Masterman, a dab hand at the business, has been allowed to publish his official record of just how this double-cross system functioned in the 1939–45 war. Here again, as he points out, the Bletchley material was invaluable, if not essential, since it enabled the credibility in the enemy's estimation of agents under our control to be continually checked, and any tricks they might try to engage in to be at once detected. It was astonishing how, on both sides in the war, agents continued to be believed in even when they had been under control for years, and regularly sending grossly misleading information. The reason was, I think, that the officers controlling double-cross agents became in time very fond and proud of them. After all, they gave them their words, and built up their fictitious characters, so that they were as much the creation of their officer-controllers as the characters in a novel are the novelist's. If one of them was awarded an enemy decoration – as sometimes happened, again on both sides – it added lustre to the whole operation; and when the time came to blow a double-cross agent for some ulterior purpose, the controlling officers were as grieved as Dickens was when he felt bound to kill off Little Nell. In time, as Sir John shows, all the enemy agents in the United Kingdom were brought under control and turned round, so that, in effect, he and his colleagues were running the *Abwehr's* British service for them. My impression is that they ran it

better, and transmitted higher-grade material, than ever the *Abwehr* would have been able to manage on its own account. Which side in the war gained thereby is a difficult equation to work out.

In North Africa we had a number of turned-round enemy agents under control. There was, for instance, a well-born English beach-comber in Tangier who was so well in with the Germans that they continued to believe his reports even after he had persuaded them that the Allies' North African expedition was making for Dakar. Also, a French colonel stationed near Algiers who continued to function successfully right up to the end of the war, and who could today, if he cared to, wear an Iron Cross in one lapel and a *Croix de Guerre* in the other. An aspect of this use of turned-round agents which greatly appealed to our French colleagues was that it could be made to pay for itself, if not yield a handsome profit. There was nothing they liked better than getting our double-cross colonel to apply to his *Abwehr* masters for money, to be dropped by parachute in specie rather than notes, which, they made him say, were dangerously detectable. They also, at one point, being short of motor tyres, induced him to apply for some on the ground that if he were to try and buy them locally at the then prohibitive price, it would draw attention to him undesirably. A set duly arrived in an air-drop, which proved, incidentally, to be Dunlops. I made the suggestion that the colonel should send a message complaining of being troubled by his sexual appetites, to the point that it was impossible for him to concentrate on his work, and that he hesitated to avail himself of local facilities for fear of giving himself away. I had a picture in my mind of Rhine maidens floating down from the sky, but our French colleagues were more sceptical. The most that could be expected by way of response, they insisted, would be a supply of bromide.

War, Napoleon is alleged to have remarked, is a matter of mobility. This, I discovered, applies especially to Intelligence officers, who are always on the move; liaising, getting into and out of the picture, bustling about, here, there and everywhere, with their maps, their talcum, their coloured chalks. A stationary Intelligence officer is a contradiction in terms, like a sedentary eagle; he moves, therefore he is. As the Allied forces pressed forward in Italy, the area for roaming steadily enlarged. Thus, I visited Brindisi, where Marshal Badoglio set up his brief Government in the Hotel Imperiale, which likewise had to accommodate civil servants, service chiefs, advisers, envoys ordinary and extraordinary; all the miscellaneous camp-followers who

go racing after authority in all its guises, and however transitory its
tenure. Just as an alcoholic will, in the last resort, drink anything,
down to and including methylated spirits or surgical spirit, so the
power-addict will procure his fix on any terms. Governments on the
run, governments in exile, shadows of shadow-cabinets, all have their
jackals whose hands reach up for coloured ribbons, honorific titles,
imaginary portfolios and other such offerings of the great. At his trial,
Laval was able to point to one of the presiding judges, and recall that
the last time he had seen him was outside his office at Vichy, where
he was waiting to solicit a favour.

So, the Imperiale was teeming; under-secretaries sleeping in bath-
rooms, monsignoris dossing down on a couple of arm-chairs in the
hotel lounge, ambassadors-to-be with nowhere to lay their heads, and
carrying their sashes and their orders and their letters of credence
about with them for lack of anywhere to stow them safely away. Italian
officers in prodigiously wide breeches and jack-boots gleaming like a
seal's back, wandered hither and thither looking for someone to
interrogate them; war correspondents – including the inseparable trio,
Alan Moorehead, Christopher Buckley and Alex Clifford – likewise
questing; in their case, for communiqués, hand-outs, interviews, any-
thing to tap out and dispatch, datelined Marshal Badoglio's Head-
quarters. I spent some pleasant hours with them. An amiable Air
Force officer, who was acting as Badoglio's interpreter-in-chief, took
me to pay my respects to the Marshal. He was accommodated in what
must have been one of the Imperiale's best rooms, with a view of the
sea and a bathroom of its own, and seemed, I thought, rather dazed
as he sat there, as though wondering what had happened, and who he
was supposed to be. There were others waiting to see him, and after a
brief exchange of courtesies I withdrew, to listen to the ecomiums of
the Air Force officer. A truly outstanding man! What a remarkable
intelligence! How understanding! Ciano in his *Diary* describes how,
when Goering and his retinue waited upon Marshal Pétain, they were
all vying with one another to get a word with Laval. Sycophancy, like
other frailties, in the last resort has no standards.

That evening, a radio link with Rome – still under German military
occupation – was being tried out, to see whether our man there was
operating freely or being controlled. It was rather exciting, waiting to
pick up his signal. What would he send? Details of German troop
movements and installations? Something about Italian morale? What
was happening in the entourage of King Victor Emmanuel? When he

finally came through, it was to tell us that we must not suppose that all the good democrats and patriots were in Marshal Badoglio's Government; there were others, as good, and better, in Rome. I voted that the link was evidently not under control; no *Abwehr* officer, I argued, would have had the wit to invent so authentic a message. So it was agreed.

In Brindisi I acquired a car and a driver. It was an ancient vehicle, but with one inestimable advantage – above its number-plate a notice bearing the legend: INTERNATIONAL CONTROL COMMISSION. When and how this notice had been acquired, who the International Control Commission were, and what, if anything, they were controlling, I never found out; but the effect of ostensibly travelling under their auspices was magical. We were never held up, or asked for papers, or in any way interfered with. The roads were crowded with military vehicles of one sort or another, and in an appalling state; the bridges had nearly all been blown up and replaced by temporary structures; the villages were largely deserted. The war seemed to have laid a particularly heavy hand on this landscape and its people. In the cities bombardment brought great misery and destruction, certainly, and the wasteland left behind was desolating; but still it was somehow inherent in them. They contained so much violence and conflict anyway, that their destruction was more like a volcano erupting from within than an attack coming unaccountably and savagely from without; whereas there seemed no place for marching men and rolling vehicles and prowling aircraft in the countryside of Southern Italy, so poor and so everlasting, cultivated over the centuries with such loving care, enshrined for me in the descriptions of Silone, dug out of his heart in love and fury.

In Naples one bright afternoon the whole population were evacuated in order that booby traps and other devices left behind by the Germans when they withdrew might be dismantled without risk to the inhabitants. A vast concourse gathered on the hills around the city; like a vision of the Last Day, when all the dead arise. In Naples, too, I was taken to a house lately occupied by the Gestapo. It was a scene of squalor and disorder; the lavatory bunged up, everything broken and torn, the grate piled high with burnt paper, books on the floor, a desk, once elegant, with inlaid wood and brass fittings, dragged halfway to the door as though to take it away, and then abandoned; in one of its pigeon-holes a family group – all in Bavarian costume – plump mother, father smoking a curved pipe, two sons wearing student caps, three

daughters in dirndl dresses, and written at the bottom some illegible
inscription in old Gothic characters, and in one of the drawers, an
illustrated erotic book, with pictures of elephantine women and bestial
men. Violence, sentimentality and porn, and finally, to round things
off, sheer imbecility, in the form of a propaganda record lying about
which played a Lili-Marlene-type song into which a soft, persuasive
voice broke from time to time, saying, in English: 'You know you're
losing the war . . . You'd far better give in. . . .' So short a while before
the others had been there, living presences; and now, surveying the
debris they had left behind, came the realisation that these ashes were
still warm. Capri abandoned; Pompeii, too, with fresh bullet marks
on its crumbling masonry. After the great eruption of two thousand
years ago, this supererogatory, man-made one scarcely showed – ruins
to ruins. At Caserta another huge headquarters was in course of
preparation, where the enemy's final surrender in the Italian campaign
would take place.

My last visit to Italy ended in Rome, which had lately fallen to the
Allies. I was lodged in the Banco di Roma; a vast marble structure for
the accommodation and celebration of money, not men. Now, it
seemed, the god had failed; its temple was empty and chill, like a tomb
full of battle-dressed intruders. Elsewhere, the presses were rolling
off Occupation money at top speed, with, on the back of the notes,
Roosevelt's Four Freedoms printed, including Freedom from Want,
which, it must be admitted, this particular currency did little to sustain.
Peeping into the Banco di Roma some years later, at the time of the
Second Vatican Council, the rites seemed to be in full swing again;
the god was back, and the battle-dressed ghosts had long since departed.

At dawn on the morning of 12 August 1944, we took off for France in a
small plane piloted by a Canadian. Besides the pilot and myself, there
were Paiolle and Pelabon, whom I had met from time to time with
Soustelle; both in uniform, the latter as a naval officer. I had not known
he was in this service; in his new, unfamiliar uniform, he looked
younger than his years. We flew low enough to follow our course – over
the Downs, then Dover and the white cliffs, the Channel, and, finally,
France. It surprised me that, seen from above, the countryside looked
exactly as it had four years before. Yet, after all, why not? What did we
expect? I scarcely knew, but not assuredly, those familiar little towns and
villages grouped so serenely around their churches; those tidy fields and
massive horses, that I remembered so well from times past. There

ought, surely, to have been a haze of smoke, gutted houses, refugees on the roads, troops and military aircraft. Our troops, I heard, when they landed suffered a similar disappointment at finding only a surly, well-fed prosperous-looking peasantry when they had been led to expect a starving, desperate population overjoyed to see them. The worst feature of propaganda, advertising, or any form of organised lying, is that, try as one will, one comes to believe it; as press lords come to believe what they read in their own newspapers, and television producers what they see on the screen.

None of the four of us said anything, or looked particularly uplifted or moved. I as, in a sense, the host, belonging, anyway, to the country which had provided the aircraft and facilities, felt I ought to utter, and tried desperately to think of suitable words. About how, at this historic moment . . . privilege of sharing together . . . resolved never again to allow . . . sectarian or selfish interests. . . . It was another of those fraudulent sentences which will never end, carrying me back to leader-writing days. Put into French it seemed even worse. I decided to stay silent. Only Paiolle, who had kept his fore-and-aft cap on, saluted, murmuring what sounded like: '*Je salue mon pays.*' Pelabon, who had taken off his peaked naval hat, which seemed to bear rather heavily upon his head, looked uncomfortable at this gesture, as though he felt he, too, should have responded in some way; but by then it was too late, and whatever he did would have looked like following Paiolle's lead. Apart from my abortive effort to bring out an appropriate sentence, I had no particular sense of drama. It is the words that make the drama, rather than the other way round; 'Now he belongs to history,' establishing, rather than defining, Lincoln's part.

Our pilot, his headphones on, indicated that we shouldn't be able to land as planned at Le Bourget, where there was still fighting going on, and he landed finally on an air-strip some seventy miles from Paris. There was a good deal of confusion there, too, and no one took much interest in us. We gathered our luggage together, and managed to get a lift in a military truck loaded with miscellaneous regular and irregular French troops, some of them with FFI (*Forces Françaises de l'Intérieur*) arm-bands. As we had an air of being senior officers, we were put up in front, with the result that, as we went along, whenever we passed through cheering crowds – which happened all the way to Paris, getting thicker and noisier the nearer we got – we responded officially, saluting and waving like royalty, on behalf of the others, many of whom were already fairly drunk, and very wild and excited; shouting, dancing about, and

even occasionally letting off a gun. In time, we, too, became infected with the prevailing excitement; the more so because, every time we were brought to a halt, swigs of cognac and glasses of champagne were pressed upon us.

As a British officer I had a certain rarity value. The Americans had insisted that, because of El Kebir, not to mention the Battle of Trafalgar and Crécy, the British were unpopular among the French, and should as far as possible be kept out of sight; whereas, because of Lafayette, the Americans were correspondingly beloved. I never myself came across anyone among the French, military or civilian, with whom such considerations weighed. They belonged only to the calculations of public relations experts, whose divorcement from the world around them is vastly greater than anything of the kind achieved by the most resolute hermits; a St Simon Stylites lives in close contact with his fellows compared with the Madison Avenue men. In this particular case, the moment it became known that there was *un officier Anglais* aboard our lorry, the offerings of champagne and cognac became ever more pressing; as did my readiness to accept them, and to exchange embraces with any agreeable females in the vicinity. In this exalted frame of mind, I gradually, as it were, got integrated into the show; until I really became convinced that I was a liberator being received with love and gratitude by the liberated.

By the time we arrived in the centre of Paris, and our truck put me down at the Petit Palais, where Allied Forces had their headquarters, I was in a very exalted state indeed, and parted from my fellow-travellers with many protestations of affection and esteem. Paiolle went off to find his wife, whom he had not seen since he left France; Pelabon made his way somewhere or other – anyway disappeared. The Petit Palais was a scene of great confusion; there was no electric light or water, Paris being then without any municipal services. Occasional electric torches or hurricane lamps showed up shadowy figures among the statuary, sleeping GI's stretched out under some Perseus or Venus, or, seated, sending up Lucky Strike oblations to a Pallas Athene. A cultural bivouac which might have been compèred by Kenneth Clark. With some difficulty I managed to find Trevor Wilson; he was in his element, having acquired a long *poilu* greatcoat which swept the ground, making him seem even smaller than he naturally was. A cigarette was, as usual, more or less permanently attached to his lower lip, and occasionally smouldering, making his always indistinct speech more so than ever. He was the perfect companion for a Liberation; I greeted him warmly and affection-

ately, and he responded in the same spirit. He would, I knew, combine his seemingly surrealist manner with a magical cunning in procuring food and shelter, and in finding his way to exactly the right places at the right time.

First he took me to an American mess, where we ate baked beans washed down with coffee; then on to a haunt of his on the Left Bank – already, in some miraculous way, he had procured a vehicle and a driver – packed out, mostly with civilians, and thick with tobacco smoke. Trevor, of course, knew the *Patron*, and a place was found and a bottle put before us. There were only flickering candles to light the tiny stage, where a man, completely bald, with a large, sad clown's face, was intoning a soliloquy, in which he recalled all the terrible things that had happened to him since the Germans came to Paris. *Et maintenant*, he concluded, with an expression of infinite woe, through which he struggled, to break into a wry smile – *Et maintenant, nous sommes libérés!* The audience roared their approval, and looked quizzically at Trevor and me. Somehow it seemed the most perfect comment on the situation, and ever after, when I have thought of the Liberation, I have seen again the solemnity of his vast expanse of face, and heard his woeful declaration. Only clowns and mystics ever speak the truth.

The next morning we went to a Requiem Mass for six heroes of the Resistance, their coffins side by side, and covered with flowers, each one bearing the Cross of Lorraine. Mourners processed by, shaking Holy Water over them as they passed. Trevor Wilson, still wearing his *poilu* greatcoat, did this with particular zest, to the point that I feared he might have emptied the receptacle used, leaving nothing for the next-in-line who took it off him. I had not previously known that he was a Roman Catholic, as he now appeared to be from his familiarity with the order of service and ceremonial usages. At Nôtre Dame, there was a special thanksgiving service attended by de Gaulle. The cathedral was packed tight, with a great array of cardinals and archbishops at the altar. The choir sang melodiously, and up in front the heads of the General and his associates could just be seen. It was at this point that someone fired a pistol; as was subsequently discovered, by mistake. The effect was fantastic; the huge congregation who had all been standing suddenly fell flat on their faces, supposing that some plot – Communist, Pétainist, Nazi, maybe even Gaullist – was about to be put into operation. There was a single exception; one solitary figure still standing, like a lonely giant. It was, of course, de Gaulle. Thenceforth, that was how I always saw him – towering and alone; the rest, prostrate.

As things turned out no posture could have been more appropriate. In those first days after the German withdrawal, without a doubt, de Gaulle's presence alone prevented a total breakdown, probably followed by a Communist takeover. As soon as he appeared on the scene, Allied plans, so painstakingly worked out, for setting up a military government, prior to the holding of elections, all ran into the sand; the brigadiers who had assembled at embarkation ports, putative gauleiters, lawyers, men from the city and of a certain age, briefed in the *Code Napoléon* and other lore for taking over their allotted districts, stole silently away, unwanted. Wherever de Gaulle appeared, he was the government, and recognised as such. Witnessing this performance I realised that it was not just his political acumen, and the undoubted charisma of his weird angular disposition, which made him the unquestioned master of the situation. Rather, he had some second sense arising out of his complete confidence in himself and in his destiny, which guided his steps, fed out those rumbling and so telling words of his, and showed him exactly where he should be and what he should say. He was like, I decided, one of those circus clowns who ride a bicycle clumsily into the ring, seeming always about to fall off, until you realise that they are in fact consummate riders, who will always recover their balance and end up standing majestically on the saddle and saluting a wildly applauding audience.

From this time on I always assumed that he must win, however strange and self-defeating his tactics at a particular moment might seem to be. When, for instance, in 1946 – Soustelle, then one of his Ministers, vividly described the scene to me – he brusquely ended his first brief spell of being head of the government by coming into a cabinet meeting and, without any prior warning, banging the table and exclaiming: '*J'en ai marre!*' I felt quite sure that the move, though inexplicable at the time, would prove to have been correct from the point of view of his larger purposes. As, indeed, it did, since it left the ghosts of the Third Republic, still extant when the Pétain Government expired, to give a public demonstration of their inability to rule France, thereby providing him with an opportunity, in due course, to take over on his own terms, and to shape a regime in accordance with his own notions of durability.

This conviction served me well when, after the war, I became a journalist again. Thanks to Soustelle, I was able to interview de Gaulle at the lowest point in his political fortunes – the only circumstances in which men of action are at all informative. At the time, he had only some six members of the *Assemblée Nationale*, one of them being Soustelle; in the Crillon Bar the foreign correspondents were unanimous that de

Gaulle was finished, and the French press was either against him, or dubious about his prospects. I, remembering my circus trick-cyclist image, thought otherwise. He received me in his office in the Rue Solférino; seated at a desk that was much too small for him, so that he seemed, at the same time, to bulge out of it and to tower above it. His stomach already protruded noticeably, his complexion was muddy and his breath bad; yet, as always, I found in him a nobility, a true dis-interestedness, even a sort of sublime absurdity, which overcame his physical and mental gaucherie. We spoke in French, of course; to the best of my knowledge, during the years he spent in London he failed to acquire one single word of English. On the occasions that he uttered a few words in a foreign language, he always had to learn them pho-netically beforehand. The encounter remains memorable; more so, I think, than any other of the kind I ever experienced, not so much be-cause of what was said – predominantly by him; I scarcely spoke, a somewhat unusual experience for me – as because of the sense that I had of being in the presence of someone of enormous significance, who was, at once, as such men are, the hero and the victim of the times we were living through.

Our conversation began with one of his tirades about the *pourriture* of French politics, and ended with my asking him what he proposed to do now, to which he replied with a majestic: *'J'attends!'* At the time I wrote an account of what he said, as exactly as I could remember it, in the *Daily Telegraph*, whose deputy-editor I then was. At one point I summoned up my courage to ask him why, if the present regime was so abhorrent, he had not tried to fashion a better one himself when, just after the war, he dominated France as no one else had since Napoleon, or even *le Roi Soleil*. He glowered at me for this, indicating, as I thought, by the very intensity of his reaction that it was something he had asked himself from time to time; then rumbled out his answer: *'Ce n'était pas l'heure.'* I had to leave it at that; the timing would have been wrong – as, indeed, one can see now, it would have been.

The only other contact I had with him was to write to him after his retirement suggesting that, as his astonishing career as a world figure had, in effect, begun with a broadcast on BBC Radio in 1940, he might consider it fitting to conclude it with a last word on the same channel. I quoted the case of Tolstoy who, in the very last sentences he wrote, concluded: 'That, my dear brothers, is what I have been trying to say.' How wonderful to have a similar last word from de Gaulle! He replied very charmingly that he appreciated the suggestion, but had resolved

not to venture upon the air (*utiliser les ondes*) again. There was one other tiny connection; when I became a waxwork in Madame Tussaud's I was put in a room between Twiggy and the Burtons, with a massive de Gaulle staring down upon the four of us. Not a sparrow can fall to the ground, we are told, without concern in Heaven; so, likewise, the *placement* of waxworks.

Soon after arriving in Paris I looked in at the Hotel Scribe where the war correspondents were accommodated, and found one or two old acquaintances among them. How familiar a scene! The fingers questing over a typewriter keyboard, the faces momentarily pulled together to concentrate wavering attention, the cigarette pulled at for inspiration, the glass to hand to fuel the motor when it faltered. TONIGHT TRICOLORE BRAVELY OVERFLYING PARISES FAMOUS ARCDETRIOMPHE FIRST TIME SINCE GERMANS UNDERGOOSE-STEPPED . . . 'Hey! can anyone tell me, is there a flag over the Arc de Triomphe? Not! Well, what about the Eiffel Tower?' A centre of attention was Hemingway, fairly drunk, surrounded by admirers, and hung round with hand-grenades like monstrous beads – which everyone hoped had been immobilised, since, as he lurched about, one might so easily have gone off. Occasionally, he doubled up as for a fight, fists clenched and beating the air; the beard surrounding the face like an artist's shading, making it nebulous, indefinite. Looking at him, there was some comparison I was reaching after; someone he closely re-sembled. Then I remembered; it was the beard which gave me the clue – of course, Walt Whitman. A similar ribald figure, boozy, preoccupied with the image rather than the reality. Music in *muzak*, speed in a speedometer, beauty in cosmetics; virility in the pederastic posturings of a Whitman and strength in a Hemingway's fists beating the air – these two, pre-eminently, the dreamers and the dream.

I spent the next few days wandering about in liberated Paris in varying states of intoxication, having, in the confusion which reigned, nothing particular to do and nowhere particular to be. My French colleagues had not yet surfaced, and the *Services Spéciaux* not yet taken down the shutters and opened for business. A British uniform continued to procure friendly smiles, embraces, bed-fellows even, as and when required, as well as limitless hospitality; food, in so far as supplies were available (which they only were, for the most part, in rather dubious company), and, more plentifully, drink. For what must have been the one and only time in French history, the more expensive paris res-taurants like Maxim's refused to present a bill to Allied officers, doubtless

hoping thereby to *épurer* themselves from having been, during the occupation, similarly attentive to German officers. It was after benefiting from this unusual dispensation that Trevor Wilson, Victor Rothschild (who had now turned up in Paris), and I, a substantial luncheon under our belts, decided to make contact for the first time with a British Forces Headquarters which we heard had been set up in the Roger et Gallet building in the Rue St Honoré. Thither we repaired, in high good humour, to be told that the brigadier who was then in charge had not yet returned, but that we might wait for him in his office, which we did, our high spirits noticeably diminishing as the minutes passed. A project entertained at a festive meal, needs, like Brutus's plot, to be taken at the flood if it is to lead on to victory.

By the time the brigadier turned up we were decidedly deflated; he, clearly, found us an astonishing, if not distasteful, spectacle. It was not difficult to see why. He looked particularly smart in his service dress, his buttons shining, his red-tabs glowing; whereas we presented, from his point of view, a lamentable appearance. Trevor had on his *poilu* greatcoat, which had not improved with the wearing; the stub of a Gaulois cigarette still clung tenaciously to his lower-lip. Rothschild was a massive, but scarcely a soldierly figure; and I doubtless bore marks of my Liberation celebrations. The situation was not made easier when it came out the lieutenant-colonel among us (Trevor and I were majors) was none other than Lord Rothschild; a name that clearly represented, in the brigadier's eyes, all that was most alluring and splendid on earth. Could this be he? And in such company? Clearly not; they must be impostors. His hand, I thought, began to move towards the bell on his desk, no doubt to summon an orderly and have us removed, when Trevor once again made himself master of a difficult situation.

We were, he explained to the brigadier, cloak-and-dagger men, leaving him to assume that what he had taken to be uniforms were, in fact, an ingenious and carefully devised disguise for some purpose of our own. He was further mollified when Trevor went on to say that we had merely come to report to him as our, pro-tem, commanding officer, with no requirements in the way of billets or rations or pay. Trevor, I should add, by this time, had moved into an elegant apartment in the Rue de la Paix, formerly occupied by an *Abwehr* officer, and I was shortly going to move into the Rothschild mansion in the Avenue Marigny, prudently requisitioned on Victor Rothschild's behalf, in which he had kindly offered me accommodation. When we got up to go, our relations with the brigadier had become positively cordial, which led me to remark that if

at any time there was anything we could do for him, he had but to mention it. At this, he looked suddenly thoughtful. Yes, he said, there was one thing over which we might be able to help. He had been asked to procure a white Rolls-Royce for an air marshal's wife. Could we possibly lay hands on one? Trevor had the air of a man with a whole fleet of Rolls-Royces in all colours at his disposal; it was just a matter of picking the right one. I murmured weakly that we would keep our eyes open. Rothschild, I thought, looked a little surly; he, after all, might well have had a white Rolls-Royce.

In these first days after the Liberation, France (apart from the war-zone itself), and more particularly Paris, was in a virtual state of breakdown, without organs of authority or law. The police, heavily tainted with Pétainism, if not collaboration, were lying low for the time being, until it became clear who was going to emerge to give orders and command obedience. By day, it was not so noticeable, though even then in places like the Palais de Justice and the prisons, which I had occasion to visit, there was total confusion; the judges having mostly disappeared or been arrested themselves, and the prisons being glutted with alleged *collaborateurs*, brought along by no one knew who, and charged with no one knew what. It was when darkness began to fall that one became aware of the breakdown; with no street-lighting, and the tall houses all silent and locked and boarded up, like sightless eyes. Inside them I imagined cowering figures, hopeful of surviving if they remained perfectly still and hidden. Then, as night came on, sounds of scurrying feet, sudden cries, shots, shrieks, but no one available, or caring, to investigate. It is unknown to this day how many were shot down, had their heads shaved, piteously disgorged their possessions in return for being released, but certainly many, many thousands. Outside Paris – for instance, in Orleans, where I spent a week-end in a country house – the situation was even more drastic. Our host had to make his terms for us to come and go with the local FFI, who terrorised the district. There, too, many were shot down or summarily executed and never accounted for. We dined by candle-light; the meal dished up and served by one or two old servants. Afterwards, we played parlour games and danced, talking a little too eagerly, and laughing a little too shrilly, to be convincing; most of us full of thoughts of 1789.

In Paris I spent several evenings with an FFI band, accompanying them on some of their nocturnal expeditions. We first met at a parade at the Arc de Triomphe, when Churchill and de Gaulle laid wreaths on the Unknown Warrior's Tomb, and then marched side by side down the

Champs Elysées. A curious pair, the one so rotund and merry, the other so tall and grave; like Mr Pickwick and Don Quixote. I struck up a friendship with the FFI band then and there, and they invited me along to an apartment they had taken over in the Avenue Foch, formerly occupied by the Gestapo; large and elegantly furnished, well stocked with champagne, and, like the *Abwehr* house in Naples, with erotica. They were a mixed lot who had come together by chance; the leader, I was told, an actor of sorts, and certainly given to striking attitudes – for instance, one arm in a sling, and flourishing a revolver with the other. His second-in-command was, I should say, an Algerian; rather vicious-looking, and probably a figure from the underworld. I never knew any of their names, except that the actor-leader was called Alain and the Algerian, Marc. There was also a girl named Chantal; pretty, but ravaged looking, in a khaki drill skirt and tunic, and wearing a cartridge belt. The others – some seven or eight – I scarcely distinguished from one another. They were mostly very young, with that curious hunted animal look that street life gives. One of them spoke in a more cultivated way, and might well have been at a Lycée. Today, one would take them to be students; or *Bezprizoray* who had stepped straight out of *The Clockwork Orange*.

I was never able to decide whether they were just a marauding gang, or whether patriotism or ideological fervour played some part in their activities and antics. They certainly took things from people – cigarette cases, jewels, money; anything like that – but for my benefit made a great point of handing them over to Alain, who kept them in a box, which he locked up, and whose contents he carefully listed, to be handed over, so he said, to his superiors. Equally certainly, they were given assignments; to go to such a house, conduct a search, interrogate such a person, make an arrest, and even – as they boasted, but I never saw them do it – carry out an execution. If a door was not opened to them, they would batter it down; everyone cowered before them, and did what they were told. Considering their youth, they behaved with horrifying callousness, arrogance and brutality, recalling a saying of Tolstoy to the effect that revolutionaries in authority always behave worse than those they replace because they come fresh to it. In the years ahead, I was often to be reminded of this. After I stopped seeing them, I vaguely heard that Alain had been arrested, and found to have a collaborationist record.

I got another glimpse of the dark face of Liberation, though this time from the other side of the fence, in connection with a notorious

Paris gangster named Laffont, who during the occupation, in his sinister establishment in the Rue Lauriston, worked closely with the Germans. In return for his services, they tolerated his nefarious activities, and provided him with many amenities and privileges. It was by making use of such criminal elements that the Germans were able, despite the Resistance, to maintain their position in France with very few troops, and those often elderly reservists. Laffont, I should say, was about the most hated and wanted man in Paris when his German protectors disappeared, and it is not surprising that quite soon he was caught and taken into custody. The police hoped to get a lot of information out of him about other underworld operators, and used the usual methods, with the result that he was soon in very poor shape, to the point that he threatened suicide. They particularly did not want this to happen, not, it goes without saying, out of any consideration for Laffont, but because his public trial and execution might help in restoring their morale and prestige. Laffont himself knew quite well that his situation was desperate, but had got it into his head that somehow, if he tried hard enough, the French might be induced to hand his case over to the Allied military authorities for them to deal with it. The police encouraged him in this totally impractical, not to say nonsensical, notion in order to counteract his suicidal tendencies, and wanted a British officer – as Serge would have put it – to *jouer la comédie* with him, and go through the motions of listening sympathetically to his plea. Through the *Sécurité Militaire*, the unappetising task fell to me.

My rendezvous with him was a room at the Sûreté; one of those impersonal, stale rooms in walnut and black leather, that you find in police stations all over the world. Two officers brought him up from the cells, handcuffed, and looking very pale and battered; a dark, sallow man, his black hair brushed, reasonably well shaved, and wearing his own clothes, but with no collar or tie. I could imagine him as something of a dandy in his time; fond of a manicure, silk shirts, well-cut suits. His dossier indicated that he had been a great womaniser. He struck me as being rather slight in stature; but others who had seen him before the police got to work on him said he was burly. Obviously, the purpose of our talk could not be achieved if the two officers remained in the room. Their withdrawal had been arranged beforehand; also the removal of his handcuffs. I hadn't liked to ask if they had facilities for keeping us under close observation, but assumed they must have. All the same, it was an eerie moment when I found myself alone with him. I felt more embarrassed than afraid of anything he might do, to me or to himself;

he seemed so listless and broken and dumb. To start the conversation I tried to put on an impersonation of a brisk staff-officer, and for the purpose had a briefcase with me from which I took out a paper or two. I gathered, I said, that he considered his case should be an Allied, rather than a French, responsibility. Why precisely? His voice, when he spoke, was flat. I thought I could detect a Midi accent. Because, he said, the offences that he was charged with took place during the German occupation. How, then, could his guilt be investigated by French police who had themselves continued to function under the occupation authorities? Or, for that matter – and here his flat voice acquired a touch of animation – how could he be tried by some upstart Gaullist military court whose members had been in exile when his alleged crimes were committed?

It was not very convincing, especially in the light of his dossier, which I had, of course, read, outlining his criminal record, going back to long before 1940. Continuing my role as a brisk staff-officer, I said that I assumed he wanted me to put this to the Allied Command, which of course I would do, though with what result I naturally could not foretell. Yes, he said, he wanted it put to General Eisenhower personally. Suddenly the overweening vanity of the criminal mind showed; he had seriously persuaded himself, it was clear, that once Eisenhower heard of his predicament, he would bang the table, and insist on the French handing him over – 'Bring me Laffont!' Now, perhaps calculating that as a British officer I might resent this undue preoccupation with an American Commander-in-Chief, he went on to tell me how he had hidden RAF pilots who had baled out over France, and helped them to escape to Spain. This had become almost a routine reaction by now; I scarcely ever met a Frenchman who had not, at some point or other in the war, had at least one RAF pilot hidden in his attic. If there had been as many RAF pilots as these revelations would seem to suggest, I often reflected, our Air Force would have been so huge that we should have won the war almost before it had begun.

Laffont's anglophilia was not exhausted by his efforts on behalf of RAF pilots; he went on to tell me that the only woman he had ever loved – this, with a dim smile, as though to say that he had known a woman or two in his time – lived in Hull, and he had sent her food parcels all through the war. However had he managed that? I asked him. Again, that atrocious vanity of his manifested itself. Oh, he said, he could do anything he liked in that line through the Swiss Red Cross. It was true, as a matter of fact, that even before the war he was on amicable terms

with senior police officers, and during the occupation with leading political figures as well, including Pierre Laval, who actually visited him in the Rue Lauriston. The only comparable egomaniac I have encountered was Hitler's banker, Hjalmar Schacht, who told me, when I interviewed him in Düsseldorf, where he opened a bank after his Nuremburg ordeal, that during the war he had received food parcels from Montague Norman, also via the Swiss Red Cross, sent on the theory, presumably, that bankers, whoever they might be, should in no circumstances be allowed to go hungry. With his rimless pince-nez gleaming, his hair *en brosse*, his tall stiff collar and air of impeccable rectitude, he seemed astonished that I should find anything bizarre in this. It would be interesting to have a look at the Swiss Red Cross records for 1939–45 – if any such exist – to see just who sent parcels to whom.

Laffont seemed reasonably content with our talk, from which I deduced that it had served its purpose, and got up to go; whereupon the two officers came back into the room, and handcuffed him again. In their presence he visibly wilted; the bounce that had been stirred up in him by his talk of his lady friend in Hull, and of what a master-hand he had been at dealing with the Swiss Red Cross, dissolved under their iron gaze. Perhaps, after all, he didn't really have much hope of escaping from their clutches. It was a relief to get away, and out into the street, but the memory of my macabre encounter with him continued to haunt me; not because I had any particular pity for his plight, or sense of horror at what he had done. Rather, at the thought of that ego of his, lifting up its head, and darting out its cobra tongue; that vanity, emerging, inviolate, fresh and new as a Pharaoh's treasure after centuries in a dark tomb, from the beatings and thumpings at the Sûreté, the questionings and shoutings, the bright lights shining and the dead hours passing. Above all, at the thought that this ego and vanity could so easily, so neatly and aptly, be related to my own. As for his crimes – in the confessional, if I ever found my way there, I should have to confess that there is no crime, however unspeakable, that I have not either contemplated, or know myself to be capable of having committed.

I read in the *Figaro* that he had been tried, found guilty and executed; not by a firing-squad, as he would undoubtedly have preferred, but guillotined – neat, sallow head with the blunt Mediterranean back to it, sliced off like a thistle's. I doubt if anyone mourned for him, unless the lady in Hull, and perhaps, in some perverse way, myself. It's a pity, maybe, that I didn't ask him for her name, for then I could have sought

her out and found out what her feelings were, if any. I expect, though, that the real reason I didn't try to track her down was the certainty of discovering that she did not exist.

By this time I was settled in the Rothschild mansion in the Avenue Marigny. It was a huge, dark, sombre house, with a courtyard and a massive door opening into the street, which could be operated from the porter's lodge, where sat M. Félix, the *maître d'hôtel*. To get in or out one required M. Félix's co-operation; at his, or one of his underling's touch, the great door could be swung open, and then inexorably shut – as it seemed, excluding or imprisoning one for ever. The furniture was in keeping with the house and the gate; also heavy and sombre. Even the pictures, some of them by old masters, and, presumably, immensely valuable, hung, as it seemed to me, lifelessly on the walls; the life and light somehow drained out of them. It astonished me, when we first moved into the house, to find its contents intact and undamaged. As belonging to one of the most famous Jewish families in Europe, one would have expected it to have suffered. During the German occupation, it was taken over by a *Luftwaffe* general, who, according to M. Félix – he continued to function as a matter of course – behaved impeccably; not only refraining from tampering with the house and its contents himself, but also preventing others from doing so. When I got to know M. Félix better, I asked him how he accounted for the general's good behaviour, he being, after all, a Nazi. His reply was interesting; Hitlers come and go, he said, but Rothschilds go on for ever. He said it with a droll smile; not a man, I concluded correctly, to tell me that he had hidden RAF officers in the Rothschild cellar, along with the Mouton Rothschild. Someone, clearly, with his wits about him. We often had chats together after that.

To me, there always seemed to be a shadow hanging over the house in the Avenue Marigny, as over the Kremlin – in the one case, of money, in the other of power; though, of course, ultimately, they amount to the same thing, money being a pasteurised form of power. This shadow, I confess, is something that has haunted all my days. Seen first, perhaps, in those Doré illustrations of Dante which so fascinated me as a child; there, hanging over the nether regions where poor lost souls await release from the chains they have forged for themselves on earth. Likewise, hanging over all Kremlins everywhere – the City, Wall Street, the Vatican, the Houses of Parliament, the Pentagon, Capitol Hill, and that Krupps sanctum at whose monstrous desk I once sat shivering through a thunderstorm; hanging over all the frozen corridors along which feet tramp

incessantly on their way to war, to vote, to applaud and to decry, to work
and to play, to victory and to defeat. The same shadow that I envisaged,
when, between Jericho and the Dead Sea, I tried to reconstruct forty
days and forty nights in the wilderness, dogged by the Devil making his
offers – of plenty, a Gross National Product without end; of wonders
illimitable, reaching to the moon and beyond; of the kingdoms of the
earth, to have and to shape. This shadow was the Devil's own, darkening
the golden sand. The sun could not reach it; only another Light, not
of this world, would suffice to abolish it.

For Rothschild himself, of course, the Avenue Marigny house was a
home from home, but at the same time, I felt, a prison. Installed there,
he was the *de facto* if not *de jure* head of the family. Other Rothschilds
appeared from time to time, and offered obeisance. He both liked to
feel they were looking to him, and abhorred their presence; his dis-
position was a curious, uneasy mixture of arrogance and diffidence.
Somewhere between White's Club and the Ark of the Covenant, between
the Old and the New Testament, between the Kremlin and the House of
Lords, he had lost his way, and been floundering about ever since.
Embedded deep down in him there was something touching and vulner-
able and perceptive; at times lovable even. But so overlaid with the
bogus certainties of science, and the equally bogus respect, accorded
and expected, on account of his wealth and famous name, that it was
only rarely apparent. Once when I was going to London he asked me to
take over a case of brandy, addressed in large letters to him at his English
address. In the guard's van where it was put, among the porters who
carried it, wherever it was seen or handled, it aroused an attitude of
adoration, real or facetious, as though it had been some holy relic – the
bones of a saint or a fragment of the True Cross. Even I partook of its
glory, momentarily deputising for this Socialist millionaire, this Rab-
binical sceptic, this epicurean ascetic, this Wise Man who had followed
the wrong star and found his way to the wrong manger – one complete
with chef, central heating and a lift. I think of him in the Avenue Marigny
dictating innumerable memoranda, as though in the hope that, if only
he dictated enough of them, one would say something; on a basis of the
philosophical notion that three monkeys tapping away at typewriters
must infallibly, if they keep at it long enough, ultimately tap out the
Bible. Rothschild, anyway, did not lack for monkeys. After the war I
caught glimpses of him at Cambridge, in think-tanks, once in the
Weizmann Institute in Tel Aviv, still dictating memoranda.

*

The *Services Spéciaux* were now installed in the Boulevard Suchet, having taken over several houses requisitioned and camouflaged by the Germans during the occupation for some sort of naval headquarters. It was an ultra-fashionable neighbourhood, where, later, the Duke and Duchess of Windsor were to reside. I had an office looking out on the Bois de Boulogne; very agreeable and convenient. Some of the original elegant furniture belonging to the dispossessed occupants remained; but when the cold, fuel-less winter months came along, in which even M. Félix had difficulty in getting supplies, a lot of this found it way into the fireplaces. I remember cheerfully consigning to the flames the carved legs of chairs and tables, which may for all I knew have been priceless antiques. At first we had 'SS' for *Services Spéciaux* on the number plates issued to us for our cars. This, with memories of the German SS troops during the occupation, soon became a subject for newspaper ridicule and abuse, so we changed to DGER – *Directorat-Général des Études et Recherches*, whatever that may have meant. Now that all the different branches, including Paiolle's, were under one roof, with Soustelle as the boss, the role of MI6, which I represented, necessarily declined. This was not a process I sought to impede, since it resulted, to my great satisfaction, in a steady diminution in the amount of paper that came my way. Most of what I had to do consisted in trying to sort out the position of purported British agents who had been arrested as collaborators by the French police. For obvious reasons, their work for us had often necessitated their being ostensibly on good terms with the German occupation authorities, for which they now found themselves under the threat of severe punishment, if not execution.

Looking back, it seems as though trying to help these people was about the only worthwhile thing I did in the whole war. It involved my visiting prisons quite a lot, especially Fresnes, and appearing in law courts which were hopelessly biased, and often dominated by Communist zealots. In Fresnes there were an extraordinary collection of alleged collaborationists, consisting of former eminent politicians, *Préfets* and other senior civil servants, officers from the three services, diplomats, writers and journalists, as well as riff-raff from the streets accused of having been informers, *agents-provocateurs* or pimps for the Germans. They were all packed tight, five or six to a cell originally intended to accommodate a single prisoner. It was a kind of Beggar's Opera scene, in which it was difficult to distinguish between some immensely distinguished admiral or general, dishevelled, but still wearing his uniform and decorations, and rogues of the Laffont type; between some famous

actress from the *Comédie Française* and prostitutes who had found a lucrative clientele among German officers and other ranks. The only faces that were vaguely familiar to me were the politicians, and they mostly managed to get transferred to the infirmary, where one caught an occasional glimpse of them, seated with blankets round their shoulders like stalactites, and treated now with some degree of deference by the warders, even called M. le President again, as being on their way back to freedom and their former status.

The name of the prisoner I had come to see would be called out in stentorian tones, and down he would come, often in a state of furious indignation, which I would do my best to soothe down, explaining that I was working for his release, and needed for that purpose to ask certain questions. I made the fatal mistake of asking one of them, who I knew had been in Fresnes during the occupation, how conditions compared with the previous occasion. He laughed uproariously at my question; why, he said, under the Germans it was a *vie de château* compared with now. As for the warders, he went on, looking savagely at the one who was hovering round us – they don't change, except that now, when they went to bawl you out, they call you *tête de Boche* instead of *tête d'Anglais*. I'm glad to say he did get released, quite soon after this encounter, and managed to make his way abroad, where, as I heard, he became a very successful picture-dealer.

As it became known that I was concerned with such cases, I received appeals for help from numerous quarters, some of them very moving ones. Thus I saw a good deal, one way and another, of the *Épuration* process; described in great and truthful detail in the definitive work on the subject, M. Robert Aron's *Histoire de l'Épuration*. It was, all things considered, one of the more squalid episodes in France's history, with, as it sometimes seemed, everyone informing on everyone else. The préfectures and police stations were stuffed with accusatory letters; some even found their way to the Boulevard Suchet. A whole people's sense of guilt found expression in this unedifying passion to accuse and to punish others, which, of course, also opened the way to a great deal of working off of private grudges and envies. The truth is that under the German occupation everyone who did not go underground or abroad was in some degree a collaborator and could be plausibly accused as such. The barber who cropped the bullet heads of German soldiers, the greengrocer who sold them fruit, the waiter who served them meals, the whore who went to bed with them, the entertainer who sang to them, the clown who made them laugh, were all collaborating.

I felt desperately sorry for the individuals who were picked on for this *soi-disant* crime, especially when, as sometimes happened, I actually saw the pack going after their victim – shaving the head of some wretched girl, hunting down a German soldier who had got left behind, carrying some gibbering, trembling creature off to prison.

One case that came to my notice particularly held my attention. It concerned a French girl who had fallen in love with a German soldier compulsorily billeted on her family. First of all she had turned away whenever he spoke to her in good *Silence de la Mer* style; but in time his kindliness and good-nature had broken down their resistance, and they had all grown fond of him; she, ultimately, as a lover. After all, she said to me, his being a German didn't make him not a man, nor her being French make her not a woman. The sentiment was commonplace enough in itself, but her words continued to echo in my mind. Now, she went on, he had disappeared; an information had been laid against her as someone who consorted with German soldiers (to add to her distress, she feared that this might have been by her brother who had joined the FFI), and she lived in terror of being taken away and having her head shaved, and other horrors. 'What a Liberation for me!' she said, beginning to cry. Perhaps because she was so sweet and pretty, and, even in her sorrow, still elegant in a French way, I brooded over her case longer and more intensely than over others ostensibly more important. It seemed to me that her plight was a true image of the war, unlike those fabricated at the Ministries of Information or in the studies of statesmen; reflecting, as it did, her actual feelings, her true state of mind, rather than some fraudulent version designed to generate alternative bellicosities and bigotries to the Nazi ones.

In the end I became so preoccupied with the subject that, after the war, I wrote a play about it, called *Liberation*, partly based on this girl's story, and trying to show that through her love for her German, she really was liberated, whereas the so-called liberating armies – the Red Army fighting, looting and raping its way across Eastern Europe, the Allied Forces raining down death and destruction on Berlin and Dresden, on Hiroshima and Nagasaki – were liberating no one and nothing, but rather, bringing new servitudes in their train. By the time I had finished the play, the point I was trying to make almost ceased to have any meaning in the light of a myth that had been created, whereby Paris was liberated by French patriots to the unanimous delight of its population, apart from a few *mauvais sujets* who were faithfully dealt with. Eisenhower gave this myth a great push forward when he

publicly stated that the French Resistance was the equivalent of putting into the field some twenty divisions – that is, rather more than the British contribution to the Normandy landings. I may add that I was able to help the heroine of my play a little in real life by affording her some protection, and after the war she doubtless married her German lover. In the play she fares worse; her German lover stays behind in Paris, to be shot down by the FFI with the connivance of her brother. She is left to grieve alone; but in the knowledge that she, at any rate, has been liberated.

Perhaps, especially today, the myth, as always, reigns supreme. In the case of the liberation myth, it has been possible to watch its growth; like a coral reef, gaining accretions all the time. Marcel Ophuls's film, *Le Chagrin et la Pitié*, is, perhaps, the myth's final apogee. It has been acclaimed all over the world, and received numerous awards. In it, the single intimation of any help in the way of personnel, supplies and money by the Allies is the appearance on the screen of an avowed English pederast, who describes a love affair he had in Paris with a German officer subsequently killed on the Eastern Front. The only heroes are the Communists, who are not asked to account for what they were doing during the first twenty months of the war, when the Nazi–Soviet Pact was in operation, and their party did everything possible to procure the defeat of France and a Nazi victory. If collaboration is to be regarded as a crime, then of all collaborators, the Communists bore the heaviest guilt. Criticism like mine, as I am well aware, can have absolutely no effect in counteracting the impact of M. Ophuls's film; any more than the scholarly researches of a Robert Aron. The camera has spoken, and before it tongues and pens are powerless. No instrument hitherto devised has been a thousandth part as effective in the creation and propagation of instant myths, often, as in the case of *Le Chagrin et la Pitié*, out of the most implausible material. We are far more likely to perish of a surfeit of celluloid than in consequence of any subversive conspiracy of nuclear explosion.

Another case that I got involved in, though in itself serious enough, was, because of the indomitably cheerful temperament of its central character, much less harrowing. About the third day after I arrived in Paris Trevor Wilson muttered to me, as we were walking along the Champs Élysées together, that he had just received instructions from London to keep an eye on P. G. Wodehouse, who was staying at the Bristol Hotel. Would I take this on? I agreed with indecent alacrity; not because I was an ardent Wodehouse reader, or even because of a

burning desire to make up for the shabby treatment he had indubitably received at the hands of his fellow-writers at the time of his notorious broadcasts from Berlin, but, primarily, out of curiosity; to see just how he had reacted to suddenly becoming a national villain after having been for so many years a national hero, or class totem.

I made my way to the Bristol Hotel that same day in the early evening, and as I walked along I tried to remember the details of Wodehouse's alleged misdemeanour, which had occurred when I was at GHQ Home Forces. I had not, as it happened, taken much account of the broadcasts themselves at the time, but I remembered something of the row they caused – letters in *The Times* signed by A. A. Milne and others, suggestions that his honorary degree at Oxford should be rescinded, a ferocious outburst by Cassandra (Bill Connor) in the *Mirror*, expulsion from the Beefsteak Club, and – as I learnt subsequently, the only thing Wodehouse really minded – being expunged from some sort of roll of honour at his old school, Dulwich College.

At the Hotel Bristol reception desk a sleek man in a black cutaway coat gave me the number of Wodehouse's suite without displaying the slightest embarrassment or curiosity about my visit, though I suppose it must have occurred to him that, in all the circumstances, a visit by a British officer probably boded no good for him. An odd, and for obvious reasons little publicised, feature of war is how much goes on unchanged despite it. This receptionist knew better than the rest of us that when all the excitement had died down, and all the arm-bands and cartridges had been handed in, there would still be expensive hotels and their clients to whom politeness was due; Wodehouse being indubitably one such.

Nothing was working in the hotel, but the receptionist must have found some way of letting Wodehouse know that I was on my way up to his suite, because he seemed to be expecting me. 'Oh, hullo!' he said when I opened the door and stepped inside. He was standing by the window; a large, bald, amiable-looking man, wearing grey flannel trousers, a loose sports jacket and what I imagine were golfing shoes, and smoking a pipe; a sort of schoolmaster's rig. He might, I suppose, easily have been a schoolmaster if he hadn't taken to writing – Wooders. Our meeting seemed so natural that it only occurred to me afterwards that he may have thought I had come to put him under arrest. If so, he showed no signs of anxiety, but seemed perfectly at ease. When I got to know him better I asked him what sort of person he had expected to come into his room. 'Oh, I don't know,' he said, 'but not you.' This, I must say, greatly pleased me.

I should, of course, before coming to see Wodehouse, have got hold of a dossier from somewhere – there always is a dossier – and studied the text of the offending broadcasts, generally familiarising myself with the case. In fact, I had made no sort of preparation for my visit, and had no plan as to how I should approach Wodehouse. So I began with the banal observation that his books had given me great pleasure. Even this was not strictly true. In my Socialist home Bertie Wooster and Jeeves were as reprehensible figures as Sade and Casanova in a Methodist one. My feelings about him on first making his acquaintance, were, I should say, that he was a distinguished and original writer who had given a great deal of pleasure to a great many people, and that, as such, he was entitled to be kept clear of the monstrous buffooneries of war. Otherwise, I had no strong sense of partisanship one way or the other.

There was still a lot of rushing about and shouting in the street outside; even an occasional pistol shot. Wodehouse turned away from the window, and we both sat down. Then, after a short silence, I made a hesitant approach to the business in hand. I had no idea, I said, to what extent he had been able to follow what was going on in England, but there had been quite a public row about his broadcasts – a row which I personally considered to be unwarranted. All the same, in order to clear matters up, questions would have to be asked and the legal position gone into. I slipped in the reference to the legal position (about which, of course, I knew nothing) in order to stress the gravity of Wodehouse's plight – in the circumstances then prevailing, decidedly serious. Judges are as prone as anyone to swim with the tide – perhaps a bit more so – and the English, too, as the trial of William Joyce (Lord Haw-Haw) showed, were in a mood for sacrificial victims, though in their case, particular ones, rather than, as with the French, in bulk. Wodehouse might well have fared ill if he had come before a British court at that time.

From numerous talks I had with him, sometimes on walks that we took together through the streets of Paris, sometimes sitting and chatting, I was able to piece together what happened to him in the war years. When in the summer of 1940 the Germans arrived at Le Touquet, where Wodehouse and his wife Ethel had a villa in which they were living at the time, he was taken into custody as an enemy alien and transported to a prison camp at Tost in Poland. The building in which they were lodged, to his great satisfaction, turned out to have previously been a lunatic asylum. Here he lived relatively contentedly, though food was decidedly short; he found, he told me, that nourishment could be

got out of match sticks if assiduously sucked. He had brought his type-
writer with him, and, marvellous to relate, he continued to turn out his
daily stint of words. When the war ended he had five novels, all up to his
usual standard, ready for publication. I asked him whether the guards
at Tost took any interest in his writing. Yes, he said, very markedly so;
they would stand and watch him tapping with awe and fascination. I
could quite believe it. Wodehouse has written an entertaining account
of his life at Tost – what he calls his Camp Book – which he gave me to
read. It must be unique in prison literature as minimising the miseries
of captivity, and stressing the pleasant relations he had even with the
guards, as well as with his fellow-captives, and the solaces they found
to alleviate their boredom and privation.

The normal procedure is to release civilian internees when they are
sixty; Wodehouse was released some months before his sixtieth birthday
as a result of well-meant but ill-advised representation by American
friends resident in Berlin, America not being then at war with Germany.
He made for Berlin, where Ethel (who had not been interned) was
awaiting him. Hearing of his presence there, the Berlin representative
of the Columbia Broadcasting System, an American named Flaherty,
asked him if he would like to broadcast to his American readers. For
professional reasons, if for no others, the idea appealed to Wodehouse,
who did not want to be forgotten in his most lucrative market. So he
foolishly agreed to Flaherty's proposal, not realising that the broadcasts
would have to go over the German network, and therefore were bound to
be exploited in the interest of Nazi propaganda. It has often been
alleged that there was some sort of bargain whereby he agreed to
broadcast in return for being released from Tost. This has been denied
again and again, and is in fact totally untrue, but nonetheless continues
to be widely believed. Lies seem to have much greater staying power
than truth.

Naturally, the broadcasts were gone through minutely by more expert
eyes than mine, but no one has ever been able to find them other than
blameless. They are, like everything Wodehouse writes, accomplished;
in his own special vein, an amusing, wry, and well-observed account of
his journey to Tost and life there – a sort of preliminary sketch for his
Camp Book. Ironically enough, they were subsequently used at an
American political warfare school as an example of how anti-German
propaganda could be subtly put across by a skilful writer in the form of
seemingly innocuous light-hearted descriptive material. The broadcasts,
in point of fact, are neither anti- nor pro-German, but just Wodehousian.

He is a man singularly ill-fitted to live in a time of ideological conflict, having no feelings of hatred about anyone, and no very strong views about anything. In the behaviour of his fellow-humans, whoever they may be, he detects nothing more pernicious than a kind of sublime idiocy, and in commenting on public affairs rarely goes further than expressing the hope that this or that august personage might be induced to return to his padded-cell. I never heard him speak bitterly about anyone – not even about old friends who turned against him in distress. Such a temperament does not make for good citizenship in the second half of the twentieth century.

As we went on talking evening shadows began to fill the room we were sitting in. There was no electricity, and so no possibility of turning on a light. I have always loved sitting in a darkening room and talking with someone sympathetic; it takes the sharp edge off the exigencies of time, and, one may dare to hope, is a little like dying. The experience was sharpened in Paris on that particular evening because of the contrast between our tranquillity together and the mounting confusion and shooting outside. Wodehouse sent down for a bottle of wine which we consumed as we talked; royalties on Spanish, Swedish and other trans-lations of his books provided him with adequate funds during the war years. Our conversation soon moved on from his Berlin misdemeanour and its repercussions. Were things still ticking along? Did clubs go on? And *The Times Literary Supplement*? Alas, yes, I had to tell him. And A. A. Milne? And *Punch*? Yes, again. Wodehouse wanted to know what books had been published and how they had sold, what plays had been put on and how long they had run, who was still alive and who dead. I satisfied him as best I could on these points, hampered, in the case of the last, by a morbid tendency to believe I had read the obituary of practically everyone; especially women novelists, eminent Quakers, popular clergymen, famous Shakespearean actors and Governors of the BBC. Bernard Shaw, I told him, was certainly alive; the news, I fancy, fell a little flat. 'And Wells?' he asked eagerly. 'He might be dead,' I said, leaving him to extract whatever joy or grief he might from my uncertainty.

The room was quite dark now, and I got up to go, promising to come again soon, if I might, to make the acquaintance of Ethel. On the way back to the Avenue Marigny I looked in at the *Cercle Interallié* where one could always find a cluster of American colonels, some with their ladies, as well as a one-armed Pole ingeniously playing snooker, and a King's Messenger or two resting between journeys. At the

Avenue Marigny I rang the bell, and after a discreet interval for inspection the great door swung open to let me in. In passing, I asked M. Félix if he had heard of P. G. Wodehouse. Yes, he had, he said; in fact he had dined at the house some years before, as the guest of M. Robert, or maybe M. Edmond. Wasn't he *un écrivain humoristique bien connu*? Correct I said, and went on to describe how I had just been to see him at the Hotel Bristol. 'They say it's a very comfortable and well-run hotel,' M. Félix sagely observed, and there the matter rested. I wish I could have presented M. Félix to Wodehouse; he would, I felt, have fitted in well with his galaxy of heroes as a sort of Gallic Jeeves.

In the following days I saw a lot of Wodehouse and Ethel, who turned out to be a spirited energetic lady trying as hard to be worldly wise as Wodehouse himself to be innocent. A bad sleeper, accustomed to wander about during the night, polishing tables and planning to pull down whatever house they happened to be occupying and re-build it nearer to her heart's desire; a mixture of Mistress Quickly and Florence Nightingale, with a touch of Lady Macbeth thrown in – I grew to love her.

When I had occasion to go over to London for a few days, Wodehouse asked me to get him some Three Nuns tobacco, and to find out from his agent, Watt, how his books had been selling. The former commission was easily fulfilled; more particularly as I had also to get some shag for George Orwell – who had turned up in Paris, to my great satisfaction, as *Observer* correspondent – of a kind that he considered to be genuinely proletarian, and so suitable for him to smoke in the cigarettes he made inexpertly for himself. The latter, however, presented unexpected difficulties; for when I called upon Mr Watt in his office in one of those little streets running between the Strand and the Embankment – a sort of no-man's land where the Savoy, Fleet Street and the Temple impinge – I found him decidedly reticent and evasive. Maybe he supposed I was collecting information to Wodehouse's discredit on behalf of MI5 or the Inland Revenue, or just considered it best, in the circumstances, to keep quite quiet about what must have been one of his most lucrative clients. There, anyway, he sat: a large sullen-looking man in an office which – to add an extra macabre touch to the scene – was lined with metal boxes bearing the names in white lettering of famous writers like Rider Haggard and Rudyard Kipling, who were all dead. In the end, with enormous difficulty, and the exercise of much persuasion, I did manage to extort from Mr Watt the information that Wodehouse's books during the war years had been having record sales,

and that a large sum in accumulated royalties stood to his account, which, however, as of then, was blocked by the authorities. It pleased me, I must say, to know that all the abuse heaped on Wodehouse had only served to increase the demand for his books, providing one more illustration of how public obloquy is as much a myth as public adulation; the hisses and cheers are taped, as in recorded broadcasts.

Orwell was a great admirer of Wodehouse's writing, and I was happy to arrange for them to meet. The essay he wrote following their meeting provides, I should say, about the best treatment of the subject there is, apart from Waugh's elegant broadcast tribute on Wodehouse's eightieth birthday. The two of them got on very well, though afterwards Wodehouse said to me that Orwell seemed a gloomy sort of chap. He did give this impression at first, but, on closer acquaintance it became clear that he was really, in his own odd way, quite a happy man; as I am sure Don Quixote was, even though known as the Knight of the Woeful Countenance. We talked a lot about Wodehouse, and I mentioned, as an example of how little writers can judge their own work, that Wodehouse had told me he considered his best book to be *Mike* – an early, and, as I think, immature, school story, which first appeared in my childhood days as a serial in *The Captain*. Of it, Wodehouse said in all seriousness that it recaptured 'the ring of a ball on a cricket bat, the green of a pitch, the white of flannels and the sound of schoolboy cheers' – or words to that effect. Orwell to my surprise, said that Wodehouse was perfectly right. *Mike*, he insisted, *was* his best book.

Orwell was delighted to be in Paris in uniform, wearing it so as to give as close an impression as possible of being in a Pioneer battalion. He tried desperately hard to enlist at the very beginning of the war, but his poor physique led to his being turned down, and he had to content himself with the Home Guard. As a veteran of the Spanish Civil War, he was considered to be a gunnery expert, but someone in the same Home Guard platoon told me that in this capacity he represented a greater danger than anything they had to fear from the enemy. It was while he was in Paris that I heard of the recent death of his first wife in hospital in Glasgow, and attempted some lame conventional remarks by way of sympathy; but he brushed them aside. It was difficult to know what he felt about anything personal, though about impersonal matters no one could be more explicit. His sister Avril told me that he inherited this enormous reticence about his own emotions from his father, who had been just the same. Under his reserve, he was, I believe, absolutely shattered by his wife's death.

Early one morning, shortly after my return from London, I got a message from Jacqueline de Broglie, whom I had met with the Wodehouses, telling me that the previous night they had been arrested by the French police. Jacqueline was the daughter of Daisy Fellowes, an American Singer sewing machine heiress, and – what interested me far more – on the de Broglie side, almost certainly a descendent of Benjamin Constant via Mme de Staël. It seemed that at a dinner party given by the then *Préfet de Police*, Luiset, an English guest had remarked on how scandalous it was that two such notorious traitors as the Wodehouses should be at large in Paris; whereupon Luiset gave orders there and then that they should be arrested, and four men with sub-machine guns and wearing black leather jackets duly appeared in their bedroom at the Bristol Hotel and took them off.

I located them at a police station on the Quai d'Orléans. No one seemed to know why M. and Mme Wodenhorse (as they appeared on the warrant) were there, and I had no difficulty in arranging for Ethel's immediate release. It appeared that, using her highly individual and idiosyncratic French at its shrillest, she had reduced the whole station to a condition of panic; aided and abetted by her peke, Wonder, whom she had insisted on taking with her when she was arrested. By the time I arrived on the scene, the police, I could see, were desperately anxious to get Ethel and Wonder off the premises as soon as possible. Getting permission for Wodehouse to have his razor returned to him was more difficult, and involved filling in an enormous form whose items I only imperfectly understood. However, with some help, I managed it, and he was able to have a shave. Then I went out and bought some food, and we all cheerfully lunched together, after which I saw Ethel and Wonder into a cab, and turned my attention to ameliorating Wodehouse's lot. It appeared that the only basis on which he could be moved straightaway was if he was ill. This presented difficulties; despite his arrest and night in the cells, he looked pink and well. However, an amiable prison doctor took his pulse, shook his head, and decided that he should be transferred to a clinic. The only one with an available bed proved to be a maternity home, with mothers having babies all round him. Each day his temperature was taken, and proved to be normal; there were two guards posted at his door, with whom he played cards in the evenings. His mornings were spent, as always, at his typewriter.

Wodehouse's release from the maternity home came sooner than expected; more, I should suppose, because of the shortage of maternity beds than as a result of representations on his behalf – though these

were made. After his release I took him and Ethel out to a hotel near Fontainebleau, where they lived fairly contentedly till the end of the war, when they settled in America. By this time the Wodehouse case had long since been taken out of my hands (in so far as it could be said ever to have been in them), and put into those of an inestimable barrister named Cusden, sent over to Paris by MI5 for the purpose. Cusden, in the way barristers do, went into everything with great care, treading systematically and purposefully along the paths I had so cursorily explored, and arriving, I was relieved to learn, at the same conclusion – that Wodehouse must be exonerated of everything except foolishness and one or two minor technical offences. This conclusion was weightily and lucidly set forth in a large file which Cusden produced to show for his labours. Nonetheless, blowing down his nose in a legal way, he delivered himself of the opinion that for the time being Wodehouse 'should be kept out of the Jurisdiction'; meaning, I assumed, out of England. It reminded me of Mr Jagger's advice, similarly delivered, regarding Pip's benefactor in *Great Expectations* – to secure the portable property. Out of the Jurisdiction Wodehouse was duly kept, and subsequently stayed; being always in a state of meaning to come to England, but never coming. His attitude has been like that of a man separated in painful circumstances from someone he loves, whom he both longs and dreads to see again. Perhaps it is as well; there would be little to please, and much to sadden, him in contemporary England, where, from his point of view, as he put it to me once, in a totally a-political observation, the cads have taken over.

I discussed the Wodehouse case with Duff Cooper, who was now comfortably settled with Lady Diana in the old British Embassy in the Rue St Honoré. There, they had raised the banner of pre-war smartness, and many flocked to it, some of whom for various reasons had been lying low since the Liberation. Every social situation produces its appropriate phraseology, and any vague – or, for that matter, actual – anxieties felt by millionaires, actors, writers, dress-designers, *vicomtesses* and others, coming into the gossip-writer's category of *tout Paris*, about their behaviour during the occupation, were described as *des ennuies*. The Duff Coopers' salon was a great place for shedding *ennuies*, and was much frequented accordingly. Though the guest-list caused some head-shaking and eyebrow-raising in the Boulevard Suchet, as I tried to explain to my colleagues there, the Embassy was only reacting like Maxim or Cartier, or, for that matter, the Hotel Bristol, and welcoming old clients. I was surprised, on the only occasion

I went myself, to find Picasso in this throng, looking like some strange wild ape who had strayed into a film-set where the ball on the eve of the Battle of Waterloo was being filmed. Already, he wore the look of an astute old comedian who would know how to turn even his doodles to account in augmenting the great cascade of gold which the *bourgeoisie* he so abominated and ridiculed were to rain down upon him. Picasso can scarcely have been seriously afflicted with *ennuies*, but even he may have been glad to take a purificatory dip at the British Embassy. During the occupation years, it seemed, his Paris studio had been warmed – a rare privilege – and visited by German officers; such minutiae, as I was all too well aware at the Boulevard Suchet, being collected, tabulated and seriously deliberated upon in that strange time.

Duff Cooper, as Minister of Information, had led the pack against Wodehouse, but now he showed a creditable disinclination to follow up the attack with a kill. On the contrary, he was ready to help in easing the Wodehouses' path. Wodehouse's trouble, he contended, was that all his life he had successfully evaded reality and his responsibilities as a citizen. Even paying his taxes was something about which he took a decidedly casual attitude, and when his country was fighting for its life his heart continued to be in Blandings Castle rather than on the beaches of Dunkirk or in blitzed London. This, despite the adulation, the honours and the wealth showered upon him by his fellow-countrymen. It might be so, I replied, but surely there were different sorts and levels of reality. Could we be sure, for instance, that Hitler's ravings and Churchill's rhetoric and Roosevelt's Four Freedoms would seem more real to posterity than Blandings Castle? I rather doubted it. As Evelyn Waugh put it in his broadcast tribute, in Wodehouse's world 'there has been no Fall of Man, no aboriginal calamity; the gardens of Blandings Castle are that original garden from which we are all exiled.'

Duff Cooper had a useful propensity, which now afflicted him, of seeming to fall asleep, or perhaps actually falling asleep, when a conversation went on too long, or failed to hold his attention. One became aware that his eyes had closed, his chin fallen onto his chest, his breathing become audibly regular. Then, suddenly, he would come to. When he did, I made one last point. Though so dyed-in-the-wool a noncombatant, Wodehouse had, all unconsciously, made at least one useful contribution to the war effort. The Germans, in their literal way, took his works as a guide to English manners, and used them when briefing their agents for a mission across the Channel. Thus it happened that an agent they dropped in the Fen country was wearing spats – an

unaccustomed article of attire which led to his speedy apprehension. Had he not been caught, he would, presumably, have made his way to London in search of the Drones Club, and thought to escape notice by throwing bread about in restaurants in the manner of Bertie Wooster. Duff Cooper agreed that this was a notable service deserving of an OBE, but did not feel that, in the circumstances, he could recommend Wodehouse for one.

Nothing impresses the English more than to live to a ripe old age, something that sufficed to make even so ill-tempered an old lady as Queen Victoria popular. As the years have passed, Wodehouse has increasingly come to be regarded as a Grand-Old-Man-of-Letters. His stories have appeared on the television screen, his books continue to be popular, his ninetieth birthday was an occasion for public acclamation, and it may confidently be anticipated that on his hundredth he will be knighted. Whether, and if so to what extent, he remembers his time of distress, he keeps as his own secret. As with all imaginative people, there is an area of inner reserve in him which one never penetrates. The scars of his time in the stocks are doubtless hidden there. In one of his rare references to the experience, he said to me that it made him feel like a music-hall comedian, accustomed always to applause, who suddenly gets the bird. This, I think, is what it signified to him, and I daresay, what it signifies.

By this time Graham Greene had left MI6 and joined the publishing firm of Eyre & Spottiswoode, calculating – as it turned out incorrectly, as far as he personally was concerned – that the aftermath of the war would be a time of great difficulty for writers, in which it would be well to have some secure economic base. The precise occasion of his leaving MI6 was very characteristic; as part of his machinations inside Section Five, Kim Philby wanted to promote him – something that Greene considered an outrage, and indignantly refused to countenance, to the point of resigning. At the Eyre & Spottiswoode office in Bedford Street, he sat in a room with Douglas Jerrold, where I several times visited them. It would be difficult to imagine two more strangely assorted human beings; both Catholic converts, certainly, but Jerrold induced thereby to move to the extreme Right, as a supporter of General Franco, and Greene to move ever further Leftwards as a fervent advocate of Catholic–Marxist dialogue. If I had occasion to talk with one of them, I was keenly aware of the other's presence; a telephone call by either produced a sort of anguished silence in which a third person found himself listening intently to every word spoken into the receiver,

however softly. Even their appearance made a striking contrast. Jerrold gave an impression of being enormous. He dressed in an old-fashioned conventional way – black coat, striped trousers, stiff collar, foot-wear noticeably hand-made for him by Lobb. His head was tiny, thinly covered with sparse hair, and altogether he looked, as Kingsmill used to say, like an inflated *hors d'œuvre*. Greene, on the other hand, was tall and slight, with the look of a perennial undergraduate engaged in working out some ingenious joke or impersonation. It is a tribute to both their characters that they managed to survive this strange proximity without a serious quarrel.

Knowing that I was going to Paris, Greene asked me to seek out François Mauriac and get him to agree to English translations of his books, to be brought out in a uniform edition by Eyre & Spottiswoode. This I gladly agreed to do, and in the very early days of the Liberation made a special point of calling at the office of Mauriac's publisher, Grasset, which I found to be in a condition of confusion. Grasset himself was suffering from acute *ennuies*, having published during the occupation numerous volumes with a decidedly collaborationist flavour, and had retired for the time being, I was given to understand, to some sort of a psychiatric institution. The firm was left in charge of his red-haired wife; a fiery lady with whom, nonetheless, I was able to establish friendly relations. Only afterwards did it occur to me that in the circumstances my appearance, unannounced and in uniform, may well have created some consternation in the Grasset office; though, actually, my mood was one of considerable diffidence. I stood for quite a while in the street outside before I could nerve myself to go in at all. Mme Grasset pronounced herself wholly in favour of the translation project, which she commended to Mauriac, and it was arranged that I should go to see him. In due course Mauriac's novels appeared under the Eyre & Spottiswoode imprint, brilliantly translated into English by Gerard Hopkins, and proved a great success.

Mauriac proved to be a frail, intense man of a kind often found among French writers and intellectuals, who seem to shake themselves to pieces with the vigour and urgency of their thoughts and words; like some ancient ricketty old car which shakes and shivers when the engine is started up, so that one constantly marvels that it can hold together at all. In his case, the impression was intensified by some impediment in his throat which caused him to speak always in a hoarse whisper, and made talking with him on the telephone an agony. Despite this, his company was enormously stimulating, and, at times hilariously

funny. Once when I called to see him he was striding up and down dictating the obituary of a distinguished friend, who, I gathered, had just died. He was obviously deeply moved, and, between each rotund phrase, delivered in his breathless whisper, he would pause to get up steam for the next – '*Encore un de la petite bande des vraiment grands* . . . *pour moi désolant* . . . *pour la France une perte irréparable* . . .' As an obituary connoisseur myself, who has enjoyed few journalistic tasks more than fixing a sheet of paper in his typewriter, and beginning, of some politician still very much alive: 'The death of X deprives the Labour (Conservative) party of one of its leading figures in the House of Commons (Lords) . . .' I rated his performance highly. It was only because of his whispering voice, he told me, that he was elected to the French Academy; the Academicians calculating that he must have cancer of the throat, and so would only be briefly among them. His stories about this august body were endlessly diverting, especially the ones relating to General Joffre, who had sat among them, largely in impenetrable silence. There was only one word, he said, which should be emblazoned in letters of fire on the Academy's walls, and he brought it out with immense zest and verve – the word PROSTATE. Once I asked him if it was true that André Gide was about to become a Catholic; a look of anguished horror spread over his face as he said he prayed heaven, if he ever did, that it would be a few seconds before he expired.

His own Resistance record was, of course, impeccable; but what I particularly admired was that, instead of luxuriating in this, he used the position of authority it gave him to protest against the intolerance and vengefulness which the Liberation had released in many of his fellow-countrymen; especially in the irregular formations like the FFI and FTP (*Franc-Tireurs Partisans*) who, in Paris and in many parts of the country, were behaving as terrorists, having taken over the role, and sometimes the actual premises and sinister gear, left behind by the Gestapo. His articles in the *Figaro* on this theme delighted and heartened me as they appeared. Like Alexander Solzhenitsyn's speech on the occasion of his being awarded the Nobel Prize for literature— an award which, incidentally, Mauriac ardently promoted shortly before he died – they raised a lone but influential voice against the destruction of literature and art by making them an instrument of power rather than of truth. Applying his own principles, he defended his arch-enemy Charles Maurras, against the vilification to which he was subjected in the press and at his trial, and pointed out that a

Liberation which applied to the victor, but not to the vanquished was a mockery. He also did everything in his power, including a personal approach to General de Gaulle, to save the poet Robert Brasillach, who was nonetheless executed as a collaborator on 6 February 1945. When Mauriac died, I was asked by the representatives of a French newspaper if I had any particular memory of him. Yes, I had, I said, and recalled how once, when I was at Fresnes Prison, someone begged me to get in touch on his behalf with *St François des Assises* (St Francis of the Assizes), meaning Mauriac. What a marvellous nick-name to die with!

Through my contact with Mauriac and his publisher, I got to know Henry Muller and his most charming wife, at whose house I met numerous French writers many of whom were having *ennuies*, of different degrees of seriousness, as a result of what they had written, or not written, during the Occupation. One I took a special fancy to was Fabre-Luce, who boasted that he had been put in prison, successively, by Daladier, Pétain, the Germans and the Gaullists. When he went in for his Liberation stretch, the warders greeted him like an old friend; the moment he got out, he started a clandestine press with a view to exposing the absurdities of the Gaullists in power. Another French writer I particularly wanted to meet was Montherlant, whose novel, *Les Célibataires* (first translated into English, badly, as I considered, with the title *The Death of the Upper Classes*; followed, later, by an excellent translation, properly entitled *The Bachelors*, by Terence Kilmartin), I greatly admired. He, I gathered, was having really quite serious *ennuies*, and for the time being was lying very low, if not actually in hiding. Before the war, he had specialised in denouncing French degeneracy, and when France collapsed in 1940 could not forbear pointing out that it was just what he would have expected from so run-down and decadent a nation. This displeased not only the French, but the Germans as well, who felt that it belittled their victory. So he was forced to adjust his position accordingly, indicating that, after all, the French had put up a good fight. One way and another, when the Liberation came, he found himself in a difficult situation.

Nonetheless, the Mullers were able to produce him for dinner one evening. He turned out to be a taciturn taut sort of man, who had little to say, and gave an impression of being under great strain; not just because of *ennuies* – which I really don't think bothered him too much, though, other things being equal, he preferred keeping out of Fresnes to going in – but rather of some inner tension, reminding me, of all people, of Enoch Powell. He was, as I learnt, another Nietzsche admirer, though

not, like Powell, to the point of emulating his soup-strainer moustache. The spiritual children of Nietzsche are mostly benighted; when I was editing Ciano's Diaries I was fascinated to find that, with his crazed sense of the fitness of things, Hitler sent Mussolini for his sixtieth birthday present a splendidly bound edition of Nietzsche's works, which the Duce opened, surely with a sinking heart, when he had become the prisoner of his despised Italian fellow-countrymen, before Skorzeny came – I was going to say, to rescue him, but, more appropriately, to take him away.

When I complimented Montherlant, too fulsomely perhaps, on *Les Célibataires*, he was not particularly pleased; the book of his that he took most pride in was *Pitié pour les Femmes*, which I considered to be an essay – and rather an unconvincing one – in that most ridiculous of all vanities, phallic exhibitionism; D. H. Lawrence being, of course, the prize exhibitor in this field. I gathered from Montherlant that he lived like a monk (France Muller confirmed this), dedicating himself wholly to his chosen work of writing; unconcerned about comfort, or food, or even heating; just sitting doggedly at his desk, and with infinite care and pains shaping words to his purpose. His taut face bore witness to this dedication; he looked like a monk – but one without laughter, bowing down in wilfulness rather than surrender, burrowing into the ego rather than escaping from it. After the war I had some correspondence with him *à propos* an article I had written on him and his work in the *TLS*, when he was little known in England, which seemed to please him. I even made some desultory efforts to promote a collected edition of his works in English, like Mauriac's – a project that met with his warm approval, if only because he was so passionately opposed to anything of the kind being undertaken in America, of which he had an obsessive hatred. Nothing, however, came of the project.

It did not surprise me that, when his *ennuies* had been dispersed – which they soon were – Montherlant's fame grew apace. The greatest craving of a scared *bourgeoisie* is for writers like Montherlant who make their secret authoritarian cravings intellectually respectable. (Their children, incidentally, achieve the same purpose by including in their proletarian fancy-dress, military tunics, German helmets and swastika arm-bands.) Thus Chesterton, Belloc and T. S. Eliot gave anti-semiticism literary credentials, as Pound did racialism – in his case, of so extreme a nature that it was calculated to make even a backwoods Afrikaner uneasy. Yeats, likewise, brought comfort and joy by writing the marching song of Franco's Irish contingent, and Lawrence by

commending thinking with our blood, producing on this theme, *Apocalypse*, with its strong affinity with *Mein Kampf*. Not to mention Céline, who carried his ravings, not just to the end of the night, but to the end of the world, and still died in his bed; while Orwell's brilliant send-up of a broiler-house state was taken as applying specifically to the USSR, instead of, as was the case, to contemporary authoritarianism in all its guises. In the end, Montherlant, like Hemingway, took his own life; they were both bull-fight fanciers – that sick resort of the weak and solace of the timid.

At the Boulevard Suchet, I heard much talk, mostly cynical and facetious, about the different grades and categories of *ennuies* then being endured, and gleaned a good deal of information on the subject, of varying degrees and reliability; not least about the famous Mme Coco Chanel. As it happens, I was to be taken to see her by an old friend of hers, F, who had appeared in Paris, covered in gold braid, as a member of one of the numerous liaison missions which by now were roosting there. So I went along with F to Mme Chanel's lavish *haute-couture* and perfume emporium with a sense of being on duty as well as pleasure bent. My first impression of her was of someone tiny and frail, who, if one puffed at her too hard, might easily just disintegrate; her powdery frame collapsing into a minute heap of dust, as those frail houses had in the London Blitz. She seemed to have various pieces and shapes of shining metal about her person; like Earl Attlee in old age when he went to a ceremonial dinner, or one of the ancient men-at-arms at Windsor Castle who appear in breast-plate and armour at gatherings of Knights of the Garter. It seemed extraordinary that she should be able to support this extra weight. By way of attendant, she had with her, not, as might have been supposed, some elegant young girl, but a grey-haired lady who looked as aged as herself, to whom she gave instructions quite softly but containing a hidden note of authority which sent her scuttling off to do her mistress's bidding.

If Mme Chanel felt any uneasiness at my presence, she gave no indication of it; towards F she adopted an attitude of old familiarity, as though to say: 'Don't imagine, my dear F (she addressed him by his surname), that your being dressed up in all that gold braid impresses me at all. I know you!' Nor had she, as a matter or fact, any cause for serious anxiety, having successfully withstood the first *épuration* assault at the time of the Liberation by one of those majestically simple strokes which made Napoleon so successful a general; she just put an announcement in the window of her emporium that scent was free for GI's, who

thereupon queued up to get their bottles of Chanel No. 5, and would have been outraged if the French police had touched a hair of her head. Having thus gained a breathing space, she proceeded to look for help *à gauche et à droite*, and not in vain, thereby managing to avoid making even a token appearance among the gilded company – Maurice Chevalier, Jean Cocteau, Sacha Guitry, and other worthies – on a collaborationist charge.

The three of us – gold-braided F, Mme Chanel and I – sat side by side on a particularly soft settee, in near darkness, two candles our only illumination, and were served an excellent dinner. The filet mignon was exquisitely tender, the red wine soft and mellow, the cognac silky, with other delicacies virtually unobtainable in Paris at that time, to all of which F did full justice, while Mme Chanel and I only nibbled. The elderly attendant was not permitted to sit down with us, but hovered round in case anything was required of her. Even in this dim twilight, Mme Chanel seemed immensely old and incorporeal; I had the feeling almost that she might expire that very evening, seated between F and me, and we just tiptoe away, leaving her there with the debris of our meal – the coffee cups, the billowing brandy glasses, the cigarette ends, hers stained a deep red. Actually, of course, she lived on for years and years, growing ever richer and more famous. I even had a glimpse of her villa looking down on the Mediterranean, all done up in shades of lavender-pink. Someone who worked there remarked of it: '*C'est une vie en rose là haut.*' So, I am sure it was, and for all I know still is, wherever she may now be.

During the dinner she and F reminisced about old times. At the slightest hint of patronage in his manner, she brought him up sharply, as it were looking through his gold braid at another F she remembered, speaking and behaving in a very different style, thus effectively putting him in his place. I had heard that for a number of years she had been the regular companion of an English duke, and asked her if she often saw Churchill in those days. Oh, yes, she said, she knew dear Winston well, and used to play piquet with him, making a point, of course, of always losing, as otherwise he'd be in a bad temper (*mauvaise humeur*). She felt sure, she said, that he'd never come to Paris without seeing her. I didn't say so, but I felt equally sure that he would; in fact, had. Afterwards, I tried to draft some sort of report on my evening with Mme Chanel, but really there was nothing to say except that I was sure the *épuration* mills, however small they might grind, would never grind her – as indeed, proved to be the case. If only I had been Cusden,

I reflected, I might have found out all sorts of things – how she managed to get to and from Spain during the occupation, whether she also offered free scent to the German troops, who were her clients, associates and intimates in those years. Alas, all I had done was to listen; fascinated, and even a little awed, at the masterly way she harpooned and skinned the braided F.

When I had been in Paris some months, a directive came from London about a new MI6 department which had been set up to deal specifically with Soviet Intelligence activities, including sabotage and subversion. The directive had been drafted by Philby, who, as he recounts in his book, *My Secret War*, had managed to get control of the department in question, the person he ousted being none other than my old Lourenço Marques friend and colleague, Steptoe. It remains a nice point as to whether Soviet Intelligence had more to gain from having its own man, in the person of Philby, or Steptoe in this post – like considering whether it is more advantageous, in a football match, to bribe a man on the other side to kick balls into his own goal, or to arrange for them to choose a goal-keeper who may be relied on to let every ball through, while supposing he is valiantly keeping them out. Contrary to what was, and probably still is, believed in the Kremlin, up to this point nothing much had been done about the field covered by Philby's new department, apart from giving diplomats going to Communist countries an article to read, which had once appeared in the *Spectator*, on the Intelligence and ideological hazards likely to confront them. As the original cutting got dog-eared through passing from hand to hand, it was cyclostyled, the copies being carefully marked 'Most Secret'. The article was later expanded into a handbook, undertaken by an estimable don named Carew-Hunt. When surveys, studies, analyses and other presentations of the subject began to proliferate, especially across the Atlantic, Carew-Hunt was allowed to publish his handbook, and it duly appeared under his name.

I was supposed to refer any queries I might receive from Philby or his staff to Soustelle, and had a discussion about it with him, Passy being also present. I could see that they did not like the idea at all, and it was not difficult to guess why. The DGER – as we had at last got into the way of calling the *Services Spéciaux* – was already under heavy attack as an organ of crypto-Fascism (quite unjustly, I may say); if it came out that it was supplying anti-Soviet material to Allied Intelligence agencies, these suspicions would seem to be confirmed. At the same

time, of course, I knew quite well that in the reconstructed French counter-espionage services, Soviet activities were by no means being overlooked. Philby's department sent me two token questions to put to the French: Where was the headquarters of the French Communist Party? and, Who was its effective boss? I showed the questions to Soustelle and Passy, just as they had come to me, as an example of the kind of information we should be seeking. Passy found them highly amusing; after all, he said, the answers could be got from the Paris telephone directory. I protested that this was a preposterous argument; if Intelligence agents were not to go sleuthing after information which was available in telephone directories, what future had the profession got? Soustelle and Passy assumed, of course, that we were hard at work finding out, with our usual skill, everything there was to know about Soviet espionage, and that these naïve questions were just a bluff. Whether other channels with the French were opened up, or, more probably, given that a Soviet agent was in charge of the department concerned with uncovering Soviet agents, whether the whole initiative was dropped, I have no idea, but I personally never heard any more about it.

One consequence of this abortive *demarché* for me personally was that I became acquainted with Colonel A, and, through him, was thenceforth to be a welcome visitor at a small convent in the neighbourhood of the Rue du Cherche-Midi, where my happiest hours in Paris in that last year of the war were spent. The Colonel called to see me at my office shortly after my talk with Soustelle and Passy, having somehow got to know what had passed between us. He was a large vigorous man, who stumped about energetically despite a severe leg wound received in the 1914–18 war; gruff and hearty and rumbustious. In my experience rumbustiousness is easier to bear in a foreign language than in one's own; anyway, the Colonel's did not unduly trouble me. He wanted, he said, to have a serious talk with me, but not there in the Boulevard Suchet, where – winking and looking round knowingly – *les murs ont des oreilles*. If I wanted to know more about him he would refer me to – and he mentioned numerous eminent personages whom I could not possibly have approached, as he must have known. He himself, he went on, was connected with French Intelligence, but not with these amateurs and adventurers in the Boulevard Suchet; with *les gens vraiment du métier*, to whom in due course he would be happy to present me. The rendezvous he suggested – safe, discreet, and quiet – was the little Cherche-Midi convent, and I agreed to meet him there for dinner

the following evening. A few discreet enquiries about the Colonel disclosed that his Resistance record was impeccable, that he was an industrialist of sorts, in a small way, and altogether a good fellow, though with some pretty lunatic ideas, to the point of being maybe a little off his head (*un peu détraqué*), which was just about what I had thought myself from meeting him.

When I arrived at the convent I was taken straight to the Reverend Mother, who had lately been awarded the *Croix de Guerre* by General de Gaulle for her part in the Resistance, especially in hiding people on the run. Her reputation was very high at that time, so much so that when, after the Liberation, milk was exceedingly scarce, and it was decided to allocate most of what there was to nursing mothers, her nuns were entrusted with the distribution, as being, in everyone's eyes, beyond any suspicion of corruption or partiality. Their house had the particular shining cleanliness religious houses have; the Avenue Marigny shadow being noticeably absent. I noticed the same thing when Mother Teresa's Sisters of Charity took over the upper part of a condemned house in Notting Hill. It was not just that they swept and scrubbed and polished, which, of course, they did to a high degree. Somehow they made the place luminous, so that visiting there was like climbing up to Heaven. The convent in the unsalubrious Cherche-Midi district seemed likewise to have caught the light of some sun outside the universe.

It was obvious, when the Colonel arrived, that he was a favoured visitor. He cracked jokes, took liberties and paid compliments, pretending that he only entertained his guests in the convent because of the excellence of the food and wine provided, and of his stinginess, which made him appreciate not having to pay. Before sitting down to eat we attended the evening office in the chapel; the Colonel groaning and puffing as he got with difficulty onto his knees, and then when I looked sidelong at him, his old worldly, weather-beaten face wearing so serene and joyful an expression, I found myself envying him, and staring, as I so often have, at the altar, as though I hoped that enlightenment would come visibly out of it to me; maybe as a voice, or a dove descending from Heaven. This, as I well know, can never be. The process is the other way round; a purified heart has to be offered to the altar, rather than the altar dispensing purification.

The Colonel and I sat down to dinner together – an excellent dinner of fish, it being a Friday. A nun served us, and the Reverend Mother stood talking with us for part of the time, but declined to join us at table.

In her face I noted the special kind of sagacity and sense of the absurd that comes of understanding the world without being in it; of knowing within the Cloud of Unknowing – what might appropriately be called, in her case, the coquetry of Christ. I greatly appreciated her company, and was sad when she left us, the Colonel having, presumably, given her instructions that he had private matters to discuss with me. What he had to tell me was a detailed story, naming names, of ostensible Communist infiltration of the French Government, administration and security services. As he went on, I confess that my heart sank; not so much because I necessarily disbelieved him – though I largely did – as because, in my mood of contentment, I did not particularly care whether what he said was truth or fantasy. He went on and on, and finally I got up to go, promising that – for what it was worth, which wasn't much – I would send on to London the information he had given me. This I did, in a very abbreviated version, with many reservations of my own, and giving full weight to the possibility that he was a bit cracked.

From Philby I got back a contemptuous dismissal of the Colonel's allegations as so much poppycock, and a recommendation to put any further offerings from this source straight into the w.p.b. (I particularly remember the newspaper-style use of initials; as scrawled editorially on some proffered news item or syndicated feature.) Coming from such a source, the judgement might almost seem like an endorsement of the authenticity of the Colonel's disclosures. After all, from a Soviet agent's point of view, if they were purely nonsensical, the obvious tactic would be to let them seem to be taken seriously and filed away. Then, when, in due course, they were discredited, other similar reports which might have some truth in them would be automatically devalued with them. As it happens, too, one or two stories I read after the war of scandals that came to light in the French Intelligence services seemed to me to lend some support to the Colonel's allegations. Perhaps, after all, he did know something; if so, it was lost, more through my fault than Philby's. I have always been glad in any capacity – as editor, publisher's reader, journalist – to put any document in the w.p.b., since thereby I am let off having to read it. So, for this inglorious reason, if for no other, Philby's instruction about communications from the Colonel was scrupulously observed by me. Into the w.p.b. they went, unread.

All the same, I did go on seeing him, and visiting the Cherche-Midi convent, where for a while he lay quite seriously ill and in considerable

pain. I would sit beside his bed, usually with one of the sisters present in case he needed anything – medicine, or a bed-pan, or to have his temperature taken. Sick and weak as he was, he managed to go on complaining, with such voice as he could muster, about France's steady decline since the Dreyfus case, if not since the Revolution, Blum's *Front Populaire* Government being a significant milestone on this road to ruin. He imagined a vast, elaborate international network of financiers, Communists, Free Masons, Leftist intellectuals and Americans, whereby a spell had been cast over Christendom, making fair foul and foul fair – as those three notable precursors of Women's Lib, the Horrid Sisters in Macbeth, put it. England alone, the Colonel considered, could break the spell, and Churchill alone lead Christendom back to its true path and destiny. I must be the intermediary, and *l'Intelligence Service* the instrument, for bringing about this splendid transformation. Without delay, I should go to London; to 'C', to Buckingham Palace, to Downing Street, to Westminster, bearing the message. It was useless trying to explain that I should make a ludicrous emissary – as though Noah, instead of sending out a dove from the Ark to see if the floods had subsided, had sent a frog to croak and enjoy the high water.

When the Colonel was better, I brought Duff Cooper to dine with him at the convent, first picking him up at the British Embassy where Lady Diana had a little group of worshippers gathered round her, she statuesque among them, like her namesake of the Ephesians – dons, photographers, dress-designers, film-makers, wits and wisecrackers, with a place, albeit lowly, for the merely rich. Duff Cooper extricated himself from this company, not too unwillingly, I thought, and we reported together in an Embassy car.

The dinner at the convent was not a success; the Reverend Mother was not as impressed as I hoped she might have been with a visit from the British Ambassador, and indirectly with me for bringing him, and the Colonel, having started by being excessively flattering and affable, got involved in a tirade about Yalta, which touched off in Duff Cooper one of his sudden spasms of rage – the counterpart of his equally sudden bouts of falling asleep – when his usually mild and genial features became distorted with fury, the veins standing out, the eyes misted over, if not slightly bloodshot, the teeth grinding, the voice rising to shrill heights. All this, of course, in French, which he knew well, but which, as he spoke it, was ill-suited to such stridency.

We left early, and I looked in at the Embassy for a farewell drink. Duff Cooper spoke of his political future, about which he had obviously

been thinking a lot. His assumption was that Churchill must win a general election when it came, and would offer him, at best, only a mediocre job. Why not, then, stay on in Paris, where he was well content? It seemed like a sound argument at the time, and in Paris he stayed. If, of course, he had known that the cards would fall the other way, he would have given up his Paris job, returned to the House of Commons, and been an important figure on the Opposition Front Bench, with a good chance of a major post when the next Conservative Government came to be formed. In politics, as in playing patience, a single mistake is usually ruinous – though in this particular case ruinous is a relative term, involving, as it did for Duff Cooper, trivial but lucrative duties on behalf of the *Wagons-Lits* and Sir Alexander Korda, rather than, say, becoming Home Secretary.

An encounter at the convent that passed off more satisfactorily was with a certain M. Jacques, about whom the Colonel and the Reverend Mother frequently spoke, as someone who stayed there from time to time, and whom they would particularly like me to meet. This was duly arranged, and I went to the convent one evening to dine with him. He was obviously in some sort of disguise; his long hair and moustache did not fit his face, and his clothes – old and shabby – seemed wrong. He turned out to be Paul Baudouin, first de Gaulle's colleague in the Ministry of Defence under Paul Reynaud, and then Pétain's Foreign Minister. I enormously admired the Reverend Mother for hiding him, as she had hidden people in the Resistance during the German occupation. To take risks for a particular cause by providing sanctuary for its fugitives can be heroic, but to take risks on behalf of all fugitives, whoever they may be, and whatever the cause, is the prerogative of saints rather than of heroes. I was also greatly flattered that the Reverend Mother should have considered it perfectly safe to present me to M. Jacques, thereby disclosing his identity to me, when he was very much on the run.

He struck me as being a cool, able, managerial sort of man, who by accident had strayed into the world of politics and power; like a well-trained circus lion straying into the jungle. Even now he seemed somehow bewildered; as though he still could not understand how he, who sat so contentedly in board-rooms and in ministries, should have come to find himself, shabbily dressed and with unbecomingly abundant whiskers and hair, lurking in a convent near the Rue du Cherche-Midi, with a prison conveniently at hand into which he might so easily, at any moment, be popped. About Pétain, the author of his misfortunes,

he spoke with a kind of wonder; as it might be an accomplished steeple-chaser brooding over a pedigree horse which, instead of winning the Grand National, had thrown him at the first fence. The Marshal, he said, still dropping his voice respectfully in mentioning his name, was unfortunately only lucid for certain periods during the day, which grew shorter and shorter as time passed. I imagined Baudouin lurking in his ante-room with carefully prepared documents in his hand, hoping to catch the Head of State during one of his moments of lucidity. Subsequently, he was arrested and imprisoned briefly in Fresnes.

After the war, when he published a volume of reminiscences of his political life, he asked me to write a Foreword to the English edition, which I did. For some reason, Professor Namier was very taken with the book, and asked me for a specimen of Baudouin's handwriting, which I provided. This he submitted to some necromancer, who specialised in deducing people's characters from their handwriting. To my considerable surprise Namier attached great importance to his findings, which he incorporated in a long front article he wrote in the *TLS* on the book. It was this article that he read aloud to me in a slow flat voice, with the deliberation of an artillery barrage; which, however, I endured with such cheerfulness as I could summon up, out of affection for the dear, solemn, preposterous man. I saw Baudouin once more, in paris, at an office he then occupied in the Boulevard Victor Hugo. We had a somewhat distant chat from which it did not emerge what precisely his office was concerned with, though I assumed it was something to do with money. He told me that he had received several feelers from de Gaulle about joining him, but always declined. About this, I was, and remain, dubious. I think his vague embarrassment when I was with him was due to the fact that my presence reminded him of a time which he wished to forget. Shortly afterwards I read he had died. He was a man I should, perhaps, have found more interesting than I did.

It was around this time I received an intimation that Kim Philby was coming over to Paris in connection with his new duties as head of the department concerned with Soviet espionage, and that he wanted to see me. He stayed in the Avenue Marigny house, and we arranged to dine together. This proved to be a very strange, though by no means unhappy, evening; certainly, it is one that I can never forget. We went to a restaurant to eat, and Kim, being very fond of food, ordered a lot of exotic dishes; whereas I, never having taken the slightest interest in gastronomy ordered my usual melon, omelette and fruit and cheese. I drank a fair amount, however, as also did Kim, and whether as a result

of this, or for some other reason, for once we felt at ease with one another. Kim's stutter was less marked than usual, which of course made things easier; I asked about his family, especially his wife Eileen, and he responded in the style of an affectionate father and husband. Then I asked about people in the office, and we laughed over some of the famous comics; like Colonel Vivien; who had actually given me an account – which I imitated – of how one of his agents, executed by the Turks, had managed to send a message: 'Tell the Colonel I kept the faith.' I regret to say that I also threw a lot of ridicule on poor Steptoe, whom Kim had just scuppered and sunk without trace. The ostensible reason for our getting together – Kim's new job, and what might be expected of me and my contacts with the French in connection with it – remained virtually unmentioned. This, in my experience, often happens when a meeting has been arranged for a particular purpose; like seeking someone out with a view to borrowing money, or effecting a seduction, and then finding oneself talking loquaciously about everything under the sun to avoid coming to the point.

When we left our restaurant in the Champs Élysées (HMG footed the bill), the evening seemed very mild and agreeable, the lights very bright, the people strolling about and sitting in the cafés, very delightful. It was one of those occasions when you seem to hear, underlying the noise of life, music mysteriously playing in the far distance – a kind of heavenly *muzak* coming from loudspeakers posted along the Milky Way, and you wonder how it has come about that there are so many beautiful women in the world. Instead of returning to the Avenue Marigny, we strolled by the river, and Kim pointed up to a block of flats, saying that he had lived there with his first wife. This was the first time he had ever mentioned a previous wife to me; and it was only afterwards, when his past came to be minutely explored, that I learnt that she had been a German Jewess and Communist Party member, whom he had met while covering the Spanish Civil War on the Franco side for *The Times*, and who was generally assumed to have played an important part in his development into a party activist and Soviet agent.

Quite suddenly Kim said: 'Let's go to the Rue de Grenelle.' I didn't know then (though I should have) that this was where the Soviet Embassy was situated, and supposed he might have in his mind some favourite café or night-spot. Anyway, I was in a mood to go anywhere, so we set off. Kim now began at last to talk about his new responsibilities, and I realised, at the time without any particular amazement, that we were making for the Soviet Embassy. How are we going to

get in there? Kim kept saying, and went on to expatiate upon the special difficulties of penetrating a Soviet embassy as compared with others – no chance of planting a servant when all the staff, down to the lowliest kitchen-maids and porters and chauffeurs are imported from the USSR, and sometimes, in reality, hold quite senior positions in the Intelligence *apparat*. Tremendous obstacles, too, in the way of bugging the place; they never let foreign electricians or builders, anyone like that, into the embassy. Listening devices, observation posts, inside agents, all ruled out; the staff themselves, high and low, rigidly controlled, only certain picked members allowed to circulate freely, and even they are often kept under surveillance. Look at it! – by this time we were in the Rue de Grenelle – every blind drawn, every door locked, every window with its iron grating, the very fire-escape contained in steel-netting; even so, behind the doors and windows, round-the-clock guards, burglar alarms, every imaginable and unimaginable security precaution.

He carried on like this in an almost demented way; not exactly shaking his fists, but gesticulating and shouting at the hermetically sealed embassy, standing so insulated and isolated in a Paris street, as though it had been just dropped there out of the sky, to be removed, intact, when its purpose had been served. While all this was going on, we were in full sight of the embassy, and of the two *flics* posted at its main entrance. Despite my fuddled state, I had my wits sufficiently about me to register in my mind that this was most irregular, if not reprehensible, behaviour on the part of a senior MI6 officer, to whom we were not allowed to refer by name, but only by symbol, even in a coded message. When I awoke the following morning I saw it as, not only irregular or reprehensible, but inconceivable. Had it really happened? I was forced to conclude that it had; I had neither dreamed nor imagined it – the two of us in the Rue de Grenelle, loitering there in so noticeable a way, and Kim behaving so strangely and uncharacteristically.

Even now I have no convincing explanation to offer. That Kim was just drunk and didn't know what he was doing? – quite ruled out; if he had been subject to that sort of thing he would have given himself away long before, and anyway, back at the Avenue Marigny, he was perfectly calm and collected. That he had some special purpose? – but what? To exhibit me to his pals at the Embassy? My ego, inflated as it easily becomes, wouldn't stretch to that supposition; I was, as they say in the trade, 'known' to the Soviet security services as a result of my time in Moscow, and of things I had written, but there was no reason on earth why so strange a procedure should be followed just to take a look

at me. That Kim wanted to test me out, with a view perhaps to using me and my connections with the DGER in some way?–I scarcely think so; after all, it was not as though we didn't know one another, and anyway, he was my boss, and could give me instructions. Was there even, perhaps, some vague notion in his mind that I might be involved in his double-cross? This, on consideration, seemed absurd, if only for the reason that Kim was sufficiently familiar with my record as an Intelligence officer to know that I should be worse than useless in such a role. Even Burgess, for whom Kim nourished a romantic admiration – disastrously for him, as it turned out – in the end proved a liability. So did Whitaker Chambers. The best traitors are the most ostensibly diligent and attentive to their betters – like Donald Maclean and Alger Hiss, and, for that matter, Kim himself. Set an Establishment to catch an Establishment.

No, the only convincing explanation I can find for an otherwise inexplicable incident is that in some peculiar way it arose out of the seeing double which is inescapable in the role Kim had taken on. To an infinitely less degree than he, I experienced the same sort of thing in Lourenço Marques as a result of the various stratagems and masquerades I involved myself in there; all that *jouant la comédie*, as Serge put it. Thus, I well remember vaguely considering whether, if I went home via Lisbon, I might not look in at the German Embassy there – they would certainly have heard of me from Wertz's reports – with a view to making my number with them. To what end? None, actually, though I could easily have worked out something that would have satisfied Section Five – or so I thought. It was not that I wanted to be a traitor, or, for that matter, a patriot or hero; just that establishing contact with the German Embassy in Lisbon would give a new twist to my script, introduce some fresh characters, and open up the possibility of quite new episodes. When I spoke to Johann about this notion, he looked, for once, really agitated. 'You mustn't think of such a thing,' he said: 'you simply don't understand. Our people mean business, they'd skin you alive, they'd have you talking as you've never talked before.' He spoke obviously from experience, and I promised to heed his words of warning. Anyway, I didn't go home via Lisbon.

What happens, as it seems to me, in playing the double-agent game, is that the magnetic field of one's mind gets dispersed, with the particles flying here, there and everywhere. Instead of straining after an integral self, one becomes first two, then maybe several selves, functioning independently. Which of them happens to be uppermost at a particular

moment depends on circumstances; on the chance of a mood, whimsical or otherwise, pushing one in this, that or the other direction. It is rather like living, instead of writing, a novel; being each character in turn, experiencing their adventures, their hopes and disappointments and moments of exaltation, as, for instance, Dickens did when his novels – sometimes two or three at a time – were being serialised while he was writing them. Indeed, the nearest I came to getting back into the double-agent state of mind after the war was when I used to walk round Regent's Park most afternoons with Tony Powell at the time he was writing the first volume of his *Music of Time*, and we would discuss, as we went along, the forthcoming adventures of his characters. Had the time come for A to seduce B? And if C got to know, how would he react? And D – what, if anything would she feel if C, as he was bound to, told her about it? By the time our walk was over, I had to jerk myself back into my own identity, so absorbed had I become in these fictional beings.

If one sees Kim's double-cross in these fictional rather than ideological terms, an episode like the one in the Rue de Grenelle becomes more comprehensible – as an interlude, perhaps even comic relief, in a plot moving majestically on to its *dénouement*, with Kim not just the author and only begetter, but the villain and the hero as well, whichever might be which. He, the hawk-eyed Secret Serviceman, infinitely resourceful and audacious, and also the star Soviet agent, one day to have his head on a Russian postage-stamp, like the famous Sorge. Dedicated, ruthless, inscrutable, with all sorts of minor roles as well – Bohemian boozer and amorist with Burgess, Arabist and persona-grata in mysterious Mecca like his father, and so on, including the brief essay in pure farce in the Rue de Grenelle.

As it happened, quite a number of dossiers of double-cross practitioners, both French and British, passed through my hands while I was in the Boulevard Suchet with the DGER, the problem in each case being to decide whether the double agent in question leant more heavily on our or the enemy's side. In most instances, it was an impossible problem to resolve for the very simple reason that the agent himself, by virtue of his circumstances, never had occasion to decide definitely where his allegiances lay. Like a man with a wife and a mistress, he maintained a position of fluidity, giving his heart to both – or to neither. One particular dossier, relating to a certain P von Q, an Austrian attached to the *Abwehr* in Paris, has stayed in my mind as a perfect example of the *genre*. The dossier could have been published

as a novel almost as it stood, so vividly did the central character, von Q himself, emerge, as well as the nature of his various relationships with subsidiary characters, such as his superior officers in the *Abwehr*, representatives of the Resistance and of Allied Intelligence services, fashionable and aristocratic French ladies for whom he had a great fancy. At *Abwehr* headquarters they were clearly dazzled by his exalted social connections; his command of travel facilities was a boon to Resistance fighters and Allied prisoners-of-war on the run, and the fashionable and aristocratic ladies found him, as far as one could judge, an agreeable and effective lover. His own central purpose, as it seemed to me, was just to remain in Paris with his charming circle of friends rather than be sent to the Eastern Front, where he would almost certainly be killed. To this end, he skilfully leant, now in this direction, now in that, concerned only to remain on his feet; the most subtle fidometer (if there were such a thing) would have been unable to indicate any marked preference for one loyalty over another. Had the Nazis won the war instead of the Allies, I felt quite sure that an *Abwehr* officer would have been thumbing over more or less the same dossier as I was, probably also in the Boulevard Suchet, and finding it equally impossible to exonerate or to accuse von Q. In the end, he would doubtless have been permitted to return to his native Vienna, as happened as a result of our side's inconclusive scrutiny, there, as I should suppose, to live out his days cheerfully enough. If anyone ever asked him what happened to him in the war, he could say with the Abbé Sieyès: '*J'ai vécu!*'

Would Kim perhaps have preferred the cards to have fallen this way for him? His 'K' and his Order of Lenin simultaneously awarded; an honoured visitor at Lords and at Lubianka, in the Royal Enclosure and in the Kremlin. It is possible. If so, he was more unfortunate than von Q. Or possibly just less adroit. To judge from his dossier, I cannot imagine von Q considering it expedient to associate with Burgess, as Kim did. In any case, it is easy to see why both of them, in their different ways, are in the category of folk heroes today, this being the age of Hamlet rather than of Henry V, of Judas rather than of his Master. Our contemporary Casabianca is the first, not the last, to leave the burning ship; if, indeed, it is not he who set fire to it.

The Liberation by now belonged to yesterday. All the lights had gone on, water flowed from the taps, and the *flics* had recovered their assurance, blowing their whistles, directing traffic and grabbing miscreants with their accustomed verve and venom. Bicycles had

given way to cars, heat had come back to icy rooms and offices, the Bourse reopened, and the newspapers sorted themselves out – *Temps* into *Monde*, *Peuple* into *Combat*, and so on; only the ultra-bourgeois *Figaro* and ultra-Communist *Humanité* remaining unchanged. Bank accounts were unblocked, villas unshuttered along the Côte d'Azur, restaurants refurbished, and the gaols delivered up their notabilities – M. le President presidential again, songsters clearing their throats, comedians dusting down their jokes, and whores reappearing in their familiar haunts, the shaved ones wearing wigs. The old Chamber of Deputies was reborn as the National Assembly, with veterans like Mm. Herriot, Léon Blum and Vincent Auriol back at the rostrum, their voices a shade hoarser than heretofore and occasionally quavering, but still able to hold forth vociferously and interminably. Mme Coco Chanel discreetly removed from her window the notice announcing that scent was *gratuit pour les GI's*, while M. Félix, hearing that a move was afoot in the Air Ministry to take over the house in the Avenue Marigny, waited upon the then Minister, a Communist. Whether as a result of his representations, or of other pressures, Rothschild remained securely in possession.

The war was still going on, of course, but as far as Paris was concerned, ever receding. At the time of the Ardennes offensive there was a momentary recurrence of panic, and once again cars loaded with mattresses and other household goods were to be seen headed south. I even heard it suggested in the Boulevard Suchet that de Gaulle should be given command of the Allied forces 'to finish the job'. This crisis, however, proved short-lived; the Ardennes offensive soon spent itself, and at last the day came when General Eisenhower's elephantine headquarters laboriously removed itself from Versailles, and was soon lost to view, moving in the direction of Germany. By then it was clear that the war was as good as over, and though young Frenchmen continued to be mobilised and sent to the front ('*ne te fais pas casser la figure,*' I heard a mother say to her son as she saw him off), Parisians were chiefly concerned to resume their peacetime existence, and forget both the occupation and the Liberation – two almost equally distasteful memories.

There remained the drama's centrepiece – blitzed Berlin. Who that set eyes on this extraordinary spectacle can ever forget it? The vast expanse of rubble, with the Brandenburg Gate rising up, stark, amidst it; a wasteland of utter desolation, like the Mountains of the Moon, which at first sight gave an impression of being denuded of all life – no

living creatures great or small, no birds, no insects even, no branch
or leaf or anything growing, nothing that could possibly associate the
scene with our human condition or existence. Just the grotesque hulks
of what had once been buildings – maybe the Adlon Hotel, Unter den
Linden, the Reichstag, who could tell? – and hanging over it all, long
after hostilities had ceased, a stench of rotting corpses, sickly-sour;
the cadaver side of our mortality, and stinking at that. Closer inspection
revealed that, contrary to the first impression, there were actually
human beings burrowing into this rubble like badgers, constructing
for themselves little rickety shelters out of it; as you sometimes find
in some grim, forgotten cave that bats have made a home there, blindly
flying to and fro and emitting tiny squawks. The rubble-dwellers were
the liberated citizens of Berlin, who in some mysterious way managed
to acquire food of a sort to sustain life, engaging in a weird kind of
commerce, with Lucky Strike and Players cigarettes for small change,
Spam for the larger pieces, and their bodies, if presentable enough,
for currency notes of varying denominations.

Was all this, I asked myself, the realisation of our war aims – on
the one hand, getting the *Banco di Roma* going again; on the other, the
creation of a non-place where once Berlin had been? Did it represent
the triumph of good over evil? In Paris, the shavers of heads chastising
the sinful, and the shaved chastised for their sins? The Red Army
coming in from the East bringing freedom on its wings; the Allied
forces coming in from the West with enlightenment on theirs? Was
Paris, now that it had a *Monde* instead of a *Temps* to read, an Assembly
instead of a Chamber to debate in, a de Gaulle instead of a Daladier or
Laval to preside over the Government, full of renewed zeal for liberty,
equality and fraternity? Had Berlin, in being reduced to rubble,
become a citadel of democracy? Or were there, as before, just victors
and vanquished, with some uncertainty as to which was which, and
justice once more a fugitive? I inclined to the latter view, myself, and
doubted very much whether restoring the *Banco di Roma* was going to
underwrite Roosevelt's Four Freedoms, any more than being liberated
by the Red Army was going to seem, in the eyes of the beneficiaries
at any rate, readily distinguishable from a new and harsher servitude.
A Restoration that restored the *Banco di Roma*, but not Rome, would
not, in my opinion, amount to much; any more than would a Liberation
that liberated governments (Herr Ulbricht's, for instance), but not the
governed.

*

There was really nothing more for me to do in the Boulevard Suchet, or anywhere else that I could see. The house in the Avenue Marigny, in any case, would soon be reverting to its rightful owners; it was time for me to go, as even M. Félix, in the nicest possible way, indicated. At this point I did something which strikes me now as altogether extraordinary, but at the time seemed the most natural thing in the world. Acting on an impulse, I simply went home, took off my uniform, got a job in Fleet Street, and resumed my peacetime life, without reference to anyone in MI6 or the DGER, or trying in any way to regularise my position as a serving officer by getting myself posted anywhere or put on anyone's strength, however nominally, or even looking in on Section Five to see Cowgill or Philby. I just wound up my military service myself, becoming, I suppose, technically a deserter, until some months later, I received my demobilisation papers, went along to Chelsea Barracks and collected my discharge and civilian suit and message of appreciation from the King, as though, like everyone else, I had come there from some military posting in which I had been impatiently awaiting this joyous deliverance.

Thus, my war service, such as it was, ended as irresponsibly as it began. Looking back on it, I cannot join the chorus of regrets at five years lost; they were just lost years in a lost life, indistinguishable, essentially, from the five preceding and the five succeeding ones. I might, it is true, have improved my French, which remained as execrable when I was demobilised at Chelsea Barracks as when I enlisted at Mytchett Hutments. Or kept a regular journal instead of scribbling down a few very occasional notes. Or cultivated less fitfully the literary figures I met at the Mullers'; perhaps even, as it were, buying up some Sarrautes and Robbe-Grillets at the bottom of the market with a view of disposing of them later at a substantial profit. (The only venture of the kind was to send a copy of Camus's *l'Étranger* to Eyre & Spottiswoode, but by that time Graham Greene had ceased to be active in the firm, and it fell on stony ground.) Altogether, I might have spent less time and energy in foolish pursuits and self-indulgences, and more in wresting some mental or professional benefit from the barren fatuities of war. Otherwise, the difference between writing leading articles in the *Guardian* or propaganda ones in the Ministry of Information, between walking about the streets of wherever I happened to be and marching up and down the barrack-square at Mytchett, between news-gathering in Moscow or Intelligence-gathering in Lourenço Marques, seemed no more than a nuance.

As for the war itself, just as it had no beginning, so it had no end. V-E Day, when it came – a two-day event, as though extending its duration might somehow enhance its significance – was a repeat performance. Remembering so vividly the first production in 1918, the 1945 version had, for me, a nightmarish quality about it. The abandonment more unrestrained, but also more desperate; faces more lavishly made-up, bodies heavier and ampler; a middle-aged bacchanalia – as, indeed, it very largely was, the young still being called-up and kept in the forces. On the former occasion, I had been a schoolboy; now I was middle-aged and white-haired, well past my half-way mark. In my forty-two years, there had been two wars, with an uneasy interlude in between. Or rather, one war that was still continuing. I saw little to rejoice over.

It happened that, at the *Daily Telegraph* where I was now working, I got hold of some tickets to take my family to a production of *As You Like It* at the Old Vic. We had moved up to London from Whatlington, sold our house there, and found very cramped accommodation in a flat in Buckingham Street looking onto Temple Gardens and the Embankment. I gave Kitty the tickets for herself and the children, but was only able to get to the theatre myself after the performance had begun. Not wanting to create a disturbance by making my way to my seat, I stood at the back waiting for the end of the first act. I could see Kitty and the children quite clearly. In that perspective, the four of them seemed to be grouped round her rather than seated side by side in a row; their faces riveted by what was happening on the stage, not just attentive, but utterly absorbed. There they were, caught up, compacted, by the enchantment of Shakespeare's comedy; and there was I, looking at them, and recalling that it was thirty years since I had likewise sat in that auditorium as a child, and been enthralled by *As You Like It*. On this occasion, the theatre was still very battered from the Blitz; part of the auditorium roped off as dangerous, and the stage similarly restricted, the roofing reinforced by a tarpaulin, but in places the sky and the stars nonetheless clearly visible. A very gallant and splendid effort, I thought, to have a performance at all; like a ship limping into port after battling its way through a terrific storm. The actors were very young – they might even have been RADA students – but they spoke the lines charmingly, bringing the Forest of Arden to pass in Waterloo Road, and Rosalind to life amidst the debris of a war fought and a victory celebrated. After all, then, something *had* been salvaged from the world's wreck, as there still might be something to

salvage from my life's wreck. At the back of the Old Vic auditorium, I had my own private V-E day, and then, when the lights went up, joined the others.

The office of the *Daily Telegraph* in Fleet Street, where I now worked, seemed oddly detached and secluded from the turbulent, confused world – the raw material which we were required to process and package for distribution to our readers. Each edition of the paper, as it came out, I used to think, might be compared with an eminently respectable man, wearing a bowler-hat and carrying an umbrella, who went racing after a furiously driven bus; just managing to jump aboard, and then settling into his seat, a shade breathless, but otherwise unruffled. Travelling each morning, as I did, from Battle to Charing Cross, I could observe our readers for myself; especially the large contingent that got in at Tunbridge Wells. How they opened the paper with great placidity, sipping its columns like a cup of hot cocoa rather than quaffing them like a glass of champagne, or gulping them down like a bloody Mary. News on the *Guardian* was script-material for yet another instalment in an interminable western, in which, for the umpteenth time, the Good Guy and the Bad Guy confront one another. On the *Evening Standard* it was fed back to our little old reader, cooked and garnished, as we hoped, to his taste; on the *Daily Telegraph* it blew where it listed, except that we had double-glazing and air-conditioning to ensure that no one was incommoded.

This atmosphere of serenity and detachment was reflected in the character, and even the appearance, of our editor, Arthur Watson; brother, incidentally of the Alfred Watson who had been shot at when he was editor of the *Calcutta Statesman*. He was a large, benign man, with a shining, pink face, abstemious in his ways and measured in his speech; a superb newspaper technician, with, beyond a vague liberalism, no particular views on anything. He had never travelled, sought no tête-à-têtes with the great, wrote legibly, read little, and sat patiently in his editorial chair without a break from the early afternoon till he had seen the first edition through the press. I met with nothing but kindness and consideration at his hands, and remained always devoted to him. Each day some three or four of us would gather round him for an editorial conference to consider possible subjects for comment. The space at our disposal was very limited owing to paper rationing, which was still in force – a restriction I could endure with equanimity. Our discussions were not particularly lively, and sometimes I found myself dozing off as they proceeded. The weighty political leaders were undertaken by

Colin Coote, a migrant from *The Times*, and later Watson's successor; the ones about economic matters by J. C. Johnstone, a survivor from the *Morning Post*, which by this time had been taken over by the *Daily Telegraph*, and I usually dealt with out-of-the-way topics – like an old man in Georgia who claimed to be 130, or the elimination of the Tsetse fly in Africa, which would make available vast new supplies of frozen meat. My copy invariably came at the bottom of the leader columns – sometimes column – and so was convenient for cutting as and when required.

I shared a room with Johnstone, who, despite a boyish, easy-going appearance, held to his old-fashioned conservative opinions with ferocious tenacity and expounded them with steely implacability. Composing a leader or feature article, he would pace up and down our room with a rapt expression on his face, oblivious to all interruptions; then sit at his typewriter and tap out his piece without a pause, only breaking off when he needed to make use of his slide-rule. He applied the same concentration of purpose to edging a lawn or verge in his own or anyone else's garden; an occupation to which he was greatly addicted. Though, in sharing a room in a newspaper office, there are infinite possibilities of strife, I cannot recall a single cross, or even irritable, word ever passing between us. To my great distress he died of cancer in 1954, when I was editor of *Punch*. I visited him in hospital shortly before his death, and even then he sternly corrected me when I was imprudent enough to refer carelessly, in my hit-or-miss way, to an approximate date.

Watson's editorial authority was strictly limited, the effective control of the paper being in the hands of the Berry family, who owned it, and under whose direction its circulation had climbed from a hundred thousand to over a million. This meant, in those days, Lord Camrose, with, for supernumaries, his two sons, always referred to in the office, in true Victorian-patrician style, as Mr Seymour and Mr Michael. Sometime after our editorial conference, Watson would be summoned to the fifth floor to give an account of his editorial intentions, and receive his instructions. Later, the news-editor would be similarly briefed. In this way, the two satrapies were kept separate and independent of one another. Occasionally, I ran into Watson in the lift on his way up to the fifth floor, looking for all the world like a trusted family solicitor called in for consultation by some wealthy client. The notes he brought back with him for guidance often included an actual phrase to be worked verbatim into a leader.

Later, in America, when I was *Daily Telegraph* correspondent in Washington, and on my return when I was made deputy-editor of the paper, I got to know Camrose quite well, and to like him. Compared with the two other newspaper magnates I worked for – C. P. Scott and Beaverbrook – he was straightforward and honest; altogether a simpler person. His aspirations had been well satisfied by becoming rich and a lord, whereas the other two continued, till the days of their deaths, to be tormented by unrealised hopes and unaccountable fears. Camrose, it is true, might have liked to go a notch or two up in the peerage, or accumulate another million or two, but as long as his brother and former associate, Lord Kemsley, didn't, it bothered him little. This contentment with his achievement and status made him seem more like a lord than most lords. He told me once how, travelling in an American plane, a fellow-passenger, hearing he was a lord, asked him where his castle was. I could see the questioner's point; Camrose looked like a man who lived in a castle. The nearest he got to actually living in one was to acquire Curzon's former residence; a huge, rambling house near Basingstoke called Hackwood. In my experience, aspirants quite often make more convincing versions of what they aspire to be than the originals they copy – for instance, Isaiah Berlin as a don, Evelyn Waugh as a country gentleman, Orwell as a proletarian and Camrose as a lord. For one thing, they take more trouble over their costumes and getting word perfect.

During the election campaign of July 1945, my services were in little demand on the paper, which, of course, campaigned hotly for a Conservative victory and Churchill's return to power. Practically everyone expected this to happen, including the numerous Labour supporters on the staff. When it didn't, there was great consternation. Even Watson seemed troubled; not in himself – I don't think he cared much either way – but at the thought of having to venture up to a stricken fifth floor. My own feelings were very mixed. It was the moment my father and his friends had dreamed of and lived for – a Labour Government in power with a huge majority, and here was I in the office of a Conservative newspaper, and taking no joy in the occasion beyond a certain satisfaction at the confusion of all the pundits and the overthrow of a government in office. I cannot recall a single election in which I have not hoped for the defeat of the incumbent side. This might seem a very negative and irresponsible attitude, and the only justification I can offer for it is that, since being able to turn a government out is almost the only advantage parliamentary democracy offers, one might as well

enjoy it as often as possible. As for the sense of being in the enemy camp – it didn't weigh much with me, since I had no expectation that Attlee and his colleagues would be able, or even seriously try, to achieve the things that had seemed so wonderful a prospect when I was lurking in the red cosy-corner in our Croydon sitting-room to avoid being sent to bed, and listening enthralled to the Saturday evening talk of my father and his friends. Moreover, a good many of the likely candidates for posts in Attlee's Government – John Strachey, for instance – had been foremost in believing the lies of the Soviet bosses and covering up their evil deeds. Of them I could expect nothing good.

A figure whose part in the campaign and in the victory fascinated me was Harold Laski, whom I had vaguely known in Manchester, where his father, Nathan Laski, was a highly respected orthodox Jew and resident on Cheetham hill. Later, when I began to work for the BBC, I quite often encountered him, and we became in a sort of way friends. What I found very endearing in him was something which many of his admirers either did not notice, or, if they did, tried to overlook – a Walter Mitty-ish strain, whereby he would invent incidents and personal relationships, and quote from purely imaginary conversations and even letters, all designed to make him seem important; as hob-nobbing with the great, consulted by them, and the recipient of their confidences. He was liable, for instance, when he had gone out of the room to take a telephone call, to say on his return: That was Stanley Baldwin, or Bob Cecil, or Lloyd George – almost anyone of eminence. There were no ideological implications. He would as readily recount, in direct speech, a conversation with Lord Halifax as with Stalin; and his long correspondence with the American Supreme Court Judge, Oliver Wendell Holmes, is laced with obviously mendacious stories. Holmes himself, who seems to have been a pompous, self-consciously erudite, rather asinine figure, no doubt, on his side of the correspondence, engaged in his own kind of fantasy; the unwritten, unspoken bargain between them being to believe each other's, which they did, most earnestly, over the years. Such bargains are common enough in all sorts of human relationships, including matrimony.

The difference was that, whereas the judge's fantasy was plausible, and as habitual with him as wearing his Supreme Court gown, Laski's was poetic, variegated, Chaplin-esque. Indeed, with his hat always a shade too large so that it was well down on his ears, his little moustache and large spectacles, he looked a bit like a campus Charlie, and continued, despite all his fame and success, to convey some of the other's

woebegone air. In his company, one would wait for it – how he had just come from the Foreign Office, where Anthony Eden had called him in to ask his advice. Or about how that very morning he had received a long letter from F.D.R., even, maybe, quoting a bit from it; about how the President hoped to be in London before long, when they'd have a chance of getting together, but adding that he wasn't going to 'eat any of your damned brussels sprouts'. Even before I was editor of *Punch* I had a fancy for old chestnuts, and I found it touching that Laski should have fallen back on the sprouts to give his Roosevelt letter verisimilitude.

In all follies there is always an appropriate pay-off lurking about somewhere, and in Laski's case it was that, as he grew to be more and more of a celebrity, life had a disconcerting way of catching up with – even overtaking–his fantasies. As an American lawyer named Thurman Arnold put it to me once in Washington, he was becoming so important that he was getting to know some of the people he'd known all his life. I caught a glimpse of him once in the British Embassy in Washington standing at the foot of the large stairway and looking up at a portrait of a past ambassador – I think Bryce. It made me realise how he would have loved to be the Ambassador himself. The only thing he ever asked Attlee for was a life peerage, which, however, was refused him. Thinking of the people who have been given life peerages, I confess I can't see why. It was typical of Churchill, who was capable of such brilliant leadership, and, at the same time, could be so politically inept, to mistake an aspiring poor man's Disraeli like Laski for a dangerous revolutionary. When he accused him, in an election broadcast, of wanting to set up a Gestapo, it must have lost him a lot of votes.

It was from Arthur Watson that I first heard the news of the dropping of atomic bombs on Hiroshima and Nagasaki. He was walking along a corridor in the direction of the news-room, at what was, for him, an accelerated pace, with a news-agency flash in his hands. Without a word he showed it to me, and I read it – the bare announcement of what had happened. It meant nothing to me except that a new powerful weapon had been developed which was calculated to bring the war in the Far East to a speedy end. This, I think, was most people's reaction; I personally came across no one in any walk of life who had moral qualms at the time. Attlee subsequently disclosed the fact that he had never, in all the War Cabinet's deliberations, heard talk of fall-out. Truman was in an even worse case, Roosevelt having told him nothing about the war-time atomic weapons programme. I remember seeing a memorable

newsreel of Truman, shortly after he became President, reading a statement about dropping the bomb in the monotonous tone of voice of a village policeman giving evidence at a court of petty sessions. A primary school doomsday.

Later, the hysteria was worked up, and in some degree affected almost everyone. I myself had perfectly sensible friends who sold up their homes and left their jobs to settle in some outlandish place, there to await the inevitable nuclear apocalypse. Others, given to dissolute behaviour, found an excuse in the dreadful potentialities of nuclear weapons, which, they were liable to say in their cups, 'caused something inside them to snap'. As they had behaved in very much the same way before the alleged snapping, I was unimpressed. For some reason I never experienced this particular *bouleversement*. It seemed to me that just having an enormously more powerful weapon altered nothing; it was the will to destroy rather than the means which mattered, and if human destructiveness had reached the point that our very earth itself could be turned to dust, this danger would not be averted by agitating for nuclear disarmament, any more than poor Arthur Henderson's Disarmament Conference at Geneva had averted the danger of Nazi aggression. I remember reading a statement from the Vatican at the time of the invention of the cross-bow to the effect that Christian men never would, or should, use so diabolically destructive a weapon; but, of course, it was used, even to settle disputes between Christians. The cross-bow is only different from nuclear weapons in degree, not in kind. Nonetheless, it became increasingly clear that for some time to come the mushroom cloud was to be the most favoured backdrop to the contemporary scene, and I was correspondingly thankful that my first introduction to it should have been under the cool, professional aegis of Arthur Watson, rather than of some *Guardian* or other *exalté*.

The Watson, as distinct from the Bertrand Russell, attitude was sustained by a visit I paid to Hiroshima in 1946. I went there from Tokyo, along with other journalists, in a special train in which the Emperor Hirohito and his suite were travelling; this being the first time he had visited the city since the atomic bombing. The Emperor wore a trilby hat, which, whenever he appeared in public, he continuously raised, his American advisers having told him that he was no longer a Sun God but a democratic monarch, and that democratic monarchs wore ordinary hats which they raised. They neglected to point out, at the same time, that hats should thus be raised only for a particular reason, as in response to cheers; and he just raised and lowered his all the time – like

working a pump-handle. His suite consisted of some twenty or thirty seemingly identical men in black cutaway coats and white gloves, who on all possible occasion⌐ clapped their hands and shouted '*Banzai!*' in unison. When we got to Hiroshima we all climbed to the top of a tower, which was almost the only edifice still standing. There, the Emperor was shown a blue-print of the town as it was going to be rebuilt. While he was examining it, the men in cutaway coats kept up a non-stop chorus of *Banzais*, but failed thereby to give this weird occasion a touch of drama. My persistent efforts to have a sight of some of the strange phenomena widely publicised in alleged eye-witness accounts of what happened when the bombs were dropped – for instance, the outline of an incinerated hand on a stone wall, and of an incinerated body on one of the bridges – were all fruitless. The only survivor of the raid I have actually talked with is the present General of the Jesuit Order, who happened to be in Hiroshima at the time; and he, too, failed to notice many of the high-lights in the vast literature on the subject.

As a basis for studying the shaping and propagation of a modern myth, some of this material is incomparable. Particularly interesting is the tragi-comedy of Claude Eatherly, billed as a much decorated American Air Force major who led the raids on Hiroshima and Nagasaki; then repented of what he had done, couldn't face a hero's welcome in his native Texas town, turned to a life of petty theft in the hope of getting punished and so drawing attention to his contribution over what he now saw as a monstrous crime, and ended up in a military psychiatric institution. The story was publicised and embellished all over the world; poems celebrating it were recited on the BBC, best-selling books written about it, and a film based on the theme was made and shown. Then it turned out that Eatherly didn't lead the raid, hadn't had any combat experience, wasn't decorated, and hadn't – at least, not until psychiatrists told him he had – experienced any remorse about the raids on Hiroshima and Nagasaki. It was all pure fantasy. The interesting thing was that no one invented the story. It just emerged, ready-made; begotten by the Media out of the prevailing nuclear hysteria.

Kitty's father and mother were living near us in Whatlington, having settled there in 1939, when once more, as in 1914, the exigencies of war brought to an end their nomadic life between Swiss mountain resorts, sea cruises and picturesquely placed *pensions* offering advantageous out-of-season terms, and forced them to return to their native land and the extortions of the Inland Revenue. As it turned out, their wanderings

were never to be resumed; Whatlington was their positively last port-of-call. For Mr Dobbs this meant being subjected to his wife's cooking, housekeeping and company without a break. There was no longer the possibility, which his job with Lunn's Tours had always provided, of being able to disengage from time to time, and, as it were, retire to a rest-camp where he could re-equip and recover his morale. I must say, he stood up manfully to a situation which might well have broken a lesser man; concentrating his efforts on maintaining a small, limited area of order of his own in their disorderly household, from which he would emerge as spry, well-groomed and turned out, as ever.

For her part, Mrs Dobbs, in so far as it was possible in their new circumstances, resumed her habitual ways. She could no longer paint her favourite subjects, like the Chateau de Chillon and the Dent du Midi, in situ, but she could, and did, make copies of past water-colour sketches of them. She also did some local painting, seated on her camp-stool and dipping her brushes in the cup of water from which she occasionally absent-mindedly took a sip to drink. Her efforts in the kitchen produced the familiar concoctions, with safety pins and other foreign bodies liable to turn up in her cakes and puddings. There was little neccessity now for her essays in dilution – water in the soup and the marmalade – as guests were increasingly a rarity. Her familiars were dying off, and old age and the strain of war made the survivors less able to face the rigors of her household. One thing that she did I found very appealing – the portraits she painted in oils of our eldest son Leonard and youngest son Charles. The one of Leonard is particularly striking, and quite different from the general run of her work. There was something even then – he was about twelve at the time – in his character akin to hers, but purified, transfigured, to which she responded. He was the only one of us never to be exasperated by her; whose amusement at her antics was never unkind, and who was able by his mere presence to pacify her. When I saw this happening, I used to think of David similarly pacifying with his music a troubled Saul. Her portrait of Charles is not so good, as a portrait, but precious to us because he was killed in a ski-ing accident when he was just about to be twenty-one.

In the village Mrs Dobbs became a familiar and much-liked figure. Her eccentricities – like stretching out for a nap wherever and whenever she felt like it; under a hedge or by the road-side, and once on a tomb-stone in Battle churchyard – caused fewer stares among country-people than they would have in a town. Likewise, her weird apparel – like an old gipsy-woman's – which, when she was travelling on the bus

to Battle or Hastings, often led some kindly fellow-passenger to offer to pay her fare – an offer she readily accepted. Actually, her wardrobe had been augmented substantially when her sister, Beatrice Webb, died in 1943, bequeathing her all her clothes. These consisted mostly of elegant dresses, coats and suits, cut to her taste, and mostly in grey – Mrs Webb's favourite colour. Mrs Dobbs soon made them her own by wearing them constantly, often back-to-front or upside-down, spilling food and paint over them, and generally assimilating them, thereby pulling off one of her unconscious parodies; in this case, of the kind of high-minded elegance her famous sister practised. Her capacity for producing such parodies amounted to genius.

With Beatrice's death, Mrs Dobbs was the last remaining Potter sister; the last exponent of their explosive combination of passionate living and dedication to good causes. Only, in her, the mixture was so weirdly blended that the result was more bizarre than, as with the others, either tragic or farcical. During Beatrice's last months the two sisters drew together. That is to say, Mrs Dobbs would descend upon Passfield Corner at fairly regular intervals, to be received affectionately by Mrs Webb, and stoically by Sidney, who was still partly incapacitated as a result of a stroke he suffered in 1938. She had various techniques for disconcerting them; one being to borrow Mrs Webb's spectacles (Mrs Dobbs could, seemingly, see through anyone's, and when hard-pressed would buy a pair for herself at Woolworth's); and another, to sit in Sidney's chair, specially low-built so that his short legs did not dangle. To take some of the sting out of her presence, she was lodged in a nearby inn rather than in the house.

It was always a nice question, with Mrs Dobbs, whether it was more painful when she agreed with one or when she disagreed. I myself, as it happened, was nearly always in the latter case; try as I would, I very rarely achieved even a show of agreement, and this only by advancing on a very wide philosophico-mystical front – as that I was confident all life would ultimately become one. Developing this point with her once in Kingsmill's presence, he let out a strangled: 'Yes, but not for a very long time!', appalled at the prospect, in any measurable future, of becoming one with Mrs Dobbs through all eternity. The Webbs had to bear the full force of Mrs Dobb's eager accord. This was particularly burdensome to Mrs Webb when applied to their views on politics, as she considered her sister to be, politically speaking, a kind of imbecile. At the same time, she had an uneasy feeling that Mrs Dobbs might have chosen the better part in her wilfulness and easy surrender to sensual

living, which, after all, had left her with a tribe of children and grand-
children, as against the row of what Mrs Webb always referred to as her
and Sidney's unreadable books. She even remarked to me once, out of
the blue, that perhaps Rosy had been right – an enigmatic observation
which might as well have related to the much-frowned-upon period
between her marriages, when, in the outraged estimation of the Potter
family, she was considered to have lived loosely, as to the years of
troubled but fruitful domesticity which followed.

Even Mrs Dobbs, I think, realised that Beatrice's last months were
deeply melancholic, and that she longed to die. In the last entries in her
immense journal, written during the sleepless hours of the night, she
poured out her misery, seriously considering taking her life – VWL, she
called it, or Voluntary Withdrawal from Life – only refraining out of
consideration for Sidney. A veiled suggestion that they might make it a
joint enterprise met with no response. Nor, in her secret communings
with herself, did she derive any comfort from either the new civilisation
in the USSR that she and Sidney had proclaimed (though she recorded
with satisfaction the continued attentions of the Soviet Ambassador,
M. Maisky), or from the launching of the Beveridge Plan, which was
generally considered to be the implementation of their ideas. Whatever
she might say in public, doubts assailed her, when she was alone with
herself, as to whether the fulsome adulation of Stalin, obligatory among
his subjects, and enforced by ever more through-going and brutal
terrorism, really amounted to a flowering of socialist brotherliness and
humanistic virtue. As for the Beveridge Plan – her severely practical
side, inherited from her father, made her realise at once that handing
out unconditional largesse to the citizenry of a universal suffrage
democracy would have grave moral and social implications. Also, I
think, very humanly, she felt some heart-burning at the limelight
which shone upon Beveridge himself, who, in his London School of
Economics days, had so often pained and irritated the Webb Partner-
ship as they toiled away on behalf of notions which, as embodied in his
Plan, now bore his name, not theirs. In the very last entry in her journal
she describes her sense of melting away into nothingness ('The garden
will disappear and all our furniture, the earth and the sun and the
moon. God wills the destruction of all living things, man and even a
child . . . we shall not be frozen or hurt, but merely not exist'); and
shortly afterwards, I am sure to her infinite relief, she participated in
this process.

What exactly Sidney felt at being deprived of his companion and

partner over so many years, could not, with his stumbling speech and partially paralysed faculties, find any clear expression. At one point, when Mrs Dobbs was staying with him, he gave her quite a turn by suddenly remarking: 'That's Beatrice, you know!', at the same time, pointing excitedly at what seemed to be a large vase placed over the fireplace, which turned out, on closer inspection, to be the urn containing his late wife's ashes. One odd consequence of finding himself on his own was that he started signing his letters 'Passfield' in the style of his peerage; during Beatrice's lifetime he had stuck to 'Sidney Webb'. Another was that he took to eating a hearty breakfast of bacon-and-egg, which, during the years of matrimony, had been prohibited. Who knows what, if anything went on behind that still placid exterior – goatee beard, pince-nez on a black ribbon, abundant hair carefully brushed, tiny feet in well-made boots, neat suit; all just as when, in 1929, as the first, and only, Lord Passfield, he settled into the late Joseph Chamberlain's seat at the Colonial Office. A laconic exchange with Kitty when she visited him, reflects something of his state of mind:

'What are you reading, Uncle Sidney?'
'I am reading the novels of Walter Scott.'
'Do you like them?'
'No!'

Some four years after Beatrice's death, a second urn containing his ashes was placed beside hers in a little shrine set up at a spot in their garden that she had designated for the purpose. There they would have remained, becoming, perhaps, the focus of a minor cult, with ageing Fabians, visiting American liberals and an odd attaché from the Soviet and satellite embassies putting in an appearance from time to time to honour their memory, and maybe lay a wreath. This was not to be, due largely to the efforts of Bernard Shaw, who wrote a letter to *The Times* urging that they should be re-interred with due ceremony in Westminster Abbey.

As was so often the case with Shaw, his precise motives for promoting this strange happening, are not easy to discern. Was it, perhaps, a kind of Shavian joke, aimed, equally, at the Abbey's Dean and Chapter, and Attlee's Labour Government; at the old and new Establishment? In his letter to *The Times* he argued that, although the Webbs, admittedly, had expressed a wish to be buried in their garden, where, in fact, their ashes then lay, the nation owed it to itself to have them disinterred and brought to the Abbey. Furthermore, that whatever objections the Dean

and Chapter might raise, the reason for their transfer was not to honour Sidney and Beatrice Webb (they being beyond being pleased or displeased by anything of the kind), but to confer an additional distinction on the Abbey itself. Anyway, his persuasion, specious or seriously intended, proved acceptable, and arrangements were made for a reburial in the North Aisle of the Nave, at the foot of the memorial to Charles James Fox, at whose roystering ways Mrs Webb would surely have sniffed as noisily as she did at mundane contemporaries like Margot Asquith, the first Lord Birkenhead, and even the sometime fellow-Fabian to whom she invariably referred as 'poor little Wells'. Another near-by memorial might be considered more appropriate – that of Joseph Chamberlain, the only man with whom she could be said ever to have been, in ordinary terms, in love.

I should very much have liked to be present at the deliberations of the Dean and Chapter on the matter. Did one of them, I wonder – if only some doddering old Canon soon to retire – raise the question of Webb's atheism, and intense dislike of what he sibilantly called 'spiritual exercises'? Or even of his and Beatrice's ardent joint adulation of the world's first professedly atheistic State, in which the practice and propagation of the Christian religion had been put down so ruthlessly and rigorously? If so, no word of it got out; and no serious objections were publicly raised to Shaw's proposal, in the columns of *The Times*, or anywhere else. Few can have known, or anyway remembered, how, in her younger days, Mrs Webb used quite often to turn into the Abbey, from her restless pacing along the Embankment, to wrestle there in peace and quietness, quite often on her knees, with the questions that so insistently intruded themselves upon her other preoccupations – the Why? questions, as distinct from the How? ones.

No such considerations arose on this occasion, when her ashes, along with Sidney's, were brought to the Abbey. Despite the ecclesiastical setting, the proceedings were almost exclusively secular, with a little sacerdotal dressing provided by hymns (Scott Holland's 'Judge eternal, throned in splendour', and G. K. Chesterton's 'O God of earth and altar', with its, in the circumstances, particularly appropriate line 'The walls of gold entomb us'), and carefully chosen readings – from Ecclesiasticus: 'Let us now praise famous men . . .'; and from the First Epistle of Peter: 'But the end of all things is at hand . . .', which might be considered as providing a scriptural basis for revolutionary sentiments. On one side of the aisle there were distinguished visitors, led by the Prime Minister, Mr Attlee, and a contingent from his Government, including

the Chancellor of the Exchequer, Dr Dalton, who, of course, unlike others present, knew from his early Windsor days how to come in strong with the responses. Fabians and London School of Economics alumni were present in strength. On the other side of the aisle there was a large turnout of members of the family. Sir Stafford Cripps, as a nephew and President of the Board of Trade, could legitimately have taken his place on either side, but chose to sit with the Government. It was altogether a goodly company, with no evident intimations of proletarian affiliations. Not a single cloth cap; no red ties even, – that convenient slide from 'Forty Years On' to 'The People's Flag'. Bourgeois through and through, a casual observer would have concluded. The organ notes swelled loudly, the Dean was especially unctuous as he intoned: 'Like as a father pitieth his own children; even so is the Lord merciful unto them that fear him.' It was the Abbey at its glorious best – re-bury the great Webbs with an empire's lamentation.

There was one notable absentee – the compère, G.B.S. Never mind! a worthy stand-in was at hand. With her familiar shuffling step, attired in Mrs Webb's best grey costume, now decidedly the worse for wear, strands of disorderly hair breaking out of a tall straw hat decorated with bunches of artificial fruit, and perched on the very top of her head, Mrs Dobbs, as the only surviving sister, made her way to the front of the family reservation, announcing in a loud grating voice: 'Well here I am!' A seat was hurriedly found for her. The address, as was fitting, was delivered by the Prime Minister. His tiny figure in its black cutaway coat perched in the pulpit was like some strange, shrilly twittering little bird. Everything the Webbs worked for, he said, looking down complacently on his Chancellor of the Exchequer, his President of the Board of Trade, and the rows of lesser colleagues, had now come to pass. Someone less attuned to the occasion might have considered the then parlous state of the world – the millions of still displaced persons, the new frontiers savagely drawn without reference to history, geography or even ethnic considerations, the widespread famine and disorder, the menacing rival power line-ups – and wondered just what the speaker had in mind. It is doubtful if any among those present so reflected. They knew perfectly well what he meant – that what the Webbs had worked for was the coming to power of himself and his colleagues. And there they were – His Majesty's Government. Was that not an achievement worthy of a place in the Abbey? He went on to say that millions were now living fuller and freer lives thanks to the Webb Partnership; not, however, adding that its crowning achievement had

been to commend to their fellow-countrymen and the whole world as a new civilisation a system of servitude more far-reaching and comprehensive than any hitherto known.

His little words seemed to be swallowed up in the swelling organ notes that followed, and, in due course, the more eminent members of the congregation made their way to the grave that had been prepared to receive the two urns. It was here that Mrs Dobbs made her only contribution to the proceedings; looking at the urns, she asked in a troubled voice: 'Which is Sidney and which is Beatrice?' Then, recollecting herself, she added that her sister's urn must be the little dirty one, which had stood so long beside Beatrice's herbal cigarettes on the mantelpiece in the Passfield sitting room. Her final comment, muttered but perfectly audible, was: 'They should have left them where they were.'

Such scenes as this pin-point history; like the tiny aperture in a camera taking in a wide scene. Doubtless they occur to help us to understand – a sort of tabloid parable. And as with parables, they disintegrate in your hand the moment you try to explain them. *Vide* St Augustine's rather enchantingly laboured exposition of the parable of the Good Samaritan – 'The inn is the Church. . . . The two pence are either the two precepts of love, or the promise of this life and that which is to come. . . . The Innkeeper is the Apostle Paul. The supererogatory payment is either his counsel of celibacy, or the fact that he worked with his own hands. . . .' Let me, then, content myself with saying that the set – the Abbey – seemed as perfectly chosen as the characters – including the two off-stage, Sidney and Beatrice – were perfectly cast. Where was there a better compère, even *in absentia*, than Shaw, the old Irish jester? What better musical accompaniment than the great organ? Who more appropriate than the Dean to give his blessing to the materialist conception of history as expressed in two urnsful of ashes, to be deposited with all the other illustrious bones and ashes in his Abbey. Or than Mr Attlee to pronounce the eulogy of two such estimable upholders of Stalinist dictatorship? Above all, than Mrs Dobbs, after her superb entry, to ring the curtain down with her riveting last line. For me, the story that began on those walks with my father through Park Hill Recreation Ground to East Croydon Station, was now, once and for all, over. Another Way had to be found and explored.

Chronicle III:

THE
RIGHT
EYE

The created soul of man hath two eyes. The one is the power
of seeing into eternity, the other of seeing into time and the
creatures, of perceiving how they differ from each other as
afore-said, of giving life and needful things to the body, and
ordering and governing it for the best. But these two eyes of
the soul of man cannot both perform their work at once; but
if the soul shall see with the right eye into eternity, then the
left eye must close itself and refrain from working, and be as
though it were dead.

—*Theologica Germanica*

The Right Eye

Previously unpublished,

the start made to Vol. 3 of *Chronicles of Wasted Time*

AFTER THE end of the war my life fell into the only continuing routine it has ever known – the bringing out of a newspaper. This feeding of rotary presses day by day follows the same essential pattern in all circumstances and places. The languid beginning among the debris of the night before's endeavour, the littered copy and old galleys scattered around, the tickertapes only half awake as yet, spluttering and coughing and scratching and spitting like someone coming to after sleep, the cleaners still at work gathering up tea trays with tannin stained cups and saucers of cigarette ends. Advertising men arriving brushed and better dressed, the early editions of the evening papers to be cursorily scanned, the programme of the day's events and reporters sent on their way. Someone arriving, someone departing, someone helping police with their enquiries, a statement expected, a press conference announced, sport, city news, women's pages all beginning to take shape. Now the senior executives carrying briefcases, and finally the Lord himself who owned it all.

The war whose ending had been celebrated had really not ended, if indeed it had ever begun. Victory celebrations this time had been even less convincing than in 1918, the ennobled soldiers, the triumphant Churchill, the cheering crowds. Sir James Grigg told me that he and Alanbrooke looking at Churchill marching in a victory procession down Whitehall discussed whether they hated him more than they loved him, or vice versa and came to the conclusion they hated him. The Queen and her Consort somehow gave the impression of having walked out of Madame Tussauds.

I have found that one of the diversions of old age is provided by historical or documentary accounts of happenings in which I

personally participated or, for one reason or other, otherwise found myself involved. For instance, the depression, when I was living in Manchester working on the *Guardian*, Or the British Raj, of which I saw quite a lot in two spells of residing in India in the early twenties and thirties. Or the liberation of Paris in 1944 at which I was present in my capacity of Liaison Officer with the French Sécurité Militaire. What is so fascinating is that the picture given diverges totally from the original as I remember it. This is not due, I hasten to add, to deliberate distortion – or at least only very rarely, and then rather obviously. Nor to lack of research and pain-staking scholarship, indeed, I would say that in general, the more thorough the research and scholarship, the more is publicity false as a result. Availability of still pictures only added to the possibilities of distortion, the more effective because of a prevailing illusion that the camera cannot lie. Not only *can* the camera lie, it invariably *does* by its very nature; with words, written or spoken, it is possible to get somewhere near the inner significance of a person, an event or situation. With the camera, never. Its sphere of operation is at life's surface, and insofar as it tries to use this as symbolising or imagining reality, it increases in fraudulence. I mention by way of illustration two books by joint authors Larry Collins and Dominique Lapierre *Is Paris Burning?* and *Freedom at Midnight.* One is about the liberation of Paris and the other about the ending of the British Raj in India. In each case, the authors diligently and conscientiously sifted through the masses of available material only to produce something that seemed to an eye-witness like myself wider of the mark than the wildest imaginings. It is, of course, purely egotistic to suppose that one's own chronicles do not suffer from such distortions; as a man can sit quite serenely in his own stench while sniffing fastidiously in someone else's. The moral is merely that there is no such thing as objective truth in summoning up the past and that the talk of "going to the basic documents" or of "checking and cross checking the facts" is merely another fantasy since the basic documents are themselves fallacious, or there are no facts to check or cross-check. The computer, which one might suppose ultimate in research for the truth, finally explodes it.

Witness *Time on the Cross: The Economics of American Negro Slavery* (Robert William Fogel and Stanley L Engelman 1974). This study of slavery in America is based on feeding into a computer every single piece of data available on the subject. The answer turns out

to be a lemon, in the sense that it invalidates every single conclusion hitherto accepted about slavery, demolishing (and greatly) the Uncle Tom, Black Power and the Ku Klux Klan attitudes. God is not mocked, and ensures that He will not be, by sooner or later reducing every human proposition to absurdity. Yes, the great reduction *ad absurdum* of history.

It was a bleak time. The lights went on but not very brightly; food was more plentiful but rationing continued. Germany was defeated but other more sinister enemies were at hand. Mr. Attlee's Government fitted into the picture, the deepest and most lasting recollection I have of life is of the appropriation of everything; like a beautiful stage set whose designer has worked everything out down to the smallest detail to express the relevant period, no ash tray, no wallpaper, flowers or even a vase or book, no speck of dust even, which is not appropriate to the time. The human scene is an everlasting parable, so cogent if we have eyes to see that we shall have no excuse for having failed to draw its correct moral. This applies particularly to Government; I have never seen one, whether autocratic, authoritarian, democratic, paternalistic, bureaucratic, oligarchic, or whatever, and God knows there have been many varieties in our time, which, as long as it exists, did not have a valid relationship with the people on whom it was set. When this is ruptured, the Government in question is fated to fall, sooner or later, and sooner rather than later. There is as little point, therefore, in overthrowing Governments as the blowing up of the walls of Jericho; the trumpets will sound, and they will fall of themselves.

The Apostle Paul, as usual, was right when he told the early Christians that all earthly authority must be accepted since it could only exist to the degree that it was acceptable to God – that is to say, appropriate. When it ceased to be so, it would collapse.

Successful revolutions only push over what is falling anyway, or conversely, unsuccessful ones fail in the same sort of way that even fierce winds only succeed in bending willow trees.

I used in these post-war months, whenever an opportunity offered, to go along to the press gallery of the House of Commons, ostensibly to gather ideas and atmosphere for pontificating in the editorial columns of the *Daily Telegraph*. Looking down on the Government benches gave me, as did Wordsworth, the nearest flower that blows – thoughts that did often lie too deep for tears. There they were, rows upon rows

of them, the begetters of those evening discussions by my father and his cronies in our Croydon sitting room, of that outdoor oratory in Surrey Street on a Saturday evening, all the election addresses posted in envelopes licked down. Many of the heads, seen from above, were oddly similar, sparse dark or greying hair, sometimes dishevelled and sometimes carefully arranged to make as good a parting as possible. Thinkers' heads, reasoning screwed-on heads, knowing, questioning, dialectical heads. A good proportion LSE-trained as staff and men who had rubbed shoulders with Laski, listened to Tawney, sat at Beveridge's feet or sported with Kingsley Martin. I felt as though I knew them all. I suppose, in the back of my mind was the thought that I might have been one of them. There, squeezed into one of the back benches was my doppelgänger, myself. It was the early days of the Attlee Government. They were all full of beans, the new masters getting into their stride. Attlee himself looked so very tiny; when he nonchalantly got up on his little legs he scarcely reached the dispatch box. He seemed visually to get smaller and smaller, and by the same token his Foreign Secretary, Ernest Bevin, swelled up to get bigger and bigger – the last of the true proletarians just as Attlee was the last truly bourgeois Prime Minister. Thenceforth, the pattern was to be shattered for ever, except for lingering in BBC documentaries and other social pieces.

Legislatures have always fascinated me. Where others seek out museums and art galleries and whore houses, I make for the local parliament and have been fortunate enough, in the course of my wanderings about the world, to see and listen to a large variety. From the Supreme Soviet with Stalin leading in a little group of grey Commissars-in-waiting and all the honourable members rising to their feet and cheering under the watchful eye of the C.P.U. who timed their applause to see that it lasted the regulation nine minutes, to the latest Westminster style African variety, white wigs on dusky heads, and Black Rod, black indeed, carrying the mace as if it might be a gilded blunderbuss. Taking in, as well, Asian versions, as India's Lok Subhta, where silken tongued Brahims in spotless kadi pour out endless rhetoric, presided over by Mohammed Mussadeq, or in Capitol Hill, those majestic senators, spittoons beside them, deliberating on the affairs of their country. And – a collector's item – the Canberra Parliament at about 7.30 in the evening, when proceedings are being broadcast, as Hon. Members gather around the microphones like flies

around carrion, to demonstrate their alertness to their constituents and even shout ribald messages to this or that crony at home.

It seems to me that representative institutions based on universal suffrage reveal the last disrepresentation of power. They are the converse face of the total despot – the elected people slobbering and drivelling to some old potentate, some Sultan on a peacock throne or Grand Mogul – or mad Stalin in the Kremlin, each meditating yet another mighty purge.

Yelling and gesticulating whether in unison or in contradiction, no matter, sometimes coming to blows even, processing through division lobbies or just raising their arm to press a button, the ayes have it, the noes have it, ayes and noes ultimately indistinguishable. If we take power as being to the collectivity what sex is to the individual, then the parliamentary orgies may be compared to the perverse, requiring strange titillations to give even the hint of arousal, albeit weird and often disgusting. All carried out to put some stiffening however briefly into flagging appetites. The pathology of sex is best studied in such sick exercises; likewise the pathology of power in bawling legislators, debating furiously about nothing or else passing laws which never come into effect and in any case have no relevance to anything that ever was, is, or can be.

I don't believe in good or bad governments, but in bearable or unbearable ones. This is the only valid distinction to be made between one government and another. And when I say 'bearable', I mean by the people governed. Attlee's government was to me, decidly more bearable than, say, Tito's of Yugoslavia, but in terms of other categories – just or unjust, egalitarian or elitist, representative or unrepresentative – I can see nothing to distinguish one from another. I would much prefer to live in America than in USSR, in Japan than in Communist China but in other terms, I can find nothing to concern one government about another.

We had part of a flat at the bottom of Buckingham Street overlooking the Embankment Gardens and the River. On the South Bank we could see the Festival of Britain. It was the celebration of a death-wish, or so it seemed to us.

It was one of those macabre enterprises to which declining regimes are addicted; rather like the champagne suppers followed by a night at the Ritz that married couples tired of one another resort to with a view to stimulating declining appetites. The guiding government

spirit, Herbert Morrison, the Home Secretary, a substantial squat man with a false eye who had impressed Mrs. Webb by continuing to read a book when on the platform of a political meeting they were both to address. It seemed to her to show a dedicated and industrious spirit in a similar vein to her Sidney. As became known subsequently, under the studious, resolute exterior, there beat an amorous heart, not just in relation to fellow toilers in the Vineyard like Ellen Wilkinson, one of the few women MPs and Minister of Education, but to ladies of fashion. One revealed that in making tentative approaches to her, he had commended himself as being a man of destiny. The expression is Napoleonic, of course, and has been taken up by many more aspiring Bonapartiste amorous seekers after top leadership.

The Festival itself, in its final shape, was decidedly Morrisonesque; a strange unedifying mix of old fashioned English pride with neo-national diffidence about its more robust certainties. The Festival lions had silly faces and the straw stuffing was showing. Looking at them I remembered the Prince of Wales in New Zealand butter at the earlier Empire Exhibition. Somehow it seemed preferable. I wandered round with Kitty and the children. Lighting was still being economised and so, drifting with the crowd, we seemed to be groping our way. My mind went back to my perambulations through the streets of Moscow, and the conviction I had so very powerfully then that this was to be the future – an unending procession of anonymous people processing, shuffling through twilit streets. Certainly, there was very little expression of festivity. Just curiosity and something to do. The celebration a dream that had come true, the Holy Grail found, the pot of gold at the rainbow's end distributed, the Never-Never land surveyed and parcelled out.

In his editor's chair at the *New Chronicle* Gerald Barry conceived the idea, the Government approved it, and old Jack Priestley threw in his blessing, a land of real hope and true glory. Now, Gerald Barry, Herbert Morrison and the cohorts of liberal minds; the *Manchester Guardian*, the *News Chronicle*, *Morning Post* and *Observer*, strutted along beside the Queen on opening day.

It was a strange twilit time immediately after the 1939-1945 war; for me personally and for the country. There had been a victory, duly celebrated but it did not produce even the spurious exhilaration of the one in 1918. The war had been, compared with the previous one, without tears, and the peace was likewise without cheers. I recall those

first months of peace as somewhat shapeless; a foretaste of the years of Century that lay ahead. Our deposed leader, when he appeared in public, had the air of a frowsty lion, a zoological specimen out of condition, but still going through the motions of roaring as of old; our new one, Major, later to be Earl, Attlee, belonged to Gulliver's travels, reproducing all the ways of authority, and still sporting all its insignia – tiny morning coat for ceremonial occasions, shrill staccato voice for national broadcasts, and little legs which somehow failed to reach the ground.

ENDS

Index

(This index does not include *The Right Eye*)

Lightning Source UK Ltd.
Milton Keynes UK
UKOW03f1150040117
291337UK00001B/70/P